EUROPE

AFRICA

International Visual
Dictionary

WRITTEN AND EDITED BY **Leo Francis Daniels**
ILLUSTRATED BY **Fernando Burgos Pérez**

CLUTE INTERNATIONAL INSTITUTE

LOS ANGELES   MEXICO   BUENOS AIRES

THE INTERNATIONAL VISUAL DICTIONARY

published by

CLUTE INTERNATIONAL INSTITUTE
Los Angeles, California 90017

Library of Congress Catalog Card Number: 70–124162

International Standard Book Number: 0–88217–001–5

Clute International Institute, Los Angeles – Mexico – Buenos Aires

Printed in the United States of America

CONTENTS

ADVISORY BOARD

FOREWORD

Dictionaries are in many ways the most precious of learning tools. Opening an unabridged dictionary one seems to be entering a world of supreme authority. It takes on the flavor of a decision of the Supreme Court of the United States, almost as if it were Holy Writ itself. There is precision and comprehensiveness and exhaustive detail. If I look up the word "flat," I find that it has sixteen meanings as an adjective; seventeen as a noun; six as an adverb; eight as a verb—with a number of variants. Such are the tortuous involutions of the English language.

Of course, for a child or a young adult who is learning the English language this will not do at all. Nor will a mere abridgement and simplification in the same general format provide the answer. What is needed in making a dictionary for children and the foreign born is a device for revealing the definition of a word by showing how it is used in sentences. In a complicated language like English, the use of a word is the most important factor for the beginning learner. If this can be accomplished by the aid of outstanding illustrations that bring out the significance of the word, a most useful learning tool has been created. When a child or the student in Caracas, New York, Miami or Los Angeles, for example, can see easily how a word is used in various ways, he owns that word even more than if he were given a stodgy definition.

Lexicographer Leo Daniels has an uncommon talent for carrying out this task. He attacks the problem joyfully by putting together a collection of words and exposing their meaning by delightful and unusually clever sentences. With the truly superb full color drawings of the Mexican artist, Fernando Burgos Pérez, and a collection of fine quotations, the book can be a gratifying and enjoyable experience for the student either with or without an instructor. And it goes without saying that the adult who is learning the English language can get the same satisfaction from this welcome addition to our bank of good reference resources.

WILLIAM J. ROEHRENBECK
Director, Jersey City Free Public Library

INTRODUCTION

The International Visual Dictionary is a tool for learning the English language. Designed for children in the early grades of elementary school and for adults learning English, this book aims to help (1) to improve one's vocabulary, (2) to express oneself more easily and confidently in English, (3) to develop certain dictionary skills, (4) to find one's way in the informative and fascinating world of words, and finally, (5) to develop one's personality by self-direction in the mastering of a difficulty.

Word Meanings

The International Visual Dictionary offers its readers an opportunity to increase their vocabulary either alone or with a teacher. With a wordlist of over 2,800 entries, preschool children, elementary school children, and students of foreign-language background can add to their vocabulary new words whose spelling and space-age meaning are interestingly presented with hundreds of illustrations. Older English-speaking readers will, of course, already be familiar with many of the words in *The International Visual Dictionary* wordlist. For them this book offers the opportunity to increase their understanding of these words.

Word Usage

The International Visual Dictionary not only defines words simply, but also uses them in uncomplicated ways. This allows students to discover new word relationships. It helps them, moreover, gradually grow in understanding more clearly how words sometimes change when they are used in various ways, e.g., an awareness of multiple meanings and of how words will take different forms as their tense, number, mood, person or case may change.

Thus, *The International Visual Dictionary,* simply organized and colorfully illustrated, encourages students to learn words and their usage independently and to develop an interest in words through browsing. It is especially useful, moreover, in helping adults of foreign-language backgrounds to learn and use English words and idioms correctly.

Dictionary Skills

The International Visual Dictionary is also very useful in introducing a child to certain dictionary and encyclopedia skills. Besides serving as an aid in learning the names of letters and in recognizing each letter in its uppercase and lowercase forms, this book helps children to learn the alphabet in its consecutive arrangement of letters and to become familiar with the location of the letters in the alphabet in relationship to each other. Finally, *The International Visual Dictionary* can help the child appreciate the dictionary as a tool and as an interesting source of information, and can serve as an excellent classroom textbook introducing the student into the use of the dictionary.

The healthy pride of having a dictionary of one's own will not only motivate the child to use this new possession to uncover words, but the very adventure of word discovery will also spark or strengthen a determination to master the contents of *The International Visual Dictionary*.

Understandable, indeed, is the discouragement or frustration which can result from a student's finding a definition whose terms are not clear enough to comprehend the word being defined. To meet this problem the student should be instructed in the dictionary skill of looking up the meaning of those unclear words. Only if each word in every definition is also defined (as the limits and design of this kind of book will allow) in the same volume, can this procedure be implemented. It is for this reason that *The International Visual Dictionary* defines in some way all the words used in the dictionary and "Word-Usage Finder" sections.

Wordlist

Before *The International Visual Dictionary* wordlist took its final form, the author studied many published wordlists along with their related research (e.g., Buckingham, Dale, Dolch, Fitzgerald, Gates, Horn, Rinsland, Spache, Stone, etc.); he also consulted with many elementary school teachers, teachers of the English language, and school librarians; furthermore, he examined closely both children's textbooks and professional language art textbooks for the early elementary grades; and finally, he used his own personal experience as teacher and as director of guidance in an elementary school. Although the resulting wordlist can nowise be considered any kind of ideal vocabulary for the early elementary school grades, it can certainly be accepted as a basic wordlist adequate for achieving to a significant degree the abovementioned goals of this book.

Techniques

The International Visual Dictionary uses the following techniques to bring the meaning and usage of words to its reader: the simple explanation of the meaning of a word; illustrations; sentences providing contextual, experience, and summary clues; examples; synonyms and antonyms; synonymous phrases and antonymous phrases; and finally, time-honored nursery rhymes along with many original rhymes. The use of these techniques are often found in combinations of two or more.

For the most part, noun, verb, adjective, and adverb entries in *The International Visual Dictionary* are found respectively in their singular, infinitive, and positive forms (root forms). Commonly used inflectional or variant forms, however, are also presented as entries when these differ significantly from their root form.

Word-Usage Finder

Very often the meaning and usage of a word can be found outside its main entry. For example, the word "week" can be found not only under the entry *week* but also under the entries *be, calendar, check, day, event, fifth, first, Friday, got, hour, in, knew, last, make, Monday, move, order, past, picnic, Saturday, second, sheet, Sunday, Thursday, Tuesday, wages, wear,* and *Wednesday.* Being able to locate a word within entries different from its own main entry can direct the reader to other contexts within which further elucidation of meaning and more examples of usage can be found. It is precisely for this reason that an index called the "Word-Usage Finder" has been compiled.

The "Word-Usage Finder," besides indicating to the reader pages where a particular word can be found, provides other helpful information such as parts of speech (a special section on the sentence and parts of speech is provided after the "Word-Usage Finder" section); various senses; plural of nouns; past tense, past participle, and present participle of verbs; comparative and superlative degrees of adjectives; idiomatic usages; and cross-references to variant and inflectional forms.

Parents, teachers and adults of foreign-language background can use the "Word-Usage Finder" to locate for their children, for their students or for themselves, respectively, more examples of a particular word's usage. If, moreover, *The International Visual Dictionary* is used as a supplementary classroom textbook in the early elementary grades, the "Word-Usage Finder" can serve as an excellent introduction into the use of a book's index.

Cooperative Effort

It is not possible here to mention everyone who shared in the work of producing *The International Visual Dictionary.* Particular mention must be made, however, of a few whose patient and competent cooperation brought this book to completion: Jorge E. Cuellar, Efren Calderon Guzman, John Carroll, Alberto Herrmann, Rita Romagosa, Frances England, Barbara E. Wallace, Shirley Shipley, Phyllis Whetsel, Raymond Soria, Eugene Marino, Anthony Prosen, Robert DaVola, John Gallagher, Timothy Sullivan, Glenda Rollins, and Dan McMillan.

L.F.D.

This is the first letter of the alphabet.

A B C D E F G H I J K L M N O P Q R S T U V W X Y Z
a b c d e f g h i j k l m n o p q r s t u v w x y z

a John has **a** ball.
John has **one** ball.

---

able I **am able to** read.
I **can** read.

---

aboard

Peter is getting **aboard** the ship.
Peter is getting **on** the ship. Peter likes to travel. He has been aboard a train, a bus, and an airplane.

Aboard the boat, aboard the ship,
The whistle whistles, "Pip! Pip! Pip!"
Aboard the plane, aboard the car,
Propeller, wheel turn fast and far.

Aboard the bus, the motor sighs,
With lights like big wide-open eyes.
Aboard the train, the engine howls,
With loud and sad and sudden growls.

---

about Daddy told me a story **about** a horse.
Daddy told me a story **of** a horse.

The dog is **about** the house.
The dog is **somewhere near** the house.

When Mary came home, it was **about** three o'clock.
When Mary came home, it was **close to** three o'clock.

The wind blew the newspapers **about** the street.
The wind blew the newspapers **all over** the street.

James is **about** as tall as his father.
James is **almost** as tall as his father.

above The squirrel is **above** the boy.
The squirrel is **higher than** the boy. The bird is above both the squirrel and the boy.

> Above the boy up in the sky,
> A bluebird flies up there so high;
> Above the fence, above the wall,
> We see the squirrel's tail rise and fall.

---

absent

Thomas is **absent from** the table.
Thomas is **not present at** the table.
His father, mother, and sister are present at the table, but Thomas is not there. He is sick in bed.

---

accident Joan dropped a cup on the floor. The cup broke. She did not want to break the cup. It was an **accident.**

Mr. Smith's car ran into my father's car. Mr. Smith did not want to hit my father's car. It was an **accident.**

---

ache I have an **ache** in my back.
I have a **pain** in my back.

When my stomach **aches,** mother sometimes asks the doctor to come.

When my stomach **hurts,** mother sometimes asks the doctor to come.

3

acorn This is an **acorn**.  It is a seed from an oak tree.

---

across I ran **across** the street.
I ran **to the other side of** the street.

The pencil is lying **across** the ruler.

---

act Mother told Jimmy to **act** like a good boy.
Mother told Jimmy to **behave** like a good boy.

Mary puts on her mother's clothes and **acts** like a grown-up. Mary plays that she is a grown-up.

Joan **acted** the part of a clown in the school play.

Walking, jumping, eating, and all things that we do are called **acts**.

---

add If you **add** one apple to two apples, there will be three apples.

One apple **added to** two apples are three apples.
One apple **put together with** two apples are three apples.

$1 + 2 = 3$

We use this sign $+$ to show that we are **adding** things.

address   I wrote the **address of my friend Richard Smith** on a postcard.

I wrote the **place where my friend Richard Smith lives** on a postcard. The **address** will tell the postman where Richard lives. This is what I wrote on the postcard.

Dear Richard,
I am having a
good time at the
beach. I wish
you were here.
Your Friend,
Bob

POST·CARD

Richard Smith
43 Elmhurst St.
Unionville, Connecticut
06085

---

admire   Most girls **admire** pretty dresses.
Most girls **like** pretty dresses.

---

advice   My father gave me some good **advice** on how to play baseball better.
My father gave me some good **suggestions** on how to play baseball better.

---

afraid   The woman is **afraid** of the mouse.
The woman is **scared** of the mouse.

A girl's afraid of a little mouse
That runs around the floor and house;
A boy's not scared of mouse or rat,
He'll even put one in his hat.

Are you afraid of a mouse?
Does a mouse frighten you?

Africa

Africa is a land on the other side of the ocean. Most of the people who live in Africa have dark brown skin. This is a map of Africa.

---

after   The cat is running **after** the mouse.
The cat is running **behind** the mouse. Cats like to catch mice.

Richard came home **after** Judy did.
Richard came home **later than** Judy did.

Mother said to Richard, "Come home **right after school.**"
Mother said to Richard, "Come home **as soon as school is over.**"

---

afternoon   We eat lunch at twelve o'clock noon. After twelve o'clock noon is **afternoon.** Afternoon ends at sunset.

---

afterward   We must go to school first, but **afterward** we will go swimming.
We must go to school first, but **later** we will go swimming.

Both **afterward** and **afterwards** mean *at a later time.*

---

again   Please tell me that story **again.**
Please tell me that story **one more time.**

Margaret likes the story very much. She wants to hear it another time.

against   The ladder is leaning **against** the tree. One end of the ladder touches the tree. The other end of the ladder touches the ground.

William and Robert played **against each other** in the baseball game.

William and Robert played **on different teams** in the baseball game.

---

age   Carol asked, "What is your **age**, Tom? How old are you?"

Tom answered, "My **age** is ten. I am ten years old. When my next birthday comes, I shall be eleven years old."

---

ago   Grandmother was a little girl many years **ago**.

Grandmother was a little girl many years **in the past**.

The Bible was written a long time **ago**.

The Bible was written a long time **before now**.

I had a birthday five days **ago**.

I had a birthday five days **before today**.

---

agree   Both Sally and Mary like the doll.

Sally and Mary **agree**.

Sally and Mary **think alike**.

Sally likes the doll, but Bob does not like the doll.

Sally and Bob **do not agree**.

Sally and Bob **do not think alike**.

Will Sarah **agree** to come?

Will Sarah **be willing** to come?

Too much candy will not **agree with** me.

Too much candy will not **be good for** me.

ahead

The rabbit is **ahead of** the dog.
The rabbit is **in front of** the dog.

Paul's baseball team is **ahead.**
Paul's baseball team is **winning.**

---

aim I **aim** to work hard in school.
I **try** to work hard in school.

The hunter **aimed** the
gun at the tiger.
The hunter **pointed** the
gun at the tiger.

---

air There is **air** all over the earth. We breathe air. Birds and
airplanes fly through the air. We blow air into balloons.

My father puts air into the
automobile tires. Sometimes
Mother opens the window to
let some fresh air into the
house.

airplane An **airplane** is a flying machine with wings. An airplane must have an engine to make it fly. Some airplanes have engines with propellers. Other airplanes have jet engines without propellers. Jet engines make airplanes go very fast. There are many different kinds of airplanes.

---

airport

An **airport** is a place where airplanes take off and land.

When father travels by airplane, he goes to the airport where he buys his ticket and gets on an airplane.

---

alarm The **alarm** clock made a loud noise at seven o'clock in the morning. This noise lets us know it is time to get out of bed.

The alarm clock helps us to get to school on time. Here is an alarm clock.

A fire **alarm** warns people that there is a fire. A fire alarm calls the firemen to put out the fire.

If you yell, you will **alarm** your mother.
If you yell, you will **scare** your mother.

Alarm everyone that the house is on fire.
Warn everyone that the house is on fire.

alfalfa   **Alfalfa** is a plant with leaves like clover and with purple blossoms. Cattle and horses eat alfalfa.

---

alike   Robert and his father walk **alike**.
Robert and his father walk **in the same way.**

The lamps are **alike.**
The lamps are **the same.**

---

alive   The fish in the aquarium is **alive.**
The fish in the aquarium is **living.**

Fish must live in water. One fish jumped out of the water. It is now on the table. The fish on the table is not alive. The fish on the table is dead.

---

all   Someone ate **all** the pie.
Someone ate **every bit of** the pie.

I gave my mother **all** my pennies.
I gave my mother **every one of** my pennies.

It rained **all** day.
It rained **during the whole** day.

Billy has four birds, but there are only three birds in the cage. One bird flew away. Billy's birds are not **all** here.

alley

An **alley** is a narrow street which is between buildings. We have an alley on the side of our apartment building. There are garbage cans in the alley. We put our garbage in these cans.

An alley is a narrow street,
Where children go to play and meet,
Where boys play ball on the alley wall,
And girls jump rope and sing and call.

---

alligator

This is an **alligator.** Alligators live in water. They live where the weather is warm. Did you ever see an alligator at the zoo?

---

allow

I will **allow** Philip to ride my bicycle.
I will **let** Philip ride my bicycle.

---

almost

Henry has ten pennies. Albert has nine pennies.
Albert has **almost** as many pennies as Henry.
Albert has **nearly** as many pennies as Henry.

alone

Alice is **alone** in the empty room.
Alice is **not with anyone** in the empty room. She is by herself.

John can fix the table **alone**.
John can fix the table **by himself**.

Two and three are five. $2 + 3 = 5$

Sam asked his teacher, "Can two and three be four?"
The teacher answered, "No, five **alone** is the answer. There is only one answer. It is five."

---

along

Trees are planted **along the street**.
Trees are planted **from one end of the street to the other end of the street**.

Let us walk **along**.
Let us walk **forward**.

When Father goes fishing, I like to go **along**. I always ask if I can go.

---

alphabet

There are twenty-six letters in the **alphabet**. Here is the alphabet printed in capital letters.

A B C D E F G H I J K L M N O P Q R S T U V W X Y Z

The alphabet can also be printed in small letters.

a b c d e f g h i j k l m n o p q r s t u v w x y z

We put the letters of the alphabet together to make words. We read words in this book.

already Louise is not home.

She went to school **already**.
She went to school **before this time**.

It is very late.

We should be home **already**.
We should be home **by this time**.

Have you read the book **already**?
Have you read the book **so soon?**

---

also Sebastian has a bicycle.

Jane has a bicycle **also**.
Jane has a bicycle **too**.

I have a bright red bicycle;
Sebastian has one too.
My bicycle is fast and clean,
And also very new.

---

although **Although** it rained all day, we went on the picnic.
Even though it rained all day, we went on the picnic.

Although Patrick likes candy very much, he gave his candy to his baby sister.

---

aluminum **Aluminum** is a dull silver-colored metal. It is light in weight, but it is very strong. Airplanes are made of aluminum. Some pots and pans are made of aluminum, too.

---

always When the sun is shining, it is **always** light.
When the sun is shining, it is **at all times** light.

Night **always** follows day.

A a

am Paul said, "I **am** hungry. Are you hungry, Jack?" Jack answered, "Yes, I am hungry. Mary is hungry too." Mary said, "Since we are hungry, maybe we can eat dinner together."

Mother came into the room and said to Paul, Jack, and Mary, "Since you are hungry, I will prepare dinner for you." Paul, Jack, and Mary ate together. They are hungry no longer.

I **am** hungry.	We **are** hungry.
You **are** hungry.	You **are** hungry.
He **is** hungry.	They **are** hungry.

America This is a map of **America.**

The upper part of America is called North America. The lower part of America is called South America. The narrow part which joins North America and South America together is called Central America.

There are many countries in America. The United States of America is in North America. The United States is at times called **America.**

American I was born in America. I live in America too. I am an **American.**

The people of the United States are called **Americans.**

This is the **American** flag. It is the flag of the United States of America.

among  The dog is **among** the sheep. The dog has many sheep all around him. The sheep are in the pasture. They are eating the grass.

Some weeds are **among** the flowers in our garden.
Some weeds are **mixed with** the flowers in our garden.

Henry divided his candy **among** his three sisters. He gave some of his candy to each of them.

---

amount   John said, "I have some money."
Mary asked, "**What amount of money** do you have?"
Mary asked, "**How much money** do you have?" John answered, "The amount is five dollars. Five dollars is how much I have."

---

an   Mother gave me **an** apple.
Mother gave me **one** apple.

---

ancient   The castle is **ancient.**
The castle is **very old.**

---

and   We dance, **and** we sing.
We dance, **also** we sing.

One **and** two are three.
One **added to** two are three.

Jack **and** Jill went up the hill.
Jack **together with** Jill went up the hill.

angry   If you pull the dog's tail, he will become **angry**. He will growl and show his teeth. He might even bite you.

When someone stole my bicycle, I became very **angry**. Now I have no bicycle.

animal   My dog is an **animal**. My goldfish is an animal too. Animals are living things that move and breathe and eat. They have children like themselves.

Here are some animals that we can find on a farm.

Here are some animals that we can find in the forest.

Not all living things are animals. Plants are living. But they do not move about like animals. Plants are not animals.

ankle   My **ankle** is that part of my body between my foot and my leg. Bill hurt his ankle. He has a bandage around it.

annoy Does the noise **annoy** Eloise?

Does the noise **bother** Eloise? Can she read her book with all the noise?

---

another Susan asked, "May I have **another** apple?"

Susan asked, "May I have **one more** apple?"

Edward lost his pencil. He had to get **another**.

He had to get **a different one**.

Mother and Father are talking to **one another**. Mother is talking to Father, and Father is talking to Mother.

---

answer Mother asked this question, "Where is the cat?" John gave his Mother the **answer**, "The cat is in the kitchen."

When the teacher asks me my name, I will **answer** her, "My name is Martha Bradley."

Mother called to Ellen, but she did not **answer**. Ellen was sleeping.

Please **answer** the telephone. When the telephone rings, find out who is calling.

Please **answer** the door. Find out who is knocking at the door.

---

ant An **ant** is an insect. There are red ants, black ants, brown ants, and yellow ants. They are sometimes called bugs. Some ants live in the ground. Other ants live in wood.

any   There are ten books on the shelf.
You may take **any book.**
You may take **the one book that you want.**

Have you **any** money?
Have you **some** money?

---

anybody   I did not see **anybody** in the room.
I did not see **a person** in the room.

Anybody can come to Fred's party.
Any person can come to Fred's party.
Anyone can come to Fred's party.

Fred is going to have a big party. He said that anybody can come to it.

---

anyone   The old lady needs some help.
Is there **anyone** to help her?
Is there **somebody** to help her?

Yes, there is someone to help the old lady.
Here comes Edward. He will help her.

---

anything   Is there **anything** on the table?
Is there **something** on the table? Yes, there are many things on the table. The table has toys on it.

You may take **anything** from the table.
You may take **any one of the things** from the table.

Joan's toy does not look **anything** like Tom's toy.

Joan's toy does not look **at all** like Tom's toy. They are not alike.

anyway   It is cold outside, but we will go for a walk **anyway.**

---

anywhere   My dog wants to go **anywhere** I go.
My dog wants to go **any place** I go. He cannot go
everywhere I go. He cannot go to school with me.
He cannot go to church with me.

---

apart

Alice is standing **apart** from
the other children. She is
not near them.

Timothy took his bicycle **apart.** It is now in
many parts. Timothy's bicycle has many
pieces.

The dish fell **apart** when Sally dropped it on
the floor. The dish broke into many
pieces.

---

apartment   My family lives in an **apartment**. It has four rooms.
Our apartment is our home. Our apartment is in a big
apartment building.

---

apartment building

An **apartment building** is a
big house where many
families live. Each family
has rooms of its own.
These rooms are called an
apartment. This is an
apartment building.

ape   An **ape** is a kind of monkey. An ape does not have a tail.

appear   When the door opens, Sally will **appear.**
When the door opens, Sally will **come where she can be seen.**

When spring comes, the leaves will **appear** on the trees.
When spring comes, the leaves will **come out** on the trees.

Nick **appears** sick.
Nick **seems** sick.

apple    This is an **apple.** An apple is a fruit which grows on an apple tree. Apples are good to eat. Mother makes good apple pies.

April   **April** is the fourth month of the year. There are thirty days in April.

apron   Mother wears an **apron** when she works in the kitchen. An apron keeps the front part of her dress clean.

aquarium   The goldfish are in an **aquarium**.
The goldfish are in a **glass tank or bowl filled with water**.

Some aquariums are round. Others are in the shape of a box.

---

are   Patty asked, "How **are** you, David? How do you feel?" David answered, "I am well, thank you."

David and Patty **are** friends. They often go to school together. David said to Patty, "We **are** going to be late for school. We must hurry."

---

aren't   The children **aren't** home.
The children **are not** home.

---

arm

Robert is holding up one **arm**.
Loretta is holding up two arms.

Two arms I have—indeed it's so:
  They're plainly in my sight;
But not so clearly do I know
  My left one from my right.

The red and yellow chair has **arms,** but the black chair does not have arms. We can put our arms on the arms of the chair.

armchair   An **armchair** is a chair with arms on its sides.

---

army   There are many soldiers in the **army.** An army keeps us safe in our country. The soldiers in the army will fight in a war to protect us from an enemy.

---

around   Peter ran quickly **around** the house.
Peter ran quickly **along all sides of** the house.

The store is **around** the corner.
The store is **on the other side of** the corner.

The boys are **around** the fire.
The boys are **near** the fire.

The airplane flew **around and around** in the sky.
The airplane flew **in a circle** in the sky.

Ellen is coming home **around** six o'clock.
Ellen is coming home **about** six o'clock.

Daniel was walking away from me.
   He then turned **around** and looked at me.
   He then turned **in the opposite direction** and looked at me.

---

arrival   Our **arrival** surprised Grandmother.
Our **coming** surprised Grandmother.

---

arrive   The bus will **arrive** at ten o'clock.
The bus will **come** at ten o'clock.

We shall **arrive at** the party early.
We shall **get to** the party early.

arrow  This is an **arrow**. It is a pointed stick that is shot from a bow.

This is also an **arrow**. This arrow is a sign which tells us where the zoo is.

---

art The **art** teacher shows the students how to draw and paint pictures. She teaches **art**.

My mother took me to the museum where there are many beautiful statues and paintings. They are works of **art**.

Playing the piano and sewing are **arts**.

---

as Albert laughed **as** he always laughs.
Albert laughed **in the way that** he always laughs.

Patricia sings **as** she works.
Patricia sings **while** she works.

We arrived at school **as** the doors were closing.
We arrived at school **when** the doors were closing.

John ran **as** quickly **as** he could. He could not run any faster.

---

ashamed Albert hit his baby sister, and he made her cry. She is just a little girl and she cannot protect herself. Albert knows he did something wrong. He is unhappy because he did wrong. He is **ashamed** that he hit his baby sister and made her cry.

---

ashes **Ashes** are what is left after something has been burned. Grandfather took the ashes out of his pipe.

aside

When the very angry dog entered the room, the children moved **aside**.

When the very angry dog entered the room, the children moved **away**.

Jane puts **aside** her pretty dress for going to church. She only wears her pretty dress to church.

---

ask Henry wants a cookie. He will **ask** his mother for it. He will say, "Mother, may I have a cookie?"

Mary likes to **ask** her mother questions about cooking food. She wants to be a good cook. Her mother is always happy to answer Mary's questions.

---

asleep The girl is **asleep**. She is sleeping in her bed. The dog is asleep too. Both the girl and the dog are not awake.

---

astronaut An **astronaut** is a pilot or passenger on a spaceship. This is an astronaut. He is floating in space outside his spaceship.

at Father asked, "Where are the children?"
Mother answered, "They are still **at** school."
Father then asked, "When will they come home?"
Mother replied, "They will come home **at** four o'clock."

Paul threw a stone **at** the bird.
Paul threw a stone **in the direction of** the bird.

---

ate Yesterday Tommy **ate** ice cream for dessert. He likes to eat dessert. Today he is eating cherry pie for dessert. Tommy does not know what he will eat for dessert tomorrow.

---

atoms **Atoms** are the smallest possible bits that all things are made of. They are so tiny that we cannot see them.

---

attention Patty yelled to get Mary's **attention**.
Patty yelled to get Mary **to look at her**.

To **pay attention** means to *notice and think carefully about what is being said or done*. The teacher says to the children, "Pay attention to what I am teaching you."

---

attic The **attic** is the space or room just under the roof of a house. This is an attic.

Have you an attic in your house,
Where many things are kept:
A dusty room that's near the roof;
A place that's seldom swept?

August   **August** is the eighth month of the year. There are thirty-one days in August.

---

aunt   My father's sister is my **aunt.** My mother's sister is also my **aunt.** My uncle's wife is my **aunt,** too.

---

auto   **Auto** is a short word for automobile. I like to ride in an auto.

---

automobile   This is our **automobile.** It is red. We often ride in our automobile. An automobile does not have to be pushed or pulled. It has a motor to make it go. Somebody must drive an automobile to make it go. Daddy drives our automobile.

---

autumn   **Autumn** is the season between summer and winter. It is the time of the year between the warm weather and the cold weather. Autumn is also called fall. There are four seasons of the year: summer, autumn, winter, and spring.

---

avenue   An **avenue** is a wide street.

aviator An **aviator** is a man who flies an airplane. An aviator is also called a pilot.

awake At what time do you **awake** in the morning?
At what time do you **wake up** in the morning?

Yesterday Priscilla **awoke** at seven o'clock.

Henry is **awake.**
Henry is **not asleep**.

away The dog ran **away.**
The dog ran **to another place.**

Mary is **away.** She is not home.
Mary is **in another place.** She is not home.

Go home **right away** before it starts raining.
Go home **immediately** before it starts raining. If you do not leave here at once and without delay, you will get wet.

awhile Billy stayed **awhile** at our house.
Billy stayed **for some time** at our house. He likes to visit our family.

ax

This is an **ax.** It is used for cutting wood. An ax has a heavy metal part and a long wooden part. The metal part is very sharp. The wooden part is the handle. Some people spell ax this way: **axe.**

This is the second letter of the alphabet.

ABCDEFGHIJKLMNOPQRSTUVWXYZ

abcdefghijklmnopqrstuvwxyz

baa   A sheep says, "**Baa, baa.**"

---

babies   Nancy has two new **babies** in her house. One baby is named Albert. The other baby is named Anthony. They are her new twin brothers.

---

baby    Mother is holding a **baby.** A baby is a very young child who cannot walk or talk.

Where should a baby rest?   Lulla, lulla, lullaby,
Where but on its mother's arms?   Softly sleep, my baby.
Where can a baby lie   Lulla, lulla, lullaby,
Half so safe from every harm?   Softly sleep, my baby.

---

back   Jimmy is riding on the pony's **back.**

Danny likes to ride on Daddy's **back.**

Look at how the car is in the garage. Father cannot turn the car around in the garage. He must **back** the car out of the garage.

Mother will **be back** soon.
Mother will **return** soon.

B b

backward Robert is falling backward off the stool. He will fall on his back.

Andrew can walk backwards. He walks with his back first. It is not safe to walk backwards.

Nancy can count **backwards.** She says, "10, 9, 8, 7, 6, 5, 4, 3, 2, 1."

Nancy can also count forward. She says, "1, 2, 3, 4, 5, 6, 7, 8, 9, 10."

Backward and **backwards** mean the same thing.

---

bacon **Bacon** is a meat that comes from the side of a pig. The meat is first covered with salt. Then it is kept in a smoky room for a while. In the morning I have bacon and eggs.

---

bad David did a **bad** thing because he told his mother a lie. He did not do a good thing in telling a lie.

This apple is **bad.** It is becoming brown and soft. This apple is old and spoiled. It is not good to eat.

This apple is good. It is red and hard. This apple is fresh. It is good to eat.

Green apples are **bad** for you. They make you sick.

---

badly Annette sings **badly.** She does not sing well. Annette does not have a good voice. When she sings, it is not pretty music.

30

bag   A **bag** is used for carrying things. There are many kinds of bags. Mother carries her money in a handbag. She carries food from the grocery in a paper bag. Sand is often put in a cloth bag.

baggage

Trunks, suitcases, and bags are called **baggage.** We put clothes and other things in them when we take a trip. The porter is putting our baggage on the train.

bait   When Ralph goes fishing, he puts **bait** on his fishhook. He puts a worm as bait on his fishhook. Fish like to eat worms. When a fish tries to eat the worm, it gets caught on the fishhook. This is how Ralph catches fish.

bake   Mother will **bake a cake.**
Mother will **cook a cake in the oven.** She **baked** some cookies for us yesterday.

31

B b

baker A **baker** makes cookies, bread, pies, and cakes. He cooks them in a big oven. The baker sells what he bakes. We often buy bread at the bakery.

We ordered a birthday cake from the baker.

---

bakery A **bakery** is a place where cookies, bread, pies, and cakes are made and sold. I like to go to the bakery to buy some cookies.

---

balance This man is walking on a rope which is made very tight. He is trying to keep his **balance**. If he does not keep his balance, he will fall.

Both sides of the scale **balance**.
Both sides of the scale **weigh the same**.

Can you **balance** a stick on the tip of your finger?

---

bald Father's head is **bald**.
Father's head is **without hair**.

---

bale  A **bale** of cotton is a big bundle of cotton tied tightly together.

Wool and hay are also made into **bales**.

ball   Each **ball** in this picture is round. There are many kinds of balls. Most balls are round.

balloon

Oscar has a red **balloon.** Martha's balloon is floating away. Sometimes balloons are filled with a gas. The gas makes them rise and float. Sometimes balloons are filled with air. Balloons with air in them do not rise and float.

banana   This is a **banana.** It is a fruit. Bananas grow in large bunches on trees. Bananas cannot grow where the weather gets cold.

band

These men playing music are a **band.**

Father's hat has a red **band** around it.

B b

bandage

A **bandage** is a band or strip of cloth used to wrap around cuts and other wounds. Harold cut his finger. Mother put a bandage around his finger to keep the cut clean.

---

bang   Betty closed the door with a **bang.**
Betty closed the door with a **loud noise.**

---

bank   A **bank** is a place to keep money.
I keep my money in a piggy bank.

Mother and Father keep their money in the city **bank.** It is a big building.

The ground at the edge of the river is called the **bank** of the river.

We stood on the **bank** of the lake.
We stood on the **shore** of the lake.

---

bar   Father is lifting the lid of the box with a metal **bar.**

Here is a **bar** of soap.

Here is a **bar** of chocolate candy.

---

barber   A **barber** cuts hair. When my hair gets too long, I go to the barber to have it cut. The barber sometimes shaves my daddy.

bare   Frank's feet were **bare** when he took off his shoes and socks.

The cupboard is **bare**.
The cupboard is **empty**.

---

barefoot   John walked around **barefoot.** He walked about without shoes or stockings on.

---

barely   We had **barely** enough wood to make the birdhouse.
We had **scarcely** enough wood to make the birdhouse.

---

bark   **Bark** covers the outside of a tree. Bark is very hard. It protects the tree. Bark is like a coat for a tree.

Dogs **bark.** They make loud sounds. Seals bark, too. My dog barks, "Bow-wow."

---

barn   A **barn** is a building on a farm. In the barn, the farmer keeps his horses and cows. He also puts food for his animals in the barn.

In many barns, hay is stored on the second floor. Animals are kept in stalls on the first floor.

---

barnyard   The yard around the barn is called the **barnyard.** Sometimes the cows and horses come out of the barn into the barnyard.

B b

barrel

This is a **barrel.** It is round and made of wood. There are metal strips wrapped around the barrel to hold it together.

A barrel is flat on the ends and a little larger in the middle than at the ends. Some people keep pickles in a barrel.

---

baseball

Baseball is a game. You need a bat and a ball to play baseball. These boys are playing baseball.

A **baseball** is also one kind of a ball.

---

basement

The lowest part of a building is called a **basement.** Usually it is partly below the ground. The basement is sometimes called a cellar. The furnace is in the basement of our house. Not every house has a basement.

---

basket

This is a **basket** filled with apples. We put our Easter eggs in a basket. Many baskets are made of wood or twigs or grasses. Sometimes baskets are made of wire.

basketball

These boys are playing the game called **basketball.** There are two teams. At each end of the playing space, there is a basket. Each team tries to get the ball in its own basket.

The basket is placed high over the heads of the players. The baskets do not have any bottoms.

The team that gets the ball in its own basket the most times wins the game.

The ball they play with is called a **basketball.**

---

bat A **bat** is a furry little animal that flies at night. It looks like a mouse with wings. Some bats eat fruit. Other bats eat insects. A bat is not a bird.

In playing baseball, a **bat** is used to hit the ball.

It is Bob's turn to **bat.** It is Bob's turn to try to hit the ball with the bat. In the game of baseball, Bob likes to bat.

B b

bath Ralph is taking a **bath** in the bathtub. He is washing his body with soap and water.

---

bathroom This is a **bathroom.** In the bathroom there is a bathtub, shower, sink, and toilet.

Scrub, scrub, in the tub,
  And wash with soap and water.
Splash, splash, in the bath;
  Be clean, oh, son and daughter.

---

bathtub We take a bath in a **bathtub.** The bathtub is in the bathroom.

---

bay A **bay** is part of the sea. It is water with much land around it. A lake has land all around it.

A bay does not have land all around it. It has an opening to the sea. From the sea, the boat sailed into the bay.

be   Mother said, "**Be** a good boy, Charles." "I will be good, Mother," Charles answered. Charles has **been** good all week. When Charles is **being** good, he is making his mother and father very happy. Everybody should be good.

I am good.   We are good.
You are good.   You are good.
He is good.   They are good.

---

beach   A **beach** is the flat, sandy land at the edge of the water. There are beaches next to oceans, rivers, and lakes. The children like to play in the sand on the beach.

---

bead   A **bead** is a small round ball with a hole in it. A string is put through the hole in the bead. Nancy likes to put many beads on a string. Mother sometimes wears beads around her neck.

When the string of Mother's beads broke, the beads rolled off in many directions. Her string of beads is called a necklace.

---

bean

A **bean** is the seed of a bean plant. Beans are a vegetable. They are good to eat. Beans grow in a pod. These are pods with beans in them.

Sometimes we eat only the beans. Sometimes we eat both pods and beans.

Did you ever hear the story of *Jack and the Beanstalk?*

B b

bear

A **bear** is a large wild animal. It is covered with much hair. A bear's tail is very short. Its paws are large and flat.

Bears are white, brown, or black. Did you ever see a bear at the zoo?

---

beard

This man has **a beard.**

This man has **hair growing on his chin and face.**

My father shaves his beard every day.

---

beast

A **beast** is an animal with four feet. Lions and elephants are beasts. At the zoo, there are many wild beasts.

---

beat

Hubert likes to **beat** his drum.
Hubert likes to **strike** his drum.

The bad boy **beats his dog.**
The bad boy **hits his dog again and again.**

Tim **beat** Dick in the race. Tim won the race. Dick lost the race.

Mother will **beat** the eggs. She will put the eggs into a bowl. Then she will mix them together very fast.

Did you ever hear a heart **beat?** It goes, "Thump, thump." Sometimes I put my ear to Mark's chest and listen to his heart **beating.**

beautiful The flower is **beautiful.**
The flower is **nice to look at.**

---

beaver

A **beaver** is an animal with brown fur and a flat tail. It lives in ponds and streams.

Beavers cut down trees with their teeth. They use the trees to make their homes in the water.

The fur of the beaver is used for coats and hats. These are beavers.

---

became The acorn **became** a tree.
The acorn **grew into** a tree.

The weather **became** cold.
The weather **turned** cold.

What **became** of my book? What happened to it? Where can my book be?

---

because Why didn't David go to school? David didn't go to school **because** he was sick. **"Because"** tells why.

---

become If you eat too much candy, you will **become** sick.
If you eat too much candy, you will **come to be** sick.

I must stop eating candy because I am **becoming** sick.

John **became** sick because he ate too much candy.

B b

bed   This is a **bed.** We sleep in beds.

Mother has a **bed** of tulips in her garden. She has a part of her garden just for tulips.

---

bedroom   A **bedroom** is a room for sleeping. My bed is in my bedroom.

---

bedtime   Susan's **bedtime** is at nine o'clock.

Susan's **time to go to bed** is at nine o'clock.

---

bee

A **bee** is an insect with wings. A bee buzzes when it flies. A bee will sting us if it thinks that we are going to hurt it. Some bees make honey. They keep the honey in their home. Their home is called a hive.

Buzz, buzz, the busy bee,
  Working for many hours
Honey to make for you and me
  By gathering from the flowers.

---

beef   **Beef** is meat from cattle. For dinner mother cooked us a roast of beef.

---

been   John **has been** a good boy today.

John **was** a good boy today.

beet  A **beet** is a plant that has green leaves and a large red root. It is a vegetable. We call the roots of beet plants beets. Mother often cooks beets for dinner. Some people cook and eat the leaves of the beet plant.

Some sugar is made from sugar beets. Sugar beets have white roots.

---

beetle A **beetle** is an insect with four wings. The top pair of wings are small and hard. They are not used for flying. They cover and protect the other pair of wings which are used for flying.

Farmers do not like many beetles because they eat leaves, fruits, and vegetables. Beetles destroy plants in the farmer's garden.

Birds like to eat beetles.

---

before Philip arrived **before** Terence did.
Philip arrived **earlier than** Terence did.

I never played baseball **before**.
I never played baseball **at any time in the past**.

Majorie went **before** Helen.
Majorie went **in front of** Helen.

---

beg Do not **beg Mother** for candy.
Do not **ask Mother again and again** for candy. She will give you some candy after dinner.

Yesterday the dog sat up and **begged** for something to eat. Now he is **begging** again.

B b

began   The baby **began** to cry.
The baby **started** to cry.

---

begin   **Begin** to run when I say, "Go!"
Start to run when I say, "Go!"

The baby **began** to cry when she heard the loud noise.

Mother said, "Be quiet. Judy is **beginning** to awake."

I haven't **begun** cleaning my room.

---

beginner   A **beginner** is a person who tries to do something for the first time.

Ralph has taken piano lessons for three years, but Barbara is just a beginner. She just started taking lessons today.

---

behave   Father says that a boy must **behave** like a gentleman.
Father says that a boy must **act** like a gentleman.

The teacher told the children to **behave**.
The teacher told the children to **act well**.

---

behind   The mailman is **behind** with his mail.
The mailman is **late** with his mail.

Mildred walked **behind** Gerald.
Mildred walked **in back of** Gerald.

Little Bo-peep has lost her sheep,
And doesn't know where to find them;
Leave them alone, and they'll come home,
Wagging their tails behind them.

---

being   Mother gave Paul some candy for **being** good. He behaved. He did what his mother told him. He was a good boy.

44

belief A **belief** is anything we think is true.

It's Paul's **belief** that it is going to snow. He thinks that it will snow.

I have a **belief** in God. I know that there is a God. I know that God will take care of me.

---

believe We **believe** what Fred told us. We think that what Fred told us is true.

I **believe** that Harriet is smart.
I **think** that Harriet is smart.

I **believe in** my mother and father.
I **trust** my mother and father. I know that they will do what is best for me.

When Sarah **makes believe** that she is a nurse, she acts like a nurse. She only plays that she is a nurse. Sarah pretends that she is a nurse. Sarah is not really a nurse.

---

bell This is a **bell.** The bell in the church tower rings on Sunday.

When people come to visit us, they ring our doorbell.

Hear the church bell in the tower
　Calling us to prayer.
Hear it ringing on the hour:
　Now thank God for his care.

---

belong To whom does this book **belong?** Who owns this book?

This book **belongs** to Bob. It is owned by Bob.

The broom **belongs** in the kitchen.
The broom **is kept** in the kitchen. When we are not using the broom, its place is in the kitchen.

B b

below The earth is **below** the clouds. The clouds are above the earth.

Ann's grade was **below** sixty.
Ann's grade was **less than** sixty. Ann got a grade of fifty on her test.

I have a pain **below** my eye.
I have a pain **in a place lower than** my eye.

---

belt A **belt** is a strip of leather or cloth. Father wears a belt around his waist. He wears a belt to keep up his trousers.

Belts are used on some machines. Machine belts make wheels turn.

---

bench

The lady is sitting on a **bench.**

My father has a long table in the basement. He calls the table a **bench.** On this table he makes things, and he fixes things. Sometimes he calls this table a workbench.

bend There was a **bend** in the road.
There was a **curve** in the road.

Jack is trying to **bend** the metal bar.
Jack is trying to **make crooked** the metal bar.

It is hard for a fat boy to **bend over.** Ernest is trying to tie his shoe.

Yesterday Eugene **bent** the stick and broke it.

---

beneath The rat is **beneath** the chair.
The rat is **under** the chair.

Beneath the chair, so frightened there,
  Is a shivering little rat,
Who fears to meet and be the treat
  Of the hungry pussy cat.

---

bent Yesterday William **bent** the long stick and broke it. You cannot **bend** a stick too much without breaking it.

---

berry A **berry** is a small juicy fruit with many seeds. There are many kinds of berries. Here are some blackberries and strawberries.

BLACKBERRY

STRAWBERRY

B b

beside   The dog is sitting **beside** Charles.
The dog is sitting **at the side of** Charles. The dog loves Charles very much. He likes to sit close to Charles.

I put my shoes **beside** my slippers.
I put my shoes **close to** my slippers.

---

besides   Vegetables are good for me. I like them **besides**.
Vegetables are good for me. I like them **also**.

Patrick got a bicycle for his birthday, **besides** a baseball and other presents.
Patrick got a bicycle for his birthday, **also** a baseball and other presents.

Besides the apples, Mother also bought some pears and oranges.

---

best   Sally got a good grade on her test. She got eighty on her test. Marvin got a better grade. He got ninety on his test. Ruth got the **best** grade. She got a hundred on her test. Nobody else in the class got as good a grade as Ruth.

Ruth got the **best** grade of all the children. She got a better grade than Marvin. She got a better grade than Sally.

I like candy, cake, and ice cream, but I like candy **best**.
I like candy, cake, and ice cream, but I like candy **the most**.

---

bet   Joe **bet** five cents that Jim's team would win. Tom bet five cents that Jim's team would lose. Jim's team won; so Joe paid Tom five cents.

better Milton fishes **better** than John. Milton caught ten fish. John only caught two fish. Milton has more fish than John. Milton is the better fisherman.

Joan was sick yesterday, but now she is **better.**

Joan was sick yesterday, but now she is **not so sick.**

---

between

There is a fence **between** the two houses.

There is a fence **which separates** the two houses.

Father divided the candy **between** Gordon and Ralph. Father had ten pieces of candy. He gave Gordon five pieces of candy. He gave Ralph five pieces of candy.

---

beyond The town is **beyond** the hill.
The town is **on the other side of** the hill.

Billy walked **beyond** the store.
Billy walked **farther than** the store.

---

bib A **bib** is a napkin for babies. It is a piece of cloth which covers the front part of Baby. Mother ties a bib around Baby's neck. A bib keeps Baby clean when she eats.

B b

Bible   The **Bible** is a book. God speaks to us when we read the Bible. In church we read the Bible. The Bible has two parts: the Old Testament and the New Testament.

---

bicycle   George is riding his **bicycle.** A bicycle has two wheels.

I learned to ride a bicycle
When I was very small.
Said I before, and say I still,
"How often I did fall!"

---

big

The elephant is **big.**
The elephant is **large.**

There is a bird on the elephant's back. The bird is very small. There is a horse near the elephant. The elephant is **bigger** than the horse. The elephant is the **biggest** of the three.

---

bill   The bird has a worm in his **bill.** The bill is the bird's mouth. The bird uses his bill to pick up food.

A **bill** is a piece of paper which tells us how much money we must pay for something.

A dollar **bill** is paper money. It is worth one hundred cents.

bird   A **bird** is an animal with wings and feathers. Most birds can fly. They fly with their wings.

---

birdhouse

There is a **birdhouse** in our yard.
There is a **house for the birds** in our yard.
Some birds build their nests in a birdhouse.

> A sparrow's in the birdhouse;
> It's there he'll make his nest.
> He'll work all day with straw and hay,
> And then at night he'll rest.

---

birthday   John is eight years old today. It is his **birthday**. John was born eight years ago on this same day in this same month. Do you know when your birthday is?

---

biscuit   A **biscuit** is a small cake of bread.

Sometimes Mother bakes biscuits for us. We love to eat hot biscuits with butter spread on them.

---

bit   Teresa gave Judy a **bit** of candy.
Teresa gave Judy a **small piece** of candy.

Yesterday Sarah **bit** into a bad apple. Did you ever bite into a bad apple?

B b

bite  Carl asked Stephen for a **bite** of his apple. Carl put his teeth into Stephen's apple and took away a piece of it. Look at Stephen's apple. Carl took a bite out of it.

Be careful! That dog will **bite you in the leg.**
Be careful! That dog will **put his teeth into your leg.**

Yesterday the dog **bit** Harold. Two days ago Sally was **bitten** by the same dog.

I got a mosquito **bite** on my arm. A mosquito gave me a sting on the arm.

---

bitten Kenneth was **bitten** on the leg by the angry dog. Ronald saw the dog bite Kenneth.

---

bitter **Bitter** things do not taste good. The outside of an orange is bitter. Some medicines are bitter.

There were **bitter** cries from the children when they could not watch the movie.
There were **unhappy** cries from the children when they could not watch the movie.

---

black **Black** is a color. Coal is black. My father is wearing a black tie. He has a piece of coal in his hand.

The words in this book are printed in **black.**

When the lights went out, it was **black** in the room. It was very dark. The room was without lights.

blackberry A **blackberry** is a dark purple fruit that grows on a bush. Blackberries are small and juicy. They have many seeds. These are blackberries.

---

blackbird This is a **blackbird.** Most blackbirds are all black. Some blackbirds have some red on their wings.

Sing a song of sixpence,
  A pocket full of rye;
Four and twenty blackbirds
  Baked in a pie.

When the pie was opened,
  The birds began to sing;
Was not that a dainty dish,
  To set before the king.

---

blackboard

A **blackboard** is a smooth, dark board that you can write on with chalk. Some blackboards are black. Other blackboards are green. At school the teacher writes on the blackboard.

---

blade The **blade** of the knife is sharp. The silver part of the knife is the blade.

The part of the knife that you hold is the handle. The blade of the knife cuts through the pie.

A long and flat leaf is called a **blade.** We gave the cows blades of grass to eat.

B b

blame   Who is **to blame** for breaking the vase?
Who is **at fault** for breaking the vase? The cat is to be blamed for breaking the vase. The cat pushed the vase onto the floor. Joan said, "Do not put the blame on me. Blame the cat."

---

blanket

The blue **blanket** on Tony's bed keeps him warm.
The blue **cover** on Tony's bed keeps him warm.

In the winter the snow covers the ground like a **blanket.**

---

blaze   When wood burns, it makes a **blaze.**
When wood burns, it makes **bright flames.**

Did you see the big fire **blaze** high into the air?
Did you see the big fire **burn with bright flames** high into the air?

---

blew   The fan **blew** the papers off the desk.
The fan **made the air push** the papers off the desk. Put something heavy on the papers so that the fan will not blow them off the desk again.

When Daddy **blew** the horn of the car, it made a loud noise.

Jimmy **blew** his whistle.

When I had a cold, I **blew** my nose often.

Patrick **blew up** his balloon.
Patrick **put air into** his balloon.

blind   If you look at the bright sun too long, it will **blind** you. You will not be able to see for a while.

The old man **is blind.**
The old man **cannot see.**

---

blink   I had to **blink** when the bright light shined in my eyes.
I had to **open and close my eyes quickly** when the bright light shined in my eyes.

---

block   Paul holds a **block** in each hand.
He likes to play with blocks.
Paul builds things with blocks.

The tree fell across the street. It **blocked** the street so that the cars could not pass.

There are stores and houses in our **block.**

B b

blood **Blood** is a liquid that goes through my body. The moving blood keeps my body alive. My heart keeps my blood moving. Blood is red when it is in the air. When Judy cut her finger, blood came from the cut.

---

bloom Flowers **bloom** in the spring.
Flowers **come out of buds** in the spring.

When a plant has flowers, we say it is in **bloom.**

---

blossom This is a **blossom.**
This is a **flower.** It is a rose.

Flowers **blossom** in the spring.
Flowers **come out of buds** in the spring.

---

blow Let the fan **blow into** my face.
Let the fan **make air move against** my face.

When I get a cold, I
blow my nose often.

Nancy is **blowing** out the candle.

Philip will **blow up** the balloon.
Philip will **put air into** the balloon.

Daddy **blew** the horn of his car.

blue   **Blue** is a color. Sally is wearing a blue dress.

> A little girl named Sally Sue
>   Liked to dress in the color blue.
> To read a book, she loved to do,
>   And the more she read the more she knew.

Kevin feels **blue** today.
Kevin feels **sad** today.

---

bluebird

This bird is a **bluebird.** It has a blue back and blue wings. A bluebird's breast is orange.

---

blue jay   This bird is a **blue jay.** It is mostly blue. But a blue jay has also some white and black on its feathers. Blue jays are noisy birds.

---

board

A **board** is a flat piece of wood cut from a log. The carpenter nails the boards to the side of the house.

B b

boast   Shirley likes to **boast**.

Shirley likes to **talk very much about herself**. She likes to tell people about the good things she can do. People do not like to hear her boast.

---

boat   We ride on the water in a **boat**. A large boat is called a ship. There are many kinds of boats. This is a rowboat.

---

body   All the parts of a human being or an animal are called a **body**. Hubert's body is dark brown. Hubert lives in Africa. Carl's body is light pink. Carl lives in Holland.

A **body** is an amount of something all together.

An ocean is a large **body of water**.
An ocean is a large **amount of water all together**.

---

boil   When water gets very hot, it will **boil**.
When water gets very hot, it will **steam and bubble**.

Mother sometimes **boils** eggs.

The pot has **boiling** water in it.

Charles has a **boil** on his arm.
Charles has a **sore** on his arm.

bone

The dog likes to chew a **bone.** Bones are hard. Animals have bones in their bodies. People have bones in their bodies, too.

---

bonnet

Baby has her blue **bonnet** on.
Baby has her blue **hat** on.

Babies and little girls often wear bonnets.

---

book   This is a **book.**

The dictionary you are now reading is a book. It has sheets of paper which are fastened together at one side. The sheets of paper are called pages.

There is a hard cover at the beginning and at the end of this book.

Alice is reading a book. Her book tells a story. Some books have pictures in them.

---

bookcase   A **bookcase** is a cupboard for putting books in. Paul puts the book in the bookcase.

Some bookcases have glass doors.

B b

boom   A **boom** is a loud sound. The children heard the boom of the thunder.

---

boot   A **boot** is a kind of shoe. Some boots are made of rubber. Other boots are made of leather. There are several kinds of boots. We wear boots in snow and water. We also wear boots when we ride horses.

---

border   Janet's yellow handkerchief has a red and white **border** around it.
Janet's yellow handkerchief has a red and white **edge** around it.

A road **borders** the field.
A road **is next to** the field.

---

born   Ann's new baby brother was **born** this morning.
Ann's new baby brother was **brought into the world** this morning. Yesterday Ann did not have a baby brother. He was born today.

Ann was **born** eight years ago.
Ann was **brought into the world** eight years ago.

---

borrow   I will **borrow** Gerald's bicycle. I will use Gerald's bicycle for a time, and then I will give it back.

both John has an apple in **both his** hands.

John has an apple in **his two** hands. He has one apple in each of his two hands. John is holding two apples.

Henry and Paul came into the kitchen. **Both** of them came into the kitchen to get some milk and cookies.

---

bother If my dog jumps up and barks, it will **bother** Mother. She does not like to see the dog get excited.

We did not **bother** to look for the hat.
We did not **take the trouble** to look for the hat.

---

bottle  This is a **bottle**. Most bottles are made of glass.

Mike drank a small bottle of orange juice. He drank all the orange juice that was in the small bottle.

---

bottom Mary is standing at the **bottom** of the ladder. Mary's daddy is at the top of the ladder. Mary's daddy is painting the house.

Jack got a small nail in the **bottom** of his shoe.
Jack got a small nail in the **under part** of his shoe.

The book is on the **bottom** shelf.
The book is on the **lowest** shelf.

B b

bough   The bird is on the **bough** of the tree.
The bird is on the **branch** of the tree.

---

bought   Helen **bought** some candy for five cents. Helen paid five cents and got some candy. Helen likes to **buy** candy.

---

bounce   Timothy likes to **bounce** his rubber ball. When he drops his ball, it bounces up and down. His rubber ball jumps up and down.

Bill **bounces** out of bed in the morning.
Bill **jumps** out of bed in the morning.

---

bounded   Tommy **bounded** out of his chair when he heard the telephone ring.
Tommy **leaped** out of his chair when he heard the telephone ring.

---

bow

Rebecca has a red **bow** in her hair.

The Indian is pulling the string of his **bow.** He is going to shoot an arrow.

bow   The children **bow** their heads when they say their prayers. The children **bend down** their heads when they say their prayers.

---

bowl   A **bowl** is a deep, round dish. We eat soup from a bowl. Jack is eating soup out of a red bowl.

Jack likes to eat a bowl of soup for lunch. Mother fills up the red bowl, and Jack eats all the soup in it.

---

bow-wow   When the dog barks, he says, "**Bow-wow.**"

---

box      Some shoes are in the brown **box.** A hat is in the red box. These are boxes.

---

boy   Jimmy is a small **boy.** His daddy is a man. When Jimmy grows up, he will be a man. All men were boys at one time.

> What are little boys made of, made of?
> What are little boys made of?
> Frogs and snails and puppy dogs' tails;
> And that's what little boys are made of, made of.

---

branch   A **branch** is a part of a tree. Branches grow out of the trunk of a tree. Leaves grow on the branches of a tree. The squirrel is sitting on the branch.

B b

brass   **Brass** is a metal. It is yellow. Sometimes bells and bowls are made of brass.

---

brave   Policemen are **brave**.
Policemen are **not afraid**.

---

bread   This is a loaf of **bread**. Bread is made from flour. It is baked in an oven. Mother sometimes gives me a slice of bread with butter on it. I like to eat bread and butter.

---

break   Peter did not mean to **break** the dish. It was an accident. Peter dropped the dish on the floor and it came apart into many pieces.

The children sometimes **break** the rules of the school.
The children sometimes **do not keep** the rules of the school.

Stanley **broke** his glass. Some of the cups were **broken,** too.

---

breakfast   **Breakfast** is the first meal of the day. When I get up in the morning, I eat my breakfast.

---

breast

Richard put his hand on his **breast**.
Richard put his hand on his **chest**.

breath A **breath** is air which you take in and let out through your nose and mouth. Did you ever blow out a candle with your breath?

---

breathe You **breathe** when you take in air and then let it out again through your nose and mouth. When you run, you breathe fast.

---

breeze A **breeze** is a little wind. The breeze blew the leaves around.

---

brick This is a **brick.** It is made from clay or mud. Bricks are baked in an oven to make them hard. Some houses are made of bricks.

Did you ever see a brick wall? Can you name some other things that are made from brick?

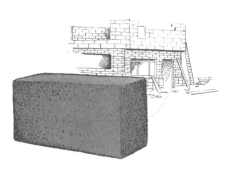

---

bridge

This is a **bridge.** It is built over water. Automobiles and people cross over the water on the bridge.

B b

bright   The sun is **bright.**
The sun is **very shiny.**

Sometimes the moon **is bright.**
Sometimes the moon **gives much light.**

Milton is a **bright** boy.
Milton is a **smart** boy.

---

bring   Susan will **bring** the book to us.
Susan will **carry** the book to us.

Clouds often **bring** rain.
Clouds often **cause** rain.

---

broad   The blue book is **broad.**
The blue book is **wide.** The yellow
book is narrow.

---

broadcast

Mr. Smith will **broadcast** the news. He will send
out the news by radio and television. We can
hear and see the broadcast of the news on our
radio or television.

The man broadcasting the news is far away.
He is in the broadcasting station. Still, we
can hear him talk over our radio. We can
see him on our television.

---

broil   John likes to **broil meat.**
John likes to **cook meat over a fire.**

broke Mother dropped the cup and **broke** it. The cup came apart into pieces when it fell on the floor. Mother did not want to **break** the cup.

Albert **broke** a rule of the school.
Albert **acted against** a rule of the school. He came late for school.

broken All the windows of the house were **broken.** Johnny said, "I did not break the windows."

Mr. Danielson said, "Someone broke all the windows with rocks yesterday."

brook

A **brook** is a small stream of water. The man is fishing in a brook.

Did you ever go fishing in a brook?

broom A **broom** is a stiff brush with a long handle. We sometimes use a broom to sweep floors, rugs, and walks. Mother is sweeping the floor with a broom.

B b

broomstick A **broomstick** is the handle of a broom.

When the broomstick broke, we threw the broom away.

---

broth **Broth** is the water in which meat or fish has been boiled.

When Ellen was sick, Mother gave her some chicken broth to drink.

---

brother Mr. and Mrs. Jones have two children. Their names are Janice and Richard. Janice says, "Richard is my brother. He is my brother because we have the same father and mother." Janice is Richard's sister.

Mr. and Mrs. Smith have two children. Their names are Alfred and William. William is Alfred's brother. Alfred is William's brother. They are brothers because they have the same father and mother. Mr. and Mrs. Smith are the father and mother of Alfred and William.

---

brought Mother **brought** the food to the table.
Mother **carried** the food to the table.

Sometimes I help mother bring the food to the table.

---

brown **Brown** is a color. This pig is brown.

Chocolate is brown. Coffee is brown, too.

The boys and girls like to brown themselves on the beach beneath the hot sun. They like to make their skin tan.

---

brownie A **brownie** is a flat chocolate cake with nuts in it.
Sometimes Mother bakes brownies for us.

brush   Father is painting the table with a **brush.**
He is painting with a paintbrush.

Eileen is cleaning her teeth with
a **brush.** Mother wants Eileen
to brush her teeth often.
Eileen is **brushing** her teeth
with a toothbrush.

Mother is **brushing** her hair with
a **brush.** She is using a hairbrush.

---

bubble   Rita is blowing a **bubble** with her bubble
pipe. To blow bubbles you need soap,
water, and a bubble pipe.

When mother washes dishes, the sink is full
of **bubbles.** Soap makes many bubbles in
the water.

---

bucket

Charles is carrying water in a **bucket.**
Charles is carrying water in a **pail.**

B b

bud

When a flower **bud** opens, it will be a flower.

Leaves also have **buds.** When leaf buds open, they become leaves.

When the weather gets warm the trees and bushes will **bud.**

When the weather gets warm the trees and bushes will **make buds.**

---

buffalo A **buffalo** is a kind of wild ox. These are buffaloes.

About a hundred years ago there was a great number of buffaloes in the United States. Most of them were killed by hunters. Today it is against the law to hunt buffaloes in the United States.

WATER BUFFALO

AMERICAN BISON

---

bug A **bug** is a small animal. Some bugs walk. Some bugs hop. Some bugs fly. Ants, grasshoppers, and butterflies are bugs. Bugs are sometimes called insects.

---

buggy Mother pushes the baby in a baby **buggy.**
Mother pushes the baby in a baby **carriage.**

---

bugle A **bugle** is a small brass horn.

The bugler in the army blew the bugle in the morning to wake up the soldiers.

---

bugler A **bugler** is a person who blows the bugle.

build

Birds **build** nests.
Birds **put together** nests.

The men are **building** a house.

Last year the men **built** our house.

A house is built of nails and wood,
Of glass and screws and bricks;
A bird he builds his nest of straw,
Of grass and mud and sticks.

---

building   Our house is a **building.** A church is a building. A store is a building. A garage and a barn are buildings. There are many other kinds of buildings. Can you name some?

---

built   Yesterday my father **built** a dog house.
Yesterday my father **put together** a dog house.

---

bulb   A **bulb** is a thick root of some plants. Some plants grow from seeds. Some plants grow from bulbs. Onions, tulips, and lilies grow from bulbs. These are onion bulbs.

An electric light **bulb** is a glass ball with a very thin wire in it. When electricity goes through the wire, it becomes very hot and bright. When this happens the bulb lights up.

B b

bumblebee

A **bumblebee** is a large bee. A bumblebee has yellow and black stripes across it. Bumblebees buzz loudly when they fly.

Bumblebee, bumblebee,
  Buzzing around,
There in the flower bed
  Only a sound.
A buzzing I hear,
  But you I don't see;
I bet in some flower
  At work you must be.

---

bump   Mike has a **bump** on his head.
Mike has a **lump** on his head. Mike has a swollen place on his head where he hit a branch.

Do not **bump** your head on the branch.
Do not **hit** your head on the branch. Mike did not see the branch, and he **bumped** his head on it.

---

bun   A **bun** is a very small loaf of bread. Sometimes buns are called rolls. Some buns are sweet. Mother bakes buns in the oven.

---

bunch

A **bunch** is many things put together.

Alice has a **bunch of flowers.**
Alice has **many flowers put together.**

Regina has only one flower. It is in her hair.

bundle Larry carried a **bundle** of books to school.
Larry carried a **package** of books to school.

Dick will **bundle up** the old newspapers. He will tie the old newspapers together with cord.

Mother said, "**Bundle up** before going outside where it is cold."

Mother said, "**Dress up in warm clothes** before going outside where it is cold."

---

bunny

A **bunny** is a pet rabbit. Ed has a bunny. It is white. He likes his bunny. Gloria has two bunnies. They are gray. She likes her bunnies, too.

A bunny has long ears and a very short tail.

---

burn Mother touched the stove and got a **burn**.
Mother touched the stove and got a **sore made by something very hot**.

The paper is **burning**.
The paper is **on fire**. We watched the paper **burn**.

The house was completely **burned**.
The house was completely **destroyed by fire**.

Children who play with fire may be **burned**.
Children who play with fire may be **hurt by fire**.

Salt **burns** when you put it in a wound.
Salt **stings** when you put it in a wound.

Do not **burn the food**.
Do not **cook the food too much**.

B b

burst   Did you see the balloon **burst?**

Did you see the balloon **break open?** Raphael blew so much air into the balloon that it burst.

Did you see the boy **burst** into the room?

Did you see the boy **rush quickly and suddenly** into the room?

---

bury   Dogs **bury bones.**

Dogs **put bones into the ground and cover them up with earth.**

When our cat died, we **buried** it in the yard.

Stanley's hat was **buried under** the leaves.

Stanley's hat was **completely covered by** the leaves.

---

bus   A **bus** is a big automobile with many seats and windows. A bus is able to carry many people at one time.

---

bush

A **bush** is a plant. It is not very high. A bush has many branches near the ground.

Martha is picking some blueberries from a blueberry bush. Most trees are bigger than bushes.

bushy   The squirrel has a **bushy tail.**
The squirrel has a **tail that is thick with hair.**

---

business   A **business** is the work a person does to get money to live. Baking is a baker's business. Delivering the mail is a mailman's business. What is your father's business?

---

busy   Father is often **busy.**
Father is often **working.**

---

but   All the children are home **but** one.
All the children are home **except** one. Frederick, Mary, and Pamela are home. Timothy did not come home yet.

Tommy is tired, **but** he is happy.
Tommy is tired; **still** he is happy.

Jerome has **but** one pencil.
Jerome has **only** one pencil.

---

butcher   A **butcher** is a man who cuts up meat and sells it for food. We buy meat from the butcher.

butter   **Butter** is made from cream. When you beat cream for a long time, it becomes butter. Sally said, "I like bread and butter."

I asked my mother to **butter** my bread.

Grandmother makes **butter** in a wooden churn.

B b

butterfly

A **butterfly** is an insect with four large wings and with a tiny body. Butterflies very often have beautiful wings. Butterflies fly among the flowers. They fly in the daytime.

Butterflies were at one time caterpillars. A caterpillar builds a covering for himself which is called a cocoon. While the caterpillar lives in his cocoon, he changes into a butterfly.

---

buttermilk

Buttermilk is the milk that is left after butter has been made from cream. Buttermilk is sometimes sour. Buttermilk is good to drink.

---

button

Helen will sew a **button** on her dress.

Christopher has yellow **buttons** on his blue jacket.

Mother will **button my coat** before I go outdoors.

Mother will **fasten my coat with buttons** before I go outdoors.

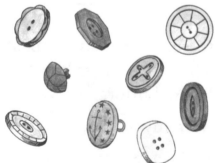

There are many different colors, shapes, and sizes of **buttons.**

Here are some buttons.

buy   Nancy wants to **buy a new dress.**
Nancy wants to **get a new dress by paying money for it.**

Yesterday Timothy **bought a pencil.**
Yesterday Timothy **got a pencil by paying some money for it.**
He paid five cents for a pencil, and he got it.

---

buzz   A bee says, "**Buzz, buzz.**" Bees and other insects buzz. The mosquito **buzzed** around Henry's head all night. Mother said, "I hear the fly **buzzing** in the room."

> As I lay there in my bed,
>   So quiet in the room,
> I heard a buzzing near my head.
>   "A noise," I asked, "from whom?
> Mosquito? fly? or bumblebee?
>   Just what could make this sound?"
> And turning on the light to see,
>   All three was what I found!

---

by   Albert sits **by** Jack.
Albert sits **near** Jack.

The window was broken **by** a rock.
The window was broken **with** a rock.

We are going to New York **by** train.
We are going to New York **using a** train.

Harry came home **by** a different street.
Harry came home **along** a different street.

We will be at the party **by** seven o'clock.
We will be at the party **not later than** seven o'clock.

I watched the parade go **by** the house.
I watched the parade go **past** the house.

Edward painted the picture. The picture was painted **by** Edward. Edward paints well.

This is the third letter of the alphabet.

ABCDEFGHIJKLMNOPQRSTUVWXYZ

abcdefghijklmnopqrstuvwxyz

cabbage

Cabbage is a vegetable. It grows in a tight ball. This ball of cabbage is called a head of cabbage. Cabbage looks like lettuce. Cabbage is red, white, or green.

cabin A **cabin** is a small house. Many cabins are built of logs.

cage A **cage** is a space with sides made of wire or bars. At the zoo we saw a lion in a cage.

At home we have a bird in a cage.

cake Mother baked a **cake** for my birthday. To make the cake mother used flour, eggs, butter, sugar, and other things.

A piece of soap is sometimes called a **cake** of soap.

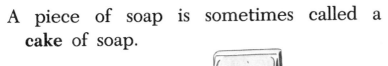

calendar   A **calendar** helps to tell which month and day it is.

A calendar shows us
the months of the year,
the weeks of the year,
the days of the month, and
the number of days in each month.

This is a **calendar**.   It shows us the month of May for the year 1971.   Do you know today's date?

---

calf

A **calf** is a baby cow.   The calf is standing next to its mother.

---

call   We heard a robin's **call**.
We heard a robin's **cry**.

There was a **call** for help from the burning building.
There was a **shout** for help from the burning building.

Sandra paid us a short **call**.
Sandra paid us a short **visit**.

Father will **call** me soon.
Father will **shout for** me soon.

Richard said, "**Call** me Dick."
Richard said, "**Name** me Dick."

Mother **called Rita for** dinner.
Mother **asked Rita to come to** dinner.

I **called** Philip yesterday.
I **telephoned** Philip yesterday.

came   The dog **came to** me.

The dog **moved toward** me. If I whistle, my dog will come to me.

---

camel

A **camel** is an animal with a hump on its back. Some camels have two humps.

Camels can travel for a long time without drinking water. A man can ride on a camel.

---

camera   A **camera** is a machine for making pictures of things we see. Daddy is taking a picture with his camera.

When we go on vacation, we bring along a camera so that we can take pictures.

---

camp   A **camp** is a place in the country where people live in tents. In some camps there are buildings instead of tents.

We like to **camp** outdoors. We like to **live in a tent** outdoors. Have you ever been **camping?**

can   Sally **can** read and write.
Sally **knows how to** read and write.

Father **can** push our automobile.
Father **is able to** push our automobile.

---

can

A **can** is used to hold things. Some cans are like jars made of metal. Most cans have round bottoms and tops. There are many different kinds of cans.

To **can** means to *put in cans or jars and to close the cans and jars so well that no air can get in.* Grandmother **canned** twenty-five jars of tomatoes. We went to the **canning** factory and saw peaches being put into tin cans.

Canada   Canada is a country in North America. Here is a map of Canada. We can see that Canada is next to the United States.

Canada and the United States are neighbors.

---

canal

A **canal** is a way of water. A canal looks like a river, but it has been dug by men. Canals are deep enough for boats to sail through them.

candle A **candle** is a stick of wax with a string through it. When fire is put to the string, the flame burns slowly through the wax. Candles give off light.

We burn candles at Christmas time, on birthday cakes, and in church.

candy

Most **candy** is made from sugar. Candy is sweet. There are many different kinds of candy.

Some candy is made with a chocolate covering. Candy can be hard or soft or sticky.

cane Grandfather uses a **cane.**
Grandfather uses a **stick to help him walk.**

My grandpa has a big red cane;
My grandma has one, too.
But mine is just a candy one
On which I lick and chew.

cannot Dogs **cannot** fly.
Dogs **are not able to** fly. Birds can fly.

canoe

A **canoe** is a light, narrow boat that is pointed at both ends. This is a canoe.

The Indian pushed the canoe swiftly through the water by using a paddle.

---

can't   Babies **can't** read and write.
Babies **cannot** read and write.

---

cap   A **cap** is a small hat.   Billy is wearing a cap. Soldiers, sailors, nurses, and cooks wear special caps made for them.

Tommy put a **cap** on the bottle.
Tommy put a **cover** on the bottle.

Mother will **cap** the fruit jars.
Mother will **put covers on** the fruit jars.

---

cape

Martha is wearing a red **cape.**   She wears it over her other clothes.   A cape does not have sleeves.   It hangs from Martha's shoulders over her arms and body.   Some capes are long. Some capes are short.

I wear my cape when it is cool,
When on my way to church or school;
And though I like my cape, so red,
I sometime wear my coat instead.

captain A **captain** is a leader. Robert is the captain of our football team.

There are **captains** in the army and navy. Many soldiers and sailors must obey their captains.

---

car

A **car** is a carriage, a cart, or anything which moves on wheels for carrying people and things. Our automobile is a car.

The engine can pull many railroad **cars.** We walked through the cars of the train to find a seat.

---

card A **card** is a stiff piece of paper. Cards are used for many things.

Aunt Sarah sent us a post**card** from Washington.

The teacher gave us our report **cards** today.

My family likes to play **card** games. I have a pack of playing cards.

cardboard   Cardboard is heavy, stiff paper.   Some boxes are made out of cardboard.

---

care   Judy does not have a **care** in the world.
Judy does not have a **worry** in the world.

Daddy has many **cares.**
Daddy has many **worries.**   Mother broke her arm and the car will not go.

The children did their work with **care.**
The children did their work with **serious attention.**

I **care for** my dog.
I **look after** my dog.   I like to **take care of** my dog.

Fred does not **care for** cabbage.
Fred does not **like** cabbage.

I don't **care** to go to the party.
I don't **want** to go to the party.

Mother does not **care** if you have dinner with us.
Mother does not **mind** if you have dinner with us.   Mother will permit you to have dinner with us.   She will allow it.

---

careful   Paul was not **careful** when he used the knife.   He did not pay attention, and he cut his hand.   We must be full of care when we use a sharp knife.   We must be careful.

---

careless   Samuel is **careless** when he crosses the street.
Samuel is **not careful** when he crosses the street.

---

cargo   Cargo is a load of anything which is carried by a ship, an airplane, a truck, or a train.

carol   A **carol** is a song of joy.

The children sang Christmas carols.

---

carpenter   A **carpenter** is a man who builds things from wood. The carpenter is making a table out of wooden boards.

A carpenter uses many tools to make things out of wood. He uses a hammer, a saw, a plane, a drill, some nails, some screws, and many other things.

---

carpet   Mother bought a **carpet** to cover the whole parlor floor.

Mother bought a **rug** to cover the whole parlor floor.

---

carriage

These people are riding in a **carriage.** Two horses are pulling the carriage. Today people use automobiles instead of carriages.

Mother pushes my baby brother in a baby's **carriage.**

carrot   A **carrot** is a vegetable with an orange root. We eat the root of the carrot. Carrots grow in the ground in the same way as beets do.

> A carrot is a vegetable
> Which grows within the ground:
> This orange root that's good to eat
> In soup is often found.

Some farmers raise carrots to feed to their cattle.

---

carry   The children **carry** their books home from school every day.
The children **take** their books home from school every day.

Susan **carries** the dishes to the table.
Susan **brings** the dishes to the table.

The teacher said, "**Carry on** your work."
The teacher said, "**Continue** your work."

The general told the soldiers to **carry out** his orders. The general told the soldiers to do what he told them.

Yesterday John **carried** the heavy box by himself.

Our car can **carry** six people.

---

cart

A **cart** is a wagon with two wheels. Carts carry people or heavy things. Sometimes carts are pushed by people. Sometimes they are pulled by a horse or a donkey.

The man will **cart the apples** to the market.
The man will **carry the apples in a cart** to the market.

carton A **carton** is a box made of stiff paper. Liquid is put into cartons which are covered with plastic or wax. When mother went shopping, she bought a carton of eggs and a carton of milk.

case A **case** is a kind of box. We put things in cases.

In case of rain, we will stay home.
If it rains, we will stay home.

BOOKCASE   SUITCASE

castle

A **castle** is a large building. A long time ago, people used to build castles. Castles had high walls and towers. Very often there was water around the castle.

A castle has a big, tall tower;
  It has a thick, tall wall.
And people used to dance and sing
  In every castle hall.

Now castles are all old and still
  With dirt and dust and cold,
With cracks and very crooked doors,
  Gray broken walls so old.

cat A **cat** is a small animal with fur. Cats are tame. Many people have cats as pets. Cats catch mice and rats. My cat says, "Meow, meow."

C c

catch   Bill is going to **catch** the ball.

George is running after Peter.   He is trying to **catch** Peter.

Terence is fishing.   He is trying to **catch** fish.   David has finished fishing.   He has already **caught** three fish

Robert wants to **catch** the train for New York.
Robert wants to **get aboard** the train for New York.

Do not play with matches, for your clothes may **catch fire.** Your clothes may start burning.

Henry **caught** a cold.
Henry **got** a cold.

---

caterpillar   A **caterpillar** is an insect.   It looks like a furry worm. Caterpillars build cocoons to live in. When caterpillars go out of their cocoons, they are butterflies.

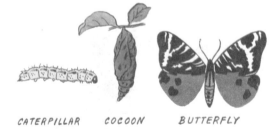

CATERPILLAR   COCOON   BUTTERFLY

A caterpillar, furry worm,
  Crawls high on tree and wall;
This worm will be a butterfly
  In summer or in fall.

90

cattle
The pasture is full of **cattle.** When we went for a ride in the country, we saw some cattle in a field. The cattle were brown cows.

Some farmers raise grain. Other farmers raise cattle.

caught
Gregory threw the ball to Albert. Albert **caught** the ball with his hands. Albert took the ball out of the air as it came toward him. Albert likes to **catch** balls.

cause
Rain **was the cause of** the wet ground. Rain made the ground wet.

Fred will **cause** the balloon to break. He is going to stick a pin into the balloon.

The bee's sting **caused pain for** the boy. The bee's sting **hurt** the boy.

cave

A **cave** is a big hole under the ground.

Many animals live in caves. Here is a cave that goes into the side of a hill. The children are looking into the cave.

We must behave
And stay outside;
In a dangerous cave
We should not hide.

caw A crow says, "Caw, caw, caw."

---

ceiling A **ceiling** is the top of a room. Bobby said, "I cannot touch the ceiling. It is too high."

---

celery

Celery is a vegetable. The celery plant has long stems with green leaves at the tops. We eat the stems of celery. We can eat them raw or cooked.

Celery has long, long stems,
   And green leaves at the top.
We eat them raw; we eat them cooked;
   And when they're gone we stop.

---

cellar The room under a house is a **cellar.** Our furnace is in the cellar of our house. A cellar is also called a basement.

---

cent A **cent** is one penny. There are five cents in a nickel. There are ten cents in a dime. There are a hundred cents in a dollar.

---

center The **center** is the place in the middle.

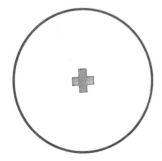

The bowl of fruit is in the **center** of the table.
The bowl of fruit is in the **middle** of the table.

The cross is in the **center** of the circle.

Central America

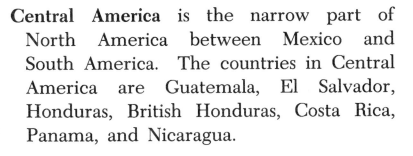

Central America is the narrow part of North America between Mexico and South America. The countries in Central America are Guatemala, El Salvador, Honduras, British Honduras, Costa Rica, Panama, and Nicaragua.

---

cereal   **Cereal** is made from grain such as rice, oats, wheat, and corn. Many people eat cereal for breakfast.

---

certain   I am **certain** that the earth is round.
I am **sure** that the earth is round.

It is possible that it may rain, but I do not know it **for certain.**

Certain foods make me sick.
Some foods make me sick.

---

certainly   Daniel will **certainly** come to the party.
Daniel will **surely** come to the party.

---

chain   A **chain** is many rings fastened together.

Father's watch chain is made of gold.

Did you ever make a chain out of colored paper?

chair

A **chair** is a piece of furniture. It has four legs, a seat, and a back. We sit in a chair.

A chair, with legs and seat to sit,
Is good for you and me:
For school, for games, for lots of fun,
For rest, and for T.V.

---

chalk **Chalk** is a stick of material which is made from soft stone. We write on the blackboard with chalk.

---

challenge The little boy will **challenge** the big boy to a fight.
The little boy will **dare** the big boy to a fight.

---

champion A **champion** is a person who wins. Milton won all the games. He is the champion.

---

chance Margaret saw her teacher by **chance**.
Margaret saw her teacher by **luck**. She did not look for her teacher. It was by accident that Margaret saw her teacher.

There is a **chance** that it will snow today. It seems as if it will snow. The weather man said that it is possible that it will snow today.

I like to go swimming when **I have a chance**.
I like to go swimming when **it is possible for me**.

Peter will have a **chance** to play with the ball. The time will come for Peter to play with the ball. It will be his turn to play with the ball.

change Jack had ten cents. He bought a piece of candy for five cents. The man gave Jack five cents **change.**

      10 Jack had ten cents.
     −5 The candy cost five cents.
      5 Jack's **change.**

Mother will **change** the baby's dress. The baby got her dress very dirty. Mother will put a new dress on the baby.

The weather **changed.** The weather became different. Yesterday was sunny and warm. Today is rainy and cold.

Jeffery **changed** his seat. He moved to a different chair.

---

chase My dog likes to **chase** cats.
My dog likes to **run after** cats.

> My dog can chase a rabbit;
> My dog can chase a cat.
> My cat can chase a ball of yarn,
> Or even chase a rat.

---

chat Susan had a **chat** with Linda. Susan and Linda had a friendly talk about little things. The things they talked about were not important.

Susan and Linda like to **chat.** They **chatted** for an hour.

---

chatter The teacher said, "Stop that **chatter.**"
The teacher said, "Stop that **quick, silly talk.**"

We could hear the girls **chatter** in the other room.
We could hear the girls **talking fast** in the other room.

---

cheap Harry bought a **cheap knife.**
Harry bought a **knife that cost only a little money.**

cheat   A **cheat** is a person who is not honest.

Patrick **did not cheat** on his test.
Patrick **was honest** on his test. He did not copy his answers from anybody.

---

check   A **check** is a piece of paper for which we can get money. Father gets paid by check every week. At the bank he will get money for the check.

A **check** is a mark. It looks like this ✓ . Mother put checks after the fruit on her grocery list.

soap
apples ✓
meat
cookies
pears ✓
butter
grapes ✓

This towel is made of green and white **checks.**
This towel is made of green and white **squares.**

Sally's spelling words **check with** mine.
Sally's spelling words **are the same as** mine.

---

cheek   We have a **cheek** on each side of our face. Cheeks are below the eye and on the side of the mouth. The baby has pink cheeks. He has his finger on one of his cheeks.

A cheek's a place upon a face
That's just below the eye.
It's where the tears go falling down
Whenever I do cry.

cheer   When our team won the baseball game, we gave a **cheer**.

When our team won the baseball game, we gave a **happy shout**.

We are **full of cheer**.
We are **very happy**.

The people will **cheer** when the president goes by.
The people will **shout happily** when the president goes by.

The toy **cheered up the sick boy**.
The toy **made the sick boy happy**.

---

cheerful   John is a **cheerful** person.
John is a **happy** person.

A sunny day makes us **cheerful**.
A sunny day makes us **feel good**.

Mary has a **cheerful** smile.
Mary has a **pleasant** smile.

Red is a **cheerful** color.
Red is a **bright** color.

---

cheese   **Cheese** is made from milk. There are many kinds of cheese. Sometimes we have cheese for lunch. Did you ever have a cheese sandwich.

---

cherry   A **cherry** is a small, round fruit that grows on a tree. **Cherries** grow on cherry trees. Some cherries are sweet and some are sour. Some cherries are red and some are white. In each cherry there is a hard seed. The seed is sometimes called a stone.

chest   A **chest** is a large box.   Daddy's tool chest is heavy.

Your **chest** is part of your body. Thomas has his hand on his chest.

---

chew   Mother said, "Eat slowly and **chew your food.**"
Mother said, "Eat slowly and **make the food into tiny bits with your teeth.**"

We chew with our teeth.   Baby cannot chew.   He has no teeth.

---

chick   A **chick** is a baby chicken.   Little birds are also called chicks.

A chick goes peep, a hen goes cluck,
A cock goes cock-a-doodle-doo.
A barnyard makes a lot of noise,
And a hen makes eggs for you.

---

chicken

HEN AND CHICKS   ROOSTER

A **chicken** is a bird.   A mother chicken is called a hen.   Hens lay eggs.   A father chicken is called a rooster.   Baby chickens are called chicks.   The meat of a chicken is good to eat.

chief   Pontiac was an Indian **chief.**
Pontiac was an Indian **leader.**

The **chief** man in the United States is the president.
The **most important** man in the United States is the president.

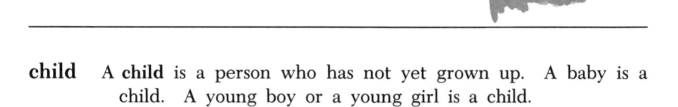

child   A **child** is a person who has not yet grown up. A baby is a child. A young boy or a young girl is a child.

children   The three **children** are playing in the yard. John is a child. Peter is a child. Mary is a child. John, Peter, and Mary are children. They are playing in the yard.

chill   A **chill** is a shivering feeling of cold.

John will **chill** the milk. He will make it cool by putting it in the refrigerator.

chimney   Our house has a **chimney.** A chimney lets the smoke from our furnace go outside. Buildings which have furnaces and fireplaces also have chimneys. Some factories have very tall chimneys.

C c

chin Your **chin** is the lowest part of your face. When you chew or talk, your chin moves up and down.

Frank is touching his chin.

China

China is a large country far away in the East. Here is a map of China.

The Chinese grow and eat much rice. They also raise the worms which make silk thread. These worms are called silkworms.

The Chinese also grow tea plants. The leaves of the tea plant are used to make tea.

Chinese The people of China are called **Chinese.**

---

chip A **chip** is a small piece broken or chopped off something.

While the man was chopping down the tree many **chips** of wood fell to the ground.

While the man was chopping down the tree, many **small pieces** of wood fell to the ground.

Mother said, "Please do not **chip** the cup."

Mother said, "Please do not **break a small piece from** the cup."

chipmunk

A **chipmunk** is an animal which looks like a small squirrel. Because chipmunks live in the ground, they are sometimes called ground squirrels. A chipmunk has black and white stripes on its back.

---

chocolate

Chocolate comes from a bean which grows in a tree. It has a dark brown color. We like to eat chocolate candy. Sometimes Mother makes chocolate cake. Her chocolate cake tastes good. Sometimes Mother puts chocolate in our milk.

---

choose

Mother said to Tom, "**Choose** the toy you want."
Mother said to Tom, "**Pick out** the toy you want." She said that Tom could take from the shelf the toy he wanted.

Yesterday Mary **chose** a doll on the shelf. The toy boat was **chosen** by Tom.

---

chop

Sometimes I have a pork **chop** for dinner. A pork chop is meat that comes from the side of a pig. Chops also come from the meat of lambs and cows. Chops from a young cow are called veal chops.

Billy is watching his father **chop** down the tree. Billy's father is using an ax to cut down the tree. Soon the tree will fall.

Mother **chopped** cabbage for a salad.
Mother **cut into small pieces** cabbage for a salad.

chose Yesterday my mother **chose** her black hat. Mother has a red hat, a blue hat, and a black hat. Yesterday she took her black hat from the closet and wore it to the store. Today she will **choose** her red hat.

---

chosen John was **chosen** by his class to give the gift to the teacher. John did not know that the class was going to pick him.

Christmas

Christmas is the birthday of Jesus. Christmas is on December 25.

On Christmas we receive presents. We have a Christmas tree, too.

> Little Jack Horner
> Sat in a corner,
> Eating a Christmas pie;
> He put in his thumb,
> And pulled out a plum,
> And said, "What a good boy am I!"

---

chum Edward is my **chum.**
Edward is my **friend.** I have known Edward for a long time.

---

church A **church** is a building where people go to worship God.

> Church is where we go to pray,
> As sister and as brother,
> To learn of God whom we obey;
> Who helps us love each other.

churn

A **churn** is a machine or long narrow tub for making butter from cream.

Kevin helped Grandmother to **churn** the butter. He used to shake cream rapidly in a churn to make butter.

---

cigar

A **cigar** is made from leaves of a tobacco plant. The leaves are rolled tightly into a large solid roll.

Uncle Ben is smoking a cigar.

---

cigarette

A **cigarette** is a small roll of chopped up tobacco leaves. The chopped up tobacco is rolled up in a thin piece of paper. Father smokes cigarettes. This is a pack of cigarettes.

It is not good for your health to smoke cigarettes.

---

circle

A **circle** is shaped like a ring. The dot in the circle is exactly in the center. If you draw many straight lines from the dot in the center to the edge of the circle, every line will be the same length.

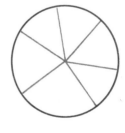

The airplane will **circle** around the airport before it lands. The airplane will **move in a circle** around the airport before it lands. The airplane will fly in a ring around the airport.

Cc

circus A **circus** is a show with clowns, horses, elephants, lions, tigers, and other animals. At the circus men and women swing from very high swings. Sometimes they walk and ride bicycles on very high ropes or wires.

Circuses travel from one town to another. Very often they have their shows in big tents.

---

citizen Mary was born in the United States. She is a **citizen** of the United States. José was born in Mexico. He is a **citizen** of Mexico. Charles was born in Canada. He is a **citizen** of Canada.

A person who was born in and who belongs to a certain country is a citizen of that country. What country are you a citizen of?

---

city A **city** is a large town. It is a place where many people live close together. New York, Chicago, and London are large cities.

---

clang When the metal pot fell on the floor, it made a **clang**.
When the metal pot fell on the floor, it made a **loud ringing sound.**

Did you hear the fire bells **clang?**
Did you hear the fire bells **making loud ringing sounds?**

clap   The **clap of** thunder frightened us.
The **loud noise from the** thunder frightened us.

We should **clap** when Mary finishes singing.
We should **hit the palms of our hands together** when Mary finishes singing. The noise we make by **clapping** tells Mary that we like her singing.

---

class   The teacher divided the students into two **classes.**
The teacher divided the students into two **groups.** She will teach one **class** today. She will teach the other **class** tomorrow.

The children study art in art **class.** In art class the students come to learn art.

---

classmate   A **classmate** is a person in the same class with another person.

Sandra and Betty are classmates. They are in the same class together. Sandra and Betty are in the second grade at the same school.

---

classroom   A **classroom** is a room in a school where students are taught.
We are taught music in one classroom, and we are taught English in another classroom.

---

clatter   When Sandra dropped the pans and dishes, there was a **clatter.**
When Sandra dropped the pans and dishes, there were **mixed up noises like that of many plates being struck together.**

---

claw   A **claw** is one of the sharp nails on the foot or paw of certain animals. Cats have sharp claws. Eagles have sharp claws, too.

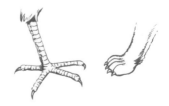

clay

Clay is a kind of earth that can easily be made into many shapes. Bricks are made from clay. Some pots and dishes are made from clay.

After bricks, pots, and dishes are shaped and dried, they are baked hard. American Indians made dishes of clay.

---

clean   Ann's white dress was **clean.**
Ann's white dress was **not soiled.**

Mother will **clean** the floor.
Mother will **remove the dirt from** the floor.

---

cleaner   A **cleaner** is a person who cleans something. Father sent his suit to the cleaner.

A cleaner is also something to remove dirt. Soap is a cleaner.

---

clear   Martha will **clear** the table.
Martha will **remove the things from** the table.

The water in the lake was **clear.**
The water in the lake was **not muddy or dirty.**

The day was **clear.** There was not one cloud in the sky.

The teacher is teaching the children how to add. She says, "One apple and two apples make three apples."
The teacher's lesson is **clear.**
The teacher's lesson is **easy to understand.**

Paul's voice was **clear.** Everybody in the room could hear and understand him.

clerk   My big sister is a **clerk** in a store.   She sells the things in the store.

Jane's big sister is a **clerk** in an office.   She uses the typewriter and answers the telephone.   She also puts important papers away, so that the office will be neat.

---

clever   John is a **clever** artist.   He can draw quickly and well.   John can draw and paint beautiful pictures.

---

click   A **click** is a short, sharp sound.   I heard the click of the key turning in the lock.

Did you hear the key **click** in the lock?
Did you hear the key **make a short, sharp sound** in the lock?

---

climb   Grandmother does not like to **climb** the stairs.
Grandmother does not like to **go up** the stairs.

Father **climbed** the ladder to fix the roof.

The morning glory plant **climbs** on the fence.   It grows along the fence.

---

clip      This is a paper **clip.**   It is made of wire.   A paper clip holds papers together.   The teacher put a clip on the papers.

In the warm weather, my father will **clip** the dog's hair.
In the warm weather, my father will **cut off some of** the dog's hair.

cloak   A **cloak** is a loose coat.   Some cloaks have sleeves.   Other cloaks do not have sleeves.

A cloak is like a cape.   Miss Smith is a nurse.   She is wearing a blue cloak.

clock   A **clock** tells what time it is.   Some clocks use electricity to make them go.   Other clocks use springs to make them go.   There are many kinds of clocks.

Hickory, dickory, dock,
The mouse ran up the clock;
The clock struck one,
Down he did run;
Hickory, dickory, dock.

close   Mother said, "Please **close** the door."
Mother said, "Please **shut** the door."

close   The dog sits **close to** Fred.
The dog sits **near** Fred.

Sam and Andy are **close** friends.
Sam and Andy are **very good** friends.

closet   A **closet** is a small room.   We keep our clothes in the closet.

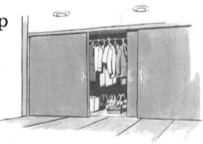

cloth Sally's dress is made of **cloth.** Billy's pants are made of cloth. Clothes are made of cloth. Our curtains are made of cloth, too.

---

clothes Clothes are the things we wear to cover our body. Timothy is putting on his clothes.

Stockings and sweaters, socks and skirts,
Slips and slippers, shoes and shirts,
Pants and pajamas, hats and hose,
Coats and cloaks, are all called clothes.

---

clothesline Mother hangs the wet clothes on the **clothesline.** After mother washes our clothes, she hangs them on the clothesline to dry.

---

clothing **Clothing** is another name for clothes.

---

cloud Rain comes from a **cloud.** Some clouds are white. Clouds float high up in the sky. The wind pushes the clouds along. Sometimes airplanes fly through the clouds.

clover

A **clover** is a small plant with three leaves. The flower of the clover plant can be pink or white or yellow. Horses and cows eat clover.

Sometimes you can find a clover with four leaves. Did you ever find a four-leaf clover?

---

clown

This is a **clown**. His face and clothes are funny. At the circus, the clown did many things to make me laugh.

A clown has a funny face,
  And he does such funny things;
You may see him jump, or skip, or race,
  Or hear him when he sings.

A clown's a very silly man,
  But that's not bad, you see,
For he acts as silly as he can,
  So happy you will be!

---

club

The policeman is holding a **club**.
The policeman is holding a **heavy wooden stick**.

This is a golf club.

Mother went to a meeting of her sewing **club**.
Mother went to a meeting of her sewing **group**.

---

cluck

A hen says, "**Cluck, cluck.**"

Hens **cluck** when they call their baby chicks.

coach   A **coach** is a carriage which is pulled by horses. A long time ago people used to travel in coaches instead of automobiles.

Today we call a railway car that carries people a **coach.**

A teacher is sometimes called a **coach.** Mary is learning how to sing better from her coach. The coach of the football team shows the boys how to throw the football.

Mary will **coach John in** music.
Mary will **help John to learn** music.

coal   **Coal** looks like black rocks. It comes from under the ground. We burn coal in a furnace to keep buildings warm. Coal is also burned in furnaces to run big machines. Some train engines run by coal. Our electricity comes from a big machine which is run by coal.

Coal is found beneath the ground,
In caves where picks and drills do sound,
Where chunks of coal from mines are got
To keep our furnace very hot.

coast   The land along the ocean or sea is called the **coast.**

Some people live on the **coast.**
Some people live on the **seashore.**

The children like to **coast** down the hill on their sleds.
The children like to **slide** down the hill on their sleds.

C c

coat　Terence is putting on his blue **coat.** It is cold outside. Terence is putting on his coat to keep warm. In winter, Terence wears his heavy coat.

My cat has a **coat** of gray fur. The fur all over an animal is called a coat.

Frank put a **coat** of white paint on the chair. He painted the chair once with white paint.

---

cob

A **cob** is a long, hard center on which corn grows. Did you ever eat corn on the cob?

Corn grows on a cob;
Peas grow in a pod.
But beets grow in the ground,
Where radishes are found.

---

cock　There is a **cock** in the chicken house.
There is a **rooster** in the chicken house.

A daddy chicken's called a cock;
　He's called a rooster too.
We hear him as the sun comes up,
　Crowing, "Cock-a-doodle-doo!"

---

cock-a-doodle-doo　Very early in the morning the rooster crows, **"Cock-a-doodle-doo."**

---

cocoa　**Cocoa** is chocolate which is made into a powder. Children like to drink hot cocoa. It is made from cocoa, sugar, and hot milk.

112

cocoon A caterpillar will make a **cocoon.** It will live in a cocoon for a while. When it comes out of the cocoon it will be a butterfly or a moth.

---

codfish A **codfish** is a fish that is found in the North of the Atlantic Ocean. A codfish is also called a cod.

Many people eat cod. We get a special oil from the codfish that is used as a medicine. It is called cod liver oil.

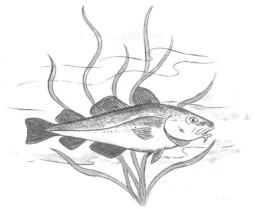

---

coffee **Coffee** is a drink which is made from the seeds of the coffee plant. The seeds are called beans. The seeds are dried, roasted, and ground.

COFFEE PLANT   COFFEE BEANS   COFFEE POT   COFFEE CUP

Mother made us some coffee by putting ground coffee beans and water into the coffee pot. My mother and father drink coffee for breakfast.

---

coin A **coin** is a piece of metal money. Here are some coins which are used in the United States of America.

Fifty cents
(half a dollar)

Twenty-five cents
(a quarter)

Ten cents
(a dime)

Five cents
(a nickel)

One cent
(a penny)

cold   Helen has a **cold.**   She sneezes, coughs, and blows her nose.

Ice is **cold.**
Ice is **not warm.**

In Canada it is very **cold** in the winter.

Margaret is holding some snow in her hands.   Snow is very **cold.**   Margaret wears mittens when she plays with snow.

Mr. Jackson is **cold.**
Mr. Jackson is **not friendly.**

---

collar   Angela has a blue **collar** on her orange dress.   The dog has a red **collar** around his neck.

---

collect   The teacher will **collect** our papers.
The teacher will **take up** our papers.

Leaves **collect** on the sidewalk in fall.
Leaves **gather together in a pile** on the sidewalk in fall.

---

college   When Teresa finishes high school, she will go to **college.**
When Teresa finishes high school, she will go to a **higher school.**

Daddy went to grade school first.   Then he went to high school.   Finally, Daddy went to **college.**

---

collide   Did you see the two cars **collide?**
Did you see the two cars **crash against each other?**

color   These are **colors.**

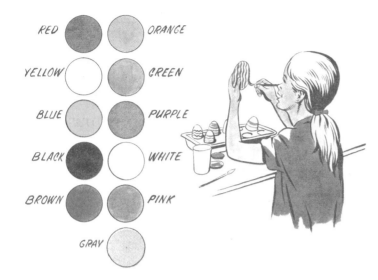

RED   ORANGE
YELLOW   GREEN
BLUE   PURPLE
BLACK   WHITE
BROWN   PINK
GRAY

Alice likes to color eggs for Easter. She likes to make the white eggs different colors.

---

colt   A **colt** is a baby horse.

---

comb   We put a **comb** through our hair to make it smooth and to put it in place. Ellen is **combing** her hair with a comb. She likes to **comb** her hair. Ellen wants to look neat.

Bees keep their honey in a kind of box made of wax. It is called a **honeycomb.**

A rooster has a red piece on the top of his head. It is called a **comb.**

115

Cc

come   The dog will **come to** you if you show him the bone.
The dog will **move toward** you if you show him the bone.

Sally will **come to** the party.
Sally will **arrive and stay at** the party.

Christmas **comes** once each year.
Christmas **happens** once each year. When Christmas **came** last year, Santa Claus brought me many presents.

---

comfort   Milton's dog was a great **comfort** to him. The dog helped to make Milton happy.

The Garcia family lives in great **comfort**. They have plenty of money, food, and clothes.

The policeman tried to **comfort the lost child**.
The policeman tried to **make the lost child happy**.

---

comfortable   My new bed is very **comfortable** to sleep in. It helps very much to give rest and peace to my body.

---

comic   The clown was a **comic** sight.
The clown was a **funny** sight.

Comics are funny pictures. They are also called funnies. The Sunday newspaper has comics in it.

---

command   The soldiers obeyed the captain's **command**.
The soldiers obeyed the captain's **order**.

The general said, "I will **command** the soldiers to stop."
The general said, "I will **order** the soldiers to stop."

116

company   Yesterday we had **company** at our house.
Yesterday we had **people visiting** at our house.

The captain leads a **company** of soldiers.
The captain leads a **group** of soldiers.

I like **company**.
I like **being with other people**.

Father works for a big **company**. His company makes automobiles.

---

complete   Mother did not **complete** her work.
Mother did not **finish** her work.

Ed has a **complete** set of tools for making a dog house.
Ed has a **full** set of tools for making a dog house. He has all the tools he needs.

---

conductor   Billy is the **conductor** of a small band. He leads the band by making signs with his hands and arms. The conductor helps the band to make beautiful music.

A **conductor** on a train asks everybody for a ticket. He also looks after the passengers on the train. Buses and streetcars have conductors too.

C c

cone   A **cone** is a long figure that is round at one end and pointed at the other end.

This is a cone with ice cream in it. It is called an ice cream **cone.**

The seeds of some trees are found in **cones.**

This is a pine cone.

---

contented   Baby is **contented** since she has her milk and her Teddy bear.

Baby is **pleased** since she has her milk and her Teddy bear. Baby is satisfied with her food and her toy bear.

---

continue   Father said, "**Continue** walking until you see the park."

Father said, "**Do not stop** walking until you see the park."

---

cook   A **cook** gets food ready for us to eat. The cook at the restaurant wears white clothes. He wears a tall white cap.

Mother is a good **cook.**

You can **cook** food
   (1) by boiling it,
   (2) by broiling it,
   (3) by baking it, or
   (4) by frying it.

We sometimes say we roast meat when we bake it.

cookie A **cookie** is a small, thin, sweet cake. Sometimes **cookie** is spelled **cooky.** Children like cookies.

---

cool John put ice in the water to **cool it.**
John put ice in the water to **make it less warm.**

We **cooled** the pie in the refrigerator.

The day was warm, but the night was **cool.**
The day was warm, but the night was **not very warm.**

---

coop A **coop** is a small pen that looks like a cage. The farmer keeps his chickens in a chicken coop.

---

copper **Copper** is a metal. Its color is red mixed with brown. Most electric wire is made of copper.

---

copy My dress is a **copy of** Mary's dress.
My dress is a **dress made exactly like** Mary's dress.

Susan will try to **copy the picture** in the book.
Susan will try to **make a picture just like the one** in the book.

---

cord A **cord** is a heavy, strong string. Mother will tie the package with cord.

Stanley put a new cord on his kite.

C c

corn

The **corn** plant is tall. On the corn plant ears of corn grow. This is an ear of corn. There are grains of corn on the ear of corn. The grains of corn are good to eat.

An ear of corn is sometimes called a cob of corn. When the grains of corn are taken from the ear, the ear is called a cob, or a corncob.

---

corner   The grocery store is on the **corner** of two streets. The corner of the street is where two streets come together.

The table is in the **corner** of the room. The corner of the room is where two walls come together.

---

corral   A **corral** is a space with a fence around it. Cattle and horses are kept in a corral.

---

correct   Helen gave the **correct** answer.
Helen gave the **right** answer.

cost   Father wants to know the **cost** of the chair.

Father wants to know **how much money is needed to buy** the chair.

Those diamonds **cost** much money.
Those diamonds **are worth** much money.

It **cost** my father much money to travel to Africa. He had to pay a lot of money to go to Africa.

---

cottage   A **cottage** is a small house.

In the summer we go to our cottage at the lake. Our cottage has only three rooms.

---

cotton   **Cotton** is a fluffy white ball that grows around the seeds of the cotton plant.

Cotton is made into threads. Cotton cloth is made from cotton threads.

---

cough   A **cough** is a sudden, rough noise that comes from your throat.

When Mary had a cold, she often used to **cough.**
When Mary had a cold, she often used to **make sudden, rough noises from her throat.**

You should put your hand over your mouth when you cough.

could Margaret **could** swim when she was five years old.
Margaret **was able** to swim when she was five years old.

---

couldn't Baby **couldn't** talk when she was one year old, but now
she can.
Baby **could not** talk when she was one year old, but now
she can.

---

count  David said, "I can **count** the birds on
the fence: One, two, three, four, five,
six."

Judy said, "I can **count** to ten: One,
two, three, four, five, six, seven,
eight, nine, ten."

---

country Which **country** do you live in?
Roberto says, "I live in Mexico."
John says, "I live in the United States."
Marie says, "I live in Canada."

Farms and woods are in the **country**. They are outside
the city.

---

couple Sandra has **a couple of** apples.
Sandra has **two** apples.

Father will **couple** the trailer to the automobile.
Father will **join** the trailer to the automobile. The
automobile will then pull the trailer.

course   **Of course** we are going to the party.

Surely we are going to the party. We always go to the party when we are invited.

Did you ever see a **golf course?**

Did you ever see **the land on which the game of golf is played?**

The airplane is flying **on the right course.**

The airplane is flying **in the right direction.**

---

cousin   My aunt and uncle have two children. Their names are Edward and Patricia. Edward is my cousin. Patricia is my **cousin,** too. The children of my aunts and uncles are my cousins. How many cousins do you have?

---

cover   Mother is putting a **cover** on the pot.

Mother is putting a **top** on the pot.

When my baby brother goes to bed, my mother will **cover** him with a blanket. She will put a blanket over him to keep him warm.

Mother **covered** the bed with a blanket. She spread a blanket on the bed.

The dog put his bone in a hole in the ground. The dog then **covered** up the bone with dirt.

Kathleen is **covering** her doll with a blanket.

Something that covers is a covering.

---

covering   A covering is something that covers.

cow   A **cow** is a large farm animal that gives us milk. The cows eat the grass in the pasture.

Grandfather milks the cows each evening. He gets milk from the cows. Did you ever see anyone milk a cow?

---

cowboy   A **cowboy** is a man who rides horses. He looks after cows and other cattle on a ranch.

Did you ever see a movie with some cowboys and Indians in it? Cowboy movies are interesting.

---

cozy   Sally likes to sit in a **cozy** corner by the fireplace.
Sally likes to sit in a **warm and comfortable** corner by the fireplace.

---

crack

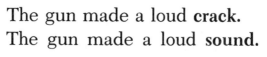

The gun made a loud **crack.**
The gun made a loud **sound.**

This cup has a **crack** in it.

Wind came through the **crack** in the wall.
Wind came through the **long, thin hole** in the wall.

Squirrels can **crack** nuts with their teeth.
Squirrels can **break open** nuts with their teeth.

The plate **cracked,** but it did not break into pieces.

cracker

A **cracker** is a thin and crisp little piece of bread. Crackers look like cookies, but crackers are not sweet. We buy crackers in a box. Sometimes people eat crackers with soup.

---

cradle

A **cradle** is a bed for a small baby. A cradle has sides on it so that the baby will not fall out. Mother rocks the cradle to put the baby to sleep.

---

crawl

Babies **crawl** before they learn to walk.

Babies **move about on their hands and knees** before they learn to walk.

---

crayon

A **crayon** is a little stick made from colored wax. I have a box of crayons. My crayons are of many different colors. I use my crayons to color the pictures in my coloring book.

Ruth likes to **color** pictures with colored crayons.

cream   **Cream** is a thick, yellow part of milk. We let the milk stand and the cream came to the top. Butter is made from cream. Did you ever have whipped cream on ice cream?

---

creature   A **creature** is any living person or animal. All creatures need food to keep themselves alive.

---

creek   A **creek** is a small stream of water. The boys like to go swimming in the creek.

---

creep   The baby can **creep** across the floor.
The baby can **crawl** across the floor.

---

crept   Yesterday the baby **crept** on the floor and got very dirty. Don't let him creep on the floor today.

---

cried   Peter **cried** when he cut his finger. He showed that his finger hurt by the tears in his eyes. Did you ever cry?

---

crooked   Paul has a stick which is **crooked.**
Paul has a stick which is **not straight.**

cross

A **cross** is a mark + made by putting one line across another line.

There is a red **cross** on the truck.

Be careful when you **cross the street.**
Be careful when you **go from one side of the street to the other side.**

Alice is **cross** today.
Alice is **angry** today.

---

crow   A **crow** is a large black bird. A crow says, "Caw, caw, caw."

Crows eat the farmer's corn. This makes the farmer very angry.

Did you ever hear the rooster **crow** early in the morning?
He says, "Cock-a-doodle-doo." When the rooster **crows,** the farmer wakes up.

---

crowd   A **crowd** came to see the movie.
A **large group of people** came to see the movie.

The seven children tried to **crowd** through the door at one time.
The seven children tried to **push** through the door at one time.

The little room is **crowded.**
The little room is **filled very full.**

Cc

crown

A **crown** is a fancy band which is worn on the head. Here is a king wearing a crown on his head. A crown is worn by a king or a queen.

Someone will **crown** the new queen soon.
Someone will **put a crown on the head of** the new queen soon.

---

cruel

The man is **cruel.** He likes to see other people and animals in pain. Father became very angry when he saw the cruel man hitting the dog.

---

crumb

A **crumb** is a small bit of bread or cake.

When Ethel ate the cake, many **crumbs** fell on the table.
When Ethel ate the cake, many **small bits of cake** fell on the table.

Birds like to eat **crumbs.**

---

cry

We heard a **cry** from the dark woods.
We heard a **shout** from the dark woods.

The **cry** of the robin is cheerful.
The **call** of the robin is cheerful.

When we hurt ourselves, we sometimes **cry.**
When we hurt ourselves, we sometimes **shed tears and make a noise showing pain.**

Fred **cries** when his mother punishes him.

When Ethel cut her foot, she **cried.**

The baby kept **crying** until his mother gave him more milk.

cub   A baby lion is called a **cub.** A baby bear
is called a cub, too.

---

cucumber

A **cucumber** is a long, green vegetable that
grows on a vine close to the ground. The
outside of a cucumber is green. The inside
of a cucumber is white.

> Cucumber, cucumber, long and green,
> Seen in salad and in jar,
> Into a pickle you soon do turn
> When in vinegar you are.

---

cuddle   My baby brother likes Mother to **cuddle**
him. He likes Mother to hold him
close in her arms. My baby brother
likes Mother to show her love for
him.

> Does your mother cuddle you,
> And hold you to her breast?
> Does she love you with a hug,
> Your head on her to rest?

---

cup

COFFEE CUP

MEASURING CUP

This is a **cup.** A cup has a handle on it. We
drink out of this kind of cup. In the
morning, my father drinks a cup of coffee.

Here is a cup to measure with. When my
mother makes a cake, she uses this cup to
measure the things that go into the cake.

cupboard   A **cupboard** is a small closet with shelves and drawers in it. We keep dishes and food in our cupboard.

> Old Mother Hubbard
> Went to the cupboard
> To get her poor dog a bone;
> When she got there
> The cupboard was bare,
> And so the poor dog had none.

---

cure   A **cure** is something that makes you well. Medicine is a cure for some sicknesses.

If you are sick, the doctor will **cure you.**
If you are sick, the doctor will **make you well.**

---

curious   Small children are **curious**
Small children are **eager to learn.** They want to know many things. They ask many questions.

We found some **curious** coins in the box. They were not like the other coins. They were different from the coins that we know.

---

curl   I wind hair around my finger to make a **curl.**

Helen has **curls** in her black hair.

Brenda does not have curls in her hair. Her hair is straight.

curly Margaret's hair is **curly**
Margaret's hair is **full of curls.**

---

curtain A **curtain** is a cloth hanging over a window or a door. Mother is putting up a curtain at the window.

A curtain is also a heavy cloth covering to hide a stage from the people watching the show.

---

curve

This road has a **curve** in it.
This road has a **bend** in it. The road is not straight.

Around the curves our car does go;
It moves from left to right;
Around each bend please travel slow;
I'm holding on so tight.

The road **curves.** It bends in a curve.

---

cushion Sally is sitting on a **cushion.**
Sally is sitting on a **pillow.**

The cushions on the chair are filled with feathers.

---

customer A **customer** is one who buys something. My mother is a customer at Mr. Brown's grocery store. She buys her groceries there.

cut  Frank fell on a sharp piece of glass and got a **cut** on his hand. The sharp glass made a small hole in the skin of his hand.

My father **cut** the meat into small pieces. With a knife he made the big piece of meat into many small pieces.

---

cute   My little dog is **cute**.
My little dog is **little and pretty.**

---

cyclone   A **cyclone** is a very strong, fierce windstorm. The cyclone destroyed many houses.

This is the fourth letter of the alphabet.

ABCDEFGHIJKLMNOPQRSTUVWXYZ

abcdefghijklmnopqrstuvwxyz

dad   Some children call their father **Dad.**

---

daddy   Sally's name for her father is **Daddy.**

---

daily   Tom brings the newspaper to our house **daily.**
Tom brings the newspaper to our house **every day.**

---

dairy   A **dairy** is a building where milk is kept.   Butter, cheese, or ice cream are made from milk at some **dairies.**

The store where we buy milk, butter, cheese, and ice cream is also called a **dairy.**

---

daisy    A **daisy** has white petals and a yellow center. **Daisies** grow in fields.   There are also pink and yellow daisies.   These usually grow in flower gardens.

Dandelions and daisies,
  Oh what pretty flowers,
Coming in the springtime
  To tell of sunny hours.
While the trees are leafless,
  While the fields are bare,
Dandelions and daisies
  Spring up everywhere.

---

dam   A **dam** is a wall built across a river or a stream to hold the water back.

damp   The clothes on the clothesline are **damp.**
The clothes on the clothesline are **a little wet.**

---

dampen   Carol will **dampen** the cloth. She will wet it a little.

---

dance   Mary did a little **dance.** She took pretty steps and moved her arms about to music.

Margaret likes to **dance** as music plays.
Margaret likes to **take pretty steps and move her arms about** as music plays.

Father and Mother were invited to a **dance.**
Father and Mother were invited to a **party for dancing.**

The lambs **danced** in the field.
The lambs **jumped about and played** in the field.

---

dancer   A **dancer** is a person who dances. My sister is a good dancer. She dances well.

---

dandelion   A **dandelion** is a plant with a yellow flower. These are dandelions.

When a dandelion is ready to spread its seeds, it is soft and white. The wind carries the seeds to many places.

135

D d

danger   When our house caught on fire, **we were in danger.**
When our house caught on fire, **there was a chance that we would get hurt.**

Do not cross the street when the light is red.
It means **danger.**
It means **that you may get hurt.**

---

dangerous   That old car is **dangerous.**
That old car is **not safe.**

---

dare   Albert says to Peter, "I **dare** you to jump into the water."
Albert thinks that Peter is afraid to jump into the water.
Albert wants Peter to show him that he is not afraid to jump into the water.

---

dark   At night the sky is **dark.**
At night the sky is **without light.**

The dirt is **dark** brown. The sky is light blue.

---

darkness   **Darkness** filled the room. The room was without light.

---

darling   A **darling** is someone who is loved very much. Mother often calls me her darling. Jack is Grandmother's darling boy.

dash   Mother put a **dash** of pepper in the soup.
Mother put a **tiny bit** of pepper in the soup.

I saw Billy **dash** after his dog.
I saw Billy **hurry** after his dog.

Father will **dash** water on the fire.
Father will **throw** water on the fire.

---

date   The teacher asked for the **date.**
The teacher asked for the **day, the month, and the year.**

The teacher asked Billy, "Can you tell me the **date** for George Washington's birth?" Billy answered, "The date for George Washington's birth is February 22, 1732."

A **date** is a small brown fruit that grows on a palm tree. A date has a long seed through the middle. Dates are very sweet.

---

daughter   Barbara is a girl. She is the **daughter** of her mother and father. Robert is a boy. He is the son of his mother and father.

---

dawn   **Dawn** is the time of day when it begins to get light.

---

day   The **day** is the time from morning till night. It is dark at night and light during the day.

Sometimes night and day together are called **day.** There are twenty-four hours in a day. There are seven days in a week. These are the days of the week: Sunday, Monday, Tuesday, Wednesday, Thursday, Friday, and Saturday.

daytime   **Daytime** is the time when it is light. We sleep at nighttime. We work and play during the daytime.

---

dead   The bear is **dead.**
The bear is **not alive.** The hunter killed the bear with the gun.

The town is **dead** on Sundays.
The town is **quiet and dull** on Sundays.

---

deaf   The old man is **deaf.** He cannot hear well. Some people are so deaf that they cannot hear anything.

---

deal   Mother spends a great **deal** of her time taking care of Baby.
Mother spends a great **amount** of her time taking care of Baby.

Matthew likes to **deal** the cards when we play cards.
Matthew likes to **hand out** the cards when we play cards. Mary dealt the cards the last time. Now it is Matthew's turn.

---

dear   My baby brother is **dear to** me.
My baby brother is **loved by** me.

When I write to my grandfather, I begin the letter with these words: "**Dear** Grandfather."

When something is wrong, my mother says, "Oh **dear!**"

death   Death is the end of life.   After the **death** of Ed's dog, his father got him another dog.   Did you ever have a pet that died?

December   December is the twelfth month of the year.   December has thirty-one days.

---

decide   Father will **decide** whether to go to the party.
Father will **make up his mind** whether to go to the party. He will tell us if he is going to the party when he comes home from work.

---

deck      The floor of a boat is called a **deck.**   The boat we were on had three decks.

A pack of playing cards is also called a **deck.**   Matthew took the deck of cards and dealt seven cards to each person at the table.

---

decorate   The children like to **decorate** the Christmas tree.   They like to put things on the Christmas tree to make it gay and pretty.   They like to trim the tree.

deed   Helping your mother wash dishes is a good **deed**.

Helping your mother wash dishes is a good **thing to do**.

---

deep   A **deep** hole goes far down into the ground. Father is digging a deep hole.

Our water well is very deep. It is a hole which goes far down into the ground. At the bottom there is water.

---

deer   A **deer** is a pretty animal that lives in the woods. Deer run very fast. Some deer have horns. This is a deer.

---

delay   There was a **delay in** the traffic, because a tree had fallen across the road.

There was a **stopping of** the traffic, because a tree had fallen across the road.

When my father was sick, we called the doctor **without delay**.

When my father was sick, we called the doctor **right away**.

Do not **delay** me, for I must hurry to school.

Do not **stop** me, for I must hurry to school.

delicious This is a **delicious apple.**
This is an **apple that is very good to eat.** It tastes very good.

---

delight Rebecca gets **delight** in seeing the monkeys at the zoo.
Rebecca gets **great pleasure** in seeing the monkeys at the zoo. Rebecca says, "It is fun to watch the monkeys play."

---

deliver The mailman will **deliver** the letter to us.
The mailman will **bring** the letter to us.

---

demand My mother will **demand** that I clean up my room before going out to play. She asks me to clean my room, and she wants me to obey her.

The policeman **demanded** that my father stop the car. We must obey policemen.

---

den A **den** is a place where a wild animal lives. The squirrel has his den in a hole in a tree. A rabbit's den is a hole in the ground.

My father's **den** is a small room with many books and a big soft chair in it. He goes to the den to sit in his big chair and read. Sometimes he falls asleep.

dentist A **dentist** is a doctor who fixes and cleans your teeth. You should visit your dentist at least twice a year.

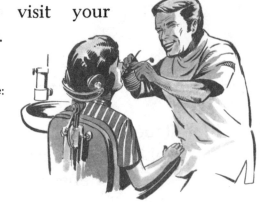

> My dentist gives me good advice
> To keep my teeth so clean and nice:
> I brush them after I do eat,
> Especially when the food is sweet.

---

describe Tom wanted to **describe** his visit to New York.
Tom wanted to **tell about** his visit to New York. He wanted to give a picture of New York in words.

---

desert A **desert** is a large, sandy place. Because a desert has very little water, few plants and trees grow there. Camels travel through the desert.

---

deserve Paul said, "I worked hard in the yard. I **deserve** a rest."
Paul said, "I worked hard in the yard. I **ought to have** a rest."

---

desire I **desire** to be happy.
I **want** to be happy.

---

desk 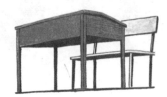 I sit at my **desk** when I read and write.
This is a desk and chair.

dessert   Dessert is the part of the meal eaten after the main part. It is usually something sweet.

---

destroy

Did you see the fire **destroy** the house?

Did you see the fire **put an end to** the house?

---

dew   In the early morning, there **is dew** on the grass in the yard. In the early morning, there **are tiny drops of water** on the grass in the yard.

---

diamond   A **diamond** is a very pretty stone. It is bright, shiny, and clear. My mother wears a diamond ring.

This playing card has eight red **diamonds** on it. It is called the eight of diamonds.

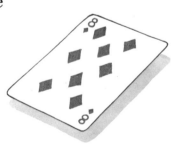

---

dictionary   A **dictionary** is a book of words. A dictionary teaches us how to use words well. You are reading a dictionary now.

D d

did I **did** my work early in the morning. Mary is **doing** her work now. Bill will **do** his tonight. Bill **does** not work now because he is sick.

---

didn't Milton said, "I **didn't** break the cup."
Milton said, "I **did not** break the cup."

---

die The ant will **die** if you step on him.
The ant will **stop living** if you step on him.

When my cat **died** we buried him. When I heard of my cat's death, I was sad. I liked my cat very much. I didn't want him to die.

---

different

Mary's hat and Judy's hat are **different**.
Mary's hat and Judy's hat are **not alike**. Mary's hat is red with blue feathers. Judy's hat is brown with flowers.

Joe has been absent from school two **different** times. He was absent yesterday, and he was absent last Tuesday.

---

dig

Did you ever see a dog **dig** a hole for his bone? He makes a hole in the ground with his front paws. Then, he puts his bone in the hole. Finally, he covers the bone with dirt. Dogs like to bury bones.

Yesterday we **dug** a hole in the ground to plant a tree.

dime   A **dime** is money. It is a coin. Ten pennies make a dime. Two nickels also make a dime.

Bob bought two apples for a **dime.** Each apple cost five cents. Together the two apples cost a dime.

---

dine   We **dine** at six o'clock every evening.
We **eat dinner** at six o'clock every evening.

---

ding dong   When the big bell rings, it says, "**Ding, dong.**"

Ding, dong, bell
Pussy's in the well.
Who put her in? Little Tommy Green.
Who pulled her out? Little Tommy Stout.
What a naughty boy was that
To drown poor pussycat,
Who never did him any harm,
But killed the mice in his father's barn.

---

dining room   The room where we eat dinner is called the **dining room.**

---

dinner   **Dinner** is the biggest meal of the day. We eat dinner in the evening, but some people eat dinner at noon.

---

dip   There was a **dip** in the road.
There was a **low place** in the road.

We went for a **dip** in the lake. We went into the lake. In the lake we played and swam in the water.

Grandmother used a cup to **dip** the soup from the kettle. She put the cup into the soup and lifted some out.

direction   North, south, east, and west are the main **directions**.

Mary asked, "Could you please **give me directions for** the hospital?"

Mary asked, "Could you please **tell me the way to** the hospital?"

Stephen was going **in the wrong direction**.
Stephen was going **the wrong way**.

---

dirt   Terence put some **dirt** in the flower pot.
Terence put some **earth** in the flower pot.

Mother said, "Do not get **dirt** on your clothes. Keep your clothes clean."

---

dirty   Harry's hands are **dirty**.
Harry's hands are **not clean**.

---

disagree   Gus and Sam **disagree**. They do not think alike. Gus thinks it will rain, but Sam does not think it will rain.

---

disappear   Did you see the airplane **disappear** into the clouds?
Did you see the airplane **go out of sight** into the clouds?

The snow **disappeared** when spring came.
The snow **went away** when spring came.

---

discover   **Discover** means *to find*. Christopher Columbus discovered America in the year 1492.

disease   Because Patty had a serious **disease,** she went to the hospital.

Because Patty had a serious **sickness,** she went to the hospital.

---

dish   I eat my food from a **dish.** Plates, cups, and saucers are **dishes.** The table has dishes on it.

Roast beef is my favorite **dish.** I like to eat a dish of roast beef better than anything else.

---

distance   The **distance** between our house and the school is very long.

The **space** between our house and the school is very long.

We saw the airplane in **the distance.**
We saw the airplane in **a far away place.**

---

ditch

A **ditch** is a long narrow hole in the ground. The man is digging a ditch.

When I'm digging in the ground,
My shovel makes a scraping sound;
With each scoop of earth I pitch
I make a neat and narrow ditch.

divide Father will **divide** the candy.

Father will **separate** the candy into parts. Each of the children will get some of the candy.

To **divide** means to *separate into parts.*

---

dizzy Sharon is **dizzy.** She feels that she is whirling around. If you keep turning around fast, you will get dizzy.

---

do **Do** you like ice cream? Yes, I **do.**

Mother will **do** her work in the morning. If mother **does** her work in the morning, she can take us to the circus in the afternoon.

Jane asked, "**Do** you have a penny, Robert?" Robert answered, "No, but I **did** have a penny yesterday."

Helen asked, "What are you **doing**, Martha?" Martha answered, "I am doing my work."

Albert's work is **done.**
Albert's work is **finished.**

---

doctor

A **doctor** helps us when we are sick. A doctor knows how to make us well.

To the doctor, doctor,
  Quick, quick, quick,
Send Suzanne who's
  Sick, sick, sick.
He'll help her, yes, sir,
  I know, know, know,
To the doctor, doctor,
  Go! Go! Go!

doe   A mother deer, or she-deer, is called a **doe.**

---

does   Mother **does** her work every day. Did you ever see Mother do her work?

---

doesn't   Father **doesn't** work on Sundays.
Father **does not** work on Sundays.

---

dog   A **dog** is an animal with four legs. Many people have dogs for pets. Do you have a dog for a pet? Some dogs learn how to look after sheep. Other dogs learn how to hunt. Dogs say, "Bow-wow." There are many different kinds of dogs.

---

doing   Edward asked, "What are you **doing,** John?" John answered, "I am doing my work. I always do my work at this time."

---

doll   A **doll** is a toy that looks like a person. Susan likes to play with her doll. Her doll's name is Laura.

Children play with dolls. They pretend that dolls are people.

dollar   A **dollar** is money. A dollar is one hundred cents. Four quarters make one dollar. Ten dimes make one dollar. Twenty nickels make one dollar. This is a dollar sign $.

---

dollhouse   A **dollhouse** is a house made for dolls.

---

done   Helen's work is **done.**
Helen's work is **finished.**

The teacher said, "Do your work, Laurence."
Laurence answered, "My work is already **done.**"

We will eat dinner when the meat is **done.**
We will eat dinner when the meat is **completely cooked.**

---

donkey   A **donkey** is an animal that looks something like a horse. It has long ears. When donkeys bray, they make a loud, rough cry. A donkey goes, "Hee-haw!"

Donkey, donkey, old and gray,
Open your mouth and gently bray,
Lift your ears and blow your horn,
To wake the world this sleepy morn.

---

don't   **Don't** means *do not.*

I **don't** want to go to bed.
I **do not** want to go to bed.

door   Mr. Brown has his hand on the **door** handle. He is pushing the **door** open.

We sometimes call a doorway a door. Mr. Brown will go through the door.

How many doors do you have in your house? Can you count them?

---

doorbell

Mary is ringing the **doorbell** of Mr. and Mrs. Smith's house. She is pushing a button which will ring a bell inside of the house. This will tell Mr. and Mrs. Smith that there is somebody who wants to see them.

If a house does not have a doorbell, we knock on the door.

---

doorstep   A **doorstep** is the step that goes from the outside door of a building to the ground. Mother swept the doorstep.

---

doorway   A **doorway** is an opening for going into a room or a house. We go into a house through a doorway.

We have ten doors in our house. We also have ten doorways. There is one doorway for each door.

D d

dot

A **dot** is a very small round mark. The dots on Ellen's dress are green.

The small letter *i* and the small letter *j* have dots over them.

The dot at the end of a sentence is called a period.

---

double
Double the candy in the bag.
Make two times as much the candy in the bag.

There are five pieces of candy in the bag. Sam wants five more pieces of candy in the bag. He wants ten pieces of candy. He wants the candy **doubled.**

5 **doubled** is 10
5 **two times** is 10
$5 + 5 = 10$

Our garage has **double** doors.
Our garage has **two** doors.

---

dough
Grandmother mixed together flour, salt, butter, water, and other things to make bread. All these things mixed together are called **dough.**

---

dove
A **dove** is a bird. It is sometimes called a pigeon.

down   When you go **down,** you go from a higher place to a lower place.

Billy came **down** the ladder.   He was at the top of the ladder, but he went to the bottom of the ladder.

---

downstairs   Ruth is coming **downstairs.**
Ruth is coming **down the stairs.**

We have two floors in our house.   The floor that is near the ground we call **downstairs.**   Downstairs we have our kitchen, our living room, and our dining room.   Upstairs is the floor above the ground. Upstairs we have our bedrooms.

---

downtown   **Downtown** is that part of a town where most of the stores and offices are.

---

downward   The balloon floated **downward.**
The balloon floated from a **higher place to a lower place.**

---

doze   I took a **doze** after school.
I took a **little nap** after school.

Grandmother sits in her chair and **dozes.**   She likes to take little naps during the day.

---

dozen   David bought **a dozen** oranges.
David bought **twelve** oranges.

D d

drag   Look at Timothy **drag his sweater** on the ground.

Look at Timothy **pull his sweater behind him** on the ground.

Yesterday George **dragged** his little brother along by the hand.

---

drank   Yesterday I **drank** all my milk. Today I will drink all my milk again.

---

draw   Raymond likes to **draw.**

Raymond likes to **make pictures.** Yesterday he **drew** a picture of a boat.

The horse can **draw** the wagon.
The horse can **pull** the wagon.

---

drawer   A **drawer** is a box which slides in and out of cupboards, desks, tables, and many other things.

We keep clothes in the drawers of our dresser. We keep napkins, table coverings, knives, forks, and spoons in the drawer of our cupboard.

Father is putting some papers in the drawer of his desk.

drawing   A **drawing** is a picture. Clarence made a pencil drawing of a horse. Clarence can draw very well with a pencil.

---

drawn   Yesterday Ann had **drawn** a picture of a horse. We saw her draw the picture. Ann drew it well.

---

dreadful   Something **dreadful** happened.
Something **terrible** happened. Father broke his leg. He had to go to the hospital.

---

dream   Jimmy had a **dream** last night. While he was sleeping, he **dreamed** that he was in a rocket on his way to the moon. Do you ever dream? What do you dream about?

---

dreary   It was a **dreary** winter's day.
It was a **dark and sad-looking** winter's day.

---

dress   This is a dress. Girls wear dresses.

I will **dress** quickly, so that I will not be late for school.
I will **put on my clothes** quickly, so that I will not be late for school.

Yesterday I **dressed** slowly, and I was late for school.

dresser

This is a **dresser.** In the dresser there are drawers. Above the dresser there is a mirror.

I have a dresser in my bedroom. I keep my brush and comb on my dresser. In the morning when I comb my hair, I look at myself in the mirror on my dresser.

---

drew Yesterday I **drew** three pictures. Today I will draw five pictures.

When Mother **drew** the candy out of the paper bag, I was so happy.

When Mother **pulled** the candy out of the paper bag, I was so happy.

I saw Mother put her hand in the paper bag and draw out some delicious candy.

---

dried The heat of the sun **dried** the clothes on the clothesline.

The heat of the sun **took the wetness out of** the clothes on the clothesline.

The clothes are wet, but the sun will **dry** them.

---

drift The children played in the snow**drift.**

The children played in the snow **which the wind blew into a pile.**

We let our boat **drift** toward the shore.

We let our boat **float along without steering it** toward the shore.

drill

Daddy is making a hole in the board with a **drill**.

The football player will **drill** every day, so that he will play football well.

The football player will **practice** every day, so that he will play football well. He will play football often.

---

drink   A **drink** is liquid food. A drink can be swallowed without chewing. Milk, coffee, and tea are drinks.

Baby **drinks milk.**
Baby **puts milk into her mouth and swallows it.**

Baby cannot chew food. She has no teeth. Baby must **drink** liquid foods. Milk is a liquid food.

Yesterday I **drank** three glasses of milk.

Peter has **drunk** all his milk.

---

drive   We went for a **drive** in our automobile.
We went for a **ride** in our automobile.

A street is sometimes called a **drive**. The name of our street is Oak Drive.

We saw the farmer **drive** the cows into the pasture.
We saw the farmer **guide** the cows into the pasture.

Father is teaching Mother to **drive.**
Father is teaching Mother to **make an automobile go.** She is learning how to steer an automobile and make it go.

Last night Father **drove** the car home from work.

Yesterday the car was **driven** by my brother.

driven   Father has **driven** the car to the store.   When he returns, he will drive us to the park.

---

driver   A **driver** is a person who drives.   A driver of a truck is a truck driver.   A driver of a bus is a bus driver.

Mother is the driver of the red car.

---

driveway

A **driveway** is a road that goes from a street to a house or a garage.   Our driveway leads to a garage.

---

drop

A **drop** is a little bit of liquid which becomes a tiny ball when it falls.

The rain falls in **drops.**

The doctor told me to put three **drops** of medicine in a glass of water.

Billy saw the limb **drop** from high up in the tree.
Billy saw the limb **fall** from high up in the tree.

Do not **drop the cup.**
Do not **let the cup fall.**

Edward **dropped** the cup, but it did not break.

drove   Yesterday Henry **drove** the car home. Today I will drive the car home.

---

drown   If you do not get the cat out of the lake, it will **drown**.

If you do not get the cat out of the lake, it will **die under the water**.

People and many other animals need air to breathe. If they are put under the water, they cannot get air to breathe. They will **drown** if they stay under the water too long. They will die under the water.

---

drowsy   After working very hard, Daddy became **drowsy**.

After working very hard, Daddy became **sleepy**.

---

drug   When I was sick, the doctor gave me **a drug** to help me get well.

When I was sick, the doctor gave me **medicine** to help me get well.

---

drum   Gerald has a blue **drum**. He likes to beat his drum.

At Christmas time when Santa does come,
I hope he brings me a bright blue drum,
So when I learn how it is played,
I'll beat my drum in a big parade.

drummer   A **drummer** is a person who beats a drum.   Stephen is a drummer in the school band.

---

drunk   Alice has **drunk** three glasses of milk today.   Tomorrow she will drink three more glasses of milk.

---

dry   Ma will **dry** her clothes on the clothesline.
Ma will **take the water out of** her clothes on the clothesline.

The ground is **dry**.
The ground is **not wet**.

Mary **dries** the dishes for her mother.

Sally is **drying** her hair in front of the fan.

Billy said, "I am **dry**."
Billy said, "I am **thirsty**."

---

duck   A **duck** is a bird with a flat bill.   A duck can swim and walk.   Some ducks can fly.   This is a duck.

A **duck** says, "Quack, quack."

John will **duck** if I throw a stone at him.
John will **get down and out of the way** if I throw a stone at him.

dug   Two days ago we **dug** a hole in our yard and planted a tree. Tomorrow we will dig a hole for another tree.

---

dull   The knife is **dull**.
The knife is **not sharp**.

Some people are **dull**.
Some people are **stupid**.

The tramp's coat was **a dull** color.
The tramp's coat was **not a bright** color.

The book I am reading is **dull**.
The book I am reading is **not interesting**.

---

dumb   Animals are **dumb**.
Animals are **not able to talk**.

---

during   **During the ball game,** it started to rain.
While the ball game was going on, it started to rain.

---

dusk   **Dusk** is the time of evening just before it gets dark. The street lights come on at dusk.

---

dust   **Dust** is very, very small bits of dirt and other things. The wind very often blows dust around. The wind blew dust into my eyes.

Patricia has to **dust** the furniture every day.
Patricia has to **wipe the dust from** the furniture every day.

D d

dusty   The furniture in the old house is **dusty**.
The furniture in the old house is **covered with dust**.

Dutch   Amsterdam is a **Dutch** city. It is a city in Holland. People who are citizens of Holland are called Dutch people. Hans was born in Holland. He is Dutch. The language he speaks is Dutch.

---

dwell   Mr. and Mrs. Brown **dwell** in a brick house.
Mr. and Mrs. Brown **live** in a brick house.

---

dying   When they pulled the cat out of the lake, they thought it was **dying**. But the cat did not die. It lived.

This is the fifth letter of the alphabet.

ABCDEFGHIJKLMNOPQRSTUVWXYZ

abcdefghijklmnopqrstuvwxyz

E e

each   **Each boy** has a bicycle.

Everyone of the boys has a bicycle. There are four boys in the group. There are also four bicycles. Each one of the four boys owns a bicycle.

---

eager   John is **eager** to go on the picnic.

John is **wanting very much** to go on the picnic. He is very excited about going on the picnic.

---

eagle   An **eagle** is a large bird that eats other birds and animals. This is an eagle.

High in the sky do eagles fly
  To find some food below;
Their eyes like telescopes look down
  And tell them where to go.

The eagle's wings are very fast
  To chase a tasty treat;
Its claws reach out and quickly snatch
  An animal to eat.

---

ear

An **ear** is part of the body which hears sounds. Albert is pointing to one of his ears.

Some dogs have **ears** that stand up. Other dogs have ears that lie down.

Did you ever eat corn off the **ear**?
Did you ever eat corn off the **cob**?

early   Father is expecting an **early** telephone call.   He is waiting for someone to call him very soon.

The milkman comes **early** in the morning.   He comes before I get out of bed.

I went to school **early**.   I went to school before it opened.

Early to bed and early to rise
Makes a man healthy, wealthy and wise.

---

earn   If I work in the yard, I will **earn** five dollars for my work.
If I work in the yard, I will **be paid** five dollars for my work.

---

earth   This is the **earth**.   We live on the earth.
It is like a ball.

Charles digs in the **earth**.
Charles digs in the **ground**.

---

earthworm   An **earthworm** is a long worm that lives in the ground. Earthworms crawl about in the ground and make tunnels.   The tunnels keep the earth loose.

---

easily   Paul lifted the box **easily**.
Paul lifted the box **with no trouble**.

---

east   The sun comes up in the **east**.   If you look at the sun early in the morning, you will be looking east.   Do you know the other directions?

E e

Easter   **Easter** is a Sunday in spring. On Easter many people go to church. They thank God for the good things he has done for them. Do you know what they are?

We color eggs on **Easter.** We put them in an Easter basket.

Here is an **Easter** lily.

---

easy   Mildred said, "It is **easy** to skip the rope."
Mildred said, "It is **not hard** to skip the rope."

---

eat   When we **eat,** we take food in our mouth and swallow it. Cows eat grass. People eat vegetables, fruits, and meats.

Yesterday Raymond **ate** two pieces of cake.

After I had **eaten** dinner, I went to play.

I try to be polite when I am **eating.**

---

edge  The glass is on the **edge** of the table. If you do not move the glass from the edge of the table, it will fall on the floor.

The **edge** of the knife cuts through the bread.
The **sharp side** of the knife cuts through the bread.

---

education   We go to school to get **education.** We learn many things at school. The teachers at school teach us many things that we should know.

effort **Effort** means *trying hard.* Patrick put much effort into learning English. He tried hard to learn English. Patrick worked hard to know English well.

---

egg The bird laid an **egg** in the nest. A little bird will come out of the egg.

Chickens lay the eggs that we eat. Do you sometimes have eggs for breakfast?

Hickety, pickety, my black hen,
She lays eggs for gentlemen;
Gentlemen come every day,
To see what my black hen does lay.
Some days five and some days ten,
She lays eggs for gentlemen.

---

eight  Here are **eight** buttons. Can you count them?
1 2 3 4 5 6 7 8 9 10

One, two, three, four,
Mary at the cottage door,
Five, six, seven, eight,
Eating cherries off a plate.

---

eighteen Eight added to ten is **eighteen**
8 + 10 = **18**

Can you count to eighteen?
1 2 3 4 5 6 7 8 9 10 11 12 13 14 15 16 17 **18** 19 20

---

eighteenth Jerome is the **eighteenth** person standing in a line. There are seventeen people standing in line in front of Jerome.

E e

eighth

John is the **eighth** boy in the row. There are seven people in the row before him. Do you know which person John is?

The seventh person in the row is sitting in front of John.

---

eighty

Ten 8's are **eighty**.

$8 + 8 + 8 + 8 + 8 + 8 + 8 + 8 + 8 + 8 = 80$

Eight times ten is **eighty**.

$8 \times 10 = 80$

Billy got eight marbles each day for ten days. At the end of eight days, he had **eighty** marbles.

---

either

I have two pieces of candy. You may have **either** of them. You may have one or the other of them. Take the piece of candy that you want.

On **either** side of the path there were oak trees. There were oak trees on both sides of the path.

---

elbow

Timothy has a hole in his sleeve. His **elbow** is coming out of the hole in his sleeve. Do you see Timothy's elbow?

Timothy's **elbow** is between the upper part and lower part of his arm. He can bend his arm by using his elbow.

elect   We will **elect** someone to be our leader.

We will **choose** someone to be our leader. We can elect our leader either by voting or by just picking him out.

electric   An **electric** lamp makes a light to see by. An electric iron makes heat to press clothes by.

An electric motor makes the electric washing machine go. Electric things work by electricity.

electricity   **Electricity** is able to do work for us. It travels through wires. Electricity can make heat. In toasters it can toast bread for us.

Electricity can make light. In lamps it can make light for us.

Electricity can make motors go. In a washing machine it can wash our clothes.

Electricity can send pictures and sound through the air. In radios and televisions we can hear voices and see pictures from far away.

elephant

An **elephant** is a very large animal with gray skin and big ears. An elephant has two long teeth on each side of his mouth. His nose is so long that he can pick up food and other things with it.

An elephant's nose is like a hose,
A nose that's called a trunk,
To pick up straw that he does eat
And water that is drunk.

elevator   An **elevator** is a little room that goes up and down to the floors of a building. It brings people upstairs and downstairs. People use an elevator instead of stairs.

A tall building where grain is stored is also called an **elevator.**

---

eleven   Philip sees **eleven** birds. Do you see them too? Can you count them?

Ten and one make eleven.
10 + 1 = 11

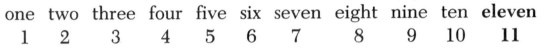

one two three four five six seven eight nine ten **eleven**
1   2   3   4   5   6   7   8   9 10 **11**

Do you know what number comes after eleven?

---

eleventh   "K" is the **eleventh** letter of the alphabet.

A B C D E F G H I J **K** L M N O P Q R S T U V W X Y Z

The first letter of the alphabet is "A." "Z" is the twenty-sixth letter of the alphabet. "Z" is also the last letter of the alphabet. Do you know what the seventeenth letter of the alphabet is?

---

elf   In fairy tales, a naughty little fairy is called an **elf.** Did you ever hear a story about elves? Elves are not real.

elm   An **elm** is a large tree. The branches of an elm tree spread out. At home we have an elm tree whose top is like an umbrella.

There is much shade under an elm tree. People like to sit in the cool shade of an elm tree when it is sunny and hot.

---

else   What **else** do you have in your pocket?
What **other thing** do you have in your pocket?

Who else will be coming to the party?
What other person will be coming to the party?

Let's go to **some place else** now.
Let's go to **some different place** now.

Be good; **else** you will be punished.
Be good; **if not** you will be punished.

---

embrace   Mother likes to **embrace** the baby. She likes to hold the baby in her arms to show love.

---

empty   Judy will **empty** the basket.
Judy will **take everything out of** the basket.

The box is **empty.** It has nothing in it.
The bowl is full. It has fruit in it.

E e

end ══════════ One **end** of the stick is red. The other **end** of the stick is green.

The **end** of the story was very sad.
The **last part** of the story was very sad.

Martin stayed until the **end** of the baseball game.
Martin stayed until the **finish** of the baseball game.

Mother said to the children, "**End** your loud noise."
Mother said to the children, "**Stop** your loud noise."

The noise **ended.**
The noise **stopped.**

---

endless A circle is **endless** because it has no end. A circle meets itself everywhere.

---

enemy An **enemy** is someone who does not like you and may hurt you.

A soldier fights his **enemies.** Patty said, "I wish I could have all friends and no enemies."

---

engine An **engine** makes things go. Our car has an engine to make it go.

Airplanes need **engines** to fly. Can you find the engines on these airplanes? All those engines without propellers are jet engines. Jet engines make airplanes go very fast.

Can you find the airplanes with jet engines?

engineer An **engineer** is a man who takes care of engines and makes them go.

Uncle David is a train engineer. He drives and takes care of a train engine.

England **England** is a country on the other side of the Atlantic Ocean. England is an island. It is a country with water all around it.

England is a country
  That's far across the sea.
England is an island,
  A place I'd like to see.

England has a queen, sir,
  But sometimes has a king.
England is so green, sir,
  It's what the rains do bring.

English London is an **English** city. It is a city in England. People who are citizens of England are called English people. Wilfred was born in England. He is English. The language he speaks is English.

enjoy We **enjoy** going on a picnic.
We **like** going on a picnic.

When you **enjoy** a thing, you like it. It makes you feel happy. I enjoy music. I enjoyed going to the beach.

enough I have **enough apples** for the twelve boys.
I have **as many apples as are needed** for the twelve boys.
I have twelve apples in my bag. I can give an apple to
each boy.

---

enter You **enter** the room through the doorway.
You **go into** the room through the doorway.

---

entire Paul ate the **entire** pie.
Paul ate the **whole** pie. The complete pie was eaten by
Paul.

---

envelope

An **envelope** is like a flat paper bag. We put
letters in envelopes when we send them through
the mail.

Milton put his letter in an **envelope**. He wrote an
address on the envelope. Then he put a stamp
on it. Finally, he gave the letter in the envelope
to the mailman. Milton wrote the letter to his
friend Bob. Milton put Bob's address on the
envelope.

---

equal Ruth and Margaret are **of equal** weight.
Ruth and Margaret are **the same** weight.

This pie is cut into **equal** parts. Each
piece is the same size.

Ten pennies **equal** one dime.
Ten pennies **are worth as much as** one dime.

This sign = means **is equal to.**   3 + 3 = 6.

equally   The two kittens are **equally** pretty.   One kitten is just as pretty as the other kitten.   Both are pretty.

---

erase   Sally will **erase** the writing from the blackboard.
Sally will **rub out** the writing from the blackboard.

---

eraser   An **eraser** is anything to rub out a mark.   There is a rubber eraser on the end of my pencil.

---

errand   William did an **errand** for his mother.   He went to the store and bought his mother some things.   William likes to do errands for his mother.   Very often William takes little trips to do things for his mother.

---

error   Joe made an **error** in spelling.
Joe made a **mistake** in spelling.   He spelled the word *cat* in this way: "kat."   This spelling is not correct.

---

escape   I put my bird in a cage so that he would not **escape.**
I put my bird in a cage so that he would not **get away.**   If I did not keep my bird in a cage, he would then fly away and never come back again.   I like my bird.   I do not want him to escape.

Eskimo   An **Eskimo** lives in the north of North America.   There is much ice and snow in the land of the Eskimos.   It is very cold there.

Eskimos are not very tall. They have straight black hair.   Most Eskimos get their food by hunting and fishing.

especially   I **especially** like apples.   I like them in a special way.   I enjoy eating apples very much.

---

even   Mother will **even** the frosting on the cake.
Mother will **make smooth** the frosting on the cake.

The ground is **even** along the river.
The ground is **flat** along the river.   The ground has no hills.

Jimmy and Bob are playing in the sand at the beach.

They made two **even** piles of sand.
They made two **equal** piles of sand.

Both piles of sand are the same size.   They are even.

It is eleven o'clock, and David has not **even** eaten breakfast.
It is eleven o'clock, and David has not **yet** eaten breakfast.

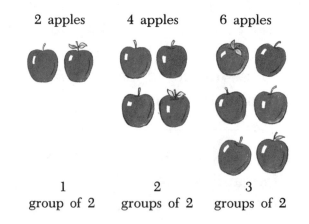

2 apples	4 apples	6 apples
1 group of 2	2 groups of 2	3 groups of 2

You can make groups of 2 in **even** numbers and not have anything left over.   Two, four, and six are even numbers.

---

evening   **Evening** is the end of the day and the beginning of the night.

event   An **event** is anything that happens. Yesterday I went to a party; it was a happy event. A week ago my father fell and hurt himself; it was a sad event.

In the event of rain, there will be no baseball game.
If it rains, there will be no baseball game.

---

ever   Have you **ever** seen an elephant?
Have you **at any time** seen an elephant?

Alice is **ever** ready to help her mother.
Alice is **always** ready to help her mother.

---

evergreen   An **evergreen** is a tree or a plant that has green leaves during the whole year. Pine trees are evergreens.

---

every   **Every** person in the room got a piece of candy.
Each person in the room got a piece of candy. There were five children in the room. **Each** one of the five children got a pice of candy.

---

everybody   **Everybody** eats and breathes.
Every person eats and breathes. All people must eat and breathe to live.

---

everyone   Julia invited **everyone** in our class to her party.
Julia invited **each person** in our class to her party.

---

everything   The house and **everything** in it burned down.
The house and **all the things** in it burned down.

everywhere   Paul looked **everywhere** in the house for his ball.
Paul looked **in every place** in the house for his ball.

---

evil   When I am selfish, I am doing something that is evil. It is bad to be selfish. I do not want to do something that is wrong.

The **evil** man beat his little dog for no reason.
The **bad** man beat his little dog for no reason.

---

exact   The **exact** price of this dress is five dollars. Mother said, "I will pay the exact price. I will pay five dollars. I will not pay a penny more or a penny less."

Mary bought some apples for fifty cents. Fifty cents was the **exact** price of the apples. Mary gave the man the exact money. She gave the man fifty cents, not one penny more nor one penny less.

---

exactly   It is **exactly** three o'clock. It is not earlier than three o'clock. It is not later than three o'clock.

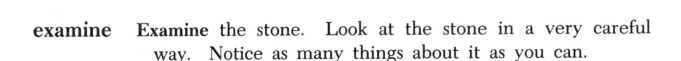

---

examine   **Examine** the stone. Look at the stone in a very careful way. Notice as many things about it as you can.

---

except   All **except** two children came to the party.
All **but** two children came to the party. Two children did not come to the party.

excess   Mother used the **excess** dough for cookies.
Mother used the **extra** dough for cookies.

---

exchange   Joseph will **exchange** his shoes because they are too small. Joseph will go to the shoe store and give his shoes back to the man. The man at the shoe store will give Joseph new shoes that will fit. Joseph and the man at the shoe store will make an **exchange.**

---

excited   The children are **excited** about going to the beach. They are so happy they are going to the beach that they are jumping up and down, clapping their hands, and singing.

---

exclaim   To **exclaim** means to *cry out.* When Bobby saw all the presents under the Christmas tree, he exclaimed, "Santa Claus has come!"

---

excuse   An **excuse** tells why you have done something wrong.

Mother wrote an **excuse** for Tom. She wrote the excuse to his teacher. The excuse was a note telling Tom's teacher why Tom was absent from school.

Bill said, "**Excuse** me, please. I must go home now."
Bill said, "**Pardon** me, please. I must go home now."

It is polite to say "Excuse me" if you hit or bump somebody by accident. If you are talking to somebody and if you must leave, it is polite to say, "Excuse me, but I must go."

179

exercise

Exercise is doing something over and over again. We do exercises to become strong. We also do exercises to be able to do things well.

Fred is doing **exercises** to make himself strong.

Nancy has **exercises** to practice on the piano. She has to play the exercises many times.

---

exist Witches do not **exist.** They are not real. There are no persons who are real witches. Some people only pretend that they are witches.

---

expect We **expect** a letter from Aunt Martha.
We **are waiting for** a letter from Aunt Martha.

---

explain The teacher will **explain to us** the story.
The teacher will **try to make us understand** the story.

Mike **explained** the word.
Mike **told the meaning of** the word. This book explains words.

---

express Teresa can **express herself** well.
Teresa can **say what she wants to say** well.

extra   Do you have **extra money?**
Do you have **more money than you need?**

Mother has to do **extra work.**
Mother has to do **more work than usual.**

---

eye   An **eye** is that part of a person or animal by which things can be seen. We see with our eyes.

Ann has her **eyes** open. Her eyes are blue. Ronald has his eyes closed. We cannot see his eyes.

What color are your eyes?

---

eyebrow   An **eyebrow** is the hairs that grow above your eye.

---

eyelash   An **eyelash** is one of the long hairs that grows on the edge of your eyelid.

---

eyelid   An **eyelid** is the part of your eye that opens and closes. When you are asleep, your eyelids are closed.

This is the sixth letter of the alphabet.

ABCDE**F**GHIJKLMNOPQRSTUVWXYZ

abcde**f**ghijklmnopqrstuvwxyz

face A **face** is the front side of somebody's head. Your face is your chin, cheeks, nose, mouth, eyes, and forehead.

The teacher said, "**Face** the blackboard." She said, "Look toward the blackboard."

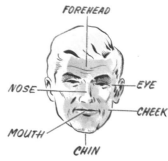

---

fact A **fact** is a thing that is true. It is a fact that spring comes after winter. Do you know some more facts?

---

factory A **factory** is a large building where things are made. Automobiles are made in a factory. Airplanes are made in a factory. My father works in a factory where they make tractors. They have many big machines in that factory.

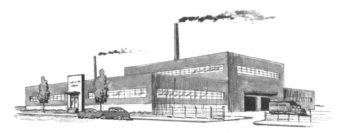

---

fade The red dress will **fade**.
The red dress will **lose some of its color.** The red dress will become pink, or less red.

 This is the red dress.

 This is the red dress after it faded.

Flowers **fade.** They dry up and die.

F f

fail   Because John is walking so slowly, he will **fail** to get to school on time.

Because John is walking so slowly, he will **not be able** to get to school on time.

Timothy **failed** in school because he did not work hard. He did not go on to the next grade. Timothy was sad because he did not pass.

---

faint   The picture on the page is **faint.** It is not clear. The picture is very dull.

The sick old lady spoke with a **faint** voice.
The sick old lady spoke with a **weak** voice.

I saw a lady **faint.** She suddenly fell down and acted as if she were sleeping. The lady was sick.

---

fair   Mother and Father took me to the **fair.** At the fair we saw cows, horses, pigs, and many other animals. People were also selling many things which they had made. There was also a merry-go-round at the fair. There were many games to play at the fair.

Sheila has **fair** hair.
Sheila has **light** hair.

Yesterday was a **fair** day. The sun was shining with no clouds in the sky.

Al is always **fair** in playing games
Al is always **honest** in playing games. Al always tells the truth.

fairy

This is a **fairy**. **Fairies** are not real people. They use magic to make people happy or unhappy. Do you like to read fairy stories?

Did you ever read the story of Cinderella? In this fairy story, Cinderella's fairy godmother changes a pumpkin into a beautiful coach. She does many other good things for Cinderella.

---

faithful   Jerome is my **faithful** friend. He is an honest person. I can trust him. When I have trouble or when I need something, Jerome will always try to help me.

---

falcon   A **falcon** is a kind of hawk. A falcon can be taught to catch other birds.

---

fall   **Fall** is one of the seasons of the year. Summer is the season before fall. Winter is the season after fall. Fall is also called autumn.

We watched the leaves **fall** from the tree.
We watched the leaves **come down** from the tree.

The man **fell** from the horse. The man suddenly came down from the horse, so that his body hit the ground.

Humpty Dumpty sat on a wall;
Humpty Dumpty had a great fall;
All the king's horses and all the king's men
Cannot put Humpty Dumpty together again.

Humpty Dumpty is an egg. He has **fallen** from the wall.

false   Gordon told a story that was **false.**
Gordon told a story that was **not true.**

Grandfather has **false** teeth.   He has teeth that are not real.

---

family   A **family** is a father, a mother, and their children.   There are five people in the Smith family: Mr. Smith, Mrs. Smith, Judy, Richard, and Joel.

Sometimes when we talk about our family, we mean our grandfather, grandmother, our aunts, our uncles, and our cousins.

---

fan   A **fan** is something that makes a breeze.

 This is an electric fan.    This is a paper fan.

Sally will **fan** herself when it becomes hot.

Terence is a baseball **fan.**   He likes baseball very much.

---

fancy   Can you **fancy** Daddy with a beard?
Can you **imagine** Daddy with a beard?

 I **fancy** having my hair long.
I **like** having my hair long.

Mary got a **fancy** dress for her birthday.
Mary got a **beautifully trimmed** dress for her birthday.
Mary wears a plain dress to school.   But she wears a fancy dress to church on Sunday.

186

far   The lake is **far** away.
The lake is **a long distance** away.   The lake is not near.

How **far** is it to your house?   Is it a long way or a short way
to your house?

Daddy's shirt is **far** too big for little Billy.
Daddy's shirt is **much** too big for little Billy.

---

fare   We have to pay **fare** on the bus.
We have to pay **money to ride** on the bus.

---

farm   My aunt and uncle live on a **farm** in the country.   On their
farm there is a big garden.   In the garden many kinds of
fruits and vegetables grow.   There are also many animals
on the farm.   There are cows, horses, pigs, sheep, chickens,
ducks, cats, and dogs.

---

farmer   A **farmer** is a person who lives and works on a farm.

---

farmyard   The yard or space around the barn or other buildings on a
farm is called the **farmyard**.   The chickens and ducks
are in the farmyard.

farther　Martin walked two miles to the school.　Norman walked three miles to the lake.

　　Norman walked **farther** than Martin.
　　Norman walked **for a longer distance** than Martin.

---

farthest　Martin walked two miles.　Norman walked three miles. Stanley walked four miles.

　　Stanley walked the **farthest**.
　　Stanley walked the **longest distance**.

---

fast　The dog runs **fast**.
　　The dog runs **quickly**.

Grandmother cannot walk **fast**.　She must walk slowly.

The car goes **fast**.
The airplane goes **faster**.
The rocket goes **fastest**.

---

fasten　Rosemary will **fasten** the door.
　　Rosemary will **lock** the door.

Mother helps Brenda to **fasten** her dress.
Mother helps Brenda to **button** her dress.

I will **fasten** the letter on the package.
I will **put** the letter on the package.　I will use glue to fasten the letter on the package.

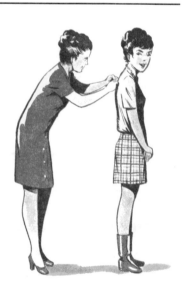

fat   This man is **fat**.    This man is thin.

FAT

THIN

Mother bought a roast with much **fat** on it.   When we cook fat, it becomes grease.

---

father   My **father** and my mother are my parents.   My father is married to my mother.   He takes care of our family.   He works to get money for us.   I call my father "Daddy."

---

faucet   This is a water **faucet**.   We turn the handle of the faucet one way to allow the water to come out.   We turn the handle of the faucet the other way to stop the water from pouring out.

---

fault   It was my **fault** that the window was broken.
It was my **mistake** that the window was broken.

Some people have many **faults**.   They do many things that are wrong.

---

favorite   This is **my favorite book**.
This is **the book which I like best**.

fear   Birds **fear** cats.

Birds **are afraid of** cats.   They are scared of cats because cats like to eat birds.

---

feast

On Thanksgiving Day we had a **feast**. On Thanksgiving Day we had a **big dinner.**

We **feast** on Christmas Day. We eat very much on Christmas Day.

---

feather   This hat has a big blue **feather** in it. The feather comes from a bird. Birds are covered with feathers.

Feathers are soft and light. They are used in pillows.

February   **February** is the second month of the year. February has twenty-eight days. Every four years February has twenty-nine days.

---

fed   The mother robin **fed** the baby robins.
The mother robin **gave food to** the baby robins.

Did you ever see a robin feed its chicks?

---

feeble   The old lady is too **feeble** to walk any faster.
The old lady is too **weak** to walk any faster.

feed   Mother will **feed** my baby brother.
Mother will **give food to** my baby brother.

Our dog has already been **fed** today.

We watch them **feeding** the elephants at the zoo.

---

feel   Eric likes to **feel** the cat's soft fur.
Eric likes to **touch** the cat's soft fur.

When you **touch** things, they may feel soft or hard, smooth or rough, warm or cold.

I **feel** sad today.
I **am** sad today.

Yesterday Sandra **felt** her baby sister's smooth, soft cheek.

---

feet

I have two **feet**. I put shoes and socks on my feet. I walk and run on my two feet.

Horses have four feet.

Billy hopped on one foot. He held one foot in the air and jumped with the other foot. Can you hop on one foot?

A **foot** is twelve inches long.
Father is six **feet** tall.

---

fell   The baby **fell** down, but she was not hurt. Did you ever fall down?

---

fellow   Peter is a happy **fellow.**
Peter is a happy **man.**

F f

felt   Mary **felt** the soft, fluffy fur of the kitten.
Mary **touched** the soft, fluffy fur of the kitten.

I **felt** sick because I ate too much candy.
I **was** sick because I ate too much candy.

---

fence

Farmer Brown put a **fence** around the cow pasture. A fence will not let the cows run away.

There are many kinds of fences. Some fences are made of wood. Other fences are made of wire.

---

fender   We find a **fender** over a wheel. Very often cars, bicycles, and other things which have wheels also have fenders. A fender keeps dirt from spreading all over when the wheel turns.

---

ferry   A **ferry** is a boat which carries people, automobiles, trucks, and buses across a river or a lake.

---

fetch   Mother said, "Please **fetch** the broom."
Mother said, "Please **get and bring back** the broom."

---

few   There are **a few** fish in our little fish bowl.
There are **not many** fish in our little fish bowl. There are many fish in the big ocean.

fiddle   This is a **fiddle.**

This is a **violin.**   Daniel makes beautiful music with his fiddle.

Old King Cole was a merry old soul,
And a merry old soul was he;
He called for his pipe,
And he called for his bowl,
And he called for his fiddlers three.

Each fiddler he had a fiddle,
And the fiddles went tweedle-dee;
Oh, there's none so rare as can compare
With King Cole and his fiddlers three.

---

field   A **field** is much land where there are no trees.   Sometimes there is a fence around the field.

The cows eat the grass in the cow field.   There is a fence around the cow field.

The farmer grows corn in the corn field.   He grows wheat in the wheat field.

---

fierce   Lions are **fierce** animals.

Lions are **wild** animals.   They are dangerous.

---

fifteen   Five pennies and ten pennies make fifteen pennies.

A nickel and a dime make fifteen cents.

$$5 + 10 = 15$$

Can you count to fifteen?

1 2 3 4 5 6 7 8 9 10 11 12 13 14 **15**

fifteenth There are fifteen houses on our street. Our house is the last house on the street. When you are counting the houses on our street, our house will be number fifteen. Our house is the **fifteenth** house on the street.

---

fifth Thursday is the **fifth** day of the week.

Sunday	Monday	Tuesday	Wednesday	Thursday	Friday	Saturday
first	second	third	fourth	**fifth**	sixth	seventh
1st	2nd	3rd	4th	**5th**	6th	7th

---

fifty Ten nickels make **fifty** cents.

.05 + .05 + .05 + .05 + .05 + .05 + .05 + .05 + .05 + .05 = .50

Five dimes make **fifty** cents.

.10 + .10 + .10 + .10 + .10 = .50

10   20   30   40   **50**

Can you count to fifty?

---

fig A **fig** is a small fruit that has the shape of a pear. Figs have tiny round seeds in them. They grow where it is warm.

---

fight

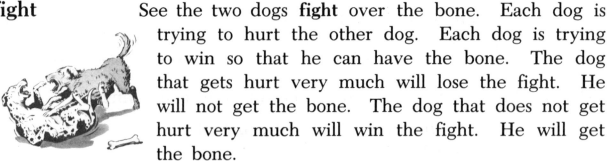

See the two dogs **fight** over the bone. Each dog is trying to hurt the other dog. Each dog is trying to win so that he can have the bone. The dog that gets hurt very much will lose the fight. He will not get the bone. The dog that does not get hurt very much will win the fight. He will get the bone.

When there is a war, soldiers **fight** for their country.

Yesterday the cat and dog **fought** in our yard.

figure   Each number is a **figure.**

        1 2 3 4 5 6 7 8 9 10

        The teacher is drawing two **figures** on the blackboard.

        The teacher is drawing two **shapes** on the blackboard. She is drawing a circle and a square.

---

file   A **file** is a long piece of metal with rough sides. A file makes things smooth.

        This is a nail **file.** It is used for making your fingernails smooth.

        This is a wood **file.** It is used for making wood smooth.

The children walked in **single file.**

The children walked in **one line each behind the other.**

---

fill   Edward will **fill** his bucket with water. He will put water into the bucket until there is no more room for water. The bucket will hold no more. It will be full.

Mary **filled** the basket with cherries.

Mother is **filling** the bathtub with water.

---

finally   **Finally** Billy came home.

        At last Billy came home. He was away at the beach for a whole month.

F f

find   Where can I **find** my dog?
Where can I **look for and get** my dog?

Tommy lost his dog. He is sad. Tommy is trying to find his dog.

Did you **find** the book interesting? Did you discover that it was a good book? I read it and saw that it was a very good book.

Yesterday he **found** his dog sleeping under the car.

---

fine   Daddy had to pay **a fine** for driving the car too fast.
Daddy had to pay **money** for driving the car too fast.

Mr. Jones is a **fine** carpenter.
Mr. Jones is a **good** carpenter.

The silk thread is **fine.**
The silk thread is **very thin.**

The salt is **fine.**
The salt is **in very small bits.**

The day is **fine.**
The day is **sunny and clear.**

---

finger

Paul is pointing with his **finger.**

We have five fingers on each hand. With our fingers we pick things up, we turn pages, we write, and we do many other things.

---

fingernail   I have a **fingernail** at the end of each finger. When my fingernails get too long, I must cut them. I must also keep my fingernails clean.

finish   Father will **finish** the work soon.
Father will **come to the end of** the work soon.

Jack **finished** his dinner.   Now he can go out to play.

---

fire

There was **a fire** in the house.
There was **something burning** in the house.

Fire can help us.   Fire can make us warm.   It can cook food.   Fire can make a light for us if we put it to a candle.

Fire can also do harm.   It can destroy houses and other buildings.   Fire can burn our skin.   We must be very careful when we use fire.

The boys are sitting around the fire.

---

fire alarm

We use a **fire alarm** to call firemen.   When we see that a house or building is going to be destroyed by fire, we ring the fire alarm.

The firemen will come quickly and put out the fire.   There is a fire alarm at the corner of my street.

---

firecracker   This is a **firecracker**.   A firecracker makes a loud noise.   On the Fourth of July we had many firecrackers.

fire engine

This is a **fire engine**. It carries a ladder and a hose. The fireman uses the hose to throw water on the fire.

"Fire! Fire!" said Mrs. Dyer;
"Where? Where?" said Mrs. Dare;
"Up the town," said Mrs. Brown;
"Any damage?" said Mrs. Gamage;
"None at all," said Mrs. Hall.

---

firefly

A **firefly** is a small insect that gives off little flashes of yellow light when it flies at night. Did you ever catch fireflies and put them in a jar? Fireflies are sometimes called lightning bugs.

A firefly's a tiny bug
  That makes a little light;
We catch and put them in a jug
  To make it shine so bright.

---

fireman A **fireman** helps us by putting out fires. The firemen are carrying hoses. They will put water on the fire.

fireplace

We have a **fireplace** in our house. Our fireplace is made of brick. Sometimes we make a fire in our fireplace. It makes the room warm.

---

fire truck   A **fire truck** is a fire engine.

---

firm   The brick wall is very **firm**.
The brick wall is very **strong and solid.**

---

first   January is the **first** month of the year.

Patricia is the **first** person in line. There is no one in front of her.

Sunday is the **first** day of the week.

Sunday	Monday	Tuesday	Wednesday	Thursday	Friday	Saturday
first	second	third	fourth	fifth	sixth	seventh
1st	2nd	3rd	4th	5th	6th	7th

At first Victor could not play the piano well.
In the beginning Victor could not play the piano well. Now, however, he plays well because he practiced much.

---

fish   A **fish** lives in water. Some fish are good to eat.

Dick likes to **fish**.
Dick likes to **catch fish.**

Little Tommy Tittlemouse
Lived in a little house;
He caught fishes
In other men's ditches.

fisherman

A **fisherman** is a man who fishes.

One, two, three, four, five,
Once I caught a fish alive,
Why did you let it go?
Because it bit my finger so.

Six, seven, eight, nine, ten,
Shall we go to fish again?
Not today, some other time,
For I just broke my fishing line.

---

fishhook   We catch fish with a **fishhook.**

Fishie, fishie, in the brook,
Daddy catch him with a hook,
Mama fry him in a pan,
Baby eat him like a man.

---

fit   Peter wants his shoes to **fit.**
Peter wants his shoes to **be the right size for him.**   Peter does not want his shoes to be too small or too big for his feet.

No more apples will **fit** in the basket.   The basket is full.   You cannot put one more apple in the basket.   There is no more room in the basket for another apple.

---

five   Here are the numbers from one to **five.**
Can you count to **five?**   How many fingers do you have?

1 2 3 4 **5**

Two added to three are **five.**
2 + 3 = **5**

Do you know what number comes after five?

fix   Albert broke the leg off the chair.
Father will **fix it.**
Father will **put it together again.**

The farmer is fixing the fence.

fizz   We opened a bottle of soda, and it started to **fizz.**
We opened a bottle of soda, and it started to **bubble up and make a hissing sound.**   It went, "Sssss!"

flag

This is an American **flag.**   It has three colors: red, white, and blue.

The American flag is sometimes called the "Stars and Stripes."

The policeman will flag down the car. He will give a signal to the driver of the car to stop by waving a flag.   The policeman wants the car to stop.

flake   A **flake** is a very small, thin piece of anything.

There were many snow**flakes** on Percy's jacket.

Mother put soap **flakes** in her washing machine.

flame   We saw the **flame** from the fire.
We saw the **colored light** from the fire.

flap   John has a **flap** on the pocket of his jacket. The flap is that part that folds over. The flap on John's pocket buttons to the pocket.

John is licking the glue on the flap of his envelope. With his tongue he is making the glue on the flap wet.

Birds **flap their wings** when they fly.
Birds **wave their wings up and down** when they fly.

The flag **flapped** in the breeze.
The flag **waved back and forth** in the breeze.

---

flash   A **flash** is a light that comes on suddenly and lasts a very short time. We saw a flash of lightning in the sky.

The accident happened in a **flash.**
The accident happened in a **short time.**

---

flashlight   A **flashlight** is a small electric light that you carry in your hand.

---

flat   Our automobile had a **flat.** The air went out of one of the tires.

The top of the table is **flat.**
The top of the table is **straight and even.**

Terence lay **flat** on his back and looked at the sky. He lay spread out on his back while he looked at the sky.

flea A **flea** is a small insect. A flea does not have wings, but it can jump. Fleas hide in the hair of animals and people. Fleas bite to get blood. My dog scratches because he has fleas.

---

fleece A **fleece** is a coat of wool on an animal. The farmer cut the fleece from the sheep's back.

---

flew The eagle **flew** over the hills.
The eagle **went through the air** over the hills.

---

flicker A **flicker** is a kind of woodpecker. Flickers have red and yellow on the underparts of their wings. Flickers like to eat ants.

We saw the flames of the fire **flicker** a few times before going out.
We saw the flames of the fire **move quickly** a few times before going out. The fire fluttered.

---

flies **Flies** are insects. Don't let a fly land on your food, for **flies** carry many diseases.

The bird **flies** in the sky.

---

float A boat can **float on** water.
A boat can **stay on top of** water.

Wood floats on water, but a rock sinks.

flock   A **flock** is a group of animals of one kind.

A **flock** of birds flew over our house.
A **group** of birds flew over our house.

People will **flock** to see the big train accident.
People will **come together in groups** to see the big train accident.

---

floor   The **floor** is the bottom of the room.   The ceiling is the top of the room.   We have a rug on our parlor floor.   Mother sweeps the kitchen floor every day.

Our house has three **floors.**   The first floor is near the ground.   The kitchen, the dining room, and the parlor are on the first floor.   The bedrooms and bathroom are on the second floor.   The attic is on the third floor.

---

flour   Flour is grain which is made into a powder.   Bread is made from flour.   Most of our bread is made from wheat flour. At the mill they grind wheat into flour.

Flour is also made from corn and rye.

---

flow   There is a **flow** of water coming out of the hydrant.
There is a **stream** of water coming out of the hydrant.

The children watched the water **flow** out of the pipe.
The children watched the water **run** out of the pipe.

flower   A **flower** is a blossom of any plant. Here is a bunch of flowers. Roses, lilies, pansies, tulips, daisies, apple blossoms, and jonquils are some flowers.

---

flown   The robins **have flown** south for the winter.
The robins **flew** south for the winter. They fly south every winter.

---

fluffy   My kitten's fur is **fluffy.**
My kitten's fur is **soft and smooth.**

---

flutter   The wind makes the clothes **flutter** on the clothesline.
The wind makes the clothes **move quickly back and forth** on the clothesline.

---

fly   A **fly** is an insect. It has two wings. Flies spread diseases. We must try to keep flies away from our food.

Harold likes to watch the birds **fly.**
Harold likes to watch the birds **go through the air.**

Did you ever see a jet plane **fly?**

Yesterday an owl **flew** over my house.

The pilot has **flown** many miles in his airplane.

The eagle is **flying** high up in the sky.

fold   Harriet must **fold** her letter so that it can fit into the envelope.

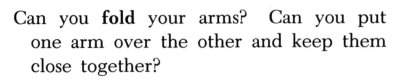

Mother is **folding** towels and sheets.

Can you **fold** your arms? Can you put one arm over the other and keep them close together?

---

folk   Our neighbors are friendly **folk.**
Our neighbors are friendly **people.**

---

follow   Dick's dog likes to **follow** him.
Dick's dog likes to **come after** him.

---

fond   Rebecca **is fond of** her baby brother.
Rebecca **likes** her baby brother.

---

fondle   Betsy likes to **fondle** her kitten gently. She likes to handle it with love.

---

fondness   James has a great **fondness** for art.
James has a great **love** for art.

---

food   **Food** is something we eat or drink. Vegetables, meats, fruits, nuts, and milk are foods.

fool   A **fool** is someone who is not wise.   Stanley was a fool.   He did not use good sense.

Did you ever **fool** anybody?
Did you ever **trick** anybody?

---

foolish   It is **foolish** to eat so much candy that you will get sick.   It is not wise to do such a thing.   It is not good sense.

---

foot   A **foot** is part of the body on which we walk or stand.   We have two **feet.**   We have five toes on each foot.   A dog has four feet.   Billy hurt his foot when he kicked the rock.

Twelve inches make a **foot.**
12 inches = 1 foot

---

football

Football is a game played between two teams.   Each team has eleven players.

Here is a **football.**

In many countries, the game of soccer is called football.   This game is played with a round football that is kicked or hit with any part of the body except the hands or arms.

---

footpath   A **footpath** is a path for people to walk on.   The children walked on the footpath.

---

footprint   Did you ever make a **footprint** in the sand?
Did you ever make a **mark with your foot** in the sand?

for   I know that Rita has a doll, **for** I saw it.
I know that Rita has a doll, **because** I saw it.

Mother left **for** New York.
Mother left **to go to** New York.

We used boxes **for** chairs.
We used boxes **in place of** chairs.

It is a good day **for** a picnic.
It is a good day **to have** a picnic.

Mary swept the floor **for** her mother. Mary's mother did not have to sweep the floor because Mary did it.

Tim is looking **for** his ball. Tim wants to find his ball.

How long can you play in the park? Can you play **for** ten minute more?

---

forehead   My **forehead** is that part of my face between my eyes and my hair.

> There was a little girl, and she had a little curl
>   Right in the middle of her forehead;
> When she was good, she was very, very good,
>   But when she was bad, she was horrid.

---

forest   There are many animals in the **forest.**
There are many animals in the **woods.**

---

forget   If I **forget** to bring my umbrella, I will get wet in the rain.
If I **do not remember** to bring my umbrella, I will get wet in the rain.

Tommy **forgot** his money when he went to the store.

I have **forgotten** where I put my book.

fork

This is a **fork**. We eat meat, vegetables, salad, and pie with a fork.

With a knife I cut my meat
Preparing it in bits to eat;
Be it beef or lamb or pork,
To pick it up I use a fork.

---

form   Sal will **form** a bowl out of a ball of wet clay.
Sal will **make** a bowl out of a ball of wet clay. With his hands, he will make the clay take the shape of a bowl.

---

forth   Mother rocked the baby **back and forth**.
Mother rocked the baby **in a backward direction and then in a forward direction**.

---

forty   Ten 4's are **forty**.

$4 + 4 + 4 + 4 + 4 + 4 + 4 + 4 + 4 + 4 = 40$

Four dimes make **forty** cents.
$10¢ + 10¢ + 10¢ + 10¢ = 40¢$
10   20   30   **40**

Can you count to forty?

---

forward   Richard walked to the **forward** part of the bus.
Richard walked to the **front** part of the bus.

The soldiers marched **forward**.
The soldiers marched **ahead**.

When Dad was parking the car, he made it go **forward** and backward.

fought   Yesterday my cat and dog **fought**. I will not let them fight today.

The soldiers fought in the war.

Father said, "I do not like to see people fighting."

---

found   Teresa **found** her hat.
Teresa **looked for and got** her hat.

Teresa said, "I do not always find everything that I lose."

---

fountain   A **fountain** is a place where water is made to squirt up.

There is a **fountain** in the park.

Susan is drinking water from a drinking **fountain**.

---

four   There are **four** ducks in the pond.
Can you count them?

One, two, three, four;
What's the matter? Count some more!
Five, six, seven, eight;
It's getting late and we can't wait!

Two and two are four.
$2 + 2 = 4$

fourteen   **Fourteen** is the number which comes after thirteen and before fifteen.   Can you count to fourteen?

1 2 3 4 5 6 7 8 9 10 11 12 13 **14** 15 16 17 18 19 20

Ten and four are **fourteen.**

$10 + 4 = 14$

---

fourteenth   There are fourteen people standing in a line.   Barbara is the last person in the line.   She is number fourteen in the line.   Barbara is the **fourteenth** person standing in line.

---

fourth   April is the **fourth** month of the year.   January is the first month.   February is the second month.   March is the third month.

first	second	third	**fourth**
1st	2nd	3rd	**4th**

Fourth of July   On the **Fourth of July** in the year 1776, the people of the United States of America told the world that they were a separate country.   They said that they did not belong to any other country.   They said that they were free.

In the United States, the fourth day of the month of July is sometimes called Independence Day.

---

fowl   Birds are called **fowl,** especially birds that we eat.   Geese, chickens, ducks, and pigeons are fowl.

fox

A **fox** is a wild animal. It looks like a dog. Some foxes are gray. Other foxes are red.

Foxes are sly. Their fur is used for coats and collars. Sometimes clothes are trimmed with fox fur.

---

frankfurter

A **frankfurter** is a roll of meat which is shaped like a sausage. Frankfurters have spices in them. They are sometimes called "hot dogs."

---

freckle

A **freckle** is a tan spot on the skin. Paul has red hair on his head, and freckles all over his face.

---

free

The water in the drinking fountain **is free.**
The water in the drinking fountain **costs no money.**

The bird outside the cage is **free.** It can fly and go where it wants.

The bird in the cage is not free. It must stay in the cage. It cannot fly and go where it wants.

---

freeze

Water will **freeze** when it gets very cold.
Water will **change to ice** when it gets very cold.

It was so cold outside that I almost **froze.**

The water in the refrigerator is **frozen.** It has become ice.

freight　The train is carrying coal, automobiles, and oil.　The things which the train brings from one city to another are called **freight.**　A train that carries freight is called a freight train.

Trucks, airplanes, and boats carry freight.

---

fresh　The tomatoes are **fresh.**　Grandmother just got them from the garden.

The bread is **fresh.**　Mother took it out of the oven a minute ago.

Annette put on a **fresh** dress.　The dress was clean and ironed.

The **fresh** air made Robert feel good.

The **clean and cool** air made Robert feel good.

Friday　**Friday** is the sixth day of the week.

Sunday	Monday	Tuesday	Wednesday	Thursday	Friday	Saturday
first	second	third	fourth	fifth	sixth	seventh
1st	2nd	3rd	4th	5th	6th	7th

---

friend　William is my **friend.**　I know William very well.　I like him very much.　William is good to me.

---

friendly　Sam treated me **friendly.**

Sam treated me **like a friend.**　He was very good to me.

frighten   Did the thunder **frighten** you?
Did the thunder **scare** you?

When the dog growled, it **frightened** me.   I was afraid of the dog.

---

frog   This is a **frog**.   It is a small animal that lives in or near the water.

---

from   The ball is coming **from** Richard.   It is going to Mary.

Tim took the apples **from** the basket.
Tim took the apples **out of** the basket.

An oak tree grows **from** an acorn.

Do you know that red is different **from** yellow?   It is not difficult to tell red **from** yellow.

---

front   Frank is washing the **front** of the car.   Susan is washing the back of the car.   The front of the car is the forward part of the car.

Louis is sitting **in front of** Peter.
Louis is sitting **before** Peter.

frost   **Frost** is frozen dew.   There was frost on the grass in the morning.

        Frost is frozen steam.   The frost on the window made a pretty picture.

        Mother will **frost** the cake.   She will put frosting on the cake.

---

frosting   Mother is covering the cake with **frosting.**   Frosting is sweet.   It is made from sugar.

> Mother makes some tasty cakes
> With frosting that's so sweet;
> I'm so happy when she bakes,
> For soon I'll eat a treat.

---

frosty   The windows are **frosty.**
The windows are **covered with frost.**

---

froze   Yesterday it became so cold that the water **froze.**
Yesterday it became so cold that the water **changed to ice.**

        It **froze** last night.   The frost came last night and killed the flowers.

        Mother **froze** the ice cream in the refrigerator.

---

frozen   The pond is **frozen.**   It is covered with ice.   The water in the pond freezes when it gets cold.

fruit

There are many kinds of **fruit.** Fruits grow on bushes, trees and vines. Apples, bananas, oranges, grapes, strawberries, and peaches are fruits.

---

fry We **fry** potatoes when we cook them in a little butter in a pan on top of the stove. Ma fried chicken in cooking oil.

---

full The glass is **full** of milk. It cannot hold any more milk. No more milk will fit into the glass. When something is full, it cannot hold any more.

Billy worked for a **full** hour.
Billy worked for a **complete** hour.

---

fun The children are having **fun** at the beach. They are having a good time playing.

Do you know some other ways for having fun?

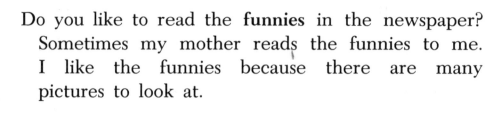

---

funnies Do you like to read the **funnies** in the newspaper? Sometimes my mother reads the funnies to me. I like the funnies because there are many pictures to look at.

funny My dog is **funny.** He makes me laugh.

---

fur My cat has **fur.**
My cat has **a lot of hair all over his body.**

Dogs, squirrels, beavers, and many other animals are covered with fur.

My mother has a **fur** coat. Her coat is made from the skin of an animal which has fur.

---

furnace We heat our house with a **furnace.**
We heat our house with a **big stove.**

Some **furnaces** burn coal. Some furnaces burn oil. Some furnaces burn gas. What kind of furnace do you have?

Our furnace is in the basement of the house.

---

furniture   The chairs, tables, and beds in our house are **furniture.** The bookcases and desks in the library are furniture too.

---

furry The kitten is **furry.**
The kitten is **covered with fur.**

This is the seventh letter of the alphabet.

ABCDEF**G**HIJKLMNOPQRSTUVWXYZ

abcdef**g**hijklmnopqrstuvwxyz

gain There is a **gain** of ten people at the meeting.
There is an **increase** of ten people at the meeting.

John will **gain** money by selling his bicycle. He will get more money than he paid for his bicycle.

Our clock gains. It runs too fast.

---

gallon

There are four quarts in a **gallon.**

We took a gallon bottle of lemonade to the picnic. My father put ten gallons of gasoline in the automobile's gas tank.

---

gallop We watched the horse **gallop.**
We watched the horse **leap into the air while running.**

---

game A **game** is a kind of playing. A game has rules. We must follow the rules of the games we play. Baseball and basketball are games.

---

gander A father goose is called a **gander.** William said, "We call a he-goose a gander."

---

garage A **garage** is a building to keep cars in. At night we keep our car in the garage.

garbage **Garbage** is food which has to be thrown away. Potato peels, corn cobs, meat bones, and spoiled food are garbage.

---

garden

A **garden** is a piece of ground where flowers or vegetables are grown.

Mary has a flower garden. She is watering her flowers.

I have a vegetable garden
   Of corn and peas and beets,
Of beans and squash and spinach,
   And other table treats.

---

gas **Gas** has no shape. Gas is not solid like a rock. It is not liquid like water. Air is a kind of gas. There are many kinds of gas.

The stove in our kitchen burns **gas.** This kind of gas is very dangerous. It must be used with great care. The gas in our kitchen stove burns very quickly. If we breath too much of this gas, we can die.

Gas is a short word for gasoline.

---

gash A **gash** is a long, deep cut. Tim fell and cut a gash in his leg.

---

gasoline **Gasoline** is a liquid which makes our automobile go. Gasoline is very dangerous. It catches fire very easily and burns very fast.

gate

A **gate** is like a door. It is part of a fence or wall. A gate opens and closes.

Helen is opening the gate.

---

gather

Susan will **gather** some flowers for her teacher.

Susan will **pick up and put together** some flowers for her teacher.

Many people **gathered** to see the accident.

Many people **came together** to see the accident.

---

gave

Yesterday Paul **gave** me a piece of candy. Today I will give Paul an orange.

---

gay

We had a **gay** time at the party.

We had a **merry** time at the party.

Mary's new dress is **gay.** It is bright and cheerful. Mary's dress has bright colors in it.

G g

geese   Herbert saw fifteen **geese** flying in the sky. Catherine saw only one goose. Did you ever see a goose?

---

general   Frank's father is a **general** in the army. The general is the head man in the army. Paul's father is a captain in the army. A general has a more important job than a captain.

---

generally   **Generally** we eat fish on Friday.
Usually we eat fish on Friday.

---

generous   Cora is **generous**. She is willing and glad to share her things with others. She allows other children to ride her bicycle.

---

gentle   My teacher is very **gentle**.
My teacher is very **kind and nice**.

Mary's voice is **gentle**.
Mary's voice is **soft and pleasant**.

My father gave me a **gentle** pat.
My father gave me a **soft, light** pat.

---

gentleman   A **gentleman** is a man who is kind and polite.

---

gently   Terence picked up the kitten **gently**.
Terence picked up the kitten **in a careful, soft, and tender way**.

genuine The diamond is **genuine.**

The diamond is **real.** Mother has a ring with a genuine diamond in it.

---

germ A **germ** is a tiny plant or animal that cannot be seen with our eyes alone. We need a microscope to see germs. Some germs are called diseases. Germs can make us sick.

---

get I **get** a new book every month from my Aunt Alice.
I **receive** a new book every month from my Aunt Alice.

Harry **gets** two dollars for cleaning the garage.
Harry **earns** two dollars for cleaning the garage.

When we **get** home, I shall watch television.
When we **arrive** home, I shall watch television.

Sally **gets up** early in the morning.
Sally **wakes up and leaves her bed** early in the morning.

The baby is **getting** big.
The baby is **becoming** big.

I **got** a cold because I **got my feet** wet.
I **became sick with** a cold because I **allowed my feet to become** wet.

---

giant A **giant** is a very large and strong man. In fairy stories we read about giants. Do you know the story of *Jack and the Bean Stalk?* There is a giant in this story. Fairy story giants are not real.

When something is larger than other things of the same kind, we call it **giant.** Mary said, "That tree is a giant. It is taller than all the other trees in the park."

gift

A **gift** is something that a person gives you because he likes you. At Christmas time Rose received many gifts. Her mother and father gave her a doll. Her Aunt Ann gave her a new dress. Rose got many other gifts. See Rose's gifts under the Christmas tree.

We also get gifts on our birthday. A gift is sometimes called a present.

---

giggle

The teacher told the girls not to **giggle**.
The teacher told the girls not to **laugh in a light and silly way.**

---

ginger

Ginger is a spice which is made from the root of the ginger plant. Ginger is used in cooking, in medicine, and in soda.

Gingerbread is cake made with ginger. Mother made me a gingerbread man.

---

giraffe

A **giraffe** is an animal with long legs and a very long neck. Giraffes can eat leaves from tall trees. Giraffes come from Africa.

A giraffe's neck is long and thin,
　As tall as many trees,
And since his head's among the limbs,
　He eats the tasty leaves.

girl A **girl** is a young woman. My little sister is a girl. She is ten years old. When my mother was little, she was a girl. When little girls become grown-ups, they are called women.

Teresa, Mary, and Patricia are girls. They are playing with their dolls.

> What are little girls made of, made of?
> What are little girls made of?
> Sugar and spice and all that's nice;
> And that's what little girls are made of, made of.

---

give Peter will **give** his book to Thomas. The book will then belong to Thomas. It will not belong to Peter anymore. Peter will give his book to Thomas to keep.

Yesterday Alice **gave** Catherine a pencil. Alice allowed Catherine to use the pencil. Today Catherine will give back the pencil to Alice. Alice gave Catherine her pencil to use.

Rebecca was **given** a puppy for her birthday.

Daddy is **giving** me a box of candy.

---

glad Mike is **glad** to be at the party.
Mike is **happy** to be at the party.

---

glance Every time the fire truck goes by, I **glance** out of the window.
Every time the fire truck goes by, I **look quickly** out of the window.

glass   Windows are made of **glass.** We can see through glass. Glass is hard, but it breaks very easily.

Some dishes are made of glass. Sandra is drinking her strawberry soda from a **glass.**

Glass is made by melting very fine sand with other materials. The soft heated glass can then be blown, pressed, or formed into different shapes.

---

glasses

These are my **glasses.** I wear them to help me see better. Sometimes glasses are called eyeglasses.

Some people cannot see far away. They need glasses to help them see in the distance. Some people cannot see near. They need glasses to help them see up close.

---

glossy   My father washed and put wax on the car.
He rubbed the wax on the car until the car became **glossy.**
He rubbed the wax on the car until the car became **smooth and shiny.**

---

glove

The man has a green **glove** on each hand.

A glove has a place for each finger and the thumb.

Richard sometimes wears mittens. A mitten has a separate place for the thumb, but it does not have separate places for each finger.

glue We use **glue** to stick things together. Frank used glue to fix the broken chair. In school we use glue to stick papers together.

Father will **glue** the leg on the table. He will stick the leg on the table with glue.

---

glum Gabriel is **glum** because he couldn't go to the picnic. He is quiet and sad.

---

gnaw Dogs like to **gnaw** the meat from bones.
Dogs like to **chew** the meat from bones.

We do not pronounce the *g* in "gnaw." We say, "–naw."

---

go John will **go** from his house to school when he finishes his breakfast.
John will **move** from his house to school when he finishes his breakfast. Do you go to school?

What makes the engine **go?**
What makes the engine **work?** The engine needs gasoline to make it go. The engine must have gasoline to make it run.

The children will **go** home at four o'clock.
The children will **leave for** home at four o'clock.

The ice cream **is gone.**
The ice cream **has disappeared.** The children have eaten it.

The hat **goes** in the closet.
The hat **belongs** in the closet. Its place is in the closet.

Tim is going to the party.
He **is going to** have fun there.
He **will** have fun there.

Yesterday, I **went** to see my grandmother.

goat   A **goat** is an animal with horns and a beard. The milk from goats is good to drink. This is a goat.

> Did you ever see some goats
>   With horns and beard and tail?
> Did you ever feed them oats
>   You carried in a pail?

---

gobble   Our turkey says, "**Gobble, gobble.**" Did you ever hear a turkey gobble?

Eugene was in such a hurry to go to the park that he gobbled his dinner. He ate his food too fast. He put too much food in his mouth at one time.

God   **God** made all things. He made the world, the stars, the moon, and the sun. He made all people. God is our Father. He is also the ruler of the world.

---

goes   The airplane **goes** very fast.
The airplane **moves forward** very fast.

The car **goes** if there is gasoline in it.
The car **works** if there is gasoline in it.

The book **goes** on the shelf.
The book **belongs** on the shelf.

The song **goes** like this. This is the way the song is sung.

Donald **goes** to school in the morning and comes home in the afternoon.

Do you know where this path **goes**.
Do you know where this path **leads**.

Susan likes to **go** swimming.

gold

Gold is a shiny, yellow metal. Gold comes from a mine. A mine is a deep hole in the earth. My father has a watch made out of gold. My mother's ring is made from gold, too.

---

goldenrod

Goldenrod is a plant that has yellow flowers. The yellow flowers grow on tall stems with leaves all along them.

> Goldenrod are flowers
>   That grow high in the meadow
> Above the green like towers
>   So bright and golden yellow.

---

goldfish

A **goldfish** is a small fish. It is the color of gold. We have two goldfish in a glass bowl. I like to feed our goldfish.

---

golf

Golf is a game. We play golf with a little white ball and with golf clubs. We must hit the little ball into a small hole with the golf clubs.

Golf is played on a large outdoor golf course. A golf course is a large field of grass. On this golf course, there are little holes. You must hit the little golf ball a long distance to get it into the little holes.

gone   We tried to catch the butterfly, but it was **gone.**

We tried to catch the butterfly, but it was **not there.**

Where has Samuel **gone?** Did he go to the park?

---

good   Mary is a **good** girl.

Mary is **not a bad** girl. She does her school work. She helps her mother. She obeys her mother and father. Mary tries to do what is right.

Edward's school work is **good.** He works very hard in school. He gets high grades. Edward is the smartest boy in his class.

This is a **good** day.

This is a **pleasant** day.

It was **good** of Aunt Martha to give me a gift.

It was **kind** of Aunt Martha to give me a gift.

Aunt Eleanor's diamond is **good.**

Aunt Eleanor's diamond is **real.** It is not false. Her diamond is not just a piece of glass. It is a jewel that is worth much money.

---

good-by   When we are going away from somebody, we say **good-by.** "Good-by" means "I hope that you will be very happy."

We sometimes spell "good-by" in this way: **good-bye.**

When we left Aunt Sophie's house, we said, "Good-by, Aunt Sophie!"

---

good morning   When we see somebody in the morning, we say **good morning** to them. "Good morning" means "I hope you will have a pleasant morning."

When Paul came to the breakfast table, he said, "Good morning, Mom and Dad!"

good night   Eileen says **good night** to her mother and father when she goes to bed at night. "Good night" means "I hope you sleep well during the night."

---

goody   Something very good to eat is called a **goody**. Candy and cookies are **goodies.**

---

goose   A **goose** is a large bird. It looks like a duck with a long neck. My uncle has three **geese.** Geese are good to eat. This is a goose.

> If I bought one goose on Monday,
> And on Tuesday did increase
> Its number by two, I could say,
> "Right now I own three geese."

---

gorgeous   The flowers in the garden were **gorgeous.** They were of many different and pretty colors. The flowers in the garden were very beautiful.

---

got   Yesterday I **got** a book from my Aunt Ann.
Yesterday I **received** a book from my Aunt Ann.

I **got** a cold last week.
I **caught** a cold last week.

I **got up** early this morning
I **woke up and left my bed** early this morning.

When we went for a walk, Grandmother **got** tired.
When we went for a walk, Grandmother **became** tired.

Today I will **get** a new coat.

gown  A **gown** is a long dress. My mother is wearing a gown to the party.

Some people wear a nightgown when they go to bed at night. A nightgown is like a long, loose dress.

---

grab **Grab** that book before it falls off the table.
Quickly take that book before it falls off the table. Peter **grabbed** the book before it hit the floor.

---

graceful The dancers are **graceful.** They dance in a beautiful way. We enjoy watching them dance.

---

grade Mary is in the third **grade** in school.
Mary is in the third **year** in school.

I got a good **grade** on my test.
I got a good **mark** on my test. I studied very hard. I answered all the questions on my test. All my answers were correct. My grade was 100. This is the highest grade.

---

grade school We go to **grade school** first. Then we go to high school. After high school, we go to college. Grade school is sometimes called elementary school or grammar school.

grain

Grain is the seeds of certain plants. We cannot eat the seeds of all plants. Some grains that we can eat are wheat, corn, rye, and oats. Flour comes from grain. Cereal comes from grain, too.

Dick got a **grain** of sand in his eye.
Dick got a **tiny piece** of sand in his eye. It hurt his eye. He tried to wash it out.

---

grand Our church is a **grand** building.
Our church is a **big and beautiful** building.

There's a grand old house
  Not far away
Where I'd like to be
  This very day,
With Grandpa and Grandma
  Two folk you'll find
So happy and gentle
  And, oh, so kind!

---

grandfather My father's father is my **grandfather.** My mother's father is my **grandfather,** too.

---

grandma **Grandma** is a name I give my grandmother. I love my grandma very much.

---

grandmother My father's mother is my **grandmother.** My mother's mother is also my **grandmother.**

233

G g

grandpa **Grandpa** is a name I give my grandfather. I love my grandpa very much.

---

grant The king will **grant** the soldier his wish.
The king will **give** the soldier his wish.

---

grape

A **grape** is a small round fruit. Grapes are found in bunches on grapevines. Grapes are good to eat. They can be green, red, or purple.

---

grapefruit A **grapefruit** is a large, sour fruit. A grapefruit looks something like an orange. But it is yellow and larger than an orange. Grapefruit is good to eat for breakfast.

Grapefruits, oranges, and lemons
Are fruits that grow on trees,
In places where the weather's warm,
And where it does not freeze.

---

grass Green **grass** grows in our yard. The grass in our yard is called our lawn. Father cuts the grass when it grows too high.

Plants that have grain are called grasses. Rye, wheat, and oats are grasses.

Cows like to eat grass.

234

grasshopper

A **grasshopper** is a bug. It has two very long legs. Grasshoppers can jump very high. Grasshoppers eat the things farmers grow. Farmers do not like grasshoppers.

---

grassy   The meadow is **grassy.**
The meadow is **covered with grass.**

---

gravel   **Gravel** is small stones. We have gravel in our driveway.

---

gray   Gray is a color. The gray dog is chasing the black cat.

---

graze   The cows **graze** in the meadow.
The cows **eat the grass from the ground** in the meadow.

---

grease   **Grease** is oil or fat. Butter, lard, and margarine are some greases.

---

great   George Washington was a **great** man.
George Washington was a **very important** man. He was the first president of the United States.

Elephants are **great,** heavy animals.
Elephants are **very big,** heavy animals.

greedy   We must not be **greedy** when we are eating.

We must not **want more than our share** when we are eating.

The big dog was **greedy** and ate all of the little dog's food.

---

green   **Green** is a color.   Grass is green.   The leaves of the trees are green.   Mary is wearing a green dress.

If you mix blue paint and yellow paint together you will get green paint.

---

greet   It is polite to **greet** people when you see them.

Pamela says, "Good morning, Mr. Smith.   How are you this morning?"   Pamela is **greeting** Mr. Smith.

Arthur said, "Good evening, Mrs. Lopez.   I hope you are well."   Arthur has **greeted** Mrs. Lopez.

Walter will greet his Aunt Helen.   He will say, "Hello, Aunt Helen.   It is so good to see you again."

---

grew   The little plant **grew** until it was a big bush.
The little plant **got bigger** until it was a big bush.

---

grind   Yesterday we saw the man **grind** coffee beans.   He put the coffee beans into a machine.   The machine cut the coffee beans into tiny pieces.   The man **ground** coffee beans so that we could make coffee in our coffee pot.

Father made the knife sharp by **grinding it**.
Father made the knife sharp by **rubbing it against a stone**.

groceries   **Groceries** are foods bought at a grocery. Apples, coffee, crackers, and a jar of pickles are all groceries.

---

grocery   A **grocery** is a store where we can buy food. Mother often sends me on an errand to the grocery store.

---

ground   Billy is digging into the **ground** to get some dirt.

Billy is digging into the **earth** to get some dirt. He will put the dirt into a flower pot. Billy's mother will plant a flower in the flower pot.

Yesterday the man at the grocery store **ground** coffee beans for us. He used a machine to chop the coffee beans into little bits.

Ground coffee beans which have been used are called coffee **grounds.** Mother took the coffee grounds out of the coffee pot.

---

group   A **group** is several people together. A group of men were washing the car.

A **group** is several things of the same kind together. We saw a group of bicycles in front of the school.

---

grove   A **grove** is a group of trees. There is a beautiful grove in the middle of the pasture.

grow   Plants, animals, and people **grow.**

Plants, animals, and people **become larger.** A little plant can grow to be a big plant. A puppy can grow to be a dog. A kitten can grow to be a cat. A little boy can grow to be a man.

The little plant **grew** all summer. Now it is a big plant.

We know that the plant is **growing** because it is getting bigger and bigger each day.

The tree has **grown** much this year.

Harry **grows** fast because he eats food that is good for him.

---

growl   Did you ever hear a dog **growl?** When a dog gets angry, he **growls.** He makes an angry sound in his throat. He says, "Grrrr." We should not go near a dog when he is **growling.**

---

grown   Mary has **grown much** during the year.
Mary has **become much bigger** during the year.

---

grown-up   My father is **grown-up.** He is big. He will not grow any more. My mother is a grown-up, too. She will not grow any more.

Helen is just a little girl. She must grow some more. She is not a grown-up. Little boys and girls will become grown-ups.

---

grumble   Some children **grumble** about everything they have to do. They are not happy about what they are told to do. In a low voice, they say they do not want to do what they should do.

grunt   The pig made a **grunt** when I gave him food.   He made a deep, quick noise in his throat.

We heard the pigs **grunt.**
We heard the pigs **make a deep, quick noise in their throats.**

---

guard   The soldier will **guard** the gate.   He will watch so that no one will go in through the gate.

The dog is **guarding the little baby.**
The dog is **watching the little baby so that no one will hurt him.**

Guard against catching cold.   Be careful so that you will not catch cold.

The United States Coast **Guard** protects the shores of the United States.

---

guess   Paul had some apples in a bag.   He said to Frank, "**Guess** how many apples are in my bag.   Try to tell me the number of apples in my bag."

Frank did not know how many apples were in Paul's bag, but Frank made a guess anyway.   He said, "I guess there are ten apples in your bag."   Paul said, "Your guess is wrong, Frank.   There are nine apples in my bag."

---

guest   We had **a guest** at our house.
We had **someone visiting** at our house.

A person who pays to live in a hotel is called a **guest** of that hotel.   We were the guests of a hotel when we went to New York.

guide A **guide** is a person who shows people the way.

Will you **guide me** through the forest?
Will you **show me the way** through the forest?

---

gum Did you ever chew chewing **gum?** We chew gum, but we do not swallow it. Chewing gum is sweet. It tastes good.

---

gun We shoot with a **gun.** Guns are very dangerous. The hunter is shooting the duck with his gun. The gun will kill the duck.

The policeman has a gun. Can you see where the policeman keeps his gun?

This is the eighth letter of the alphabet.

ABCDEFG**H**IJKLMNOPQRSTUVWXYZ

abcdefg**h**ijklmnopqrstuvwxyz

H h

ha When Stanley laughed, he said, "**Ha,** ha!"

---

habit A **habit** is the usual thing to do. I have the habit of brushing my teeth after each meal. Every time I eat a meal, I brush my teeth afterward.

I am **in the habit of** saying my prayers before I go to bed. Every night before I go to bed, I say my prayers.

---

had Teresa **had** a green dress.
Teresa **owned** a green dress. A green dress belonged to Teresa. Now the dress is torn and worn out. Teresa does not have the dress anymore.

Mother **had** the baby in her arms.
Mother **held** the baby in her arms.

We **had to** eat our vegetables. Mother said that we could not go out and play unless we ate our vegetables.

Yesterday at six o'clock, my mother **had** dinner ready.
Yesterday at six o'clock, my mother **made** dinner ready.

Patricia came to see me, but I **had** gone to the park.

---

hail **Hail** is frozen raindrops. The hail beat on the tin roof. It made a loud sound.

Did you ever see it **hail** in the summer?

---

hair My father has black **hair** on his head. My Uncle Stephen does not have any hair on his head.

My cat is covered with hair. The cat's hair is called fur.

242

half   Mother cut the pie in **half.**

Mother cut the pie in **two parts.**   Each
part is the same size.

One half of ten is five.
$$5 + 5 = 10$$

---

hall   In the **hall,** there are many doors.   The doors open into
rooms.   The hall is narrow.   I must walk through the hall
to go to my bedroom.   Margaret said, "We have long halls
in our school."

A very big room is also called a **hall.**   We had a meeting in a
large hall.

Halloween   **Halloween** is the last night in October.   On
Halloween children dress in funny clothes.
They also wear masks.

On Halloween some children carry jack-o'-lanterns.

---

ham   A **ham** is a piece of meat that comes from a pig.   Ham
comes from the upper part of
the pig's back leg.

On Easter we had ham for dinner.

H h

hamburger   Hamburger is beef that is ground up. Mother went to the butcher to buy some hamburger.

A **hamburger** is also a name for a sandwich made from hamburger meat which is pressed flat like a small saucer and cooked. It is then eaten between two sides of a bun or roll.

---

hammer

A **hammer** is used to put nails into wood. The top part of a hammer is made of metal. The handle of the hammer is usually made of wood.

Fred likes to **hammer.** He is **hammering** nails into the box.

In his toolbox, the carpenter had a hammer, a drill, a saw, a plane, and many other tools.

---

hand   This is a **hand.** We have two hands. Fingers are part of each hand. Each hand has five fingers. One of our fingers is called a thumb. Do you know which one it is?

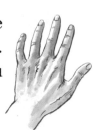

A clock has hands to point to the hour and the minute. Can you tell what time it is from the hands of the clock?

Sally will **hand me the book.**
Sally will **give me the book with her hand.**

Thomas will **hand out** the cards. He will give cards to everyone who is playing cards.

---

handbag   A **handbag** is a small bag which a woman holds in her hand. My mother carries her money in a handbag.

handful Patrick has a **handful** of pennies. He has as many pennies in his hand as he can hold. He cannot hold any more pennies in his hand.

---

handkerchief A **handkerchief** is a small square piece of cloth. I use a handkerchief for wiping my face. I also blow my nose in my handkerchief. Jimmy keeps a handkerchief in his pocket.

---

handle Grandfather is holding the ax by its **handle.** Grandmother is holding the cup by its handle.

Many things have handles. We hold them by their handles. Cups, pitchers, pots, and pans have handles.

I turn the handle of the car door to open it.

Jeannette will **handle** the kitten gently.
Jeannette will **hold and touch** the kitten gently.

---

handle bars The curved bar in the front part of a bicycle is called **handle bars.** I steer my bicycle with the handle bars.

---

handsome My father is **handsome.**
My father is **pleasant to look at.**

hang **Hang** your coat on the hook. Fasten your coat on the hook and let it fall loosely.

Yesterday Donald **hung** from a limb with both arms.

The picture was **hung** on the wall by a wire.

---

hangar A **hangar** is a building to keep airplanes in.

---

hangs The jacket **hangs** on the hook. **Hang** your hat near the jacket.

---

happen Martha asked, "When did the accident **happen?**" She wanted to know when the two cars bumped into each other.

Gertrude said, "The accident **happened** at two o'clock."
Gertrude said, "The accident **took place** at two o'clock."

Something has happened to Father's car. It will not run. Father's car will not go. It has stopped working.

---

happening It was an unusual **happening** when ten kittens were born. It was a strange event when our cat had ten baby kittens. Usually cats don't have as many kittens as that.

---

happily The children went to the party **happily.**
The children went to the party **with much joy.**

happiness   We have **happiness** when we are glad and merry.

---

happy   Bernard is **happy.** He is glad. When Bernard is happy, he smiles and laughs.

---

hard   A rock is **hard.** The kitten's fur is soft.

It is **hard** to swim ten miles.
It is **not easy** to swim ten miles.

John worked **hard.**
John worked **very much.**

---

harden   The ice cream will **harden** when it freezes.
The ice cream will **become hard** when it freezes.

---

hardly   We **hardly** had time to play one game.
We **only just** had time to play one game.

I **could hardly** see the airplane because it was so far away.
I **almost could not** see the airplane because it was so far away.

---

hare   A **hare** is an animal that looks like a rabbit. But it is bigger than a rabbit. Hares are gray or brown. A hare can run very fast.

Long ears, short tail, and rapid start
  Are shared by hare and rabbit;
So, you cannot tell them apart,
  Unless you're in the habit.

harm Vincent said, "My dog will not **harm** you."
Vincent said, "My dog will not **hurt** you."

---

harness A **harness** is straps which we put on a horse so that he can pull a wagon or a carriage. There is a yellow harness on the horse.

The farmer will **harness** the horse and hitch it to the wagon.
The farmer will **put a harness on** the horse and hitch it to the wagon.
Did you ever see a horse **harnessed?**

---

has Jerry **has** a red ball.
Jerry **owns** a red ball. Do you have a red ball?

Jerry **has** the ball in his hand.
Jerry **holds** the ball in his hand.

Ellen **has to** go home for dinner.
Ellen **must** go home for dinner.

Billy **has** a good time when he goes to the park.

Paul **has** worked all day.

---

hat I wear a **hat** on my head. There are many kinds of hats.

There are so many kinds of hats
  For any time or weather:
Some made of cloth; some made of straw;
  Some even with a feather.

hatch   The hen will **hatch** the eggs by sitting on them.

She will keep them warm until **they hatch**.
She will keep them warm until **little chicks
   come out of them.**

---

hate   Some people **hate** to work.
Some people **do not like** to work.

Mary hates snakes.   She is very much afraid of snakes.

---

haul   The donkey is carrying a big **haul** of sticks on his back.   He is
   carrying a big load of sticks.

The dog will **haul** the sled over
   the snow.
The dog will **pull** the sled over
   the snow.

The man **hauled** the load of sand from the beach to my
house.   The man carried the load of sand in his truck.

---

have   I **have** a puppy.
I **own** a puppy.   It belongs to me.

I **have** a button in my hand.
I **hold** a button in my hand.

We **have to** go to school at eight o'clock.
We **must** go to school at eight o'clock.

Jack will **have** fun at the party.

James and Peter **have** walked home from school.

Timothy **had** a ball, but he lost it.   Now he **has** none.

haven't   Mary and Judy **haven't** any money.
Mary and Judy **have not** any money.

---

hawk

A **hawk** is a large, strong bird. A hawk eats other birds and animals. This bird is a hawk.

> A hawk's in the sky
> With a very good eye,
>   Looking for some kind of treat:
> A wren or a rat,
> Or something like that,
>   Animals he'd like to eat.

---

hay   **Hay** is dried grass. The farmer cuts long grass to make hay. When the grass has dried in the sun, it becomes hay. Horses and cows eat hay. The farmer is putting the hay in the barn.

---

haystack   A **haystack** is a pile of hay. The farmer has a haystack in the field.

---

he   My father is working in the yard. **He** is cutting the grass. My brother Billy is helping my father. **He** is watering the flowers. **"He"** is a word we use instead of the name of a boy or a man.

head The **head** is the top part of your body. Ears, eyes, nose, and mouth are part of your head. Hair grows on your head. Your face is part of your head.

Susan is **at the head of** the line.
Susan is **in the front of** the line. She is the first one in the line. All the other children are behind her.

---

headache I have a **headache.**
I have a **pain in my head.** My head hurts.

---

health Sam is in good **health.** He is not sick. Rita is in bad health. She is sick. When you have nothing wrong with your body, you are in good health. When you have something wrong with your body, you are in bad health.

---

healthy Ellen is **healthy.**
Ellen is **not sick.**

---

heap There is a **heap** of bricks in the yard.
There is a **pile** of bricks in the yard.

---

hear I **hear** with my ears. I hear Mary singing a song. With my ears I know that Mary is singing a song.

Peter asked, "Did you **hear** the thunder, Martin?" Martin answered, "Yes, I **heard** the thunder. It was a loud sound."

I **heard** that John is sick.
I **learned from someone** that John is sick.

heart   Your **heart** pushes your blood through your body. If you put your head against someone's chest, you will hear his heart beat. You will hear his heart go, "Thump, thump." Can you hear your heart beat?

There are red hearts on this Valentine's Day card.

We sometimes use red hearts to show love. We send Valentine's Day cards to people whom we love.

---

heat   **Heat** makes us feel warm. We can feel the heat from the sun.

The **heat** made my grandmother very tired.
The **hot weather** made my grandmother very tired.

The fire will **heat** the soup.
The fire will **warm** the soup.

---

heavy   The piano is **heavy.**
The piano is **not easy to lift.** We need five men to move our piano.

A feather is not heavy. It is light.

hedge   A **hedge** is a row of bushes.   We use a hedge like a fence.

Can you see the hedge around this house?   A hedge is made of many plants.   They must be cut when they grow too tall.

---

heel   Your **heel** is the back part of your foot.   You have two heels because you have two feet.   You can see one of Jack's heels because he has a big hole in his sock.

Shoes have **heels** too.

The brown shoe has a heel, but the red shoe does not have a heel.   The heel of the shoe is on the bottom of the shoe.

---

held   Judy said, "Billy **held** the kitten yesterday.   Please let me **hold** the kitten today."

---

helicopter

This is a **helicopter**.   It is a machine that flies in the air.   A helicopter has a big propeller on its top part.   A helicopter can go straight up in the air and then come straight down again.   Do you know the difference between a helicopter and an airplane?

H h

he'll   **He'll** visit us tomorrow.
He will visit us tomorrow.   *He'll* also means *he shall.*

---

hello   When we greet someone, we often say "**hello.**"   Tommy said,
"Hello, Sally."   Sally said, "Hello, Tommy."

---

help   Betty gave her mother some **help.**   Betty did some work for
her mother.   This made the work easier for Betty's mother.
Betty's mother was very happy.

Do you sometimes **help** your mother?
Do you sometimes **do some work** for your mother?

Johnny **helped** his father by sweeping the garage floor.

Vincent said, "I cannot play now.   I am **helping** my father
cut the grass."

I cannot **help** sneezing.   I sneeze even if I do not want to.

---

helpful   Bob is **helpful** at home.   He does things to help.   Are you
helpful at home?   What do you do to help?

---

hen   A **hen** is a mother chicken.   The hen is sitting on the nest.
She is sitting on her eggs.
Hens lay eggs.   A rooster is
standing near the hen.   He is
bigger than the hen.   Roosters
do not lay eggs.   A hen and a
rooster are chickens.

254

her   Mary brought **her** doll. The doll belonged to Mary.

I gave my pen to Mary. I gave my pen to **her** when she needed it. I saw **her** looking for a pen.

---

here   Martin sat **here**.
Martin sat **in this place**.

Father mailed the package **here**.
Father mailed the package **to this place**.

The children said "**here**" when the teacher called their name. *Here* means *I am present.*

---

hers   This is Mary's hat.
This hat **is hers**.
This hat **belongs to her**.

---

herself   Sally dressed **herself**. She put on her own clothes.

Ruth cut **herself** with a piece of glass. Some blood came out from the cut on her finger.

My teacher **herself** told me that.

Patricia was standing **by herself**.
Patricia was standing **alone**. There was no one near her.

---

hid   Yesterday my brother **hid** under the bed. I wonder where he will **hide** today.

Let us look for my brother. Let's see if we can find him.

hidden   My Christmas present was **hidden** under the bed. It was a good place to hide it, because I did not find it.

The sun was **hidden** by the clouds. The clouds moved in front of the sun, so that we could not see it.

---

hide   **Hide** is skin that comes from an animal. Al's belt is made from the hide of a cow. His belt is made of cowhide.

---

hide   Billy said, "I am going to **hide** this ball. You will not find the ball easily. I will try to hide the ball where you cannot see it.

Billy will hide the ball where Johnny will not find it. He will put the ball in the closet. Yesterday Billy **hid** the ball in a box. Johnny said, "I wonder where the ball is **hidden**."

---

high   The jet airplane flies **high**.
The jet airplane flies **far above the ground.**

Nancy cannot get the book on the shelf. The book is too **high**. Nancy is too small to reach the book. She is not tall enough to get the book.

---

higher   Father is high on the ladder. The kitten is **higher**. The kitten is on the roof.

---

highest   The bird is **highest** of all. The bird is flying in the air.

high school   **High school** is the school above grade school.

---

hilarious   The Christmas party was **hilarious.**
The Christmas party was **merry.** We had a lot of fun at the party.

---

hill   A **hill** is land that is higher than the other land around it. Our house is on a hill. Mountains are bigger than hills.

---

hillside   A **hillside** is the side of a hill. The children slid down the hillside on the sled.

---

him   I gave a pencil to the boy. I gave the pencil to **him** when he wanted to write. I saw **him** looking for a pencil.

---

himself   Albert cut **himself** with a knife. He cut his finger. Albert put a bandage on his finger.

The president **himself** came to our town.

Ronald walked down the street **by himself.**
Ronald walked down the street **alone.**

hind  My dog can walk on his **hind** legs.
My dog can walk on his **back** legs.

Rabbits have strong hind legs. They can take big jumps with their big hind legs.

---

his This is Paul's coat. Please give Paul **his** coat.
This coat **is his.**
This coat **belongs to him.**

---

history **History** is a story of the past. The teacher told us the history of Mexico.

---

hit David **hit** the ball with his bat. David plays baseball well. He **hits** the ball often with his bat.

The carpenter **hit** the nail with his hammer.

The bad boy **hit** the baby.

I saw the car **hit** the tree. It was a bad accident.

---

hitch  See Father **hitch** the boat to the post.
See Father **tie** the boat to the post.

Hitch the boat to the post;
Don't let it float away:
Fasten it well; tie it tight;
We do want it to stay.

hive   A **hive** is a box or small house in which bees live.

---

ho   When Santa Claus laughs, he says, "**Ho,** ho."

---

hoarse   John's voice was hoarse. When John talked, he made deep and rough sounds.

---

hoe   A **hoe** is a tool which we use in the garden. A hoe has a long handle and a wide blade at one end. A farmer uses a hoe to take the weeds out of his garden. Sometimes he digs potatoes out of the ground with a hoe.

I will **hoe** the garden.
I will **dig with a hoe in** the garden.

---

hog   A **hog** is a large pig.

---

hold   I will **hold** your package while you put on your coat. I will take your package into my hands and keep it there. Now you can put your coat on. After you put your coat on, I will give you back your package.

The bottle **holds** one quart of milk. One quart of milk is able to go into the bottle. One quart of milk fits in the bottle.

Yesterday I **held** my baby sister.

hole

There is a **hole** in the blanket.
There is an **opening** in the blanket. I can put my arm through the hole in the blanket.

> In the hole in the ground
> I'm sure can be found
>   Some animal living inside.
> It's too small for a hare,
> And also a bear,
>   There chipmunks, I bet, do reside.

---

holiday A **holiday** is a day when we play and do things we want to. Christmas and the Fourth of July are holidays in the United States. A vacation is sometimes called a holiday.

Holland **Holland** is a country on the other side of the ocean. It gets cold in Holland in the winter. Another name for Holland is the Netherlands. The people who live in Holland are called Dutch people.

---

hollow The squirrel went into the **hollow** in the tree.
The squirrel went into the **hole** in the tree.

We picked violets in the **hollow.**
We picked violets in the **little valley.**

A pipe is **hollow.** It is not solid. A pipe has a hole running through the center. Balloons are hollow, too. They are empty in the middle.

home   Sandra is going **home**.

Sandra is going **to the place where she lives**.

---

honest   My father is **honest**. He is fair. My father does not lie. He always tells the truth. My father does not steal. He does not take what is not his.

---

honey   **Honey** is a food which is made by bees. It is sweet and sticky. Honey is like syrup. Did you ever have honey on pancakes?

---

honeybee   A **honeybee** is the kind of bee that makes honey. The honeybees stored honey in the honeycomb.

---

honeycomb   A **honeycomb** is a place where bees store honey. A honeycomb has many little hollow boxes. These boxes are fastened together and are made of wax.

---

honk   The wild goose said, "**Honk, honk.**"

The driver of the car will **honk** at the boy riding the bicycle.

The driver of the car will **blow his horn** at the boy riding the bicycle.

---

honor   We must **honor** our mother and father. We must be kind to them. We must do good things for them. We must take care of them. We must show our mother and father that we love them.

hood

Mary has a red **hood.**
Mary has a red **covering that goes over her head.**

Father lifted **the hood of the car.**
Father lifted **that part of the car that covers the motor.**

---

hoof   A **hoof** is the hard covering on the foot of horses, cows, deer, pigs, and some other animals.   Hoofs are like shoes for these animals.

---

hook   A **hook** is a piece of metal that is curved at one end.   We use hooks to hold or catch things.

We use a coat hook to hang coats on.   We use a fishhook to catch fish.

FISHHOOK   COAT HOOK

---

hoop   A **hoop** is a circle of wire, metal, or wood.   Vincent likes to play with a hoop.

Hoops are used around wooden buckets and barrels.

---

hop   Stanley made a big **hop.**
Stanley made a big **jump.**

Did you ever **hop** on one foot?
Did you ever **jump** on one foot?

The rabbit **hopped** across the field.

hope   I **hope** that I can go to the party.
I **wish** that I can go to the party.

horn

My uncle makes music on a **horn.** My little brother has a toy horn. He can make loud noise on his toy horn.

My father's automobile has an electric **horn.** Electricity makes the automobile horn work.

Some animals have **horns** on their heads.

horse

A **horse** is a large animal with four legs. A horse is used for working and for riding.

The horse is pulling the cart.

hose   A **hose** is a long tube. Water, or some other liquid, flows through a hose. Hoses are usually made of rubber or plastic. Albert is watering the lawn with a hose.

David will **hose** the lawn when the weather is dry. He will use the hose to sprinkle the lawn with water.

Stockings are sometimes called **hose.**

H h

hospital   A **hospital** is a place where sick people go to be helped. My father went to the hospital when he was sick. The doctors and the nurses in the hospital made my father well.

hot   The pot is **hot**.
The pot is **very warm**.

Fire is hot. Ice and snow are cold.

hotel   A **hotel** is a place to live when you are away from home. You can eat and sleep in a hotel. A hotel has many rooms. Many people live in a hotel. People pay money to live in a hotel.

hour   An **hour** is a measure of time. There are sixty minutes in an hour. There are twenty-four hours in a day. Can you tell what hour it is by the clock? Time is measured by years, months, weeks, days, hours, minutes, and seconds.

hourly   The bells ring **hourly**. The bells ring once every hour.

house   A **house** is a building in which people live. There are many kinds of houses.

how   Mary asked, "**How** did you make that cake, Mother?"
Mary asked, "**In what way** did you make that cake, Mother?"

The teacher asked, "**How** are you today?" She wanted to know if I was well. I said to my teacher, "I am well. How are you?"

How is it that Daddy is putting on his coat?
Why is it that Daddy is putting on his coat? Is he going to the store?

How much candy did Marvin eat? What was the number of pieces of candy that Marvin ate? He ate ten pieces of candy.

---

however   The sky looks clear. **However,** I shall take an umbrella in case it rains.
The sky looks clear. **But anyway,** I shall take an umbrella in case it rains.

You may work **however** you want to.
You may work **in any kind of way** you want to.

However cold it is outside, it will be warm in the house.
It does not matter how much it is cold outside, it will be warm in the house.

---

howl   Did you hear the dog **howl?**
Did you hear the dog **make a long, sad cry?**

---

hug   Mother gave me a big **hug.** She put her arms around me and held me tight. My mother loves me.

My grandmother will **hug me.**
My grandmother will **hold me tight in her arms.**

huge   An elephant is a **huge** animal.
An elephant is a **very big** animal.

---

hum   Keep your mouth closed and say the letter "m." The sound you make is a hum.

Can you **hum?**
Can you **make a sound with your voice with your mouth closed?**

---

human   People are **human.** A person is a human. Men, women, and children are human beings.

My dog almost acts **human.**
My dog almost acts **like a person.**

---

hump   The camel has a **hump** on his back.
The camel has a **raised place** on his back.

Some camels have two humps on their back.

---

hundred   One dollar equals one **hundred** cents.

Ten 10's is a **hundred.**
$10 + 10 + 10 + 10 + 10 + 10 + 10 + 10 + 10 + 10 = \mathbf{100}$

10   20   30   40   50   60   70   80   90   **100**

Ten times ten is a **hundred.**
$10 \times 10 = \mathbf{100}$

hung   The monkey **hung** from a tree by its tail.   Did you ever see a monkey hang by its tail?

hungry   The baby **is hungry**.
The baby **wants something to eat.**

hunt   My father likes to **hunt**.   He likes to go out to find and catch animals.

The man goes out to **hunt** deer.
The man goes out to **find and kill** deer.   He is **hunting** with a gun. He will shoot the deer with his gun.

We **hunted** for my lost book, but we could not find it.
We **looked** for my lost book, but we could not find it.

hunter   A **hunter** is a man who hunts animals.   He tries to find and kill animals.

hurrah When our team won the baseball game, we shouted, "Hurrah!" Hurrah is a cry of joy.

---

hurricane A **hurricane** is a very strong windstorm.

---

hurry We must **hurry** if we want to arrive at school on time.
We must **move fast** if we want to arrive at school on time.

We **hurried** the sick boy to the doctor.
We **quickly took** the sick boy to the doctor.

Mother is **in a hurry** to go home. She wants to go home as soon as possible. She wants to leave for home now.

---

hurt A **hurt** is something that gives us pain. Cuts, burns, scratches, and other wounds are called hurts.

I **hurt the dog** when I step on his tail.
I **make the dog have pain** when I step on his tail. The dog cries when I step on his tail.

John's head **hurts.** He has a pain in his head. Yesterday my head hurt. I suffered with an ache in my head. I had a headache.

The frost **hurt** the flower garden. The frost killed all the beautiful flowers. Yesterday the flowers were beautiful. Last night there was a frost. Today the flowers are brown. The flowers are dead.

---

husband A **husband** is the man to whom a woman is married. My father is my mother's husband. My father and mother are husband and wife. My grandfather and my grandmother are husband and wife, too.

hush When the teacher came into the room, there was a **hush.**
When the teacher came into the room, there was a **silence.**

Mother told me to **hush.**
Mother told me to **keep quiet.** She did not want me to make noise. Mother told me to stop talking.

The teacher **hushed** the children. She made the children be quiet.

---

hut A **hut** is a very small house. The hunters lived in a hut in the woods.

---

hydrant There is a **hydrant** in front of our house. Water comes out of a hydrant. When a hydrant is open, water comes out into the street. Firemen get water from hydrants to put out fires.

This is the ninth letter of the alphabet.

ABCDEFGHIJKLMNOPQRSTUVWXYZ

abcdefghijklmnopqrstuvwxyz

I **I** is a word used to mean myself. I am reading the *Visual Dictionary.* I am learning how to use words. *Me* is another word used to mean myself. *Me* is used in a different way in a sentence: Mother teaches *me* new words each day.

ice **Ice** is frozen water. When water becomes very cold, it becomes ice. We went skating on the ice.

Mother will **ice the cake.**
Mother will **cover the cake with frosting.**

Aunt Helen **iced the lemonade.**
Aunt Helen **made the lemonade cold with ice.**

ice cream **Ice cream** is made from cream, milk, eggs, and sugar. Ice cream is frozen. Did you ever have an ice cream cone? Do you like chocolate or strawberry ice cream?

I eat ice cream, smooth and sweet,
    Frozen and so cold;
It's a very tasty treat,
    Liked by young and old.

idea An **idea** is a thought. When I am thinking I get ideas. Here are some ideas that I have in the morning when I get out of bed. I must get dressed quickly so that I will not be late for school. I will wash myself and brush my teeth.

At other times during the day, I have different ideas. What are some of your ideas?

if I do not know **if** John will come to school today.

I do not know **whether** John will come to school today. It is possible that John will come to school, but I do not know it for sure.

Even if it rains, we shall play baseball.

Even though it rains, we shall play baseball. We like to play baseball so much that we will even play in the rain.

---

igloo

An **igloo** is a house made of snow and ice blocks. An igloo is an Eskimo's house.

Did you ever try to make a house out of snow?

---

ignore The teacher said, "**Ignore** the noise outside."

The teacher said, "**Do not notice** the noise outside." She did not want us to pay attention to the noise out in the street.

---

ill When Jack had a bad cold, he was **ill**.

When Jack had a bad cold, he was **sick.** He was not well. Jack was in bad health.

I'll I'll means *I will* or *I shall.* I'll go to the birthday party this afternoon, if I finish my work.

I'm I'm means *I am.* I'm going to the zoo on Saturday.

imagine I sometimes **imagine** that I am a great doctor. I make a picture in my mind of how I can help people. I think of things I would do if I were a doctor.

I **imagine** that my father will be late for supper, since he is usually home by now.

I **suppose** that my father will be late for supper, since he is usually home by now.

---

immediately Father wants me to go home **immediately**.
Father wants me to go home **without waiting**. He wants me to leave for home at once. He told me to leave right away.

---

important To go to school is **important**.
To go to school is **helpful and valuable**. If we go to school we will learn much. We will be able to get a good job. Going to school will help us to live better.

George Washington was an **important** person. He was the first president of the United States. He worked hard to help make the United States a strong country.

---

in The yellow bird is **in** the cage. The blue bird is outside the cage.

There are seven days **in** a week. A week has seven days.

Come **in** the house where it is warm.
Come **inside** the house where it is warm.

I will be home **in an hour**.
I will be home **before an hour goes by**.

Sam will be home **in a minute**.
Sam will be home **in a little while**.

inch   This line is one **inch** long. ——————— There are twelve inches in a foot. There are thirty-six inches in a yard.

---

increase   Did you notice the **increase** in size of the plant? Did you notice how much bigger the plant became?

The number of my marbles will **increase** if I get more.
The number of my marbles will **grow larger** if I get more.

My balloon **increased** when I blew more air into it.
My balloon **became larger** when I blew more air into it.

---

indeed   **Indeed,** I would like to go to the circus.
Really, I would like to go to the circus. Yes, indeed, I would like to go.

Indian   Did you ever see an **Indian?** The Indians were in North America, Central America, and South America before other people came.

The Indians are really the first Americans. There are many kinds of Indians. Here are some pictures of two kinds of Indians found in the Americas.

ink **Ink** is a liquid used with a pen. We need ink for writing when we use a pen. Ink can be red, blue, black, green, or purple.

---

inn An **inn** is a house where travelers stop to eat and rest for the night.

---

insect An **insect** is a tiny animal with six legs. Sometimes insects have wings. Ants, bees, butterflies, grasshoppers, and moths are insects. Insects are sometimes called bugs.

Insects are everywhere, it seems to me:
Beetle and butterfly and moth and flea.
Why do they want in the house to hide
When there's plenty of room for them outside?

---

inside  The **inside** is the side that is in. It is not the side that is out. The inside of the cupboard is painted red. The outside of the cupboard is painted yellow.

Billy went **inside** the house. He opened the front door and went into the house.

---

instantly Come here **instantly**!
Come here **immediately**! Do not wait! Come here at once!

instead   Margaret is writing with a pen **instead of** a pencil.
Margaret is writing with a pen **in place of** a pencil.

Susan came **instead of** Rita.
Susan came **in place of** Rita. Rita did not come. Susan came instead.

---

interest   Mildred has an **interest** in dogs. She wants to know about dogs.

The story about cowboys and Indians will **interest** the boys.

The story about cowboys and Indians will **get the attention of** the boys. They will like the story. The boys will want to hear the story.

Peter is interested in airplanes. He wants to know about airplanes.

---

interesting   The book is **interesting.** It is an interesting story about a horse. I want to keep reading the book. I want to know what will happen to the horse. I do not want to stop reading until I come to the end of the book.

---

international   It was an **international** meeting. At the meeting there were people from many nations.

---

into   Edward went **into** the house.
Edward went **toward and in** the house.

Henry is running **into** the water.

If you keep mixing cream, it will change **into** butter. The cream will turn **into** butter. The cream will become butter.

invite   I will **invite my teacher** to my house for dinner.

I will **ask my teacher to come** to my house for dinner.   I also invited Sally, but she could not come.

---

iron   **Iron** is a metal.   Mother has a heavy pan made of iron.

My mother uses an **iron** to make my clothes smooth.   An iron takes the wrinkles out of clothes.

My mother presses clothes with a hot iron. She has an electric iron.   The electricity makes the iron hot.

Ruth helped her mother **iron** the clothes.
Ruth helped her mother **press** the clothes.

Marjorie **ironed** my shirt.

---

ironing board   An **ironing board** is a board on which clothes are ironed.

---

is   Barbara **is** home.   Thomas is at school.   It is time for supper. I am home.   You are home.   We are ready to eat.   Tom will be late.

---

island   An **island** is a piece of land that has water all around it.

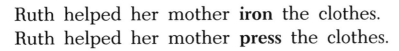

isn't   My dog **isn't** in the house.
My dog **is not** in the house.

---

it   We use "**it**" when we speak about a place, an animal, or a thing.
I went to New York. It is a big city. Rebecca has a cat. It
is white. Stanley has a new wagon. Stanley gave me a ride
in it.

---

its   Jane has a rabbit. **Its** ears are long. The ears of the rabbit are
long.

---

it's   **It's** going to rain.
It is going to rain.

---

itself   The bird hurt **itself** when it flew into the glass window.

The dog is in the room **by itself.**
The dog is in the room **alone.**

I've   **I've** means *I have.*

I've seen that picture already.
I have seen that picture already.

This is the tenth letter of the alphabet.

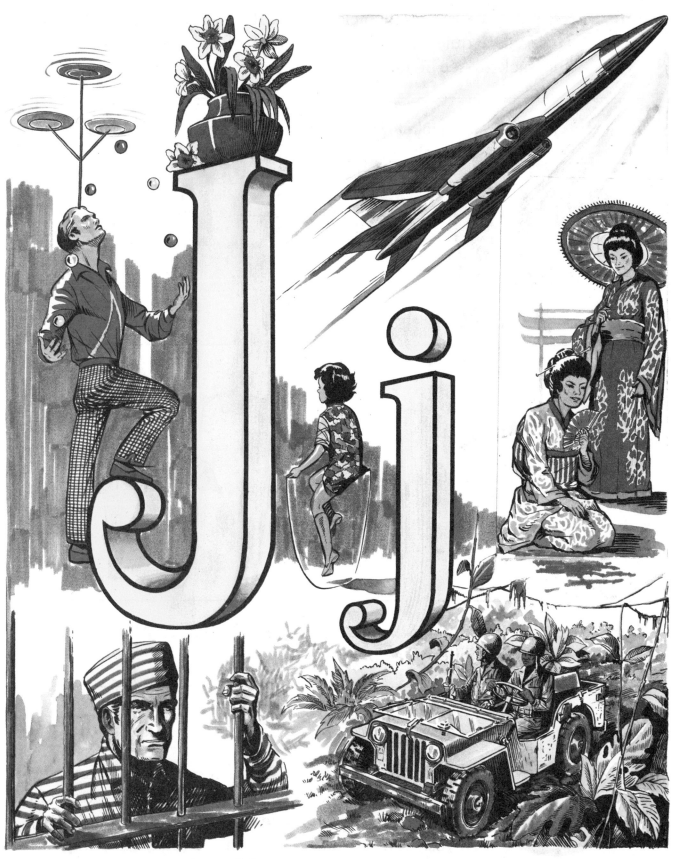

ABCDEFGHIJKLMNOPQRSTUVWXYZ

abcdefghijklmnopqrstuvwxyz

Jj

jab Fred will give the cloth sack a **jab** with his stick. He will give the sack a quick push with the end of his stick. He will **jab** the sack to see if there is a rat inside.

---

jacket A **jacket** is a short coat. Mary is wearing a red coat, but John is wearing a blue jacket.

John has a jacket which is blue;
He likes it since it's very new;
He wears it when the weather's cool,
And when he's on his way to school.

---

jack-in-the-pulpit

A **jack-in-the-pulpit** is a flower.

Here is a jack-in-the-pulpit.

---

jackknife A jackknife is a large knife which folds. Allen carries a jackknife in his pocket.

---

jack-o'-lantern A **jack-o'-lantern** is a funny face which is made out of a pumpkin.

Tommy made a jack-o'-lantern for Halloween. He took the seeds out of the inside of the pumpkin. Then he cut into the pumpkin and made two eyes, a nose, and a mouth. Finally, Tommy put a light inside the pumpkin.

jagged Kenneth cut his hand on a **jagged stone.**
Kenneth cut his hand on a **stone which had rough edges.**

---

jail People who do not obey the law are put into **jail.** The policeman put the robber in jail. The robber tried to steal money from the bank.

Jail is a place where bad men are locked behind walls made of bars.

---

jam Jam is made from fruit and sugar. The fruit and sugar are cooked together until everything becomes thick. The jam is then put into jars to cool. Billy likes strawberry jam on bread. Nancy likes grape jam on toast.

Did you see the boys **jam** into the small room?
Did you see the boys **crowd into** the small room? There were too many boys in the small room.

---

janitor A **janitor** is a man who takes care of a building, an apartment house, or a school. Mr. Smith is the janitor in our school. He keeps our school building clean.

January **January** is the first month of the year. January has thirty-one days. New Year's Day is the first day of January.

Jj

Japan   **Japan** is a country which is far away in the East.   Japan is a country of islands.   It is a country with water all around it.   The Japanese people like rice very much. Much rice is grown in Japan.

Japanese   The people of Japan are called **Japanese.**   Kazuko was born in Japan.   She lives in a Japanese city called Tokyo.   Kazuko is Japanese.   She is wearing Japanese clothes.

The Japanese are very nice,
  So kind and gentle and polite,
A people known for liking rice
  And clothes that are a pretty sight.

---

jar   This is a **jar** of pickles.

This is a jar of grape jam.

There are cookies in this jar.   It is a cookie jar.

Mother said, "Do not **jar** the baby's carriage."
Mother said, "Do not **shake** the baby's carriage."

The baby woke up when Jimmy **jarred** the carriage.

jaw   My **jaw** is the lower part of my face.   My jaw moves when I talk and when I chew.

jay

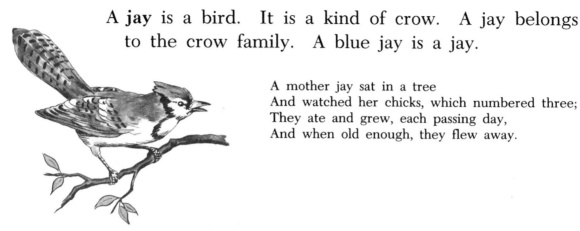

A **jay** is a bird.   It is a kind of crow.   A jay belongs to the crow family.   A blue jay is a jay.

A mother jay sat in a tree
And watched her chicks, which numbered three;
They ate and grew, each passing day,
And when old enough, they flew away.

jeep   A **jeep** is a small automobile.

When my father was in the army, he used to drive a jeep.

jelly   **Jelly** is made from fruit juice and sugar.   Rita likes grape jelly on bread.   Kathy likes apple jelly on toast.

jerk   A **jerk** is a quick pull.

Patrick gave the rope a **jerk.**
Patrick gave the rope a **quick pull.**   He was trying to get the rope out of the tree.

The drawer will not open.
   Jerk the drawer and it will open.
   Quickly pull the drawer and it will open.

Bobby **jerked** the wagon and the blocks fell out.

jet engine A **jet engine** is a machine which quickly pushes hot air and gas out of the rear of the machine. When a jet engine is put on an airplane, it makes the airplane go very fast.

---

jet plane A **jet plane** is an airplane with jet engines. Jet planes are sometimes called *jets*. They are also called jet airplanes.

---

jewel A **jewel** is a beautiful stone. A jewel costs much money. A diamond is a jewel. The rich lady wears many jewels.

---

jewelry My mother put her diamond ring with her other jewelry. Her gold pin and her diamond ring are in a jewelry box. We wear jewelry. Jewelry is made of gold, silver, and jewels.

---

jingle A **jingle** is a tinkling sound. Listen to Sam **jingle** the pennies in his pocket. Hear the tinkling sound.

---

job Marie's **job** was to sweep the floor.
Marie's **work** was to sweep the floor.

join   Father will **join** the two pieces of wood with some glue.
Father will **fasten together** the two pieces of wood with some glue.

Ronald **joined** the two ends of the rope by tying them together.

My Uncle David **joined** the United States Army.   He belongs to the army.   Now my Uncle David is a soldier in the United States Army.

---

joke   Albert told me **a joke.**
Albert told me **something funny which made me laugh.**

We sometimes **joke** with Daddy.
We sometimes **have fun** with Daddy.

The children **joked** with the policeman.   The policeman is very kind.   He often jokes with the children.

---

jolly   Sarah is **jolly.**
Sarah is **happy and gay.**

---

jolt   The train stopped with a sudden **jolt.**
The train stopped with a sudden **jerk.**

---

jonquil   A **jonquil** is a flower which grows in the early spring.
Jonquils are white and yellow.   Jonquils smell sweet.

Jonquils are flowers, yellow and white,
  Blossoming early in spring,
When sun and warm showers, for many hours,
  Life to my garden do bring.

Jj

journey   My Uncle Harry took a long **journey** to Japan.
My Uncle Harry took a long **trip** to Japan.

We will **journey** far to see the people of Africa.
We will **travel** far to see the people of Africa.

The astronauts **journeyed** far to get to the moon.

---

joy   The little puppy brings much **joy** to the children.
The little puppy brings much **happiness** to the children.   The children are so glad that they have a puppy.

---

judge   A **judge** is a person who tells us how good or how bad something is.

The artist will **judge** your picture.   He will tell you how good or how bad it is.

The artist **judged** Jerome's picture.   He decided that it was painted well.   The artist judged that it was a beautiful picture.

---

juggle   Did you see the clown **juggle** the balls?   The clown was doing tricks with the balls.

He threw many balls into the air at one time.   But the clown did not drop one ball. The clown juggled well.   The clown had to practice much to do such good tricks.

---

juggler   A juggler is one who **juggles**.   The clown is juggling the balls.

juice   Juice is a liquid which is in fruit, vegetables, or meat. Mother squeezed the orange until all the juice came out of it. Michael likes tomato juice and carrot juice.

When my mother cooked the roast beef, there was juice at the bottom of the pan. The juice was from the roast beef.

---

juicy   Peaches are **juicy.** They have much juice in them. I like juicy peaches. They are soft and sweet. They are not dry.

July   **July** is the seventh month of the year. July has thirty-one days.

---

jumble   Mother's sewing box was in a **jumble.** The cat got into her sewing box and mixed up the many spools of thread and the buttons.

Did you see the cat **jumble up** her sewing box?
Did you see the cat **mix up** her sewing box?

---

jump   Did you see David's **jump** over the big rock?
Did you see David's **leap** over the big rock?

David can **jump** over the big rock. He can quickly throw himself into the air with his legs. He can push himself over the rock without using his hands to help. David jumped high into the air.

June   **June** is the sixth month of the year. June has thirty days.

Jj

jungle   A **jungle** is land with many trees, vines, and bushes on it. It is hard to travel in the jungle.

We find jungles in countries where the weather is hot most of the time. It rains often in the jungle. Apes, lions, monkeys, tigers, and other wild animals live in jungles.

---

just   My father is a **just** man.
My father is an **honest** man.

My shoes **just** fit me. They fit me perfectly. My shoes are exactly the right size. They are not too big. They are not too small.

It is **just about** time to eat dinner.
It is **almost** time to eat dinner.

Billy **just** left for school. He left for school only a minute ago.

This is the eleventh letter of the alphabet.

ABCDEFGHIJKLMNOPQRSTUVWXYZ

abcdefghijklmnopqrstuvwxyz

K k

kangaroo

A **kangaroo** is a large animal. It has short front legs and very large back legs. A kangaroo has a long, thick tail.

A kangaroo leaps something like a rabbit. Kangaroos can go very fast. The mother kangaroo carries her baby in a pocket on her front side.

---

keep

My Aunt Ann gave me a pen to **keep.**

My Aunt Ann gave me a pen to **have for my own as long as I want.** I do not have to give the pen back to my aunt.

My Uncle Leo **keeps** chickens.
My Uncle Leo **takes care** of chickens.

I will **keep** your key until you come home. I will hold your key for a time until you come home. Then I will give you back your key.

Keep to the right side of the street.
Stay to the right side of the street.

Rita did not pass her test at school. She failed. She did not get a good grade.
The teacher said, "**Keep** trying to pass your test, Rita."
The teacher said, "**Do not stop** trying to pass your test, Rita."

We **keep** the broom in the kitchen closet.
We **usually put** the broom in the kitchen closet. The broom belongs in the kitchen closet.

Mother said, "Please **keep quiet** in church."
Mother said, "Please **do not talk** in church."

Judy has **kept** her doll since she was a baby.

290

kettle   A **kettle** is a metal pot with a cover. Mother boils water in the kettle.

Polly, put the kettle on,
Polly, put the kettle on,
Polly, put the kettle on,
We'll all have tea.

Sukey, take it off again,
Sukey, take it off again,
Sukey, take it off again,
They've all gone away.

---

key    A **key** is a piece of metal made to fit into a lock. We lock and unlock doors with keys.

A piano has many black and white **keys.** We strike the piano keys when we play the piano.

---

keyhole   A **keyhole** is the hole in a lock into which a key is put.

---

kick   Andrew gave the box a hard **kick.** He hit the box hard with his foot.

Simon can **kick the football well.**
Simon can **hit the football with his foot well.** He can make the football go far.

The horse **kicked** the man.

---

kid   A **kid** is a baby goat.

Billy said, "The **kids** are coming to my house to play."
Billy said, "The **children** are coming to my house to play."

kill   The cat will **kill the bird** if it catches the bird.
The cat will **make the bird die** if it catches the bird.

Yesterday the cat **killed** a mouse.

---

kind   What **kind** of animal do you like best for a pet? In the pet store there are many different kinds of animals. There are cats, dogs, fish, rabbits, birds, and many other kinds of animals. The kind of animal that Billy likes best is a dog. Billy likes to play with dogs.

My teacher is **kind** to me.
My teacher is **gentle and good** to me.

---

kindergarten   A **kindergarten** is school for young children. In kindergarten children learn to play and work together.

Kindergarten is the grade before first grade.

---

kindly   Joseph has a **kindly** face.
Joseph has a **friendly** face. He looks kind.

---

kindness   Mary has much **kindness.** She is very good to other people. Mary very often helps others.

---

king   Some countries have a **king.** The king is the head of all the people in his country.

In the United States of America we do not have a king. We have a president.

kingdom   A **kingdom** is a country that has a king or a queen.

---

kiss   My mother gives me a **kiss** on the cheek before I go to sleep.

My mother also will **kiss me on the cheek** before I go to school.

My mother also will **press her lips against my cheek** before I go to school.

I **kissed** my grandmother when I saw her. When we kiss people, we tell them that we love them.

---

kitchen   A **kitchen** is a room where our food is prepared and cooked.

---

kite   A **kite** is made of light wood covered with paper. A kite flies in the air. The wind carries the kite through the air. We hold on to the kite by a string which is tied to the kite.

kitten   A **kitten** is a young cat.

---

kitty   **Kitty** means *kitten*.

---

knee   My **knee** joins the upper part of my leg with the lower part of my leg. Barbara hurt her knee. Her mother is putting a bandage on her knee.

When we walk up stairs, we bend one knee at a time.

My baby brother crawls on his hands and knees.

---

kneel   Martin had to **kneel** to look into the cave.
Martin had to **go down on both knees** to look into the cave.

Last night Martha **knelt** near her bed to say her prayers.

---

knew   Tom **knew how** to swim.
Tom **was able** to swim.

Jack **knew** Sally. He met Sally a week ago. Jack talked to Sally then. Yes, Jack had Sally for a friend for a whole week already.

Nancy **knew** the story about the black horse. Nancy had heard the story before. Now she will tell us the story that she knows.

knife   We use a **knife** for cutting things.   There are many kinds of knives.

We use this knife for cutting meat.

We use this knife for peeling fruits and vegetables.

We carry this knife in our pocket.   You must hide the blade of this pocket knife before you put it into your pocket.   This kind of knife is called a jackknife.

---

knives   Mother has many **knives** in the kitchen.   Each knife is sharp.

---

knock   Albert got a **knock** on the head with a ball.
Albert got a **hard hit** on the head with a ball.

I will **knock** on the door.
I will **hit** on the door.   When I knock on the door I will make a noise.   Then someone will know that I want to come inside.

Stanley **knocked** the ball to Timothy.

---

knot   You make a **knot** by tying together the ends of thread, rope, ribbons, or some other cord.

Helen tied a string around the box and made a knot with the string.

K k

know   I **know how** to play the piano.

I **am able** to play the piano.

Jack **knows** Brenda. He goes to school with Brenda. Both Brenda and Jack are in the same class. Brenda is Jack's friend.

Philip **knows** what happened at the baseball game. He will tell you about the baseball game.

I told Peter, Rita, and George about my trip to England. The story of my trip is **known** by three people.

---

knowledge   All the things that we know are called **knowledge**. Knowledge is everything that we have learned.

Ann has much **knowledge** of birds.

---

known   I have **known** the alphabet ever since I was six years old. Do you **know** the alphabet? When did you learn the alphabet?

This is the twelfth letter of the alphabet.

ABCDEFGHIJK**L**MNOPQRSTUVWXYZ

abcdefghijk**l**mnopqrstuvwxyz

lace A **lace** is a cord for tying things together.

Billy knows how to **lace** his shoes.
Billy knows how to **tie the lace on** his shoes.

Bernice has a handkerchief with **lace** around the edges. The lace is made from thread which is tied together so that it looks pretty.

---

lad A **lad** is a boy. My brother Hugo is a small lad.

---

ladder We climb a **ladder** to reach high places. My father is climbing the ladder. He wants to get on the roof of our house.

My daddy has a ladder tall
  For reaching places high;
If he did have one long enough,
  I think he'd reach the sky.

---

lady My mother is a **lady.**
My mother is a **woman.** A lady is polite and kind.

Three **ladies** came to see my mother.

---

laid Bob **laid the book** on the table
Bob **put the book down** on the table.

lain   The tired dog has **lain** on the rug all day. The dog likes to lie there. He slept on the rug all day.

---

lake   A **lake** is water with land all around it. In summer we go to the lake. I like to swim in the lake. My father likes to fish in the lake.

---

lamb   A **lamb** is a baby sheep.

> So glad I am
> To have a lamb,
> So woolly white,
> To cuddle tight!

---

lamp   A **lamp** gives light.

This is an oil lamp. In this kind of lamp, light comes from a flame. When the oil in the lamp burns, it gives a flame.

This is an electric lamp.

In an electric lamp, light comes from a tiny wire which gets so hot that it turns bright white. The electricity going through the wire makes the wire become white hot.

land   An automobile goes on **land,** but a boat goes in water.

An automobile goes on **ground,** but a boat goes in water. I run on land, but I swim in water. The farmer used his land for planting corn. He grew corn in his garden.

The United States of America is **our land.**
The United States of America is **the country we live in.**

We went to the airport to watch the airplanes **land.**
We went to the airport to watch the airplanes **come to the ground.**

The giant jet **landed** like a beautiful bird.

---

landscape   A **landscape** is a view of land. We stood on a hill and saw a beautiful landscape below.

---

lane   Mary is walking down the **lane.**

A lane is a path or a road that is narrow
With a hedge or a fence on each side;
It's a way that is curved or straight as an arrow,
A walk that is truly not wide.

---

language   When we talk or write words, we are talking or writing a **language.** Language is for letting people know what we want to say. There are many languages.

In the United States, the Americans speak the English language. In Mexico, the Mexicans speak the Spanish language. In Brazil, the Brazilians speak the Portuguese language.

lantern   A **lantern** gives light. My grandfather lives on a farm. He carries a **lantern** at night.

He carries a **light** at night. My grandfather holds the lantern by its handle.

> I take a lantern in my hand
>   To rid the black of night;
> To let me see just where I stand,
>   By giving helpful light.

---

lap   Susan is holding the cat in her **lap.** You only have a lap when you sit down. Your lap is the front part of your body from your waist to your knees.

Watch my cat **lap up the milk** from the dish.

Watch my cat **drink the milk with its tongue** from the dish. This is the way some animals drink.

The thirsty dog **lapped** up the water.

---

lard   **Lard** is fat. It comes from pigs. We use lard for cooking.

---

large

An elephant is **large.**
An elephant is **big.**

An elephant is larger than a horse. A horse is larger than a dog.

An elephant is the largest of the three animals.

lark  A **lark** is a bird. It sings a pretty song.

---

larva A **larva** is an insect. Larvae look like worms. Caterpillars are larvae.

---

lass A **lass** is a girl. Sarah is a small lass.

---

last The moving picture will **last** two hours.
The moving picture will **go on for** two hours. The movie will continue for two hours.

I saw James **last** night.
I saw James **yesterday** night.

The crow is the **last** one to land on the fence. Three birds landed on the fence. A robin landed on the fence first. A sparrow landed on the fence second. Finally, a crow landed on the fence third. The crow landed on the fence last.

Halloween is the **last** day in October. There are no more days in the month of October.

I went to the movies **last week**.
I went to the movies **this past week**.

---

late William was **late** for school.
William was **tardy** for school. He did not arrive at school on time.

Rebecca stayed up **late** last night. She did not go to bed as early as she usually goes to bed.

later   Anthony was late for supper, but Mary was **later**.   Mary came to supper after Anthony.

You go to the party now.
I will go to the party **later**.
I will go to the party **after a while**.

---

laugh   Regina gave a short **laugh** when she heard the funny story.

When we are merry we **laugh**.   We make sounds that tell everybody that we are happy.   Tommy **laughed** at the joke.   Sally said, "I like to hear people **laughing**."

---

launder   Mother will **launder** the dirty clothes on Monday.
Mother will **wash** the dirty clothes on Monday.

---

law   A **law** tells us what to do.   Laws are made to keep us from harm.   The laws of our country should protect us.   That is why we should obey the laws of our country.

It is a law that cars must stop for red traffic lights.   This law helps us to cross the street safely.

It is a law that people must pay taxes.   Tax money pays for our parks, our policemen, our libraries, and for many other things.

---

lawn   Harry is cutting the **lawn**.
Harry is cutting the **grass in the yard**.

lawyer A **lawyer** is a person who has gone to school to learn about laws. Father paid a lawyer to help him use laws better.

---

lay **Lay your book** on the table.
Put your book down on the table.

Hens **lay** eggs.
Hens **give** eggs.

Yesterday my dog **lay** on the kitchen floor all day.
Yesterday my dog **was lying** on the kitchen floor all day. He was sleeping near the kitchen stove.

---

lazy Margaret is **lazy.** She does not want to work. A person who is lazy does not want to work.

Bruce walked home from work in a **lazy** way.
Bruce walked home from work in a **slow-moving** way.

---

lead Joe and Bob were running in a race. During the race, Bob took the **lead.** Bob ran ahead of Joe.

The teacher will **lead** us through the rooms of the school.
The teacher will **guide** us through the rooms of the school. She will show us the way.

Yesterday the farmer **led** the gray horse into the barn.

Our team **leads** in the football game.
Our team **is first** in the football game.

---

lead **Lead** is a heavy metal. Lead is used to make some water pipes.

We sometimes write with a **lead** pencil. The lead in a lead pencil is soft and black. This lead is not a metal, but it has the same name as the metal.

leader   A **leader** is a person who leads. He shows other people how to do things. The leader showed us the way through the woods.

---

leaf   A **leaf** is a part of a tree, plant, or a bush. Leaves are usually green. These are leaves.

OAK LEAF
MAPLE LEAF
WILLOW LEAF
ELM LEAF

The page of a book is sometimes called a **leaf.**

---

lean   **Lean** is the red part of meat.
The roast **was lean.**
The roast **had very little fat.**

I am tired of standing up. I will **lean** against the wall. When I lean, I stand at a slant. My feet are on the ground and my back is pushing against the wall.

The tree **leaned** when the wind blew hard.
The tree **was at a slant** when the wind blew hard.

My mother **leaned** over to pick up the baby's toys.
My mother **bent** over to pick up the baby's toys.

leap　The horse made a high **leap.**
The horse made a high **jump.**

Watch the dog **leap** over the fence.
Watch the dog **jump** over the fence.

---

learn　In school we **learn** to read and write.
In school we **find out how** to read and write.

Patrick **learned** that his sister was ill.
Patrick **came to know** that his sister was ill.

---

leash　A **leash** is a leather strap fastened to an animal's collar or harness. Sam holds his dog's leash when he walks with him.

Donald will **leash** his dog. He will put his dog on a leash, so that his dog will not go about loose.

---

least　Ruth has fifty cents. Billy has twenty-five cents. Brenda has ten cents. Brenda has the **least** of all. Ruth has more money than Brenda. Billy has more money than Brenda.

Uncle Peter wanted **the least** bit of sugar in his coffee.
Uncle Peter wanted **a very little** bit of sugar in his coffee.

You should sleep for **at least** eight hours each night.
You should sleep for **not less than** eight hours each night.

---

leather　**Leather** is made from the skin of an animal. My shoes are made of leather. Some suitcases are made of leather. My father's belt is made of leather.

leave Mary had to **leave** before school was over.
Mary had to **go away** before school was over.

Harold will **leave** his bat and ball at our house. He will allow his bat and ball to stay at our house.

Susan **left** her pen at school. She went home without taking her pen.

---

leaves In autumn the **leaves** of some trees turn many colors. In autumn these colored leaves fall from the trees. Did you ever try to find a very pretty autumn leaf?

The pages of a book are sometimes called **leaves.**

---

led Terence **led** his horse into the barn. He went ahead of the horse and showed him the way into the barn. I will lead my horse into the barn later.

---

ledge A **ledge** is a narrow shelf.

There was a **ledge** outside the window of the building.

---

left  Jim is holding up his **left** hand. Do you write with your left hand or your right hand?

The **left** side of your body is the side that points north when you face the rising sun.

Rita **left** from home very early this morning. Rita **went away** from home very early this morning. I saw her leave about six o'clock in the morning.

leg  The dancer is holding one **leg** in the air. She is standing on one leg.

A dog has four legs. A bird has two legs. An ant has six legs. Most tables have four legs.

---

lemon  A **lemon** is a fruit. It is yellow. Lemons have a sour juice. The juice of the lemon is used in drinks, pies, candy and in many other things.

---

lemonade **Lemonade** is a drink made with lemon juice, water, and sugar.

---

lend Joan will **lend** me her pencil. She will let me use her pencil for a while. I lent Joan my pencil yesterday.

---

length Mark wants to know the **length of the boat.**
Mark wants to know **how long the boat is.**

The **length** of the ruler is twelve inches. The ruler is twelve inches long.

What is the **length** of the moving picture: How long will the moving picture last?

less   I have **less** money than Paul. I do not have as much money as Paul. Paul has fifty cents. I only have ten cents. Paul has more money than I have.

Three **less** two is one.
Three **take away** two is one.
$3 - 2 = 1$

---

lesson   A **lesson** is something that someone teaches us. The teacher taught us a lesson in reading. We learned how to read from the lesson.

---

let   **Let me** help you with your work.
Allow me to help you with your work.

---

let's   **Let's** go to the park today.
Let us go to the park today.

---

letter   There are twenty-six letters in the English alphabet:

A B C D E F G H I J K L M N O P Q R S T U V W X Y Z.
a b c d e f g h i j k l m n o p q r s t u v w x y z

These letters make up all our words.

I wrote a **letter** to my grandmother. I took a piece of paper and wrote the things that I wanted to tell her. I told my grandmother that I love her. I told her that I will come and see her soon.

I put my letter in an envelope. On the envelope I wrote my grandmother's address. I put a stamp on the envelope. Then I mailed the letter to my grandmother.

lettuce   **Lettuce** is a green vegetable that is used in salads. Some lettuce grows in heads.

---

library   A **library** is a place where many books are kept. Our town has a library. I go to the library to read books.

Sometimes I borrow some books and bring them home. I must bring the books back to the library when I finish reading them.

---

lick   The mother cat gave her kitten a **lick.**
The mother cat gave her kitten a **rub with her tongue.**

The dog will **lick** the milk from his dish. The dog will drink all the milk in his dish by rubbing it with his tongue.

---

lid   Mother put the **lid** on the pot.
Mother put the **top** on the pot.

---

lie   Bernard told a **lie** to his father. Bernard told his father something that was not true. Bernard knew that it was not true. Bernard did a bad thing in telling a lie.

We should not **lie.**
We should not **tell a thing that we know is not true.**

Bernard said, "Yesterday I **lied,** but now I will stop **lying.**"

lie

I like to **lie** on the rug near the fireplace.
I like to **stretch my body out flat** on the rug near the fireplace.

The baby has **lain** down to take a nap.

Yesterday my dog **lay** on the kitchen floor all day.

Today my dog is **lying** on the front lawn.

---

life   Plants, animals, and people have **life.**   The earth and rocks do not have life.   An elephant has a long life.   He lives a long time.   A butterfly has a short life.   It lives a short time.

The fireman saved my grandmother's **life.**   He helped my grandmother get out of the burning house.

---

lift   Frank can **lift** the big box.
Frank can **raise** the big box.   He is able to pick the box up from the floor and put it in a higher place.   He can put the big box on the table.

David **lifted** the heavy suitcase.

---

light   The sun gives **light.**   At night it is dark.   In the day it is light.

The **lights** on the Christmas tree are red, white, green, and blue.

Uncle Joe wants a match to **light** his cigar.
Uncle Joe wants a match to **put fire to** his cigar.

Sally **lighted** the Christmas tree.   She turned the Christmas tree lights on.

A feather is **light.**
A feather is **not heavy.**

Yellow is a **light** color.   Brown is a dark color.

lightly   Ronald knocked on the door **lightly.**
Ronald knocked on the door **gently.**

---

lightning   **Lightning** is a bright, quick light in the sky. Lightning is caused by electricity. Usually there is thunder after there is lightning. Lightning and thunder often come when we have a rain storm.

---

like   The two dogs look **like** each other.
The two dogs look **the same as** each other.

I **like** ice cream.
I **get pleasure from** ice cream. I enjoy eating ice cream.

Roberta said she **liked** the pudding that her Aunt Helen gave her.

---

lily   A lily is a flower. Easter **lilies** are white. Tiger lilies are orange.

EASTER LILY

TIGER LILY

---

limb   The squirrel is sitting on the **limb** of the tree.
The squirrel is sitting on the **branch** of the tree.

A leg or an arm are sometimes called **limbs.**

line   This is a **line.** ————————————

These are telephone **lines.**

This is a fishing **line.**

This is a **line** of people.

This is a clothes **line.**

The children will **line** their paper.
The children will **put lines on** their paper.

---

lion

A **lion** is a large wild animal. A lion belongs to the cat family. Lions live in Africa. They eat other animals. Did you ever hear a lion roar?

---

lip   I have an upper **lip** and a lower **lip.** My lips are the edges of my mouth. When I open my lips, you can see my teeth.

liquid Water is a **liquid.** Milk is a liquid. Oil is a liquid. Liquid does not have a shape of its own. Liquids flow easily. We pour liquids.

---

list A **list** is a row of words or numbers.

The teacher will **list** ten names on the blackboard.
The teacher will **write in a row** ten names on the blackboard.

---

listen **Listen to** what the teacher is saying.
Try to hear what the teacher is saying.

We **listened** to the beautiful music on the radio.

---

listener A **listener** is a person who listens. He tries to hear something.

---

lit Yesterday my father **lit** a fire in the fireplace.
Yesterday my father **lighted** a fire in the fireplace.

---

literature Poems, stories, and other writings are **literature.** I love to study literature in school.

---

little My father is big, but my baby sister is **little.**
My father is big, but my baby sister is **small.**

live Plants, animals, and people **live.** Things that live can grow and have babies or seeds. People can have babies. Dogs can have baby dogs. Plants have seeds, so that they also can make more plants.

Rocks do not live. Rocks do not grow. They cannot have babies or seeds.

We **live** in a house. A bird lives in a nest.

The Smith family **lived** in the same house for fifteen years.

President John Kennedy is not **living.** He is dead.

---

load A **load** is something that is carried. The truck carried a load of bricks.

The men will **load** the truck with stones. The men will put a load of stones on the truck.

---

loaf A **loaf** is a large piece of bread baked in one piece. Here is a loaf of bread.

---

loan Uncle John gave us a **loan** of his car. He let us use his car for awhile.

Harry will **loan** me his bicycle.
Harry will **lend** me his bicycle. He will let me use his bicycle for a while.

---

loaves My mother baked two **loaves** of bread. She baked one loaf for today and one loaf for tomorrow.

lock A **lock** is used to keep things fastened. Doors and drawers are closed with locks. When we close a door or a drawer with a lock, we need a key to open it.

We **lock our doors** at night.
We **fasten our doors with locks** at night.

The farmer **locked** the horse in the barn. He put the horse in the barn and locked the door.

---

log A **log** is part of a tree after the tree has been cut down. The trunk of a tree is a log. Large branches of a tree are also logs. This truck is hauling logs.

---

lollipop A **lollipop** is a large lump of hard candy on a stick. We lick a lollipop.

---

lone A **lone** wolf is a wolf that travels by himself. He does not travel with other wolves. He goes alone.

---

lonely Monica feels **lonely** because the other children are in school. Monica is sad because she is alone.

---

lonesome Grandfather lives in a very big house all by himself. He gets very **lonesome**. He becomes sad from being alone. Grandfather becomes lonely.

long Bob's stick is **long.** Regina's stick is short.

The ruler is twelve inches **long.** The distance from one end of the ruler to the other end is twelve inches.

How long will you be in New York?
For how much time will you be in New York? I shall be in New York for two days.

In the winter the days are short. In the summer the days are **long.**

I **long** to go on a vacation.
I **want very much** to go on a vacation.

---

longer The black car is **longer** than the red car.

Ed waited for Tim a long time. Still he did not come.

Ursula will wait for Ernest **a little longer.**
Ursula will wait for Ernest **for a little more time.**

---

look Christopher has a sad **look** on his face. He is crying because he lost his puppy.

Look at the beautiful rainbow.
See the beautiful rainbow.

Jane **looked at** the window.
Jane **turned her eyes toward** the window. She tried to see the birds which she heard singing outside.

Stephen lost his book. He will **look for** it.
                              He will **try to find** it.

Carl **looks like** his father. Carl is like his father. In many ways Carl and his father look alike.

looking glass I look into a **looking glass** when I comb my hair.
I look into a **mirror** when I comb my hair.

---

loose My shoe is **loose.**
My shoe is **not tight.** I must tie my shoe lace so that my shoe will not be loose.

The button on my jacket is **loose.** It is not fastened well. My mother will sew the button on tight.

The bird got **loose** and flew away.
The bird got **free** and flew away.

---

loosen **Loosen the collar** around the dog's neck.
Make the collar loose around the dog's neck. The collar is too tight. The dog can hardly breathe.

---

lopsided The table is **lopsided.** The table is uneven. It leans to one side because two of the legs are shorter than the other two. The table is crooked.

---

lose Do not **lose** your pen. Do not put your pen where you cannot find it. Jerome lost his pen while he was in the park. He does not know where in the park to find his pen.

That team will **lose** the baseball game.
That team will **not win** the baseball game.

Hansel and Gretel were **lost** in the woods. They did not know how to get home.

---

lost Alice was **lost** in the forest. She could not find her way out of the forest. Alice did not know how to get home.

lot   A **lot** is a piece of land. The men are going to build a house on the empty lot near our house.

There are **a lot of** birds in the tree.
There are **very many** birds in the tree.

---

loud   The music was **loud.**
The music was **not soft.** Billy played the piano. Jack beat his drums. Margaret and Susan sang a song. Their music was loud. It was not quiet.

---

love   I have a great **love** for my father and mother. I like them very much. I like to be with my father and mother. I show my love for my mother and father by helping them and being good to them.

My father and mother **love me.**
My father and mother **like me very much.**

Baby **loves** mother. He kisses her because he loves her.

I love you well, my little brother,
And you are fond of me;
Let us be kind to one another,
As brothers ought to be.

---

lovely   Aunt Clara has a **lovely** hat.
Aunt Clara has a **beautiful** hat.

low

The airplane is flying high.
The bird is flying **low.**
The bird is flying **near the ground.**

Mother spoke in a **low** voice.
Mother spoke in a **soft** voice. She whispered. She tried to be as quiet as she could.

Anita bought a dress for a very **low** price.
Anita bought a dress for a very **small** price. She did not have to pay much money for the dress.

Please **lower** the window shade.
Please **pull down** the window shade.

The stool is **lower than** the table.
The stool is **not as high as** the table.

---

luck   Edward found ten dollars. He did not look for it. It was **luck** that he found the ten dollars.

Edward threw a rock into the air. Edward caught the rock in his hand with his eyes closed. He did not try to catch the rock. It was luck that Edward caught the rock. Edward has good luck.

---

lucky   Eddie is **lucky.** He has a lot of good luck. Many good things happen to Eddie.

---

luggage   Suitcases, trunks, and bags are **luggage.** Mother packed our luggage for the trip.

lullaby   Mother sang a **lullaby** to the baby.   Mother softly sang a song to help the baby to sleep.   I like to hear my mother sing lullabies.

---

lump   The baby fell out of bed and got a **lump** on his head.
The baby fell out of bed and got a **bump** on his head.   Where the baby hit his head, he got a raised place.   The lump hurt.

I gave the horse a **lump** of sugar.
I gave the horse a **small piece** of sugar.

A **lump** of dirt fell out of the truck.

---

lunch   We eat **lunch** at noon.
We eat **a small meal** at noon.   We do not eat as much for lunch as we do for dinner.   I carry my lunch to school in a lunch box.   When we go on a picnic, we carry our lunch in a lunch basket.

---

lying   The brown dog is **lying** down.   The white dog is standing up.

---

lying   The naughty boy is **lying**.
The naughty boy is **saying things that are not true**.   We should not lie.

This is the thirteenth letter of the alphabet.

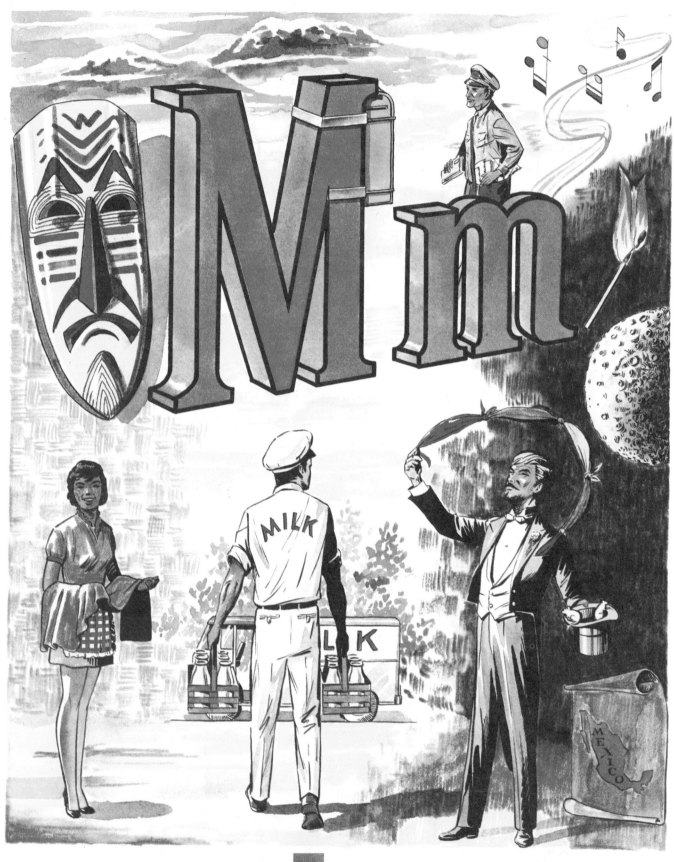

ABCDEFGHIJKL**M**NOPQRSTUVWXYZ

abcdefghijkl**m**nopqrstuvwxyz

ma   Some children call their mothers **Ma.**

---

machine   A **machine** does work faster and better than people do.

This machine cuts the grass. It is called a lawn mower.

This machine writes letters. It is called a typewriter.

An airplane, a helicopter, and a vacuum cleaner are machines. Can you name some more machines?

---

mad   Some people say **mad** when they mean angry.

Our neighbor became **mad.**
Our neighbor became **sick in his mind.** He did not have good sense. He did not know the right thing to do. The mad man went to the hospital to get better.

Herbert was **mad** because he could not go swimming.
Herbert was **angry** because he could not go swimming.

---

made   Yesterday Carl **made** a desk.
Yesterday Carl **built** a desk. He will make a chair today.

Alexander **made** much noise with his drum.
Alexander **caused** much noise with his drum.

The furnace **made the house** warm.
The furnace **caused the house to become** warm.

Mr. Smith **made** a good teacher.
Mr. Smith **was** a good teacher.

When I worked in the office, I **made** ten dollars each day.
When I worked in the office, I **earned** ten dollars each day.

magic We saw a man pull a rabbit out of a hat. He pretended that he was able to pull a rabbit out of a hat. We know that it was only a trick. He calls his trick **magic.**

The man's hand worked so fast and so well that it seemed that he was taking a rabbit out of the hat.

---

magician A **magician** is a person who does tricks that are a puzzle or a mystery to the people who watch him. He calls his tricks magic.

---

maid Gertrude is a pretty **maid.**
Gertrude is a pretty **young woman who is not married.**

Mother has a **maid** to help her do the work at home.
Mother has a **servant girl** to help her do the work at home.

---

mail Letters, postcards, and packages are called **mail.** Yesterday the mailman brought us some mail. He brought my mother a letter from Grandmother. He brought me a postcard from my friend Raymond. He brought my father a package of tobacco which was sent from a store.

Freddie will **mail** his letter. He will drop the letter in a mailbox. Freddie sometimes **mails** his letters at the post office. Yesterday Freddie **mailed** a package to Grandmother.

---

mailbox The box that mail is put into is called a **mailbox.**

mailman   A **mailman** delivers mail from the post office to our house. He also picks up mail from mailboxes. He is sometimes called a postman.

---

main   We eat our **main** meal at noon.
We eat our **largest and best** meal at noon.

---

mainly   The things on the table were **mainly** books. Most of the things on the table were books.

---

make

The boys like to **make** a tree house.
The boys like to **build** a tree house.

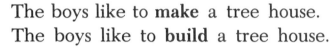

The girls will **make** some candy.
The girls will **prepare** some candy. They made some good candy yesterday.

Mother can **make** a dress.
Mother can **sew** a dress.

Mrs. Jones **makes** a good teacher.
Mrs. Jones **is** a good teacher.

The furnace **makes the house** warm.
The furnace **causes the house to be** warm.

Donald can **make** much noise with his drum.
Donald can **cause** much noise with his drum.

Edwin **makes** ten dollars each week for delivering the newspaper.
Edwin **earns** ten dollars each week for delivering the newspaper.

Louis likes to **make believe** he is an astronaut.
Louis likes to **pretend** he is an astronaut.

Mother **makes Alice** brush her teeth.
Mother **tells Alice she must** brush her teeth.

mall   A **mall** is a shaded walk. We walked down the mall. We enjoyed walking in the shade of the mall.

---

mamma   **Mamma** is a child's word for mother.

---

man   My father is a **man**. My little brother is a boy. My little brother will grow up to be a man like my father.

Man sometimes means all human beings.

---

mankind   All **mankind** wants peace. All people want peace. All human beings want to live in peace. The human race wants peace.

---

manner   Mother holds the baby in a gentle **manner**.
Mother holds the baby in a gentle **way**. She handles the baby gently.

---

manners   "**Manners**" means ways of doing things. Edith has good manners. She is kind and polite to everybody.

---

mansion   A **mansion** is a large and beautiful house. The rich family lived in a mansion.

---

many   There are **many** birds in that tree.
There are **a great number of** birds in that tree.

map   A **map** is a flat picture which shows you where countries and oceans are. A map shows you where cities, towns, lakes, and rivers are. This is a map of North America.

maple

A **maple** is a kind of tree. Maple syrup and sugar are made from the sap of a maple tree. This is a leaf from a maple tree.

> I really like the maple tree
> Which gives so many things to me:
> Leaves that bring a cooling shade,
> And wood from which my table's made;
> Sap which makes some syrup sweet
> And sugar candy that's a treat.

marble   **Marble** is a hard stone which is used for statues and big buildings. Much marble is white.

A **marble** is a small ball which is usually made of glass. We play games with marbles. Do you ever play with marbles?

March   **March** is the third month of the year. March has thirty-one days.

march   A **march** is music which is played while we are walking. It is walking music. The band played a march in the parade.

The soldiers **march.**
The soldiers **walk in steps with each other.** They are walking together. The soldiers are taking steps of the same length. It is a pleasure to watch the soldiers march.

margarine   **Margarine** is a food made of fat and vegetable oil. We sometimes spread margarine on our bread instead of butter.

marigold   A **marigold** is a flower with many yellow, red, and orange petals.

mark Evelyn made a **mark** on the sidewalk with chalk. Her mark was a circle. Peter made a mark also. His mark was a cross.

Janice got a good **mark** on her paper.
Janice got a good **grade** on her paper. She did not make any mistakes on her paper. Janice's mark was 100. Janice was very happy.

Mark the oak trees with a spot of yellow paint. Show which trees are oak trees by putting a spot of yellow paint on them.

Mother **marked** the Christmas presents.
Mother **put names on** the Christmas presents.

Mark a straight line on your paper.
Write a straight line on your paper.

The teacher just finished **marking** our papers.
The teacher just finished **putting grades** on our papers.

---

market A **market** is a place where people buy things. Mother goes to the market to buy fruits and vegetables.

My mother will **market** tomorrow.
My mother will **shop for food** tomorrow.

---

marry When a man and woman **marry,** they become husband and wife. John **married** Alice in church.

We saw the man **marry** John and Alice.

mask   Bernard is wearing a **mask.**
Bernard is wearing a **false face.**   The mask covers Bernard's real face.

---

master   The dog knows **his master.**
The dog knows **who owns him.**

Geraldine will **master** the alphabet.   She will learn the alphabet very well.

---

mat   Brenda wiped her shoes on the **mat.**
Brenda wiped her shoes on the **small rug.**

Jane put a **mat** under the very hot dish.
Jane put a **small pad** under the very hot dish.   She did not want the hot dish to burn the table.

The dog's long hair will **mat** if he plays in the mud.
The dog's long hair will **tangle and stick together** if he plays in the mud.   Sally sometimes combs the dog's **matted** hair.

---

match   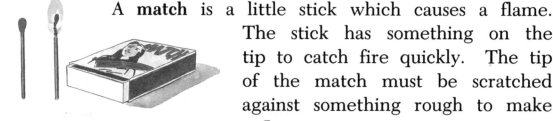   A **match** is a little stick which causes a flame. The stick has something on the tip to catch fire quickly. The tip of the match must be scratched against something rough to make a flame.

The buttons **match.**
The buttons **are alike.**

Stanley wants a tie to **match** his shirt.   He wants a tie that will look good with his shirt. Patty thinks a light blue tie will go well with Stanley's dark blue shirt.

material   **Material** is what things are made of.   Brick is the material we used to build the house.   Wood is the material we used to make the table.

Cloth is sometimes called **material.**

---

matter   What is the **matter,** Sophie?
What is the **trouble,** Sophie?   What is wrong with you?

What **matter** will we talk about?   What are we going to talk about?

Matter is what things are made of.

Does it **matter** to you if we borrow your car?
Does it **make a difference** to you if we borrow your car?
   I didn't think you would mind if we borrowed your car.
   Do you care if we use it for an hour?

May   **May** is the fifth month of the year.   May has thirty-one days.

---

may   **May I** have some candy?
Am I allowed to have some candy?

It **may** rain today.
It **is possible that it will** rain today.

May you have a merry Christmas!
Let it be that you have a merry Christmas!

---

maybe   **Maybe** I can go swimming, but I am not sure.
Perhaps I can go swimming, but I am not sure.

me Sarah said, "I want the ball. Give the ball to **me.** Please give **me** my ball."

---

meadow A **meadow** is a field where grass grows. The cows eat grass in the meadow. The children like to pick wild flowers in the meadow.

---

meal We eat three times a day. Breakfast is our first **meal.** Lunch is our second meal. Dinner is our third meal.

---

mean I do not understand what you **mean.**
I do not understand what you **want to say.** Please tell me again what you have in mind.

A dictionary tells us what words **mean.** Big **means** large. Gloria did not know what that word **meant.**

Ralph was **mean** to the dog.
Ralph was **not kind** to the dog.

---

measure A **measure** tells how much of something. Inches, feet, hours, years, pounds, and tons are measures.

The children will **measure** some things.

Nancy is measuring the table. She wants to know how long it is.

Danny is measuring the bag of flour. He wants to know how heavy it is.

Later Nancy will measure the door. She wants to know how high it is.

meat   **Meat** is food. It comes from animals. Beef is meat that comes from cows. Pork is meat that comes from pigs.

---

mechanic   A **mechanic** is a person who makes or fixes machines. A mechanic fixed our car.

---

medal   The soldier got a **medal** for being brave in the war. The general put the medal on the soldier's jacket.

> Many men are very brave,
> Fighting so hard our country to save:
> Soldiers, sailors, so we are told,
> Honored by medals of silver and gold.

---

medicine   I take **medicine** to make me well. The doctor gives me medicine to make me well. Medicines can be pills, tablets, powders, or liquids. The doctor gave my mother a bottle of medicine to stop her from coughing.

---

meet   Mother will **meet** Judy at school.
Mother will **come to** Judy at school.

Yesterday I **met** my teacher in the store.

I want to **meet** our new neighbors. I want to see them and to know their names. I will tell them my name. I will also tell our neighbors that I am happy to know them.

meeting   There was a **meeting** of my mother's friends at our house. There was a **coming together** of my mother's friends at our house. They gathered at our house. My mother's friends often meet at our house.

---

melody   A song has words and a **melody**. The melody of a song is the part that we can hum.

---

melon   A **melon** is a large juicy fruit that grows on a vine. Melons are sweet inside. A watermelon is a kind of melon that is red inside.

---

melt   Ice will **melt** if it gets warm.
Ice will **become liquid** if it gets warm. Ice becomes water when it melts.

Sugar will **melt** if we heat it in a pan. Sugar will also melt if we put it in water.

The butter **melted** because it was left in the sun.

---

men   My father and my Uncle Eugene are **men**. My grandfather is also a man. Boys grow up to be men.

---

mend   Alfred tore a hole in his shirt. Mother will **mend** Alfred's shirt. She will sew the shirt so that there will not be a hole in it.

The leg of the table broke off. Father **mended** the leg with glue. He put the leg back on the table.

meow   A cat says, "**Meow,** meow."

---

merchant   A **merchant** is a man who buys and sells things. My Uncle Hugo owns a store. He buys many things for his store. My uncle then sells these things for more money than he paid for them. My Uncle Hugo is a merchant.

---

mere   It was **mere** luck that I found my watch.
It was **only** luck that I found my watch. It was nothing more than luck.

---

merrily   Judy skipped **merrily** down the street. She skipped down the street in a merry way. Judy was very happy.

---

merry   I hope you have a **merry** Christmas.
I hope you have a **happy** Christmas.

> Merry are the bells, and merry would they ring,
> Merry was myself, and merry could I sing;
> With a merry ding-dong, happy, gay, and free,
> And a merry sing-song, happy let us be.

---

merry-go-round

This is a **merry-go-round.** There are wooden horses and seats on the merry-go-round. Some horses go up and down as the merry-go-round goes around and around. Music plays as the merry-go-round turns.

message   Bill whispered a **message** into my ear. He told me something he wanted me to know.

Shirley wrote her mother a **message** on a piece of paper. I gave the message to Shirley's mother.

> Dear Mother,
> I shall be late for supper tonight.
> Love,
> Shirley

---

met   I **met** Tommy in the park. While I was in the park I saw Tommy and talked to him. Did you also meet Tommy in the park?

---

metal   **Metal** is a hard material. Metal is usually found in mines. Iron, lead, gold, and silver are metals. Most metals are heavy.

---

mew   Our kitten says, "**Mew,** mew." Our kitten **mews** when it is hungry.

Mexico   **Mexico** is a country in North America. The United States is the country north of Mexico. Central America is south of Mexico. The people in Mexico speak Spanish.

mice   We saw three **mice** in the barn.   The cat caught one mouse. The other two mice ran away.

microphone

People talk into a **microphone** when they broadcast on the radio.   The microphone helps to send sounds from the radio station to your radio.

A **microphone** is used to make the sound of a voice louder.

microscope   We use a **microscope** to see very small things which we cannot see with our eyes alone.

midday   **Midday** is noon, or the middle of the day.   We eat our lunch at midday.

middle   I drew a line down the **middle** of the paper.
I drew a line down the **center** of the paper.

There is a dot in the **middle** of this circle.

midnight   **Midnight** is the middle of the night.   It is twelve o'clock at night.   A new day begins at midnight.

might   We **might** go to the lake tomorrow.
We **will perhaps** go to the lake tomorrow.

Bill **might** have won the race if he had not stumbled.
Bill **could** have won the race if he had not stumbled.

---

mile   It is a distance of one **mile** from my house to the school. It is a long walk for me to go to school. It takes me twenty minutes to walk a mile. It is almost fifty miles to my grandmother's house. I never walk to her house. It is too far.

Father sometimes drives our car at sixty **miles** an hour. This means that we can travel sixty miles in one hour.

---

milk   **Milk** is a white liquid food. Some mother animals give milk to feed their babies. The milk that we get in bottles or cartons comes from cows.

Did you ever see anybody **milk** a cow? Yesterday the farmer **milked** the cow.

---

milkman   A **milkman** is a man who sells or delivers milk.

---

mill   A **mill** is a machine for grinding coffee, corn, or other grains or seeds. Wheat is ground into flour at a flour mill.

A **mill** is also a factory where things are made. In our town we have a cotton mill. Cotton is made into cloth in a cotton mill.

Did you see the miller **mill** the grain?
Did you see the miller **grind** the grain?

miller   A **miller** is a person who owns or works at a mill.

---

million   A **million** is one thousand thousands.

    100 is one hundred, or ten tens.
    1,000 is one thousand, or ten hundreds.
    1,000,000 is one million, or one thousand thousands.

---

mind   A person thinks with his **mind.** He knows with his mind. A person learns with his mind. His mind tells him what he must do.

Do you **mind** your mother and father?
Do you **obey** your mother and father?

Mary **minded** the baby while Mother went to the store.
Mary **took care of** the baby while Mother went to the store.

Mind what the teacher says.
Pay attention to what the teacher says.

Do you mind if I turn on the television set?
Will it bother you if I turn on the television set? If you do not like the noise from the television set, I will turn it off.

---

mine   A **mine** is a large and deep hole in the earth. Coal and diamonds come from mines.

The men **mine** coal in a coal mine. The men dig coal from the earth.

This ball is **mine.** This ball belongs to me. I own it.

minus   Six **minus** two leaves four.
Six **less** two leaves four.

$6 - 2 = 4$

Two taken away from six equals four.

---

minute   A **minute** is a measure of time. There are sixty seconds in a minute. There are sixty minutes in an hour.

David will be here in a **minute.**
David will be here in a **very short time.**

This clock tells us that it is fifteen minutes after seven o'clock.

---

mirror

A **mirror** is a glass in which you can see yourself. Father looks at himself in a mirror when he shaves. A mirror is sometimes called a looking glass.

I look in the mirror and what do I see?
A person who's standing there looking at me!
It's I in the looking glass; my face is seen,
A face I keep washing until it is clean.

---

mischief   Tim often gets into **mischief.** He often does bad things. He doesn't obey his parents. He is often naughty.

---

misery   War causes much **misery.**
War causes much **pain and unhappiness.**

Miss   My aunt's name is **Miss** Clark. She is not married; so we call her Miss.

miss   I try to hit the ball with my bat.
Sometimes I **miss** the ball.
Sometimes I **do not hit** the ball.

Uncle John **missed** the train.
Uncle John **did not catch** the train. The train had already left the railroad station before he was able to get aboard it.

I was sick and had to **miss** church last Sunday. I was not at church last Sunday.

I **miss** my grandmother and grandfather. I am very sad that they are not here with me.

---

mistake   When you do something wrong without really wanting to do it, it is a **mistake.** Paul took Edward's hat by mistake. Paul really wanted to take his own hat.

Sally did not add the numbers in the correct way.
3 + 2 = 4   This is a mistake.
3 + 2 = 5   This is correct.

---

mitten    This is a **mitten.** We wear mittens to keep our hands warm. A mitten does not have a place for each finger. It has a place for the thumb. A glove has a place for each finger and the thumb.

---

mix   I **mix** chocolate, milk, and sugar to make a chocolate drink.
I **stir together** chocolate, milk, and sugar to make a chocolate drink.

Robert **mixes up** his words when he talks too fast. He doesn't say his words in the correct way. I didn't understand Robert when he mixed up his words.

moccasin   A **moccasin** is a soft leather shoe. American Indians wore moccasins.

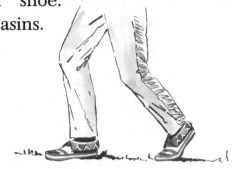

> Moccasins of leather brown
>   Are what the Indian wears,
> While hunting in the forest deep
>   For rabbits, deer, or bears.

moment   Jerry will be home in a **moment**.
Jerry will be home in a **very short time**.

Monday   **Monday** is the second day of the week.

Sunday	Monday	Tuesday	Wednesday	Thursday	Friday	Saturday
first	second	third	fourth	fifth	sixth	seventh
1st	2nd	3rd	4th	5th	6th	7th

money   We buy things with **money**. Pennies, nickels, dimes, quarters, half-dollars, and dollar bills are American money. Do you have enough money to pay for a coat?

monkey   A **monkey** is an animal that climbs trees. It has a long tail. The paws of a monkey look like a human being's hands.

month A **month** is a part of a year. There are twelve months in a year. These are the months of the year: January, February, March, April, May, June, July, August, September, October, November, December. Here is a little poem to help us to remember how many days there are in each month.

> Thirty days has September,
> April, June, and November;
> All the rest have thirty-one;
> February has twenty-eight alone,
> Except in leap year, that's the time
> When February's days are twenty-nine.

---

moo The cow says, "**Moo,** moo."

---

moon The **moon** is a large round ball of matter in space. The moon travels around the earth. We see the moon shining.

It does not have any light of its own. The sun lights up the moon with sunlight. On the moon there is no air. Two Americans were the first human beings to land on the moon.

---

moonlight **Moonlight** is light from the moon. The sun shines on the moon and gives us moonlight.

---

more Eric ate one apple. James ate three apples.
James ate **more** apples than Eric did.
James ate **a greater number of** apples than Eric did.

Daniel can walk **more** quickly than Joan. Joan does not walk as quickly as Daniel.

morning   **Morning** is the first part of the day.   Morning begins at twelve o'clock midnight.   It ends at twelve o'clock noon.   I get up at seven o'clock in the morning and eat breakfast.

---

morning glory   A **morning glory** is a flower which blossoms early in the morning.   Morning-glory flowers grow on a vine.   We have some blue morning glories growing on our fence.

> Morning glories of summertime
> Pretty on my fence do climb,
> Specially when the sun does shine,
> Opening them on their twisting vine.

---

morsel   A **morsel** is a tiny piece of something.   Not a morsel of food was left after the hungry children finished eating.

---

mosquito   A **mosquito** is a small insect which flies.   When mosquitoes bite us, they drink some of our blood.

> Bad little mosquito, do bite if you will!
> But if I catch you, be sure I will kill.

---

moss   **Moss** is a bunch of tiny, green plants.   These plants are so close to each other that they look like a green carpet.   Moss grows on trees, on rocks, and on the ground.   Moss is soft like velvet.

most   Stanley has two marbles. Allen has ten marbles. Louis has fifty marbles.

Louis has **the most** marbles.

Louis has **the greatest number of** marbles.

The baby drank **most of** her milk.

The baby drank **almost all** of her milk.

Anita's dress is the **most** beautiful of all the dresses. No other girl is wearing a dress as beautiful as Anita's dress.

---

motel   A **motel** is a hotel for travelers going by car. Motels have space for parking cars. Motels also have rooms for sleeping.

---

moth   A **moth** is an insect that looks like a butterfly. Moths fly at night.

---

mother   A **mother** is a woman who has a child or children. I love my mother. She takes care of me. My parents are my mother and father.

---

motion   Did you see Frances **make a motion?**

Did you see Frances **move?**

Terence will **motion** to me with his hand when he wants me to come.

Terence will **make a signal** to me with his hand when he wants me to come.

I **motioned** to Terence, but he did not see me.

motion picture   A **motion picture** is a moving picture.   Motion pictures are sometimes called movies.

---

motor   A **motor** is an engine.   A motor is a machine that makes other machines work.   Our washing machine is run by an electric motor.   Our automobile goes by a gasoline motor.

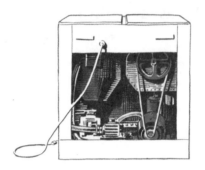 

---

motorboat   A **motorboat** is a boat which runs by a motor.

---

mountain   A **mountain** is a very high hill.   These are mountains.

---

mouse   A **mouse** is a little animal that lives in people's houses or in barns.   Some **mice** live in the field or woods.

mouth   I eat and talk with my **mouth.**   My tongue and my teeth are in my mouth.

---

mouthful   Steve could not talk because he had a **mouthful** of candy. His mouth was full of candy.

---

move   Will you help me to **move this table?**
Will you help me to **put this table in a different place?**

Our neighbors will **move** next week.
Our neighbors will **go to a different place** next week. They are going to live in a different city. Our neighbors are moving to New York.

Sally's turtle **moves** slowly.
Sally's turtle **goes** slowly.

Wilbur's leg is not broken. He **moved** his leg easily. He lifted his leg and put it down again. He can walk with his leg. Wilbur can **move** his leg without having pain.

---

movie   A **movie** is a moving picture.

---

moving picture   My father showed us a funny **moving picture.**
Moving pictures are sometimes called movies.

mow   Farmer Brown will **mow** the hay in the field. He will cut down the hay.

---

mower   A **mower** is a machine for cutting grass, weeds, hay, and other plants.

Mr.   Our mailman's name is **Mister** Adams. This is the way to write his name: **Mr.** Adams.

Mrs.   My mother is **Mrs.** Ricardo. A woman who is married writes **Mrs.** before her last name.

---

much   Philip asked, "How **much** money do you have? Do you have five dollars? Do you have more money than five dollars?" Elizabeth answered, "I have twenty dollars. I have much more money than five dollars."

Please don't give me **much** pie. I don't want a very big piece of pie.

I have **too much candy.**
I have **more candy than I need.**

James is **much** stronger than Alfred. James can lift bigger and heavier boxes than Alfred can lift.

---

mud   **Mud** is wet and sticky earth. Mud is dirt and water mixed together. Our car got stuck in the mud.

---

muddy   Carl's shoes are **muddy.**
Carl's shoes are **covered with mud.**

mule   A **mule** is an animal which is half horse and half donkey.

> If I had a mule, sir, and he wouldn't start
> Do you think I'd harness him up to a cart?
> No, no, I'd give him oats and hay
> And let him stay there all day.

mumble   Please do not **mumble.**   Please do not speak with your mouth almost closed.   Be so kind as to speak clearly so that I can understand you.

museum   A **museum** is a building where there are many interesting things.   There are paintings, statues, machines, and many other things in the museum.   We learn much by going to the museum.

music   Clara makes **music** by singing.   Jeff makes music by playing the piano.   Jeff plays the piano while Clara sings.   They are making music.   Music is pleasant sounds.   A band makes music.

must   We **must** eat in order to stay alive.
We **have to** eat in order to stay alive.

We **must** hurry.
We **should** hurry.

my   This is **my** book.   This book belongs to me.   I own the book.   It is mine.   This book is not yours.

myself I cut **myself** with a sharp knife. I cut my hand with a knife. I will put a bandage on my hand.

I **myself** will cook dinner.

I cooked dinner all **by myself.**
I cooked dinner all **alone.** Nobody helped me cook dinner.

---

mysterious My father's watch is gone. How my father could have lost his watch is **mysterious.** Nobody can tell how my father lost his watch.

---

mystery A **mystery** is a secret or a problem.

What could have happened to the lost puppy was a mystery to Tim. He couldn't understand where the little dog could have gone.

This is the fourteenth letter of the alphabet.

ABCDEFGHIJKLMNOPQRSTUVWXYZ

abcdefghijklmnopqrstuvwxyz

nail   You have a **nail** at the end of each of your fingers and your toes.   They are called fingernails and toenails.   They are hard.   Fingernails protect the ends of your fingers.   They also help you to pick up small things.

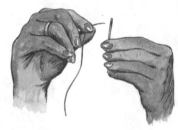

Father hammered a **nail** into the box.   A nail for hammering is a thin and smooth piece of metal.   It is pointed at one end and flat at the other.   Nails are hammered into boards to keep them together.

Ted will **nail** those two boards together.   He will fasten those two boards together.

---

naked   The baby was **naked.**
The baby was **without clothes.**   He was not wearing any clothes.

---

name   My **name** is Kevin Kelly.   The name of what I am reading is book.   We know persons and things by their names.

My first name is Kevin.   My last name is Kelly.   My last name is sometimes called a family name.   It is the name of my family.   My father, mother, sisters, and brothers have the same last name.   We have different first names.

I will **name** my puppy Skippy.   Kim named her kitten Puff.

nap   My baby sister takes a **nap** each afternoon.
My baby sister takes a **short sleep** each afternoon.

I like to **nap** when I am sleepy.   Daddy **napped** yesterday afternoon.

---

napkin   A **napkin** is a square piece of cloth.   You use a napkin at the table to wipe your mouth and fingers while eating. You should keep your napkin in your lap while you are at table.   Some napkins are made out of paper.

---

narrow   The road will **narrow** after about a mile.
The road will **become less wide** after about a mile.

The sidewalk was **narrow.**
The sidewalk was **not wide.**

---

nasturtium   A **nasturtium** is a plant that has yellow and red flowers.   The leaves of the nasturtium plant are round and shiny.

---

nation   A **nation** is a country in which people live with the same laws.   Mexico is a nation.   Canada is a nation.   The United States of America is a nation.

---

native   A person is a **native** of the place in which he was born. Carol is a native of Canada.   She was born in Canada. Stephen is a native of Sacramento, California.   He was born in Sacramento, California.   Margarita is a native of Puebla, Mexico.   She was born there.

nature   **Nature** is the whole world we live in. Nature is the trees, the clouds, the rivers, the lakes, the animals, and everything that God has made for us.

---

naughty   Harry is a **naughty** boy.
Harry is a **bad** boy. He is bad in many little ways.

> Naughty boy that stole a pie,
> Broke a plate, and told a lie.

---

navy   A **navy** is all the fighting ships of a country and the men who run them. The men in the navy are called sailors.

---

near   The tree is **near** the house.
The tree is **close to** the house.

As we **near** the airport, we very often see giant airplanes come in for a landing. As we get close to the airport, we are able to see very big airplanes ready to land.

---

nearly   It is **nearly** three o'clock.
It is **almost** three o'clock. It is two minutes to three o'clock.

---

neat   Susan is a **neat person**.
Susan is a **person who likes to keep things clean and in order.**

Mother's cupboards are **neat**.
Mother's cupboards are **clean and tidy.**

neck   Your **neck** joins your head to your body. Ann is putting some beads around her neck.

---

necktie   A **necktie** is a band of cloth which is worn around a person's neck. A necktie is tied in front. My father is wearing a green necktie. My brother Alexander is wearing a red bow tie.

---

need   We **need** milk to feed the baby.
We **must have** milk to feed the baby.

You **need** a bigger shovel to dig that big hole.
You **should have** a bigger shovel to dig that big hole.

Do you **need** to work so much?
Do you **have** to work so much?

---

needle   Mother sews with a **needle** and thread. A needle is a very thin, round piece of metal. One end of the needle has a sharp point. In the other end of the needle, there is a hole through which thread is put.

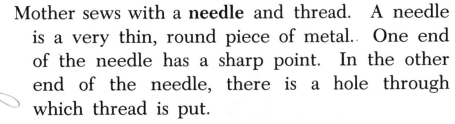

The leaves of a pine tree are called **needles**.

N n

neighbor A **neighbor** is a person who lives near to me. Mr. and Mrs. Lopez live in the house next to my house. They are my neighbors.

---

neither **Neither** Paul nor Frank want to sweep the kitchen floor. Paul did not want to sweep the floor. Frank did not want to sweep the floor either.

Mary and Judy went to the store, but **neither of them** bought anything.

Mary and Judy went to the store, but **not either one** bought anything.

---

nest Birds build a **nest** for their home. The mother bird lays her eggs in a nest. When the eggs hatch, the baby birds live in the nest until they can fly.

---

net There are many kinds of **nets.** This is a butterfly net. It is used for catching butterflies.

Below is a tennis net.

Above is a fish net.

356

Netherlands Netherlands is another name for the country of Holland.

The people who live in the Netherlands are called Dutch people.

---

never I **never** saw a giraffe.

I **did not ever see** a giraffe. I did not see a giraffe at any time in my life.

---

new Mary is wearing a **new** dress. Mary bought her new dress this morning. Louise is wearing an old dress. Louise bought her dress a year ago.

I will read a **new** book when I finish reading this book.
I will read a **different** book when I finish reading this book.

Father listens to the radio to find out the **news**
Father listens to the radio to find out the **story of what has happened.** Father also reads the **news**paper to learn the news.

---

newspaper We get the **newspaper** every day at our house. The newspaper tells people what is happening in the world. It tells them what they can buy in stores.

The newspaper has pictures in it. It has funnies in it, too.

New Testament The **New Testament** is part of the Bible. The New Testament tells us about Jesus.

New Year's Day   New Year's Day is the first day of January. It is the first day of a new year.

New York   New York is a city in the United States. New York City is in the state of New York. New York City is one of the largest cities in the world.

There are many skyscrapers and large buildings in New York.

---

next

Mr. and Mrs. Adams live in the house **next** to our house.

Mr. and Mrs. Adams live in the house **nearest** to our house.

The squirrel is **next** to the bird.
The squirrel is **near** the bird.

Milton's turn is **next.**
Milton's turn is **right after this one.**

---

nibble   The cat watched the mouse **nibble the cheese.**
The cat watched the mouse **eat the cheese in small bits.**

Paul got fat because he **nibbled** candy between meals.

---

nice   Yesterday was a **nice** day. The sun shone. It was neither too hot nor too cold. The air was fresh and clean. It was a pleasant day.

Regina is a **nice** person. We like to be with Regina. She is a pleasant person.

Kenneth is a **nice** worker. His work is careful and neat.

nickel   A **nickel** is money. It is worth five cents. Five pennies are five cents also.

1¢ + 1¢ + 1¢ + 1¢ + 1¢ = 5¢   .01 + .01 + .01 + .01 + .01 = .05

Nickel is a metal that looks something like silver.

---

night   **Night** is the time between evening and morning. It is dark at night. During the day it is light. Most people sleep during the night and stay awake during the day.

---

nightgown   A **nightgown** is a long and loose dress. Some people wear a nightgown at night when they sleep.

Grandpa wears a nightgown
When sleeping in his bed
Of soft and fluffy goose down
On which he rests his head.

---

nighttime   **Nighttime** is the time between evening and morning. It is dark at nighttime.

---

nine   There are **nine** cows in the meadow. Can you count them?

1 2 3 4 5 6 7 8 9 10

N n

nineteen   The number **nineteen** comes after number eighteen and before number twenty. Can you count from one to nineteen?

1 2 3 4 5 6 7 8 9 10
11 12 13 14 15 16 17 18 **19** 20

---

nineteenth   Billy is the **nineteenth** (19th) person standing in the line. There are eighteen people standing in line in front of Billy. He is number nineteen in the line.

Today is Cynthia's nineteenth birthday. Today she is nineteen years old.

---

ninety   Nine dimes make **ninety** cents. If I add together nine 10's, I will get ninety.

10 + 10 + 10 + 10 + 10 + 10 + 10 + 10 + 10 = **90**

Nine times ten is **ninety.**

9 × 10 = **90**

10 20 30 40 50 60 70 80 **90** 100

---

ninth   Edward is the **ninth** person standing in line. There are eight people standing in front of Edward. He is wearing a green shirt with red and white stripes. Can you find Edward in the line?

no   **No** is the opposite of yes.   Mother asked Helen and Peter if they wanted some cabbage.   Helen said, "Yes, I like cabbage. I want to eat some."   Peter said, "No, I do not like cabbage. I do not want to eat any."

Carl has **no** candy.
Carl has **not any** candy.

---

nobody   **Nobody** saw the accident.
No one saw the accident.   Not even one person saw the accident happen.

---

nod   A **nod** is a bend of the head.

The teacher will **nod** when she wants me to help her.   She will say yes by bending her head forward and down.

When Johnny asked if he might go to the movies, Mother **nodded.**   Mother said yes by moving her head up and down.

When Daddy is sleepy, his head will **nod.**

---

noise   **Noise** is loud, unpleasant sounds.   Did you hear the noise that people made at the baseball game?   They were yelling and screaming.   They wanted their team to win.

---

noisy   The children were **noisy.**
The children were **making many loud noises.**

---

none   **None** of the boys is in the room.
Not one of the boys is in the room.

noon   We eat our lunch at **noon.**
We eat our lunch at **twelve o'clock in the middle of the day.**

---

no one   I saw **no one** in the hall. I didn't see one person in the hall. There was nobody there.

---

nor   Neither Stanley **nor** Harry heard the bell ring. Stanley didn't hear the bell, and Harry didn't hear the bell. They were too busy playing.

---

north   **North** is a direction. If you look toward the sun as it comes up in the morning, your left shoulder will be pointing north, and your right shoulder will be pointing south.

In the United States of America, it is cold in the North in winter. It is warm in the South.

North America   This is a map of **North America.** Canada, the United States, and Mexico are in North America. The United States is sometimes called U.S.A.

---

nose   You breathe and smell through your **nose.**
The baby has a finger on his nose.
There is a bee on the dog's nose.

not   A bird has wings. It can fly. I do **not** have wings. I can **not** fly.

---

note   A **note** is a short letter. Dick wrote a note to his mother.
In his note, he said:

Dear Mother,

I will be late for supper tonight.

Love,
Dick

Mother **made a note of** what she needed at the store.
Mother **wrote down** what she needed at the store.

Did you **note** that the television is not here.
Did you **notice** that the television is not here.

---

nothing   The dog ate all his food.
There is **nothing** in his dish.
There is **not anything** in his dish.

Five taken away from five is **nothing.**
Five taken away from five is **zero.**
$5 - 5 = 0$

---

notice   The teacher put a **notice** on the blackboard. The notice said:

To all the children:
There will be no school on Wednesday.
Miss Smith

Did you **notice** that Rita is wearing a new dress?
Did you **see** that Rita is wearing a new dress?

November   **November** is the eleventh month of the year. November has thirty days.

---

now   We must go to school **now.**

We must go to school **at this time.** If we do not leave for school now, we will be late.

---

nowhere   I can find my hat **nowhere.** I looked all over the house and I cannot find my hat in any place.

---

nudge   Terence gave me a **nudge.**

Terence gave me a **gentle push.** Terence wanted to get my attention. He wanted me to notice him.

---

number   A **number** tells how many. The farmer counted his hens to find out their number. He counted, "One, two, three, four, five, six." Then the farmer said, "The number of hens that I have is six."

Here are the numbers from 1 to 6:   1 2 3 4 5 6

My telephone **number** is 427-8667.

A number of people came to visit us.
Some people came to visit us.

nurse   A **nurse** takes care of sick people, babies, and old people. Some nurses take care of people in hospitals. Other nurses take care of people in their homes. Rose wants to be a nurse. She must go to school to learn how to be a nurse.

---

nut   A **nut** is the fruit of certain trees. Nuts have hard shells. We must crack open the shell of the nut to get the meat of the nut inside. These are nuts. The meat of the nut is good to eat.

This is the fifteenth letter of the alphabet.

ABCDEFGHIJKLMN**O**PQRSTUVWXYZ

abcdefghijklmn**o**pqrstuvwxyz

oak   An **oak** is a kind of tree. An oak tree has very hard wood. The seeds of the oak are called acorns. These are some leaves from oak trees.

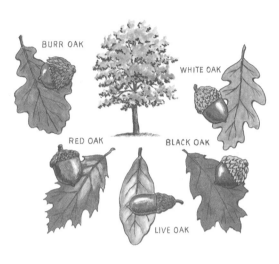

BURR OAK

WHITE OAK

RED OAK   BLACK OAK

LIVE OAK

---

oar   An **oar** is a long wooden pole which is flat at one end. We row a rowboat with a pair of oars.

---

oatmeal   **Oatmeal** is ground oats. Mother cooks oatmeal with water and a little bit of salt. We eat hot oatmeal for breakfast. Did you ever eat oatmeal cookies?

---

oats   **Oats** are a kind of grass. We can eat the seeds of oats. These seeds are also called oats. They are a grain. Oatmeal is made from oats.

---

obey   Clement always tries to **obey** his father and mother. He tries to do what they tell him. A good boy always minds his parents.

O o

object An **object** is a thing that you can see or touch. Books, pencils, tables, chairs, desks, or anything else you can see or touch are objects.

---

observatory

An **observatory** is a place that has telescopes for looking at stars, planets, and other bodies far out in space.

---

obvious It is **obvious** that it is snowing.
It is **easy to see** that it is snowing.

---

ocean An **ocean** is the largest body of water there is. The two largest oceans are the Atlantic Ocean and the Pacific Ocean. The Atlantic Ocean touches the east coast of the United States. The Pacific Ocean touches the west coast of the United States.

In the ocean there is salt water: the water is salty. In lakes and rivers there is fresh water: the water is not salty.

---

o'clock School begins at nine **o'clock**.
School begins at nine **by the clock**.

October **October** is the tenth month of the year. October has thirty-one days.

octopus   An **octopus** is a sea animal that has eight arms.

---

odd   You can make groups of 2 in even numbers and not have anything left over. Two, four, and six are even numbers.

2 APPLES	4 APPLES	6 APPLES
ONE GROUP OF 2	TWO GROUPS OF 2	THREE GROUPS OF 2

If you make groups of 2 with **odd** numbers, you will always have one left over. Three, five, and seven are **odd** numbers.

3 APPLES	5 APPLES	7 APPLES
ONE GROUP OF 2 ONE LEFT OVER	TWO GROUPS OF 2 ONE LEFT OVER	THREE GROUPS OF 2 ONE LEFT OVER

Do you know some more odd numbers?

The clown has an **odd** face.
The clown has a **queer-looking** face.

---

odor   The rose has a pleasant **odor**. When I sniff the rose, I like the way it smells. The smell of the rose is pleasing to me.

O o

of   This is a story **of** a black horse.
This is a story **about** a black horse.

Albert made a game **of** his work.
Albert made a game **out of** his work. He made his work seem like a game.

Mary has a dress **of** silk.
Mary has a dress **made from** silk.

Samuel is a boy **of** good sense.
Samuel is a boy **who has** good sense.

The people **of** the town are very busy.
The people **in** the town are very busy.

Some **of** us should help Mother wash the dishes.
Some **among** us should help Mother wash the dishes.

It is ten minutes **of** ten.
It is ten minutes **before** ten.

New York City is west **of** Boston.
New York City is west **from** Boston.

The stories **of** Mark Twain are interesting.
The stories **by** Mark Twain are interesting.

---

off   The man jumped **off** the galloping horse.
The man jumped **from** the galloping horse.

The canary flew **off**.
The canary flew **away**.

Raymond took **off his coat**.
Raymond took **his coat from his body.**

One leg is **off** the table. There are only three legs on the table. One leg is not there.

Turn the water **off**. Turn the handle of the faucet so that the water will stop pouring out.

offer   **Offer** our guests some ice cream and soda.   Show our guests that we want to give them some ice cream and soda.

---

office   An **office** is a place where some people do their work. Some doctors do their work in an office.   Have you ever been to a doctor's office?

My sister works in an **office** with other people.   My sister uses a typewriter in the office.

Mother mailed a letter at the post **office**.

---

often   I brush my teeth **often**.
I brush my teeth **many times**.   I brush my teeth after I eat something.

---

oh   Marie was so happy to see the pretty roses.   She said, "**Oh,** how beautiful!"

---

oil   **Oil** is grease or fat.   Oil can come from plants, from animals, or from the ground.   Some margarine is made from corn oil. We take the oil of a codfish for medicine.   Gasoline is made from oil that comes out of the ground.   Some oil is used to make machines run more smoothly.

old   Grandfather is **old.**

Grandfather is **not young.** He has lived a long time. His hair is gray. He has many wrinkles in his face. Grandfather cannot run and walk as quickly as young people.

Larry is seven years **old.**
Larry is seven years **of age.** Larry has lived seven years.

I am wearing **old** shoes. These shoes are not new.

---

older   I am six years old. James is eight years old. James is **older** than I. He has lived more years than I have.

---

oldest   Judy is six years old. Walter is seven years old. Vincent is eight years old. Vincent is **oldest.** He has lived longer than both Walter and Judy.

Old Testament   The **Old Testament** is part of the Bible. The Old Testament tells us the story of how God taught His people.

---

on   Where is the clock? The clock is **on** the shelf. Where is the picture? The picture is **on** the wall.

When are you going to the movies?
I am going **on** Tuesday.

I have a book **on** cats.
I have a book **about** cats.

The lights were off, but Marvin turned them **on.** He made the lights work by turning on the electric light switch.

I will **go on** painting the chair until I finish.
I will **continue** painting the chair until I finish.

Timothy has a hat **on.** He is wearing a hat.

once   Mary has been in an airplane **once**.
Mary has been in an airplane **one time**.

Once I had a blue kite.
At one time in the past I had a blue kite.

Everybody started speaking **at once**.
Everybody started speaking **at the same time**.

Go to school **at once**!
Go to school **right away**!

Once upon a time there was a young girl named Cinderella.
A long time ago there was a young girl named Cinderella.

---

one   A man has only **one** head.

This is how the number one is written: **1**
1 2 3 4 5 6 7 8 9 10 11 12 13

The **one** sweeping the sidewalk is Mary.
The **person** sweeping the sidewalk is Mary.

One must eat to stay alive.
Each person must eat to stay alive.

Everybody was walking in **one** direction.
Everybody was walking in **the same** direction.

---

one hundred   Ten 10's are **one hundred**.
$10 + 10 + 10 + 10 + 10 + 10 + 10 + 10 + 10 + 10 = \mathbf{100}$
Fifty plus fifty is **one hundred**. $50 + 50 = \mathbf{100}$
One hundred cents is a dollar: $1.00

---

onion   An **onion** is a vegetable that grows in the ground. When you peel onions tears come from your eyes.

O o

only   Andrew lost his **only** coat.   He lost the one coat he had. Andrew has no other coat.

It is **only** a short walk to school.
It is **just** a short walk to school.   It is no more than a short walk to school.

I would go swimming, **only** I am sick.
I would go swimming, **except that** I am sick.   I can't go.

---

onto   The farmer threw the bundles of hay **onto** the wagon.
The farmer threw the bundles of hay **on top of** the wagon.

---

open   The red door is **open**.
The red door is **not closed**   The green door is closed.

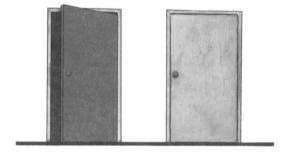

Jane will **open** the box.
Jane will **take the top off** the box.

The package has been **opened.**

---

opening   There is an **opening** in the wall.
There is a **hole** in the wall.

374

opposite If a thing is as different as it can be from something else, it is **opposite.**

Black is the opposite to white.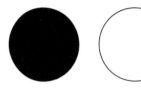

Large is opposite to small.

Tall is opposite to short.

Fat is opposite to thin.

Martha was **opposite** to Raymond at the dinner table. Martha sat in a chair across the table from Raymond. While they were eating, Raymond and Martha could look across the table at one another.

---

or Will you drink milk **or** hot chocolate? Which would you like to drink?

Will you come home on Sunday, Monday, **or** Tuesday. Will you return home on Sunday? **Or** will you return on Monday? **Or** will you return on Tuesday? On which day will you return home?

---

orange An **orange** is a fruit. Oranges are round. They grow on orange trees. My mother squeezes oranges to make orange juice.

This is the color **orange.** It is the same as the fruit.

O o

orbit

The moon has an **orbit** around the earth.
The moon has a **path through space** around the earth.

The earth is **in orbit** around the sun. The earth travels around the sun.

It takes 365 days for the earth to **orbit** the sun once.
It takes 365 days for the earth to **travel around** the sun once. It takes a year for the earth to go around the sun one time.

---

orchard   An **orchard** is a piece of land where fruit trees are grown. We like to play in Grandfather's apple orchard.

---

order   In what **order** are the days of the week? How do the days of the week follow one another? The days of the week are in this order: Sunday, Monday, Tuesday, Wednesday, Thursday, Friday, Saturday.

The policeman works to **keep order.**
The policeman works to **give us peace.**

The captain gave the soldiers an **order.** The captain told the soldiers what they had to do.

Mother called the grocery store and gave the man an **order** for some food. This was Mother's order: sugar, coffee, cream, apples, meat, lettuce, and cookies.

Mother will **order** meat from the butcher. She will ask the butcher to bring the meat to our house.

The captain **orders** the soldiers to march. The captain told the soldiers that they must march.

Mother said, "Put your room **in order,** Jimmy. Put things back where they belong."

We must eat **in order to** live.
We must eat **so that we can** live.

376

organ 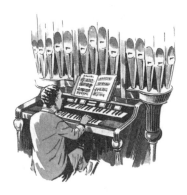 My father plays the **organ**. He makes beautiful music when he plays the organ.

---

other I will read this book at some **other** time.
I will read this book at some **different** time.

Are there any **other** chairs in the house?
Are there any **more** chairs in the house?

Every **other** child standing in line was a boy.
Every **second** child standing in line was a boy. The children stood in line in this order: Jane, Peter, Mary, Joseph, Gloria, Edward, Susan, Richard.

I waited for Billy, but all the **other** children went to the picnic.
I waited for Billy, but all the **rest of the** children went to the picnic.

---

ouch When Sarah hurt her finger, she said, "**Ouch!**"

---

ought We **ought to** help our mother and father.
We **should** help our mother and father. This is one way of showing them that we love them.

---

our This is **our** house. This house belongs to us. We own this house.

O o

ours   This car is **ours.**   It belongs to us.   We own it.

---

ourselves

Sally and I bent over at the same time, and we bumped our heads together.   We hurt **ourselves** when we bumped our heads.

Kathleen and I made the cookies **ourselves.**   We ourselves made the cookies.

Denis and I were standing **by ourselves** away from all the other children.

Denis and I were standing **alone** away from all the other children.

---

out   Mother let the dog go **out.**

Mother let the dog go **outside.**   Now the dog is not inside the house.

We went to visit Aunt Helen, but she was **out.**

We went to visit Aunt Helen, but she was **not at home.**

Speak **out** if you want someone to hear you.

Speak **aloud** if you want someone to hear you.   Your voice must be loud.

Mother told me to pick **out** those vegetables that I like best.

Mother told me to pick **from the others** those vegetables that I like best.

We are **out of** bread.   We no longer have any bread.   We don't have any more bread.

---

outdoors   When the sun is shining, we like to play **outdoors.**

When the sun is shining, we like to play **outside the house.**   We like to be out in the open air.

outside The **outside** of the cupboard is blue. The inside of the cupboard is white.

The children like to play **outside**.
The children like to play **outdoors**. They like to be where there is sun and fresh air.

---

oven My mother cooks roasts in the **oven**. She cooks bread, cakes, and pies in the oven, too.

---

over Father held an umbrella **over** my head.
Father held an umbrella **above** my head.

Donald jumped **over** the brook.
Donald jumped **across** the brook.

While I was sleeping, Mother put a blanket **over** me.
While I was sleeping, Mother put a blanket **on top of** me.

When the movie was **over**, we went home.
When the movie was **at an end**, we went home.

Over thirty children were at the party.
More than thirty children were at the party.

The cat knocked the vase **over**.
The cat knocked the vase **down**. The cat hit the vase so that it fell from the table onto the floor.

We looked for my hat **all over** the house.
We looked for my hat **everywhere in** the house.

I talked to my Aunt Rita **over** the telephone.
I talked to my Aunt Rita **using** the telephone.

O o

overalls   Overalls are loose trousers with a bib in front. Father wears overalls when he works.

> Whenever I go out to play,
>   My overalls I wear,
> To keep my good clothes neat and clean
>   And free from any tear.

---

owe   I got a book from Ernest.

I **owe** Ernest for the book.

I **have to pay** Ernest for the book.   I owe Ernest fifty cents for the book.   I must pay him fifty cents.

---

owl    An **owl** is a large bird with large eyes.   Owls eat mice and other small animals.   Owls fly at night. An owl says, "Whoo, whoo."

> An owl is a kind of bird;
>   Large are his head and eyes;
> And when from treetops he is heard,
>   "Whoo! Whoo!" is what he cries.

---

own   I **own** the blue kite.   The blue kite belongs to me.   It is mine.   The blue kite is my **own.**

---

owner   An **owner** is a person who owns things.   Patrick is the owner of the blue hat.   The blue hat belongs to Patrick.

ox An **ox** is an animal that looks like a cow. An ox is often used for plowing, for pulling loads, and for doing other heavy jobs. We saw two **oxen** working in the field.

oxen More than one ox are called **oxen.** The two oxen pulled a heavy load in a wagon.

oxygen **Oxygen** is a gas which you cannot see, taste, or smell. Air has oxygen in it. People, animals, and plants need oxygen to live.

This is the sixteenth letter of the alphabet.

ABCDEFGHIJKLMNO**P**QRSTUVWXYZ

abcdefghijklmno**p**qrstuvwxyz

pa **Pa** is another name for father.

---

pack A **pack** is a bundle of food, blankets, and other things needed for camping or for a long walk in the woods.

This man is carrying a **pack** on his back.
This man is carrying a **bundle** on his back. He is going to camp in the woods.

I will **pack the books** in the box.
I will **put the books** in the box.

James **packed** his suitcase for his vacation.

---

package

A **package** is a bundle which is wrapped up. Mother came home from the store with many packages. I was so happy because she gave me a package. In my package, there was a toy airplane.

My package is a mystery;
  I wonder what's inside.
I'll open it so I can see
  What does the covering hide.

---

pad I have a **pad** on my chair.
  I have a **thin pillow** on my chair.

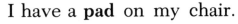

There is a **pad** on the desk.
There is a **book of paper** on the desk. I use the paper in the pad for writing letters.

paddle   A **paddle** is a stick which is flat at one end.   The Indian moved his canoe through the water with a paddle.

Did you ever see an Indian **paddle** a canoe?   I paddled a canoe once.

---

page   I am reading from a **page** in a book.   Books have pages in them.   The book that I am reading is the *Visual Dictionary*.   Most of the pages have pretty pictures on them.

---

paid   Uncle Wilbur **paid me** for cutting the lawn.
Uncle Wilbur **gave me money** for cutting the lawn.

---

pail   Father is carrying a **pail.**   In the pail there is water.   A pail is also called a bucket.

Jack and Jill went up the hill,
   To fetch a pail of water;
Jack fell down, and broke his crown,
   And Jill came tumbling after.

pain We have **pain** when we get sick or when we get hurt. When George had a cold, he had a pain in his throat. When Kenneth cut his finger with a knife, he had pain in his finger. A toothache is pain in a tooth.

---

paint **Paint** is a liquid which is used for covering and coloring things. Paint becomes hard when it is dry. Father has many different colors of paint.

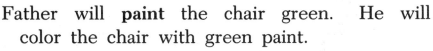

Father will **paint** the chair green. He will color the chair with green paint.

Don't bother Ann. She is **painting** a picture.

When Ann finishes, she will have a beautiful painting of a horse.

---

paintbrush We paint things with a **paintbrush.** We use one kind of paintbrush for painting chairs, tables, houses, and other big things. We use another kind of paintbrush for painting pictures. We paint pictures with a very small paintbrush.

---

painter A **painter** is a person who paints. The artist who paints pictures is a painter. The man who painted our house is a painter.

painting   A **painting** is a painted picture.   We saw some beautiful paintings in the art museum.

---

pair   A **pair** is two things of a kind that go together.   I have a pair of black shoes.   My black shoes are made to be worn at the same time by the same person.   I have a pair of brown gloves.   How many pairs of socks do you have?

---

pajamas   **Pajamas** are a shirt and pants which we sleep in.   Kevin has his pajamas on.   He is ready to go to bed.

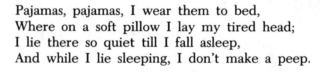

Pajamas, pajamas, I wear them to bed,
Where on a soft pillow I lay my tired head;
I lie there so quiet till I fall asleep,
And while I lie sleeping, I don't make a peep.

---

palace   The king and queen live in a **palace**.
The king and queen live in a **large and beautiful house.**

pale   Mary was so frightened by the spider that her face became **pale**. Mary was so frightened by the spider that her face became **very white**.

---

palm

Your **palm** is the inside of your hand.

A **palm** is a kind of tree that grows where it is warm. The leaves of the palm tree are long and flat. They grow in bunches near the top of the tree.

---

pan

Mother cooked the soup in a **pan**. There are many kinds of pans. Cake is baked in a cake pan. Pie is baked in a pie pan.

---

pancake   A **pancake** is a flat and round cake. Pancakes are fried in a pan. A pancake is made of milk, eggs, and flour.

---

panda   A **panda** is a large black and white animal that looks like a bear.

He's black and he's white,
A bear to the sight,
   But don't say a bear too soon;
      For actually,
      He's cousin, you see,
To Mr. and Mrs. Raccoon.

P p

pansy

A **pansy** is a flower with wide petals. Pansies are small plants. They grow close to the ground. There are many beautiful colors in one pansy.

---

pant   My dog will **pant** if he runs too much.
My dog will **breathe hard and fast** if he runs too much.

---

pantry   A **pantry** is a small room near the kitchen where food and dishes are kept.

---

pants   Charles is putting on a pair of **pants**.
Charles is putting on a pair of **trousers**.

Charlie has some trousers:
    Pants both long and blue;
Charlie likes his trousers,
    Because they're clean and new.

---

papa   Some children call their father **papa**.

---

paper   The pages of this book are made of **paper**. Paper is made from ground wood or rags. We write on paper. We wrap things in paper. We read the news**papers**.

The paper hangers will **paper** the walls of my bedroom.
The paper hangers will **put paper on** the walls of my bedroom.

parachute

A man uses a **parachute** if he wants to jump out of an airplane. When the parachute opens, the man floats slowly and safely down to the ground. The parachute is fastened to the man's body.

parade   In a **parade,** people and animals pass by for everybody to see. Sometimes soldiers march in a parade. Did you ever see a circus parade? In a circus parade, there is a band which plays music. There are also animals, clowns, and many other interesting things.

parakeet

A **parakeet** is a small thin parrot with a long pointed tail.

My parakeet's a tiny bird
From whom real words are sometimes heard;
Yes, I mean we hear him speak
Human words right from his beak.

pardon Mary's father was talking to her mother. Mary wanted to talk. She said, "I beg your **pardon,** Daddy. May I ask you a question?" *I beg your pardon* is a polite way of talking to a person when he is already talking to someone.

I beg your pardon also means *I am sorry I did that* or *I didn't mean to.* John stepped on Alice's foot by accident. He said, "Oh! I beg your pardon." *Pardon me* means the same thing as *I beg your pardon.*

---

parent Your mother is your **parent.** Your father is your parent, too. Joan's parents are very kind.

---

park A **park** is a place outdoors for people to visit and to have fun. In the park there are many trees and much green grass. We have picnics and we play games in the park. In the park we have a good time.

Father will **park** the car in the garage. Father will put the car in the garage and leave it there.

parlor   A **parlor** is a room where guests come when they visit. We sat in the parlor when the company came.

---

parrot    A **parrot** is a bird whose feathers are of bright colors. Some parrots can be taught to say words. I heard a parrot say, "Polly wants a cracker."

---

part   Mother gave me a small **part** of the cake.
Mother gave me a small **piece** of the cake. She kept the rest of the cake for supper.

Howard always does his **part** of the work.
Howard always does his **share** of the work.

In the play, Mary acted the **part** of Snow White. Mary pretended that she was Snow White in the play.

A clock has many **parts**. Stan is trying to put the pieces of the clock back together again.

Part the two boys who are fighting there. Separate them. Push the boys away from each other so that they will not fight.

Richard will **take part** in the baseball game.
Richard will **join** in the baseball game.

---

partly   The house is **partly** finished. There is still work to be done on it. The house is not completed.

party   Jack had a birthday **party**. All Jack's friends came to his party. Everybody had fun. They played games and had ice cream and cake to eat. Jack said, "I like to have **parties**."

---

pass   We saw the parade **pass** the school.
We saw the parade **go on by** the school.

Please **pass** me the bread.
Please **hand** me the bread.

Irene worked hard in school so that she would **pass**.
Irene worked hard in school so that she would **go on to the next grade**.

I **passed** the test. I got a good grade on the test.

The clouds quickly **passed,** and the sun began to shine.
The clouds quickly **moved on,** and the sun began to shine.

---

passenger   A **passenger** is a person traveling in a plane, a train, a bus, a boat, or a car. I took a train to Chicago. I was a passanger in a train that went to Chicago.

---

past   **In the past** we ate dinner at five o'clock, but now we eat dinner at six o'clock.
In time gone by we ate dinner at five o'clock, but now we eat dinner at six o'clock.

Grandfather told us stories of his **past**.
Grandfather told us stories of his **life up to now**.

It is **past** three o'clock.
It is **after** three o'clock.

Ed washed the cars during the **past week**.
Ed washed the cars during the **week that has just gone by**.

paste   We use **paste** to stick things together. In school we use paste to stick pieces of paper together. You can make a kind of paste by mixing flour and water together.

Sally will **paste pictures in a book.**
Sally will **stick pictures in a book with paste.**

---

pasture   A **pasture** is a field where there is much grass. The cows eat the grass in the pasture.

---

pat   I sometimes **pat my dog.**
I sometimes **give my dog a gentle tap with my open hand.**

---

patch   Mother sewed a **patch** on my trousers. The patch covers a hole that I tore in my trousers.

I fell on the ground,
And suddenly found
  The seat of my pants had a tear,
To which Mother did sew
A patch; now I know
  My trousers again I can wear.

---

path   There is a **path** to the house. The path leads to the front door of the house. The cows made a **path** to the barn.

The earth follows the same **path** around the sun each year.

P p

patter   We heard the **patter** of the baby's feet.
We heard the **gentle tapping** of the baby's feet.

Listen to the rain **patter** against the window.
Listen to the rain **tap gently** against the window.

The dog's feet **pattered** across the kitchen floor.

---

paw   A **paw** is the foot of an animal with claws. The kitten hit the ball with her paw. Cats and dogs have four paws. Many other animals have paws.

---

pay   On Friday my father gets his **pay.**
On Friday my father gets his **money for working.**

I will **pay** for the candy.
I will **give money** for the candy.

The teacher told us to **pay** attention to what she is saying.
The teacher told us to **give** attention to what she is saying. She wants us to listen to her with care.

We will **pay** Aunt Gertrude a call. We are going to visit Aunt Gertrude.

Mrs. Smith **paid** me for sweeping her sidewalk.

---

pea  A **pea** is a small and round green seed. It is eaten as a vegetable. Peas grow in pods on vines.

peace   I enjoy the **peace** of the country.

I enjoy the **quiet** of the country. There is less noise in the country than there is in the city.

The United States and Canada are **at peace.**
The United States and Canada are **not at war.**

All good people **want peace.**
All good people **do not like war.**

---

peach   A **peach** is a round fruit. It is yellow and juicy. In the middle of a peach there is a peach stone. The peach stone is a seed. Peaches grow on trees.

---

peanut   A **peanut** is a plant. The seeds of the peanut plant grow under the ground. We eat the seeds of the peanut plant. We call the seeds peanuts.

---

pear   A **pear** is a sweet and juicy fruit. Some pears are yellow. Some pears are green. Some pears are brown. Pears grow on pear trees.

---

peas   Green **peas** are a vegetable. Peas are the seeds of the pea plant.

---

pebble   A **pebble** is a small round stone. Ann picked up pebbles along the seashore.

peck Did you ever see a chicken **peck at its food?**
Did you ever see a chicken **strike at and pick up** its food **with its bill.**

A woodpecker can **peck** a hole in a tree. A woodpecker can make a hole in a tree with its bill.

The hen **pecked** Frank.

---

peel A **peel** is the outside part of a fruit or vegetable. Banana peels are yellow. Orange peels are orange. Potato peels are brown.

Mother will **peel** the apples.
Mother will **take the skin off** the apples.

I **peeled** the rind off my orange.

---

peep Mother took a **peep** at the cake in the oven.
Mother took a **quick look** at the cake in the oven.

The little chick said, "**Peep,** peep."

Let us **peep** through the hole in the fence to see if anybody is coming.
Let us **look through** the hole in the fence to see if anybody is coming.

The boys **peeped** through the hole in the fence to see if the angry dog was there.

---

pen A **pen** is a small yard with a fence around it.
The pigs are in the pen.

Henry writes with a **pen** and ink.
There are different kinds of pens.

pencil   A **pencil** is a long stick of wood that has a long thin piece of lead through the middle. We write with a pencil.

---

penguin   A **penguin** is a bird that can swim, but cannot fly. Penguins live near the South Pole where it is very cold.

> In lands of cold and ice and snow,
> There lives a silly bird, I know,
> Who's dressed in suit of black and white,
> Which he even wears to bed at night.

---

penny   A **penny** is money. It is a coin. A penny is worth one cent. There are a hundred pennies in a dollar.

---

people   There were many **people** in the park.
There were many **persons** in the park.

---

pepper   A **pepper** is a vegetable. Peppers can be green or red.

Some peppers and their seeds are ground up and put into food. Ground pepper helps food to taste better. We keep salt and pepper on our kitchen table.

perch   A **perch** is a kind of fish. Perch live in lakes, rivers, and ponds.

---

perfect   Ted's spelling paper was **perfect.**

Ted's spelling paper **had no mistakes on it.** He spelled every word the correct way.

Would you get me a **perfect apple?**
Would you get me an **apple that has nothing wrong with it?**

---

perfectly   Jane played the piano **perfectly.**
Jane played the piano **without any mistakes.**

---

perhaps   **Perhaps** Uncle John will visit us tonight.
It may be that Uncle John will visit us tonight. It is possible that he will come.

---

period   We put a **period** at the end of the sentence.
We put a **small dot** at the end of the sentence.

The teacher divided the school day into five **periods.**
The teacher divided the school day into five **parts.** During each period we did a different thing.

---

person   A **person** is a human being. I am a person. You are a person. All people are persons.

pet   A **pet** is an animal that you take care of and play with. Harold has three pets. He has a dog, a cat, and a pony. Do you have a pet?

petal

A **petal** is the colored part of a flower. A petal looks something like a leaf. The petals fall off when a flower dies. The petals are falling off of this red rose.

petunia   A **petunia** is a kind of flower. Petunias have many pink, purple, or white blossoms.

pharmacy   A **pharmacy** is a store where medicine and drugs are sold. A pharmacy is also called a drugstore.

phone   Leland will answer the **phone**.
Leland will answer the **telephone.**

photograph   A **photograph** is a picture made by a camera.

piano   Donald plays the **piano.**   He can make music on the piano. To play the piano Donald strikes the keys.   Donald played the piano while the other children sang.

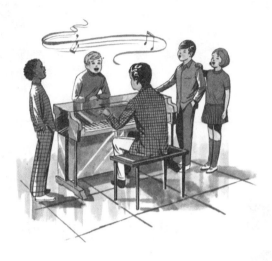

---

pick   The man used a heavy **pick** to dig into the hard earth.

Mother used an ice **pick** to break the ice for the lemonade.

Pick the kind of candy that you like.
Choose the kind of candy that you like.   Pick out any candy.

Jean likes to **pick** flowers in the meadow.
Jean likes to **gather** flowers in the meadow.

Mother **picked up** the spoon that was on the floor.
Mother **bent over and took up in her hand** the spoon that was on the floor.

The man **picked a hole** in the ground.
The man **dug a hole with a pick** in the ground.

The sled **picked up** speed as it slid down the hill.
The sled **gained** speed as it slid down the hill.

pickle   A **pickle** is a cucumber that has been kept in vinegar or salt water. Usually spices are added to the vinegar or salt water. Some pickles are sour. Some pickles are sweet. Here is a jar of sliced pickles.

---

picnic   A **picnic** is an outdoor party with food.

We like to **picnic** in the woods. Last week we picnicked in the park. Mother said, "I like **picnicking** at the beach, too."

---

picture

A **picture** is a painting, a drawing, or photograph of something. Rachel is looking at a picture of a sailboat.

Martha said that she could not **picture** Sam as a clown. She could not imagine what Sam would be like as a clown. Martha could not see in her mind Sam as a clown.

---

pie   Mother can bake a good **pie.** She baked an apple pie, a blueberry pie, and a strawberry pie.

piece   I would like a **piece** of the strawberry pie.
I would like a **part** of the strawberry pie.

May I have a **piece** of your paper.
May I have a **sheet** of your paper.

Jenny gave me a **piece** of her candy bar.
Jenny gave me a **bit** of her candy bar.

Can you **piece** together the broken cup? Can you take the pieces of the broken cup and join them together? If I get some glue, will you try to put the cup together again?

---

pierce   George will **pierce** the paper box with a knife.
George will **put a hole** in the paper box with a knife.

The arrow **pierced** the tree.
The arrow **went into** the tree.

---

pig      A **pig** is a young hog. Pork is meat from pigs.

---

pigeon   A **pigeon** is a large bird of the same kind as a dove.

I had two pigeons bright and gay;
They flew from me the other day.
What was the reason they did go?
I cannot tell, for I do not know.

---

piggy bank   A **piggy bank** is a bank for coins. A piggy bank is shaped like a pig.

pile   A **pile** is many things put into one place.   Here is a pile of sand, a pile of wood, and a pile of books.

Billy will **pile the boxes** in the corner of the room.
Billy will **put the boxes in a pile** in the corner of the room.

Father **piled** the wood in the yard.

---

pill   A **pill** is medicine made into a small ball.   The doctor gave Mother some pills.   A pill is easy to take.

---

pillow   A **pillow** is a bag filled with something soft.   Some pillows are filled with feathers.   Some pillows are filled with cotton.   I sleep with my head on a pillow.

A cushion is sometimes called a **pillow.**

---

pilot   A **pilot** is a person who guides or drives an airplane, a boat, or a spaceship.   Here are pilots of an airplane, of a boat, and of a spaceship.

pin

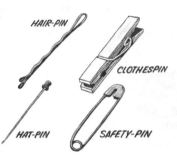

HAIR-PIN · CLOTHESPIN · HAT-PIN · SAFETY-PIN

A **pin** is used to fasten things together. Here are some pins.

---

pine   A **pine** is a kind of tree.   A pine tree stays green all the year round.   The leaves of a pine tree are called needles.   A pine cone is the fruit of a pine tree.

---

pineapple   A **pineapple** is a large and juicy fruit.   The skin of a pineapple is rough.   Its leaves are stiff with sharp points along the edges.   Pineapples grow where the weather is warm all the year round.

---

pink   **Pink** is a color.   These flowers are pink.

Kathleen has a **pink** dress.
Kathleen has a **light red** dress.

---

pint   We can measure liquid by the **pint**.   There are two cups in a pint.   There are two pints in a quart.   I bought a pint of milk at school.

pipe   Father smokes a **pipe.** He puts tobacco in his pipe. Father then lights the tobacco with a match. He sucks the smoke into his mouth and then blows it out again.

A pipe is a metal tube through which the water or gas can flow. Water comes into our house through pipes. The faucet in our kitchen is joined to a water pipe.

---

pitch   The baseball player will **pitch** the ball.
The baseball player will **throw** the ball.

---

pitcher

We pour liquid from a **pitcher.** Mother is pouring water in the glass from a pitcher.

The baseball pitcher will throw the ball.

---

place   The book is in its **place.** The book is where it belongs.

One **place** in the apple was rotten.
One **part** in the apple was rotten.

The people in the airplane took their **places.**
The people in the airplane took their **seats.**

I scratched my arm in two **places.**
I scratched my arm in two **spots.**

Washington is a **place** I would like to visit.
Washington is a **city** I would like to visit.

Santa Claus will **place** the gifts under the Christmas tree.
Santa Claus will **put** the gifts under the Christmas tree.

plain   A **plain** is smooth and flat country.   In the West of the United States, cattle live on the plains.

The teacher spoke in **plain** words.
The teacher spoke in **simple and easy** words.   Her words were easy to understand.   The teacher spoke plainly.

In the dark room, the candle was quite **plain** to everybody.   Everybody in the dark room could easily see the candle.

Eileen's dress is **plain.**   Her dress is not trimmed enough to be pretty.   Eileen's dress is not fancy.

The girl is **plain.**   She is not pretty.

---

plan

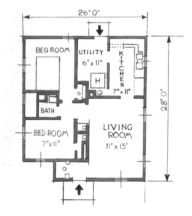

This is a **plan** for a house.   It shows us how the house is to be built.

We made our **plans** for the picnic.   We know where we are going.   We know how many people will be going.   We know what kind of food we will have.

We **plan** to go to the picnic.
We **expect** to go to the picnic.

Mother and Father **planned** the picnic yesterday.
Mother and Father **thought out** the picnic yesterday.

---

plane   The carpenter uses a **plane** to make wood even and smooth.

The carpenter will **plane a board.**
The carpenter will **make a board smooth with a plane.**

An airplane is sometimes called a **plane.**

planet   A **planet** is a large solid body that travels around the sun. The earth is a planet. There are nine planets which travel around the sun. They are Mercury, Venus, Earth, Mars, Jupiter, Saturn, Uranus, Neptune, and Pluto.

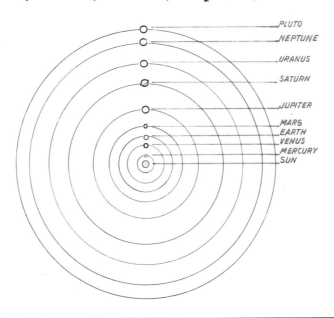

plant   A maple tree is a **plant.** A rosebush is also a plant. Trees, grass, flowers, vegetables, grain, bushes, weeds are all called plants. Animals are not plants.

The farmer will **plant corn seeds.**
The farmer will **put corn seeds into the ground to grow.**

In the spring, Mother **planted** some petunia seeds. When summer came the seeds had become beautiful flowers.

Factories are sometimes called **plants.**

planter   A **planter** is a person or a machine that plants seeds.

plastic   **Plastic** is a material which can be shaped into many things. Judy has a comb which is made from plastic. Jimmy has a plastic pen. Father has a plastic raincoat. Can you name some other things that are made out of plastic?

plate   A **plate** is a dish.   We eat from plates.
Pauline put four plates on the table.

A thin, flat piece of metal is also called
a plate.   Daddy covered the hole in
the wall with a tin plate.

platform   The teacher spoke to us from a **platform**.
The teacher spoke to us from a **raised floor**.   A platform
is like a stage.

play   We went to see the **play** about Cinderella.
We went to see the **show** about Cinderella.   We saw the
story of Cinderella acted out by actors.

Donald is going to **play that he is** a fireman.
Donald is going to **act like** a fireman.

Peter is learning to **play** the piano.
Peter is learning to **make music** on the piano.

Leo likes to **play baseball**.
Leo likes to **take part in the game of baseball and have fun.**

Mary likes to **play**.   She likes to have fun.

player A **player** is a person who plays a game. Ben plays football. He is a football player.

---

playful Simon's dog is **playful.**
Simon's dog is **full of fun.** He likes to have children play with him.

---

playground A **playground** is a piece of ground used for playing. In our town there is a playground at school and in the park. On the playground the children play on the seesaws, on the swings, and on the slide. They like to play in the big box of sand, too. The children have a lot of fun on the playground.

---

playhouse A **playhouse** is a small house for children to play in.

---

playmate Your **playmate** is the boy or girl with whom you play.

---

plaything A **plaything** is something to play with. A toy is a plaything.

pleasant   We went for a **pleasant ride** in the car.
We went for a **ride that pleased us** in the car.

Yesterday was a **pleasant** day.
Yesterday was a **fair and bright** day. The sun was shining, and it wasn't too hot or too cold.

Aunt Ruby is a **pleasant person**.
Aunt Ruby is a **person you like to be with**.

---

please   When we want something, we should say "**please.**" When Mary wanted some milk she said, "Mother may I have some milk, please." It is polite to say please when we ask for something.

I will **please Angela** if I give her some candy.
I will **make Angela happy** if I give her some candy.

Daddy **pleased** me when he took me to the movies. The movie was very **pleasing**. I enjoyed it very much.

---

pleasure   It was a **pleasure** to see Grandfather and Grandmother again.
It was a **joy** to see Grandfather and Grandmother again. We are always happy to see them.

---

plentiful   Peaches are **plentiful** this year. Very many peaches grew this year. The weather was just right for growing peaches. So, now that the peaches are ripe, there is plenty of them.

---

plenty   There is **plenty of meat** on the table.
There is **all the meat that is needed** on the table.

plow   A **plow** is a farm tool that cuts into the earth and turns it over, so that seeds can be planted. A plow has a sharp blade for cutting into the ground. Plows are pulled by horses, oxen, or tractors.

The farmer will **plow** his field.
The farmer will **turn over the earth with a plow** in his field.

Last year the farmer **plowed** with a tractor plow.

The truck is **plowing** the snow from the street.

---

plum      A **plum** is a fruit that grows on a tree. Plums are red, green, purple, or yellow. They are good to eat.

---

plumber   A **plumber** is a person who puts in and fixes pipes in homes and other buildings.

plump The baby is **plump**.
The baby is **a little bit fat.**

---

pocket Danny is putting some marbles into his **pocket**. His pocket is a small bag which is sewed into his clothes. Danny has four pockets in his clothes.

My pocket is a secret place,
  Where there are special things,
Like frogs and stones and marbles bright,
  Some pennies, gum, and strings.

---

pocketbook A **pocketbook** is a purse. Mother carries money in her pocketbook. A lady's handbag is often called a pocketbook.

---

pod A **pod** is a shell in which seeds grow. The seeds of peas and beans grow in pods.

---

poem This is a **poem** by Sarah Josepha Hale.

Mary had a little lamb,
Its fleece was white as snow;
And everywhere that Mary went
The lamb was sure to go.

point   A needle has a sharp **point.**
A needle has a sharp **end.** The needle has a very narrow tip.

One end of a cone is **pointed.**
One end of a cone is **very narrow.** It comes to a point.

When we write one dollar in numbers, we must put a **point** after the one and before the two zeros: $1.00

I asked Sally to **point** to her dog. She is showing me her dog by holding her finger in the direction of her dog.

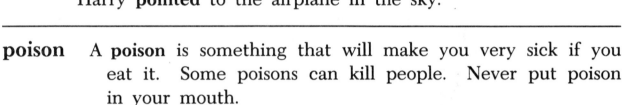

What is the **point** of the story?
What is the **meaning** of the story?

We stopped at different **points** along the road.
We stopped at different **places** along the road.

Harry **pointed** to the airplane in the sky.

---

poison   A **poison** is something that will make you very sick if you eat it. Some poisons can kill people. Never put poison in your mouth.

---

poke   Peter gave Bill a **poke** with his finger.
Peter gave Bill a **push** with his finger.

---

polar bear   A **polar bear** is a large white bear. Polar bears live in the far North where it is very cold.

In the North where it is cold
There lives a beast, so I am told,
Who's very large and has white hair,
An animal called the polar bear.

pole   A **pole** is a long stick. Here are three kinds of poles: a telephone pole, a flag pole, and a fishing pole.

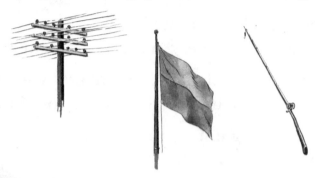

police   The **police** are a group of men who help us. They protect us and keep us safe by making people keep the law. Do you know a policeman?

policeman

A **policeman** helps us. He keeps us safe by making sure that people obey the rules of the country.

polite   Harold is **polite.**
Harold is **kind and thoughtful.** He has good manners. Harold thanks people who do things for him.

pond   A **pond** is a little lake. Children often sail their toy boats on the pond.

pony A **pony** is a small horse. Children like to ride **ponies.**

> I had a little pony
>   His name was Dapple Gray;
> I lent him to a lady
>   To ride a mile away.

---

pool A **pool** is a small body of still water. After it rained, there were small pools of water on the ground.

In summer we often go to the swimming **pool.**

---

poor **Poor** people do not own very much. They have very little money. Poor people often cannot buy enough food to eat.

Kevin did **poor** work in school.
Kevin did **bad** work in school. He did not pay attention to the teacher.

Daddy is sick. I feel sorry for Daddy. **Poor** Daddy is sick.

The people who have few things or nothing are called **the poor.** We should always try to help the poor.

P p

pop   If we put a pin in the balloon, it will **pop.**

If we put a pin in the balloon, it will **burst and make a noise.**

Pop is also a kind of drink.

---

popcorn   **Popcorn** is a kind of corn that bursts open when it is heated.

---

poplar

A **poplar** is a kind of tree. The leaves of a poplar tree are in the shape of a heart.

The leaves of the poplar tree tremble at the smallest breeze. Poplar trees grow very fast.

---

poppy   A **poppy** is a kind of flower. The seeds of poppies are sometimes sprinkled on bread and rolls.

---

popular   Mike is **popular** in school.

Mike is **well known and liked** in school.

---

population   Do you know the **population** of England? Do you know how many people live in the country of England?

The population of my town is 10,000. Ten thousand people live in my town.

porch   We have a **porch** outside our house.   Our porch has a roof on it.   We have to go onto the porch to get to the door of our house.

pork   **Pork** is the meat of a pig.

porridge   We sometimes have hot **porridge** for breakfast.   We sometimes call cooked oatmeal porridge.

> Peas porridge hot,
>   Peas porridge cold,
> Peas porridge in the pot,
>   Nine days old.
>
> Some like it hot,
>   Some like it cold,
> Some like it in the pot,
>   Nine days old.

porter   A **porter** is a man who carries other people's baggage.   The man who helps passengers on a train is also called a porter.

possible   I will go to the movies if it **is possible.**
I will go to the movies if it **can be done.**   I do not know if my mother will let me go.

Father worked as quickly as possible.   He could not work more quickly.

possibly   **Possibly** Jim will want to go to the movies.

            Perhaps Jim will want to go to the movies. Or maybe he will just want to stay home.

---

post   A fence **post** holds up a fence.

        A sign **post** has a sign on it.

        Ralph will **post** the letter.

        Ralph will **mail** the letter.

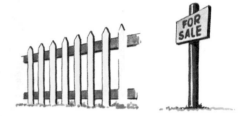

---

postcard   A **postcard** is a small card that may be sent through the mail.

---

poster   A **poster** is a sign. In our school there is a poster which says, "Never cross the street between parked cars."

---

postman   **Postman** is another name for mailman. The postman brings letters, magazines, and bills to our house. He brings us the mail.

---

post office   A **post office** is a place where letters and packages are mailed. Mail goes to our post office before the postman brings it to our house. We buy stamps at the post office, too.

pot Do you have a **pot** in your house? Here are some pots.

Some pots are used for cooking. Some pots are used to hold flowers.

---

potato  A **potato** is a vegetable. Potatoes are white with brown skin. Sweet potatoes are yellow or orange. Potatoes grow in the ground.

---

pound A **pound** is a measure of weight. Bernadette bought a pound of butter and a pound of coffee at the store. A pound of butter is as heavy as a pound of coffee.

Harry will **pound** the nail with a hammer.
Harry will **hit** the nail with a hammer.

Yesterday Father **pounded** a post into the ground with a hammer. Now he is **pounding** another post into the ground.

---

pour Gail helps her mother **pour** fruit juice into the glasses on the dinner table.

My father turned the handle of the faucet of the kitchen sink, and then the water **poured** out.

The water kept **pouring** out of the broken pipe.

powder   **Powder** is like dust. Mother puts face powder on her face before she goes out. She puts powder on her face so that it will not be shiny.

Flour is a fine powder.

Mother will **powder the baby's skin** after the baby's bath. Mother will **sprinkle the baby's skin with powder** after the baby's bath.

---

practice   Tony will **practice his piano lesson.**
Tony will **play his piano lesson over and over.**

---

praise   The teacher will **praise your work** if you try hard.
The teacher will **speak well of your work** if you try hard.

---

pray   Gregory will **pray** before he goes to bed tonight.
Gregory will **speak to God** before he goes to bed tonight. He will say this prayer.

Now I lay me down to sleep,
I pray the Lord my soul to keep.
And if I should die before I wake,
I pray the Lord my soul to take.

---

prayer   A **prayer** is what we say to God when we pray.

---

prepare   Mother will **prepare supper** early today.
Mother will **get supper ready** early today.

Yesterday Susan **prepared** the table for supper.

present   Emma received a birthday **present**.

Emma received a birthday **gift**. Someone gave Emma something nice because it was her birthday.

John is **present** in this room.
John is **here** in this room.

---

president   The **president** of the United States is chosen by the people.

The **leader** of the United States is chosen by the people. George Washington was the first president of the United States.

---

press   A printing machine is called a **press**. City newspapers are printed on big presses. This book was printed on a press.

Rosalie will **press** her dress.
Rosalie will **iron** her dress. She will make her dress smooth with an iron. Rosalie will take the wrinkles out of her dress by **pressing** it.

Hector **pressed** the door shut.
Hector **pushed** the door shut.

---

pretend   Ned likes to **pretend** that he is a policeman.

Ned likes to **make believe** that he is a policeman. Ned acts as if he is a policeman. He plays that he is a policeman. Ned really is not a policeman.

---

pretty   My baby sister is **pretty**.
My baby sister is **very beautiful**.

price A **price** is the amount of money a thing costs. Matthew asked, "How much did your kite cost, Harry?" Harry answered, "The price of my kite was twenty-five cents."

---

prince The son of a king is a **prince**.

---

princess The daughter of a king is a **princess**.

---

print A **print** is a line or mark made by pressing one thing against another. These are footprints, or tracks, in the snow.

Words stamped on paper by a printing press are called **print**. You are reading print in this book.

Printing presses **print** books. They stamp the letters and pictures onto the pages with ink.

Jane Smith's name is printed in this way: J A N E S M I T H

She writes her name in this way: *Jane Smith*

---

prison A **prison** is a place where people are punished. They are punished because they have broken the law.

---

prize Tom won a **prize** for writing the best story. All the children in Tom's class wrote a story. The teacher said that Tom's story was best. It was written very well. It was a very interesting story. The teacher gave Tom a new pen as a prize.

promise   Gerald made a **promise** to Jeffery. Gerald told Jeffery that he would buy him a candy bar.
Gerald always **keeps his promise.**
Gerald always **does what he says he will do.**

I **promise** to buy a bar of candy for you.
I **am making a promise** to buy a bar of candy for you.

Yesterday I **promised** Ma to sweep the floor.

---

promote   If you have good marks in school, the teacher will **promote you.**
If you have good marks in school, the teacher will **put you in a higher grade.** Jerome was promoted from the first grade to the second grade.

---

prompt   Chester is always **prompt.**
Chester is always **on time.** He is never late for school.

---

pronounce   The teacher said to **pronounce each word** slowly and plainly.
The teacher said to **speak the sounds of each word** slowly and plainly.

---

propeller   This airplane has a **propeller** in front. The propeller goes around and around. An engine makes the propeller go very fast. The propeller pushes the air and moves the airplane.

P p

proper   It is **proper** to say "Excuse me" when you leave the dinner table.

It is **right** to say "Excuse me" when you leave the dinner table. It is the correct thing to do.

---

protect   My father will **protect** me.

My father will **take care of** me. He will keep me from danger.

---

proud   Mother was **proud of me** when I sang so well.

Mother was **very pleased with me** when I sang so well. She was glad to say that I am her daughter.

---

proudly   John was so happy that his sister played the piano so well. **Proudly** he said, "That is my sister."

With great pleasure he said, "That is my sister."

---

prune   A **prune** is a plum that has become very dry. Prunes are good to eat.

---

pudding   **Pudding** is a sweet and soft food. We usually eat our pudding last at dinner or supper. Mother makes many kinds of pudding. She makes rice pudding, bread pudding, chocolate pudding, and many other kinds.

---

puddle   A **puddle** is a small pool of water. After the rain there were many puddles on the ground.

puff   Mother is putting powder on her face with a powder **puff.**

A **puff** of white smoke came out of the chimney.
A **little cloud** of white smoke came out of the chimney.

Mark blew out the candles with one **puff.**
Mark blew out the candles with one **quick, hard breath.**

Grandfather will **puff** after he walks up the hill.
Grandfather will **breathe hard and fast** after he walks up the hill.

---

pull   I gave the string a **pull** and the kite came out of the tree. I kept bringing the string in my direction until the kite came out of the tree.

I will **pull** Raymond in a wagon. I will move the wagon toward me. When I walk forward, I will bring the wagon behind me.

---

pump   Irene is working a water pump. A water pump is a machine for bringing water up from the ground.

Irene likes to **pump** water from Grandmother's well. She is pumping water into a bucket. Have you ever **pumped** water from a well?

pumpkin   A **pumpkin** is a large orange fruit.   Pumpkins grow on vines on the ground.

Peter, Peter pumpkin eater,
Had a wife and couldn't keep her:
He put her in a pumpkin shell
And there he kept her very well.

punish   Some parents **punish** their children by spanking them. Other parents punish their children by taking away something the children like.   We are punished when we know something is wrong, and when we do it anyway.

pupil   A **pupil** is a boy or a girl who is in school.

puppet   A **puppet** is a doll moved by strings or by hand.   We watched a puppet show on the tiny puppet stage.   The puppets were moved by strings.   Harold has a puppet which he works by putting his hand in it.

puppy   A **puppy** is a baby dog.   Our dog has three **puppies.**

pure   The water is **pure.**
The water is **clear and clean.**

---

purple   **Purple** is a color. We make purple by mixing red and blue together. These flowers are purple.

---

purr   Did you hear the **purr** of the cat?
Did you hear the **humming sound** of the cat?

A cat will **purr** when it is pleased.
A cat will **make a humming sound** when it is pleased. My cat **purred** when I scratched the back of its neck.

---

purse   A **purse** is a small bag to carry money and other things in. A purse is sometimes called a pocketbook. Here are some purses.

---

push

The men are trying to **push** the car. The men want to move the car away from themselves.

I **pushed** my baby brother in a wagon.

P p

pussy We sometimes call our kitten a **pussy.**

> I love little pussy, her coat is so warm;
> And if I don't hurt her she'll do me no harm.
> I'll sit by the fire and give her some food,
> And pussy will love me because I am good.

pussy willow A **pussy willow** is a plant whose flowers do not have any petals. The flowers of pussy willows are soft like a pussy's fur.

put **Put** the dish on the table.
Lay the dish on the table. Place the dish on the table where the other dishes have been set.

Stephen will **put out** the fire in the fireplace. He will pour water on the fire. The fire will then be dead. There will be no more fire in the fireplace.

Mother **put the cat out** an hour ago.
Mother **made the cat go outside** an hour ago.

Yesterday John **put** the chair back together. The chair was broken in many parts. John glued the parts back together.

I **put on** my new shirt.
I **dressed myself in** my new shirt.

putter A **putter** is a golf club. In the game of golf it is used to hit the golf ball into a hole.

Father likes to **putter** in the garden.
Father likes to **keep busy but not get very much done** in the garden.

puzzle A **puzzle** is a picture cut into many pieces. Sam is trying to put the pieces of the puzzle together. If he fits the pieces together in the right way, he will have a beautiful picture.

A riddle is a **puzzle** with words. This is a riddle.

Question: The more you take from it, the bigger it grows. What is it?

Answer: A hole.

This is the seventeenth letter of the alphabet.

ABCDEFGHIJKLMNOPQRSTUVWXYZ

abcdefghijklmnopqrstuvwxyz

quack A duck says, "**Quack,** quack." Did you hear the duck **quack.** He quacked twice.

---

quail A **quail** is a plump bird. Hunters like to shoot quails. Quails are good to eat.

---

quarrel We should not **quarrel.**
We should not **say angry words to each other.** Billy and Bobby quarreled, but now they are friends. Mother does not like to hear us quarreling.

---

quarry A **quarry** is a large hole in the ground from which stone is taken. Much stone was cut into blocks and taken from the quarry to build our church.

---

quart We can measure liquid by the **quart.** Two pints make a quart. Four quarts make a gallon. Mother bought a quart of milk.

---

quarter When you divide anything into four equal parts, you call each part one **quarter.** This pie is divided into quarters.

A **quarter** is money. It is a coin. A quarter is worth twenty-five cents. Four quarters make a dollar.

Qq

quartet   A **quartet** is a group of four persons or four things.

---

queen   A **queen** is a woman ruler.   The queen is the wife of a king.

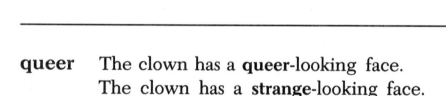

---

queer   The clown has a **queer**-looking face.
The clown has a **strange**-looking face.

We have had **queer** weather this winter.
We have had **odd** weather this winter.   It is usually cold.
But this winter has been warm.

---

question   A **question** is a sentence that asks something.   These are questions: Where are you going?   What is your name?   How is your mother?   Do you know how to swim?

Mother will **question** us about the broken dish.
Mother will **ask** us about the broken dish.   She already questioned Harry.

---

quick   My dog is very **quick.**
My dog is very **fast.**   My dog chased and caught a rabbit.

quickly   Nelson cleaned his room **quickly**.
Nelson cleaned his room **with great speed**. He put his room in order in only ten minutes.

quiet   There is **quiet** in the forest.
There is **little noise** in the forest. Frank likes the peace of the forest. It is not quiet in the city. There is much noise in the city.

quietly   Amy opened the door **quietly**.
Amy opened the door **without making a noise**.

We sat **quietly**.
We sat **without moving**.

quill   A **quill** is a large, stiff feather. A long time ago people used quills for pens.

quit   **Quit** talking in the library.
Stop talking in the library.

Father **quit** working at seven o'clock.
Father **stopped** working at seven o'clock.

quite   The story is not **quite** finished.
The story is not **all** finished.

Mary's cold is **quite** bad.
Mary's cold is **really** bad.

This coat is **not quite** large enough to fit me.
This coat is **almost large** enough to fit me.

This is the eighteenth letter of the alphabet.

A B C D E F G H I J K L M N O P Q **R** S T U V W X Y Z

a b c d e f g h i j k l m n o p q **r** s t u v w x y z

rabbit   A **rabbit** is an animal with long ears and a short tail. It has strong hind legs for jumping. Rabbits run and jump very fast.

race   Nick and Tony ran a **race.** They started running together to see who could run the fastest. They wanted to see who could run to the tree first.

Nick won the race. He ran to the tree first. Nick can run faster than Tony.

NOBUTAKE   HAROLD   PETER

These three boys belong to different **races.** Peter is from England. Harold is from Africa. Nobutake is from Japan.

racoon   A **racoon** is a small furry animal. Racoons live in trees. Racoons move about the forest at night.

Sometimes racoon is written in this way: raccoon.

435

R r

radio We hear people say many interesting things over the **radio**. We also hear music on the radio. The sound comes through the air to our radio without wires.

---

radish  A **radish** is a vegetable. Radishes grow in the ground. The part of the radish that we eat is the root. Some radishes are white. Some radishes are red.

---

rag A **rag** is a small cloth. Mother washed the dishes with a dish rag.

The poor little girl was dressed in **rags**.
The poor little girl was dressed in **old and torn clothes**.

---

ragged After the football game was over, William's clothes were all **ragged**.

After the football game was over, William's clothes were all **torn in pieces**.

rail Fred is sliding down the **rail** along our stairs.

There was a **rail** on the bridge so that no one would fall off into the water.

A train runs on **rails.**

A train runs on **bars of steel laid on the ground.**

The rails for a train are sometimes called tracks.

---

railroad A **railroad** is a road made of rails. The rails are fastened to heavy pieces of wood. Trains travel on railroads.

When we speak of **railroad** we sometimes mean the train tracks, the trains, the railroad stations, and the men who take care of all these things.

---

railway A **railroad** is also called a railway.

rain **Rain** is water which falls from the clouds. Rain comes down in drops. The rain got me all wet.

Do you think **it will rain?**
Do you think **water will fall in drops from the clouds?**

The ground is wet because it **rained.**

Wait inside the house until it stops **raining.**

> Rain, rain go away,
> Come again another day;
> Little Tommy wants to play.

---

rainbow A **rainbow** is a part of a circle which we see in the sky. There are seven colors in a rainbow. A rainbow is caused by the sun's light shining through raindrops.

Martin and his mother are looking at a beautiful rainbow in the sky.

---

raincoat A **raincoat** is a coat which you wear when it rains. Rain will not go through a raincoat. You wear a raincoat to keep your clothes dry.

---

raindrop A **raindrop** is one drop of water falling from the clouds. Milton said, "I think a raindrop fell on my head."

---

rainy Yesterday was a **rainy** day. It rained all day yesterday.

raise   Nora will **raise** her hand if she wants to say something to the teacher.

Nora will **put up** her hand if she wants to say something to the teacher.

Carl will **raise** the rock to see what is under it.

Carl will **pick up** the rock to see what is under it.

My mother **raises** flowers in her garden.

My mother **grows** flowers in her garden.

Grandfather **raises** cows. He takes care of the cows and their calves. He feeds the cows and helps them to grow. Last year Grandfather raised sheep.

---

raisin   A **raisin** is a dried grape. Mother put raisins in the cookies.

---

rake   A **rake** is a tool for working in the garden or in the yard. We gather things together on the ground with a rake.

Rita likes to **rake** the leaves in the yard. She likes to gather together the leaves in the yard with a rake.

---

ran   Betty **ran** all the way home. Betty said, "I had to run from school because it was raining. I did not have a raincoat or an umbrella."

R r

ranch   A **ranch** is a large farm for raising cattle, sheep, or horses. The cowboy lives on a ranch.

---

rang   The doorbell **rang** a minute ago. Did you hear it ring? I do think there is someone waiting at the door.

---

rap   I heard a light **rap** on my window.
I heard a light **hit** on my window.

Rap on the door so that we will not frighten Grandmother.
Hit the door lightly and quickly so that we will not frighten Grandmother. She gets scared if she hears a sudden, loud knock.

Billy already **rapped** on the door.

---

rapid   After the race, Larry felt the **rapid** beating of his heart.
After the race, Larry felt the **quick** beating of his heart. He could hear his heart pounding very fast.

We watched the **rapid** flow of the river.
We watched the **swift** flow of the river.

---

raspberry

A **raspberry** is a fruit that grows on a bush. Raspberries are usually red, but there are also black, purple, or yellow raspberries.

Did you ever eat raspberry jam? Raspberry jam has many little seeds in it.

rat

A **rat** looks like a mouse, but it is much larger. Rats can be brown, black, gray, or white. Rats often carry diseases with them. We don't like rats in our house.

rather   I would **rather** have ice cream than pudding. I like ice cream better than pudding.

rattle   A **rattle** is a baby's toy. A rattle makes noise when the baby shakes it. Baby likes to shake her rattle. She likes to hear the noise. Sue is holding her baby sister's rattle.

raven   A **raven** is a very shiny black bird that looks like a crow. A raven is larger than a crow, though.

raw   We sometimes eat **raw cabbage** in a salad.
We sometimes eat **cabbage that is not cooked** in a salad.

At the zoo we saw the lion eat **raw** meat. The meat was not cooked.

razor   My father shaves his face with a **razor**. He cuts the whiskers off his face with a razor. My Uncle Peter has an electric razor.

reach The red plate is on the top shelf of the cupboard.
Paul will try to **reach the plate.**
Paul will try to **get the plate by stretching.**

Baby **reached** to Mother.
Baby **pushed out her arms** to Mother. Baby stretched out her arms so that Mother would pick her up.

---

read Margaret can **read a book to us.**
Margaret can **look at the words in a book and tell us what they say.**

---

ready When Daddy came home, the dinner was **ready.** The dinner was already cooked. The table was set and the food was on the table. Everything was prepared for dinner.

Are you ready for your ice cream now?
Do you want your ice cream now?

---

real George Washington is a **real** person. He lived in America many years ago. He was the first president of the United States. These things are true. They are facts about George Washington.

Cinderella is not a real person. She is a person in a fairy tale. Cinderella never lived. The story about Cinderella is not true. It is false.

---

really I **really** want to fly in an airplane. I would like very much to fly in a jet airplane. I am not joking with you. It is true.

reason   What **is the reason for your** going to the store?
Why **are you** going to the store?

Jason did not use **reason** when he stole the pen.
Jason did not use **good sense** when he stole the pen. Jason was foolish to do such a bad thing.

You must use your **reason** to add and subtract numbers.
You must use your **mind** to add and subtract numbers. We can add and subtract numbers because we can think.

---

receive   Judy hopes she will **receive** many presents for Christmas.
Judy hopes she will **get** many presents for Christmas. She wants many things for Christmas.

---

recess   At school we have a **recess** in the morning. During the recess, we play in the school yard. Recess is a time when school work stops.

---

red   **Red** is a color. The fire truck is red.

---

refrigerator

A **refrigerator** is a box for keeping food cold. Our refrigerator is run by electricity. Some refrigerators run on gas.

Refrigerators are used to help keep food from spoiling. Mother said, "Put the milk in the refrigerator so that it will not go bad."

refuse   If you ask Albert if he wants some cabbage, he will **refuse.**
If you ask Albert if he wants some cabbage, he will **say no.**

---

reindeer   A **reindeer** is a kind of deer. Reindeer live in the North
where it is very cold. Reindeer pull Santa Claus's sled.

---

remain   **Remain** in the house until it stops raining.
Stay in the house until it stops raining.

There were three pieces of candy in the box. I ate two
pieces of candy.
    Only one piece of candy **remained.**
    Only one piece of candy **was left over.**

---

remember   I **remember** the birthday party I had last year. I can
bring back into my mind the things that happened at
my birthday party a year ago. There were many
children at my party. We had a good time. I like
to think about my birthday party.

remove **Remove** your coat and visit with us awhile.
Take off your coat and visit with us awhile.

Please **remove** the dirty dishes from the table.
Please **take away** the dirty dishes from the table.

Jack **removed the gum from** his mouth.
Jack **took the gum out of** his mouth.

---

rent Daddy pays **rent** each month so that we can live in our apartment.
Daddy pays **money** each month so that we can live in our apartment.

We **rent** our house from Mr. Smith. We pay Mr. Smith money each month, so that we can live in our house. Mr. Smith owns our house.

---

repeat Please **repeat that poem.**
Please **say that poem again.**

Polly can dance well. She danced for Mother.
Mother asked, "Please **repeat that,** Polly."
Mother asked, "Please **do that again,** Polly." Mother wanted Polly to dance another time.

---

reply I will give Jack a **reply** to his question.
I will give Jack an **answer** to his question. Jack will ask me if I am going to the movies. I will reply that I cannot go because I must help Father. I will answer Jack in this way: "I cannot go to the movies, Jack, because I have work to do."

Yesterday when Father asked me to help him, I **replied,** "Yes, Daddy, I will be glad to help you."

R r

report   The children gave a **report** of their trip to the zoo.
The children gave a **story** of their trip to the zoo.

The teacher said, "Please **report to us** what you saw at the zoo."
The teacher said, "Please **tell us** what you saw at the zoo."

---

reside   We **reside** in the city.
We **live** in the city.   We have our home in the city.

---

resident   Who is the **resident of** this house?
Who is the **person who lives in** this house?

---

rest   Gerard ate the **rest** of the meat.   He ate the meat that was left over.   Everybody had some meat, but there was still some meat in the plate.   Gerard ate the rest.

Father worked all day.   Now he must have some **rest**.   Now he must not do any work.

Rest now.   You have worked hard all day.
Do no work now.   You have worked hard all day.   After you have rested, you will feel much better.

---

return   I will **return** to school after I eat lunch.
I will **come back** to school after I eat lunch.

---

rhyme   A **rhyme** is a poem.   This is a rhyme.

> Georgie Porgie pumpkin pie,
> Kissed the girls and made them cry.
> When the girls came out to play,
> Georgie Porgie ran away.

The last words of some of these lines **rhyme.**
The last words of some of these lines **sound alike.**   Do you know which words rhyme?

446

ribbon A **ribbon** is a narrow band of cloth. Nancy has two pink ribbons in her hair.

> I have some ribbons in my hair:
> They make me look so pretty;
> It was my mom who put them there,
> For we're going to the city.

---

rice **Rice** is a plant. It is a kind of grass. The seeds of the rice plant are used for food. We call this food rice. Rice grows where the weather is warm. The people in Japan eat a lot of rice.

---

rich Mr. Clark is **rich.** He has much money. He lives in a big house. He has three big cars. Mr. Clark has many servants and maids. The opposite of *rich* is *poor.* Do you know what *poor* means?

---

rid I will **rid** the house of the old furniture. I will take the old furniture out of the house.

---

ridden The horse was **ridden** by me until it started to get dark. I rode the horse until night came. Did you ever ride a horse?

---

riddle A **riddle** is a puzzle with words.

ride   Yesterday we went for a **ride** in our car.
Yesterday we went for a **trip** in our car.

Edward likes to **ride** a horse.

Helen likes to **ride** a bicycle.

Yesterday we **rode** on a boat, on a train, and in an airplane.

The white horse was **ridden** by my father.   My brother likes **riding** in a bus.

You ride behind and I'll ride before
And trot, trot away to Baltimore.
You shall take bread and I will take honey,
And both of us carry a purse full of money.

---

ridiculous   Billy looks **ridiculous** in Mother's hat.
Billy looks **silly** in Mother's hat.   Billy looks foolish.

---

right   Carl found five dollars in the school.   Carl did the **right** thing. He tried to find out who lost the five dollars.   Carl wanted to know the owner of the five dollars he found.   Carl did what he should have done.   He did the proper thing.

Sandra is holding a flag in her **right** hand.

My watch gives the **right** time.
My watch gives the **correct** time.

Pamela told me that you have a new dress.
  Is that **right?**
  Is that **true?**

I will do that **right now.**
I will do that **immediately.**   **Right away** means the same thing as **right now.**

rind   The skin of an orange is called a **rind.** There is also a rind on melons and grapefruit. What else has a rind?

---

ring      This is a **ring.** It is made of gold. The ring has a red stone in it. I wear it on my finger.

The children held hands and made a **ring.**
The children held hands and made a **circle.**

Patricia hears the **ring** of the doorbell.
   Did you hear the doorbell **ring?**
   Did you hear the doorbell **make a sound?**

When Mother dropped the pan, it **rang** throughout the house.
When Mother dropped the pan, it **made a sound like a bell** throughout the house. Did you hear the pan **ringing?**

The school bell has **rung,** and I must go to my class.

---

ripe   We pick the peaches when they are **ripe.**
We pick the peaches when they are **ready to eat.** We pick them when they are soft, juicy, and sweet.

---

rise   Please **rise** when you speak in class.
Please **stand up** when you speak in class.

We watched the balloon **rise** into the air.
We watched the balloon **go up** into the air.

Did the price of apples **rise?**
Did the price of apples **increase?** Do they cost more?

The pupils **rose** when the teacher came into the room.

river A **river** is a large brook or stream. We traveled up the river in a canoe.

road Cars travel on a **road**. Roads are usually smooth. In the country the roads are sometimes rough.

Do you know the **road** to Grandmother's house?
Do you know the **way** to Grandmother's house?

roar Did you hear the **roar** of that big airplane?
Did you hear the **loud noise** of that big airplane?

The lions at the zoo **roar**.
The lions at the zoo **make a loud deep sound**.

roast A **roast** is a piece of meat which is cooked in the oven.

Mother can **roast beef** very well.
Mother can **cook beef in the oven** very well.

Has the meat been roasted yet?

---

rob The thief tried to **rob me of my money.**
The thief tried to **take my money away from me.**

Yesterday the thieves **robbed** Daddy of his wallet.

---

robber A **robber** is a person who robs or steals.

---

robin A **robin** is a bird. It has a red breast.

The north wind does blow,
And we shall have snow,
And what will poor robin do then, poor thing?
He'll sit in a barn,
And keep himself warm,
And hide his head under his wing, poor thing.

---

rock A **rock** is a large stone. The meadow had many rocks in it.

Mother will **rock** the baby to sleep. Mother will move the baby from side to side until she goes to sleep.

rocket

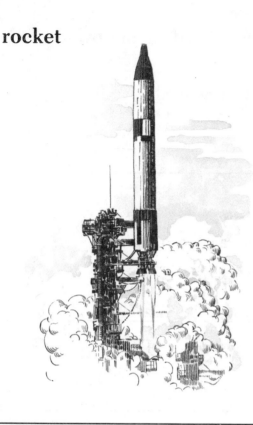

A **rocket** is an engine that puts things high into the sky or far into space.

This rocket will send men to the moon. On the very top of the rocket there is a space capsule.

On the top of this rocket, there is also a machine for landing on the moon.

---

rod   Frank has a fishing **rod**.
Frank has a fishing **pole**.

---

rode   Yesterday I **rode** on a train.   I like to ride on trains.

---

role   Christina plays **the role of a queen**.
Christina plays **that she is a queen**.

In the school play Christina pretends that she is a queen.

roll   Here are two rolls: a roll of paper
       towels and a **roll** of film.

       Can you name some other things
       that come in a roll?

       A very small loaf of bread is called a **roll**. We had hot rolls
       for dinner.

       The children like to **roll the snowball down the hill.**
       The children like to **turn the snowball over and over down
       the hill.**

       Mother **rolled up the carpet.**
       Mother **wrapped the carpet around and around itself.**

---

roller   A **roller** is anything that rolls. Eugene likes to
       skate on roller skates. On each skate there
       are little wheels that go around and around.

       There are rollers on the legs of my bed. I can move my
       bed very easily.

---

roof   A **roof** is the top of a building.
       There is a cat on the **roof** of our house.
       There is a cat on the **top** of our house.

---

room   The **room** my mother cooks in is called the kitchen. The
       inside of our house is divided into rooms. We
       have six rooms. We have a parlor, a dining
       room, a kitchen, and three bedrooms.

       There is no more **room** in the box.
       There is no more **space** in the box. Nothing
       else will fit in the box. The box is full.

rooster   A **rooster** is a father chicken.   A hen is a mother chicken.   A rooster crows early in the morning.   He says, "Cock-a-doodle-doo."

root   A **root** is the part of a plant that grows under the ground. Roots hold a plant in its place.   Roots also feed plants water and give them food from the earth.   We eat some roots. Carrots, beets, and radishes are some roots that we eat.

rope

A **rope** is a strong and heavy cord.   Rope is made by twisting together many smaller cords.   Clarence is tying a knot in a piece of rope.

Children like to jump the **rope.**

rose

A **rose** is a flower.   Roses have a pleasant smell. The stem of a rose has many thorns.

rosebush   Roses grow on a **rosebush.**

---

rotten   The apple is **rotten.**
The apple is **soft and spoiled.**

---

rough   The **road** was rough.   It was made only of dirt.   It had many rocks on it.   There were many holes in the road, too.   The dirt road was not smooth.   There were many bumps in the road.

Mother said, "Billy!   Do not play **rough** with your baby sister.   Be gentle with her."

---

round   A circle is **round.**   A ball is round.
Round also means *around.*

---

row      Teresa put the blocks in a **row.**
Teresa put the blocks in a **line.**

Daddy knows how to **row a boat.**
Daddy knows how to **move a boat with oars.**

rowboat A **rowboat** is a small boat which is moved by oars. Daddy is rowing a rowboat.

---

rub When your hands are cold, **rub** them together and they will become warm. Press your hands together and move them back and forth; then they will get warm.

Mother **rubs** my back when it aches.

Alice **rubbed** the silver dish with a cloth until it shined.

Keep **rubbing** the stove with a rag until it is clean.

---

rubber **Rubber** is made from the sap of the rubber tree. Automobile tires and balloons are made from rubber. Can you name some other things that are made from rubber?

---

rubbers

We wear **rubbers** when it rains. They cover our shoes and keep them dry. Most rubbers are made from rubber. Some rubbers are made from plastic.

---

rude Jeffery is **rude**.
Jeffery is **not polite**. He does not have good manners.

ruffle   A **ruffle** helps to make a dress look fancy.   Mary is wearing a green dress with ruffles.

Carla is wearing a light red dress without ruffles.

rug   We covered the parlor floor with a green **rug.**   A rug is soft.   It is made with many little threads standing up very close together.   Mother cleans the rug with a vacuum cleaner.

ruin   If you step on Baby's rattle, you will **ruin** it.
If you step on Baby's rattle, you will **destroy** it.

Irene **ruined** her new dress by getting paint on it.   She spoiled her pretty dress.

rule   The teacher has made a **rule:**   If you want to speak, you must first raise your hand.   We should obey our teacher.   We should keep her rule.

When we play games we follow the **rules.**   The rules tell us what we may do and what we may not do.

A king can **rule** his country.   He can tell the people of his country what they must do.

ruler   A **ruler** is a stick for measuring how long a thing is.

A king is a **ruler.**   He rules the people of his country.

run When you **run,** both of your feet go off the ground at the same time with each step. Tommy can run fast.

The dog **ran** after Tommy.

The car **runs** quietly.
The car **works** quietly.

The water **runs** from the faucet.
The water **flows** from the faucet.

The refrigerator **runs** by electricity. Electricity makes the refrigerator go. The refrigerator will not work without electricity.

Sarah can **run** the sewing machine. She knows how to make the sewing machine work.

---

rung I think the doorbell has **rung.** Did you hear it ring? It rang about two minutes ago.

---

rush David is in a **rush** to go to school. He doesn't want to be late.
David is in a **hurry** to go to school. He doesn't want to be late.

The fire truck will **rush** to the burning building.
The fire truck will **go fast** to the burning building.

Do not **rush** through your supper. Do not eat your supper so quickly.

---

rye **Rye** is a grain. Rye is made into flour. Rye bread is made from rye flour.

This is the nineteenth letter of the alphabet.

A B C D E F G H I J K L M N O P Q R S T U V W X Y Z

a b c d e f g h i j k l m n o p q r s t u v w x y z

S s

sack   A **sack** is a large bag. Some sacks are made of paper. Other sacks are made of cloth.

The farmer put grain in cloth sacks.

Mrs. Smith carried the food home from the store in a paper sack.

---

sad   Jane is **sad.**
Jane is **not happy.** She has a feeling of sorrow. Jane lost her pet dog. Jane misses her dog.

---

saddle   A **saddle** is a seat for a person riding a horse. Saddles are made of leather. This man is putting a saddle on the horse's back.

Sometimes the seat of a bicycle is called a saddle.

---

sadly   Gerald told his story **sadly.**
Gerald told his story **in a sad way.**

---

safe   A **safe** is a heavy metal box with a door. We lock things in a safe so that nobody will steal them.

Cross the street when the light is green.
    You will **be safe** then.
    You will **not be in danger** then.

safely   The policeman told Uncle Simon to drive **safely**.

The policeman told Uncle Simon to drive **so that nobody would get hurt**.

---

safety   The policeman helps us to cross the street **for our safety**.

The policeman helps us to cross the street **so that we will not be in danger**.

---

said   Martha **said** something to me.

Martha **spoke** something to me.

Yesterday Paul said hello to me. Today I will say hello to Paul.

---

sail   A **sail** is a large piece of heavy cloth on a boat. When the wind blows on the sail, it pushes the boat. Sailboats have sails.

We went for a **sail**.

We went for a **trip in a sailboat**.

We saw the boat **sail** down the river.

We saw the boat **move along** down the river.

---

sailboat   A **sailboat** is a boat which has a sail. The wind blows against the sail and moves the boat. The wind pushes the boat.

Some sailboats have many sails on them.

sailor A **sailor** is a man who sails on a boat or ship.

sake The soldiers fought in the war **for the sake of** our country.
The soldiers fought in the war **to help** our country.

salad Sometimes my mother makes a **salad** for us to eat. A salad is made with raw vegetables or fruits. I like cabbage salad, lettuce and tomato salad, potato salad, and apple and walnut salad. Sometimes my mother mixes eggs, meat, or fish into our vegetable salads.

sale Herbert earned ten dollars **on the sale of** his bicycle.
Herbert earned ten dollars **on selling** his bicycle.

The store had a **sale** of books. The store was selling books at a lower price than usual. The books were cheaper during the sale than they are usually.

salmon A **salmon** is a large fish. It is good to eat. My mother sometimes buys a can of salmon at the store. The color of the salmon in the can is pink.

salt We use **salt** with our food to make it taste better. Sometimes we use salt with food so that it will not spoil. Salt looks like white sand. Sugar and salt look alike, but they do not taste alike. Sugar is sweet. Salt is salty. Salt is found in the earth.

---

salty The food **was salty.**
The food **had the taste of salt.** There was salt in the food.

---

same Carol wore the **same** hat to church that she wore to school. She did not wear a different hat.

Teresa's hat is **the same as** Linda's hat.
Teresa's hat is **just like** Linda's hat.

---

sample A **sample** is a small part that shows what the rest is like. The man in the candy store gave us a sample of chocolate candy. Now we know what his chocolate candy tastes like.

---

sand **Sand** is very tiny bits of stone. We often find sand at the shores of oceans, lakes, and rivers. Children like to play in the sand at the beach. Did you ever build a sand castle?

sandwich My mother made me a ham **sandwich.** She put a slice of ham in between two pieces of bread. Sometimes she puts butter on the bread. My mom makes sandwiches with many kinds of food.

She makes jam sandwiches, fish sandwiches, tomato and lettuce sandwiches, cheese sandwiches, and other kinds of sandwiches.

---

sandy The beach was **sandy.**
The beach was **covered with sand.**

---

sang Mary and William **sang together.**
Mary and William **made music with their voices** together. They like to sing.

---

sank The book **sank** into the ocean.
The book **went down** into the ocean.

Santa Claus **Santa Claus** brings children gifts on Christmas.

Santa Claus flies through the air in a sleigh. Eight reindeer pull his sleigh.

Santa Claus is sometimes called Saint Nicholas.

sap   **Sap** is a juice which flows through trees and other plants. Sap helps trees and plants to live and grow. The sap of some maple trees is made into maple sugar and maple syrup. The sap of the rubber tree is made into rubber.

---

sardine   A **sardine** is a tiny fish. I like to eat sardines.

---

sat   I **sat** in the wooden chair for two hours. I do not like to sit for such a long time.

---

satellite   A **satellite** is a body which travels around another larger body in space. The moon is a satellite. It goes around the earth.

There are also **satellites** made by man. With rockets men send satellites into space.

---

satisfy   A cookie will **satisfy** my baby brother.
A cookie will **please** my baby brother.

Saturday   **Saturday** is the seventh day of the week.

Sunday	Monday	Tuesday	Wednesday	Thursday	Friday	**Saturday**
first	second	third	fourth	fifth	sixth	seventh
1st	2nd	3rd	4th	5th	6th	7th

---

sauce   **Sauce** is a liquid put over food to make it taste better. Father likes tomato sauce on his meat loaf.

saucer   A **saucer** is a small dish used to set a cup in.   The cup and spoon are in a saucer.

---

sauerkraut   **Sauerkraut** is made from cabbage.   Sauerkraut is sour. It is good to eat.

---

sausage   **Sausage** is made from chopped meat and spices. Sausage is put into a very thin tube.

Did you ever have sausage for breakfast?

---

save   Mother said, "**Save** your money."
Mother said, "**Do not spend** your money."

The fireman **saved** the lady from the burning building.   The lady was in danger of being killed by the fire.   The fireman went up the ladder to get the lady so that she would not die.

saw   A **saw** is a tool for cutting wood. The edge of the saw has small sharp teeth.

Watch Father **saw the board.**
Watch Father **cut the board with a saw.**

---

saw   Mary **saw** that movie before. Did you see that movie?

---

sawdust   **Sawdust** is tiny bits of wood made in sawing wood.

---

say   Did James **say something?**
Did James **speak some words?** Was he **saying** something?

What does the letter say to you? What do the words written in the letter tell you?

Mother **says,** "I want you to do your school work before you go out to play."

Yesterday Father **said,** "Smart boys always do their school work."

---

scale   We use a **scale** for weighing things. There are many kinds of scales.

Barbara stood on the scale to be weighed.

467

scamper   Did you see the mice **scamper** when the cat came?
Did you see the mice **run quickly** when the cat came?

---

scarce   Oranges are **scarce** this year. It is not easy to get oranges because the weather has been bad for growing them. There are not many oranges to be sold this year.

---

scarcely   There was **scarcely** any milk in the refrigerator.
There was **hardly** any milk in the refrigerator. There was very little milk left. There was almost no milk in the refrigerator.

---

scare   The noise did not **scare my mother.**
The noise did not **make my mother afraid.** It did not frighten her.

The big dog **scared** Grandmother.
The big dog **frightened** Grandmother.

---

scarecrow   A **scarecrow** is made of sticks. It is dressed to look like a man. A scarecrow is used to scare away crows and other birds.

Farmer Brown put a scarecrow in his garden to scare away the crows. Farmer Brown does not want the crows to eat the corn in his garden.

---

scared   When the big dog growled, I was **scared.**
When the big dog growled, I was **afraid.**

scarf Vincent is wearing a **scarf** around his neck to keep his neck warm.

A **scarf** is also a strip of cloth used as a cover for furniture. Ann put a clean lace scarf on her dresser.

scatter **Scatter** the grass seed on the ground. Spread the grass seed all over the ground.

scene A **scene** is the time and place of a story. The scene of our play is a small house in the country during the summer.

A **scene** is also a part of a play. Our play has three scenes.

You can see a beautiful **scene** from the top of that hill.
You can see a beautiful **view** from the top of that hill.

scent A **scent** is a smell. The scent of frying pork chops made me feel hungry.

school A **school** is a place where teachers teach and where pupils learn. In school we learn to read and write. We also learn how to add and subtract numbers in school.

A school is a schoolhouse.

schoolhouse A **schoolhouse** is a building where teachers teach and pupils learn.

schoolroom   A **schoolroom** is a room in a schoolhouse where children are taught. Our schoolroom has desks and blackboards in it. We learn our lesson in our schoolroom.

scissors   **Scissors** are used to cut things. They have two handles and two sharp blades fastened together. The blades move against each other, and they cut whatever is in between them.

My mother uses tiny scissors to trim her fingernails.

The barber cuts my daddy's hair with scissors.

scold   Mother will **scold** me if I am bad. Mother will say angry words to me if I am bad. Yesterday when I did not do my work, my mother scolded me.

scoop   A **scoop** is like a shovel. The man in the store used a small scoop to put the peanuts into a bag.

At the ice cream store, the man used a scoop to put ice cream into a cone.

I will **scoop some flour from the bag,** and I will put it into this bowl.

I will **take some flour out of the bag with a scoop,** and I will put it into this bowl.

scooter   Alvin likes to ride his **scooter.** His scooter has two wheels. Alvin can make his scooter go very fast.

---

scour   We must **scour the pans.**
We must **rub the pans very hard to clean them.** The pans get very dirty when we cook with them. We must scrub the pans after they are used.

---

scout      Sam is a Boy **Scout.** Eve is a Girl **Scout.** There are Boy Scouts and Girl Scouts all over the world.

---

scrap   I found a **scrap** of paper on the desk.
I found a **small piece** of paper on the desk.

We fed the **scraps of our dinner** to the dog.
We fed the **bits of food of our dinner that were left over** to the dog.

---

scrape   The painter will **scrape** the loose paint off the side of the house.
The painter will **scratch** the loose paint off the side of the house. He will use a metal blade to get the loose, dry paint off the wood.

Mother **scraped** the food from the bottom of the pan.

S s

scratch   Inez has a **scratch** on her knee.
Inez has a **little cut** on her knee.

Don't let the cat **scratch you** with its claws.
Don't let the cat **dig into your flesh** with its claws. He will make little cuts with his claws.

Maurice **scratched** himself on a nail. He cut himself.

Walter **scratched** his mosquito bites with his fingernails.
Walter **rubbed** his mosquito bites with his fingernails. It is not good to scratch mosquito bites.

---

scream   I heard a **scream.**
I heard a **loud cry.** I wonder if someone is hurt or in danger.

People often **scream** when they are afraid or when they are in pain.
People often **make a loud cry** when they are afraid or when they are in pain.

The baby **screamed** when she saw the big black dog.

---

screw   A **screw** is like a nail. You put a nail into wood by hammering it. You put a screw into wood by turning it around and around.

Father will **screw the board onto the wall.**
Father will **fasten the board onto the wall with screws.**

---

scrub   Claudia will **scrub** the kitchen floor.
Claudia will **wash and rub** the kitchen floor.

Mother **scrubbed** the pans last night. Now they are shiny.

472

sea   A **sea** is sometimes called an ocean. It is salt water that covers most of the earth. Fish and other animals live in the sea. Ships sail on the sea.

---

sea gull   A **sea gull** is a large bird that lives near the sea. Sea gulls often follow ships and eat bits of food that are thrown from the ships.

Sea gulls also eat fish.

---

seal   A **seal** is a sea animal that lives near the coast. Seals swim very well. They eat fish.

---

seashore   The **seashore** is the land along the ocean or sea.

---

season   I like the **season** of summer because I can go swimming. The year is divided into four seasons. Spring, summer, autumn, and winter are seasons.

seat   Something to sit on is called a **seat.** Chairs, benches, and stools are seats.

---

second   A **second** is part of a minute. There are sixty seconds in a minute. If you count to sixty slowly, it will take you about one minute, or sixty seconds.

Sunday is the first day of the week. Monday is the **second** day of the week.

Sunday	Monday	Tuesday	Wednesday	Thursday	Friday	Saturday
first	**second**	third	fourth	fifth	sixth	seventh
1st	**2nd**	3rd	4th	5th	6th	7th

---

secret   Something that no one else knows is a **secret.** What I have in this box is a secret.

There is a **secret** safe in my room.
There is a **hidden** safe in my room. Nobody knows about my secret safe.

---

see   We **see** with our eyes. With our eyes we see shapes, shadows, and colors.

Did you **see** that big car that passed by.
Did you **notice with your eyes** that big car that passed by.

See that the window is closed before you go to bed.
Make certain that the window is closed before you go to bed.

We went to **see** Aunt Agatha last week.
We went to **visit** Aunt Agatha last week.

I don't **see** why Mark is so sad.
I don't **know** why Mark is so sad. Do you know the reason why?

We **saw** a movie yesterday.

I have not **seen** Margaret for a long time.

seed

A **seed** is part of a plant from which other plants will grow. An acorn is the seed of an oak tree. An oak tree will grow from an acorn. Here are some seeds.

Pamela planted some flower seeds in her garden. She put some petunia seeds, some marigold seeds, and some zinnia seeds into the ground. She covered the seeds with earth.

---

seem   Does Albert **seem** sick to you?

Does Albert **look** sick to you? He appears sick to me. Albert looks tired. He doesn't seem well.

Does the soup **seem** too salty?
Does the soup **taste** too salty?

This milk **seems** too cold for the baby.
This milk **feels** too cold for the baby.

Donald **seemed** angry when he dropped his ice cream cone.

---

seesaw   A **seesaw** is a game for children. A seesaw is a heavy

board. A child sits on each end of this board. Frank is riding on one end of the seesaw. Ted is riding on the other end of the seesaw. First Ted goes up in the air. Then, Frank goes up in the air.

---

seize   The hungry dog will **seize** the bone.
The hungry dog will **grab** the bone.

---

seldom   We **seldom** see Aunt Priscilla. We do not see her often. Aunt Priscilla lives far away from our house.

select   **Select** the book that you want to read.

Choose the book that you want to read. Pick out the book you like best.

---

self   Leonard had two pieces of candy. He gave me one piece of candy. Leonard ate the other piece of candy him**self**.

Myself is I. **Yourself** is you.

---

selfish   You should not be **selfish**.

You should not be **too interested in yourself**. You should not always put yourself first. You should think of other people.

---

sell   The man will **sell me a kite**.

The man will **give me a kite for some money**. The man is selling kites. He sold many kites already.

---

send   I will **send a box of candy** to my mother.
I will **have someone bring a box of candy** to my mother.

Father will **send me** to the store.
Father will **make me go** to the store.

Yesterday Father **sent** Mother some flowers. Today I am **sending** Mother some candy.

---

sense   The man is blind. He cannot see. He has lost his **sense** of seeing. We have five senses. They are the sense of seeing, the sense of hearing, the sense of smelling, the sense of touching, and the sense of tasting.

Wilbur has good **sense**. He knows the right thing to do.

sensitive   Ann's tooth is **sensitive** to heat.   Hot tea makes it hurt.

---

sent   Last year Father **sent** flowers to Mother on her birthday.
Last year Father **had someone bring flowers** to Mother on her birthday.   This year he will send her some candy.

---

sentence   A **sentence** is a group of words that tells something or asks something.

This sentence tells something: Mother has a new hat.
This sentence asks something: Where did Mother get her new hat?

---

separate   My brother Bill and I have **separate** rooms.
My brother Bill and I have **different** rooms.   Bill has a room of his own in one part of the house.   I also have a room of my own in another part of the house.

Marie will **separate** the blue buttons from the red buttons.   She will put the blue buttons in one group, and she will put the red buttons in another group.

The two houses were **separated by** a fence.
The two houses were **divided by** a fence.

September   September is the ninth month of the year.   September
has thirty days.

> Thirty days has September,
> April, June, and November.

---

serious   Richard's cut was **serious.**

Richard's cut was **dangerous.**   He had to go to the hospital
so that the doctor could take care of his cut.

---

servant   Mary is paid to cook the meals in Mrs. Smith's house.   She is
Mrs. Smith's **servant.**

Ellen is paid to wash and iron Mrs. Smith's clothes.   Ellen
is Mrs. Smith's **servant,** too.

---

serve   The servant will **serve the soup.**
The servant will **put the soup on the table.**

The president of the United States should **serve** the people
of his country.

The president of the United States should **do good for** the
people of his country.

---

set   A **set** is a group of things used together.   Mother has a new set
of dishes.   All the dishes are blue.

We got a new television **set.**

Annette will **set** the basket on the table.
Annette will **put** the basket on the table.

Ruth can **set the table** for dinner.   She puts the dishes, the
knives, the forks, and the spoons on the table.   Ruth knows
how to put everything on the table for dinner.

The sun **sets** in the west.
The sun **goes down** in the west.

settle To **settle** means to *get yourself quiet and comfortable in a place.*

Robert became **settled** in the big chair, and then he watched television.

Robert became **quiet and comfortable** in the big chair, and then he watched television.

---

seven There are **seven** birds sitting on the fence. Can you count them?

one two three four five six **seven** eight
1   2   3   4   5   6   **7**   8

$$10 - 3 = 7$$
$$7 + 3 = 10$$

---

seventeen **Seventeen** is a number which comes after sixteen and before eighteen. Can you count to seventeen?

1 2 3 4 5 6 7 8 9 10 11 12 13 14 15 16 **17** 18 19 20

Ten and seven are **seventeen.**
$$10 + 7 = 17$$

---

seventeenth There are seventeen people standing in line. Barbara is the last person in line. Barbara is the **seventeenth** person standing in line.

---

seventh Saturday is the **seventh** day of the week. Sunday is the first day of the week.

Sunday	Monday	Tuesday	Wednesday	Thursday	Friday	Saturday
first	second	third	fourth	fifth	sixth	**seventh**
1st	2nd	3rd	4th	5th	6th	**7th**

seventy   Seven tens are **seventy.**

$$10 + 10 + 10 + 10 + 10 + 10 + 10 = 70$$
$$10 \quad 20 \quad 30 \quad 40 \quad 50 \quad 60 \quad \mathbf{70}$$

Fifty added to twenty are **seventy.**

$$50 + 20 = 70$$

Can you count to **seventy?**

---

several   There is one bird in the small cage.   There are several birds in the large cage.   Five or six birds would be several birds, but a hundred birds would be many birds.

---

severe   Sally had a **severe** pain in her tooth.   The pain was very great.   Sally's tooth hurt her very much.

Frank was shivering from the **severe** cold.   It was so very cold that Frank shivered.

---

sew   I will **sew** these two pieces of cloth together.   I will fasten them together by putting thread through them with a needle.

Mother **sewed** a patch on my pants.

Anita is **sewing** a dress for her doll.   She is making a blue dress.

---

shabby   The poor boy was wearing **shabby** clothes.
The poor boy was wearing **worn and faded** clothes.   His clothes were old and torn.

shade   We ate a picnic lunch in the **shade** of a tree.   We did not sit in the sunshine.   The children played ball in the field. There was no shade in the field.   There was only sunshine.

A window **shade** keeps light out.   Mother pulled down the window shade, so that the sunlight would not shine into the room.

A lamp **shade** keeps the light out of your eyes.

Father has to **shade** his eyes with his hand.
Father has to **partly cover** his eyes with his hand.   The sun is very bright.

shadow   If you stand in the sunshine, your body will make **a shadow.** Your body will make some shade.

Tim made a **shadow** on the wall by getting in between the lamp and the wall.   Tim saw his shadow on the wall.

shake   Rose will **shake the dirty rag** out of the window.

Rose will **quickly move the dirty rag up and down** out of the window. She already shook a small rug out of the window. She shakes the rag and the rug to get the dust out of them.

Father and Mr. Smith shake hands when they see each other. They hold each other's right hand and move it up and down. This means they are happy to see each other.

---

shall   Tomorrow I **shall** visit Grandmother.
Tomorrow I **am going to** visit Grandmother.

You **shall** not take my bicycle.
You **must** not take my bicycle.

---

shamrock   A **shamrock** is a plant that has three green leaves. A shamrock looks like a clover.

The people of Ireland call the green shamrock their plant. The shamrock is the plant of Ireland.

---

shape

The **shape** of the ball is round. The shape of the box is square.

Raymond will **shape** the clay like a pancake. He will make the clay look like a pancake.

share Bruce and Henry picked a basket of apples.
Each boy took his **share** of apples.
Each boy took his **part** of apples.

Patty and Andrew will **share** the big cookie.
Patty and Andrew will **each have a part of** the big cookie.

Frank **shares** his toys with other children. Frank allows
other children to play with his toys.

---

sharp The butcher cuts meat with a **sharp** knife. His knife cuts
through meat easily. My mother has sharp scissors. They
cut cloth easily.

Pins and needles have **sharp** points.

---

shave Does your father **shave his face?**
Does your father **cut off the hair on
his face with a razor?**

My father shaves every morning. I
sometimes watch my father shave.

---

shawl  Grandmother is wearing a woolen **shawl** on her
shoulders. She sometimes wears the shawl over
her head.

The shawl helps to keep Grandmother warm.

Have you ever seen a shawl before?

she   Nancy is my sister. **She** is a good girl. I like her very much.

---

shears   **Shears** are large scissors. The man used shears to cut the wool off the sheep.

---

shed   A **shed** is a low building. Daddy keeps his garden tools in a shed in our back yard.

---

sheep   A **sheep** is an animal from which we get wool. Sheep are gentle animals. The farmer cuts the wool off the sheep with shears.

Little Bo-Peep has lost her sheep
And can't tell where to find them;
Leave them alone, and they'll come home
And bring their tails behind them.

---

sheet   A **sheet** is a big piece of cloth which covers my bed. I sleep on a sheet. I also cover myself with a sheet. Mother puts clean sheets on my bed every week.

Carl writes on a **sheet** of paper.
Carl writes on a **piece** of paper.

---

shelf   There is a clock on the top **shelf** of the cupboard. There are cups and dishes on the other three shelves of the cupboard.

shell The outside of an egg is a **shell**. The hard outside of a nut is a **shell**. The pod for peas is a **shell**.

A turtle has a **shell**. A clam has a **shell**.

---

she'll **She'll** means *she will.*

---

shelter Umbrellas **shelter** us from the rain.
Umbrellas **protect** us from the rain.

Our house shelters us from the sun, the rain, the snow, and the cold.

---

shepherd A **shepherd** is a man who takes care of sheep.

---

she's Mary is my sister. **She's** here.
She is here.

---

shine Look how the stars **shine**!
Look how the stars **give out light**!

The sun **shines** in the daytime.

William **shined** the light of the flashlight into my face. It **shone** into my eyes so that I could not see.

Richard **shined his shoes**.
Richard **made his shoes bright**.

---

shiny Daddy's gold watch is **shiny**.
Daddy's gold watch is **very bright**. When the light shines on Daddy's watch, it looks very pretty.

ship   A **ship** is a big boat that sails on the seas.

shirt

Fred is wearing a blue **shirt**.   Men and boys wear shirts.

> I have a shirt that's very blue;
>   My dad has one that's yellow.
> A shirt there is for me and you,
>   For almost any fellow.

shiver   I **shiver** when I am cold.
          I **shake** when I am cold.

shoe   Ronald is putting on his **shoe**.   We wear shoes to cover and protect our feet. Most shoes are made from leather.

shoemaker   A man who makes or fixes shoes is a **shoemaker**.

shone The moonlight **shone** on the still lake.
The moonlight **sent out light** on the still lake. We saw it shine. It was a beautiful sight.

---

shoo **Shoo** is a sound made to scare away animals. Farmer Brown says "Shoo!" when he wants to scare the chickens away.

---

shook Ann **shook the rug** to get the dirt out.
Ann **quickly moved the rug up and down** to get the dirt out.

---

shoot In the winter my father will go into the forest to **shoot** a deer with his gun. He likes to go hunting for deer. If he brings a deer home, we will be very happy. Deer meat is good to eat.

Last year Uncle John **shot** a deer.

I like **shooting** arrows into a tree.

---

shop A **shop** is a small store.

A **shop** is also a place where things are made or mended.

Mother likes to **shop**.
Mother likes to **look at and buy things in shops or stores**.

We were **shopping** all afternoon.

---

shore The **shore** is the land along the edge of an ocean, lake, or stream. We like to look for sea shells along the seashore.

S s

short   The blue pencil is **short.**
The red pencil is long.

The blue pencil is **shorter than** the red pencil.
The blue pencil is **not as long as** the red pencil.

Mark is **short,** but his father is tall.

---

shot   The hunter **shot** the rabbit. The hunter killed the rabbit with a gun. We must be careful if we shoot a gun.

---

should   You **should** obey your parents.
You **ought to** obey your parents.

If you **should** go to the store, please buy me some candy.
If you **happen to** go to the store, please buy me some candy.

---

shoulder

The man is carrying a box on his **shoulder.** Father is carrying my baby sister on his shoulder.

A **shoulder** is the part of a human body between the neck and an arm.

Did you ever carry anything on your shoulder?

---

shouldn't   You **shouldn't** walk in the rain without an umbrella.
You **should not** walk in the rain without an umbrella.

shout   We heard the boy's **shout.**
We heard the boy's **loud call.**

When children play outdoors they **shout.**
When children play outdoors they **yell.**

---

shovel   A **shovel** is a tool used to lift or move dirt, coal, snow, or other things. This is a shovel.

In the winter we **shovel snow from the sidewalks.**
In the winter we **lift up the snow from the sidewalks and put it somewhere else.**

---

show   We went to the moving picture **show.** Did you ever go to a puppet **show?**

Victor will **show me** his new bicycle.
Victor will **let me see** his new bicycle.

Mother **showed** me how to sew. She taught me how to sew.

---

shower   Do you think we will have a **shower?**
Do you think we will have a **rain that will not last too long?**

Did you ever wash yourself in a **shower?** Bob likes to take a shower.

I think it will **shower** today.
I think it will **rain for a little while** today.

---

shut   Please **shut** the door.
Please **close** the door. Lock the door after you have closed it.

sick   Diane is **sick**. She is not well. Diane is ill. She has bad health. The doctor will come and see Diane. He will give Diane some medicine to make her well.

---

sickness   **Sickness** is bad health. Joe has a cold. He has a sickness. Joe is in bad health. He is ill. Joe is not well.

---

side   There is a door on each **side** of the automobile. You have one arm and one leg on each **side** of your body.

We are playing a football game. Jerome is captain of one team. Fred is captain of the other team. Do you want to join Jerome's group or Fred's group?

Which **side** do you want to play on?

Which **team** do you want to play on?

The old lady was on one **side** of the street. Vincent helped the old lady to get to the other side of the street.

---

sidewalk   A **sidewalk** is at the side of the street. People walk on the sidewalk. Automobiles, buses, and trucks travel on the street.

sigh Do you **sigh** when you are tired? I heard Mother make a sigh. Mother sighed. She let out a very long and deep breath. Mother said, "I am glad I have finished all my work."

Do you **sigh** when you are tired?
Do you **let out long and deep breaths** when you are tired?

---

sight Harold has good **sight**. He can see well. Grandfather has bad sight. He needs glasses to help him see well.

The rocket kept going higher and higher into the sky until it **was out of sight.**
The rocket kept going higher and higher into the sky until it **could not be seen anymore.**

---

sign A traffic **sign** tells the driver of an automobile what to do. A stop **sign** tells the driver he must stop. Can you find a traffic sign in this picture?

There are many other **signs** in this picture. Can you find them? Do you know what they are telling us?

Father will **sign** the check.
Father will **write his name on** the check.

signal A **signal** is a sign which tells us to do something. A signal sometimes tells us that something will happen. A red traffic light is a signal which tells us not to cross the street.

The bell of a fire alarm is a signal that there is a fire in our building. The ringing bell tells us to leave the building.

silence There was **silence** in the church.
There was **no noise** in the church.

silent The children were **silent** while the teacher read to them. The children did not make any noise. They did not speak.

silently Mother tried to walk **silently** up the stairs.
Mother tried to walk **quietly** up the stairs. She did not want to wake the baby.

silk **Silk** is a cloth which is made from fine and shiny thread. Silk thread is made by a kind of worm. This worm is called a silkworm. Silk is soft and beautiful. Mother has a silk dress.

silkworm A **silkworm** is a caterpillar that makes a cocoon of silk thread. Silk cloth is made from this silk thread.

silly   Uncle Robert looks **silly** with Mother's hat on.   He looks very funny.   Uncle Robert does silly things to make me laugh.   I like Uncle Robert.

silver   **Silver** is a kind of metal.   Silver is white and shiny.   Some knives, forks, and spoons are made out of silver.   Some money is made of silver, too.

since   I have not seen Aunt Ruth **since Christmas.**
I have not see Aunt Ruth **from Christmas time until now.**

Since Louis was such a good boy, his mother let him go to the movies.
Because Louis was such a good boy, his mother let him go to the movies.

sing   Mother likes to **sing.**
Mother likes to **make music with her voice.**

Yesterday the children **sang** a song.   We heard them **singing** a beautiful song.   The song was **sung** very well.

singer   A **singer** is a person who sings.

sink   We have a **sink** in the kitchen. Mother washes dishes in the kitchen sink.

We also have a **sink** in the bathroom. I wash my face and hands in the bathroom sink.

I watched the rock **sink** in the water.
I watched the rock **go down** in the water.

Yesterday a ship **sank** at sea because there was a bad storm.

The canoe had **sunk** because there was a big hole in it.

---

sir   When Kenneth greeted the policeman, he said, "Good morning, **sir**." When a soldier speaks to his captain, he says, "Yes, **sir**" or "No, **sir**."

---

sister   Mary and Rita are **sisters**. They have the same mother and father. Mary says, "Rita is my **sister**." Rita says, "Mary is my **sister**, too."

---

sit   Father likes to **sit** in his big chair. Susan is sitting on a stool. Mother often sits on a wooden chair. The dog is sitting next to mother.

six   There are **six** cows in the field. Can you count them?

one two three four five **six** seven
1   2   3   4   5   **6**   7

---

sixteen   **Sixteen** is a number which comes after fifteen and before seventeen. Can you count to sixteen?

1 2 3 4 5 6 7 8 9 10 11 12 13 14 15 **16** 17 18 19 20

Ten and six are **sixteen.**
$$10 + 6 = 16$$

---

sixteenth   There are sixteen books in a pile. The book at the bottom of the pile is for Paul. The sixteenth book is Paul's.

---

sixth   Friday is the **sixth** day of the week.

Sunday	Monday	Tuesday	Wednesday	Thursday	Friday	Saturday
first	second	third	fourth	fifth	sixth	seventh
1st	2nd	3rd	4th	5th	6th	7th

---

sixty   Six tens are **sixty.**
$$10 + 10 + 10 + 10 + 10 + 10 = 60$$
10   20   30   40   50   **60**

Forty added to twenty are **sixty.**
$$40 + 20 = 60$$

Can you count to sixty?

size   **Size** means *how big or how small.*   The size of baby's shoe is small.   The size of Daddy's shoe is large.

---

skate   Michael is putting on a **skate.**   It is an ice skate.   With his ice skates he will move about on the ice.

In the winter we like to **skate** on the frozen pond.   We are so happy when the pond freezes into ice.

 These are roller skates.   Roller skates are shoes with four wheels on the bottom.   Have you ever skated with roller skates?

---

skater   A **skater** is a person who skates.   Leo is a good ice skater. Carolyn is a good roller skater.

---

skin   Your body is covered with **skin.**   When you take a bath, you wash your skin.   You feel with your skin.

The outside part of a banana is a banana **skin.**   The outside part of an orange is an orange skin.   We must peel the skin from bananas and oranges before we eat these fruits.

skip

Loretta can **skip** rope.
Loretta can **jump** rope.

Deborah **skipped** down the street. She went down the street making little hopping steps.

---

skirt A **skirt** is that part of a girl's dress which hangs from her waist. The skirt of Alice's dress is red.

Girls wear skirts of many a kind;
Just look around and you will find
Some tight, some full, some long, some short:
A skirt for church, or work, or sport.

---

sky In the daytime the sun is in the **sky.** On a clear day, the sky looks blue. Birds fly high in the sky. At nighttime the stars shine in the sky. What else do we see in the sky?

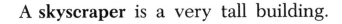

skyscraper

A **skyscraper** is a very tall building.

Guess what I saw when I went to the city.
Skyscrapers tall: some so old; some so pretty.
Oh, they were buildings that were very high,
Looking like needles just piercing the sky!

When we went to New York City, we saw many skyscrapers.

slant   The blue pole stands straight up. The yellow
pole is at a **slant**.

Donald asked, "Does the roof of your house **slant**." Patrick answered, "Yes, the roof of my house slants so that the rain will roll off it. It is a slanted roof."

slap   Mother gave the dog a gentle **slap**.
Mother gave the dog a gentle **hit with her open hand**. The dog was naughty.

When a mosquito bites me, I **slap it**.
When a mosquito bites me, I **hit it with my open hand**.

sled   After it snows, George likes to slide down the hill on his **sled**.

sleep   When I go to bed at night, I **sleep** until morning. My body needs rest at night. We must get enough sleep each night to stay healthy.

Last night I **slept** for eight hours.

Is the baby **sleeping** now?

sleepy   Helen is **sleepy**. She wants to go to sleep. She is tired.

sleet   **Sleet** is rain that freezes into tiny pieces of ice as it falls.

sleeve The **sleeve** of your coat covers your arm. Your coat has two sleeves.

---

sleigh A **sleigh** is a big sled. Sleighs are pulled over the snow by horses.

---

slept I **slept** well last night. How did you sleep?

---

slice A **slice** is a thin, flat piece of something. Mother gave me a slice of bread. I put jam on it.

Father will **slice the roast.**
Father will **cut the roast into slices.**

---

slid Yesterday Carl **slid** down the hill on his sled. I will slide down the hill on my sled today.

---

slide There is a **slide** on the playground in the park. The children like to go down the slide.

The children like to **slide** down the hill on their sleds. They like to move smoothly and easily down the hill on their sleds.

Bob said, "I **slid** down the hill three times already."

slip   Mother wears a **slip** under her dress. My mother's slip is hanging on the clothesline.

Grandmother was afraid she would **slip** on the ice.
Grandmother was afraid she would **slide and fall** on the ice. She does not like ice and snow. Grandmother is afraid that she will slip and hurt herself.

Johnny **slipped** on the ice.

---

slipper

A **slipper** is a light and low shoe. These are my slippers. I wear them when I get up in the morning.

---

slow   Robert is **slow.**
Robert is **not fast.** He will be late for school.

The driver will **slow down his car** when he sees the policeman.
The driver will **make his car go more slowly** when he sees the policeman.

Raymond writes **slowly.** Raymond does not write fast. He needs a lot of time to write a letter.

---

sly   A fox is **sly.**
A fox is **able to do things without letting others see or know.**
The sly fox stole one of the farmer's chickens.

small The mouse is **small.**

The mouse is **little.** The cow is big. The dog is smaller than the cow. The mouse is the smallest of the three animals.

---

smart Gerald is a **smart** person. Gerald has a lot of good sense. He gets good marks in school. The teacher said, "Gerald always gives me the correct answers when I ask him questions. He is a bright boy."

When Alfred cut his finger, it made his finger **smart.**
When Alfred cut his finger, it made his finger **hurt.**

---

smell The **smell** of the cigar filled the room.

Everybody in the room can **smell** the burning cigar. You smell with your nose. A rose smells good. Rotten eggs smell bad. Have you ever smelled a rotten egg?

---

smile  Martin has a **smile** on his face.
Martin has a **happy look** on his face. When we are happy, we smile. Martin is smiling.

---

smog **Smog** is smoke and fog mixed together. It is not healthy to have smog in your town or city. It is dangerous to breathe too much smog.

smoke   **Smoke** is coming out of the chimney.

Mr. Lopez likes to **smoke.** He likes to breathe in and out the smoke from burning tobacco. Mr. Lopez is smoking a cigarette. Some people smoke pipes and cigarettes.

---

smoky   The room is **smoky.**
The room is **full of smoke.**

---

smooth   My desk has a **smooth top.** It has a top without bumps or holes. It is not rough.

The pudding was **smooth.**
The pudding was **without lumps.**

---

snail   A **snail** is a soft, little animal that lives in a shell. Some snails live on land. Other snails live in water. Snails move slowly.

Some snails are good to eat.

---

snake   A **snake** is a long, thin animal without legs. Snakes move by crawling. Some snakes live on the ground. Other snakes live in the water. Some snakes can hurt you if they bite you.

snap A **snap** is a quick, sharp noise. The stick broke with a snap.

Can you snap your fingers?

Do not go near that angry dog, for he will **snap at you.**
Do not go near that angry dog, for he will **bite quickly at you.** He snapped at other children.

---

snatch A thief tried to **snatch** Mother's purse.
A thief tried to **quickly take away** Mother's purse.

---

sneeze When I have a cold, I sometimes **sneeze.**
When I have a cold, I sometimes **push air out through my nose so suddenly and quickly that I make a loud noise.**

---

sniff **Take a sniff of** this pretty rose.
Smell this pretty rose.

When a dog smells something, he will **sniff.**
When a dog smells something, he will **take little short breaths through his nose.**

---

snow **Snow** is frozen rain. A piece of snow is called a snowflake. Snow is white.

I like to watch **it snow.**
I like to watch **the snow fall.**

Because each snowflake is so light,
Falling gently to the ground,
A fluffy blanket, oh, so white,
Covers earth without a sound!

Snow is soft; sleet is hard.

---

snowball I made a **snowball** by pressing snow together in the shape of a ball.

snowflake A **snowflake** is one tiny piece of snow that falls from the sky. Each snowflake is different.

---

snowstorm A **snowstorm** is a storm during which much snow falls. We had such a bad snowstorm that we could not drive the car. The car could not go in the deep snow.

---

snug Gertrude was **snug** in her bed.
Gertrude was **cozy, warm, and comfortable** in her bed.

Billy's new shoes were **snug.**
Billy's new shoes were **not loose.**

---

so Aunt Mary's cookies were not **so** good as Mother's cookies.
Aunt Mary's cookies were not **as** good as Mother's cookies.

Do not talk **so much.**
Do not talk **as much as that.**

It is **so** hot today.
It is **very** hot today.

Mark was singing, and **so was Terence.**
Mark was singing, and **Terence was too.**

What Mother told us is **so.**
What Mother told us is **true.**

Billy wears a hat **so that** his head will be warm.
Billy wears a hat **in order that** his head will be warm. He wears a hat to keep his head from getting cold.

soap   When I take a bath, I use **soap** and water to wash myself. I take a cake of soap into the bathtub with me.

Mother uses **soap** powder to wash dirty dishes and clothes.

---

sob   When Alice lost her dog, she began to **sob**.
When Alice lost her dog, she began to **cry**.

---

sock   A **sock** is a short stocking.

---

soda   Father bought me a strawberry **soda**. Strawberry soda is strawberry syrup mixed into soda water. Soda water has hundreds of tiny bubbles in it. Soda tickles my nose when I drink it.

---

soft   A pillow is **soft**. A rock is hard. A kitten's fur is soft. The floor is hard.

Mother spoke in a **soft** voice because Baby was sleeping.
Mother spoke in a **low** voice because Baby was sleeping. She whispered.

---

soil   Father put some **soil** in the flower pot.
Father put some **earth** in the flower pot.

Mother said, "Do not **soil your clean dress**."
Mother said, "Do not **get your clean dress dirty**."

sold The man **sold me a book.**
The man **gave me a book for money.**

---

soldier

A **soldier** will fight to protect his country. A soldier is part of the army. Soldiers wear uniforms.

While the soldier did fight,
In dangerous war,
His uniform bright,
The enemy tore.

---

sole A **sole** is the bottom of a shoe. The bottom of a person's foot is also called a **sole.**

---

solid A baseball bat is solid. There is wood all the way through it. A pipe is not solid. It has a hole through it. A pipe is hollow.

Our dining room table is **solid.** It is strong. It does not shake.

---

some Pick out **some** book you want to read.
Pick out **a** book you want to read.

Some children came to the park.
A number of children came to the park.

Grandfather gave me **some** apples.
Grandfather gave me **several** apples.

---

somebody I hear **somebody** coming up the stairs.
I hear **some person** coming up the stairs.

someone   Ask **someone** to help you.
Ask **some person** to help you.

---

something   There is **something** in this box.
There is **a thing** in this box.

---

sometime   I will visit you **sometime** soon.
I will visit you **at some time** soon.

---

sometimes   **Sometimes** I play ball with my father.
At times I play ball with my father. Now and then my father plays ball with me.

---

somewhere   Aunt Sarah lives **somewhere** on this street.
Aunt Sarah lives **in some place** on this street.

Are you going **somewhere**?
Are you going **to some place**?

---

son   Mr. and Mrs. Smith have a boy of their own. He is their **son**. His name is Bobby. Mr. Smith is Bobby's father. Mrs. Smith is Bobby's mother.

---

song   A **song** is music with words to be sung. We know a song called "The Star-Spangled Banner." We know how the music of this song goes. We also know the words of this song. The teacher said, "We will now sing the song called 'The Star-Spangled Banner.'"

soon   Dinner will be ready **soon.**
Dinner will be ready **at a time not far away.**

As soon as you hear the bell, answer the telephone.
When you hear the bell, answer the telephone.

---

sore   A **sore** is a spot on your body which hurts. Carl burned his hand. It made a sore on Carl's hand. Mary fell on the sidewalk. She scraped her knee. It made a sore on Mary's knee.

Father hit his finger with a hammer.
Now his finger **is sore.**
Now his finger **gives him pain.**

---

sorrow   There is much **sorrow** in Helen's life. She is sad because many bad things happened to her: Her house burned down. She broke her leg. Her pet dog died.

---

sorry   Mother was **sorry** that Grandmother was sick.
Mother was **sad** that Grandmother was sick.

Jack is **sorry** he did wrong. He wishes he had been good.

---

sort   What **sort** of ice cream do you like?
What **kind** of ice cream do you like? I like chocolate ice cream.

Annette wants to **sort** the buttons. Annette will separate the red buttons from the green buttons. She will put the red buttons in one pile. She will put the green buttons in another pile.

soul   Not a **soul** heard the doorbell.
Not a **person** heard the doorbell.

My **soul** is that part of me which thinks, feels, and makes my body do things. My soul cannot be seen.

---

sound   The big bell made a loud **sound.**
The big bell made a loud **noise.** My watch makes a little sound. We hear sounds with our ears.

Pamela has a **sound** body and mind.
Pamela has a **healthy** body and mind.

Does Nancy **sound** sick to you?
Does Nancy **seem** sick to you?

---

soup   **Soup** is a liquid food. Soup is made by boiling meat and vegetables in water. Mother sometimes makes soup with milk. Walter likes three kinds of soup: chicken soup, vegetable soup, and cream of tomato soup.

---

sour   Sugar is sweet. A lemon is **sour.**

The milk will **sour** if you don't put it in the refrigerator.
The milk will **spoil** if you don't put it in the refrigerator.

---

south   **South** is a direction. If you look in the direction of the sun as it comes up each morning in the east, your right shoulder will be pointing south. On a map south is at the bottom.

Paul lives in the United States of America. He lives in the South. He lives in the state of Florida where it is warm.

South America

This is a map of **South America.** Some of the countries in South America are Argentina, Bolivia, Brazil, British Guiana, Chile, Colombia, Ecuador, Paraguay, Peru, Uruguay, and Venezuela.

---

sow   In the spring the farmer will **sow the wheat.**
In the spring the farmer will **plant by scattering wheat seeds.**

---

space   The earth moves through **space.** The sun, the moon, and the planets are in space. There is no air in space. Astronauts must bring air with them in space, so that they can breathe. Space has no end. There is always room for something else in space.

There is no more **space** on the shelf.
There is no more **room** on the shelf.
There are so many books on the shelf that we cannot put another one there.

---

spaceship   Astronauts travel through space in a **spaceship.**

This spaceship was put into space by means of a rocket. The spaceship was placed on the top of a rocket. When the rocket got far enough away from earth, the spaceship left the rocket.

When the spaceship could not be pulled back to earth, the spaceship travelled either around the earth or away from the earth.

spade   A **spade** is a kind of shovel.

---

spank   Father will **spank me** if I am naughty.

Father will **hit me with an open hand on my back side** if I am naughty.

---

spare   I have **a spare** pair of shoes.

I have **an extra** pair of shoes. I have one more pair of shoes than I need.

---

spark   A **spark** is a little piece or bit of fire. We saw the sparks shoot out from the burning house.

---

sparkle   The **sparkle** of Mother's diamond ring was beautiful. When the light shined on the diamond, it seemed to throw light in many directions. Her ring was so very shiny.

Did you see Mother's diamond ring **sparkle** when the sunlight shined on it?

Did you see Mother's diamond ring **throw light in many directions** when the sunlight shined on it?

---

sparrow   A **sparrow** is a small brown bird.

    Who killed Cock Robin?
      I, said the Sparrow,
      With my bow and arrow,
    I killed Cock Robin.

    Who saw him die?
      I, said the fly,
      With my little eye,
    I saw him die.

speak   My dog cannot **speak**.
My dog cannot **say words**.

Charles **spoke of** his trip to Mexico.
Charles **talked about** his trip to Mexico. He told us many
interesting things.

Mother has **spoken** to me about the picnic.

---

special   Grandmother bought presents for Peter, Terence, and
Virginia. Grandmother bought a **special**
present for Virginia. She gives Virginia
something big, because it is Virginia's
birthday. Grandmother bought Peter a
book. She bought Terence a top.

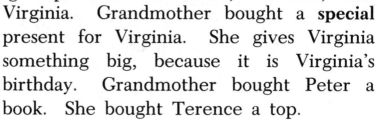

Grandmother bought Virginia a beautiful
bicycle. It is a **special** day for Virginia.
It is her birthday.

---

speck   A **speck** is a small spot or bit of something.

I washed the table because it was covered with **specks**.

---

speckle   A **speckle** is a small spot.

This is a **speckled** egg. It has little
spots all over it.

---

speed   At what **speed** is the car going?
How fast is the car going?

It is not safe to **speed** in a car.
It is not safe to **go too fast** in a car.

spell   I can **spell** words. *C* and *A* and *T* spell *cat*. I can put the letters in the right order so that they spell cat.

---

spend   I will **spend** five cents for a pencil.
I will **pay** five cents for a pencil.

George **spent** all his money.
George **used up** all his money. Now he has no money.

I will not **spend** any more time waiting for Donald.
I will not **use up** any more time waiting for Donald. If I do not leave for school now, I will be late.

---

sphere   A **sphere** is a ball. Every part of the outside of a sphere is the same distance from the center.

---

spice   Pepper is a **spice.** Spices are used to help make food taste better. Spices are made from dried leaves, seeds, or the bark of certain trees.

Mother put spices in the tomato sauce.

---

spider   A **spider** is a small animal with eight long legs. A spider is not an insect. An insect has only six legs. A spider can spin a web.

---

spike   A **spike** is a long, strong, thick nail.

The farmer hammered the spike into the post.

spill   Don't **spill the water** on the floor.
Don't **let the water fall out** on the floor.

Yesterday Baby **spilled** her milk on the table.

Spilt means the same thing as **spilled**.

---

spin   Did you ever see anybody **spin thread from** wool?
Did you ever see anybody **make thread by pulling out and twisting pieces of wool?**

Today there are machines for **spinning** thread.

A spider can **spin** its own thread. A spider makes a web with its thread.

Dick made the top **spin.**
Dick made the top **go around and around.**

Yesterday Peter **spun the top.**
Yesterday Peter **made the top go around and around.**

---

spinach   **Spinach** is a vegetable with green leaves. Mother often cooks spinach for us. Spinach is good to eat.

---

splash   Children like to **splash water** when they go swimming.
Children like to **throw water all about** when they go swimming.

---

splatter   Do not **splatter** water on the floor. Please do not splash the water in the sink too much, because you are scattering it on the floor.

splendid   Walter did a **splendid** job in painting the picture.
Walter did a **very good** job in painting the picture. He is a fine artist. Walter paints well.

split   There is a **split** in the tree where it was hit by lightning.
There is a **big crack** in the tree where it was hit by lightning.

Did you ever see Father **split** logs for the fireplace? He breaks them apart with an ax. Father split several logs so that we would have wood for the fireplace.

spoil   If you get paint on your new dress, you will **spoil** it. It will not look pretty. You will ruin your pretty dress.

If you bake the cake too long, it will **spoil**. The cake will burn and nobody will want to eat it.

When meat, fruit, and vegetables become old, they **spoil**. They become rotten, and we cannot eat them. Mother said, "Put the lettuce in the refrigerator, or it will spoil quickly."

We could not eat the meat because it was **spoiled**. It was not good to eat.

Harold is a **spoiled** child.
Harold is a **naughty** child because he has been allowed to do everything he wants to.

spoke   Paul **spoke** to his friend John yesterday.
Paul **talked** to his friend John yesterday.

Paul likes to **speak** to his friend John.

Has Paul **spoken** to John about the party?

spoken   Donald has **spoken** to me about helping him.
Donald has **talked** to me about helping him.

---

spool   A **spool** is a short, round piece of wood with a hole through it. Some spools are made of metal. Thread, cord, and wire are often wound around spools.

---

spoon   I eat with a **spoon**. Liquids and soft foods are eaten with a spoon. I eat ice cream and pudding with a spoon. We stir things with spoons, too. There are many kinds of spoons.

---

sport   Fishing is a **sport**. It is fun to go fishing. Baseball, basketball, and football are sports, too. It is fun to play these games.

---

spot   Ben got a **spot** on his new white shirt. It is dirt.

Nancy got a **spot of** ink on her new dress.
Nancy got a **mark made from** ink on her new dress.

We found a good **spot** to have our picnic.
We found a good **place** to have our picnic.

I call my dog Spot because he has **spots** all over him.

sprang   The cat **sprang** at the mouse.

The cat **jumped** at the mouse. Did you see the cat spring at the mouse?

---

spray   A **spray** is fine drops of water. The wind blew the spray from the water hose into our faces.

Mother will **spray** her flowers.
Mother will **sprinkle** her flowers. She will water them.

---

spread   Joan put the **spread** on the bed.
Joan put the **cover** on the bed. A spread for a bed is also called a bedspread.

Rachel likes to **spread jam on toast.**
Rachel likes to **cover the toast with jam.**

Did you see the bird **spread** its wings and fly away?
Did you see the bird **stretch out** its wings and fly away?

Father **spread the blanket out** on the ground.
Father **opened the blanket out flat** on the ground. Here is where we ate our picnic lunch on the ground.

spring   **Spring** is one of the four seasons of the year. The other three seasons are summer, autumn, and winter. The farmer plants his seeds in the spring.

Springs help to make my bed soft.

There is a spring in my watch.

Did you see the cat **spring** at the mouse?
Did you see the cat **jump at** the mouse? He **sprang** up very quickly.

---

sprinkle   We had a **sprinkle** this morning.
We had a **light rain** this morning.

Mother will **sprinkle** the clothes before she irons them.
Mother will **put drops of water on** the clothes before she irons them.

Frank **sprinkled** the garden with the water hose.
Frank **put drops of water all over** the garden with the water hose.

---

sprung   Martha saw the squirrel which had **sprung** from the hole in the tree. David didn't see the squirrel spring from the tree. He didn't see it jump out of the hole.

---

spun   Yesterday Clement **spun** the top. I want to spin the top today. I want to make it go around and around.

square   This is a **square.** A square has four sides. All four sides of a square are of the same length. All four corners of a square are the same.

---

squash  A **squash** is a vegetable that grows on a vine. Squash can be yellow, green, or white. Mother sometimes cooks squash for us.

You will **squash the tomato** if you step on it.
You will **make the tomato flat** if you step on it.

---

squeak   The barn door makes a **squeak** when you open it. The door makes a short sharp and high sound. The farmer will put some oil on the part of the door that squeaks. Then the door will not squeak anymore.

Did you hear the mouse **squeak?**
Did you hear the mouse **make a short sharp and high sound?**

---

squeal   The little pig will **squeal** when it is hurt.
The little pig will **make a long sharp and high sound** when it is hurt. Did you ever hear the **squeal** of a pig?

---

squeeze   We **squeeze oranges** to get juice out of them.
We **press hard on the oranges** to get juice out of them.

Mother **squeezed** the wet shirt until she got much of the water out of it. She pressed hard and twisted the shirt to get rid of a lot of the water.

Grandmother **squeezed** me. She gave me a hug.

squirrel A **squirrel** is a small animal with a long, furry tail. Squirrels live in trees. They like to eat nuts. Squirrels can be gray, black, or red.

squirt Did you see the water **squirt** out of the hole in the pipe?

Did you see the water **quickly come** out of the hole in the pipe?

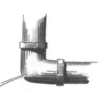

stable A **stable** is a building where horses or cattle are kept. A stable is like a barn.

stack A chimney of a large building is called a **stack**. The factory has smokestacks.

A **stack** is a large pile. There is a big stack of hay on Grandfather's farm. The children like to play in the haystack.

Please **stack the books** on the table.
Please **put the books in a pile** on the table.

staff   A **staff** is a thin pole.   Grandfather carried a staff to help him walk.

There is a **staff** of teachers working in the school.
There is a **group** of teachers working in the school.

---

stage   A **stage** is a floor which is made higher than the rest of the floor in a room.   Because a stage is made higher than the floor, everybody in the room can see what is happening on it.   We saw a play on the stage.

---

stair   A **stair** is a step in a group of steps.   All the steps are called stairs.   I have to walk up the stairs to get to my room. My room is upstairs.

---

stale   The cake is **stale**.   It is old and dry.   Billy said, "The cake was good when it was fresh, but now that it is stale, it tastes bad.

---

stalk   A **stalk** is the stem of a plant.

stall   A **stall** is a space in a barn for one horse or one cow.   Three animals are in stalls.

When the weather is cold, the motor of our car will **stall.**
When the weather is cold, the motor of our car will **stop when we don't want it to.**

---

stallion   A **stallion** is a he-horse.   My grandfather has a beautiful stallion on his ranch.   Sometimes he lets me ride on his stallion.

---

stamp   A **stamp** is a small printed piece of paper which we buy from the post office.   We glue stamps to packages and letters, so that we can mail them.   This is how we pay to send our packages and letters.   This letter has two stamps on it.

Don't **stamp your feet** on the floor.
Don't **put your feet down hard** on the floor.

---

stand   The children will **stand** when the teacher comes into the room.

The children will **get up on their feet** when the teacher comes into the room.   They will sit when the teacher says, "Please sit down."

The children **stood** until the teacher told them to sit down.

There is someone **standing** at our front door.

Mother let the pie **stand** in the kitchen until it became cool.
Mother let the pie **stay** in the kitchen until it became cool.

star The North Star is a very bright **star**. On a clear night, we can see many stars shining in the sky. Stars are really suns. They look tiny because they are so very far away.

Our sun is also a star. It looks big because it is much closer than the other stars.

The stars we draw on paper are different from the stars found in the sky. On the right side of this page are two kinds of stars we can draw.

---

starch Mother puts **starch** in Father's shirts when she washes them. Starch makes clothes stiff.

---

stare It is not polite to **stare at somebody.**
It is not polite to **look at somebody for a long time with your eyes wide open.**

---

start I **start for** school at eight o'clock.
I **begin to go to** school at eight o'clock.

Father will **start the car.**
Father will **get the car going.** He will make the car begin to move.

We **started** our walk from the school. We will end our walk at the park.
We **began** our walk from the school. We will end our walk at the park.

---

startle Don't **startle** Baby with a sudden, loud noise.
Don't **frighten** Baby with a sudden, loud noise.

starve   If you do not eat, you will **starve.**

If you do not eat, you will **die from not having food.** In some poor countries people die by starving. In these poor countries some people cannot get food.

When Henry is hungry, he sometimes says, "I am **starved!** When are we going to eat?" Henry does not mean he is dying. He only means that he is hungry.

---

state   Uncle Robert lives in the **state** of Maine. I live in the state of California. The United States is a country with fifty states.

Countries are also called **states.** England, Canada, Peru and Mexico are states.

---

station   A **station** is a place where trains or buses stop. A railroad station is a building where people wait for trains.

A bus station is a place where people wait for buses.

A gasoline station is a place where people buy gasoline for their cars.

The sounds we hear on the radio are broadcast from a radio **station.** The pictures and sounds we see and hear on the television are broadcast from a television **station.**

statue   A **statue** is the shape of a man or an animal made from stone, clay, metal, wood, or from some other material. We saw a beautiful marble statue.

stay   Paul can **stay** at the park for an hour.
Paul can **be** at the park for an hour. He can remain and play in the park for an hour.

Mildred **stayed up** until eleven o'clock.
Mildred **did not go to bed** until eleven o'clock.

steal   To **steal** means to *take something that does not belong to you.* The thieves tried to steal money from the bank.

Yesterday somebody **stole** Mother's diamond ring.

steam   **Steam** comes from boiling water. Steam is a gas which we cannot see.

When we boil water there is a white cloud which rises from the hot water. Some people call this white cloud steam.

steamship   A **steamship** is a ship which runs by steam.

steel   Steel is iron which has been made much harder and stronger. Cars are made from steel.

---

steep   We walked up the **steep** hill.

We walked up the **very slanted** hill.   The hill was almost straight up and down.

---

steer   A young ox is called a **steer.**

When I ride my bicycle I **steer carefully.**

When I ride my bicycle I **carefully make the bicycle go where I want.**   I steer with the handlebars of my bicycle.

Daddy **steers** the car with the steering wheel.

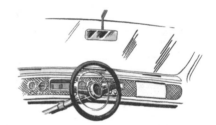

---

steering wheel   A **steering wheel** is a wheel for steering an automobile.   Ships have steering wheels, too.

---

stem   The flower and leaves are joined to the **stem** of this plant.   A stem is also called a stalk.

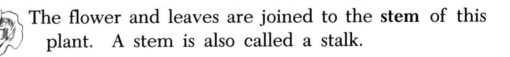

There is a little brown stem on this apple.   Can you see it?

step   When I put one foot in front of me, I take a **step.**   When I
          walk, I take one step after another.

          Step this way.
          Walk this way.

          Walter is walking up the **steps.**
          Walter is walking up the **stairs.**

          Father climbed up the steps of the ladder.

---

stepladder      A **stepladder** is a ladder with two parts
                 joined together.   A stepladder can stand
                 up by itself.

   My kitty, so frightened was she
   To be caught up so high in a tree;
     So I got a stepladder,
       And with it got at her,
   To bring her down safely with me.

---

stick   A **stick** is a long, thin piece of wood.

           Did you ever have a **stick** of candy?   It is a long, thin piece
           of candy.

           Do not **stick** the pen into your finger.
           Do not **put the sharp point of** the pen into your finger.

           Philip **stuck** a knife into the tree.   Did you see him do it?

           Stick these two pieces of paper together.   Fasten these two
           pieces of paper together with glue or paste.

---

sticky   The wet paint is **sticky.**
            The wet paint **makes things stick to it.**

stiff   My new shoes are **stiff.**   They do not bend easily.

---

still   Be **still.**   Do not make a sound.
Be **quiet.**   Do not make a sound.

The dog lay **still** for an hour.
The dog lay **without moving** for an hour.

Mother scrubbed the pot twice, and **still** it is not clean.
Mother scrubbed the pot twice, and **even now** it is not clean.

---

sting   A **sting** is the bite of an insect.   Did a bee ever **sting** you?
It feels as if you are being stuck with a pin.   Yesterday a
bee **stung** Rita on the hand.

How Luke's sore did hurt when he got salt in it!   Salt **stings**
if you get it into a sore or cut.

---

stir   Please **stir the soup** in the pan with a spoon.
Please **move the soup around and around** in the pan with a
spoon.

---

stitch   Mother makes a **stitch** with a needle and thread to sew cloth.

The needle goes through the cloth and pulls the
thread with it.   The thread holds the cloth
together in stitches.   The needle must go
through the cloth many times.

A sewing machine makes **stitches** in cloth.

Mother will **stitch** the sleeve on my shirt.
Mother will **sew** the sleeve on my shirt.

stocking   A **stocking** is a covering for the foot and the lower part of the leg. Two stockings of the same kind are called a pair of stockings.

> Deedle, deedle dumpling, my son John,
> He went to bed with his stockings on;
> One shoe off and one shoe on,
> Deedle, deedle dumpling, my son John.

---

stole   The thief was put into jail because he **stole.**
The thief was put into jail because he **took things that did not belong to him.**

It is wrong to steal.

---

stolen   Mother's fur coat was **stolen.** Nobody saw the thief steal her new fur coat.

---

stomach   When you swallow food, it goes down your throat into your **stomach.** Your stomach prepares the food so that it can feed all the parts of your body. Your stomach helps to keep you healthy.

---

stone   A **stone** is a piece of rock. I can throw this stone far because it is small. I can't throw that rock because it is too big.

My mother has a ring with a **stone** in it. The stone is a diamond.

The large seeds of some fruits are called **stones.** Mother took the stones out of the peaches before putting the peaches into jars. Peach stones are hard.

stood   I **stood** at the door for ten minutes, and no one answered the doorbell.

I **was standing** at the door for ten minutes, and no one answered the doorbell. I waited on my feet for ten minutes.

---

stool   A **stool** is a seat without a back to lean on.

---

stoop   Dad said, "Don't **stoop.** Don't stand with your head and shoulders bent forward. Stand up straight.

---

stop   The policeman said, "Stop!"
The policeman said, "**Do not go any farther!**"

Please **stop making** noise.
Please **do not make any more** noise.

Benjamin will **stop** up the hole in the wall with a piece of wood.

Benjamin will **close** up the hole in the wall with a piece of wood.

A big tree had fallen across the railroad tracks.
  The tree had **stopped** the train.
  The tree had **blocked** the train.

The cars are **stopping** because the traffic light is red.

---

store   A **store** is a place where things are sold.

We **store** potatoes in our basement for the winter. We keep potatoes in our basement, and we will use them in the winter.

stork  A **stork** is a large bird with long legs, a long neck, and a long bill. Storks can walk in deep water.

storm We had a bad **storm** yesterday. The wind blew very hard, and the rain poured down. There was also a lot of thunder and lightning.

In the winter we sometimes have a snow**storm.** The snow comes down thick and fast.

story I like Daddy to tell me a **story** about himself when he was a little boy. He tells me what he did when he was a little boy.

Mother sometimes tells me fairy **stories.** They are not true stories like Daddy's stories, but they are very interesting. Mother told me the story of Cinderella. Fairy stories are also called fairy tales.

storybook A **storybook** is a book with many stories in it.

stout The man was **stout,** but his wife was thin.
The man was **fat,** but his wife was thin.

S s

stove Mother cooks on the kitchen **stove.** Electricity makes the heat for her stove. Some kitchen stoves work with gas.

In some houses there is a stove to keep the rooms warm. In some stoves wood or coal is burned.

---

straight Ann draws a **straight** line. Al draws a curved line.

Walk straight ahead.
Walk in a straight line without turning.

---

strange We moved to a **strange** city. We were never there before.

Many things were **strange** to us.
Many things were **new** to us. We had to learn many things about the city so that it wouldn't be so strange to us.

A dragon is a **strange**-looking animal.
A dragon is a **queer**-looking animal. It is not real.

strap   A **strap** is a narrow piece of leather or of some other material that can be bent easily.

Father has **straps** around his suitcase.   There is a **strap** on the shoe.

Alfred will **strap a pack to his back** when he goes camping. Alfred will **fasten a pack to his back with straps** when he goes camping.

---

straw   A **straw** is a dry stem of wheat, rye, oats, or other grain. The farmer has a piece of straw in his mouth.

Sally is drinking through a **straw.** Drinking straws are made from paper or plastic.

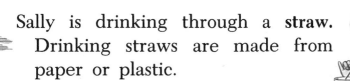

---

strawberry

A **strawberry** is a red berry that grows on a vine close to the ground.   Do you like strawberries?

---

stream   A **stream** is a small river.   Father went fishing in the stream.   The water in a stream flows toward a river, a lake, or a sea.

street A **street** is a road in a city or a town. On the street there were many automobiles, bicycles, and people.

---

streetcar A **streetcar** is like the car of a train. Many people can ride in a streetcar at one time. Streetcars travel on tracks in the streets of a city. They are run by electricity.

We must pay money to take a ride on a streetcar.

---

stretch

Father can **stretch** as high as the top shelf of the cupboard.
Father can **reach out his arms** as high as the top shelf of the cupboard.

A rubber band will **stretch** if you pull it.
A rubber band will **get longer** if you pull it.

The baby **stretched** out her hand for some milk.
The baby **reached** out her hand for some milk.

---

strike Did you hear the clock **strike** ten times?
Did you hear the clock **sound** ten times?

Nicholas will **strike** the nail with a hammer.
Nicholas will **hit** the nail with a hammer.

Michael **struck** the ball with a bat. Now he will try again.

string　Do you have a piece of **string?**
Do you have a piece of **cord?** I need some string to tie my package. When you buy string, it comes rolled up.

Sandra likes to **string beads.**
Sandra likes to **put beads on a string.**

Have you ever **strung** beads?

strip　The belt is made out of a **strip** of leather.
The belt is made out of a **long narrow piece** of leather.

Paul will **strip** before he takes a bath.
Paul will **take off all his clothes** before he takes a bath.

stripe　A **stripe** is a long, narrow band. The flag of the United States of America has thirteen red and white stripes.

stroll　Beatrice and Kim went for a **stroll.**
Beatrice and Kim went for a **slow and easy walk.** They like to **stroll** in the woods.

strong　My father is **strong.** He can lift heavy things. My father is not weak.

The **strong** wind blew the door open.

The United States has a **strong** army. It has many soldiers, many guns, and many tanks.

My swing hangs from **strong** ropes. The ropes are heavy. They will not break easily.

Some radishes have a **strong** taste. They taste hot. Some cheeses have a strong taste, too. They smell very much.

struck   Yesterday I was **struck** with a snowball.
              Yesterday I was **hit** with a snowball. Did a snowball ever strike you?

stuck   Geraldine just **stuck** a stamp on the envelope. Does she need to stick another stamp on the envelope?

       Our car got **stuck** in the mud. It sunk into the soft mud so that Father could not drive away.

stuff   Put the **stuff** in a box up in the attic.
          Put the **things** in a box up in the attic.

          Mother will **stuff** the pillow with cotton.
          Mother will **fill** the pillow with cotton.

          My bed pillow is **stuffed** with feathers.

stumble   Do not **stumble** on that rock.
             Do not **trip by hitting your foot** on that rock.

stump   A **stump** is the lower part of a tree after the top has been cut down. There is a squirrel sitting on the stump of the tree.

---

stung   A bee **stung** Carl on the arm.
A bee **bit** Carl on the arm.   Did a bee ever sting you?

---

stupid   **Stupid** means *not smart*.   A person who is stupid is not very bright.   He doesn't have good sense.

---

subtract   If we **subtract** one from four, we will have three.
If we **take away** one from four, we will have three.
$$4 - 1 = 3$$

---

succeed   If you work hard, you will **succeed.**
If you work hard, you will **do well.**

Bill **succeeded** in winning the race.   Bill tried hard to win the race, and he did win the race.

---

such   I have seen several **such movies.**
I have seen several **movies of that kind.**

Patsy is **such a** big baby.
Patsy is **a very** big baby.

Captain Brown is **such a good** soldier that he will be made a general.
Captain Brown is **so good a** soldier that he will be made a general.

sudden   Father made a **sudden** trip to New York.
Father made a **quick** trip to New York. After he found out that he had to go to New York, he had to leave immediately.

All of a sudden means *suddenly.*

---

suddenly   **Suddenly** it started to snow.
When we were not looking for it, it started to snow.

---

suds   Mother washed the dirty dishes in **suds.** She washed the dirty dishes in water with enough soap in it to make bubbles.

---

suffer   Grandfather did **suffer** when he broke his leg.
Grandfather did **feel great pain** when he broke his leg.

---

sugar   We use **sugar** to make things sweet. Sugar is made from the sugar beet plant and the sugar cane plant. Most candy is made with sugar. We put sugar in coffee, in cookies, in cakes, and in many other things.

---

suggestion   Mother wanted to make a cake for Father's birthday party. She did not know what kind of cake to make. Mother said to Susan, "What kind of a cake should I make? Do you have a **suggestion?**
Do you have an **idea?"**

Susan said, "Yes, I have a suggestion. You should make a chocolate cake with fluffy white frosting. Daddy likes that kind of cake."

suit   A **suit** is a set of clothing worn together.   Father has a new blue suit.   His new suit has a coat and trousers.

Will this tie **suit** me?
Will this tie **look good on** me?

Do these flowers **suit** you?
Do these flowers **please** you?

suitcase   A **suitcase** is a bag that is used for traveling.   Mother packed our clothes in suitcases when we went away on vacation.

summer   **Summer** is one of the four seasons of the year.   The other seasons are autumn, winter, and spring.

sun   The **sun** is the brightest body we can see in the sky.   The sun is a star which gives the earth light and heat.   The earth goes around the sun in one year.   We can see the sun shine in the daytime.

Sunday   **Sunday** is the first day of the week.   Most people do not go to work on Sunday.   They stay home and rest.   Sunday is the day of rest.   Many people go to church on Sunday.

Sunday	Monday	Tuesday	Wednesday	Thursday	Friday	Saturday
first	second	third	fourth	fifth	sixth	seventh
1st	2nd	3rd	4th	5th	6th	7th

539

sunflower

A **sunflower** is a tall plant that has a large, yellow flower. The center of the flower is large, brown, and full of seeds. Birds like to eat sunflower seeds. Sunflower seeds are good to eat.

---

sunk   The boat hit a rock and **sunk in** the water.
The boat hit a rock and **went down under** the water. We saw the boat sink.

---

sunlight   **Sunlight** is the light from the sun. Plants grow in the sunlight.

---

sunny   Monday was a **sunny day.**
Monday was a **day filled with sunshine.**

---

sunrise   I watch the **sunrise** from my window.
I watch the **light in the sky when the sun comes up** from my window.

---

sunset   Mother said that we must be in the house **at sunset.**
Mother said that we must be in the house **when the sun goes down.**

Did you see that beautiful **sunset?**
Did you see that beautiful **changing light and color in the sky when the sun went down?**

sunshine **Sunshine** is the light from the sun. When I go to the beach, I lie in the sunshine.

---

supper **Supper** is the last meal of the day. Some people have dinner at noon. In the evening they have supper.

---

suppose I **suppose** Jack will come to the party.
I **think perhaps** Jack will come to the party.

The children **are supposed to** be in bed.
The children **should** be in bed.

---

sure When I am **sure** of something, I know that it is true. I am sure that I am reading this book. I am also sure that daytime comes after nighttime. I am sure that one and one make two. I know that all these things are true.

---

surely **Surely** this pen is not mine.
I am sure this pen is not mine. I am certain of it.

---

surprise Daddy sometimes brings me **a surprise.**
Daddy sometimes brings me **something that I was not waiting for.** Yesterday he brought me a bar of candy. I did not know he was going to bring me candy. It was a surprise for me.

If I come home from school early, I will **surprise** Mother. She will be surprised because she will not be waiting for me. Mother will wonder why I am home so early.

swallow   A **swallow** is a small bird.   It can fly fast.

---

swallow   After I put milk into my mouth, I **swallow** it.
After I put milk into my mouth, **I make it go down my throat and into my stomach.**

Always chew your food well before swallowing it.

---

swam   Yesterday Billy **swam** across the lake.   I cannot swim that far.

---

swan   A **swan** is a large bird.   A swan looks something like a goose. Here is a swan.

---

swarm   A **swarm** is a large group.   A swarm of bees is a group of bees that leave their beehive and fly away together.   The bees will make a new hive somewhere else.

sweat Sweat is liquid that comes through our skin. I was so hot from running, that sweat was all over my body.

---

sweater A **sweater** is like a jacket. Sweaters are made out of yarn. Christopher is wearing a green sweater. His sweater has buttons in front. Charles is wearing a red sweater. He does not have any buttons on the front of his sweater. Charles pulls his sweater over his head to put it on.

---

sweep Mother will **sweep the floor.**
Mother will **brush the floor with a broom.** She sweeps the floor to clean it.

Yesterday I **swept** the floor for Mother.

Stanley was **sweeping** the leaves from the walk.

---

sweet Sugar is **sweet.** Lemons are sour. Anything made with sugar is sweet. Candy is sweet.

Roses have a **sweet** smell.
Roses have a **pleasant** smell.

Mother has a **sweet** voice.
Mother has a **soft and pleasant** voice.

Baby is **sweet.** We love baby very much.

swell   The bee's sting made Ed's hand **swell.**
The bee's sting made Ed's hand **become larger.**   Ed said, "My hand hurts."

When I blow air into a balloon, it **swells.**

Jack said, "That was a **swell** party."
Jack said, "That was a **very good** party."

---

swept   Yesterday Mary **swept** the sidewalk.   Today Timothy will sweep the sidewalk.

---

swift   My mother is **swift** when she sews.
My mother is **fast** when she sews.   She sews quickly.

The horse is **swift.**
The horse is **very fast.**   He can run faster than every other horse in the race.

---

swim   Neil can **swim.**
Neil can **move through the water by moving his hands and feet.**

I **swam** across the pond yesterday.

Patricia likes **swimming.**

Jeffery is tired because he has **swum** all afternoon.

swing   Janice is on a **swing.**

Janice likes to **swing.**
Janice likes to **move back and forth on a swing.** She **swung** on the swing yesterday, too.

The baseball player **swung the bat** at the ball.
The baseball player **moved the bat around** at the ball.

---

switch   We turn the electric light on and off with a light **switch.**

Please **switch the light on.**
Please **turn the light on with a switch.**

These are light switches.

A **switch** is a whip.   A switch can also be a small branch of a tree used for whipping.

The cruel man **switched** the dog.
The cruel man **whipped** the dog.

---

swollen   John's finger had **swollen** where the spider bit him.
John's finger had **become larger** where the spider bit him.
John said, "My finger hurts."

sword   A **sword** is like a long knife. Men used to fight with swords.

---

swum   Edwin is tired because he has just **swum** across the lake. I cannot swim as far as that.

---

swung   The monkey **swung** by his tail from a limb of a tree. Did you ever see a monkey swing by his tail?

---

syrup   **Syrup** is a thick, sticky, and sweet liquid. It has much sugar in it. Fruit juice is put in some syrup. Maple syrup comes from the sap of the maple tree. Chocolate syrup is made with chocolate.

Raymond likes maple syrup on his pancakes. Elizabeth likes chocolate syrup on her ice cream.

This is the twentieth letter of the alphabet.

ABCDEFGHIJKLMNOPQRSTUVWXYZ

abcdefghijklmnopqrstuvwxyz

table We sit at a **table** when we eat. The table in our dining room is called a dining room table. It has a flat top and four legs.

There are many other kinds of **tables** in our house.

---

tablecloth A **tablecloth** is a large cloth covering for a table. Sarah spread the tablecloth on the dining room table before putting the dishes and food on it.

---

tablespoon A **tablespoon** is a large spoon. Mother serves the vegetables with a tablespoon.

---

tablet Martin is writing in his **tablet**.
Martin is writing in his **pad**. A writing tablet has many sheets of paper fastened together at the top.

The doctor gave Father some **tablets**.
The doctor gave Father some **small, flat pills**.

---

tack A **tack** is a short nail with a large flat top.

Frances will **tack** the picture onto the wall with thumb**tacks**. She will fasten the picture onto the wall by pushing tacks into the wall with her thumb.

---

tadpole  A **tadpole** is a very young frog or toad. Tadpoles have tails which disappear before they are grown-up frogs or toads.

taffy   Taffy is candy which is made of sugar, water, and vinegar. The children like taffy.

---

tag   There is a **tag** fastened to the package.
There is a **small card** fastened to the package. A name and an address are on the card. The tag tells to whom the package belongs.

A price **tag** tells how much something costs.

Mother will **tag** the Christmas gifts.
Mother will **put tags on** the Christmas gifts.

There is a game called **tag.** One player chases the other players until he touches one. The player who does the chasing is called "it." William was "it." So, all the other children ran away from William.

William **tagged** Susan. Now Susan is "it."
William **touched** Susan. Now Susan is "it."

---

tail   The pig has a ribbon on his little **tail.** The monkey is hanging by his tail. The rooster's tail is made of feathers.

The last or back part of anything is also called a **tail.** The tail of the car was sticking out of the garage. The tail of the airplane was painted red.

---

tailor   The man who makes and fixes Father's clothes is called a **tailor.**

T t

take I **take** Mother's hand when we cross the street.
I **hold** Mother's hand when we cross the street.

Take the book you want.
Choose the book you want.

We **take** our lunch to school.
We **bring** our lunch to school.

Daddy will **take** us to the picnic.
Daddy will **go with** us to the picnic.

Roberta will **take** a cup from the cupboard.
Roberta will **get** a cup from the cupboard.

Mother will **take** an hour to make dinner.
Mother will **need** an hour to make dinner.

Father will **take** a train to New York.
Father will **ride on** a train to New York.

Take off your muddy rubbers when you come into the house.
Remove your muddy rubbers when you come into the house.
  Do not leave your rubbers on your shoes.

The airplane will **take off** in New York. It will land in
  Chicago.
The airplane will **go into the air** in New York. It will land
  in Chicago.

The teacher said, "**Take** your seat."
The teacher said, "**Sit down in** your seat."

Father **takes** me to the baseball game.

Terence is **taking** a ride on his bicycle.

Harry has **taken** a piece of candy.

Yesterday I **took** a walk in the park.

---

tale My father told us a **tale.**
My father told us a **story.** He told us of his trip to Africa.

550

talk   To **talk** means to *say words.* Yesterday I **talked** to my Aunt Rita over the telephone. I like **talking** to Aunt Rita. I like to tell her about the many things that I do.

tall    We went to the circus where we saw a very **tall** man. He was the **tallest** man at the circus. I never saw a man as tall as he was. There was a very short man at the circus, too.

I see a clown who's very tall,
And also one who's very small;
Not tall, not small—it is no riddle,
I'd rather be right in the middle.

tame   We have a racoon that is **tame.**
We have a racoon that is **not afraid of people.**

The lion in the zoo is wild. He is not **tame.** The lion might hurt us if we get too close to him.

tan   Stella is wearing a **tan** coat.
Stella is wearing a **light brown** coat.

The children were outdoors so much that their faces started to **tan.** Their faces started to turn a light brown color.

Martha **tanned** herself on the beach.

Did you ever get a **tan?**

T t

tangle　What a **tangle** the kitten has made with Mother's yarn! The kitten has twisted and mixed up all of Mother's yarn. Did you ever see the kitten tangle the yarn before? Look how the kitten is **tangled** up in the yarn.

---

tank　There is a **tank** for hot water in our basement. The water in the tank is heated for washing clothes and for taking baths.

A **tank** is a long, heavy machine with guns on it. A tank does not need a road to travel on. It can ride over very rough ground.

The man put gasoline in the **tank** of our automobile.

---

tap　I heard a **tap** on the door.
I heard a **light knock** on the door. Did you hear that **tapping** at the door?

Mother turned on the water **tap** to get a glass of water.
Mother turned on the water **faucet** to get a glass of water.

Tap Johnny on the shoulder.
Touch Johnny on the shoulder. I want him to turn around and look at me. Johnny said, "Who **tapped** me on the shoulder?"

---

tardy　Patty was **tardy** for dinner.
Patty was **late** for dinner. She was not on time. Patty came to the dinner table after everybody had already started to eat.

tart A **tart** is a small pie with fruit, jelly, or jam in it.

---

task A **task** is some work to be done. If a task is once begun,
Do not leave it till it's done.

---

tassel Mary's hat has a red **tassel** on it.

---

taste The **taste** of sugar is sweet. The taste of vinegar is sour.

Mother asked, "How does the soup **taste,** Al?" Al said, "The soup **tastes** salty. There is too much salt in it."

Freddy **tasted** the blueberry pie.
Freddy **took a little bite of** the blueberry pie.

---

taught When I was in first grade, Miss Smith **taught me.**
When I was in first grade, Miss Smith **helped me to learn.** Now I am going into second grade. Miss Ricardo will teach me.

---

tax Father must pay a **tax** to our country.
Father must pay **money** to our country. He must also pay taxes to our state and to our city. Tax money is used to pay for policemen, soldiers, firemen, roads, schools, parks, and many other people and things that help us.

---

taxi We took a ride in a **taxi.** A taxi is an automobile. The driver of the taxi will take us where we want to go. We must pay the taxi driver for our ride.

tea Tea is a **drink.** It is made by pouring boiling water over the dried leaves of a tea plant. Mother and Father drink tea. Did you ever see tea leaves?

---

teach Mother will **teach Martha** how to sew.
Mother will **help Martha to learn** how to sew. Grandmother **taught** Mother how to sew when Mother was a little girl.

---

teacher A **teacher** is a person who helps others to learn.

---

team A **team** is a number of people who act, work, or play together.

There are nine players on a baseball **team.** Our baseball team played against another baseball team.

Animals can work as a **team,** too. A team of four horses pulled the wagon.

---

tear I will **tear the paper** into two pieces.
I will **pull the paper apart** into two pieces.

Yesterday baby **tore** the picture in half.

Did you see Sam **tear** his jacket on that nail? Sam made a hole in his jacket by pulling it on that nail. Mother asked, "Show me where your jacket is **torn,** Sam?"

tear   A **tear** is a drop of salty water that comes from a person's eye.   When I cry, tears come from my eyes.   When Mother peels onions, sometimes tears come from her eyes.

---

tease   The children **tease Alfred** about his red hair.
The children **make Alfred angry by making jokes** about his red hair.

Jack **teased** his mother to go to the movies.
Jack **begged** his mother to go to the movies.

---

teaspoon   A **teaspoon** is a small spoon.   Mother and Father stir tea and coffee with a teaspoon.   I eat ice cream with a teaspoon.

---

teddy bear   My baby brother has a **teddy bear.**   It is a soft toy bear.   My baby brother likes to play with his teddy bear.

---

teeth   I chew my food with my **teeth.**   Each one of my teeth is called a tooth.

I brush my teeth after each meal, so that they will be white and clean.

---

telegram   When Father was away, he sent us a **telegram.**   A telegram is a written message.   It is sent over wires by electricity.

telephone   When I was in Boston, I talked to Grandmother in Los Angeles by using a **telephone.**

telescope

When you look through a **telescope,** things that are very far away seem larger and closer. People look at the stars, the moon, and the planets through a telescope.

television   We see moving pictures on our **television** set. These pictures are broadcast from far away. They are sent through the air by electricity. Sometimes television is called TV.

tell   I will **tell** Mother, "Happy Birthday!"
I will **say to** Mother, "Happy Birthday!"

I will **tell** you about my trip.
I will **speak to** you about my trip.

Tell me where you are going.
Let me know where you are going.

Father sometimes **tells** me a story before I go to bed. He **told** me a story named *The Three Bears.*

---

ten   Can you count to **ten?**

one two three four five six seven eight nine **ten** eleven
 1   2   3   4   5   6   7   8   9   **10**   11

Five and five make **ten.**
$5 + 5 = 10$

Ten 10's are one hundred.
$10 + 10 + 10 + 10 + 10 + 10 + 10 + 10 + 10 + 10 = 100$
10   20   30   40   50   60   70   80   90   **100**

---

tender   The meat was **tender.**
The meat was **easy to chew.** It was not hard and tough.

In the spring the leaves are **tender.**
In the spring the leaves are **soft.**

The mother spoke **tender** words to her baby.
The mother spoke **kind and loving** words to her baby.

---

tennis   **Tennis** is a game played by hitting a ball back and forth over a net. The ball is hit with a kind of paddle.

557

tent   When we go camping, we sleep in a **tent** at night. We put the tent up with poles and ropes.

---

tenth   The alphabet is printed in a row. "J" is the tenth letter in the row. It is number ten in the row. Can you count the letters and find the tenth one?

A B C D E F G H I **J** K L M N O P Q R S T U V W X Y Z
10th

---

tepee   A **tepee** is a pointed tent made by some Indians in North America. A tepee is made of poles. It is covered with the skin of buffaloes.

What is meant
  By tepee, called a home?
A kind of tent
  For Indians who liked to roam.

---

terrible   The storm we had yesterday was **terrible.**
The storm we had yesterday **caused great fear.** Everybody in our house was afraid. The rain came down. The wind blew hard, and there was much thunder and lightning.

test   After the teacher taught us how to add numbers, she gave us a test. She gave us some numbers and told us to add them. She wanted to see if we learned how to add. This was the test. Can you do this test?

6	8	7	11	62	10	65	10
+1	+2	+3	+34	+37	+10	+34	+11

---

than   An elephant is bigger **than** a cat.

A rabbit can run faster **than** a turtle.

Grandfather is older **than** Daddy.

I have more candy **than** Peter. I have ten pieces of candy. Peter only has two pieces of candy.

---

thank   I will **thank Grandmother** for the present she gave me.
I will **tell Grandmother that I am pleased and happy** for the present she gave me.

When someone does something for you, you should say, **"Thank you."** We should always thank people when they do nice things for us.

---

thankful   When you are **thankful** you are happy and feel like saying "Thank you."

---

thanks   Thanks means "I thank you."

Thanks for the candy.
I thank you for the candy.

We **give thanks** to God on Thanksgiving Day.
We **say thank you** to God on Thanksgiving Day.

Thanksgiving On **Thanksgiving Day** we thank God for all the good things He has given us. Thanksgiving Day comes in the month of November. We eat turkey on Thanksgiving.

---

that Billy said, "This is my coat and **that** is Daddy's coat."

Do you see **that** big bird over there?

Joan said **that** she will come to visit us.

This is the watch **that** Aunt Hilda gave me.

---

that's **That's** the last penny I have.
That is the last penny I have.

---

the I don't want a book. I don't want just any book. I want **the** book called *Black Beauty*. It is the book about a black horse.

---

their Three little kittens lost **their** mittens,
And they began to cry,
"Oh! Mother dear, we sadly fear
That we have lost our mittens."

The kittens lost **their mittens.**
The kittens lost **the mittens that belonged to them.**

---

theirs Those are Mr. and Mrs. Smith's books.
The books **are theirs.**
The books **belong to them.**

them Yesterday I saw Peter and David. I saw **them** in the park. I played ball with them.

---

themselves The three little children dressed **themselves**. Each child put on his own clothes.

Elizabeth and Kathy made the cookies **themselves**. Nobody helped them.

Herbert and Carl were standing **by themselves** away from the other children.

Herbert and Carl were standing **alone** away from the other children.

---

then A month ago I went ice skating. It was winter **then**.

It was winter **at that time**.

We arrived home, and **then** it started to snow.

We arrived home, and **afterward** it started to snow.

In the parade, first came the band, and **then** came the soldiers.

In the parade, first came the band, and **next** came the soldiers.

If Stanley broke the window, **then** he should pay for it.

If Stanley broke the window, **because of that** he should pay for it.

---

there Please sit **there**.

Please sit **in that place**.

I am going to the beach. Are you going **there**?

Are you going **to that place**?

There is one book on the table. One book is on the table.

Baby fell and scratched her knee. Mother said, "**There, there,** don't cry. I will put a little bandage on it. Soon it will be well."

therefore   It is raining and **therefore** we cannot have our picnic.

It is raining and **for that reason** we cannot have our picnic.

---

there's   **There's** means *there is.* There's a store on the corner of our street.

---

these   This green pen is mine. This black pen is also mine. **These** pens in my hand are mine. That yellow pen is yours. That blue pen is yours, too. Those pens over there are yours.

---

they   I walk to school with Henry and Donald. **They** are my friends.

They are saying that it might snow.
People are saying that is might snow.

---

they'll   The boys are coming; **they'll** be here soon.
The boys are coming; **they will** be here soon.

---

they're   **They're** going to the movies later.
They are going to the movies later.

---

thick   The stone wall is **thick.**
The stone wall is **not thin.**

Frank has **thick** hair.
Frank has **much** hair.

We walked in a **thick forest.**
We walked in a **forest with many trees growing close together.**

thief   A **thief** is a person who steals.

---

thieves   Three **thieves** stole the money, but only one thief was caught by the policeman.

---

thimble   Mother puts a **thimble** over the end of her finger when she sews. A thimble is a small cap which protects Mother's finger when she pushes the sewing needle.

---

thin   Margaret is holding a **thin** book. There are not very many pages in Margaret's book. Albert is reading a thick book. There are many pages in Albert's book.

Margaret's book is **thin**. Her book is not thick.

Uncle Frank is **thin**. He is not fat.

The grass in our yard is **thin**.
The grass in our yard is **growing far apart**. There is not much grass in our yard.

thing   A **thing** is any object, any act, or any idea.

Mother put the **things** in a box.
Mother put the **objects** in a box. She put the drinking glasses, the cups, and the plates in a box. She put other things in the box, too.

That was a good **thing** to do.
That was a good **act** to do.

That is a funny **thing** to think about.
That is a funny **idea** to think about.

Daddy put his **things** in a suitcase.
Daddy put his **clothes** in a suitcase.

think   When I **think** I use my mind.

I want to **think** about that question before I answer it.

I want to **have some ideas** about that question before I answer it.

Philip **thinks** it will rain.

Philip **believes** it will rain. He said that it looks as if it will rain.

Irene **thought** and thought, but she didn't have any idea of what to buy Father for Christmas. Irene did not know what to buy for Father.

---

third   There are five blocks in a row.

The **third** block in the row is yellow.

The **number three** block in the row is yellow

first   second   **third**   fourth   fifth
1st   2nd   **3rd**   4th   5th

---

thirst   **Thirst** is a dry feeling in your throat and mouth. You get this feeling when you need to drink liquid.

---

thirsty   Paul is **thirsty**. He wants something to drink.

---

thirteen   Seven pennies and six pennies are **thirteen** pennies.
7 + 6 = 13

Can you count to thirteen?
1 2 3 4 5 6 7 8 9 10 11 12 **13** 14 15

thirteenth There are thirteen airplanes flying in a row. My uncle is the pilot of the last airplane in the row. My uncle is flying the **thirteenth** airplane.

---

thirty Six 5's make **30**. $5 + 5 + 5 + 5 + 5 + 5 = 30$

Three dimes make **thirty** cents. $.10 + .10 + .10 = .30$

Can you count to thirty?

---

thirty-one There are **thirty-one** days in the month of January.

JANUARY						
SUN	MON	TUES	WEN	THR	FRI	SAT
						1
2	3	4	5	6	7	8
9	10	11	12	13	14	15
16	17	18	19	20	21	22
23	24	25	26	27	28	29
30	31					

---

this **This** book is mine; that book is John's.

This desk right here is mine; that desk over there is Al's.

---

thorn

A **thorn** is a sharp point on a stem or branch of a plant or a tree. Rosebushes have thorns.

When you pick the roses,
  Handle them with care;
Or else the thorns will scratch your hands,
  Or give your clothes a tear.

---

those These are my books here on my desk, but **those** are his books over there on his desk.

Do you see **those** cows over there in the field? My Grandfather owns them.

T t

though Gary will come to the party **though** he will be late.

Gary will come to the party **even if** he will be late.

---

thought Do you have a **thought** on how to fix this chair?

Do you have an **idea** on how to fix this chair?

The things we think are **thoughts.**

I **thought** I heard the telephone ring.

I **believed** I heard the telephone ring.

---

thoughtful Al is **thoughtful** about going to college.

Al is **doing a lot of thinking** about going to college.

Sally is **thoughtful.**

Sally is **careful of others.** She thinks often about doing good for others. Sally tries to do good for others.

---

thoughtless A **thoughtless** person is careless. He is always making mistakes.

Don't be **thoughtless.** Think about others. Give some thought about doing good for others.

---

thousand One hundred ten times is one **thousand.**

$100 + 100 + 100 + 100 + 100 + 100 + 100 + 100 + 100 + 100 = \textbf{1,000}$

100 200 300 400 500 600 700 800 900 **1,000**

---

thread Mother sews our clothes with **thread.** This is a spool of thread.

Did you ever **thread** a needle?

Did you ever **put thread through the hole of** a needle?

three   There are **three** donkeys in the barnyard. Can you count
them?

one two **three** four five
1   2   **3**   4   5

Do you know what number comes before three? Do you
know what number comes after three?

---

thresh   Did you ever see a farmer **thresh** wheat?
Did you ever see a farmer **take the seeds from** wheat?

---

threw   Did you see how far David **threw** the stone? Can you throw
a stone farther than that?

---

throat   Your **throat** is the front part of your neck.

The inside of your neck is also called your **throat.** It is a
tube which joins your mouth and your stomach.
Yesterday I had a sore throat. The inside of my neck
hurt.

---

throb   To **throb** means to *beat fast or hard.* Henry's heart throbbed
after he ran the race.

---

throne   A **throne** is a chair used by a king, a queen, or other ruler.

through   Father will be **through** working soon.
Father will be **finished** working soon.

Have you read the book **through?**
Have you read the book **from beginning to end?**

The train went **through the tunnel.**
The train went **in one side of the tunnel, and out the other side.**

The butterflies flew **through** the flowers.
The butterflies flew **among** the flowers.

We worked **through the** day.
We worked **all** day.

He became rich **through** hard work.
He became rich **because of** hard work.

We got a package **through the** mail.
We got a package **by** mail.

---

throughout   We knew there was a fire because there was smoke **throughout** the house.
We knew there was a fire because there was smoke **everywhere in** the house.

---

throw   The football player will **throw** the ball. He will send the football through the air so that another football player can catch it.

A little while ago I **threw** a little rock into the water. Now I will throw a bigger rock into the water.

My shoes were all worn out. I could not wear them anymore. So, I **threw my old shoes away.**

Norma has **thrown** away all her old clothes.

thumb   Your **thumb** is one of the fingers on your hand. It is the short, thick finger set apart from the other fingers.

Eileen has a bandage on her thumb.

---

thump   Did you see Mr. Clark **thump** the table with his hand?
Did you see Mr. Clark **pound** the table with his hand? Mr. Clark was angry.

Raphael **thumped** his drum.

Thursday   **Thursday** is the fifth day of the week.

Sunday	Monday	Tuesday	Wednesday	**Thursday**	Friday	Saturday
first	second	third	fourth	fifth	sixth	seventh
1st	2nd	3rd	4th	5th	6th	7th

---

tick   The sound made by a clock or a watch is called a **tick.**

The room was so quiet that we could hear the clock **tick.** The clock went, "**Tick,** tick, tick."

This small mark √ is also called a **tick.**

---

ticket   A **ticket** is a card or a piece of paper that allows you to do something.

Father bought a train **ticket.** He needs a train ticket to ride on the train.

Nora bought a **ticket** to the show. She needs a ticket to go in and see the moving picture show.

569

tickle I coughed because I had a **tickle** in my throat.
I coughed because I had a **funny feeling as if something was touching me lightly** in my throat.

Did anybody ever **tickle your feet?**
Did anybody ever **touch your feet so lightly that your feet felt funny?**

---

tidy Paula's room is **tidy.**
Paula's room is **neat and in order.**

---

tie A **tie** is a strip of cloth which is worn around a person's neck. Father is wearing a blue tie.

The race was a **tie.** Both boys ran at the same speed. They came to the end at the same time. One boy did not run faster than the other. Neither boy won the race.

Please **tie** a string around this package. Put a string around this package and fasten the ends of the string in a knot.

Yesterday Anthony **tied** the knot in his own tie. He is a big boy now.

Rachel is **tying** a ribbon in her hair.

---

tiger A **tiger** is a large wild animal. The fur of a tiger is yellow with black stripes. The tiger belongs to the cat family.

tight   The ring was **tight** on Brenda's finger. It was not loose.

Tim's shoes are too **tight**. He needs shoes of a bigger size.

Mother **held me tight** when she kissed me good night.
Mother **hugged me** when she kissed me good night.

---

tightly   Kenneth's shoes fit him too **tightly**. His shoes are too small for his feet. Kenneth has to squeeze his feet into his shoes. Kenneth's tight shoes hurt his feet.

---

till   **Till** means *until*.

Wait **till** Father comes home. Then we will eat dinner.
Wait **up to the time** when Father gets home. Then we will eat dinner.

We must wait **till** evening.
We must wait **up to the time of** evening.

---

time   We measure **time** by seconds, minutes, hours, days, weeks, months, and years.

We measure the **time** of day by a clock. The clock tells us how much of the day has gone by. There are twenty-four hours in a day. When we say that it is two o'clock in the morning, we mean that the clock has measured for us that two hours of the day have already gone by.

We measure the **time** of the year by a calendar. There are twelve months in a year. There are 365 days in a year. When we say that today is January 1, we mean that it is the first month of the year, and it is the first day of that month. Do you know all the months of the year?

Morning is a **time** of the day. Spring is a time of year.

Ed hit the ball two **times**. Ed hit the ball, and hit it again.

Betty came to the party on **time**. She was not late.

times Three **times** ten means the same as ten three times.

3 × 10 means the same as 10 + 10 + 10.

3 × 10 is a short way of writing 10 + 10 + 10.

3 × 10 = 30

10 + 10 + 10 = 30

× is a sign which tells us how many times we add a number.

2 × 10 = 20

2 $\boxed{×}$ 10 = 20

Two $\boxed{\text{times we add}}$ the number 10. The answer is 20.

---

timid Harriet is **timid.**

Harriet is **afraid of people and things.**

---

tin **Tin** is a metal. Many cans are made out of tin. Mother has a tin pan in the kitchen.

---

tinkle A **tinkle** is a soft ringing sound. We heard the tinkle of the small bell which the cow wears around her neck.

The drinking glasses **tinkle** when Mother hits them gently together.

The drinking glasses **make soft ringing sounds** when Mother hits them gently together.

---

tiny We saw a **tiny** baby chick.

We saw a **very small** baby chick.

---

tip The seal is balancing a ball on the **tip** of his nose.

The seal is balancing a ball on the **end** of his nose.

Do not **tip** the table.

Do not **slant** the table.

Bob **tipped** the small table so much that it fell over.

tiptoe   Mary walked on **tiptoe** because the baby was asleep.
Mary walked on **the tips of her toes** because the baby was asleep.

Tiptoe so that you don't wake baby.
Walk on the tips of your toes softly and with care so that you don't wake baby.

---

tire   A rubber **tire** is a band of rubber around a wheel. The tires of our automobile are filled with air. Daddy is changing the tire on our automobile.

---

tire   Hard work will **tire you.**
Hard work will **make you weary.** You will want to rest.

Lucy **tired** quickly because she ran very fast.

---

tired   Peter was **tired,** for he worked hard all day. Now he needs some rest. After Peter gets some rest, he will no longer be tired. Peter will sleep for awhile.

---

title   What is the **title** of the story you are reading?
What is the **name** of the story you are reading?

The title of this book is *The International Visual Dictionary.*

to   Go **to** the right.
Go **in the direction of** the right.

Walk **to** the window and look outside.
Walk **as far as** the window and look outside.

Mother went to the store **to buy** some bread.
Mother went to the store **for the purpose of buying** some bread.

We danced **to** the music.
We danced **along with** the music.

Fasten the coat hook **to** the door.
Fasten the coat hook **on** the door.

It is five minutes **to** three o'clock.
It is five minutes **before** three o'clock.

Give the book **to** Harold. Give Harold the book.

John likes **to** read. He wants **to** read an interesting book.

---

toad   A **toad** is a small animal that looks like a frog. Toads live most of the time on land. They eat worms and insects. Toads have rough brown skin.

---

toast   A piece of **toast** is a slice of bread which has been made brown by heating it.

I will **toast the bread.**
I will **make the bread brown by heating it.**

---

tobacco   **Tobacco** is a plant with large leaves. The leaves of tobacco are dried and used for smoking or chewing.

today   Today is "this day." I will go to the beach **today.**
I will go to the beach **on this day.**

---

toe   A **toe** is one of the five end parts of the foot. Mother played a game with Baby. She called each of Baby's toes a little pig. Mother gently pulled each toe at the words "this little pig" when she said this poem for Baby.

This little pig went to market;
This little pig stayed home;
This little pig had roast beef;
This little pig had none;
This little pig said, "Wee, wee, wee!"
All the way home.

---

toenail   A **toenail** is the hard top part of each of your toes.

---

together   James and I walk to school **together.**
James and I walk to school **with each other.**

Mother sewed two pieces of cloth **together.** She sewed two pieces of cloth to each other.

Call the children **together.** Call them into a group.

---

toilet   A **toilet** is a bathroom.

---

told   Yesterday Ed **told** a story. I will tell it today.

---

tomato   A **tomato** is a red or yellow fruit that tastes like a vegetable. Tomatoes have seeds in them.

---

tomorrow   **Tomorrow** is the day after today.

ton A **ton** is a measure of weight. In the United States, there are 2,000 pounds in one ton. Our car weighs two tons. It weighs 4,000 pounds.

---

tongue Your **tongue** is in your mouth. You taste food with your tongue. You use your tongue to speak.

This dog's mouth is open. We can see his **tongue.**

---

tonight **Tonight** is the night of this day. Mother wants to finish her work this afternoon, so that she can go to the movies tonight.

---

too We have a dog, and a kitten, **too.**
We have a dog, and a kitten, **also.**

This dress is **too long** for you.
This dress is **more than long enough** for you.

I am **only too** glad to help you.
I am **very** glad to help you.

---

took Yesterday I **took** a book from that shelf. Today I will take another book from the shelf.

---

tool A **tool** is anything used in doing work. A hammer, a saw, and nails are some of the tools a carpenter uses. Carpenters, mechanics, plumbers, and shoemakers need tools. Can you name some more tools?

tooth Each one of my teeth is called a **tooth.** I chew food with my teeth. I brush my teeth after each meal, so that they will be white and clean.

toothache Did you ever have a **toothache?**
Did you ever have a **pain in a tooth?**

toothbrush A **toothbrush** is a small brush for cleaning your teeth.

top The **top** is the highest part of anything. The bird is on the top of the post.

A **top** is a round toy. It has a point on one end. The top spins on the point. Tommy likes to spin his top.

Edward got mud on the **top** and the bottom of his shoes.
Edward got mud on the **upper part** and the bottom of his shoes.

tore Henry **tore** his jacket on the nail.
Henry **made a hole by pulling** his jacket on the nail. He was sad, because he did not want to tear his jacket.

Kevin **tore the paper** into two pieces.
Kevin **pulled the paper apart** into two pieces.

torn   Hilda was playing with her dog. By accident her dress was **torn** by the dog. Hilda said, "You naughty dog! You should not tear my dress."

---

tortoise      A **tortoise** is a turtle. A tortoise has a shell on his back.

---

toss   Vincent likes to **toss** the ball up into the air and then to catch it.

Vincent likes to **throw** the ball up into the air and then to catch it.

Bertrand and Bernard **tossed** their pillows at each other. My mother said, "Stop **tossing** the pillows."

---

touch   **Touch** is one of the senses of your body. Touch allows you to learn about things by feeling them. Do you know what the other senses of your body are?

When we let our skin come against something, we **touch** it.

Robert **touched** the cat's smooth fur with his hand.

---

tough   The meat was **tough.**
The meat was **hard to chew.** Father said, "This meat is not tender."

---

toward   The cows walked **toward** the barn.
The cows walked **in the direction of** the barn.

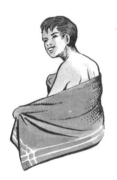

towards Towards means *toward*.

---

towel A **towel** is a piece of cloth used for wiping or drying. Stephen is drying himself with a towel.

Some towels are made of paper. They are used for wiping and drying, too.

Wipe up the spilled milk with a paper towel. You will find the paper towels on a roll hanging on the kitchen wall.

---

tower  A **tower** is a tall, narrow part of a building. The church bell is in the tower.

Up in the tower,
    Hangs a heavy bell,
Ringing on the hour,
    The time of day to tell.

---

town A **town** is a place where many people live near each other. A town is a small city. We live in a town, but Grandmother and Grandfather live in the country.

---

toy Aunt Agnes gave me a **toy**.
Aunt Agnes gave me a **thing to play with.**
    I like to play with toys.

track   A railroad **track** is the road that the trains travel on.

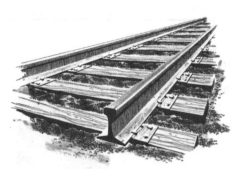

We saw a deer's **tracks** in the snow.
We saw a deer's **footprints** in the snow.

A good hunter knows how to **track** animals.
A good hunter knows how to **follow the tracks of** animals.

---

tractor   A **tractor** is a heavy machine that has a motor. It is used for pulling a plow or some other machine.

---

trade   A **trade** is the work a person does to earn money for food, clothes, and shelter. My father's trade is farming. He works on a farm.

We **trade with** Mr. Delgado.
We **buy from** Mr. Delgado. He owns a grocery store.

I **traded** books with Mildred. I gave Mildred my book, and Mildred gave me her book.

---

trader   A **trader** is a person who buys, sells, or exchanges things that people need. Mr. Jones is a horse trader. He buys and sells horses.

---

traffic   There was much automobile **traffic** on our street yesterday. There were many cars, buses, and trucks coming and going on our street.

trailer Mr. and Mrs. Davis live in a **trailer.**
Mr. and Mrs. Davis live in a **house on wheels.**

The truck pulled a **trailer** filled with furniture.
The truck pulled a **wagon** filled with furniture.

---

train A **train** is a line of railroad cars moving along together. This is a train that carries people.

This is a train that carries freight.

I will try to **train** my dog well. I will try to teach my dog many tricks.

---

tramp A **tramp** is a man who does not have a home. He travels from place to place. Daddy gave the tramp some money for food.

The children **tramp** through the halls of the school.
The children **walk with heavy steps** through the halls of the school.

trap

We use a **trap** to catch animals.

The hunter will **trap** a fox. He will catch a fox in a trap. Yesterday he **trapped** a squirrel.

---

travel   I like to **travel.**

I like to **go from one place to another.** I have traveled by car, by bus, by boat, and by airplane. I like traveling by jet airplane best.

---

traveler   A **traveler** is a person who is going from one place to another.

---

tray

A **tray** is a flat piece of metal, wood, or other material. Food, dishes, and glasses are often carried on trays. When I was sick, Mother brought me my dinner on a tray.

---

treasure   A **treasure** is money, jewels, or anything of great value that has been stored up. The boys found the hidden treasure that was buried on the beach.

treat   Father took us to the movies for a **treat.**   After the movies, he gave us another treat.   Father took us to get some ice cream.

I will **treat you to** a bar of candy.
I will **buy you** a bar of candy.

We **treat** our new baby gently.
We **act toward** our new baby gently.

Father **treated** me like a big boy when we went fishing.

---

tree   A **tree** is a very big plant.   A tree has a trunk, branches, and leaves.   Some trees lose their leaves in the winter.   Other trees have leaves throughout the year.   Three kinds of trees are a cherry tree, a maple tree, and a pine tree.   Can you name some more trees?

Wood for building houses and furniture comes from the trunks and branches of trees.

---

tremble   The dog was so cold that he did **tremble.**
The dog was so cold that he did **shake all over.**

---

trial   Father gave our new car a **trial.**
Father gave our new car a **test.**   He drove our new car for a while to see how it would run.   Father gave the new car a tryout.

triangle

A **triangle** is a flat figure with three sides and three corners.

---

tribe   A **tribe** is a group of people.   American Indians still live in tribes.

---

trick   Stanley played a **trick** on Mother.   He filled the sugar bowl with salt.   Mother did not like Stanley's trick.

The seal can do a **trick.**   He can balance a ball on his nose. The lion can do a trick, too.   He can jump through a hoop which is on fire.

I like to watch magic **tricks.**   Did you ever see a man pull a rabbit out of a hat?

---

tried   I **tried** to clean my room well.
I **worked hard** to clean my room well.

Mary **tried** on the new dress.   She put on the new dress to see if it would fit well on her.

Henry **tried** the soup.   He took a taste of the soup to see if he liked it.

trim

I like to **trim** the Christmas tree. I like to make the tree look pretty. I put lights, shiny balls, and strips of silver paper on the tree.

The barber will **trim** Daddy's hair. The barber will cut off some of Daddy's hair, so that he will look neat.

The room is **trim.**
The room is **neat.** Everything is in its place.

---

trio

A **trio** is a group of three persons or things. The trio of boys sang a song.

---

trip

To **take a trip** means to *go to a place away from home.* In the summer, we are going on a **trip** to Mexico. I like to go on journeys.

Did you **trip?** Did you catch your foot on something and start to fall. Do be careful not to stumble.

Roy **tripped** on the edge of the rug, but he did not fall.

Kevin **tripped** over the small stool, and he fell down.

---

trot

Did you ever see a horse **trot?**

When a horse **trots,** he lifts his right front foot and his left back foot at about the same time.

trouble   Mother said, "Be a good boy, and do not **make trouble for me**."

Mother said, "Be a good boy, and do not **make me worry**."

The sick children **trouble** Mother.

The sick children **worry** Mother. She hopes that they will get well soon.

We will eat dinner at your house, if it isn't too much **trouble** for you.

We will eat dinner at your house, if it isn't too much **extra work** for you.

---

trousers   Father is wearing brown **trousers**.

Father is wearing brown **pants**. Little Louis is wearing blue pants.

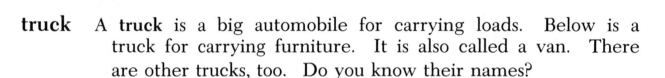

> Dad's trousers are so old and brown;
> My trousers too are old, but blue;
> We'll wear our trousers into town
>   And there buy trousers which are new.

---

truck   A **truck** is a big automobile for carrying loads. Below is a truck for carrying furniture. It is also called a van. There are other trucks, too. Do you know their names?

I. V. D.

true   It is true that sunlight comes from the sun.
It is **correct** that sunlight comes from the sun. If I say something which I know is not true, it is a lie. We should not lie.

Sometimes I think what I say is **true,** but it is false. This is called a mistake. Sometimes we make mistakes.

---

truly   I am **truly** going to the circus.
I am **really** going to the circus. It is true.

---

trunk   A **trunk** is the main stem of a tree. The squirrel is climbing up the tree trunk.

A big box to put your clothes in is called a **trunk.** When we moved to another house, we packed our clothes in a trunk.

The long nose of an elephant is called a **trunk.** The elephant picked up the log with his trunk.

---

trust   I **trust** Clarence because I know he will tell the truth.
I **believe** Clarence because I know he will tell the truth.

---

truth   We should always tell the **truth.**
We should always tell **things that are true.**

Aloysius told Helen that he can swim. But Aloysius is not able to swim. He told Helen a lie. He didn't tell Helen the truth.

T t

try The captain of the baseball team said to the players,
"**Try** hard to win the game."
"**Work** hard to win the game." The captain wanted the baseball players to do their best.

At first, Father could not fix the car. He **tried** again, and finally he made the car run.

We should keep **trying** if we do not at first succeed.

Try this cake to see if you like it.
Taste this cake to see if you like it.

Try out this bicycle to see if it rides well.
Go for a ride on this bicycle to see if it rides well. Give the bicycle a **tryout**.

---

tub Mother washes her clothes in a **tub**. This tub is called a washtub.

I take a bath in a **tub**. This tub is called a bathtub.

---

tube A **tube** is a long pipe.

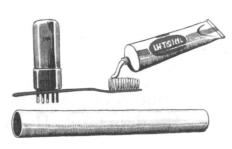

A radio tube is part of my radio. Electricity must go through the radio tubes to make the radio work.

Toothpaste comes in a tube. This kind of tube is made out of thin metal. I take the top off the tube and squeeze some toothpaste onto my toothbrush.

tuck   **Tuck the handkerchief** into your pocket.
Squeeze the handkerchief neatly into your pocket.

Mother **tucked** the baby's curls into her bonnet.

Tuesday   **Tuesday** is the day after Monday. Tuesday is the third day of the week.

Sunday	Monday	Tuesday	Wednesday	Thursday	Friday	Saturday
first	second	third	fourth	fifth	sixth	seventh
1st	2nd	3rd	4th	5th	6th	7th

---

tug   A **tug** is a small boat which pushes or pulls other boats.

Sue gave the rope a **tug.** She gave the rope a hard pull.

Tug at the wagon to get it out of the hole.
Pull the wagon hard to get it out of the hole.

Dick **tugged** at the kite's string, but he could not get the kite out of the tree.

---

tulip    A **tulip** is a flower. Tulips bloom in the spring. They are of many bright colors.

The tulips in my flower bed
Have colors gay and bright,
Cheering up my flower patch
To make a pretty sight.

tumble   Did the baby **tumble** out of bed?
Did the baby **fall** out of bed?

Sometimes I **tumble** on my bed.
Sometimes I **bounce around** on my bed.

---

tumbler   A drinking glass is sometimes called a **tumbler**.

---

tune   Rita played a **tune** for us on the piano.
Rita played a **song** for us on the piano.

We heard Mother humming a tune.

---

tunnel   The men are digging a **tunnel**.
The men are digging a **way under the ground**.

Tunnels are made through mountains and hills. Tunnels are also made under rivers. Very often roads are made in these tunnels. Automobiles travel through these tunnels. The train is going through a tunnel.

---

turkey    A **turkey** is a large bird. Mother roasted a turkey for us on Thanksgiving Day.

turn   It was Billy's **turn** to hit the baseball with the bat. Each player on the team took a turn with the bat. Each player could try to hit the ball.

The children are in a line, and each child waits his **turn** to get a drink.

We will walk straight ahead. Then we will **turn** to the right at the corner. We will change our direction by walking to the right at the corner.

The merry-go-round **turns**.
The merry-go-round **moves round as a wheel does.**

Ice **turns to** water when it becomes warm.
Ice **becomes** water when it becomes warm.

Caterpillars **turn** into butterflies. They change into butterflies.

Turn the light on. Make the light work.

My father **turned** the car around.

Sally is **turning** the pages of the book.

---

turnip   A **turnip** is a plant with a large root. The root of the turnip plant is eaten as a vegetable.

Turnips are usually boiled before they are eaten.

turpentine   Turpentine is an oily liquid that comes from trees that have cones.

Father put turpentine in the paint.   He wanted to make the paint thinner.

---

turtle   A **turtle** is an animal with a hard shell on his back.   Some turtles live in water.   Other turtles live on land.

---

tusk   A **tusk** is a long pointed tooth.   Elephants have a tusk on each side of their head.

TV   **TV** is a short name for television.

---

twelfth   The alphabet is printed in a row.   "L" is the **twelfth** letter in the row.   It is number twelve in the row.

A B C D E F G H I J K L M N O P Q R S T U V W X Y Z

12th

twelve   The mother hen has **twelve** chicks.
Can you count them?

1 2 3 4 5 6 7 8 9 10 11 **12** 13

$$11 + 1 = 12$$
$$10 + 2 = 12$$
$$9 + 3 = 12$$
$$8 + 4 = 12$$
$$7 + 5 = 12$$
$$6 + 6 = 12$$

---

twentieth   There are twenty people standing in line. Margaret is the last person in the line. She is number twenty in the line. Margaret is the **twentieth** person standing in line.

---

twenty   Ten and ten make **twenty**.
$$10 + 10 = 20$$

Can you count to twenty?

1 2 3 4 5 6 7 8 9 10
11 12 13 14 15 16 17 18 19 **20**

These numbers answer the question, "How many are there?"

21	twenty-one
22	twenty-two
23	twenty-three
24	twenty-four
25	twenty-five
26	twenty-six
27	twenty-seven
28	twenty-eight
29	twenty-nine
30	thirty

There are twenty-eight cars in a row.

These numbers answer the question, "Which one is it in the row?"

21st	twenty-first
22nd	twenty-second
23rd	twenty-third
24th	twenty-fourth
25th	twenty-fifth
26th	twenty-sixth
27th	twenty-seventh
28th	twenty-eighth
29th	twenty-ninth
30th	thirtieth

My car is the twenty-fifth car in that row of cars.

twice I caught the ball **twice.**
I caught the ball **two times.**

John has **twice** as much candy as Peter.
John has **two times** as much candy as Peter. John has four pieces of candy. Peter has only two pieces of candy.

---

twig A **twig** is a very small branch.

We stuck sausages on twigs, and cooked them over the fire.

---

twin Patty is a **twin.** Stella is Patty's twin sister. Patty and Stella were born on the same day. Patty and Stella are twins. Patty and Stella look alike. They wear the same kind of clothes.

Not all twins look alike. Wilber and Alice are twins. They do not look alike.

---

twinkle The stars **twinkle** at night.
The stars **sparkle** at night.

Twinkle, twinkle little star,
How I wonder what you are;
Up above the world so high,
Like a diamond in the sky.

---

twirl Did you notice the dancer **twirl** rapidly on her toes? She spun around and around. She whirled fast.

---

twist John will **twist** the kite string around his fingers.
John will **wind** the kite string around his fingers.

two   There are **two** eggs in the nest.   Can you count them?

one **two** three
  1   **2**   3

---

tying   Mother is **tying** the string around the package.   I will help Mother tie up the package.

---

typewriter

A **typewriter** is a machine for making letters and numbers on paper.

This is the twenty-first letter of the alphabet.

ABCDEFGHIJKLMNOPQRST**U**VWXYZ

abcdefghijklmnopqrst**u**vwxyz

ugly   Susan is wearing an **ugly mask.**

Susan is wearing a **mask which is not pretty to look at.**

Sometimes baby is **ugly** for a little while after she wakes up from her nap.

Sometimes baby is **angry and mean** for a little while after she wakes up from her nap.

---

umbrella

I carry an **umbrella** to keep the rain off me. When it is raining I open my umbrella, and I hold it over my head.

> When I see a cloudy sky—
> Especially in spring,
> To keep myself so very dry
> My umbrella do I bring.

---

uncle   Your father's brother is your **uncle.** Your mother's brother is your **uncle,** too. Your aunt's husband is also your **uncle.**

---

under   There is a lamp on the table. There is a dog **under** the table.

> I have a worry—so big a care!
> I've lost my dog, and don't know where;
> Is he under the table? behind the chair?
> I hope, I hope I'll find him there!

U u

underneath   We found the cat **underneath** the bed.
We found the cat **under** the bed.

---

understand   I do not **understand** what the teacher is saying.
I do not **know** what the teacher is saying. What do her words mean? What is she trying to say to us?

Jane **does not understand how to** add.
Jane **cannot** add. She does not know how to add numbers.

Andrew **understood** how the radio works, and he explained it to me.

---

underwear   **Underwear** is the clothes we wear under those clothes which everybody sees. Underwear is sometimes called underclothes.

---

undress   Mother will **undress Baby** for a bath.
Mother will **take off Baby's clothes** for a bath.

---

unfold   Mother will **unfold** the sheet to put it on the bed.
Mother will **open out** the sheet to put it on the bed. The sheet on the chair is **folded**.

unhappy   Richard was **unhappy** because he could not go to the football game.

Richard was **sad** because he could not go to the football game.

---

uniform   The army captain is wearing a **uniform.** He is wearing an army captain's uniform. All army captains wear the same kind of clothes.

The sailors are wearing **uniforms.**
The sailors are wearing **the same kind of clothes.**

United Nations   The **United Nations** is a group of many countries. These countries work together to help stop wars and to help each other.

The United Nations works very hard to make the world a safe and happy place to live in. The main office of the United Nations is in New York City.

United States   The **United States** is a country in North America. There are fifty states in the United States. The citizens of the United States are called Americans.

---

unkind   The bad boy was **unkind** to his dog.
The bad boy was **cruel** to his dog.   He hurt his dog.

---

unknown   The man's name was **unknown**.
The man's name was **not known**.   Tell us his name.

---

unless   You do not have to come to the park **unless you** want to.
You do not have to come to the park **if you do not** want to.

---

unlock   Father will **unlock** the door with a key.
Father will **open the lock of** the door with a key.

---

untie   Mother tied string around a package.   She mailed the package to Cora.
Cora will **untie** the package to see what is inside.
Cora will **take the string from around** the package to see what is inside.

until   James will stay in his room **until** he finishes cleaning it.
James will stay in his room **up to the time when** he finishes cleaning it.

---

unusual   The autumn snow is **unusual.** It seldom snows in fall.

---

up   The bird flew **up.**
The bird flew **to a higher place.**

We stood **up** when the teacher came into the room.
We stood **on our feet** when the teacher came into the room.

The time for playing is **up.**
The time for playing is **at an end.**

The farmer gets **up** early in the morning.
The farmer gets **out of bed** early in the morning.

The farmer pulled the weeds **up.**
The farmer pulled the weeds **out of the ground.**

The spring flowers will soon be **up.**
The spring flowers will soon be **above the ground.**

Eat your food **up.**
Eat your food **until you are finished.**

Bill went **up** the hill.
Bill went **to the top of** the hill.

Alice walked **up** the street.
Alice walked **along** the street.

---

upon   Ma set the dish **upon** the table. She put it on the table.

---

upper   The **upper** part of anything is the higher part. My head is in the upper part of my body. My feet are in the lower part of my body.

upset

Did you see the cat **upset** the vase of flowers?

Did you see the cat **tip over** the vase of flowers?

Mother was **upset** when Baby fell out of bed.

Mother was **worried** when Baby fell out of bed. She was afraid that Baby got hurt.

---

upstairs My bedroom is on the second floor of our house. I sleep **upstairs.**

I go **upstairs** to my bedroom.

I go **up the stairs** to my bedroom.

---

upward The smoke floated **upward.**

The smoke floated **to a higher place.**

---

us Us means myself and somebody else. My two brothers and I were playing outside. Mother called **us.** She wanted **us** to eat dinner. She gave delicious food to **us.**

The three of us ate all our meal. We enjoyed our dinner very much. Mom is a good cook.

---

use We have no **use** for this broken glass.

We have no **need** for this broken glass.

There is no **use** in crying over spilt milk. It won't do you any good. You can't drink that milk anymore.

use   I **use** my legs for walking. I make my legs work when I want to walk. I **use** my eyes for seeing things. I **use** my arms for throwing a ball.

I **use a spoon** to eat my soup.
I **put a spoon to work** to eat my soup. The spoon helps me to eat my soup.

I **used** my knife to cut my meat.

Mary **used to** go to that school. She went to that school for eight years. Now she goes to another school.

Grandfather **is used** to getting up early. He gets up early every morning. It does not bother Grandfather to get up early.

The paint is all **used up.** There is no more paint left.

Father bought a **used car.**
Father bought a **car which was not new.** The car belonged to someone else.

---

useful   A car is very **useful.**

A car is very **helpful.** Father travels to work in a car. Mother often goes shopping in a car. We go to see Grandfather and Grandmother in a car. Our car helps us to go to many places.

---

usher   An **usher** is a person who shows people to a seat. The usher in church showed me to a seat.

---

usual   We will eat breakfast at the **usual** time.

We will eat breakfast at the **same time.** The usual time for our breakfast is eight o'clock in the morning. Every morning we eat breakfast at eight o'clock.

usually **Usually** I come home from school at three o'clock.
    Most of the time I come home from school at three o'clock. Three o'clock is the usual time when I return from school.

---

utmost Pluto is the **utmost** planet which travels around our sun.
    Pluto is the **farthest** planet which travels around our sun.

    I had the **utmost** sadness when Grandmother died.
    I had the **greatest** sadness when Grandmother died.

---

utter Don't **utter** a word.
   Don't **say** a word.

---

utterly The house was **utterly** destroyed by fire.
    The house was **completely** destroyed by fire.

This is the twenty-second letter of the alphabet.

ABCDEFGHIJKLMNOPQRSTUVWXYZ

abcdefghijklmnopqrstuvwxyz

vacation   A child's **vacation** is the time he does not go to school. Ralph said, "My summer vacation begins in June and it ends in September."

A grown-up's **vacation** is the time that he does not work. When my daddy gets his vacation, we are going on a trip to Mexico.

---

vacuum cleaner   A **vacuum cleaner** is a machine for cleaning carpets, curtains, floors, and other things.

My dear mother, have you seen her,
Working with her vacuum cleaner;
Cleaning curtains, rugs, and walls,
Upstairs, downstairs, rooms and halls?

---

valentine   A **valentine** is a card, a letter, or a small gift which is given to somebody on Saint Valentine's Day. Saint Valentine's Day is on February 14.

By giving people valentines, we tell them that we love them, or that we are glad to be their friend.

---

valley   A **valley** is the low land between hills. A river went through the valley.

valuable My mother's diamond ring is **valuable**.
My mother's diamond ring is **worth much money**.

---

value What is the **value** of your car?
What is the **price** of your car? How much does your car cost? Can you tell me what your car is worth? The value of my car is two thousand dollars.

---

van A **van** is a large covered truck. A van is usually used for carrying furniture. A moving van carried our furniture to our new house.

---

vanish We saw the boy **vanish** into the forest. We saw him go out of our sight among the many trees and bushes. He disappeared from our view into the woods.

---

vase Mother put the flowers in a **vase**.

In the vase of flowers, gay and bright,
With cheerful colors to be seen,
The blossoms make a pretty sight
Of orange, yellow, red and green.

---

veal **Veal** is meat from a calf. Mother sometimes cooks veal for supper.

V v

vegetable A **vegetable** is a plant that is used for food. Peas, corn, lettuce, spinach, and beets are vegetables. Can you name some more vegetables?

LETTUCE
BEETS
CARROTS
PEAS CORN

---

velvet **Velvet** is a thick, soft cloth. My mother has a dress made of silk velvet.

---

verse A **verse** is a group of lines that go together in a poem or song. Can you sing the first verse of "The Star-Spangled Banner"?

---

very Betty **is very happy** because she is having a birthday party. Betty **has much happiness** because she is having a birthday party. Betty's brother is happy because he will have ice cream and cake at the party. Betty is **very** happy because she will get birthday presents, too.

The water in this lake is deep. But the water in the ocean is **very** deep.

---

vest A **vest** is like a jacket without a collar and without sleeves. Paul is wearing a vest. He will put on his suit coat over his vest.

I have a vest,
Which I like best,
To wear to school,
When it is cool.

view We stood at the top of the hill and we looked at the beautiful **view.**

We stood at the top of the hill and we looked at the beautiful **scene.** What we saw was beautiful. We saw the hills, the valleys, and the towns.

We were able to **view** our town from the top of the hill.
We were able to **see** our town from the top of the hill.

---

village A **village** is a small town.

---

vine A plant that grows along the ground is a **vine.** Some vines can climb. Climbing vines fasten themselves onto a wall, a tree, or some other thing, and then they grow upward. Cucumber vines crawl. Morning-glory vines climb.

---

vinegar **Vinegar** is a sour liquid. It can be made from apple juice and grape juice. My mother sometimes puts vinegar and oil on our lettuce and tomato salad.

---

violent The **violent** wind tore the roof off our garage. The strong and rough wind caused much harm to our garage. The violent wind, however, did not destroy our house.

V v

violet  A **violet** is a small plant with purple, blue, yellow, or white flowers.

---

violin Harry is making music on his **violin**. He likes to play his violin.

> When Harry plays his violin,
> Up and down on strings, so thin,
> He always gives us such a treat,
> Making music that's so sweet!

---

visit Grandmother will **visit** us tomorrow.

Grandmother will **come to see** us tomorrow. She will see us and stay with us awhile. Grandmother will be our guest.

---

visitor A **visitor** is a person who comes for a visit. A visitor is a guest.

---

visual **Visual** means *having to do with seeing or sight.* This book is called the *Visual Dictionary* because there are many colored pictures in it. Seeing these pictures helps us to learn words.

---

voice My **voice** is the sound I make with my mouth, with my tongue, and with my throat. Fred's voice was loud and clear. He spoke well.

vote   Our school class will choose its president.

Each pupil **has a vote** for the class president.

Each pupil **can say who he wants** for the class president. There are thirty pupils in the class. Martin received twenty votes. Paul received ten votes. Martin is the class president because he received more votes than Paul.

Whom did you **vote** for?   I **voted** for Martin. Nineteen other pupils voted for Martin, too.

---

voter   A **voter** is a person who votes.

---

voyage   Father will go on a long **voyage**.

Father will go on a long **trip across the sea**. He will travel on a big boat.

This is the twenty-third letter of the alphabet.

ABCDEFGHIJKLMNOPQRSTUV**W**XYZ

abcdefghijklmnopqrstuv**w**xyz

wade Children like to **wade** in the water.
Children like to **walk along** in the water.

---

wag Watch my dog **wag his tail.**
Watch my dog **move his tail from side to side.** My dog is happy.

---

wages Paul delivered newspapers for **a wage.**
Paul delivered newspapers for **pay.** Paul earned fifteen dollars ($15.00) a week for delivering the newspapers to homes.

Father's **wages** are one hundred dollars a week.
Father's **pay** is one hundred dollars a week. Each week Father earns $100.00.

---

wagon

My Uncle Charles has a big **wagon** on his farm. There are four wheels on this wagon. He fills the wagon with hay. A horse pulls the wagon.

I sometimes pull my friend Richard in my **wagon.**

---

waist Your **waist** is the middle part of your body. Rudolf put a belt around his waist.

wait   The train was late, so we had a long **wait** at the station until it arrived.

The train was late, so we had a long **time to stay** at the station until it arrived.

Wait here until Mother comes back.

Stay here until Mother comes back. Do not go away until she returns. Mother will return from the store in a little while.

Bob **waited** for Henry in front of the store.

Bob **stayed and looked** for Henry in front of the store.

There was a crowd **waiting** for the bus to come.

Mother **waited on** us at dinner.

Mother **served** us at dinner. She brought us the food, and she took away the dirty dishes.

---

waiter   A **waiter** is a man who serves food at table. He puts food on the table for us to eat. The waiter also takes away the dirty dishes.

---

wake   I **wake** when the alarm clock rings.

I **stop sleeping** when the alarm clock rings.

Yesterday morning the barking dog **woke me**.

Yesterday morning the barking dog **made me stop sleeping**.

---

walk   We went for a **walk** in the country.

We went for a **trip on foot** in the country.

To **walk** means to *take one step after another with your feet.*

Harold likes to go **walking** in the country. Yesterday he **walked** so much that his feet hurt.

wall   One of the sides of a room is called a **wall.**   The sides of a building are also called **walls.**   On the wall of my bedroom there is a picture of a horse.

There is a **stone wall** around our house.
There is a **fence made out of stone** around our house.

---

wallet   A **wallet** is a small case which is used to carry money or important things.

Wallets usually fold shut like a book.   They are usually made of leather or plastic.   Father carries his wallet in his pocket.

---

wallpaper   The man covered the walls of my bedroom with **wallpaper.**   He pasted pretty paper on the walls.

---

walnut    A **walnut** is a large nut with a rough shell.   Walnuts are good to eat.   They grow on walnut trees.   Some furniture is made from the wood of walnut trees.

---

walrus   A **walrus** is a large animal which looks like a seal. **Walruses** have long tusks.   They live near the sea where the weather is cold.

wander Clement likes to **wander** through the woods.
Clement likes to **walk slowly** through the woods. He enjoys looking at the plants and animals.

---

want I **want** a bicycle for Christmas.
I **would like to have** a bicycle for Christmas.

I **want** a new coat.
I **need** a new coat. My old coat has a big tear in it.

Jerry **wanted** to go to the movies.

Hilda **wants** us to come to her birthday party.

---

war A **war** is a fight between countries. Soldiers and sailors fight in a war. Nobody likes war. Everybody wants peace.

---

wares **Wares** are things for sale.

Simple Simon met a pieman
  Going to the fair;
Said Simple Simon to the pieman,
  "Let me taste your ware."

---

warm The boys sat around the fire to get **warm**. They will not sit too close to the fire because they will get hot.

Spring is **warm**. Summer is **warmer**. Winter is cold.

When I am **warm** I like to drink a cool glass of lemonade.

I wear a **warm coat** in the winter.
I wear a **coat that keeps me warm** in the winter.

616

warn   Did anybody ever **warn you about** playing with fire?

Did anybody ever **tell you about the danger of** playing with fire?   You can hurt yourself with fire.

---

was   Yesterday I **was** sick, but today I am well.

Frank **was** sleepy last night, but today he is very much awake. He is wide awake.

---

wash   I **wash my hands** before I eat my meals.

I **clean my hands with water** before I eat my meals.   I use soap, too, when I wash.

---

washing machine   A **washing machine** is a machine for washing clothes.

Washington   George **Washington** was the first president of the United States of America.

Washington, D.C., is the name of a big city in the United States. It is where the President lives.

Washington is also the name of a state in the United States of America.

---

washtub   A **washtub** is a tub to wash clothes in.

wasn't I **wasn't** hungry after I ate dinner.
I **was not** hungry after I ate dinner.

---

wasp A **wasp** is an insect. It is something like a bee. Wasps can sting you. A wasp's sting can hurt you very much.

---

waste **Waste** is anything that is left over and has to be thrown away. Garbage is waste.

Daniel put **wastepaper** into the wastepaper basket.
Daniel put **paper that has been used** into the wastepaper basket.

We must not **waste food.**
We must not **use food so that a part of it will have to be thrown away.**

---

watch A **watch** is a small clock. Daddy has a pocket **watch.** He keeps his watch in a small pocket. Mother has a wrist **watch.** She wears her watch on a strap around her wrist.

Watch me ride my bicycle.
Look at me ride my bicycle.

Watch out that you don't trip on that rock.
Be careful that you don't trip on that rock.

I **watched** for Mother coming out of the store.
I **looked** for Mother coming out of the store. She was **watching** for me, too.

---

watchful Our dog is **watchful.** He hears very well. Our dog knows when someone is coming. He barks at almost any noise during the night.

water   **Water** is a liquid. We drink water. We wash in water. Oceans, rivers, and lakes are filled with water.

Father is going to **water** the garden.
Father is going to **put water on** the garden.

---

water lily   A **water lily** is a plant that grows in the water. It has white, yellow, or pink flowers. The green leaves of water lilies are large and flat. They float on the water.

---

watermelon   A **watermelon** is a big melon filled with sweet juice. Watermelons are red or pink inside. They have a hard green rind on the outside. Watermelons grow on a vine. The vine is on the ground.

---

wave   A **wave** is made by the rising and falling of water. The small boat bounced up and down on the waves.

Mother has **waves** in her hair.
Mother has **curves** in her hair. Her hair is not straight. The curls in Mother's hair make waves.

I **wave** to my father.
I **move my hand up and down** to my father. I waved good-by to him.

wax Wax is made by bees. Bees use their wax to make their honeycomb. Bees' wax is light yellow. Wax is hard when it is cold. It is soft when it is warm. Some candles are made from bees' wax.

Not all wax is made by bees.

Mother will **wax** the floor.
Mother will **put wax on** the floor. The wax will make the floor shine.

---

way Show me the **way** to your house.
Show me the **road** to your house.

The boys went **that way.**
The boys went **in that direction.** They went toward the lake.

It is a long **way** to Grandmother's house.
It is a long **distance** to Grandmother's house. We must travel far to see Grandmother.

Do you know **of a way** to fix my bicycle?
Do you know **how** to fix my bicycle?

I wanted to go to the beach, but I didn't get **my way.**
I wanted to go to the beach, but I didn't get **what I wanted.** We did not go to the beach.

Mother used to wear her hair in one **way.** Now she wears her hair in another way.

---

we When I talk about myself and other people, I use the word **we.** Nick and I will go to the movies today. **We** will go at two o'clock. You and I will eat supper together. **We** will eat at Aunt Ruth's house.

Roberta and I are going to visit Aunt Martha. We will eat dinner there. She will feed us a good meal.

weak   Baby is **too weak** to lift the chair.
Baby is **not strong enough** to lift the chair.

George was **weak** after his sickness.
George was **not strong** after his sickness.

---

wealthy   Mr. Jones is **wealthy**.
Mr. Jones is **rich**. He has a lot of money.

---

wear   Irene is going to **wear** her new dress at the party.
Irene is going to **have on** her new dress at the party.

Today Father is **wearing** a blue shirt.

Yesterday Father **wore** a white shirt.

Sandra has **worn** her gloves every day for a whole week. It has been very cold outside.

Henry usually **wears out** his shoes very quickly. It is not long before he must buy a new pair of shoes. Soon his shoes become so damaged and ragged that they must be thrown away.

---

weary   When Dad comes home from work, he is **weary**.
When Dad comes home from work, he is **tired**. He wants to rest.

---

weather   The **weather** is cold today.
The **air outside** is cold today.

Yesterday we had bad **weather**. It was rainy and cold. The wind was blowing, too.

Today we have good **weather**. The sun is shining and the sky is clear. The air is warm and pleasant.

weave

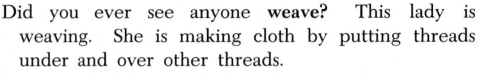

Did you ever see anyone **weave?** This lady is weaving. She is making cloth by putting threads under and over other threads.

Some people **weave** rugs with strips of cloth.

Yesterday the children **wove** baskets with palm leaves.

---

weaver　A **weaver** is a person who makes cloth, rugs, and other things by weaving.

---

web　The spider is on his **web.** If an insect goes into the spider's web, it will not be able to get free. The spider gets his food by catching other insects in his web.

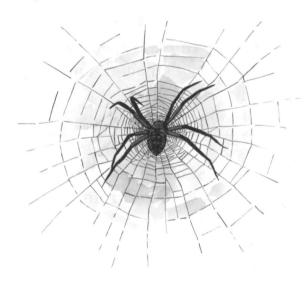

---

webbed　The feet of a duck **are webbed.**

The feet of a duck **have toes fastened together with a web of skin.** Webbed feet help ducks to swim.

wed Father and Mother were **wed** a long time ago.
Father and Mother were **married** a long time ago.

Wednesday **Wednesday** is the fourth day of the week. It is the day after Tuesday.

Sunday	Monday	Tuesday	**Wednesday**	Thursday	Friday	Saturday
first	second	third	fourth	fifth	sixth	seventh
1st	2nd	3rd	4th	5th	6th	7th

---

wee We have a **wee** kitten at our house.
We have a **very small** kitten at our house.

---

weed A **weed** is a plant that grows where it is not wanted. The vegetables in the garden will not grow well if there are too many weeds near them.

In the summer we help Daddy **weed** his vegetable garden.
In the summer we help Daddy **pull the weeds out of** his vegetable garden.

---

week A **week** is made up of seven days. The first day of the week is Sunday. The days of the week are Sunday, Monday, Tuesday, Wednesday, Thursday, Friday, and Saturday.

---

weep When Baby fell down, she started to **weep.**
When Baby fell down, she started to **cry.**

weigh   Kenneth will **weigh himself** on the scale.
Kenneth will **find out how heavy he is** on the scale.

The bag of potatoes **weighs ten pounds.**
The bag of potatoes **is ten pounds heavy.**

---

weight   A person's **weight** is how heavy he is. We measure a person's weight in pounds. Mother said, "Baby's weight is fifteen pounds."

Do you know **the weight of that turkey?**
Do you know **how much that turkey weighs?**

---

welcome   Mother told my friend Vernon, "You are always **welcome** here. We are always happy to have you come and see us."

When someone says *thank you* to you, you say, "**You are welcome.**"

When Jeff thanked Sally for her gift, she said, "You are welcome."

---

well   When we are in the country, we get water from a **well.**
When we are in the country, we get water from a **deep hole in the ground.**

Grandfather is **well.**
Grandfather is **in good health.** He is not sick.

Stewart plays the piano **well.** He is good at playing the piano.

Sometimes people say **well** when they are surprised.

Grandmother said, "Well, well, how nice it is that you have come to visit me!"

we'll   We'll means *we shall* or *we will*.   We'll play a baseball game tomorrow.

---

went   Yesterday James **went** from school to his house at three o'clock.

Yesterday James **moved** from school to his house at three o'clock.   Today he will go home at two o'clock.

The children **went** home after the party.
The children **left for** home after the party.

The car **went** well when there was gasoline in it.
The car **ran** well when there was gasoline in it.

The bus **went** down my street last year.   This year the bus goes down another street.

Do you remember how that song **went?**   I would like to know how that song goes, so that I can sing it.

---

wept   Janice **wept** when she hurt her finger.
Janice **cried** when she hurt her finger.   Mother said, "Don't weep, dear, your finger will be well soon."

---

were   Yesterday we **were** in a train.   Today we are in an airplane. **Were** you ever in a train?   Are you happy that you are in an airplane with us?

---

we're   **We're** going to the movies later.
We are going to the movies later.

---

west   If you look toward the sun as it goes down in the evening, you will be looking **west.**   The sun rises in the east, and it sets in the west.

wet   To **wet** something means to *put a liquid on it.*

      Jack **wets** his hair with water when he combs it. Mother wets bread with milk when she makes bread pudding.

      The grass is **wet with rain.**
      The grass is **covered with rain.**

      The paint is still **wet.**
      The paint is still **not dry.**

---

wetness   When I held Daddy's coat, I felt a **wetness in it.**
      When I held Daddy's coat, I felt **that it was wet.** It was raining outside.

---

whale   A **whale** is an animal that lives in the sea. A whale looks like a fish, but it is not a fish. The whale is the biggest animal in the world.

---

what   **What** is a word which is used to ask questions?
      What is your name? My name is Alice. What is that noise? That noise is from an airplane. What are you doing? I am writing a letter. What makes the kite go up in the sky? The wind makes the kite go up into the sky.

---

whatever   He may have **whatever book** he wants.
      He may have **any one of the books** he wants.

      Eat **whatever** you want.
      Eat **anything that** you want.

what's   **What's** that noise I hear?
          What is that noise I hear?

---

wheat    **Wheat** is a grain from which flour is made. Bread, cereals, and many other foods are made from wheat. Farmers grow wheat.

---

wheel   A **wheel** is round.

This trailer has two wheels. A wheelbarrow has one wheel.

---

wheelbarrow   A **wheelbarrow** has two legs and one wheel. My father is pushing some bricks in the wheelbarrow.

---

when   Do you know **when** Donald will come home?
       Do you know **at what time** Donald will come home?

---

whenever   Some children eat **whenever** they are hungry.
          Some children eat **at any time that** they are hungry.

Ww

where   **Where** did you put your hat?
In what place did you put your hat?

Where are you going?
To what place are you going?

Where did you get that coat?
From what place did you get that coat?

---

wherever   My dog follows me **wherever** I go.
My dog follows me **to any place that** I go.

---

whether   **Whether** it rains or snows, I will still visit you.
No matter if it rains or snows, I will still visit you.

I do not know **whether** Paul is home or not.
I do not know **if** Paul is home or not.

I do not know **whether** to go to the movies.   Shall I go to the movies, or shall I stay home?

---

which   **Which boy** owns this ball?   **What one of the boys** owns this ball?   There are five boys.   Who owns the ball?

There are three books on the table.   **Which** one is yours?

Sally is wearing a coat **which** I like.
Sally is wearing a coat **that** I like.

---

while   Henry waited a **while** for the school doors to open.
Henry waited a **time** for the school doors to open.

Anita sang **while** she washed the dishes.
Anita sang **during the time that** she washed the dishes.

whip   The man driving the carriage has a whip in his hand.

If he wants the horses to go faster, he will **whip the horses lightly.**

If he wants the horses to go faster, he will **hit the horses lightly with a whip.**

Geraldine **whipped** the cream in a bowl to make it thick and fluffy.

Geraldine **beat** the cream in a bowl to make it thick and fluffy.

I like **whipped** cream on my ice cream.

---

whirl   The leaves on the ground **whirl** in the wind.

The leaves on the ground **turn round and round** in the wind.

---

whisker   A **whisker** is a hair that grows on the face of a man or an animal.

My kitten has **whiskers.**

My kitten has **long stiff hairs that stick out from the sides of his mouth.**

My grandfather has **whiskers.**

My grandfather has **hair growing on his cheeks, on his upper lip, and on his chin.**

Father shaves off his **whiskers** in the morning.

whisper   Baby likes to **whisper** in my ear.
Baby likes to **talk in a low voice** in my ear.

---

whistle  These are **whistles**. A whistle makes a noise when you blow through it.

Listen to Eugene **whistle**.
Listen to Eugene **make the sound of a whistle with his mouth**. He can whistle a tune.

---

white   **White** is the color of snow. This snowman is white.

---

who   **Who** drew this very beautiful picture?
What person drew this very beautiful picture? Was it you, William?

The man **who** is painting the house is my father.
The man **that** is painting the house is my father.

---

whole   This is a **whole** cake.   This is **not a whole** cake.
This is **all of a** cake.   This is **part of a** cake.

whom   To **whom** shall I give this book?
To **what person** shall I give this book?

The man **whom** you saw in the car is my uncle.
The man **that** you saw in the car is my uncle.

---

whose   **Whose** coat is this.
Which person's coat is this? To **whom** does it belong. Is it yours, Mary?

---

why   Do you know **why** the television does not work?
Do you know **the reason that** the television does not work?

Why were you late for school?
For what reason were you late for school?

---

wicked   **Wicked** people do bad things. The wicked man stole money from a poor old lady. When he came home he beat his dog. The man does not need money. His dog is a good dog. The man did wicked things.

---

wide   Raymond is looking out the **wide** window. The window is not narrow.

wife   A **wife** is a married woman. My mother is my father's wife. A husband is a married man. My father is my mother's husband. Father and Mother are husband and wife. John said that when he is a grown-up, he will marry and have a wife.

---

wig   A **wig** is a covering of hair which is worn on the head. The man who has little hair is putting on a **wig**.

> Gregory Griggs, Gregory Griggs,
> Had twenty-seven different wigs.
> He wore them up, he wore them down,
> To please the people in the town;
> He wore them east, he wore them west,
> But he could never tell which he loved best.

---

wigwam

A **wigwam** is a hut. It is made with poles which are covered with bark from a tree. Some wigwams are covered with the skins of animals. Some Indians in North America live in wigwams.

---

wild   **Wild** animals live in the forest and fields. They are not tame. Wild animals are afraid of people. They will run or fly away when you go near them. Some wild animals will hurt you if you get too close to them.

When we went to the zoo, Mother said, "Don't get too close to that tiger. He is **wild**. He will hurt you."

Our dog is tame. He is not wild.

will   I **will** ride my bicycle to the park.
I **am going to** ride my bicycle to the park.

Randolph **will** bring me a sandwich.
Randolph **is going to** bring me a sandwich.

---

willing   Sebastian is **willing** to help us clean the yard.
Sebastian is **ready** to help us clean the yard. He is pleased
to work with us.

---

willow   There is a **willow** tree in our yard. It has thin leaves.

The branches of our willow tree bend
toward the ground.

Our kind of willow is called a weeping
willow. Its branches bow down as if
they are sad.

---

win   To **win** you must do better than anyone else who is trying to
do the same thing.

The boys are running a race to the fence. Who will **win** the
race? Who do you think will get to the fence first?

Ww

wind Wind is air that is moving. The wind blew off Father's hat.

The south wind brings wet weather,
The north wind wet and cold together;
The west wind always brings rain,
The east wind blows it back again.

wind

Harold will **wind his kite string** into a ball. Harold will **wrap his kite string around and around** into a ball.

Father **winds** the alarm clock every night. He turns part of the clock around and around so that the clock will keep running.

I like **winding** the clock.

Yesterday I **wound** the clock for my father.

windmill A **windmill** is a machine which is run by the wind. Most windmills are used for pumping water.

This is the kind of **windmill** that we find in Holland.

window   A **window** is an opening in a wall.   Air, light, and sunshine can come in through a window.   We must keep the windows closed in cold weather.   Nancy is looking out the window.

window sill   A **window sill** is a piece of wood across the bottom of a window. Some window sills are made of stone.   Nancy has a flower pot on her window sill.

windy   Saturday was a **windy day.**
Saturday was a **day with much wind.**

wing   A **wing** is part of an animal that flies.   Wings help animals to fly.   The butterfly has two wings.   The bird has two wings. The butterfly and bird must flap their wings to fly.

This airplane also has two wings.   This airplane has yellow wings.   Airplanes do not flap their wings.

wink   The bright light made me **wink.**
The bright light made me **open and shut my eyes quickly.**

winter   Winter is one of the four seasons of the year. The other three seasons are spring, summer, and autumn. Winter is the coldest season of the year.

---

wipe   When I wash my face, I **wipe** it with a towel. I make my face dry by rubbing it with a towel.

Carol **wiped** the jelly from the table. She cleaned the jelly off the table by rubbing it away.

---

wire   A **wire** is a thread of metal. Electricity goes through wires for telephones, for electric lights, and for other things.

These are telephone **wires.**

This is a **wire** fence.

---

wise   My father is very **wise.**
My father is very **smart.**

---

wish   What is **your wish?**
What is **it that you want?**

Do you **wish** to go to the lake?
Do you **want** to go to the lake? Would you like to go swimming in the lake?

I **wish you** a happy birthday.
I **hope you have** a happy birthday.

wishes Betty made three **wishes.** She wanted three things.

---

witch A **witch** is an ugly old woman. In fairy tales, witches ride on brooms. Witches are not real.

---

with I like to take a walk **with** Grandfather. He and I sometimes go walking together.

Harry is **with** his dog.
Harry is **by the side of** his dog.

Jane has a book **with** many pictures.
Jane has a book **having** many pictures.

Do you want pepper **with** your soup?
Do you want pepper **added to** your soup?

I will cut my meat **with** a knife.
I will cut my meat **using** a knife.

---

within Paul is hiding **within** the garage.
Paul is hiding **inside of** the garage.

I will be at school **within** an hour.
I will be at school **in not more than** an hour.

---

without Father left for work **without a** hat.
Father left for work **with no** hat. He forgot to take his hat.

---

woke I **woke** at eight o'clock this morning.
I **stopped sleeping** at eight o'clock this morning. I will wake at seven o'clock tomorrow.

wolf A **wolf** is a wild animal. It looks something like a big dog.

---

wolves We saw some **wolves** at the zoo. We saw a baby wolf there.

---

woman My mother is a **woman.** My father is a man. A girl will grow up to be a woman.

---

women There are two **women** in our kitchen. One woman is my mother. The other woman is my Aunt Harriet.

---

won Yesterday the boys ran a race to the fence. Who **won** the race? Who got to the fence first. Richard won the race. He got to the fence before the other boys. Albert wanted to win the race, but he got to the fence last.

---

wonder I **wonder** who could be knocking at the door.
I **ask myself** who could be knocking at the door. Could it be the mailman?

No wonder the car won't run; there is no gasoline in the tank.

It is not a surprise that the car won't run; there is no gasoline in the tank.

wonderful Our trip to the zoo was **wonderful.**
Our trip to the zoo was **full of many surprising and pleasant things.**

---

won't **I won't** eat too much pie.
I will not eat too much pie.

---

wood **Wood** is the part of a tree under the bark. It is the inside part of the tree. Furniture is made of wood. Some houses are made of wood. Can you name some other things that are made of wood?

---

woodcutter A **woodcutter** is a person who cuts down trees and chops up wood.

---

wooden Some houses are **wooden;** some are made of brick.
Some houses are **made of wood;** some are made of brick.

---

woodpecker

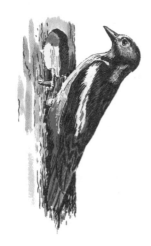

A **woodpecker** is a bird that pecks holes in the bark of trees.

Woodpeckers peck holes to get the insects that live under the bark.

A flicker is a kind of woodpecker.

woods   **Woods** is a place where many trees grow close together.

wool   **Wool** is the soft and curly hair that grows on sheep. The sheep's wool is cut off and made into yarn, cloth, and clothes.

woolen   I have a **woolen sweater.**
I have a **sweater made of wool.**

word   A **word** is a group of letters that gives us an idea. *C* and *A* and *T* are letters that give us a word when they are put together. They spell *cat.* I get an idea when I see the word *cat.* I think of a furry animal that says, "Meow, meow."

wore   Yesterday I **wore** my coat because it was cold outside.
Yesterday I **had on** my coat because it was cold outside. Today is warmer, so I shall wear my sweater.

work   Father's **work** is delivering mail to houses. He is a mailman.

Bill's **work** is to keep the yard clean.

Sometimes I help Mother do some of her **work.** I wash the dishes. I sweep the floor.

Stephen likes to **work.** Yesterday he **worked** all morning cutting the grass. On Saturdays, Stephen sometimes **works** with his dad in pulling the weeds from the garden. He enjoys **working.**

The painting is a beautiful **work** of art. Donald **worked** very hard, and he gave much time to paint that picture.

workbench   A **workbench** is a table at which a carpenter or mechanic works.   There are tools on the workbench.

Daddy has a workbench,
  On which are many tools:
A hammer, drill, and heavy wrench;
  Some nails, some screws, some rules.

---

worker   A **worker** is a person who works.   Daddy is a hard worker. He is very tired when he comes home from work.

---

workman   A **workman** is a man who works, especially one who works with his hands.

---

world   The **world** is the whole earth and the sky.   The astronauts went around the world several times in their spaceship.

---

worm   A **worm** is a small, thin animal that crawls on or through the ground.   Most worms have soft bodies and no legs.

When Edward goes fishing, he puts a worm on his fishing hook.   Fish like to eat worms.

worn Lois wears the same coat every day. She has **worn** it for a month.

My old shoes are **worn-out.**
My old shoes **have been used so much that they cannot be used anymore.** I must buy a new pair of shoes.

---

worry Frank does not have one **worry.** He has nothing to bother him. He is very happy. Norman has many **worries:** He broke his arm. His dog is sick. He lost his money.

Father is sick in bed.
  I **worry about** whether he will get well soon.
  I **am unhappy wondering** whether he will get well soon.

When Daddy was sick, Mother **worried,** too. She always **worries** whenever Daddy or I become ill. Mother will not stop **worrying** until we are better.

---

worse Father has been sick, but he is **worse** today.
Father has been sick, but he is **more sick** today.

My dog is bad, but your dog acts **worse.**
My dog is bad, but your dog acts **more badly.**

---

worship When we pray to God, we **worship** him.

---

worst Paul, Wilbur, and Hubert are sick. Paul has a bad cold. Wilbur is worse. He is sicker than Paul. Hubert is the **worst.** He is the sickest of the three boys.

worth Patricia bought ten cents **worth** of candy. The candy cost ten cents. She bought as much candy as ten cents could buy.

The book is **worth** reading.
The book is **good enough for** reading. It is an interesting story.

The toy is **worth** fifty cents. It takes fifty cents to buy the toy.

---

would Alice said that she **would** help Mother wash the dishes.
Alice said that she **wanted to** help Mother wash the dishes.

Benedict **would** go swimming every day if he could.
Benedict **is willing to** go swimming every day if he could.

In the summer, I **would** play baseball almost every day.
In the summer, I **used to** play baseball almost every day.

Would you close the window for me.
Please close the window for me.

I **would** buy that football if I had the money.

---

wouldn't Helen **wouldn't** eat her potatoes.
Helen **would not** eat her potatoes.

---

wound The soldier received a **wound** on his arm. He got a cut on his arm. Much blood came from his wound.

Peter was **wounded** by an arrow. Did you see the arrow **wound** him? It stuck into his leg.

---

wound Grandmother **wound** the yarn into a ball. She wrapped the yarn around and around until it made a ball. Did you ever see her wind the yarn into a ball?

Grandfather **wound** his watch. His watch would stop running if he did not wind it.

wove   Last year my mother **wove** a rug.   She made a rug by weaving strips of cloth.

---

wrap

To **wrap** means to *put a covering around.* Yesterday we wrapped Christmas presents. We put pretty colored paper around all the Christmas presents.

Put on your **wraps** before going outside in the cold.

Put on your **coat and hat** before going outside in the cold.

---

wreath   A **wreath** is a ring of leaves or flowers or other pretty things.   We have a Christmas wreath on our front door.

---

wreck   This is an airplane **wreck.**   The airplane did not land at the airport where it should have landed.

Did you see Father **wreck** my wagon when he drove over it with the car.   He destroyed my wagon by accident.

wren   A **wren** is a small bird. It has a thin bill and a short tail. Wrens have a sweet song. They sometimes build their nests in birdhouses which people make for them.

---

wrench    A **wrench** is a tool. Father used a wrench when he fixed the faucet in the sink. Father also uses wrenches when he fixes the motor in our car.

---

wring   To **wring** means to *twist and squeeze.* Mom **wrings out** the wet cloth. She twists and squeezes it between her hands to get the water out.

---

wrinkle   A **wrinkle** is a line made in something because it was folded. When you fold a piece of cloth and then open it up again, a line sometimes will be left where you have folded it.

Mother ironed my very pretty dress because it had many **wrinkles** in it.

The old lady has **wrinkles** in her face.
The old lady has **lines** in her face. When we become old we will get wrinkles in our face.

Do not **wrinkle** your dress.
Do not **make wrinkles in** your dress.

Baby **wrinkled** the pages of the book.

wrist   Your **wrist** is between your hand and your arm. You can turn your hand on your wrist. Father is wearing a watch around his wrist.

---

write   When you **write,** you make letters and words on paper. You can also write on a blackboard with chalk. Sometimes you write with a pen. Sometimes you write with a pencil. Can you write your name?

I am **writing** a letter to Grandmother.

Grandmother has **written** me a letter, too.

Fred **wrote** a story about a dog.

---

wrong   It is **wrong** to lie.

It is **bad** to lie. It is right to tell the truth.

This answer is **wrong.**	2
This answer is **not correct.**	+2
	3

This answer is correct.	2
	+2
	4

---

wrote   Yesterday I **wrote** a letter to Aunt Hilda. Today I will write a letter to Grandfather and Grandmother.

---

wrung   Yesterday I **wrung out** my towel, because it was so wet. I twisted and squeezed the towel between my hands to get the water out.

I do not have to **wring** out my towel today, for it is not very wet.

his is the twenty-fourth letter of the alphabet.

ABCDEFGHIJKLMNOPQRSTUVWXYZ

abcdefghijklmnopqrstuvwxyz

X x

Xmas   **Xmas** is a short way of writing Christmas. We saw a sign which said: *Xmas Trees for Sale*.

X rays

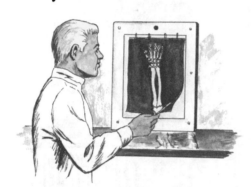

A doctor can take pictures of your bones with **X rays**. He uses an X-ray camera to take a picture of the inside of your body.

The doctor took an X-ray picture of my arm to see if any bones were broken.

Did you ever see an X-ray picture?

---

xylophone   Susan is playing music on a **xylophone.** She is making music by hitting the wooden bars with little hammers.

Did you ever see and hear a xylophone band? It makes pretty music.

This is the twenty-fifth letter of the alphabet.

ABCDEFGHIJKLMNOPQRSTUVWXYZ

abcdefghijklmnopqrstuvwxyz

Y y

yacht A **yacht** is a boat. People use yachts to have a good time. We went for a ride in my uncle's yacht. Some yachts are used for racing.

Some sailboats are called yachts.

---

yard The ground around our house is the **yard.** Grass, trees, and flowers grow in our yard.

Mother bought a **yard** of ribbon.
Mother bought **three feet** of ribbon.

A **yard** is also thirty-six inches.

---

yarn Wool is sometimes made into **yarn.**
Wool is sometimes made into **long threads.**
Cotton and silk are also made into yarn.
My mother is making me some stockings with wool yarn.

---

yawn When I am tired, I sometimes **yawn.**
When I am tired, I sometimes **open my mouth wide and take a long breath.**

year There are twelve months in a **year.** They are January, February, March, April, May, June, July, August, September, October, November, December. A year is the time it takes the earth to go around the sun.

---

yell I heard a **yell** come from the old house.
I heard a **loud cry** come from the old house.

Did you hear somebody **yell?**
Did you hear somebody **cry out with a strong, loud sound?**

Yesterday I **yelled** to you from across the street, but you did not hear me.

---

yellow **Yellow** is a color. Butter is yellow.
Some lemons are yellow, too.

---

yelp A **yelp** is a sharp cry or bark. When the dog gave a yelp, Bill came running.

When Bill heard the dog **yelp,** he knew his pet was hurt.
When Bill heard the dog **bark sharply,** he knew his pet was hurt.

---

yes Bridget asked Susan if she wanted to go to the playground. Susan said, "**Yes,** I do want to go to the playground. Let's go now."

---

yesterday **Yesterday** is the day before today. Today is Monday. Yesterday was Sunday.

Y y

yet   The train has not come **yet.**

The train has not come **up to now.** We are waiting for it.

The bells are ringing **yet.**
The bells are ringing **still.** You can hear them even now.

I don't know how to swim now, but I will learn **yet.**
I don't know how to swim now, but I will learn **at some time to come.**

I ran as fast as I could, **yet** I was late for school.
I ran as fast as I could, **still** I was late for school.

---

yolk   The **yolk** is the yellow part of an egg. My mother is frying two eggs. Can you see the yolks?

---

yonder   Look at the sunset **yonder.**
Look at the sunset **over there.**

---

you   Mother said, "Billy, are **you** ready to go to church? You must hurry, or we will be late."

The teacher said to the children, "I am going to give **you** a surprise. You all are going to see a movie this afternoon."

If **you** will go to bed early, **you** will get up early.
If **anyone** will go to bed early, **he or she** will get up early.

---

you'll   If you don't hurry, **you'll** be late.
If you don't hurry, **you will** be late.

young   Betty is **young.** She is eight years old.

My grandmother is old. She is eighty years old.

---

youngster   A **youngster** is a child or a young person. The youngsters in the park played many games. The old lady said, "I remember when I was a youngster."

---

your   Is this **your** hat? Does this hat belong to you?

Your nose, your toes, your hands are all parts of you.

---

you're   **You're** going to be late.
You are going to be late.

---

yours   That coat is **yours.**
That coat **belongs to you.**

---

yourself   Did you cut **yourself** with that sharp knife? Did you cut your hand with that knife? Let me help you put a bandage on your hand.

Mother said, "You **yourself,** Betsy, will cook dinner! I am so surprised. I didn't know that you could cook."

Did you walk home all **by yourself?**
Did you walk home all **alone?** Nobody came with you?

Y y

653

This is the twenty-sixth letter of the alphabet.

ABCDEFGHIJKLMNOPQRSTUVWXYZ

abcdefghijklmnopqrstuvwxyz

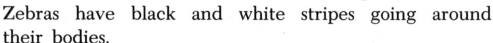

zebra  A **zebra** is a wild animal that looks something like a horse. Zebras have black and white stripes going around their bodies.

---

zero **Zero** is the number that comes before 1. This is how zero is written: **0**

0 1 2 3 4 5 6 7 8 9

When **zero** is by itself, it means none or nothing.

If there is a number in front of the zero, it tells us how many times we have "ten."

20 = 10 + 10.   The two before the zero means two tens.

30 = 10 + 10 + 10. The three before the zero means three tens.

120 = ?   How many tens are in one hundred and twenty?

When people say it is zero today, they mean that it is very cold outside.

---

zest The children ate their food with **zest**.
The children ate their food with **great joy**.

---

zinnia  A **zinnia** is a flower which has many small petals. Zinnias are of many bright colors. They last a long time.

Z z

zone   A **zone** is a special place.

The children waited for the bus in the **safety zone.**
The children waited for the bus in the **special place made
safe for them.**

---

zoo   A **zoo** is a park where wild animals are kept behind fences or
in cages.   Many people come to the zoo to look at the
animals.

Word-Usage Finder

"The Word-Usage Finder" is designed to help locate a particular word within entries different from its own main entry. Parents, teachers, older children and adults of foreign-language background studying English will find this section helpful in finding a word used within different contexts. It should be kept in mind that "The Word-Usage Finder" represents only words and word usage found in The International Visual Dictionary.

ABBREVIATIONS

adj., adjective   *interj.*, interjection
adv., adverb   *n.*, noun
art., article   *prep.*, preposition
conj., conjunction   *pro.*, pronoun
            v., verb

A

A, *adj.* or *art.*, 2 (*See also* **an**).
  n. (A's, A's) (*first letter of the alphabet*), 1, 12, 170, 309, 513, 558, 592, 640.
able, *adj.* (ABLER, ABLEST), 2, 55, 74, 82, 83, 122, 161, 169, 180, 184, 259, 273, 294, 296, 311, 324, 341, 354, 500, 587, 609, 622 (*adv.* ABLY).
aboard, *prep.*, 2, 90, 341.
about, *adv.* (*almost*), 2, 288, 353, 458, 474, 585.
  (*close to*), 2, 22, 70
  prep. (*all over*), 2, 16, 125, 135, 306, 435, 496, 514.
  (*of; concerning*), 2, 24, 25, 58, 142, 155, 170, 179, 186, 223, 238, 276, 278, 294, 296, 331, 357, 370, 372, 408, 432, 442, 444, 515, 516, 531, 532, 551, 555, 557, 560, 563, 564, 566, 578, 617, 620, 642, 646.
  (*somewhere near*), 2.
above, *prep.* (*higher than*), 3, 46, 153, 156, 181, 229, 256, 257, 379, 594, 601.
  adv., 356
absent, *adj.*, 3, 144, 179.
accident, *n.* (ACCIDENTS), 3, 64, 94, 179, 202, 204, 221, 246, 258, 361, 578, 644.
ache, *n.* (ACHES), 3, 268.
  v. (ACHED, ACHED, ACHING), 3, 456.
acorn, *n.* (ACORNS), 4, 41, 214, 367, 475.
across, *prep.*, 4, 55, 72, 126, 127, 140, 173, 262, 375, 379, 394, 530, 542, 544, 546, 611, 635, 651.

act, *n.* (ACTS), 4, 563.
  v. (ACTED, ACTED, ACTING) (*to do; to behave*), 4, 67, 110, 184, 266, 583, 642.
  (*to pretend; to take part in a play*), 4, 45, 391, 408, 421.
actor *n.* (ACTORS), 408 (*See also* **act**).
actually, *adv.*, 387.
add, *v.* (ADDED, ADDED, ADDING), 4, 15, 106, 167, 200, 341, 360, 401, 443, 469, 480, 495, 559, 572, 598, 637.
address, *n.* (ADDRESSES), 5, 174, 309, 549.
admire, *v.* (ADMIRED, ADMIRED, ADMIRING), 5.
advice, *n.*, 5, 142.
afraid, *adj.*, 5, 64, 136, 190, 214, 249, 468, 472, 500, 551, 558, 572, 602, 632.
Africa, *n.*, 6, 58, 121, 224, 286, 313, 435, 556 (*adj.*, AFRICAN).
after, *adv.* (*following the time when*) 142, 166, 183, 259, 415, 425, 436, 446, 471, 498, 537, 538, 542, 555, 559, 567, 573, 583, 618.
  prep. (*behind*), 6, 90, 95, 96, 137, 143, 206, 211, 303, 353, 384, 413, 479, 489, 495, 575, 589, 614, 623.
  (*later than; following the time of*), 6, 43, 153, 185, 392, 420, 424, 440, 555, 577, 597, 621, 625.
  look after (*to take care of*), 86, 117, 124, 149.
  right after (*immediately following*), 6, 358.
afternoon, *n.* (AFTERNOONS), 6, 148, 228, 272, 353, 487, 544, 576, 652.

afterward or **afterwards,** *adv.*, 6, 242, 561.
again, *adv.*, 6, 40, 43, 54, 154, 175, 180, 185, 200, 201, 236, 253, 291, 332, 347, 391, 393, 402, 405, 410, 438, 445, 534, 571, 588, 615, 634, 645.
against, *prep.* (*as a protection or defense from*), 239.
  (*on*), 7, 56, 114, 236, 252, 293, 305, 394, 422, 461, 470, 578.
  (*opposite; opposed to*), 7, 67, 70, 554.
age, *n.* (AGES), 7, 372.
ago, *adj.*, 7, 52, 89, 111, 161, 213, 288, 294, 357, 428, 433, 440, 442, 444, 458, 561, 568, 623.
agree, *v.* (AGREED, AGREED, AGREEING), 7.
ahead, *adj.* (*winning*), 8.
  adv. (*on; forward*), 209, 532, 591.
  ahead of (*preposition meaning* IN FRONT OF), 8, 304, 307.
aim, *v.* (AIMED, AIMED, AIMING), 8.
air, *n.* (AIRS) 8, 33, 54, 56, 65, 74, 82, 91, 159, 169, 191, 202, 203, 205, 213, 219, 220, 253, 256, 274, 284, 286, 287, 293, 308, 320, 343, 358, 378, 379, 381, 423, 436, 449, 464, 475, 503, 510, 544, 550, 556, 573, 578, 621, 635.
airplane, *n.* (AIRPLANES), 2, 8, 9, 13, 22, 27, 109, 123, 146, 147, 172, 183, 188, 205, 213, 228, 246, 247, 253, 256, 276, 284, 300, 320, 323, 354, 373, 383, 389, 403, 405, 406, 413, 423, 442, 448, 450, 549, 550, 565, 582, 625, 626, 635, 644.
airport, *n.* (AIRPORTS), 9, 300, 354, 644.

alarm, *n.* (ALARMS), 9, 492.
  v. (ALARMED, ALARMED, ALARMING), 9 (*See also* **alarm clock**).
alarm clock, *n.* (ALARM CLOCKS), 9, 614, 634 (*See also* **alarm**).
alfalfa, *n.*, 10.
alike, *adj.*, 10, 18, 144, 317, 330, 463, 594.
  adv., 7, 10, 146, 446.
alive, *adj.*, 10, 56, 126, 138, 349, 373.
all, *adj.* (*every bit of; the whole of*), 10, 13, 17, 39, 51, 61, 63, 154, 236, 238, 248, 287, 299, 304, 310, 311, 345, 349, 363, 404, 410, 439, 446, 487, 491, 506, 513, 535, 544, 552, 568, 573, 575, 620, 630, 640.
  (*everyone of*), 4, 10, 16, 22, 25, 48, 58, 75, 77, 94, 117, 126, 152, 177, 179, 185, 223, 228, 232, 233, 237, 251, 268, 292, 309, 326, 343, 354, 363, 377, 378, 392, 395, 398, 422, 437, 478, 519, 521, 529, 541, 549, 560, 571, 594, 599, 652.
  (*nothing but; only; alone*), 172, 407, 653.
  adv. (*completely*), 2, 8, 15, 38, 53, 89, 112, 173, 192, 212, 217, 239, 277, 282, 316, 350, 364, 436, 438, 469, 471, 512, 514, 516, 518, 543, 583, 603, 644.
  pro. (*everyone*), 178, 306.
  (*everything*), 225, 256.
  all of a sudden (*suddenly*), 538.
  all the way (*completely*), 506, 575.
  at all (*in the least*), 18, 198.
alley, *n.* (ALLEYS), 11.
alligator, *n.* (ALLIGATORS), 11.
allow, *v.* (ALLOWED, ALLOWED, ALLOWING), 11, 89, 223, 225, 307, 309, 331, 515, 569, 578.
almost, *adv.*, 2, 11, 212, 247, 266, 288, 338, 345, 349, 354, 433, 468, 486, 526, 618, 643.
alone, *adj.*, 12, 223, 255, 257, 278, 316, 337, 350, 378, 561, 653.
  adv., 12, 343.
along, *adv.* (*forward; onward*), 12, 154, 156, 461, 581, 613.
  (*with one; in accompaniment with*), 12, 81, 574.
  prep. (*through the length of; by; beside*), 12, 22, 77, 111, 176, 229, 404, 413, 437, 473, 487, 601, 609.
alphabet, *n.* (ALPHABETS), 12, 170, 296, 309, 330, 350, 592.
already, *adv.*, 13, 90, 191, 278, 294, 341, 390, 432, 440, 442, 476, 482, 499, 552, 571.
also, *adv.*, 12, 13, 15, 23, 26, 27, 30, 32, 35, 36, 48, 57, 60, 70, 92, 98, 99, 100, 101, 106, 107, 111, 113, 117, 131, 134, 139, 145, 164, 180, 184, 185, 187, 192, 196, 197, 224, 228, 233, 243, 245, 254, 260, 277, 284, 293, 315, 316, 325, 329, 333, 334, 336, 338, 345, 352, 357, 359, 367, 384, 389, 390, 407, 408, 416, 417, 436, 437, 440, 449, 452, 454, 465, 469, 470, 473, 477, 484, 487, 506, 507, 517, 523, 524, 526, 531, 541, 545, 549, 551, 553, 562, 567, 569, 576,

also (*Cont'd.*)
  586, 590, 597, 614, 615, 616, 635, 645, 646, 650.
although, *conj.*, 13.
aluminum, *n.*, 13.
always, *adv.*, 12, 13, 23, 24, 123, 149, 177, 184, 185, 210, 261, 367, 369, 391, 423, 467, 476, 501, 510, 542, 559, 566, 587, 610, 624, 634, 642.
am, *v.* (*first person singular, present indicative of* BE), 2, 7, 14, 21, 25, 39, 41, 93, 102, 148, 149, 160, 161, 166, 178, 191, 242, 254, 255, 256, 265, 271, 272, 273, 277, 296, 299, 305, 331, 333, 352, 353, 372, 374, 384, 390, 398, 413, 423, 428, 442, 445, 470, 476, 482, 486, 491, 511, 524, 541, 553, 559, 561, 576, 587, 616, 617, 626, 633, 642, 646, 650, 652, 653 (*See also* **be**).
America, *n.* (AMERICAS), 14, 274, 442.
American, *adj.*, 14, 106, 201, 342, 584.
  n. (AMERICANS), 14, 274, 300, 343, 600.
among, *prep.* (*in the midst of; mixed with; together with*), 15, 76, 224, 370, 568.
amount, *n.* (AMOUNTS), 15, 58, 138, 422.
Amsterdam, *n.*, 162.
an, *art.*, 15 (*See also* **a**).
ancient, *adj.*, 15.
and, *conj.*, 15.
angry, *adj.* (ANGRIER, ANGRIEST), 16, 24, 127, 128, 238, 323, 396, 431, 470, 475, 503, 555, 569, 597 (*adv.* ANGRILY).
animal, *n.* (ANIMALS), 16, 35, 37, 40, 41, 51, 58, 59, 70, 81, 89, 101, 105, 112, 124, 126, 128, 140, 141, 149, 150, 159, 161, 164, 169, 181, 184, 187, 193, 203, 204, 208, 212, 214, 217, 223, 224, 228, 235, 247, 250, 256, 260, 262, 263, 266, 267, 275, 278, 288, 290, 292, 301, 306, 311, 313, 315, 333, 338, 342, 346, 349, 354, 369, 371, 380, 381, 387, 389, 394, 399, 413, 435, 473, 484, 487, 500, 502, 513, 520, 522, 525, 532, 554, 570, 574, 580, 582, 592, 615, 616, 626, 629, 632, 635, 638, 640, 641, 655, 656.
ankle, *n.* (ANKLES), 16.
annoy, *v.* (ANNOYED, ANNOYED, ANNOYING), 17.
another, *adj.* (*different*), 17, 27, 104, 109, 127, 260, 271, 357, 383, 385, 418, 438, 477, 508, 554, 568, 576, 587, 603, 620, 625.
  (*one more*), 6, 17, 161, 419, 445, 510, 536, 583.
  pro., 17, 213, 422, 527, 582, 614.
  one another (*each other*), 17, 319, 375.
answer, *n.* (ANSWERS), 12, 17, 96, 120, 232, 429, 445, 501, 572, 646.
  v. (ANSWERED, ANSWERED, ANSWERING), 12, 14, 15, 17, 21, 24, 25, 39, 107, 137, 148, 149, 232, 251, 348, 422, 498, 508, 530, 564, 593.
ant, *n.* (ANTS), 17, 70, 144, 203, 275, 308.
any, *adj.* (*no particular one; no matter which*), 18, 19, 43, 126, 205, 207, 248,

any (*Cont'd.*)
  265, 357, 364, 400, 486, 560, 563, 626, 627, 628.
  (*some; a little; even one*), 18, 37, 145, 198, 211, 250, 329, 343, 352, 378, 380, 398, 446, 468, 492, 543, 564, 602, 648.
  adv. (*to any degree*), 23, 216, 225, 238, 242, 245, 361, 377, 513, 530.
anybody, *pro.*, 18, 96, 207, 338, 396, 514, 570, 617.
anymore, *adv.* (*now; at the present time*), 225, 242, 491, 519, 568, 602, 642.
anyone, *pro.*, 12, 18, 124, 622, 633.
anything, *adv.* (*at all; in anyway*), 18.
  pro. (*something; one thing*), 18, 85, 147, 176, 201, 356, 363, 368, 369, 431, 453, 488, 543, 549, 576, 577, 582, 601, 618, 626.
anyway, *adv.* (*no matter what happens; anyhow*), 19, 239, 265, 426.
anywhere, *adv.*, 19.
apart, *adv.* (*not near*), 19, 563, 569.
  (*one from another*), 247.
  (*to pieces*), 19, 64, 67, 515, 554, 577.
apartment, *n.* (*apartments*), 11, 19, 281.
apartment building, *n.* (APARTMENT BUILDINGS), 11, 19.
ape, *n.* (*apes*), 20, 288.
appear, *v.* (APPEARED, APPEARED, APPEARING), (*to come to be seen*), 20.
  (*to seem or look*), 20, 475.
apple, *n.* (APPLES), 4, 15, 17, 20, 30, 36, 48, 51, 52, 61, 88, 96, 106, 122, 141, 145, 174, 176, 178, 200, 214, 216, 237, 239, 283, 343, 376, 396, 398, 401, 405, 449, 455, 462, 483, 506, 526, 609.
apple blossom, *n.* (APPLE BLOSSOMS), 205.
April, *n.* (APRILS), 20, 211, 343, 478, 651.
apron, *n.* (APRONS), 20.
aquarium, *n.* (AQUARIUMS), 10, 21.
are, *pl., v.* (*plural and second person singular, present indicative of* BE), 21 (*See also* **am; be; is, was; were**).
aren't, *v.* and *adv.* (*contraction for* ARE NOT), 21 (*See also* **are**).
Argentina, *n.*, 510.
arm, *n.* (ARMS) (*limb of a person*), 21, 29, 52, 58, 84, 86, 117, 129, 135, 168, 171, 206, 207, 242, 246, 260, 265, 312, 369, 405, 442, 488, 490, 499, 534, 537, 642, 646, 648.
  (*support or side of chair*), 21, 22.
armchair, *n.* (ARMCHAIRS), 22.
army, *n.* (ARMIES), 22, 85, 222, 283, 285, 506, 535, 599.
around, *adv.* (*almost; about*), 22.
  (*in a circle*), 22, 335, 423, 453, 472, 514, 518, 528, 545, 634, 643.
  (*in every direction*), 65, 72, 161, 497, 590.
  prep. (*along all sides; so as to encircle or envelop*), 15, 16, 22, 33, 34, 35, 36, 38, 39, 46, 49, 60, 89, 114, 120, 121, 130, 131, 173, 192, 193, 197, 253, 257, 262, 265, 277, 282, 295, 298, 299, 318, 343, 355, 376, 393, 396, 407, 465, 469, 510, 516, 533, 539,

around (*Cont'd.*)
570, 572, 594, 595, 600, 604, 613, 615, 616, 618, 641, 644, 646, 650, 651, 655.
(*near*), **22,** 77, 616.
(*to the other side of*), **22.**

arrival, *n.* (ARRIVALS), **22**

arrive, *v.* (ARRIVED, ARRIVED, ARRIVING), **22,** 23, 43, 116, 223, 268, 302, 561, 614.

arrow, *n.* (ARROWS), **23,** 62, 300, 402, 487, 511.

art, *n.* (ARTS), **23,** 44, 105, 386, 640.

artist, *n.* (ARTISTS), 107, 236, 286, 385, 515.

as, *adv.* (*equally; to that or the same extent*), 2, **23,** 110, 175, 224, 300, 302, 309, 320, 321, 343, 345, 419, 488, 504, 534, 546, 594, 643, 652.
(*for instance; such as*), 93.
conj. (*as if; as though; as might be; supposing that*), 94, 184, 528, 564, 570, 633.
(*in the way or manner that*), 23, 113, 319, 591.
(*showing result or consequence with infinitive*), 349.
(*to which extent; in which degree; in or to the same degree in or to which*), 2, 11, **23,** 110, 152, 174, 175, 224, 245, 302, 309, 320, 321, 343, 345, 372, 419, 488, 504, 534, 546, 594, 643, 652.
(*when; while*), **23,** 77, 91, 112, 135, 335, 354, 362, 400, 498, 509.
prep. (*in capacity of; like*), 31, 89, 102, 300, 394, 401, 412, 422, 469, 554.
pro. (*that; which; the like of which; who*), 88, 96, 174, 193, 245, 304, 390, 402, 448, 463, 514, 572.
as . . . as possible (*to the greatest degree achievable*), 268, 417.
as long as (*for as much time as*), 290.
as soon as (*when*), 508.
as soon as possible (*immediately*), 268.

ashamed, *adj.,* 23.

ashes, *pl. n.,* 23.

aside, *adv.,* 24.

ask, *v.* (ASKED, ASKED, ASKING), 3, 7, 12, 15, 17, 21, **24,** 25, 43, 52, 75, 77, 80, 117, 130, 137, 141, 146, 148, 149, 246, 251, 265, 277, 348, 361, 376, 390, 410, 413, 422, 432, 445, 477, 498, 501, 507, 553, 554, 626, 638, 651.

asleep, *adj.,* 24, 27, 181, 573.
adv., 141, 386.

astronaut, *n.* (ASTRONAUTS), **24,** 286, 325, 510, 641.

at, *prep.* (*because of*), 303, 305, 416, 498.
(*busy with*), 624.
(*in the amount, price, speed, etc. of*), 338, 462, 512, 570.
(*in the direction of*), 8, **25,** 29, 41, 52, 55, 154, 156, 160, 165, 202, 245, 261, 317, 349, 368, 396, 438, 442, 487, 503, 517, 518, 523, 545, 556, 578, 589, 597, 616, 618, 656.
(*in the state or manner of*), 395.
(*place where*), 3, 11, 17, **25,** 32, 34, 36, 37, 39, 40, 48, 51, 53, 59, 61, 72, 77, 79, 84, 92, 96, 104, 110, 116, 117, 121, 131, 134, 139, 140, 141, 152,

at (*Cont'd.*)
153, 167, 171, 176, 179, 184, 191, 196, 197, 204, 216, 219, 221, 225, 237, 239, 251, 254, 257, 259, 262, 268, 277, 287, 290, 296, 302, 307, 324, 333, 334, 339, 341, 352, 353, 361, 363, 367, 371, 375, 379, 384, 398, 399, 401, 404, 409, 413, 418, 419, 424, 440, 441, 443, 444, 446, 450, 463, 470, 490, 494, 495, 509, 522, 525, 530, 548, 551, 552, 586, 591, 608, 609, 614, 621, 623, 637, 638, 641, 644.
(*time when*), 6, 9, 13, 22, **25,** 27, 42, 43, 63, 74, 76, 83, 127, 136, 137, 138, 145, 149, 159, 168, 177, 224, 227, 228, 231, 232, 242, 246, 249, 271, 286, 294, 301, 311, 316, 321, 325, 337, 344, 345, 357, 359, 362, 364, 377, 378, 380, 386, 392, 397, 433, 435, 458, 497, 507, 508, 534, 540, 541, 558, 560, 575, 585, 588, 594, 601, 603, 604, 620, 625, 627, 652.
at all (*in the least; in any way*), 18, 198.
at last (*finally*), 195.
at least (*not less than*), 142, 306.
at once (*immediately*), 273, 275, 373.
at times (*sometimes*), 14.

ate, *v.* (*past tense of* EAT), 10, 14, **25,** 41, 128, 166, 192, 228, 236, 242, 265, 283, 343, 363, 392, 444, 446, 476, 481, 517, 618, 655 (*See also* eat).

Atlantic Ocean, *n.,* 113, 173, 368.

atoms, *pl. n.,* 25.

attention, *n.* (ATTENTIONS), **25,** 86, 272, 276, 330, 394, 415.

attic, *n.* (ATTICS), **25,** 204, 536.

August, *n.* (AUGUSTS), **26,** 343, 651.

aunt, *n.* (AUNTS), **26,** 85, 123, 180, 186, 187, 223, 224, 230, 231, 236, 271, 290, 312, 319, 340, 378, 379, 394, 410, 474, 475, 493, 504, 507, 551, 560, 579, 597, 620, 638, 646.

auto, *n.* (AUTOS), **26.**

automobile, *n.* (AUTOMOBILES), 8, **26,** 65, 74, 82, 85, 87, 111, 117, 157, 183, 202, 213, 219, 220, 263, 283, 300, 346, 456, 490, 491, 526, 534, 552, 553, 573, 580, 586, 590.

autumn, *n.* (AUTUMNS), **26,** 185, 307, 473, 518, 539, 636.

aviator, *n.* (AVIATORS), **27.**

awake, *v.* (AWAKED or AWOKE, AWAKED or AWOKE or AWOKEN, AWAKING), 24, 27, 44, 359, 617.

away, *adj.* (*absent; distant*), 66, 187, 195, 233, 247, 264, 282, 508, 523, 555, 556, 585.
adv. (*at a distance; in or at another place*), 27, 205, 226, 378, 561.
(*from a place to another place*), 10, 22, 24, **27,** 33, 192, 226, 230, 283, 291, 307, 318, 337, 370, 391, 415, 446, 448, 468, 510, 517, 536, 539, 542, 549, 632.
(*out of one's possession; out of existence, sight, notice, etc.*) 52, 107, 146, 175, 220, 258, 309, 340, 363, 426, 438, 445, 503, 537, 568, 614, 618, 636.

away (*Cont'd.*)
from far away (*from a great distance*), 55.
right away (*immediately*), **27,** 140, 273, 373, 448.

awhile, *adv.,* **27,** 445, 583, 610 (*See also* while).

awoke, *v.* (*past tense of* AWAKE), **27** (*See also* awake).

ax, *n.* (AXES), **27,** 101, 245, 515.

axe, *n.,* **27** (*See also* ax).

B

B, b, *n.* (B's, B's) (*second letter of the alphabet*), 12, **28,** 170, 309, 558, 592.

baa, *n.* (BAAS) **29.**

babies (*See* baby).

baby, *n.* (BABIES), 13, 23, 29, 44, 49, 59, 60, 70, 80, 84, 87, 95, 96, 98, 99, 110, 115, 118, 122, 123, 125, 126, 128, 129, 138, 157, 171, 190, 191, 200, 202, 206, 209, 223, 239, 242, 246, 258, 259, 267, 290, 291, 294, 299, 311, 314, 315, 319, 321, 326, 338, 339, 345, 352, 353, 355, 356, 362, 365, 412, 421, 426, 427, 441, 442, 451, 455, 465, 472, 475, 488, 492, 498, 505, 514, 523, 534, 537, 543, 554, 555, 557, 561, 572, 573, 575, 583, 590, 597, 598, 602, 621, 623, 624, 630, 638, 645.

back, *adj.* (*at the rear*), 243, 253, 258, 290, 484, 511, 549, 585.
adv. (*in return*), 29, 60, 175, 179, 192, 225, 259, 310, 334, 376, 391, 428, 444, 446, 510, 614, 634.
n. (BACKS) (*opposite front*), 94, 214, 530.
(*part of body*), 3, 29, 30, 50, 57, 81, 101, 202, 203, 249, 266, 305, 383, 427, 460, 533, 578, 592.
v. (BACKED, BACKED, BACKING) (*to back out*), 29.
back and forth (*side to side; first backward and then forward*), 205, 209, 456, 545, 557.
in back of (*behind*), 44.

backward, *adv.* (*also spelled* BACKWARDS), 30, 209.

backwards (*See* backward).

bacon, *n.,* 30.

bad, *adj.* (WORSE, WORST) (*harmful; not good*), 30, 40, 110, 178, 208, 230, 251, 258, 272, 281, 286, 310, 340, 344, 354, 415, 433, 470, 490, 491, 494, 504, 508, 531, 600, 621, 631, 642, 646.
(*spoiled*), 30, 51, 443, 501, 521 (*adv. See* badly).

badly, *adv.,* 30, 642.

bag, *n.* (BAGS), 31, 152, 156, 174, 239, 244, 320, 332, 403, 412, 427, 460, 470, 539, 624.

baggage, *n.,* 31, 417.

bait, *n.* (BAITS), 31.

bought *(Cont'd.)*
356, 357, 404, 419, 431, 569, 603, 643, 650 (*See also* **buy**).

bounce, *v.* (BOUNCED, BOUNCED, BOUNCING), 62, 590, 619.

bounded, *v.* (*past tense and past participle of* BOUND), 62.

bow, *n.* (BOWS) (*knot with loops*), 63, 355. (*weapon used with arrows*), 23, 62, 511.

bow, *v.* (BOWED, BOWED, BOWING), 63, 633.

bowl, *n.* (BOWLS), 20, 40, 63, **64,** 92, 171, 192, 193, 209, 229, 470, 584, 629.

bow-wow, *n.* (BOW-WOWS), 35, **63,** 149.

box, *n.* (BOXES), 21, 34, 63, 86, 88, 89, 98, 115, 125, 130, 154, 165, 171, 208, 225, 244, 256, 259, 261, 284, 287, 291, 295, 311, 321, 324, 348, 352, 374, 383, 402, 403, 409, 443, 444, 453, 460, 474, 476, 482, 488, 507, 536, 563, 587.

boy, *n.* (BOYS), 3, 4, 5, 11, 22, 36, 37, 39, 40, 42, 44, 47, **63,** 66, 68, 74, 91, 94, 97, 99, 110, 126, 136, 137, 145, 164, 168, 174, 197, 238, 250, 257, 258, 261, 268, 276, 281, 298, 321, 325, 326, 334, 354, 361, 367, 370, 377, 391, 396, 409, 426, 435, 467, 471, 480, 483, 486, 489, 493, 501, 507, 531, 562, 570, 582, 583, 585, 586, 600, 607, 616, 620, 628, 633, 638, 642.

Boy Scouts, *n.,* 471.

branch, *n.* (BRANCHES), 62, **63,** 72, 74, 171, 312, 316, 545, 565, 583, 594, 633.

brass, *n.,* 64, 70.

brave, *adj.* (BRAVER, BRAVEST), 64, 333 (*adv.* BRAVELY).

bray, *v.* (BRAYED, BRAYED, BRAYING) (*loud harsh cry*), 150.

Brazil, *n.,* 300, 510.

Brazilian, *n.* or *adj.* (BRAZILIANS), 300.

bread, *n.* (BREADS), 32, 51, **64,** 72, 75, 125, 152, 166, 169, 204, 213, 281, 283, 315, 328, 378, 379, 392, 416, 424, 448, 453, 458, 464, 499, 574, 626, 627.

break, *v.* (BROKE, BROKEN, BREAKING), 3, 47, 54, **64,** 67, 74, 91, 100, 124, 128, 144, 158, 226, 400, 515, 535 (*See also* **broke; broken**).

breakfast, *n.* (BREAKFASTS), **64,** 93, 113, 167, 176, 227, 230, 234, 332, 344, 367, 417, 466, 603.

breast, *n.* (BREASTS), 57, **64,** 129, 451.

breath, *n.* (BREATHS), **65,** 220, 425, 491, 503, 650.

breathe, *v.* (BREATHED, BREATHED, BREATHING), 8 16, **65,** 159, 177, 318, 362, 388, 425, 501, 502, 510.

breeze, *n.* (BREEZES), **65,** 186, 202, 416.

brick, *n.* (BRICKS), **65,** 71, 106, 162, 199, 251, 315, 331, 627, 639.

bridge, *n.* (BRIDGES), **65,** 437.

bright, *adj.* (BRIGHTER, BRIGHTEST) (*colorful; cheerful*), 97, 221, 229, 391, 402, 412, 506, 589, 607, 635, 655.
(*shiny; giving off or reflecting light*), 13, 54, 55, **66,** 71, 143, 159, 161, 299, 312, 481, 485, 523, 539.
(*smart*), 66, 501, 537.
(*adv.* BRIGHTLY).

bring, *v.* (BROUGHT, BROUGHT, BRINGING) (*to cause to come with oneself; carry, lead, or accompany*), 66, 68, 81, 88, 134, 141, 159, 170, 192, 208, 213, 310, 376, 418, 425, 464, 476, 477, 484, 487, 510, 541, 550, 597, 633.
(*to cause something to happen*), 66, 173, 285, 286, 634.

British Guiana, *n.,* 510.

British Honduras, *n.,* 93.

broad, *adj.* (BROADER, BROADEST), 66.

broadcast, *v.* (BROADCAST or BROADCASTED, BROADCAST or BROADCASTED, BROADCASTING), 66, 337, 524, 556.

broil, *v.* (BROILED, BROILED, BROILING), 66, 118.

broke, *v.* (*past tense of* BREAK), 3, 19, 39, 47, 64, 67, 68, 86, 155, 200, 201, 334, 354, 384, 503, 508, 538, 561, 642 (*See also* **break**).

broken, *v.* (*past participle of* BREAK), 64, 67, 77, 89, 100, 189, 227, 347, 402, 419, 422, 428, 432, 602, 468 (*See also* **break**).

brook, *n.* (BROOKS), **67,** 200, 379, 450.

broom, *n.* (BROOMS), 45, **67,** 192, 290, 543, 637.

broomstick, *n.* (BROOMSTICKS), **68.**

broth, *n.,* 68.

brother, *n.* (BROTHERS), 29, 60, **68,** 87, 102, 123, 129, 138, 154, 157, 191, 206, 250, 255, 263, 294, 298, 319, 326, 352, 427, 448, 465, 477, 555, 597, 602, 608.

brought, *v.* (*past tense and past participle of* BRING), 60, **68,** 116, 255, 324, 505, 512, 541, 582, 614.

brown, *adj.* (BROWNER, BROWNEST), 6, 17, 30, 40, 41, 58, 63, **68,** 91, 101, 136, 137, 144, 247, 253, 268, 321, 342, 386, 395, 396, 419, 441, 511, 526, 540, 551, 574, 586.
n. (BROWNS), 68, 119, 311.

brownie, *n.* (BROWNIES), **68.**

brush, *n.* (BRUSHES), 67, **69,** 156, 577.
v. (BRUSHED, BRUSHED, BRUSHING), **69,** 142, 242, 271, 325, 371, 543, 555.

bubble, *n.* (BUBBLES), 58, **69,** 201, 505, 538.

bucket, *n.* (BUCKETS), **69,** 195, 262, 384, 425.

bud, *n.* (BUDS), 56, **70.**

buffalo, *n.* (BUFFALOS or BUFFALOES or BUFFALO), **70,** 558.

bug, *n.* (BUGS), 17, **70,** 198, 235, 275.

buggy, *n.* (BUGGIES), **70.**

bugle, *n.* (BUGLES), **70.**

bugler, *n.* (BUGLERS), **70.**

build, *v.* (BUILT, BUILT, BUILDING), 51, 55, **71,** 76, 87, 89, 90, 319, 325, 331, 356, 431, 463, 583, 645 (*See also* **built**).

building, *n.* (BUILDINGS), 11, 19, 34, 35, 36, **71,** 80, 81, 89, 99, 102, 111, 134, 151, 170, 183, 187, 197, 219, 233, 246, 264, 281, 307, 327, 349, 357, 411, 453, 458, 466, 469, 484, 492, 497, 520, 524, 579, 615.

built, *v.* (*past tense and past participle of* BUILD), 65, **71,** 79, 134, 323, 406 (*See also* **build**).

bulb, *n.* (BULBS), **71.**

bumblebee, *n.* (BUMBLEBEES), **72,** 77.

bump, *n.* (BUMPS), **72,** 321, 455, 502.
v. (BUMPED, BUMPED, BUMPING), **72,** 179, 246, 378.

bun, *n.* (BUNS), **72,** 244.

bunch, *n.* (BUNCHES), 33, **72,** 205, 234, 344, 383, 387.

bundle, *n.* (BUNDLES), 32, **73,** 374.
v. (BUNDLED, BUNDLED, BUNDLING), 73.
bundle up (*to dress up in warm clothes*), 73.

bunny, *n.* (BUNNIES), **73.**

burn, *n.* (BURNS), **73,** 268.
v. (BURNED or BURNT, BURNED or BURNT, BURNING), 23, 54, **73,** 80, 83, 90, 111, 177, 197, 217, 220, 299, 311, 330, 458, 466, 501, 502, 508, 511, 515, 532.

burst, *v.* (BURST, BURST, BURSTING), **74,** 416.

bury, *v.* (BURIED, BURIED, BURYING), **74,** 144, 582.

bus, *n.* (BUSES), 2, 22, **74,** 117, 158, 187, 192, 209, 392, 448, 490, 524, 580, 614, 625, 656.

bush, *n.* (BUSHES), 53, 70, **74,** 216, 236, 253, 288, 305, 407, 440, 607.

bushy, *adj.* (BUSHIER, BUSHIEST), **75.**

business, *n.* (BUSINESSES), **75.**

busy, *adj.* (BUSIER, BUSIEST), 42, **75,** 362, 370, 428.

but, *adv.* (*only*), **75.**
conj., 3, 6, 7, 10, 13, 17, 19, 48, 49, 72, **75,** 82, 93, 110, 119, 122, 124, 146, 153, 156, 158, 179, 191, 203, 226, 230, 239, 240, 242, 249, 253, 267, 277, 280, 300, 303, 304, 310, 331, 345, 356, 372, 377, 378, 387, 392, 431, 440, 521, 531, 563, 617, 620, 632, 638, 651, 652.
prep., 29, **75.**
(*used in an independent clause as a conjunctive adverb meaning* HOWEVER), 21, 57, **75,** 83, 112, 148, 234, 247, 265, 286, 344.

butcher, *n.* (BUTCHERS), **75,** 244, 376, 483.

butter, *n.* (BUTTERS), 64, **75,** 76, 79, 96, 103, 126, 134, 152, 216, 235, 276, 328, 334, 419, 464, 651.
v. (BUTTERED, BUTTERED, BUTTERING), **75.**

butterfly, *n.* (BUTTERFLIES), 70, **76,** 90, 113, 230, 275, 311, 345, 356, 568, 591, 635.

buttermilk, *n.,* **76.**

button, *n.* (BUTTONS) (*clothing*), **76,** 167, 249, 287, 318, 330, 477, 508, 543.
(*doorbell*), 151.
v. (BUTTONED, BUTTONED, BUTTONING), **76,** 188, 202.

buy, *v.* (BOUGHT, BOUGHT, BUYING), 9, 32, 62, 75, **77,** 121, 125, 131, 134, 237, 244, 329, 335, 342, 357, 415, 418, 423, 462, 487, 488, 522, 524, 535, 564, 574, 580, 586, 621, 642, 643 (*See also* **bought**).

buzz, *n.* (BUZZES), **77.**
v. (BUZZED, BUZZED, BUZZING), 42, 72, **77.**

by, *adv.* (*past; beyond*), 97, 225, 474, 571.
  prep.(*according to; by means, act, or effort of; using*), 12, 42, 66, 70, 73, **77**, 82, 84, 88, 96, 105, 113, 118, 126, 138, 154, 157, 169, 197, 231, 245, 264, 278, 285, 293, 310, 341, 346, 349, 361, 371, 399, 404, 413, 427, 438, 447, 454, 465, 480, 492, 502, 514, 525, 548, 554, 567, 582, 591, 604, 619, 620, 644.
  (*along*), **77**.
  (*near*), **77**, 378.
  (*not later than*), 13, **77**.
  (*past*), **77**.
  by myself, yourself, himself, etc. (*alone*), 378, 653, 655.

C

C, c, *n.* (C's, c's) (*third letter of the alphabet*), 12, **78**, 170, 309, 513, 558, 592, 640.
cabbage, *n.* (CABBAGES), 79, 86, 101, 361, 441, 444, 462, 466.
cabin, *n.* (CABINS), 79.
cage, *n.* (CAGES), 10, **79**, 119, 175, 212, 273, 480, 656.
cake, *n.* (CAKES) (*baked batter of flour, eggs, sugar*), 32, 48, 68, 79, 83, 101, 119, 128, 129, 166, 176, 215, 224, 265, 271, 379, 387, 391, 392, 396, 515, 521, 538, 588, 608, 630.
  (*piece*), **79**, 505.
calendar, *n.* (CALENDARS), 80, 571.
calf, *n.* (CALVES), 80, 439, 607.
California, *n.*, 353, 524.
call, *n.* (CALLS) (*contact by telephone*), 165.
  (*cry*), 80, 128.
  (*shout*), 80, 489.
  (*visit*), 80, 394.
  v. (CALLED, CALLED, CALLING) (*to ask to come*), 9, 45, **80**, 110, 140, 193, 197.
  (*to call someone's or something's name; to name*), 4, 14, 17, 19, 26, 27, 31, 34, 35, 36, 37, 42, 46, 53, 58, 59, 70, 72, 76, 79, 80, 92, 97, 98, 100, 111, 112, 113, 115, 118, 120, 129, 134, 136, 137, 139, 143, 145, 151, 152, 153, 157, 162, 163, 170, 173, 185, 189, 198, 201, 207, 211, 213, 219, 223, 224, 225, 226, 232, 234, 239, 242, 243, 244, 245, 260, 263, 268, 275, 282, 284, 295, 296, 305, 307, 312, 323, 324, 325, 331, 340, 346, 347, 352, 354, 355, 362, 367, 381, 388, 395, 404, 406, 407, 408, 412, 417, 422, 427, 428, 431, 437, 447, 449, 453, 460, 464, 473, 482, 492, 503, 506, 507, 516, 517, 520, 521, 524, 525, 526, 529, 531, 548, 549, 555, 556, 558, 560, 567, 569, 575, 577, 586, 587, 588, 590, 600, 615, 633, 650.
  (*to shout for*), **80**, 255, 602.
  (*to telephone*), **80**, 165, 367.
came, *v.* (*past tense of* **come**), 2, 6, 14, 56, 61, 64, 67, 77, **81**, 91, 116, 124, 126,

came (*Cont'd.*)
  127, 146, 153, 178, 185, 195, 215, 221, 230, 242, 255, 257, 269, 274, 276, 287, 298, 303, 306, 364, 383, 384, 391, 392, 407, 425, 442, 446, 447, 449, 468, 506, 552, 558, 561, 570, 571, 601, 631, 651, 653 (*See also* **come**).
camel, *n.* (CAMELS), 81, 142, 266.
camera, *n.* (CAMERAS) 81, 399, 648.
camp, *n.* (CAMPS), 81.
  v. (CAMPED, CAMPED, CAMPING), 81, 383, 533, 558.
can, *n.* (CANS), **82**, 572.
  v. (CANNED, CANNED, CANNING), **82**.
can, *v.* (COULD), 2, 11, 12, 14, 16, 17, 18, 20, 21, 29, 30, 32, 41, 51, 53, 58, 65, 66, 71, 81, **82**, 83, 85, 88, 89, 92, 95, 96, 106, 107, 110, 122, 124, 126, 137, 148, 151, 154, 155, 157, 160, 167, 168, 169, 170, 172, 174, 176, 178, 180, 181, 185, 186, 191, 193, 194, 196, 197, 200, 203, 206, 208, 209, 210, 211, 212, 220, 223, 224, 226, 233, 234, 235, 237, 238, 240, 244, 245, 247, 248, 252, 253, 255, 258, 259, 260, 263, 264, 266, 273, 275, 287, 290, 291, 311, 313, 315, 318, 323, 325, 331, 333, 334, 338, 340, 343, 347, 348, 349, 350, 356, 357, 360, 363, 364, 367, 368, 369, 371, 375, 376, 383, 391, 393, 396, 397, 400, 401, 402, 404, 407, 411, 413, 417, 431, 435, 441, 442, 443, 444, 445, 451, 453, 456, 457, 458, 462, 469, 471, 473, 478, 479, 480, 491, 495, 497, 501, 502, 503, 510, 513, 514, 519, 520, 521, 522, 523, 525, 526, 527, 529, 531, 533, 534, 535, 539, 542, 544, 545, 552, 554, 557, 558, 559, 564, 565, 567, 568, 576, 583, 584, 587, 593, 595, 607, 608, 609, 611, 617, 618, 625, 630, 635, 639, 646, 648, 652 (*See also* **able; cannot; can't; could; couldn't**).
Canada, *n.*, **82**, 104, 114, 122, 353, 362, 395, 524.
canal, *n.* (CANALS), 82.
canary, *n.* (CANARIES), 370.
candle, *n.* (CANDLES), 56, 65, 83, 197, 406, 425, 620.
candy, *n.* (CANDIES), 7, 13, 15, 16, 30, 34, 41, 43, 44, 48, 49, 51, 62, 83, 95, 101, 148, 152, 156, 168, 177, 192, 207, 221, 225, 231, 265, 308, 316, 325, 327, 331, 348, 361, 394, 400, 410, 423, 444, 463, 476, 477, 488, 527, 538, 541, 543, 549, 550, 559, 583, 594, 643.
  adj. or *compound noun*, **83**, 402, 423, 463, 538.
cane, *n.* (CANES), **83**, 538.
cannot, *v.*, 19, 23, 25, 29, 33, 47, 55, 83, 84, 92, 98, 157, 159, 181, 185, 188, 200, 212, 216, 223, 226, 233, 245, 247, 254, 256, 318, 337, 351, 364, 372, 381, 397, 402, 415, 445, 476, 509, 510, 512, 515, 524, 525, 542, 546, 562, 598, 642 (*See also* **can; can't**).

canoe, *n.* (CANOES), 84, 384, 450, 494.
can't, *v.* and *adv.* (*contraction for* CAN NOT), 84, 210, 374, 484, 529, 602 (*See also* **cannot**).
cap, *n.* (CAPS) (*cover*), 84, 563.
  (*hat*), 84, 118.
  v. (CAPPED, CAPPED, CAPPING), 84.
cape, *n.* (CAPES), 84, 108.
capital, *adj.*, 12.
capsule, *n.* (CAPSULES), 452.
captain, *n.* (CAPTAINS) (*leader*), **85**, 490.
  (OFFICER), **85**, 117, 222, 376, 494, 537, 588, 599.
car, *n.* (CARS) (*automobile*), 2, 3, 29, 54, 55, 56, 85, 86, 88, 114, 131, 141, 157, 158, 159, 172, 188, 192, 196, 201, 209, 214, 219, 226, 228, 237, 245, 246, 258, 261, 262, 303, 317, 331, 333, 345, 348, 378, 390, 392, 410, 418, 427, 447, 448, 450, 458, 474, 500, 504, 512, 522, 523, 524, 526, 530, 536, 549, 576, 580, 582, 583, 588, 591, 593, 603, 607, 625, 631, 638, 644, 645.
  (*train*), **85**, 534, 581.
card, *n.* (CARDS) (*greeting*), 252, 606.
  (*piece of stiff paper*), **85**, 252, 549, 569.
  (*playing*), **85**, 138, 139, 143, 244.
  (*post*), **85**, 418.
  (*report*), **85**.
cardboard, *n.*, 86.
care, *n.* (CARES) (*anxiety; worry*), **86**, 597.
  (*attention*), **86**, 220, 394, 565, 573.
  (*custody; protection*), 45, 138, 173, 189, 261, 281, 290, 339, 345, 365, 399, 424, 437, 439, 478, 485.
  v. (CARED, CARED, CARING)(*to desire*), 86.
  (*to mind*), **86**, 331.
  care for (*to like*), 86.
  care for (*to look after*) 86.
careful, *adj.*, 52, 86, 127, 197, 222, 239, 358, 488, 566, 585, 618 (*adv. See* **carefully**).
carefully, *adv.*, 25, 526.
careless, *adj.*, 86, 566 (*adv.* CARELESSLY).
carpenter, *n.* (CARPENTERS), 57, 87, 196, 244, 258, 406, 576, 641.
carpet, *n.* (CARPETS), 87, 344, 453, 606.
carriage, *n.* (CARRIAGES) (*wheeled vehicle drawn by horses*), 85, 87, 111, 248, 629.
  (*small wheeled vehicle to be pushed*), 70, 87, 282.
carrot, *n.* (CARROTS), 88, 287, 454.
carry, *v.* (CARRIED, CARRIED, CARRYING), 31, 66, 68, 69, 73, 74, 85, 88, 111, 135, 198, 202, 213, 228, 243, 244, 249, 280, 290, 293, 295, 301, 315, 321, 383, 384, 412, 417, 427, 441, 448, 460, 488, 521, 581, 582, 586, 597, 607.
cart, *n.* (CARTS), 85, 88, 263, 349.
  v. (CARTED, CARTED, CARTING), 88.
carton, *n.* (CARTONS), 89, 338.
case, *n.* (CASES) (*box*), 89.
  (*condition; instance*), 89, 265.
castle, *n.* (CASTLES), 15, 89, 463.
cat, *n.* (CATS), 6, 17, 47, 54, 74, 89, 95, 105, 112, 144, 159, 162, 187, 190, 191, 194, 210, 217, 235, 238, 242, 278,

cat *(Cont'd.)*
287, 292, 294, 301, 310, 313, 335, 337, 358, 372, 379, 394, 399, 427, 428, 453, 468, 472, 513, 517, 518, 559, 570, 578, 598, 602, 640.

catch, *v.* (CAUGHT, CAUGHT, CATCHING) *(to become tangled with),* 585.
(to get), 6, 31, 89, **90,** 198, 199, 200, 230, 239, 262, 267, 291, 320, 341, 344, 356, 568, 578, 582, 585, 622.

catch fire *(to start burning),* 220, 330.

caterpillar, *n.* (CATERPILLARS), 76, **90,** 113, 302, 492, 591.

cattle, *plural n.,* 10, 42, 88, **91,** 120, 124, 406, 440, 520.

caught, *v. (past tense and past participle of* CATCH), 31, 48, 90, **91,** 136, 199, 200, 231, 320, 337, 432, 576, 563, 582, 594 (*See also* catch).

cause, *n.* (CAUSES), **91.**
v. (CAUSED, CAUSED, CAUSING), 66, **91,** 325, 312, 323, 325, 330, 340, 438, 558, 609.

cave, *n.* (CAVES), **91,** 111, 294.

caw, *n.* (CAWS), **92,** 127.

ceiling, *n.* (CEILINGS), **92,** 204.

celery, *n.,* 92.

cellar, *n.* (CELLARS), 36, **92.**

cent, *n.* (CENTS), 48, 50, 62, 77, **92,** 95, 145, 150, 178, 193, 194, 209, 266, 306, 309, 359, 360, 373, 380, 397, 422, 431, 513, 565, 643.

center, *n.* (CENTERS), **92,** 103, 112, 134, 260, 337, 513, 540.

Central America, *n.,* 14, **93,** 274, 336.

cereal, *n.* (CEREALS), **93,** 233, 627.

certain, *adj. (some; special; particular),* **93,** 104, 105, 233, 365, 513.
(sure), 93, 474, 541 (*adv. See* certainly).

certainly, *adv.,* 93.

chain, *n.* (CHAINS), 93.

chair, *n.* (CHAIRS), 21, 22, 47, 62, **94,** 95, 112, 121, 131, 141, 142, 153, 201, 208, 217, 227, 323, 368, 372, 375, 377, 383, 385, 428, 465, 474, 479, 494, 566, 567, 597, 598, 621.

chalk, *n.* (CHALKS), 53, **94,** 329, 646.

challenge, *v.* (CHALLENGED, CHALLENGED, CHALLENGING), 94.

champion, *n.* (CHAMPIONS), 94.

chance, *n.* (CHANCES), 94.

change, *n.* (CHANGES), 95.
v. (CHANGED, CHANGED, CHANGING), 76, 95, 185, 212, 215, 276, 540, 573, 591.

chase, *v.* (CHASED, CHASED, CHASING), 95, 164, 235, 432, 549.

chat, *v.* (CHATTED, CHATTED, CHATTING), 95.

chatter, *n.,* 95.
v. (CHATTERED, CHATTERED, CHATTERING), 95.

cheap, *adj.* (CHEAPER, CHEAPEST), **95,** 462 (*adv.* CHEAPLY).

cheat, *n.* (CHEATS), 96.
v. (CHEATED, CHEATED, CHEATING), 96.

check, *n.* (CHECKS) *(mark),* 96.
(money), 96, 491.
(square), 96.
v. (CHECKED, CHECKED, CHECKING), 96.

cheek, *n.* (CHEEKS), **96,** 183, 191, 293, 629.

cheer, *n.* (CHEERS), 97.
v. (CHEERED, CHEERED, CHEERING), 97, 589.

cheerful, *adj.,* **97,** 128, 221, 607 (*adv.* CHEERFULLY).

cheese, *n.* (CHEESES), **97,** 134, 358, 464, 535.

cherry, *n.* (CHERRIES), 25, **97,** 167, 195, 583.

chest, *n.* (CHESTS) *(box),* 98.
(part of body), 40, 64, 98, 252.

chew, *v.* (CHEWED, CHEWED, CHEWING), 59, 83, **98,** 100, 157, 227, 240, 283, 542, 555, 557, 574, 577, 578.

Chicago, *n.,* 104, 392, 550.

chick, *n.* (CHICKS), **98,** 110, 190, 249, 283, 396, 572, 593.

chicken, *n.* (CHICKENS), 68, **98,** 112, 119, 167, 187, 211, 216, 254, 290, 396, 454, 487, 500, 509.

chief, *n.* (CHIEFS), 99.
adj., 99 (*adv.* CHIEFLY).

child, *n.* (CHILDREN), 29, **99,** 116, 326, 345, 377, 475, 515, 561, 591, 606, 653 (*See also* children).

children, *n. (plural of* CHILD), 11, 16, 19, 21, 24, 25, 39, 44, 45, 48, 52, 60, 63, 64, 68, 73, 75, 86, 87, 88, 91, **99,** 105, 106, 111, 112, 119, 123, 127, 130, 134, 139, 148, 149, 156, 172, 177, 178, 179, 186, 195, 204, 207, 216, 222, 227, 238, 243, 246, 251, 255, 257, 266, 269, 285, 286, 292, 313, 316, 323, 332, 344, 345, 361, 363, 377, 378, 379, 388, 400, 409, 414, 415, 422, 426, 444, 446, 449, 453, 454, 463, 464, 470, 475, 481, 483, 489, 492, 493, 499, 503, 506, 514, 520, 522, 541, 549, 551, 555, 561, 575, 581, 586, 591, 613, 625, 627, 629, 652, 655, 656 (*See also* child).

Chile, *n.,* 510.

chill, *n.* (CHILLS), 99.
v. (CHILLED, CHILLED, CHILLING), 99.

chimney, *n.* (CHIMNEYS), **99,** 425, 502, 520.

chin, *n.* (CHINS), 40, **100,** 183.

China, *n.,* 100.

Chinese, *adj.* and *n.,* 100.

chip, *v.* (CHIPS), 100.
v. (CHIPPED, CHIPPED, CHIPPING), 100.

chipmunk, *n.* (CHIPMUNKS), **101,** 260.

chocolate, *adj.,* 34, 68, 83, **101,** 271, 341, 508, 538, 546.
n. (CHOCOLATES), **101,** 112, 341, 375, 424, 463.

choose, *v.* (CHOSE, CHOSEN, CHOOSING), 101, **102,** 169, 400, 476, 550, 611 (*See also* chose; chosen).

chop, *n.* (CHOPS), **101,** 469.
v. (CHOPPED, CHOPPED, CHOPPING), 100, 101, 103, 237, 466.

chose, *v. (past tense of* CHOOSE), 101, **102** (*See also* choose).

chosen, *v. (past participle of* CHOOSE), 101, **102,** 421 (*See also* choose).

Christmas, *n.* (CHRISTMASES), 83, 87, **102,** 116, 139, 159, 179, 224, 256, 257, 260, 311, 329, 331, 335, 405, 443, 464, 493, 549, 564, 585, 616, 644, 648.

chum, *n.* (CHUMS), 102.

chunk, *n.* (CHUNKS) *(large lump),* 111.

church, *n.* (CHURCHES), 19, 24, 45, 50, 71, 83, 84, **102,** 166, 186, 233, 290, 329, 341, 431, 463, 492, 497, 539, 579, 603, 652.

churn, *n.* (CHURNS), 75, **103.**
v. (CHURNED, CHURNED, CHURNING), **103.**

cigar, *n.* (CIGARS), **103,** 311, 501.

cigarette, *n.* (CIGARETTES), **103,** 502.

Cinderella, *n.,* 185, 373, 408, 442, 531.

circle, *n.* (CIRCLES), 22, 92, **103,** 172, 195, 262, 329, 337, 438, 449, 455.

circus, *n.* (CIRCUSES), **104,** 110, 148, 274, 389, 551, 587.

cities (*See* city).

citizen, *n.* (CITIZENS), **104,** 162, 173, 600.

city, *n.* (CITIES), 34, **104,** 122, 162, 173, 213, 278, 282, 327, 347, 358, 395, 405, 421, 433, 446, 447, 497, 501, 532, 534, 553, 579, 617.

clam, *n.* (CLAMS) *(animal with two shells that lives in water),* 485.

clang, *n.* (CLANGS), **104.**
v. (CLANGED, CLANGED, CLANGING), **104.**

clap, *n.* (CLAPS), **105.**
v. (CLAPPED, CLAPPED, CLAPPING), **105,** 179.

class, *n.* (CLASSES) *(group),* **105.**
(study), 48, 102, **105,** 177, 230, 296, 422, 449, 611.

classmate, *n.* (CLASSMATES), **105.**

classroom, *n.* (CLASSROOMS), **105.**

clatter, *n.* (CLATTERS), **105.**

claw, *n.* (CLAWS), **105,** 164, 394, 472.

clay, *n.* (CLAYS), 65, **106,** 209, 482, 525.

clean, *adj.* (CLEANER, CLEANEST), 13, 20, 34, 38, 49, **106,** 146, 196, 213, 281, 340, 354, 358, 380, 388, 427, 456, 469, 484, 505, 528, 555, 577, 640.
v. (CLEANED, CLEANED, CLEANING), 44, 69, **106,** 141, 142, 223, 433, 457, 471, 543, 577, 584, 601, 606, 617, 633, 636.

cleaner, *n.* (CLEANERS), 38, **106,** 323, 457, 606.

clear, *adj.* (CLEARER, CLEAREST), **106,** 143, 184, 196, 265, 427, 497, 523, 610, 621 (*adv. See* clearly).
v. (CLEARED, CLEARED, CLEARING), **106.**

clearly, *adv.,* 21, 349.

clerk, *n.* (CLERKS), **107.**

clever, *adj.* (CLEVERER, CLEVEREST), **107.**

click, *n.* (CLICKS), **107.**
v. (CLICKED, CLICKED, CLICKING), **107.**

climb, *v.* (CLIMBED, CLIMBED, CLIMBING), **107,** 298, 342, 344, 527, 587, 609.

clip, *n.* (CLIPS), **107.**
v. (CLIPPED, CLIPPED, CLIPPING), **107.**

cloak, *n.* (CLOAKS), **108,** 109.

clock, *n.* (CLOCKS), 9, **108,** 219, 244, 264, 340, 368, 372, 391, 484, 534, 569, 571, 614, 618, 634.

close, *adj.* (CLOSER, CLOSEST), 2, 48, 104, **108,** 129, 344, 354, 388, 523, 533, 551, 556, 632 (*adv.* CLOSELY).
adv., 206, 226, 457, 562, 616, 640.
v. (CLOSED, CLOSED, CLOSING), 23, 34, 55, 82, **108,** 181, 221, 266, 316, 320, 349, 374, 474, 489, 530, 635, 643.

closet, *n.* (CLOSETS), 102, **108,** 130, 227, 256, 290.

cloth, *n.* (CLOTHS), 31, 34, 46, 49, **109,** 131, 135, 245, 248, 280, 331, 338, 353, 355, 436, 447, 456, 460, 461, 469, 480, 483, 484, 492, 528, 548, 570, 575, 579, 608, 622, 640, 644, 645.

clothes, *plural n.,* 4, 31, 73, 84, 90, 108, **109,** 110, 116, 118, 135, 146, 154, 155, 156, 160, 169, 205, 212, 243, 255, 277, 282, 303, 313, 352, 380, 414, 436, 438, 478, 480, 505, 518, 523, 535, 539, 552, 561, 563, 565, 566, 580, 587, 588, 594, 598, 599, 617, 640.

clothesline, *n.* (CLOTHESLINES), **109,** 135, 156, 160, 205, 500.

clothing, *n.,* 109, 539.

cloud, *n.* (CLOUDS), 46, 66, 106, **109,** 146, 184, 256, 354, 392, 425, 438, 525.

cloudy, *adj.* (CLOUDIER, CLOUDIEST) *(filled with clouds),* 597.

clover, *n.* (CLOVERS), 10, **110,** 482.

clown, *n.* (CLOWNS), 4, 104, **110,** 116, 286, 369, 389, 401, 432, 551.

club, *n.* (CLUBS) *(group),* **110.**
(stick), **110,** 229, 428.

cluck, *n.* (CLUCKS), 98, **110.**
v. (CLUCKED, CLUCKED, CLUCKING), **110.**

coach, *n.* (COACHES) *(carriage),* **111,** 185.
(teacher), **111.**
v. (COACHED, COACHED, COACHING), **111.**

coal, *n.* (COALS), 52, **111,** 213, 217, 339, 489, 532.

coast, *n.* (COASTS), **111,** 368, 473.
v. (COASTED, COASTED, COASTING), **111.**

coat, *n.* (COATS), 35, 41, 76, 84, 108, 109, **112,** 161, 203, 212, 217, 231, 246, 258, 259, 262, 265, 280, 342, 370, 374, 428, 433, 438, 445, 499, 529, 539, 551, 560, 574, 608, 616, 626, 628, 631, 640, 642, 653.

cob, *n.* (COBS), **112,** 120, 164, 220.

cock, *n.* (COCKS), 98, **112,** 511.

cock-a-doodle-doo, *n.* (COCK-A-DOODLE-DOOS), 98, **112,** 127, 454.

cocoa, *n.,* 112.

cocoon, *n.* (COCOONS), 76, 90, **113,** 492.

cod, *n.* (COD or CODS), **113** (*See also* **codfish**).

codfish, *n.* (CODFISH or CODFISHES), **113.** 371.

coffee, *n.* (COFFEES), 68, **113,** 129, 157, 236, 237, 306, 338, 376, 419, 538, 555.

coin, *n.* (COINS), **113,** 130, 145, 397, 402, 431.

cold, *adj.* (COLDER, COLDEST) *(not friendly),* **114.**
(not warm), 19, 26, 33, 41, 73, 95, 112, **114,** 175, 191, 212, 215, 260, 264, 271, 410, 413, 417, 443, 444, 456, 475, 486, 504, 522, 583, 615, 616, 620, 621, 634, 635, 636, 640, 655.
n. (*disease*), 54, 56, 90, **114,** 121, 223, 231, 239, 272, 385, 433, 480, 490, 503, 642.
(low temperature; not warmth), 89, 99, 397, 485, 644.
(adv. COLDLY).

collar, *n.* (COLLARS), **114,** 212, 306, 318, 608.

collect, *v.* (COLLECTED, COLLECTED, COLLECTING), **114.**

college, *n.* (COLLEGES), **114,** 232, 566.

collide, *v.* (COLLIDED, COLLIDED, COLLIDING), **114.**

Colombia, *n.,* 510.

color, *n.* (COLORS), 52, 57, 68, 76, 97, 101, **115,** 119, 125, 161, 181, 183, 201, 221, 229, 231, 235, 236, 307, 311, 375, 385, 388, 391, 404, 427, 438, 443, 462, 474, 540, 551, 589, 607, 630, 651, 655.
v. (COLORED, COLORED, COLORING), **115,** 125, 166, 385.

colt, *n.* (COLTS), **115.**

Columbus, Christopher, *n.,* 146.

comb, *n.* (COMBS) *(bird's),* **115.**
(hair), 115, 156, 407.
v. (COMBED, COMBED, COMBING), **115,** 156, 318, 330, 626.

come, *v.* (CAME, COME, COMING), 6, 7, 18, 20, 22, 30, 35, 44, 45, 56, 75, 80, 81, 93, 94, 101, 105, 109, 111, 112, 113, 116, 120, 121, 134, 139, 153, 159, 165, 167, 168, 170, 171, 175, 178, 179, 183, 185, 189, 190, 197, 200, 202, 204, 206, 211, 214, 224, 228, 229, 233, 243, 249, 253, 269, 272, 273, 275, 276, 277, 290, 295, 299, 300, 301, 309, 312, 317, 333, 334, 338, 339, 345, 354, 360, 362, 371, 373, 375, 391, 396, 398, 405, 413, 436, 438, 446, 453, 479, 484, 490, 495, 502, 506, 509, 520, 522, 525, 531, 535, 540, 541, 543, 546, 550, 555, 560, 562, 566, 567, 571, 578, 580, 583, 587, 588, 600, 604, 610, 614, 616, 618, 621, 624, 627, 635, 656.

comfort, *n.* (COMFORTS), 116.
v. (COMFORTED, COMFORTED, COMFORTING), 116.

comfortable, *adj.,* 116, 124, 479, 504
(adv. COMFORTABLY).

comic, *adj.,* 116.

comics, *n.,* 116.

coming, *n.* (COMINGS), 22 (*See also* **come**).

command, *n.* (COMMANDS), 116.
v. (COMMANDED, COMMANDED, COMMANDING), 116.

company, *n.* (COMPANIES), 117, 391.

compare, *v.* (COMPARED, COMPARED, COMPARING) *(to see how things are different or alike),* 193.

complete, *adj.,* 117, 216 *(adv. See* completely).
v. (COMPLETED, COMPLETED, COMPLETING), 117, 391.

completely, *adj.,* 73, 150, 604.

conductor, *n.* (CONDUCTORS), 117.

cone, *n.* (CONES) *(figure),* 118, 413, 470, 475.
(of seeds), 118, 404, 592.

contented, *adj.,* 118.

continue, *v.* (CONTINUED, CONTINUED, CONTINUING), 49, 88, 118, 302, 372.

cook, *n.* (COOKS), 24, 84, **118.**
v. (COOKED, COOKED, COOKING), 24, 32, 42, 43, 66, 73, 92, **118,** 150, 189, 197, 216, 224, 244, 281, 287, 293, 350, 387, 417, 441, 442, 451, 471, 478, 532, 594, 607, 653.

cookie, *n.* (COOKIES), 24, 32, 61, 96, **119,** 125, 179, 231, 282, 367, 376, 378, 439, 465, 483, 504, 538, 561 (*See also* **cooky**).

cooky, *n.* (COOKIES), **119** (*See also* **cookie**).

cool, *adj.* (COOLER, COOLEST), 84, 99, **119,** 171, 213, 280, 522, 616.
v. (COOLED, COOLED, COOLING), **119,** 281, 327.

coop, *n.* (COOPS), **119.**

copper, *n.,* **119.**

copy, *n.* (COPIES), **119.**
v. (COPIED, COPIED, COPYING), 96, **119.**

cord, *n.* (CORDS), 73, **119,** 295, 298, 454, 516, 535.

corn, *n.,* 93, 112, **120,** 127, 164, 204, 220, 233, 300, 338, 371, 407, 416, 468, 608.

corncob, *n.* (CORNCOBS), **120** (*See also* **cob**; **corn**).

corner, *n.* (CORNERS), 22, 102, **120,** 124, 197, 403, 519, 562, 584, 591.

corral, *n.* (CORRALS), **120.**

correct, *adj.,* **120,** 175, 232, 341, 398, 424, 448, 501, 587, 646.

cost, *n.* (COSTS), **121.**
v. (COST, COST, COSTING), 95, **121,** 145, 212, 284, 422, 449, 549, 607, 643.

Costa Rica, *n.,* 93.

cottage, *n.* (COTTAGES), **121,** 167.

cotton, *adj.,* **121,** 338.
n., 32, **121,** 338, 403, 536, 650.

cough, *n.* (COUGHS), **121.**
v. (COUGHED, COUGHED, COUGHING), 114, **121,** 333, 570.

could, *v.* (*past tense of* CAN), 23, 52, 55, 77, 95, 101, 106, **122,** 146, 172, 231, 236, 242, 247, 256, 267, 277, 318, 320, 323, 335, 338, 347, 350, 375, 401, 406, 417, 435, 440, 478, 485, 491, 504, 510, 515, 536, 568, 569, 588, 589, 591, 599, 632, 638, 643, 652, 653 (*See also* **can**; **couldn't**).

couldn't, *v.* and *adv.* (*contraction for* COULD NOT), **122,** 227, 350, 426, 615.

count, *v.* (COUNTED, COUNTED, COUNTING), 30, **122,** 151, 167, 170, 193, 194, 200, 209, 210, 211, 359, 360, 364, 474, 479, 480, 495, 557, 558, 564, 565, 567, 593, 595.

country, *n.* (COUNTRIES) *(land),* 406.
(land where people do not live close together), 91, **122,** 187, 395, 450, 469, 579, 614, 624.
(nation), 14, 22, 82, 93, 100, 104, **122,** 173, 194, 207, 211, 260, 273, 282, 288, 292, 293, 300, 303, 327, 333, 336, 353, 354, 357, 414, 416, 457, 462, 478, 482, 506, 510, 524, 553, 599, 600, 616.

couple, *n.* (COUPLES), **122.**
v. (COUPLED, COUPLED, COUPLING), **122.**

course, n. (COURSES) *(direction; way)*, 123. *(grounds)*, 123, 229.
  of course *(surely)*, 123.
cousin, n. (COUSINS), 123, 186, 387.
cover, n. (COVERS), 54, 59, 84, 123, 291, 469, 517.
  v. (COVERED, COVERED, COVERING), 30, 35, 40, 43, 49, 54, 74, 87, 89, 109, 123, 144, 162, 190, 215, 217, 242, 262, 271, 293, 330, 348, 385, 393, 408, 456, 457, 464, 473, 475, 481, 484, 486, 496, 499, 503, 512, 558, 607, 615, 626, 632 *(See also* covering).
covering n. (COVERINGS), 83, 76, 123, 131, 154, 262, 383, 529, 548, 632, 644.
cow, n. (COWS), 35, 53, 80, 91, 101, 110, 124, 157, 166, 184, 187, 192, 193, 234, 235, 250, 256, 262, 332, 333, 338, 343, 359, 381, 393, 439, 495, 500, 522, 565, 572, 578.
cowboy, n. (COWBOYS), 124, 276, 440.
cowhide, n. (COWHIDES), 256.
cozy, adj. (COZIER, COZIEST), 124, 504 *(adv.* COZILY).
crack, n. (CRACKS) *(hole)*, 89, 124, 515. *(pound)*, 124.
  v. (CRACKED, CRACKED, CRACKING), 124, 365.
cracker, n. (CRACKERS), 125, 237, 391.
cradle, n. (CRADLES), 125.
crash, v. (CRASHED, CRASHED, CRASHING) *(to break with much noise)*, 114.
crawl, v. (CRAWLED, CRAWLED, CRAWLING), 90, 125, 126, 165, 294, 502, 609, 641.
crayon, n. (CRAYONS), 125.
cream, n. (CREAMS), 25, 48, 75, 76, 103, 118, 126, 271, 276, 376, 470, 508, 509, 516, 546, 555, 583, 608, 629.
creature, n. (CREATURES), 126.
creek, n. (CREEKS), 126.
creep, v. (CREPT, CREPT, CREEPING), 126.
crept, v. *(past tense and past participle of* CREEP), 126 *(See also* creep).
cried, v. *(past tense and past participle of* CRY) 126, 128, 625 *(See also* cry).
cries *(See* cry).
crisp, adj. *(not soft; easily broken)*, 125 *(adv.* CRISPLY).
crooked, adj., 47, 89, 126, 318, *(adv.* CROOKEDLY).
cross, adj., 127.
  n. (CROSSES), 92, 127, 329.
  v. (CROSSED, CROSSED, CROSSING), 65, 86, 127, 136, 303, 418, 460, 461, 492, 550.
crow, n. (CROWS), 92, 127, 283, 302, 441.
  v. (CROWED, CROWED, CROWING), 112, 127, 454.
crowd, n. (CROWDS), 127, 614.
  v. (CROWDED, CROWDED, CROWDING), 127, 281.
crown, n. (CROWNS), 128, 384.
  v. (CROWNED, CROWNED, CROWNING), 128.
cruel, adj., 128, 545, 600 *(adv.* CRUELLY).
crumb, n. (CRUMBS), 128.
cry, n. (CRIES) *(call)*, 80, 128, 179. *(shout; yell)*, 52, 128, 150, 265, 268, 472, 651.
  v. (CRIED, CRIED, CRYING) *(to call)*, 380.

cry *(Cont'd.)*
  (to sob; to weep), 23, 44, 96, 126, 128, 317, 446, 505, 555, 560, 561, 602, 623, 625.
cub, n. (CUBS), 129.
cucumber, n. (CUCUMBERS), 129, 401, 609.
cuddle, v. (CUDDLED, CUDDLED, CUDDLING), 129, 299.
cup, n. (CUPS), 3, 64, 67, 100, 124, 129, 144, 145, 147, 158, 245, 402, 404, 466, 484, 550, 563.
cupboard, n. (CUPBOARDS), 35, 59, 130, 154, 275, 354, 379, 442, 484, 534, 550.
cure, n. (CURES), 130.
  v. (CURED, CURED, CURING), 130.
curious, adj., 130 *(adv.* CURIOUSLY).
curl, n. (CURLS), 130, 131, 208, 589, 619.
curly, adj. (CURLIER, CURLIEST), 131, 640.
curtain, n. (CURTAINS), 109, 131, 606.
curve, n. (CURVES), 47, 131, 619.
  v. (CURVED, CURVED, CURVING), 131, 245, 262, 300, 532, 619.
cushion, n. (CUSHIONS), 131, 403.
customers, n. (CUSTOMERS), 131.
cut, n. (CUTS), 34, 56, 132, 220, 268, 472, 478, 483, 528.
  v. (CUT, CUT, CUTTING), 27, 34, 41, 53, 57, 75, 86, 101, 107, 126, 128, 132, 166, 174, 196, 203, 209, 234, 236, 243, 250, 253, 254, 255, 257, 280, 281, 295, 303, 316, 323, 348, 350, 384, 385, 411, 429, 441, 467, 470, 483, 484, 499, 501, 537, 585, 603, 637, 640, 653.
cute, adj. (CUTER, CUTEST), 132 *(adv.* CUTELY).
cyclone, n. (CYCLONES), 132.

D

D, d, n. (D'S, D'S) *(fourth letter of the alphabet)*, 12, 133, 170, 309, 558, 592.
dad, n. (DADS), 134, 209, 230, 486, 530, 586, 640.
daddy, n. (DADDIES), 2, 26, 29, 34, 54, 56, 61, 63, 81, 86, 98, 114, 134, 157, 159, 186, 187, 189, 196, 200, 225, 265, 285, 298, 353, 361, 390, 408, 410, 415, 442, 445, 451, 455, 456, 470, 484, 485, 496, 526, 531, 538, 541, 606, 626, 642.
daily, adv., 134.
dainty, adj. *(pleasant; delicate; pretty)*, 53 *(adv.* DAINTILY).
dairy, n. (DAIRIES), 134.
daisy, n. (DAISIES), 134, 205.
dam, n. (DAMS), 134.
damage, n. (DAMAGES) *(harm)*, 198.
  v. (DAMAGED, DAMAGED, DAMAGING), 621.
damp, adj. (DAMPER, DAMPEST), 135.
dampen, v. (DAMPENED, DAMPENED, DAMPENING), 135.

dance, n. (DANCES), 135.
  v. (DANCED, DANCED, DANCING), 15, 89, 135, 232, 445, 574.
dancer, n. (DANCERS), 135, 232, 308, 594.
dandelion, n. (DANDELIONS), 134, 135.
danger, n. (DANGERS), 136, 424, 460, 461, 466, 472, 617.
dangerous, adj., 91, 136, 193, 220, 240, 478, 501, 506 *(adv.* DANGEROUSLY).
Dapple Gray, n., 415.
dare, v. (DARED, DARED, DARING), 94, 136.
dark, adj. (DARKER, DARKEST), 6, 52, 53, 58, 101, 128, 136, 137, 155, 161, 311, 330, 359, 406, 447.
darkness, n., 136.
darling, adj. and n. (DARLINGS), 136.
dash, n. (DASHES), 137.
date, n. (DATES) *(exact time)* 80, 137. *(fruit)*, 137.
daughter, n. (DAUGHTERS), 38, 137, 422, 424.
dawn, n. (DAWNS), 137.
day, n. (DAYS), 7, 10, 13, 20, 26, 40, 51, 106, 134, 137, 139, 161, 168, 184, 194, 204, 211, 233, 248, 260, 287, 302, 332, 343, 357, 364, 376, 410, 446, 512, 540, 565, 569, 573, 621, 623, 651.
daytime, n. (DAYTIMES), 76, 138, 485, 497, 539, 541.
dead, adj. *(not alive)*, 10, 138, 268, 315. *(not on fire)*, 428. *(quiet and dull)*, 138.
deaf, adj., 138.
deal, n. (DEALS), 138.
  v. (DEALT, DEALT, DEALING), 138.
dealt, v. *(past tense and past participle of* DEAL), 138, 139 *(See also* deal).
dear, adj. (DEARER, DEAREST), 138, 336, 560, 606, 625.
death, n. (DEATHS), 139, 144.
December, n. (DECEMBERS), 102, 139, 343, 651.
decide, v. (DECIDED, DECIDED, DECIDING), 139, 286.
deck, n. (DECKS), 139.
decorate, v. (DECORATED, DECORATED, DECORATING), 139.
deed, n. (DEEDS), 140.
deep, adj. (DEEPER, DEEPEST), 63, 82, 140, 220, 229, 239, 259, 339, 342, 450, 491, 504, 531, 608, 624 *(adv.* DEEPLY).
deer, n. (DEER), 140, 149, 262, 267, 342, 444, 487, 588.
delay, v. (DELAYED, DELAYED, DELAYING), 140.
delicious, adj., 141, 156, 602 *(adv.* DELICIOUSLY).
delight, n. (DELIGHTS), 141.
deliver, v. (DELIVERED, DELIVERED, DELIVERING), 75, 141, 325, 338, 613, 640.
demand, v. (DEMANDED, DEMANDED, DEMANDING), 141.
den, n. (DENS), 141.
dentist, n. (DENTISTS), 142.
describe, v. (DESCRIBED, DESCRIBED, DESCRIBING), 142.
desert, n. (DESERTS), 142.
deserve, v. (DESERVED, DESERVED, DESERVING), 142.

desire, *v.* (DESIRED, DESIRED, DESIRING), 142.

desk, *n.* (DESKS), 54, **142**, 154, 217, 323, 368, 383, 470, 471, 502, 565.

dessert, *n.* (DESSERTS), 25, **143**.

destroy, *v.* (DESTROYED, DESTROYED, DESTROYING), 43, 73, 132, **143**, 197, 457, 604, 609, 644.

dew, *n.*, **143**, 215.

diamond, *n.* (DIAMONDS), 121, **143**, 223, 230, 284, 339, 511, 525, 529, 594, 607.

dictionary, *n.* (DICTIONARIES), 59, **143**, 271, 332, 610.

did, *v.* (*past tense of* DO), 3, 6, 11, 17, 18, 23, 30, 39, 40, 43, 44, 50, 51, 65, 75, 93, 97, 114, 135, **144**, 149, 175, 184, 198, 231, 239, 251, 269, 276, 286, 298, 307, 320, 341, 357, 390, 415, 439, 449, 466, 474, 508, 514, 520, 527, 536, 540, 551, 564, 569, 577, 585, 602, 611, 620, 631, 651, 653 (*See also* didn't; do; done).

didn't, *v.* and *adv.* (*contraction for* DID NOT), 41, **144**, 331, 341, 362, 390, 518, 564, 587, 620, 653 (*See also* did).

die, *v.* (DIED, DIED, DYING), 74, 139, **144**, 159, 162, 183, 220, 262, 274, 292, 399, 420, 466, 508, 511, 524, 604.

difference, *n.* (DIFFERENCES) (*way in which people or things are not the same; being different*), 253, 331 (*See also* different).

different, *adj.*, 7, 9, 17, 76, 77, 82, 83, 95, 115, 125, 130, **144**, 149, 171, 214, 226, 231, 271, 292, 347, 352, 357, 375, 377, 385, 396, 398, 413, 435, 463, 477, 504, 523, 632 (*adv.* DIFFERENTLY).

difficult, *adj.* (*hard; not easy*), 214 (*adv.* DIFFICULTLY).

dig, *v.* (DUG, DUG, DIGGING), 140, **144**, 147, 161, 165, 237, 259, 339, 355, 400, 472, 590.

dime, *n.* (DIMES), 92, **145**, 150, 174, 193, 194, 209, 342, 360, 565.

dine, *v.* (DINED, DINED, DINING), **145**, 153, 204, 506, 548.

ding dong, *n.* (DING DONGS), **145**, 335.

dining room, *n.* (DINING ROOMS), **145**, 453.

dinner, *n.* (DINNERS), 14, 42, 43, 80, 86, 101, **145**, 150, 166, 190, 197, 228, 242, 243, 248, 277, 288, 321, 332, 350, 375, 392, 419, 424, 442, 453, 471, 478, 508, 541, 550, 552, 571, 582, 586, 602, 614, 618, 620, 653.

dip, *v.* (DIPPED, DIPPED, DIPPING), **145**.

direction, *n.* (DIRECTIONS), 22, 25, 39, 123, **146**, 165, 209, 362, 373, 413, 425, 509, 511, 573, 574, 578, 591, 620.

dirt, *n.*, 89, 106, 123, 136, 144, **146**, 161, 192, 237, 321, 348, 455, 487, 489, 516.

dirty, *adj.* (DIRTIER, DIRTIEST), 95, 106, 126, **146**, 303, 445, 471, 482, 505, 538, 614 (*adv.* DIRTILY).

disagree, *v.* (DISAGREED, DISAGREED, DISAGREEING), **146**.

disappear, *v.* (DISAPPEARED, DISAPPEARED, DISAPPEARING), **146**, 227, 548, 607.

discover, *v.* (DISCOVERED, DISCOVERED, DISCOVERING), **146**, 196.

disease, *n.* (DISEASES), **147**, 203, 205, 223, 441.

dish, *n.* (DISHES), 19, 53, 63, 64, 69, 88, 105, 106, 130, 140, **147**, 160, 226, 301, 310, 330, 363, 370, 388, 408, 425, 428, 432, 436, 445, 456, 466, 478, 484, 494, 505, 538, 548, 582, 601, 614, 628, 640, 643.

distance, *n.* (DISTANCES), **147**, 187, 188, 226, 229, 317, 338, 513.

ditch, *n.* (DITCHES), **147**, 199.

divide, *v.* (DIVIDED, DIVIDED, DIVIDING), 15, 49, 105, **148**, 398, 431, 453, 473, 477.

dizzy, *adj.* (DIZZIER, DIZZIEST), **148** (*adv.* DIZZILY).

do, *v.* (DID, DONE, DOING), 4, 7, 16, 21, 30, 44, 57, 64, 72, 80, 96, 108, 122, 136, **148**, 150, 164, 170, 189, 197, 207, 210, 230, 240, 254, 272, 282, 296, 305, 321, 339, 341, 355, 363, 371, 386, 399, 414, 424, 440, 451, 465, 475, 490, 504, 515, 528, 533, 550, 565, 571, 586, 594, 602, 614, 620, 631, 645, 651 (*See also* did; does; doing; done).

doctor, *n.* (DOCTORS), 3, 130, 140, 142, **148**, 158, 159, 264, 268, 333, 371, 403, 478, 490, 548, 648.

doe, *n.* (DOES), 149.

does, *v.* (*third person singular, present indicative of* DO), 5, 7, 17, 20, 32, 45, 61, 75, 84, 110, 129, 131, **149**, 151, 167, 185, 194, 200, 230, 242, 253, 265, 285, 304, 314, 323, 331, 340, 383, 423, 451, 456, 467, 468, 475, 493, 500, 524, 536, 543, 552, 580, 591, 603, 606, 631, 642, 653 (*See also* do).

doesn't, *v.* and *adv.* (*contraction for* DOES NOT), 44, **149**, 340, 341, 458, 475, 537 (*See also* does).

dog, *n.* (DOGS), 2, 15, 24, 35, 43, 52, 61, 71, 83, 95, 114, 123, 137, **149**, 164, 178, 187, 194, 203, 213, 227, 236, 249, 258, 265, 276, 292, 301, 311, 315, 321, 330, 362, 378, 388, 394, 409, 413, 426, 432, 460, 472, 494, 503, 516, 528, 545, 576, 581, 597, 600, 613, 628, 631, 638, 642, 651.

doing, *v.* (*present participle of* DO), 144, 148, **149**, 178, 180, 286, 326, 381, 566, 576, 626 (*See also* do).

doll, *n.* (DOLLS), 7, 101, 123, **149**, 150, 208, 224, 225, 255, 290, 426, 480, 575.

dollar, *n.* (DOLLARS), 15, 50, 92, **150**, 165, 178, 223, 266, 320, 323, 325, 342, 348, 373, 397, 413, 431, 448, 462, 607, 613.

dollhouse, *n.* (DOLLHOUSES), **150**.

done, *v.* (*past participle of* DO), 25, 148, **150**, 166, 179, 391, 417, 428, 448, 553 (*See also* do).

donkey, *n.* (DONKEYS), 88, **150**, 249, 349, 567.

don't, *v.* and *adv.* (*contraction for* DO NOT), 72, 86, 126, **150**, 203, 246, 258, 348, 378, 385, 386, 387, 428, 441,

don't (*Cont'd.*)
472, 474, 509, 514, 522, 523, 530, 560, 561, 566, 573, 597, 604, 618, 625, 632, 652 (*See also* do).

door, *n.* (DOORS), 17, 20, 23, 34, 59, 89, 108, 127, 131, **151**, 152, 167, 188, 221, 243, 245, 275, 291, 295, 312, 316, 332, 374, 393, 417, 421, 433, 440, 460, 489, 490, 519, 522, 530, 535, 552, 574, 600, 628, 638, 644.

doorbell, *n.* (DOORBELLS), 45, **151**, 440, 449, 458, 509, 530.

doorstep, *n.* (DOORSTEPS), **151**.

doorway, *n.* (DOORWAYS), **151**, 174.

dot, *n.* (DOTS), 103, **152**, 337, 398.

double, *adj.*, **152**.

v. (DOUBLED, DOUBLED, DOUBLING), **152**.

dough, *n.*, **152**, 179.

dove, *n.* (DOVES), **152**, 402.

down, *n.* (*soft feathers*), 359.

down, *adv.*, 41, 62, 63, 96, 100, 101, 108, 111, 140, **153**, 160, 164, 170, 177, 179, 184, 185, 191, 202, 253, 294, 298, 301, 304, 311, 316, 320, 321, 347, 348, 361, 363, 379, 384, 389, 420, 438, 464, 478, 481, 550, 558, 610, 619, 623, 633, 639.

prep., **153**, 257, 300, 326, 335, 337, 400, 437, 453, 461, 625.

flag down (*to give a signal with a flag to stop someone*), 201.

downstairs, *adv.*, **153**, 170, 606.

downtown, *adj.* or *adv.*, **153**.

downward, *adv.*, **153**.

doze, *n.* (DOZES), **153**.

v. (DOZED, DOZED, DOZING), **153**.

dozen, *n.* (DOZENS), **153**.

drag, *v.* (DRAGGED, DRAGGED, DRAGGING), **154**.

dragon, *n.* (DRAGONS), 532.

drank, *v.* (*past tense of* DRINK), 61, **154**, 157, 345 (*See also* drink).

draw, *v.* (DREW, DRAWN, DRAWING) (*to make lines, pictures, etc., as with a pencil*), 23, 103, 107, **154**, 155, 156, 195, 523 532.

(*to pull*), 154, 156 (*See also* drew; drawn; drawing).

drawer, *n.* (DRAWERS), 130, **154**, 156, 283, 316.

drawing, *n.* (DRAWINGS), **155**, 401.

drawn, *v.* (*past participle of* DRAW), **155**.

dreadful, *adj.*, **155** (*adv.* DREADFULLY).

dream, *n.* (DREAMS), **155**.

v. (DREAMED or DREAMT, DREAMED or DREAMT, DREAMING), **155**.

dreary, *adj.* (DREARIER, DREARIEST), **155** (*adv.* DREARILY).

dress, *n.* (DRESSES), 5, 20, 24, 57, 76, 77, 95, 106, 109, 114, 119, 152, **155**, 178, 183, 186, 224, 345, 357, 406, 575, 608, 621, 645.

v. (DRESSED, DRESSED, DRESSING), 73, **155**, 255, 271, 397, 428, 436, 468, 561.

dresser, *n.* (DRESSERS), **154**, 156, 469.

drew, *v.* (*past tense of* DRAW), 154, 155, **156**, 337, 630.

enter, *v.* (ENTERED, ENTERED, ENTERING), 24, **174.**

entire, *adj.,* **174** (*adv.* ENTIRELY).

envelope, *n.* (ENVELOPES), 174, 202, 206, 309, 536.

equal, *adj.,* **174,** 431 (*adv. See* **equally**).
v. (EQUALED or EQUALLED, EQUALED or EQUALLED, EQUALING or EQUALLING), **174,** 266, 340, 655.

equally, *adv.,* **175.**

erase, *v.* (ERASED, ERASED, ERASING), **175.**

eraser, *n.* (ERASERS), **175.**

errand, *n.* (ERRANDS), **175,** 237.

error, *n.* (ERRORS), **175.**

escape, *v.* (ESCAPED, ESCAPED, ESCAPING), **175.**

Eskimo, *n.* (ESKIMOS), **175,** 272.

especially, *adv.,* 142, **176,** 211, 597, 641.

even, *adj.,* **176,** 202, 369, 406.
adv., 13, 16, 95, **176,** 248, 254, 272, 361, 397, 528, 566, 652.
v. (EVENED, EVENED, EVENING), **176.**

evening, *n.* (EVENINGS), 124, 145, 161, **176,** 236, 359, 541, 571, 625.

event, *n.* (EVENTS), **177,** 246.

ever, *adv.,* 11, 39, 40, 51, 65, 67, 81, 93, 97, 110, 112, 123, 124, 126, 127, 139, 144, 149, 155, 164, 170, **177,** 185, 190, 198, 205, 207, 222, 228, 238, 240, 261, 267, 272, 296, 307, 327, 357, 371, 389, 396, 425, 440, 447, 463, 483, 489, 496, 501, 514, 519, 527, 535, 536, 537, 546, 551, 552, 554, 567, 570, 584, 617, 622, 625, 643, 648.

evergreen, *n.* (EVERGREENS), **177.**

every, *adj.,* 10, 29, 36, 40, 88, 89, 96, 103, 134, 145, 157, 161, 167, **177,** 178, 190, 204, 205, 223, 225, 242, 264, 357, 377, 398, 483, 484, 513, 544, 603, 621, 634, 642.

everybody, *pro.,* 39, 106, 117, **177,** 303, 326, 373, 389, 392, 406, 446, 501, 521, 552, 558, 598, 616.

everyone, *pro.,* 9, 164, **177,** 244.

everything, *pro.,* 171, **177,** 210, 238, 281, 296, 354, 442, 478, 515, 585.

everywhere, *adv.,* 19, 134, 172, **178,** 275, 379, 412, 568.

evil, *adj.,* **178.**

exact, *adj.,* **178.**

exactly, *adv.,* 103, 119, **178,** 288.

examine, *v.* (EXAMINED, EXAMINED, EXAMINING), **178.**

except, *prep.,* 75, **178,** 207, 343, 374.

excess, *adj.,* **179.**

exchange, *v.* (EXCHANGED, EXCHANGED, EXCHANGING), **179,** 580.

excited, *adj.,* 61, 164, **179.**

exclaim, *v.* (EXCLAIMED, EXCLAIMED, EXCLAIMING), **179.**

excuse, *n.* (EXCUSES), **179.**
v. (EXCUSED, EXCUSED, EXCUSING), **179,** 424.

exercise, *n.* (EXERCISES), **180.**

exist, *v.* (EXISTED, EXISTED, EXISTING), **180.**

expect, *v.* (EXPECTED, EXPECTED, EXPECTING), 165, **180,** 406.

explain, *v.* (EXPLAINED, EXPLAINED, EXPLAINING), **180,** 598.

express, *v.* (EXPRESSED, EXPRESSED, EXPRESSING), **180.**

extra, *adj.,* 179, **181,** 511, 586.

eye, *n.* (EYES), 2, 46, 55, 96, 126, 161, 164, **181,** 183, 208, 223, 233, 250, 251, 280, 317, 320, 337, 373, 380, 474, 481, 485, 511, 523, 555, 603, 635.

eyebrow, *n.* (EYEBROWS), **181.**

eyeglasses, *n.,* 226.

eyelid, *n.* (EYELIDS), **181.**

F

F, f, *n.* (F'S, F's) (*sixth letter of the alphabet*), 12, 170, **182,** 309, 558, 592.

face, *n.* (FACES), 40, 56, 96, 100, 110, **183,** 208, 212, 245, 251, 280, 283, 292, 317, 330, 340, 369, 372, 387, 420, 425, 432, 441, 483, 485, 494, 501, 517, 551, 629, 636, 645.
v. (FACED, FACED, FACING), **183,** 307.

fact, *n.* (FACTS), **183,** 442.

factory, *n.* (FACTORIES), 82, 99, **183,** 338, 407, 520.

fade, *v.* (FADED, FADED, FADING), **183,** 480.

fail, *v.* (FAILED, FAILED, FAILING), **184,** 290.

faint, *adj.* (*weak*) **184,** (*adv.* FAINTLY).
v. (FAINTED, FAINTED, FAINTING), **184.**

fair, *adj.* (FAIRER, FAIREST) (*clear and sunny*), **184,** 410.
(*honest*), **184,** 261.
n. (FAIRS), **184,** 616.

fairy, *n.* (FAIRIES), 170, **185,** 223, 442, 531, 637.

faithful, *adj.,* **185** (*adv.* FAITHFULLY).

fall, *n.* (FALLS), 26, 90, 114, **185,** 601.
v. (FELL, FALLEN, FALLING), 3, 30, 32, 50, 96, 101, 125, 140, 141, 158, 166, **185,** 191, 232, 246, 307, 386, 399, 437, 438, 498, 500, 503, 504, 514, 585, 590, 619 (*See also* **fell**).

fallen, *v.* (*past participle of* FALL), 140, **185,** 530 (*See also* **fall**).

false, *adj.* (FALSER, FALSEST), **186,** 230, 330, 442, 587 (*adv.* FALSELY).

family, *n.* (FAMILIES), 19, 27, 85, 116, **186,** 189, 283, 313, 315, 326, 352, 570.

fan, *n.* (FANS), 54, 56, 160, **186.**
v. (FANNED, FANNED, FANNING), **186.**

fancy, *adj.* (FANCIER, FANCIEST), 128, **186,** 406, 457.
v. (FANCIED, FANCIED, FANCYING), **186.**

far, *adj.* (FARTHER or FURTHER, FARTHEST or FURTHEST), **187,** 188, 338, 413, 604.
adv. (FARTHER or FURTHER, FARTHEST or FURTHEST), 2, 66, 100, 140, 147, 169, **187,** 188, 226, 233, 247, 256, 282, 286, 291, 368, 452, 475, 508, 510, 523, 529, 530, 556, 563, 567, 574, 620.

fare, *n.* (FARES), **187.**

farm, *n.* (FARMS), 16, 35, 122, 124, **187,** 301, 411, 440, 520, 580, 613.

farmer, *n.* (FARMERS), 35, 43, 88, 91, 119, 127, 157, **187,** 192, 193, 201, 203, 235, 248, 250, 259, 300, 304, 316,

farmer (*Cont'd.*)
338, 364, 407, 411, 460, 484, 500, 510, 513, 518, 519, 533, 567, 568, 601, 627.

farmyard, *n.* (FARMYARDS), **187.**

farther, *adv.* (*comparative of* FAR), **188,** 530, 567 (*See also* **far**).

farthest, *adj.* (*superlative of* FAR), **188,** 604 (*See also* **far**).

fast, *adj.* (FASTER, FASTEST), 13, 164, 432, 500, 544.
adv., 2, 9, 23, 40, 65, 95, 140, 148, 172, **188,** 190, 196, 219, 220, 228, 238, 247, 268, 284, 290, 324, 341, 388, 416, 423, 425, 435, 440, 458, 471, 512, 531, 542, 559, 567, 570, 629, 652.

fasten, *v.* (FASTENED, FASTENED, FASTENING), 59, 76, 93, **188,** 246, 258, 261, 285, 306, 316, 318, 323, 389, 404, 437, 470, 472, 527, 533, 548, 549, 570, 574, 609, 622.

fat, *adj.* (FATTER, FATTEST), 47, **189,** 375, 412, 531, 563.
n. (FATS), **189,** 235, 301, 305, 328, 371.

father, *n.* (FATHERS), 2, 3, 10, 17, 25, 26, 32, 45, 52, 68, 75, 80, 93, 103, 117, 121, 129, 132, 140, 183, **189,** 219, 222, 230, 242, 250, 262, 273, 285, 298, 304, 310, 324, 338, 340, 352, 379, 383, 390, 403, 424, 441, 446, 465, 481, 494, 505, 515, 523, 533, 534, 548, 550, 568, 580, 592, 600, 611, 619, 623, 629, 630, 634, 636, 640, 645, 646.

faucet, *n.* (FAUCETS), **189,** 370, 405, 419, 458, 552, 645.

fault, *n.* (FAULTS), **189.**
at fault (*in the wrong*), 54.

favorite, *adj.,* 147, **189.**

fear, *n.* (FEARS), 558.
v. (FEARED, FEARED, FEARING), 47, **190,** 560.

feast, *n.* (FEASTS), **190.**
v. (FEASTED, FEASTED, FEASTING), **190.**

feather, *n.* (FEATHERS), 51, 57, 131, 144, **190,** 248, 252, 311, 391, 403, 433, 536, 549.

February, *n.* (FEBRUARIES or FEBRUARYS), 137, **190,** 211, 343, 606, 651.

fed, *v.* (*past tense and past participle of* FEED), **190,** 191, 471 (*See also* **feed**).

feeble, *adj.* (FEEBLER, FEEBLEST), **190** (*adv.* FEEBLY).

feed, *v.* (FED, FED, FEEDING), 88, 190, **191,** 228, 229, 338, 355, 439, 454, 529, 620 (*See also* **fed**).

feel, *v.* (FELT, FELT, FEELING), 21, 57, 97, 99, 148, 173, **191,** 213, 252, 316, 415, 446, 460, 469, 475, 509, 528, 538, 559, 564, 570, 578 (*See also* **felt**).

feet, *n.* (*plural of* FOOT) (*part of body*), 35, 40, **191,** 200, 207, 223, 305, 394, 458, 486, 522, 530, 544, 570, 571, 601, 614, 622.
(*twelve inches*), **191,** 207, 332, 650 (*See also* **foot**).

fell, *v.* (*past tense of* FALL), 19, 55, 67, 100, 104, 128, 132, 177, 184, 185, **191,** 220, 283, 321, 379, 384, 393, 438,

fell *(Cont'd.)*
508, 561, 572, 585, 602, 623 *(See also* **fall**).

fellow, *n.* (FELLOWS), **191,** 486.

felt, *v.* *(past tense and past participle of* FEEL), 191, **192,** 440, 570, 626 *(See also* **feel**).

fence, *n.* (FENCES), 3, 49, 107, 120, 122, **192, 193,** 201, 221, 253, 300, 302, 306, 344, 396, 418, 477, 479, 615, 633, 636, 638, 656.

fender, *n.* (FENDERS), **192.**

ferry, *n.* (FERRIES), **192.**

fetch, *v.* (FETCHED, FETCHED, FETCHING), **192,** 384.

few, *adj.* (FEWER, FEWEST), 142, **192,** 203, 415.

fiddle, *n.* (FIDDLES), **193.**

field, *n.* (FIELDS), 60, 91, 134, 135, **193,** 229, 250, 262, 332, 346, 348, 381, 393, 411, 481, 495, 565, 632.

fierce, *adj.* (FIERCER, FIERCEST), 132, **193** *(adv.* FIERCELY).

fifteen, *adj.,* **193, 194,** 222, 315, 340, 624.
n. (FIFTEENS), 167, **193,** 211, 564, 593.

fifteenth, *adj.,* **194.**

fifth, *adj.,* **194,** 199, 213, 331, 342, 474, 479, 495, 539, 564, 569, 589, 623.

fifty, *adj.,* 178, **194,** 306, 309, 524, 600, 643.
n. (FIFTIES), 46, **194,** 266, 480, 495, 557.

fig, *n.* (FIGS), **194.**

fight, *v.* (FOUGHT, FOUGHT, FIGHTING), 22, 94, 172, **194,** 210, 333, 354, 391, 506, 546, 616 *(See also* **fought**).

figure, *n.* (FIGURES), 118, **195,** 584.

file, *n.* (FILES), **195.**

fill, *v.* (FILLED, FILLED, FILLING), 20, 33, 36, 63, 127, 131, 136, **195,** 403, 501, 536, 540, 573, 581, 584, 613, 619.

film, *n.* (FILMS) *(material used for taking pictures in a camera),* 453.

finally, *adv.,* 114, 144, 174, **195,** 280, 302, 588.

find, *v.* (FOUND, FOUND, FINDING), 16, 17, 44, 110, 146, 164, 172, 192, **196,** 208, 210, 233, 255, 256, 267, 288, 306, 307, 317, 318, 357, 360, 364, 448, 463, 484, 491, 497, 558, 579, 597, 624, 634 *(See also* **found**).

fine, *adj.* (FINER, FINEST) *(good),* **196,** 515.
(in very small bits), **196,** 226, 420, 517.
(sunny and clear), **196.**
(very thin), **196,** 492.
n. (FINES), **196.**

finger, *n.* (FINGERS), 32, 34, 56, 126, 130, **196,** 200, 226, 244, 255, 257, 341, 352, 353, 362, 377, 385, 413, 449, 501, 503, 508, 545, 563, 569, 571, 594, 625.

fingernail, *n.* (FINGERNAILS), 195, **196,** 352, 470, 472.

finish, *v.* (FINISHED, FINISHED, FINISHING), 90, 105, 114, 117, 148, 150, 172, **197,** 227, 272, 310, 329, 344, 357, 372, 385, 391, 433, 491, 568, 576, 601.

fire, *n.* (FIRES), 9, 22, 54, 66, 73, 83, 90, 136, 137, 143, **197,** 198, 199, 201, 203, 220, 225, 252, 264, 269, 311,

fire *(Cont'd.)*
314, 330, 428, 443, 458, 466, 492, 511, 568, 584, 594, 604, 616, 617.

fire alarm, *n.* (FIRE ALARMS), **197.**

firecracker, *n.* (FIRECRACKERS), **197.**

fire engine, *n.* (FIRE ENGINES), **198.**

firefly, *n.* (FIREFLIES), **198.**

fireman, *n.* (FIREMEN), 9, 197, 198, 269, 311, 408, 466, 553.

fireplace, *n.* (FIREPLACES), 99, 124, **199,** 311, 314, 428, 515.

fire truck, *n.* (FIRE TRUCKS), **199.**

firm, *adj.* (FIRMER, FIRMEST), **199** *(adv.* FIRMLY).

first, *adj.,* 64, 170, 194, **199,** 211, 235, 251, 273, 274, 281, 292, 304, 332, 342, 343, 344, 352, 358, 421, 423, 442, 465, 474, 479, 495, 539, 553, 564, 569, 571, 589, 608, 617, 623.
adv., 6, 30, 114, 232, 302, 435, 475, 476, 561, 633, 638.
at first *(in the beginning),* 588.

fish, *n.* (FISH or FISHES), 10, 31, 49, 90, 113, 192, **199, 200,** 229, 262, 356, 398, 462, 464, 465, 473, 626, 641.
v. (FISHED, FISHED, FISHING), 12, 31, 67, 90, 175, **199, 200,** 299, 313, 414, 452, 516, 533, 583, 641.

fisherman, *n.* (FISHERMEN), 49, **200.**

fishhook, *n.* (FISHHOOKS), 31, **200,** 262.

fit, *v.* (FITTED or FIT, FITTED, FITTING), 179, **200,** 206, 216, 259, 288, 291, 429, 433, 453, 571, 584.

five, *adj.,* 7, 15, 48, 49, 62, 77, 92, 95, 145, 152, 156, 165, 177, 178, 186, 194, 196, **200,** 207, 244, 252, 348, 359, 398, 448, 476, 480, 513, 564, 628.
n. (FIVES), 12, 122, 167, 170, **200,** 210, 211, 243, 363, 364, 479, 495, 557, 567, 575.

fix, *v.* (FIXED, FIXED, FIXING), 12, 46, 107, 142, **201,** 227, 333, 411, 486, 549, 566, 588, 620, 645.

fizz, *v.* (FIZZED, FIZZED, FIZZING), **201.**

flag, *n.* (FLAGS), 14, **201,** 202, 414, 535.
v. (FLAGGED, FLAGGED, FLAGGING), **201.**

flake, *n.* (FLAKES), **201.**

flame, *n.* (FLAMES), 54, 83, **201,** 203, 299, 330.

flap, *n.* (FLAPS), **202.**
v. (FLAPPED, FLAPPED, FLAPPING), **202,** 635.

flash, *n.* (FLASHES), 198, **202.**

flashlight, *n.* (FLASHLIGHTS), **202,** 485.

flat, *adj.* (FLATTER, FLATTEST), 36, 39, 40, 41, 53, 57, 68, 160, 174, 176, **202,** 244, 311, 327, 352, 367, 384, 387, 406, 408, 499, 517, 519, 548, 582, 584, 619 *(adv.* FLATLY).
n. (FLATS), **202.**

flea, *n.* (FLEAS), **203,** 275.

fleece, *n.,* **203,** 412.

flesh, *n.* *(part of body that covers bone; meat),* 472.

flew, *(past tense of* FLY), 10, 22, **203,** 204, 205, 278, 283, 318, 370, 402, 568, 601 *(See also* **fly**).

flicker, *n.* (FLICKERS), **203,** 639.
v. (FLICKERED, FLICKERED, FLICKERING), **203.**

flies *(See* **fly**).

float, *v.* (FLOATED, FLOATED, FLOATING), 24, 33, 109, 153, 156, **203,** 258, 389, 602, 619.

flock, *n.* (FLOCKS), **204.**

floor, *n.* (FLOORS), 3, 5, 19, 35, 54, 64, 67, 87, 104, 106, 126, 139, 153, 166, 170, **204,** 208, 232, 254, 284, 304, 311, 356, 379, 394, 400, 408, 423, 457, 472, 505, 514, 521, 522, 543, 602, 606, 620, 640.

flour, *n.* (FLOURS), 64, 79, 152, **204,** 233, 332, 338, 387, 393, 420, 458, 470, 627.

flow, *n.,* **204,** 440.
v. (FLOWED, FLOWED, FLOWING), **204,** 263, 314, 458, 465, 533.

flower, *n.* (FLOWERS), 15, 41, 42, 56, 70, 72, 76, 110, 134, 135, 144, 146, 183, **205,** 215, 220, 221, 229, 231, 237, 250, 268, 280, 285, 312, 328, 332, 344, 353, 388, 399, 400, 404, 407, 416, 419, 428, 439, 454, 475, 476, 477, 505, 517, 526, 539, 540, 568, 589, 601, 602, 607, 610, 619, 635, 644, 650, 655.

flown, *v.* *(past participle of* FLY), **205** *(See also* **fly**).

fluffy, *adj.* (FLUFFIER, FLUFFIEST), 121, 192, **205,** 359, 503, 538, 629.

flutter, *v.* (FLUTTERED, FLUTTERED, FLUTTERING), 203, **205.**

fly, *n.* (FLIES), 77, 203, **205,** 511.
v. (FLEW, FLOWN, FLYING), 3, 8, 9, 27, 37, 42, 43, 51, 70, 72, 76, 109, 123, 160, 164, 172, 175, 198, 202, **205,** 212, 222, 253, 256, 293, 320, 344, 345, 356, 380, 397, 442, 464, 497, 517, 542, 565, 632, 635 *(See also* **flew;** **flown**).

fog, *n.* (FOGS) *(cloud lying near the ground),* 501.

fold, *v.* (FOLDED, FOLDED, FOLDING), 202, **206,** 280, 615, 645.

folk, *n.* (FOLKS), **206,** 233.

follow, *v.* (FOLLOWED, FOLLOWED, FOLLOWING), 13, **206,** 219, 376, 393, 457, 473, 580, 628.

fond, *adj.* (FONDER, FONDEST), **206,** 319 *(adv.* FONDLY).

fondle, *v.* (FONDLED, FONDLED, FONDLING), **206.**

fondness, *n.,* **206.**

food, *n.* (FOODS), 24, 31, 35, 50, 68, 73, 75, 93, 98, 116, 118, 126, 130, 142, 147, 157, 164, 166, 169, 175, 190, 191, 197, 203, 205, **206,** 220, 228, 236, 237, 238, 239, 261, 293, 328, 329, 333, 338, 344, 363, 376, 383, 388, 396, 397, 401, 406, 415, 424, 428, 442, 443, 447, 454, 460, 463, 464, 465, 473, 509, 513, 524, 529, 542, 548, 555, 576, 577, 580, 581, 582, 601, 602, 608, 614, 618, 622, 627, 655.

fool, *n.* (FOOLS), **207.**
v. (FOOLED, FOOLED, FOOLING), **207.**

foolish, *adj.* **207,** 443, 448 *(adv.* FOOLISHLY).

foot, *n.* (FEET) (*part of body*), 16, 105, 128, 191, **207,** 253, 262, 274, 291, 390, 394, 506, 527, 529, 536, 575, 585, 614.
(*measurement of twelve inches*), 191, **207.**
football, *n.* (FOOTBALLS), 85, 111, 157, **207,** 291, 304, 409, 436, 490, 516, 568, 599, 643.
footpath, *n.,* (FOOTPATHS), **207.**
footprint, *n.* (FOOTPRINTS), **207,** 422, 580.
for, *conj.,* 110, 140, 203, **208,** 215, 387.
prep. (*at the price of; in exchange for*), 96, 145, 320, 380, 506.
(*because of; as a result of; out of*), 223, 325, 333, 443.
(*in honor of; on the occasion of*), 115, 167, 243, 248, 277, 391, 420, 466.
(*in its effect on*), 7, 47, 94, 576.
(*in place of*), 109, **208,** 220, 383, 433.
(*in support of; in favor of*), 611.
(*meant to be received by, to be done in the interest of, to be directed or sent to*), 14, 76, 94, 98, 118, 134, 160, 174, 200, **208,** 210, 254, 261, 341, 400, 478, 486, 515, 559, 566.
(*sentiment directed toward*), 415.
(*to the length, amount, or duration of*), 55, 60, 102, 113, 205, 208, 285, 306, 474, 498, 528.
(*with the purpose of using as, of obtaining, of going to, of serving as, of being suitable to or in*), 19, 21, 24, 41, 67, 82, 103, 117, 155, **208,** 212, 231, 271, 292, 301, 327, 352, 356, 368, 385, 409, 457, 500, 522, 545, 583, 598, 601, 617, 625, 636, 645.
ask for (*request*), 137.
look for (*search for; expect*), 178, **208,** 210, 257, 267.
wait for (*stay in expectation of*), 165, 317, 377, 652.
forehead, *n.* (FOREHEADS), 183, **208.**
forest, *n.* (FORESTS), 16, **208,** 240, 318, 342, 433, 435, 487, 562, 607, 632.
forget, *v.* (FORGOT, FORGOTTEN, FORGETTING), **208,** 637.
forgot (*See* **forget**).
forgotten (*See* **forget**).
fork, *n.* (FORKS), 154, **209,** 478, 493.
form, *v.* (FORMED, FORMED, FORMING), **209,** 226.
forth, *adv.,* 202, 205, **209,** 456, 545, 557.
forty, *adj.,* **209.**
n. (FORTIES), 209, 495.
forward, *adj.,* **209,** 214.
adv., 12, 30, **209,** 228, 361, 425, 530.
fought, *v.* (*past tense and past participle of* FIGHT), 194, **210,** 462 (*See also* **fight**).
found, *v.* (*past tense and past participle of* FIND), 77, 88, 111, 112, 113, 118, 130, 196, **210,** 234, 260, 274, 320, 335, 336, 393, 448, 463, 471, 516, 523, 538, 582, 598 (*See also* **find**).
fountain, *n.* (FOUNTAINS), **210,** 212.
four, *adj.,* 10, 19, 25, 26, 40, 43, 76, 94, 110, 191, **210,** 431, 613.
n. (FOURS), 12, 210, **210,** 211, 340, 495, 567.

fourteen, *adj.,* **211.**
n. (FOURTEENS), **211.**
fourteenth, *adj.,* **211.**
fourth, *adj.,* 20, 194, 197, 199, **211,** 213, 342, 465, 474, 495, 539, 564, 569, 589, 623.
Fourth of July, *n.* (FOURTH OF JULYS), 197, **211,** 260.
fowl, *n.* (FOWL *or* FOWLS), **211.**
fox, *n.* (FOXES), **212,** 500, 582.
frankfurter, *n.* (FRANKFURTERS), **212.**
freckle, *n.* (FRECKLES), **212.**
free, *adj.* (FREER, FREEST) (*not under the power of another; to be able to do what one wants*), 211, **212,** 622.
(*not costing*), **212,** 335.
freeze, *v.* (FROZE, FROZEN, FREEZING), **212,** 215, 234, 247, 496, 498 (*See also* **frozen**).
freight, *n.,* **213.**
fresh, *adj.* (FRESHER, FRESHEST) (*clean and cool*), 8, **213,** 358, 379.
(*newly gotten from the garden, oven, laundry, etc.*), 30, **213,** 521.
(*not salty*), 368.
(*adv.* FRESHLY).
Friday, *n.* (FRIDAYS), 137, 194, 199, **213,** 342, 376, 394, 465, 474, 479, 495, 539, 569, 589, 623.
fried, *adj.* and *v.* (*past tense and past participle of* FRY), 216, 387.
friend, *n.* (FRIENDS), 5, 21, 102, 108, 172, 174, 185, **213,** 294, 296, 324, 334, 392, 431, 515, 562, 606, 613, 624.
friendly, *adj.* (FRIENDLIER, FRIENDLIEST), 95, 114, 206, **213,** 292.
frighten, *adj.* and *v.* (FRIGHTENED, FRIGHTENED, FRIGHTENING), 5, 47, 105, **214,** 387, 440, 468, 523, 527.
frog, *n.* (FROGS), 63, **214,** 412, 548, 574.
from, *prep.* (*indicating a starting point*), 158, 213, **214,** 249, 304, 337, 360, 641.
(*indicating separation, differentiation, etc.*), 3, 22, 29, 120, 144, 179, 189, 192, 203, **214,** 264, 391, 411, 429, 445, 473, 514, 549, 567, 576, 600, 636, 640.
(*indicating source, cause, agent, or basis*), 4, 32, 43, 63, 71, 83, 97, 102, 112, 134, **214,** 224, 233, 243, 255, 281, 287, 298, 324, 343, 388, 405, 435, 454, 466, 484, 526, 535, 555, 587, 592, 620, 627, 651.
front, *adj.,* 20, 49, 144, 183, 209, 245, 275, 290, 301, 311, 522, 567, 585, 644.
n. (FRONTS), **214,** 251.
in front of (*prepositional use meaning before; ahead of*), 8, 160, 167, 168, 199, 214, 237, 256, 269, 360, 393, 527, 614, 655.
in front *or* **front** (*adverbial use meaning before; in the front*), 355, 380, 543.
frost, *n.* (FROSTS), **215,** 268.
frosting, *n.* (FROSTINGS), 176, **215,** 271, 538.
frosty, *adj.* (FROSTIER, FROSTIEST), **215.**

froze, *v.* (*past tense of* FREEZE), **212,** 215 (*See also* **freeze**).
frozen, *adj.* and *v.* (*past participle of* FREEZE), **212,** **215,** 242, 271, 496, 503 (*See also* **freeze**).
fruit, *n.* (FRUITS), 20, 33, 37, 43, 47, 53, 84, 92, 96, 97, 137, 166, 171, 187, 194, 206, **216,** 234, 281, 283, 287, 295, 308, 329, 334, 365, 375, 376, 395, 396, 404, 411, 419, 426, 440, 462, 496, 515, 529, 546, 553.
fry, *v.* (FRIED, FRIED, FRYING), 118, 200, **216,** 469, 652 (*See also* **fried**).
full, *adj.,* 53, 69, 86, 91, 97, 117, 131, 171, 195, 200, **216,** 347, 409, 448, 453, 497, 502, 540, 639.
adv., 127 (*adverb also* FULLY).
fun, *n.,* 94, 141, **216,** 227, 249, 257, 285, 390, 392, 408, 409, 516.
funnies, *n.,* 116, **216,** 357.
funny, *adj.* (FUNNIER, FUNNIEST), 110, 116, **217,** 243, 280, 285, 303, 347, 493, 563, 570.
fur, *adj.,* **217,** 529.
n. (FURS), 41, 89, 112, 191, 192, 205, 212, **217,** 242, 247, 428, 505, 570, 578.
furnace, *n.* (FURNACES), 36, 92, 99, 111, **217,** 323, 325.
furniture, *n.,* 94, 161, 162, **217,** 447, 469, 581, 583, 586, 607, 615, 639.
furry, *adj.* (FURRIER, FURRIEST), 37, 90, **217,** 435, 520, 640.

G

G, g, *n.* (G's, G's) (*seventh letter of the alphabet*), 12, 170, **218,** 227, 309, 558, 592.
gain, *v.* (GAINED, GAINED, GAINING), **219,** 400.
gallon, *n.* (GALLONS), **219,** 431.
gallop, *v.* (GALLOPED, GALLOPED, GALLOPING), **219,** 370.
game, *n.* (GAMES), 7, 36, 37, 85, 94, 97, 123, 161, 172, 177, 184, 207, **219,** 229, 247, 268, 296, 304, 318, 327, 361, 370, 390, 391, 392, 408, 409, 428, 436, 457, 475, 490, 516, 549, 550, 557, 575, 588, 599, 653.
gander, *n.* (GANDERS), **219.**
garage, *n.* (GARAGES), 29, 71, 152, 158, **219,** 223, 254, 390, 549, 609, 637.
garbage, *n.,* 11, **220,** 618.
garden, *n.* (GARDENS), 15, 42, 43, 134, 187, 213, **220,** 231, 259, 268, 285, 300, 428, 439, 468, 475, 484, 518, 619, 623, 640.
gas, *n.* (GASES), 33, 217, 219, **220,** 284, 381, 443, 525, 532.
gash, *n.* (GASHES), **220.**
gasoline, *n.* (GASOLINES), 219, **220,** 227, 228, 346, 371, 524, 552, 625, 638.
gate, *n.* (GATES), **221,** 239.
gather, *v.* (GATHERED, GATHERED, GATHERING), 42, 114, **221,** 334, 400, 439.

gave, *v.* (*past tense of* GIVE), 5, 10, 13, 15, 17, 44, 49, 51, 52, 53, 68, 85, 95, 97, 120, 128, 159, 174, 178, 190, **221,** 222, 224, 225, 239, 254, 255, 257, 265, 278, 283, 290, 291, 303, 310, 312, 315, 321, 333, 336, 364, 376, 383, 384, 391, 402, 413, 446, 476, 506, 548, 559, 581, 602, 640, 651 (*See also* give).

gay, *adj.* (GAYER, GAYEST), 139, **221,** 285, 335, 402, 589, 607 (*adv.* GAILY *or* GAYLY).

geese, *n.* (*plural of* GOOSE), 211, 222, 231 (*See also* goose).

general, *n.* (GENERALS), 88, 116, **222,** 333, 537.

generous, *adj.,* 222 (*adv.* GENEROUSLY).

gentle, *adj.* (GENTLER, GENTLEST), **222,** 233, 282, 292, 326, 364, 393, 394, 455, 484, 498 (*adv. See* gently).

gentleman, *n.* (GENTLEMEN), 44, 167, **222.**

gently, *adv.,* 150, 206, **222,** 245, 312, 326, 394, 503, 572, 575, 583.

genuine, *adj.,* 223 (*adv.* GENUINELY).

George Washington, *n.,* 137, 235, 273, 421, 442, 617.

Georgie Porgie, *n.,* 446.

germ, *n.* (GERMS), **223.**

get, *v.* (GOT, GOT *or* GOTTEN, GETTING) (*to arrive at; to go to),* 223, 318, 417, 481.
(*to become*), 38, 58, 136, 148, 159, 196, 210, 215, **223,** 260, 440, 471, 534, 616.
(*to cause to be*), 420, 482, 487, 646.
(*to come into state of having; to receive; to obtain; to acquire*), 25, 77, 113, 141, 189, **223,** 273, 290, 357, 365, 394, 443, 457, 466, 477, 498, 515, 524, 552, 573, 606, 624, 628, 639, 640.
(*to earn*), **223.**
get aboard (*to go onto an airplane, boat, bus, etc.*), 2, 90.
get away (*to escape*), 175.
get a cold (*to get sick with a cold*), 223.
get into (*to become involved in*), 340.
get on (*to go on*), 2.
get out of (*to go out of; to take out of*), 164, 311.
get up (*to wake up and leave bed; to stand up*), **223,** 344, 500, 522 (*See also* got).

giant, *adj.,* 223, 300, 354.
n. (GIANTS), **223.**

gift, *n.* (GIFTS), 224, 230, 405, 421, 464, 549, 606, 624.

giggle, *v.* (GIGGLED, GIGGLED, GIGGLING), **224.**

ginger, *n.,* 224.

gingerbread, *n.,* 224.

giraffe, *n.* (GIRAFFES), 224, 357.

girl, *n.* (GIRLS), 5, 7, 11, 23, 24, 57, 59, 68, 95, 99, 137, 155, 208, **225,** 230, 238, 302, 324, 325, 345, 373, 406, 409, 426, 436, 446, 471, 484, 497, 554, 638.

Girl Scouts, *n.,* 471.

give, *v.* (GAVE, GIVEN, GIVING), 43, 60, 64, 66, 83, 102, 124, 142, 146, 174, 179, 191, 198, 201, 221, 224, 225, 230,

give (*Cont'd.*)
233, 234, 244, 280, 290, 301, 327, 332, 333, 338, 343, 348, 349, 371, 376, 410, 428, 445, 454, 485, 490, 501, 508, 512, 539, 559, 560, 565, 566, 574, 588, 606, 610 (*See also* gave).

given, *v.* (*past participle of* GIVE), 225.

glad, *adj.* (GLADDER, GLADDEST), 222, **225,** 247, 286, 299, 424, 445, 491, 576 (*adv.* GLADLY).

glance, *v.,* (GLANCED, GLANCED, GLANCING), 225.

glass, *n.* (GLASSES) (*hard material that you can see through*), 21, 59, 61, 71, 132, **226,** 229, 230, 255, 278, 327, 340.
(*vessel for drinking*), 64, 157, 158, 160, 166, 216, **226,** 405, 419, 552, 563, 572, 582, 590, 602, 616 (*See also* glasses).

glasses, *n.* (*eyeglasses*), **226,** 491.

glossy, *adj.* (GLOSSIER, GLOSSIEST), **226.**

glove, *n.* (GLOVES), **226,** 386, 621.

glue, *n.* (GLUES), 188, 202, **227,** 285, 334, 527.
v. (GLUED, GLUED, GLUING), **227,** 428, 522.

glum, *adj.* (GLUMMER, GLUMMEST), **227** (*adv.* GLUMLY).

gnaw, *v.* (GNAWED, GNAWED *or* GNAWN, GNAWING), **227.**

go, *v.* (WENT, GONE, GOING) (*to be expressed, sung, sounded, etc.*), 252.
(*to move; to proceed; to depart; to leave for; to travel*), 6, 24, 27, 34, 67, 73, 77, 94, 107, 114, 126, 131, 141, 150, 153, 155, 174, 212, 214, **227,** 242, 243, 253, 263, 264, 265, 267, 284, 291, 294, 306, 307, 361, 364, 373, 374, 376, 378, 402, 432, 447, 449, 467, 473, 487, 488, 489, 500, 503, 525, 526, 528, 574, 575, 576, 602, 603, 626, 629, 632.
(*to work; to operate*), 9, **227,** 423, 471, 504.
go in *or* **into** (*to belong in*), 129, **227.**
go on (*to continue; to happen; to be performed*), 161, 392 (*See also* went; gone).

goat, *n.* (GOATS), **228,** 291.

gobble, *v.* (GOBBLED, GOBBLED, GOBBLING), **228.**

God, *n.,* 45, 50, 102, 166, **228,** 354, 372, 420, 559, 560, 642.

godmother, *n.* (GODMOTHERS), 185.

goes, *v.* (*third person singular, present tense of* GO), 9, 12, 24, 31, 40, 56, 71, 91, 97, 98, 123, 140, 141, 150, 151, 158, 170, 188, 225, 227, 228, 231, 248, 262, 267, 273, 296, 300, 302, 316, 329, 335, 346, 347, 418, 420, 423, 457, 465, 475, 478, 507, 528, 529, 533, 539, 540, 603, 622, 625, 636, 641 (*See also* go).

gold, *n.,* 93, **229,** 284, 333, 336, 449, 485.

golden, *adj.* (*made of gold; of the yellow color of gold*), 229.

goldenrod, *n.,* 229.

goldfish, *n.* (GOLDFISH *or* GOLDFISHES), 16, 21, **229.**

golf, *n.,* 110, 123, **229,** 428.

gone, *adj.* and *v.* (*past participle of* GO), 92, 227, **230,** 242, 271, 273, 304, 350, 392, 561, 571.

good, *adj.* (BETTER, BEST) (*beneficial*), 5, 76, 88, 94, 98, 142, 166, 185, 199, 228, **230,** 234, 365, 411, 466, 514, 540, 615.
(*enjoyable; happy; pleasant*), 20, 101, 213, **230,** 248, 390, 444, 504, 553, 621.
(*having proper qualities; being in proper condition*), 30, 196, 250, 286, 290, 323, 326, 336, 380, 392, 401, 414, 423, 456, 521, 624.
(*healthy*), 491.
(*morally sound; virtuous; kind; dutiful*), 4, 44, 140, 171, **230,** 261, 395, 428, 484, 563, 586.
(*skilled*), 58, 118, 135, **230,** 496, 515.
(*valid; real*), 207, **230,** 323, 370, 501 (*See also* better; best).

good-by, *n.* (GOOD-BYS *or* GOOD-BYES), **230,** 619.

good-bye (*See* good-by).

good morning, *n.* (GOOD MORNINGS), **230.**

good night, *n.* (GOOD NIGHTS), **231.**

goody, *n.* (GOODIES), **231.**

goose, *n.* (geese), 219, 222, 231, 261, 359, 542.

gorgeous, *adj.,* **231** (*adv.* GORGEOUSLY).

got, *v.* (*past tense and past participle of* GET), 46, 48, 52, 61, 62, 73, 77, 90, 95, 111, 126, 130, 132, 139, 168, 177, 186, 210, 223, 224, **231,** 232, 233, 236, 287, 295, 318, 321, 329, 333, 348, 354, 358, 380, 392, 438, 478, 510, 516, 519, 528, 536, 568, 576, 577, 602, 638, 643 (*See also* get).

gown, *n.* (GOWNS), **232.**

grab, *v.* (GRABBED, GRABBED, GRABBING), **232,** 475.

graceful, *adj.,* **232** (*adv.* GRACEFULLY).

grade, *n.* (GRADES) (*class; level; year*), 105, 184, **232,** 292, 423, 553.
(*mark or rating in evaluation*), 46, **232,** 290, 329, 392.

grade school, *n.* (GRADE SCHOOLS), **232.**

grain, *n.* (GRAINS), 91, 93, 120, 170, 204, **233,** 234, 338, 367, 407, 458, 460, 533, 627.

grand, *adj.* (GRANDER, GRANDEST), **233** (*adv.* GRANDLY).

grandfather, *n.* (GRANDFATHERS), 23, 83, 124, 138, 186, **233,** 234, 268, 301, 316, 334, 341, 372, 376, 491, 506, 520, 521, 522, 538, 559, 579, 565, 603, 624, 629, 637, 643, 646.

grandma, *n.* (GRANDMAS), 83, **233.**

grandmother, *n.* (GRANDMOTHERS), 7, 22, 75, 82, 103, 107, 145, 153, 186, 227, 231, **233,** 245, 252, 265, 268, 293, 309, 311, 338, 341, 410, 440, 468, 482, 483, 500, 508, 512, 519, 554, 556, 559, 579, 603, 604, 610, 620, 624, 643, 646, 653.

grandpa, *n.* (GRANDPAS), 83, **234,** 359.

grant, *v.* (GRANTED, GRANTED, GRANTING), **234.**

grape, *n.* (GRAPES), 96, 216, **234,** 281, 282, 283, 439, 609.

grapefruit, *n.* (GRAPEFRUITS), **234.**

grapevine, *n.* (GRAPEVINES), **234.**

grass, *n.* (GRASSES), 15, 36, 53, 71, 124, 143, 166, 193, 215, 229, **234,** 235, 236, 250, 254, 303, 323, 332, 348, 367, 390, 393, 407, 447, 469, 563, 626, 640, 650.

grasshopper, *n.* (GRASSHOPPERS), 70, **235,** 275.

gravel, *n.* (GRAVELS), **235.**

gray, *adj.* (GRAYER, GRAYEST), 89, 112, 150, 169, 212, **235,** 247, 304, 372, 441, 520.

   n. (GRAYS), **235.**

graze, *v.* (GRAZED, GRAZED, GRAZING), **235.**

grease, *n.* (GREASES), 189, **235,** 371.

great, *adj.* (GREATER, GREATEST), 70, 116, 138, 141, 185, 206, 220, **235,** 273, 319, 326, 343, 345, 424, 433, 480, 538, 558, 582, 615, 655 (*adv.* GREATLY).

greatness, *n.,* 604.

greedy, *adj.* (GREEDIER, GREEDIEST), **236** (*adv.* GREEDILY).

green, *adj.* (GREENER, GREENEST), 43, 53, 79, 92, 96, 129, 152, 172, 173, 177, 226, 234, **236,** 242, 275, 305, 310, 311, 344, 360, 374, 385, 390, 394, 395, 397, 404, 411, 457, 460, 482, 508, 514, 519, 543, 562, 607, 619.

   n. (GREENS), 229, **236.**

greet, *v.* (GREETED, GREETED, GREETING), **236,** 254, 494.

grew, *v.* (*past tense of* GROW), 41, **236,** 238, 283, 309, 410.

grind, *v.* (GROUND, GROUND, GRINDING), 204, **236,** 338.

groceries, *n.,* 131, **237.**

grocery, *n.* (GROCERIES), 31, **237.**

   grocery store (*store at which groceries are sold*), 96, 120, 131, 376, 580.

ground, *n.* (GROUNDS) (*land; earth*), 7, 17, 34, 36, 54, 74, 88, 91, 100, 101, 111, 112, 123, 129, 140, 141, 144, 147, 151, 153, 154, 160, 165, 176, 185, 204, 220, 235, 237, 256, 259, 260, 300, 305, 344, 371, 373, 388, 389, 393, 395, 400, 407, 409, 411, 415, 419, 424, 425, 426, 436, 437, 438, 439, 454, 458, 469, 475, 502, 503, 517, 533, 552, 590, 601, 609, 619, 624, 629, 633, 641, 650.

ground, *v.* (*past tense and past participle of* GRIND), 113, 236, **237,** 338, 367, 397 (*See also* **grind**).

grounds, *n.* **237.**

group, *n.* (GROUPS), 105, 110, 117, 127, 164, 176, 204, 237, 369, 414, 432, 477, 478, 490, 521, 542, 575, 584, 585, 599, 608, 640.

grove, *n.* (GROVES), **237.**

grow, *v.* (GREW, GROWN, GROWING), 20, 39, 53, 79, 88, 97, 100, 101, 112, 121, 134, 181, 193, 194, 216, 234, **238,** 253, 285, 326, 334, 373, 387, 394, 407, 411, 426, 440, 454, 519, 540, 563, 615, 627, 650 (*See also* **grew; grown**).

growl *n.* (GROWLS), 2.

   v. (GROWLED, GROWLED, GROWLING), 16, 214, **238,** 468.

grown, *adj.* and *v.* (*past participle of* GROW), 99, 220, **238,** 282, 376 (*See also* **grow**).

grown-up, *adj.,* **238,** 548.

   n. (GROWN-UPS), 4, 225, **238,** 606, 632.

grumble, *v.* (GRUMBLED, GRUMBLED, GRUMBLING), **238.**

grunt, *n.* (GRUNTS), **239.**

   v. (GRUNTED, GRUNTED, GRUNTING), **239.**

guard, *v.* (GUARDED, GUARDED, GUARDING), **239.**

Guatemala, *n.,* 93.

guess, *n.* (GUESSES), **239.**

   v. (GUESSED, GUESSED, GUESSING), **239,** 497.

guest, *n.* (GUESTS), **239,** 371, 391, 610.

guide, *n.* (GUIDES), **240.**

   v. (GUIDED, GUIDED, GUIDING), 157, **240,** 304, 403.

gum, *n.* (GUMS), **240,** 412, 445.

gun, *n.* (GUNS), 8, 124, 138, **240,** 267, 487, 488, 535, 552.

H

H, h, *n.* (H'S, H'S) (*eighth letter of the alphabet*), 12, 170, **241,** 309, 558.

ha, *interj.,* **242.**

habit, *n.* (HABITS), **242,** 247.

had, *v.* (*past tense and past participle of* HAVE), 7, 17, 35, 95, 117, 130, 140, 155, 168, 180, 185, 193, 197, 202, 221, 239, **242,** 247, 257, 268, 294, 305, 338, 349, 385, 393, 402, 446, 462, 476, 478, 504, 518, 531, 538, 552, 591, 614, 621, 640, 645 (*See also* **have**).

hail, *n.* (HAILS), **242.**

hair, *n.* (HAIRS), 32, 34, 40, 62, 69, 72, 75, 107, 115, 130, 131, 156, 160, 175, 181, 184, 186, 203, 208, 212, 217, **242,** 251, 318, 372, 413, 447, 470, 483, 555, 562, 570, 585, 619, 620, 626, 629, 632, 640.

hairbrush, *n.* (HAIRBRUSHES), 69.

half, *adj.,* 349.

   adv., 29.

   n. (HALVES), **243.**

   in half (*into halves; in two parts*), **243,** 554.

half-dollar, *n.* (HALF-DOLLARS), 342.

hall, *n.* (HALLS), 89, **243,** 362, 581, 606.

Halloween, *n.* (HALLOWEENS), **243,** 280, 302.

ham, *n.* (HAMS), **243,** 464.

hamburger, *n.* (HAMBURGERS), **244.**

hammer, *n.* (HAMMERS), 87, **244,** 258, 419, 508, 534, 576, 641, 648.

   v. (HAMMERED, HAMMERED, HAMMERING), **244,** 352, 472, 513.

hand, *n.* (HANDS) (*clock's*), **244.**

   (*human*), 52, 55, 61, 86, 91, 98, 105, 114, 117, 121, 125, 132, 146, 151,

hand (*Cont'd.*)

   154, 156, 179, 196, 202, 207, 209, 226, 244, 245, 248, 249, 259, 281, 287, 294, 301, 307, 320, 324, 341, 342, 345, 350, 387, 393, 400, 426, 439, 448, 449, 456, 481, 482, 494, 498, 508, 511, 528, 534, 544, 550, 562, 565, 569, 578, 617, 619, 629, 645, 646, 653.

   v. (HANDED, HANDED, HANDING), 138, **244,** 392.

handbag, *n.* (HANDBAGS), 31, **244,** 412.

handful, *n.* (HANDFULS), **245.**

handkerchief, *n.* (HANDERCHIEFS), 60, **245,** 298, 589.

handle, *n.* (HANDLES), 27, 53, 67, 129, 151, 189, 244, **245,** 259, 301, 370, 419, 470.

   v. (HANDLED, HANDLED, HANDLING), 206, **245,** 326, 565.

handle bars or **handlebars** *n.* (*sometimes written in the singular*), **245,** 526.

handsome, *adj.* (HANDSOMER, HANDSOMEST), **245** (*adv.* HANDSOMELY).

hang, *v.* (HUNG *or* HANGED, HUNG *or* HANGED, HANGING) (HANGED *is the preferred past tense and past participle when the meaning is* TO KILL BY HANGING WITH A ROPE AROUND THE NECK), 84, 109, 131, **246,** 262, 267, 497, 500, 535, 549, 579.

hangar, *n.* (HANGARS), **246.**

hanger, *n.* (HANGERS) (*one who hangs something*), 388.

hangs, *v.* (*third person singular, indicative of* HANG), **246** (*See also* **hang**).

happen, *v.* (HAPPENED, HAPPENED, HAPPENING), 41, 71, 116, 155, 177, 202, **246,** 276, 296, 320, 350, 357, 361, 444, 488, 492, 508, 521.

happily, *adv.,* 97, **246** (*See also* **happy**).

happiness, *n.* (HAPPINESSES), **247,** 286, 608.

happy, *adj.* (HAPPIER, HAPPIEST), 24, 39, 75, 97, 110, 116, 142, 156, 173, 177, 179, 185, 191, 215, 225, 230, 233, 238, **247,** 254, 285, 303, 329, 333, 335, 371, 383, 410, 424, 460, 487, 496, 501, 557, 559, 599, 606, 608, 613, 624, 625, 636, 642 (*adv. See* **happily**).

hard, *adj.* (HARDER, HARDEST) (*difficult to do, understand, or deal with*), 47, 166, **247,** 288, 573.

   (*energetic*), 641.

   (*firm, solid*), 30, 35, 43, 59, 65, 83, 97, 112, 191, 226, **247,** 262, 316, 327, 336, 352, 365, 367, 385, 400, 485, 505, 619, 620.

   (*powerful*), 291, 295.

   adv. (*energetically; with strength*), 8, 142, 159, 167, 184, 230, 232, **247,** 305, 333, 388, 392, 420, 425, 446, 471, 519, 584, 640.

   (*so as to be solid*), 106.

harden, *v.* (HARDENED, HARDENED, HARDENING), **247.**

hardly, *adv.,* **247.**

hare, *n.* (HARES), **247,** 260.

harm, *n.* (HARMS), 29, 145, 197, 303, 428.

   v. (HARMED, HARMED, HARMING), **248.**

harness, *n.* (HARNESS), **248**, 306.

    v. (HARNESSED, HARNESSED, HARNESSING), **248**, 349.

has, (*third person singular, present indicative of* HAVE), 2, 18, 33, 46, 55, 61, 74, 82, 90, 98, 101, 112, 117, 122, 126, 131, 137, 142, 147, 151, 161, 176, 181, 185, 205, 221, 231, **248**, 262, 273, 280, 296, 306, 316, 320, 331, 353, 364, 381, 407, 426, 432, 441, 447, 460, 478, 505, 520, 540, 552, 569, 578, 594, 613, 621, 632, 645, 655 (*See also* **have**).

hat, *n.* (HATS), 5, 33, 41, 59, 61, 63, 74, 84, 102, 109, 144, 190, 210, 227, 246, **248**, 255, 319, 324, 341, 364, 372, 379, 448, 463, 477, 493, 504, 553, 584, 628, 634, 637, 644, 653.

hatch, *v.* (HATCHED, HATCHED, HATCHING), **249**, 356.

hate, *v.* (HATED, HATED, HATING), **249**.

haul, *n.* (HAULS), **249**.

    v. (HAULED, HAULED, HAULING), **249**.

have, *v.* (HAD, HAD, HAVING) (*to be ill with*), 3.

    (*to experience*), 216, **249**, 312, 390, 392, 443, 466, 562, 597, 602.

    (*helping verb with past participles*), 205, 208, **249**, 350, 425, 493, 501.

    (*to hold, own, possess*), 11, 16, 21, 30, 43, 59, 68, 82, 105, 108, 125, 148, 156, 164, 171, 183, 192, 227, 235, 245, 248, **249**, 250, 266, 271, 286, 299, 331, 342, 364, 378, 384, 453, 477, 535, 548, 559, 574, 589, 615, 632, 640.

    (*must*), **249**, 521, 646.

    (*to take*), 419.

    have on (*wear*), 621.

    (*See also* **had**; **has**).

haven't, *v.* and *adv.* (*contraction for* HAVE NOT), 44, **250**.

hawk, *n.* (HAWKS), **250**.

hay, *n.*, 32, 35, 51, **250**, 348, 349, 374, 520, 613.

haystack, *n.* (HAYSTACKS), **250**, 520.

he, *pro.* (THEY), 2, 17, 23, 30, 43, 52, 61, 73, 86, 94, 101, 102, 114, 124, 136, 141, 155, 164, 179, 185, 194, 202, 217, 228, 230, 242, **250**, 263, 276, 283, 294, 304, 316, 320, 334, 345, 350, 360, 370, 383, 390, 400, 414, 415, 423, 431, 441, 454, 467, 471, 482, 493, 501, 522, 531, 541, 553, 567, 571, 582, 592, 601, 611, 624, 630, 637, 640, 644, 651 (*See also* **it**; **she**; **they**).

head, *n.* (HEADS) (*front*), **251**.

    (*leader*), 292.

    (*of lettuce, cabbage, etc.*), 79, 310.

    (*of a body*), 37, 63, 72, 77, 115, 128, 129, 183, 212, 224, 242, 248, **251**, 252, 262, 263, 268, 295, 321, 355, 359, 361, 373, 378, 379, 380, 386, 403, 438, 451, 483, 504, 530, 543, 592, 597, 601, 632.

headache, *n.* (HEADACHES), **251**, 268.

health, *n.*, 103, **251**, 272, 490, 624.

healthy, *adj.* (HEALTHIER, HEALTHIEST), 165, **251**, 498, 501, 509, 529 (*adv.* HEALTHILY).

heap, *n.* (HEAPS), **251**.

hear, *v.* (HEARD, HEARD, HEARING), 6, 39, 40, 45, 58, 66, 72, 77, 95, 104, 106, 107, 110, 112, 127, 128, 138, 164, 169, 170, 228, 238, **251**, 252, 265, 276, 284, 303, 313, 314, 321, 361, 362, 378, 389, 427, 431, 436, 440, 441, 449, 450, 458, 476, 506, 508, 509, 519, 524, 534, 552, 569, 618, 627, 648, 651, 652 (*See also* HEARD).

heard, *v.* (*past tense and past participle of* HEAR), 44, 60, 62, 77, 80, 107, 144, 239, 294, 303, 317, 362, 380, 389, 391, 394, 440, 472, 489, 491, 493, 509, 552, 566, 572, 590, 651 (*See also* **hear**).

heart, *n.* (HEARTS), 40, 56, **252**, 416, 440, 567.

heat, *n.* (HEATS), 217, **252**, 334.

    v. (HEATED, HEATED, HEATING), 156, 169, 226, **252**, 416, 477, 532, 539, 552, 574.

heavy, *adj.* (HEAVIER, HEAVIEST), 27, 54, 86, 88, 98, 110, 112, 119, 131, 235, **252**, 277, 304, 311, 332, 336, 348, 381, 400, 419, 437, 454, 460, 461, 475, 535, 552, 579, 580, 581, 624, 641 (*adv.* HEAVILY).

he'd, *pro.* and *v.* (*contraction for* HE HAD *or* HE WOULD), 250, 298.

hedge, *n.* (HEDGES), **253**, 300.

hee-haw, *n.* (HEE-HAWS), 150.

heel, *n.* (HEELS), **253**.

held, *v.* (*past tense and past participle of* HOLD), 191, 242, **253**, 259, 265, 379, 449, 571, 626 (*See also* **hold**).

helicopter, *n.* (HELICOPTERS), **253**, 323.

he'll, *pro.* and *v.* (*contraction for* HE SHALL *or* HE WILL), 5, 51, **254**, 451.

hello, *interj.*, 236, **254**.

    n. (HELLOS *or* HELLOES), **254**, 461.

help, *n.* (HELPS), 18, 80, **254**.

    v. (HELPED, HELPED, HELPING), 9, 68, 80, 83, 103, 111, 116, 140, 159, 177, 185, 197, 226, 250, **254**, 273, 277, 309, 311, 319, 321, 324, 337, 343, 347, 350, 352, 361, 370, 377, 414, 443, 445, 461, 490, 491, 507, 516, 553, 554, 561, 622, 623, 633, 635, 640, 643, 653.

helpful, *adj.*, **254**, 273, 301 (*adv.* HELPFULLY).

hen, *n.* (HENS), 98, 110, 167, 249, **254**, 304, 364, 396, 454, 593.

her, *adj.*, 4, 39, 44, 56, 115, 128, 138, 160, 210, 221, 225, **255**, 265, 294, 318, 377, 387, 390, 402, 420, 441, 469, 504, 529, 548, 555, 568, 578, 598, 618, 620, 625.

    pro., 25, 145, **255**, 324, 480.

here, *adv.*, 9, 10, 12, 16, 18, 27, 34, 47, 76, 82, 91, 100, 113, 128, 129, 167, 200, 205, 207, **255**, 271, 275, 280, 315, 340, 341, 343, 363, 364, 401, 403, 404, 414, 419, 421, 427, 453, 475, 485, 542, 562, 565, 586, 614, 624.

hers, *pro.* (THEIRS), **255**.

herself, *pro.*, 12, 23, 58, 180, 186, **255**, 500, 551.

he's, *pro.* and *v.* (*contraction for* HE IS), 112, 280, 387.

hid, *v.* (*past tense and past participle of* HIDE), **255**, 256 (*See also* **hide**).

hidden, *adj.* and *v.* (*past participle of* HIDE), **256**, 474, 582 (*See also* **hide**).

hide, *n.* (HIDES), **256**.

hide, *v.* (HID, HIDDEN *or* HID, HIDING), 91, 131, 203, 255, **256**, 275, 295, 383, 451, 637 (*See also* **hidden**).

high, *adj.* (HIGHER, HIGHEST), 3, 37, 54, 74, 89, 90, 92, 104, 109, 158, 164, 205, 229, 234, 235, **256**, 287, 298, 306, 320, 332, 346, 452, 497, 519, 534, 576, 594 (*adv.* HIGHLY) (*See also* **higher**; **highest**).

higher, *adj.* (*comparative degree of* HIGH), 3, 114, 153, 311, **256**, 257, 423, 491, 521, 601, 602 (*See also* **high**).

highest, *adj.* (*superlative degree of* HIGH), **256**, 577 (*See also* **high**).

high school, *n.* (HIGH SCHOOLS), 232, **257**.

hilarious, *adj.*, **257** (*adv.* HILARIOUSLY).

hill, *n.* (HILLS), 15, 49, 91, 111, 176, 203, **257**, 300, 346, 384, 400, 425, 453, 469, 498, 499, 526, 590, 601, 606, 609.

hillside, *n.* (HILLSIDES), **257**.

him, *pro.* (*objective case of* HE), 15, 44, 54, 66, 83, 91, 102, 106, 110, 112, 116, 123, 126, 128, 129, 136, 139, 144, 145, 154, 160, 165, 168, 169, 175, 185, 200, 206, 213, 238, 239, 255, **257**, 258, 306, 307, 324, 330, 336, 339, 349, 364, 367, 380, 423, 493, 516, 529, 552, 597, 619, 642 (*See also* **he**).

himself, *pro.*, 12, 76, 88, 177, 180, **257**, 287, 316, 340, 451, 472, 476, 531, 579, 624.

hind, *adj.* (HINDER, HINDMOST *or* HINDERMOST), **258**, 435.

his, *adj.*, 2, 13, 23, 30, 40, 44, 51, 62, 76, 91, 94, 100, 112, 123, 137, 145, 155, 164, 179, 181, 195, 200, 202, 205, 217, 224, 230, 245, **258**, 266, 281, 317, 320, 330, 341, 358, 364, 374, 463, 512, 571, 585, 625, 629, 631, 640, 651.

    pro., **258**.

hiss, *v.* (HISSED, HISSED, HISSING), 201.

history, *n.* (HISTORIES), **258**.

hit, *n.* (HITS), 440.

    v. (HIT, HIT, HITTING), 3, 23, 37, 72, 105, 128, 179, 185, 207, 229, 232, **258**, 291, 379, 440, 511, 536, 557, 571, 629, 648.

hitch, *v.* (HITCHED, HITCHED, HITCHING), 248, **258**.

hive, *n.* (HIVES), 42, **259**, 542.

ho, *interj.* (*exclamation showing joy*), **259**.

hoarse, *adj.* (HOARSER, HOARSEST), 259 (*adv.* HOARSELY).

hoe, *n.* (HOES), **259**.

    v. (HOED, HOED, HOEING), **259**.

hog, *n.* (HOGS), **259**, 402.

I

Independence Day, *n.* (INDEPENDENCE DAYS), 211.

Indian, *n.* (INDIANS), 62, 84, 99, 106, 124, **274,** 276, 342, 384, 558, 584, 632.

ink, *n.* (INKS), **275,** 396, 422, 458, 516.

inn, *n.* (INNS), **275.**

insect, *n.* (INSECTS), 17, 37, 42, 43, 70, 76, 77, 90, 198, 203, 205, **275,** 302, 344, 345, 513, 528, 574, 618, 622, 639.

inside, *adv.,* 260, 295, 365, 383, 387, 600, 619, 637.

n. (INSIDES), 129, **275,** 280, 334, 379, 453.
prep. (*also* inside of), 151, 273, **275,** 378, 438.

instantly, *adv.,* 275.

instead, *adv.,* 81, 84, 87, 111, 170, 250, **276,** 328.

interest, *n.* (INTERESTS), **276.**

v. (INTERESTED, INTERESTED, INTEREST-ING), 124, 161, **276,** 370, 476, 531.

interesting, *adj.,* 196, **276,** 349, 389, 422, 436, 512, 574, 643.

international, *adj.,* **276** (*adv.* INTERNA-TIONALLY).

International Visual Dictionary, *n.,* 573.

into, *prep.,* 3, 19, 38, 64, 89, 101, 112, 140, 167, 195, 204, 236, **276,** 280, 287, 295, 307, 318, 324, 352, 398, 407, 425, 444, 464, 475, 498, 499, 505, 522, 536, 553, 586, 607, 634.

invite, *v.* (INVITED, INVITED, INVITING), 123, 135, 177, **277.**

iron, *adj.,* 526.

n. (IRONS), 169, **277,** 336, 518.
v. (IRONED, IRONED, IRONING), 213, 277, 421, 478, 645.

ironing board, *n.* (IRONING BOARDS), 277.

is, *v.* (*third person singular, present in-dicative of* BE), 2, 9, 14, 20, 32, 65, 72, 82, 90, 100, 106, 114, 132, 140, 155, 165, 178, 184, 189, 194, 205, 216, 234, 246, 253, 260, **277,** 278, 283, 290, 295, 305, 316, 327, 365, 390, 410, 436, 463, 471, 490, 511, 548, 562, 569, 581, 587, 594, 618, 635, 641, 650 (*See also* be).

island, *n.* (ISLANDS), 173, 202, **277.**

isn't, *v.* and *adv.* (*contraction for* IS NOT), 278, 586.

it, *pro.,* 4, 16, 27, 34, 42, 57, 64, 72, 80, 89, 101, 111, 124, 138, 146, 162, 173, 186, 194, 199, 201, 220, 231, 244, 258, 275, 278, 301, 311, 320, 338, 357, 370, 381, 394, 400, 411, 421, 443, 465, 482, 498, 504, 506, 518, 541, 552, 562, 572, 578, 598, 614, 622, 626, 633, 640, 655.

its, *adj.,* 19, 22, 29, 37, 45, 57, 80, 81, 101, 119, 135, 164, 190, 227, 245, 253, 267, 278, 301, 343, 396, 404, 405, 412, 427, 454, 472, 482, 514, 517, 572, 585, 611.

it's, *pro.* and *v.* (*contraction for* IT IS), 21, 40, 45, 91, 96, 173, 210, 260, 271, 278, 280, 300, 340, 553.

itself, *pro.,* 172, **278,** 453, 527, 655.

I've, *pro.* and *v.* (*contraction for* I HAVE), 278.

J

J, j, *n.* (J's, J's), (*tenth letter of the alpha-bet*), 12, 152, 170, **279,** 309, 558, 592.

jab, *n.* (JABS), 280.

v. (JABBED, JABBED, JABBING), 280.

Jack and the Bean Stalk, 223.

jacket, *n.* (JACKETS), 76, 201, 202, 246, 280, 318, 333, 543, 554, 577, 608.

Jack Horner, *n.,* 102.

jack-in-the-pulpit, *n.* (JACK-IN-THE-PUL-PITS), 280.

jackknife, *n.* (JACKKNIVES), 280, 295.

jack-o'-lantern, *n.* (JACK-O'-LANTERNS), 243, 280.

jagged, *adj.,* 281.

jail, *n.* (JAILS), 281, 529.

jam, *n.* (JAMS), 281, 282, 440, 464, 499, 517, 553.

v. (JAMMED, JAMMED, JAMMING), 281.

janitor, *n.* (JANITORS), 281.

January, *n.* (JANUARIES or JANUARYS), 199, 211, 281, 343, 358, 565, 571, 651.

Japan, *n.,* 282, 286, 435, 447.

Japanese, *adj.,* 282.

jar, *n.* (JARS), 82, 84, 129, 198, 237, 281, 282, 401, 529.

v. (JARRED, JARRED, JARRING), 282.

jaw, *n.* (JAWS), 283.

jay, *n.* (JAYS), 283.

jeep, *n.* (JEEPS), 283.

jelly, *n.* (JELLIES), 283, 553, 636.

jerk, *n.* (JERKS), 283, 285.

v. (JERKED, JERKED, JERKING), 283.

jet engine, *n.* (JET ENGINES), 9, 172, 284.

jet plane, *n.* (JET PLANES), 205, 256, 284, 300, 442, 582.

jewel, *n.* (JEWELS), 230, 284, 582.

jewelry, *n.* (JEWELRY), 284 (*See also* JEWEL).

jingle, *n.* (JINGLES), 284.

v. (JINGLED, JINGLED, JINGLING), 284.

job, *n.* (JOBS), 222, 273, 284, 381, 515.

join, *v.* (JOINED, JOINED, JOINING) (*to be-come a member of*), 285, 391, 490.

(*to fix together; to meet or touch*), 14, 122, 285, 294, 355, 402, 405, 526, 527, 567.

joke, *n.* (JOKES), 285, 303, 555.

v. (JOKED, JOKED, JOKING), 285, 442.

jolly, *adj.* (JOLLIER, JOLLIEST), 285.

jolt, *n.* (JOLTS), 285.

jonquil, *n.* (JONQUILS), 205, 285.

journey, *n.* (JOURNEYS), 286, 585.

v. (JOURNEYED, JOURNEYED, JOURNEYING), 286.

joy, *n.* (JOYS), 87, 246, 268, 286, 410, 655.

judge, *n.* (JUDGES), 286.

v. (JUDGED, JUDGED, JUDGING), 286.

jug, *n.* (JUGS) (*a heavy container or pitcher for holding water or other liquids*), 198.

juggle, *v.* (JUGGLED, JUGGLED, JUGGLING), 286.

juggler, *n.* (JUGGLERS), 286.

juice, *n.* (JUICES), 61, 283, **287,** 308, 375, 419, 465, 519, 609, 619.

juicy, *adj.* (JUICIER, JUICIEST), 47, 53, **287,** 334, 395, 404, 449.

July, *n.* (JULIES or JULYS), 197, **287,** 343, 651.

jumble, *n.* (JUMBLES), **287.**

v. (JUMBLED, JUMBLED, JUMBLING), **287.**

jump, *n.* (JUMPS), 4, 258, 262, **287,** 306.

v. (JUMPED, JUMPED, JUMPING), 10, 11, 61, 62, 110, 135, 136, 179, 191, 203, 235, 276, 287, 370, 379, 389, 454, 497, 517, 518, 584.

June, *n.* (JUNES), **287,** 343, 478, 606, 651.

jungle, *n.* (JUNGLES), 288.

Jupiter, *n.,* 407.

just, *adj.,* 288.

adv. (*by only a moment*), 161, 200, **288.**
(*exactly; perfectly*), 119, 175, 247, **288,** 301, 410, 463, 497.
(*immediately*), 25, 96.
(*only*), 23, 42, 83, 169, 230, 238, 374, 418, 497, 536, 560.
(*very recently*), 213, **288,** 329, 392, 546.

K

K, k, *n.* (K's, K's) (*eleventh letter of the alphabet*), 12, 170, **289,** 309, 558, 592.

kangaroo, *n.* (KANGAROOS), 290.

keep, *v.* (KEPT, KEPT, KEEPING) (*to con-tinue*), 148, 276, 290, 588.

(*to have as one's own*), 225, 290.
(*to hold for a time*), 32, 290, 426.
(*to observe; to follow; to show respect for*), 64, 414, 457.
(*to preserve in a state*), 20, 22, 34, 46, 49, 54, 56, 111, 112, 123, 126, 142, 146, 196, 206, 249, 266, 269, 281, 290, 316, 340, 341, 352, 354, 376, 380, 428, 438, 443, 451, 469, 483, 529, 532, 597, 616.
(*to protect from*), 192, 303, 424, 504.
(*to put regularly; to belong; to have a place for*), 35, 36, 42, 108, 115, 119, 130, 154, 156, 175, 219, 240, 245, 246, 290, 353, 397, 530.
(*to refrain*), 205.
(*to stay; to remain*), 290.
(*to take care of regularly; to main-tain*), 290, 420.

kept, *v.* (*past tense and past participle of* KEEP), 25, 30, 35, 45, 120, 128, 134, 290, 310, 388, 391, 401, 419, 425, 426, 491, 520, 656.

kettle, *n.* (KETTLES), 145, **291.**

key, *n.* (KEYS), 107, 290, **291,** 316, 600.

keyhole, *n.* (KEYHOLES), 291.

kick, *n.* (KICKS), 291.

v. (KICKED, KICKED, KICKING), 207, 291.

kid, *n.* (KIDS) (*baby goat*), 291.
(*child*), 291.

kill, *v.* (KILLED, KILLED, KILLING), 70, 138, 145, 215, 240, 267, 268, **292,** 344, 413, 466, 488, 511.

kind, *adj.* (KINDER, KINDEST), 233, **292,** 298, 332.

    n. (KINDS), 9, 20, 31, 33, 47, 58, 60, 71, 83, 97, 106, 108, 129, 149, 187, 197, 216, 217, 220, 223, 237, 248, 264, 271, 274, **292,** 295, 299, 327, 334, 356, 385, 386, 387, 396, 399, 402, 404, 406, 414, 424, 464, 467, 492, 493, 508, 509, 516, 523, 548, 583, 634, 639 (*adv. See* **kindly**).

kindergarten, *n.* (KINDERGARTENS), **292.**

kindly, *adv.,* **292.**

kindness, *n.* (KINDNESSES), **292.**

king, *n.* (KINGS), 53, 128, 173, 185, 234, **292,** 293, 386, 422, 432, 457, 567, 615.

King Cole, *n.,* 193.

kingdom, *n.* (KINGDOMS), **293.**

kiss, *n.* (KISSES), **293.**

    v. (KISSED, KISSED, KISSING), **293,** 319, 446, 571.

kitchen, *n.* (KITCHENS), 17, 20, 45, 61, 153, 204, 220, 290, **293,** 295, 304, 311, 356, 388, 394, 397, 405, 419, 453, 472, 494, 522, 532, 572, 579, 638.

kite, *n.* (KITES), 119, **293,** 373, 380, 422, 425, 476, 589, 594, 626, 634.

kitten, *n.* (KITTENS), 175, 192, 205, 206, 217, 222, 238, 245, 246, 247, 253, 256, **294,** 310, 336, 352, 394, 428, 505, 554, 560, 576, 623.

kitty, *n.* (KITTIES), **294,** 527.

knee, *n.* (KNEES), 125, **294,** 301, 472, 508, 561.

kneel, *v.* (KNELT or KNEELED, KNELT or KNEELED, KNEELING), **294.**

knelt, *v.* (*past tense and past participle of* KNEEL), **294.**

knew, *v.* (*past tense of* KNOW), 44, 57, **294,** 310, 568, 651 (*See also* KNOW).

knife, *n.* (KNIVES), 53, 86, 95, 132, 154, 161, 166, 209, 236, 257, 280, **295,** 350, 385, 402, 478, 483, 493, 527, 546, 603, 637, 653.

knives, *n.* (*plural of* KNIFE), 154, **295,** 478 (*See also* **knife**).

knock, *n.* (KNOCKS), **295,** 440, 552.

    v. (KNOCKED, KNOCKED, KNOCKING), 17, 151, **295,** 312, 379, 638.

knot, *n.* (KNOTS), **295,** 454, 570.

know, *v.* (KNEW, KNOWN, KNOWING), 9, 21, 25, 38, 51, 93, 102, 130, 165, 167, 170, 208, 214, 228, 239, 246, 251, 265, 272, 276, **296,** 300, 318, 324, 332, 336, 352, 406, 416, 426, 446, 450, 458, 476, 507, 557, 571, 580, 597, 618, 624, 628, 653 (*See also,* **knew; known**).

knowledge, *n.,* **296.**

known, *v.* (*past participle of* KNOW), 102, 282, **296,** 416, 600, 627.

L

L, l, *n.* (L's, L's) (*twelfth letter of the alphabet*), 12, 170, **297,** 309, 558, 592.

lace, *n.* (LACES) (*cord or string for tying the parts of a thing together*), **298,** 318.

    (*thread woven together in a fancy design*), **298,** 469.

    v. (LACED, LACED, LACING), **298.**

lad, *n.* (LADS), **298.**

ladder, *n.* (LADDERS), 7, 61, 107, 153, 198, 256, **298,** 466, 527.

lady, *n.* (LADIES), 18, 46, 184, 190, 284, **298,** 412, 415, 466, 490, 622, 631, 645, 653.

laid, *v.* (*past tense and past participle of* LAY), 167, **298,** 437.

lain, *v.* (*past participle of* LIE *meaning* TO STRETCH THE BODY OUT FLAT; TO REST), **299,** 311.

lake, *n.* (LAKES), 34, 38, 39, 121, 145, 159, 162, 187, 188, 192, **299,** 327, 338, 354, 368, 398, 414, 463, 487, 533, 542, 546, 608, 619, 620, 636.

lamb, *n.* (LAMBS), 101, 135, 209, **299,** 412.

lamp, *n.* (LAMPS), 10, 169, **299,** 481, 597.

land, *n.* (LANDS) (*solid part of the earth's surface*), 38, 39, 111, 123, 193, 257, 277, 288, 299, 300, 319, 376, 473, 487, 502, 574, 592, 606.

    (*country or nation*), 6, 175, **300,** 397.

    v. (LANDED, LANDED, LANDING) (*to bring to a particular place*), 203, 302.

    (*to set an aircraft down*), 9, 103, **300,** 343, 354, 452, 550, 644.

landscape, *n.* (LANDSCAPES), **300.**

lane, *n.* (LANES), **300.**

language, *n.* (LANGUAGES), 162, 173, **300.**

lantern, *n.* (LANTERNS), **301.**

lap, *n.* (LAPS), **301.**

    v. (LAPPED, LAPPED, LAPPING), **301.**

lard, *n.* (LARDS), 235, **301.**

large, *adj.* (LARGER, LARGEST), 33, 36, 40, 43, 50, 58, 72, 76, 89, 98, 100, 103, 104, 124, 127, 142, 164, 169, 171, 183, 223, 229, 231, 234, 238, 243, 250, 259, 263, 274, 280, 290, **301,** 313, 315, 316, 325, 326, 332, 334, 339, 343, 358, 368, 375, 380, 386, 387, 402, 404, 407, 413, 426, 431, 433, 440, 441, 450, 451, 460, 461, 462, 465, 473, 480, 484, 496, 520, 529, 531, 540, 542, 544, 545, 548, 556, 570, 574, 590, 591, 607, 615, 619 (*adv.* LARGELY).

lark, *n.* (LARKS), **302.**

larva, *n.* (LARVAE), **302.**

lass, *n.* (LASSES), **302.**

last, *adj.* (*being or coming after all others in place or time*), 71, 116, 138, 144, 155, 157, 170, 172, 194, 211, 215, 231, 243, 268, 294, **302,** 352, 401, 411, 424, 439, 444, 446, 472, 474, 477, 479, 487, 498, 499, 541, 549, 560, 565, 593, 617, 625, 644.

    adv. (*after all others*), 195, **302,** 638.

    v. (LASTED, LASTED, LASTING), 202, **302,** 308, 489, 655.

late, *adj.* (LATER, LATEST) (*near the end*), 13, 210, **302.**

    (*tardy; after the proper time*), 21, 44, 67, 155, 271, 273, 277, **302,** 303, 336,

late (*Cont'd.*)

    500, 513, 552, 566, 571, 614, 631, 652, 653.

later, *adj.* (*comparative degree of* LATE), 303 (*See also* **late**).

laugh, *n.* (LAUGHS), **303.**

    v. (LAUGHED, LAUGHED, LAUGHING), 23, 110, 217, 224, 242, 247, 255, 285, **303,** 493.

launder, *v.* (LAUNDERED, LAUNDERED, LAUNDERING), **303.**

law, *n.* (LAWS), 70, 281, **303,** 304, 353, 414, 422.

lawn, *n.* (LAWNS), 234, 263, **303,** 311, 323, 384.

lawyer, *n.* (LAWYERS), **304.**

lay, *v.* (LAID, LAID, LAYING), 77, 98, 167, 202, 254, **304,** 311, 356, 386, 420, 428, 528.

lazy, *adj.* (LAZIER, LAZIEST), **304** (*adv.* LAZILY).

lead, *n.* (LEADS) (*first or front place*), **304.**

    v. (LED, LED, LEADING), 117, 158, 228, **304,** 305, 307, 393 (*See also* **led**).

lead, *n.* (*heavy, bluish-gray metallic chemical*), **304,** 336.

    (*thin stick of graphite used in pencils*), **304,** 397.

leader, *n.* (LEADERS), 85, 99, 169, **305,** 421.

leaf, *n.* (LEAVES) (*any of the flat, thin parts growing from the stem of a plant*), 53, 70, 134, **305,** 307, 327, 399.

    (*sheet of paper*), **305** (*See also* **leaves**).

lean, *adj.* (LEANER, LEANEST), **305.**

    v. (LEANED or LEANT, LEANED or LEANT, LEANING), 7, **305,** 318, 530.

leap, *n.* (LEAPS), **306.**

    v. (LEAPED or LEAPT, LEAPED or LEAPT, LEAPING), 62, 219, 290, **306.**

leap year, *n.* (LEAP YEARS) (*every fourth year, containing an extra day in February*), 343.

learn, *v.* (LEARNED or LEARNT, LEARNED or LEARNT, LEARNING), 50, 102, 105, 111, 125, 130, 149, 157, 159, 166, 167, 251, 271, 273, 292, 296, 304, **306,** 309, 330, 339, 349, 357, 365, 408, 469, 470, 553, 554, 559, 578, 610, 652.

leash, *n.* (LEASHES), **306.**

    v. (LEASHED, LEASHED, LEASHING), **306.**

least, *adv.,* **306.**

    n. 142, **306.**

leather, *n.* (LEATHERS), 46, 60, **306,** 342, 460, 486, 533, 535, 615.

leave, *v.* (LEFT, LEFT, LEAVING), 27, 44, 90, 179, 223, 227, 268, 273, **307,** 340, 364, 390, 424, 484, 492, 513, 538, 542, 550, 553.

leaves, *n.* (*plural of leaf*), 10, 20, 43, 63, 65, 70, 74, 92, 100, 103, 110, 114, 177, 185, 224, 229, 236, 305, **307,** 327, 353, 355, 367, 387, 404, 416, 439, 482, 513, 514, 526, 543, 554, 557, 574, 583, 619, 622, 629, 633, 644 (*See also* **leaf**).

led, *v.* (*past tense and past participle of* LEAD), 304, **307** (*See also* **lead**).

ledge, *n.* (LEDGES), **307.**

look *(Cont'd.)*
look after *(to care for)*, 86, 117, 124, 149.
looking glass, *n.* (LOOKING GLASSES), 318.
loose, *adj.* (LOOSER, LOOSEST) *(free from a state of confinement)*, 306.
(not rigidly fastened), 108, 165, 232, 318, 359, 380, 471, 504, 571 *(adv. See* **loosely***)*.
loosely, *adv.*, 246.
loosen, *v.* (LOOSENED, LOOSENED, LOOSENING), 318.
lopsided, *adj.*, 318.
Lord, *n.* *(God or Jesus Christ)*, 420.
Los Angeles, *n.*, 556.
lose, *v.* (LOST, LOST, LOSING) *(accidentally to drop or leave something where one cannot find it; to fail to keep)*, 183, 210, 318, 583.
(to be defeated in), 48, 194, 318.
lost, *v.* *(past tense and past participle of* LOSE*)*, 17, 40, 44, 116, 196, 249, 267, 317, 318, 350, 374, 448, 460, 476, 484, 505, 560, 597, 642.
lot, *n.* (LOTS) *(considerable quantity)*, 94, 98, 121, 217, 257, 319, 320, 409, 447, 500, 501, 519, 531, 566, 621.
(piece of ground or land), 319.
loud, *adj.* (LOUDER, LOUDEST), 2, 9, 34, 35, 44, 54, 60, 104, 105, 124, 150, 172, 197, 242, 251, 263, 319, 337, 361, 378, 440, 450, 472, 489, 503, 509, 523, 610, 651 *(adv. See* **loudly***)*.
loudly, *adv.*, 72.
love, *n.* (LOVES), 129, 171, 206, 252, 319.
v. (LOVED, LOVED, LOVING), 48, 57, 102, 136, 138, 233, 234, 265, 293, 309, 314, 319, 345, 377, 428, 543, 557, 606, 632.
lovely, *adj.* (LOVELIER, LOVELIEST), 319 *(adv.* LOVELY*)*.
low, *adj.* (LOWER, LOWEST) *(below in place)*, 14, 46, 61, 100, 153, 168, 283, 294, 313, 529, 537, 601.
(below the normal or usual surface or level), 145, 484, 500, 606.
(near the ground), 320.
(of deep pitch), 238, 320.
(small), 320, 462.
(soft), 505, 630.
(adv. LOW*)*.
lower, *v.* (LOWERED, LOWERED, LOWERING), 320.
luck, *n.*, 94, 320, 335.
lucky, *adj.* (LUCKIER, LUCKIEST), 320 *(adv.* LUCKILY*)*.
luggage, *n.*, 320.
lullaby, *n.* (LULLABIES), 29, 321.
lump, *n.* (LUMPS) *(hump; swelling)*, 72, 321.
(mass or a bit of anything that has no particular shape), 316, 321, 502.
lunch, *n.* (LUNCHES), 6, 63, 97, 321, 332, 337, 362, 446, 517, 550.
lying, *v.* *(present participle of* LIE*)* *(reclining)*, 4, 304, 311, 321.
lying, *v.* *(present participle of* LIE*)* *(telling an untruth)*, 310, 321.

M

M, m, *n.* (M'S, M'S) *(thirteenth letter of the alphabet)*, 12, 170, 266, 309, 322, 558, 592.
ma, *n.* (MAS), 160, 216, 323, 423, 601.
machine, *n.* (MACHINES), 9, 46, 81, 103, 111, 169, 183, 201, 236, 237, 253, 284, 323, 333, 338, 346, 348, 349, 371, 407, 421, 425, 452, 458, 514, 528, 552, 580, 595, 606, 617, 634.
mad, *adj.* (MADDER, MADDEST), 323 *(adv.* MADLY*)*.
made, *v.* *(past tense and past participle of* MAKE*)*, 9, 13, 23, 32, 43, 54, 60, 73, 84, 90, 103, 115, 125, 132, 150, 176, 184, 209, 215, 224, 236, 244, 254, 262, 272, 285, 295, 306, 323, 338, 353, 363, 372, 387, 399, 406, 422, 437, 449, 458, 469, 485, 492, 503, 514, 525, 535, 544, 558, 569, 579, 590, 608, 619, 623, 635, 644, 656 *(See also* **make***)*.
magazine, *n.* (MAGAZINES) *(printed soft-covered book or publication having articles, stories, poems, etc., that appears regularly)*, 418.
magic, *adj.*, 324, 584.
n., 185.
magician, *n.* (MAGICIANS), 324.
maid, *n.* (MAIDS), 324, 447.
mail, *n.* (MAILS), 44, 75, 174, 324, 325, 418, 568, 640.
v. (MAILED, MAILED, MAILING), 255, 309, 324, 371, 418, 522, 600.
mailbox, *n.* (MAILBOXES), 324, 325.
mailman, *n.* (MAILMEN), 44, 75, 141, 174, 324, 325, 348, 418, 638, 640.
main, *adj.*, 143, 146, 325, 587, 599 *(adv. See* **mainly***)*.
Maine, *n.*, 524.
mainly, *adv.*, 325.
make, *v.* (MADE, MADE, MAKING) *(to build; to cause; to prepare; to produce)*, 4, 9, 56, 70, 87, 103, 113, 121, 152, 172, 215, 238, 250, 266, 272, 284, 295, 304, 315, 323, 325, 333, 341, 346, 371, 386, 393, 400, 449, 458, 477, 486, 513, 526, 549, 555, 585, 587, 591, 595, 610, 622, 626, 630, 646, 650.
(to be; to be equal or equivalent to), 30, 68, 99, 130, 165, 179, 185, 195, 202, 223, 325, 413, 421, 468, 538, 573, 629.
(to cause someone or something to become), 30, 68, 99, 130, 165, 179, 185, 195, 202, 223, 325, 413, 421, 468, 538, 573, 629.
(to earn), 325.
(to force), 325.
(to sew), 325.
make believe, 325 *(See also* **believe***)*.
mall, *n.* (MALLS), 326.
mama, *n.* (MAMAS), 200 *(See also* **mamma***)*.

mamma, *n.* (MAMMAS), 326 *(See also* **mama***)*.
man, *n.* (MEN), 27, 32, 40, 55, 63, 66, 67, 75, 81, 87, 88, 94, 95, 99, 100, 110, 124, 128, 138, 147, 165, 173, 178, 179, 185, 189, 191, 200, 222, 223, 224, 226, 235, 236, 237, 238, 249, 267, 268, 281, 288, 291, 323, 324, 326, 329, 334, 335, 338, 370, 373, 376, 383, 460, 465, 476, 486, 525, 549, 552, 584, 614, 629, 632, 638, 641 *(See also* **men***)*.
mankind, *n.*, 326.
manner, *n.* (MANNERS), 326.
manners, *n.*, 326, 414, 456.
mansion, *n.* (MANSIONS), 326.
many, *adj.* (MORE, MOST), 7, 14, 22, 31, 42, 64, 76, 83, 91, 104, 110, 128, 135, 149, 159, 166, 174, 187, 197, 216, 239, 245, 253, 264, 281, 291, 300, 326, 328, 333, 361, 386, 387, 406, 407, 442, 443, 454, 455, 497, 510, 511, 528, 531, 532, 551, 553, 655.
map, *n.* (MAPS), 6, 14, 82, 100, 327, 362, 509, 510.
maple, *adj.*, 327, 407, 465, 546, 583.
n. (MAPLES), 327.
marble, *adj.*, 525.
n., 327.
marbles, *n.* *(plural of* MARBLE*)* *(small hard balls with which a game is played)*, 168, 274, 327, 345, 412.
march, *n.* (MARCHES), 328.
v. (MARCHED, MARCHED, MARCHING), 209, 328, 376, 389.
March, *n.* (MARCHES), 211, 327, 343, 651.
margarine, *n.* (MARGARINES), 235, 328, 371.
marigold, *n.* (MARIGOLDS), 328, 475.
mark, *n.* (MARKS) *(grade)*, 232, 329, 423, 501.
(sign), 96, 127, 152, 175, 207, 329, 422, 516, 569.
v. (MARKED, MARKED, MARKING) *(to indicate)*, 329.
(to put a grade), 329.
market, *n.* (MARKETS), 88, 329.
v. (MARKETED, MARKETED, MARKETING), 329, 575.
Mark Twain, *n.*, 370.
marry, *v.* (MARRIED, MARRIED, MARRYING), 189, 268, 324, 329, 340, 348, 623, 632.
Mars, *n.*, 407.
mask, *n.* (MASKS), 243, 330, 597.
master, *n.* (MASTERS), 330.
v. (MASTERED, MASTERED, MASTERING), 330.
mat, *n.* (MATS), 330.
v. (MATTED, MATTED, MATTING), 330.
match, *n.* (MATCHES), 90, 311, 330, 405.
v. (MATCHED, MATCHED, MATCHING), 330.
material, *n.* (MATERIALS), 94, 226, 331, 336, 407, 525, 533, 582.
matter, *n.* (MATTERS) *(material)*, 331, 343.
(subject; topic), 331.
(trouble), 210, 331.
v. (MATTERED, MATTERED, MATTERING), 265, 331.
no matter *(regardless of)*, 628.
May, *n.* (MAYS), 80, 331, 343, 651.
may, *v.* *(to be allowed or permitted)*, 17, 18, 24, 168, 265, 331, 390, 402, 410, 418, 457, 626.

679

may *(Cont'd.)*
   (to let it be that), 331.
   (possibly that it will), 73, 90, 93, 110, 136, 172, 191, **331**, 398.
maybe, *adv.,* 14, **331**, 418.
me, *pro.* (US), 2, 15, 22, 42, 52, 64, 81, 93, 116, 136, 138, 141, 159, 184, 192, 214, 217, 221, 230, 237, 244, 255, 269, 273, 285, 290, 301, 308, 315, 324, 332, 334, 338, 341, 356, 364, 378, 402, 417, 425, 438, 448, 476, 488, 498, 506, 522, 552, 559, 583, 618 *(See also* **I**).
meadow, *n.* (MEADOWS), 229, 235, **332**, 359, 400, 451.
meal, *n.* (MEALS), 64, 143, 145, 242, 321, 325, **332**, 358, 478, 541, 555, 577, 602, 617, 620
mean, *v.* (MEANT, MEANT, MEANING) *(to intend),* 6, 30, 64, 186, 271, 323, 389, 390, 524.
   (to intend to convey), 6, 25, 30, 82, 136, 148, 150, 167, 174, 179, 186, 230, 231, 254, 255, 271, 272, 278, 294, 323, 326, **332**, 338, 390, 437, 447, 448, 455, 479, 485, 496, 514, 525, 537, 538, 551, 558, 559, 562, 567, 571, 572, 579, 585, 598, 602, 614, 625, 626, 644, 645, 655.
   adj. (MEANER, MEANEST) *(not kind),* **332**, 597.
   by means of *(by the help or use of),* 510.
meaning, *n.* (MEANINGS) *(understanding of what someone wants to tell us),* 180.
meant, *v.* *(past tense and past participle of* MEAN), 332.
measure, *n.* (MEASURES), 264, **332**, 340, 419, 576.
   v. (MEASURED, MEASURED, MEASURING), 129, 264, **332**, 404, 431, 457, 571, 624.
meat, *n.* (MEATS), 30, 42, 66, 68, 75, 90, 96, 98, 101, 118, 132, 150, 166, 206, 209, 212, 220, 227, 243, 244, 287, 295, 305, 333, 365, 376, 402, 410, 417, 441, 446, 451, 462, 465, 466, 483, 487, 509, 515, 557, 578, 603, 607, 637.
mechanic, *n.* (MECHANICS), 333, 576, 641.
medal, *n.* (MEDALS), 333.
medicine, *n.* (MEDICINES), 52, 113, 130, 158, 159, 224, 333, 371, 399, 403, 490.
meet, *v.* (MET, MET, MEETING), 11, 47, 172, 333, 334, 336 *(See also* met).
meeting, *n.* (MEETINGS), 110, 219, 243, **334**.
melody, *n.* (MELODIES), 334.
melon, *n.* (MELONS), 334, 449, 619.
melt, *v.* (MELTED, MELTED, MELTING), 226, **334**.
men, *n.* *(plural of* MAN), 33, 63, 71, 82, 104, 185, 199, 237, 252, 266, 281, 315, 319, 333, **334**, 339, 354, 414, 427, 437, 452, 465, 486, 546, 590, 615 *(See also* **man**).
mend, *v.* (MENDED, MENDED, MENDING), **334**, 487.

meow, *n.* (MEOWS), 89, **335**, 640.
merchant, *n.* (MERCHANTS), **335**.
Mercury, *n.,* 407.
mere, *adj.* *(superlative degree:* MEREST), 335.
merrily, *adv.,* **335**.
merry, *adj.* (MERRIER, MERRIEST), 193, 221, 247, 257, 303, 331, **335**.
merry-go-round, *n.* (MERRY-GO-ROUNDS), 184, 335, 591.
message, *n.* (MESSAGES), **336**, 555.
met, *v.* *(past tense and past participle of* MEET), 294, 333, **336**, 616.
metal, *n.* (METALS), 13, 27, 34, 36, 47, 64, 82, 104, 113, 119, 195, 229, 244, 262, 277, 291, 304, **336**, 352, 355, 359, 405, 408, 460, 471, 493, 516, 525, 572, 582, 588, 636.
mew, *n.* (MEWS), **336**.
   v. (MEWED, MEWED, MEWING), **336** *(See also* meow).
Mexican, *adj.* and *n.* (MEXICANS), 300.
Mexico, *n.,* 94, 104, 122, 258, **336**, 353, 362, 512, 524, 585, 606.
mice, *n.* *(plural of* MOUSE), 6, 89, 145, 337, 346, 380, 468.
microphone, *n.* (MICROPHONES), 337.
microscope, *n.* (MICROSCOPES), 223, **337**.
midday, *n.* (MIDDAYS), 337.
middle, *n.* (MIDDLES) *(center),* 92, 137, 260, 337, 395, 397.
   (part or point that is the same distance from each end or side), 36, 208, 237, 337, 362, 551, 613.
midnight, *n.* (MIDNIGHTS), 337, 344.
might, *v.* *(past tense of* MAY), 16, 338, 361, 551, 562.
mile, *n.* (MILES), 188, 205, 247, **338**, 353, 415.
milk, *n.* (MILKS), 61, 76, 89, 97, 99, 101, 112, 124, 126, 128, 134, 154, 157, 160, 206, 216, 228, 259, 271, 301, 310, 314, 338, 341, 345, 355, 375, 387, 404, 410, 431, 443, 468, 475, 509, 514, 534, 542, 602.
   v. (MILKED, MILKED, MILKING), 124, **338**.
milkman, *n.* (MILKMEN), 165, **338**.
mill, *n.* (MILLS), 204, **338**, 339.
   v. (MILLED, MILLED, MILLING), 338.
miller, *n.* (MILLERS), 338, 339.
million, *adj.,* 339.
   n. (MILLIONS), **339**.
mind, *n.* (MINDS), 139, 273, 323, 339, 401, 443, 444, 509, 564.
   v. (MINDED, MINDED, MINDING) *(to obey),* 367.
   (to object), 86, 331, 339.
   (to pay attention to), 339.
   (to take care of), 339.
mine, *n.* (MINES), 111, 229, 336, 339.
   pro., 83, 96, 339, 349, 380, 541, 562.
   v. (MINED, MINED, MINING), **339**.
minus, *prep.,* 340.
minute, *n.* (MINUTES), 208, 213, 244, 264, 273, 288, 338, **340**, 354, 370, 433, 440, 458, 474, 530, 571, 574.
mirror, *n.* (MIRRORS), 156, 318, **340**.
mischief, *n.* (MISCHIEFS), **340**.
misery, *n.* (MISERIES), **340**.
Miss, *n.* (MISSES), 340, 363, 553.

miss, *v.* (MISSED, MISSED, MISSING), 341, 460.
mistake, *n.* (MISTAKES), 189, 329, 341, 398, 566, 587.
mister, *n.,* 348 *(See also* **Mr.**).
mitten, *n.* (MITTENS), 114, 226, 341, 560.
mix, *v.* (MIXED, MIXED, MIXING), 15, 40, 105, 119, 152, 236, 276, 287, 341, 348, 393, 427, 462, 501, 505, 552.
moccasin, *n.* (MOCCASINS), 342.
mom, *n.* (MOMS) *(name for mother),* 230, 447, 464, 602, 645.
moment, *n.* (MOMENTS), 342.
Monday, *n.* (MONDAYS), 137, 194, 199, 213, 231, 303, **342**, 375, 376, 465, 474, 479, 495, 539, 540, 569, 589, 623, 651.
money, *n.* (MONEYS or MONIES), 15, 18, 31, 34, 50, 75, 77, 95, 96, 113, 116, 121, 145, 150, 178, 181, 187, 189, 196, 208, 212, 219, 230, 244, 250, 264, 281, 284, 303, 306, 309, 320, 335, 342, 348, 359, 384, 394, 397, 412, 415, 422, 427, 431, 445, 447, 448, 451, 466, 476, 493, 506, 513, 525, 534, 553, 563, 580, 581, 582, 607, 621.
monkey, *n.* (MONKEYS), 20, 141, 267, 288, **342**, 546, 549.
month, *n.* (MONTHS), 20, 26, 51, 80, 137, 139, 190, 195, 199, 211, 223, 264, 281, 287, 302, 327, 331, **343**, 364, 368, 445, 478, 560, 561, 565, 571, 642, 651.
moo, *n.* (MOOS), 343.
moon, *n.* (MOONS), 66, 155, 228, 286, 343, 376, 452, 465, 510, 556.
moonlight, *n.,* **343**, 487.
more, *adj.* *(superlative:* MOST), 6, 17, 49, 128, 152, 160, 181, 183, 195, 200, 208, 216, 219, 245, 302, 306, 309, 315, 323, 335, **343**, 348, 369, 372, 377, 378, 428, 453, 510, 511, 513, 530, 559, 583, 603, 611.
   adv., 178, 222, 225, 371, 417, 500.
   n., 210, 216, 236, 238, 274, 381, 429, 576, 637.
morn, *n.* (MORNS) *(morning),* 150.
morning, *n.* (MORNINGS), 9, 27, 30, 60, 62, 64, 70, 112, 127, 129, 137, 143, 144, 148, 156, 165, 215, 223, 228, 230, 231, 236, 271, 307, 344, 357, 359, 362, 443, 454, 483, 494, 498, 500, 509, 518, 571, 601, 603, 614, 629, 637, 640.
morning glory or **morning-glory,** *n.* (MORNING GLORIES), 107, 344, 609.
morsel, *n.* (MORSELS), 344.
mosquito, *n.* (MOSQUITOS or MOSQUITOES), 52, 77, **344**, 472, 498.
moss, *n.* (MOSSES), 344.
most, *adj.* *(comparative:* MORE), 5, 6, 33, 37, 51, 53, 61, 74, 82, 83, 119, 175, 336, **345**, 359, 456, 486, 538, 539, 634, 641.
   adv., 99, 345 *(See also* **mostly**).
   n., 70, 153, 204, 288, 325, 384, 473, 574, 604.
mostly, *adv.* *(almost all),* 57 *(See also* **most**).

N

on (*Cont'd.*)

   (*with respect to; connected with*), 46, 232.

   to go on, (*to happen*), 161.

once, *adv.*, 112, 116, 200, 264, **373**, 376, 384, 553.

   at once (*right away; immediately*), 27, 273, 275, **373**.

   at once (*in accord; at the same time*), **373**.

one, *adj.*, 2, 12, 29, 50, 74, 118, 150, 228, 231, 262, 337, 352, 370, **373**, 381, 388, 403, 425, 475, 480, 490, 504, 534, 566, 576, 620, 642, 655.

   n. (ONES), 210, 364, **373**.

   pro., 96, 168, 181, 185, 244, 253, 298, **373**, 437, 551.

one hundred, *adj.* and *n.*, **373**.

onion, *n.* (ONIONS), 71, 90, **373**, 555.

only, *conj.*, **374**.

   adj., 12, **373**, **374**, 563.

   adv., 10, 24, 39, 45, 49, 72, 75, 121, 180, 222, 247, 288, 301, 309, 324, 335, 370, **374**, 433, 455, 481, 513, 524, 559, 576, 594.

onto, *prep.*, 54, **374**, 379, 417, 422, 472, 548, 588, 609.

open, *adj.*, 151, 181, 269, **374**, 378, 393, 498, 511, 523, 576.

   v. (OPENED, OPENED, OPENING) (*to begin business*), 165.

   (*to change from a shut position*), 8, 20, 55, 74, 124, 150, 181, 201, 221, 243, 245, 275, 283, 313, 316, **374**, 389, 416, 433, 519, 535, 600, 628, 635, 645.

   (*to spread out*), 70, 344, 517, 597, 598.

   (*to take apart so as to expose or show the contents*), 365, **374**, **383**.

opening, *n.* (openings), 38, 151, 260, **374**, 635.

opposite, *adj.* (*anything that is the reverse of something else*), 22, 361, **375**.

   n. (OPPOSITES), **375**, 447.

or, *conj.*, 5, 20, 34, 40, 65, 79, 83, 90, 103, 111, 126, 131, 149, 151, 169, 177, 181, 200, 214, 221, 232, 247, 259, 271, 286, 295, 305, 312, 337, 345, 350, 368, **375**, 385, 392, 401, 415, 432, 441, 472, 486, 500, 513, 525, 532, 549, 563, 574, 580, 606, 610, 619, 632, 656.

orange, *adj.*, 88, 114, 328, 426, 496, 607.

   n. (ORANGES) (*bright color made by mixing red and yellow*), 57, 312, **375**, 419.

   (*reddish-yellow fruit*), 48, 52, 153, 216, 221, 234, 287, **375**, 396, 449, 496, 519.

orbit, *n.* (ORBITS), **376**.

   v. (ORBITED, ORBITED, ORBITING), **376**.

orchard, *n.* (ORCHARDS), **376**.

order, *n.* (ORDERS) (*instruction or command*), 88, 116, **376**.

   (*request for goods one wants*), **376**.

   (*social peace*), **376**.

   (*way in which things happen*), **376**, 377, 513.

order (*Cont'd.*)

   v. (ORDERED, ORDERED, ORDERING) (*to make a request for goods*), 32, **376**.

   (*to direct; to command*), 116, **376**.

   in order (*for the purpose of*), 349, **376**, 504.

   in order (*in a neat arrangement*), 354, **376**, 433, 570.

organ, *n.* (ORGANS), **377**.

other, *adj.*, 4, 19, 29, 48, 53, 60, 77, 91, 104, 128, 149, 161, 171, 185, 192, 200, 211, 223, 244, 251, 263, 284, 295, 305, 313, 346, 368, **377**, 383, 394, 411, 428, 453, 464, 473, 490, 502, 533, 549, 606, 620, 636, 644.

   pro., 114, 328, 352, 482, 566, 599.

   each other (*compound reciprocal pronoun*), 328, 482, 579 (See also **each**).

ouch, *interj.*, **377**.

ought, *v.*, 142, 319, **377**, 488.

our, *adj.*, 11, 21, 31, 51, 66, 85, 96, 108, 111, 121, 134, 147, 153, 169, 172, 186, 192, 202, 219, 224, 235, 242, 252, 268, 298, 304, 310, 321, 332, 344, 358, 371, **377**, 385, 397, 417, 428, 431, 443, 456, 462, 475, 485, 509, 522, 543, 552, 558, 573, 583, 602, 610, 650.

ours, *pro.*, **378**.

ourselves, *pro.*, 128, **378**.

out, *adj.*, **378**.

   adv., 23, 35, 64, 102, 171, 198, **378**, 405, 420, 442, 467, 503, 514, 534, 631, 646.

   prep., 9, 56, 87, 93, 129, 160, 165, 229, 271, 389, 493, 572, 615, 623.

   out of (*lacking*), **378**.

   try out (*to test; to prove; to sample*), 588.

   wear out (*to use up*), 242.

outdoor, *adj.*, 229, 401.

outdoors, *adv.*, 76, 81, **378**, 379, 390, 489, 551.

outside, *adj.*, 151, 396, 496.

   adv., 19, 91, 99, 112, 212, 265, 378, 379, 428, 574, 602, 621, 626, 640, 644, 655.

   n. (OUTSIDES), 35, 52, 129, 379, 485, 513, 619.

   prep., 24, 122, 417.

oven, *n.* (OVENS), 32, 64, 65, 72, 213, 379, 396, 451.

over, *adj.* (*at an end*), 379.

   adv. (*above or across*), 37, 65, 262.

   (*again*), 420, 453.

   (*at or on the other side*), 560, 562, 565, 652.

   (*from an upright position*), 47, 202, 305, 378, 379, 400, 572, 602.

   (*into a inverted position*), 411.

   (*more*), 176, 369, 444, 446, 618.

   prep. (*about; concerning*), 602.

   (*on; upon; or above*), 2, 8, 84, 112, 121, 123, 152, 192, 379, 465, 483, 499, 552, 554, 557, 563, 585, 594, 597, 608, 622, 644.

   (*more than*), 379.

   (*through all parts of*), 364, 379, 469, 471, 516, 518, 543, 583.

   (*to or on the other side of*), 379.

overalls, *n.*, 380.

owe, *v.* (OWED, OWED, OWING), **380**.

owl, *n.* (OWLS), 205, **380**.

own, *adj.*, 19, 37, 255, 339, 341, 514, 561, 570.

   v. (OWNED, OWNED, OWNING), 45, 164, 231, 242, 248, 249, 330, 335, 339, 349, 377, 378, **380**, 415, 445, 565, 580, 628.

   of one's own (*belonging only to oneself*), 290, 314, 343, **380**, 477, 507.

owner, *n.* (OWNERS), **380**, 448.

ox, *n.* (OXEN), 70, **381**, 526.

oxen, *n.* (*plural of* OX), 70, **381**, 411.

oxygen, *n.*, **381**.

P

P, p, *n.* (P'S, P'S) (*sixteenth letter of the alphabet*), 12, 170, 309, **382**, 558, 592.

pa, *n.*, (PAS), **383**.

Pacific Ocean, *n.*, **368**.

pack, *n.* (PACKS), 85, 103, 139, **383**, 533.

   v. (PACKED, PACKED, PACKING), 320, **383**, 539, 595.

package, *n.* (PACKAGES), 73, 119, 188, 255, 259, 324, 374, **383**, 418, 535, 549, 568, 570, 595, 600.

pad, *n.* (PADS) (*kind of cover or flat cushion*), 330, **383**.

   (*small tablet of paper*), 548.

paddle, *n.* (PADDLES), 84, **384**, 557.

   v. (PADDLED, PADDLED, PADDLING), **384**.

page, *n.* (PAGES), 59, 184, 196, 305, 307, 384, 388, 422, 523, 563, 591, 645.

paid, *v.* (*past tense and past participle of* PAY), 48, 62, 77, 80, 96, 165, 219, 304, 335, 384, 394, 478.

pail, *n.* (PAILS), 69, 228, **384**.

pain, *n.* (PAINS), 3, 46, 91, 128, 251, 268, 340, 347, **385**, 472, 480, 508, 538, 577.

paint, *n.* (PAINTS), 112, 236, 329, **385**, 457, 471, 515, 527, 592, 603, 626.

   v. (PAINTED, PAINTED, PAINTING) (*to make a picture with paint*), 23, 107, 286, **385**, 386, 515.

   (*to spread paint on*), 61, 69, 112, 275, 372, 385, 549, 630, 640.

paintbrush, *n.* (PAINTBRUSHES), 69, **385**.

painter, *n.* (PAINTERS), **385**, 471.

painting, *n.* (PAINTINGS), 23, 349, **386**, 401, 640.

pair, *n.* (PAIRS), 43, 367, **386**, 388, 511, 529, 621, 642.

pajamas, *n.*, 109, **386**.

palace, *n.* (PALACES), **386**.

pale, *adj.* (PALER, PALEST), **387**.

palm, *n.* (PALMS) (*inside of the hand between the wrist and the fingers*), 105, 387.

   (*tree that grows in warm regions*), 137, 387, 622.

pan, *n.* (PANS), 13, 105, 200, 216, 245, 277, 287, 334, 387, 449, 471, 472, 528, 572.

Panama, *n.*, 93.

pancake, *n.* (PANCAKES), 261, 387, 482, 546.

panda, *n.* (PANDAS), 387.

pansy, *n.* (PANSIES), 205, **388.**

pant, *v.* (PANTED, PANTED, PANTING), **388.**

pantry, *n.* (PANTRIES), **388.**

pants, *n.*, 109, 386, 388, 393, 480, 586.

papa, *n.* (PAPAS), **388.**

paper, *adj.*, 31, 107, 156, 174, 186, 453.
　　n. (PAPERS) (*composition*), 114, 329, 398.
　　(*material made in thin sheets from ground wood or rags*), 50, 54, 59, 73, 85, 86, 89, 93, 96, 103, 154, 227, 293, 309, 313, 329, 336, 337, 353, 383, 388, 393, 402, 460, 471, 484, 522, 523, 527, 533, 548, 554, 565, 577, 579, 585, 595, 618, 644, 646.
　　(*printed or written legal agreement*), 107.
　　v. (PAPERED, PAPERED, PAPERING), **388.**

paper hanger, *n.* (PAPER HANGERS), **388.**

parachute, *n.* (PARACHUTES), **389.**

parade, *n.* (PARADES), 159, 328, **389,** 392, 561.

Paraguay, *n.*, 510.

parakeet, *n.* (PARAKEETS), **389.**

pardon, *n.* (PARDONS), **390.**
　　v. (PARDONED, PARDONED, PARDONING), 179, **390.**

parent, *n.* (PARENTS), 189, 340, 345, 367, **390,** 426, 488.

park, *n.* (PARKS), 118, 158, 208, 210, 223, 228, 230, 242, 248, 303, 309, 318, 336, **390,** 397, 401, 409, 499, 506, 523, 525, 550, 553, 561, 600, 633, 653, 656.
　　v. (PARKED, PARKED, PARKING), 209, 345, **390,** 418.

parlor, *n.* (PARLORS), 87, 204, **391,** 453, 457.

parrot, *n.* (PARROTS), 389, **391.**

part, *n.* (PARTS) (*each of the equal pieces into which a thing can be divided*), 431.
　　(*piece or amount; section*), 14, 16, 20, 27, 36, 38, 42, 49, 53, 61, 63, 93, 98, 100, 126, 143, 153, 164, 168, 172, 181, 202, 207, 208, 209, 214, 221, 243, 244, 245, 251, 253, 262, 283, 294, 301, 305, 316, 334, 343, 344, 357, 372, 391, 396, 399, 405, 436, 438, 454, 463, 469, 474, 475, 477, 483, 488, 496, 497, 506, 509, 537, 549, 567, 575, 577, 579, 588, 601, 613, 618, 630, 634, 635, 652.
　　(*role in a play*), 4, **391.**
　　(*share*), **391.**
　　take part (*to participate*), **391,** 408.

partly, *adv.*, 36, **391,** 481.

party, *n.* (PARTIES), 18, 22, 24, 77, 86, 93, 116, 123, 135, 139, 171, 177, 178, 221, 225, 227, 232, 246, 249, 257, 263, 272, 303, 379, **392,** 401, 444, 515, 538, 541, 544, 566, 571, 608, 616, 621, 625.

pass, *v.* (PASSED, PASSED, PASSING) (*to finish the work of a school grade or course and succeed in an examination in it*), 184, 290, 392.

pass (*Cont'd.*)
　　(*to go by; to move past*), 55, 283, 389, 392, 474.
　　(*to hand*), 392.

passenger, *n.* (PASSENGERS), 24, 117, 392, 417.

past, *adj.*, 302, 392.
　　n. (*one's life up to now*), 392.
　　(*time gone by*), 7, 43, 258, 392.
　　prep., 77, 392.

paste, *n.* (PASTES) (*any soft, moist, doughy substance*), 588.
　　(*soft substance used for sticking things together*), 393, 527.
　　v. (PASTED, PASTED, PASTING), 393, 615.

pasture, *n.* (PASTURES), 15, 91, 124, 157, 192, 237, 393.

pat, *n.* (PATS), 222, 393.

patch, *n.* (PATCHES) (*piece of cloth sewn over a hole or tear in cloth*), 393, 480.
　　(*piece of land*), 589.

path, *n.* (PATHS), 168, 207, 228, 300, 376, 393.

patter, *n.*, 394.
　　v. (PATTERED, PATTERED, PATTERING), 394.

paw, *n.* (PAWS), 40, 105, 144, 342, 394.

pay, *n.*, 394, 613.
　　v. (PAID, PAID, PAYING) (*to give money in exchange*), 50, 77, 121, 178, 187, 196, 239, 264, 303, 320, 342, 380, 394, 445, 513, 522, 534, 553, 561.
　　(*to offer; to give*), 25, 86, 272, 339, 394, 415.

pea, *n.* (PEAS), 394, 395.

peace, *n.*, 116, 326, 376, 395, 433, 616.

peach, *n.* (PEACHES), 82, 216, 287, 395, 410, 449, 529.

peanut, *n.* (PEANUTS), 395, 470.

pear, *n.* (PEARS), 48, 96, 194, 395.

peas, *n.* (*plural of* PEA), 112, 220, 394, 395, 412, 485, 608.

pebble, *n.* (PEBBLES), 395.

peck, *v.* (PECKED, PECKED, PECKING), 396, 639.

peel, *n.* (PEELS), 220, 396.
　　v. (PEELED, PEELED, PEELING), 295, 373, 396, 496, 555.

peep, *n.* (PEEPS), 98, 386, 396.
　　v. (PEEPED, PEEPED, PEEPING), 396.

pen, *n.* (PENS) (*instrument with which we write in ink*), 255, 275, 276, 290, 307, 318, 396, 407, 422, 433, 443, 527, 541, 562, 646.
　　(*small enclosed space in which animals are kept*), 119, 396.

pencil, *n.* (PENCILS), 4, 17, 75, 77, 155, 175, 225, 257, 276, 304, 308, 368, 397, 488, 513, 646.

penguin, *n.* (PENGUINS), 397.

penny, *n.* (PENNIES), 10, 11, 92, 145, 148, 174, 178, 193, 245, 284, 342, 359, 397, 412, 560, 564.

people, *n.* (PEOPLE), 6, 9, 14, 36, 43, 45, 58, 59, 65, 74, 81, 85, 88, 89, 93, 97, 100, 102, 104, 111, 113, 117, 125, 127, 128, 131, 138, 145, 149, 159, 161, 162, 166, 167, 168, 170, 171, 173, 177, 180, 184, 185, 186, 189, 192, 203, 204, 206, 207, 210, 211,

people (*Cont'd.*)
　　219, 221, 226, 228, 232, 236, 237, 238, 240, 249, 252, 260, 264, 266, 273, 274, 276, 281, 282, 286, 292, 293, 296, 300, 303, 305, 311, 313, 315, 321, 323, 326, 329, 336, 337, 346, 353, 357, 359, 360, 361, 364, 365, 370, 371, 372, 381, 389, 390, 395, 397, 398, 405, 406, 413, 414, 415, 416, 417, 421, 433, 436, 447, 457, 472, 476, 478, 479, 490, 502, 524, 525, 534, 539, 541, 551, 553, 554, 559, 562, 572, 579, 580, 581, 584, 593, 603, 606, 620, 622, 624, 631, 632, 645, 650, 655, 656.

pepper, *n.* (PEPPERS) (*kind of green or red vegetable used in salads and in seasoning*), 397.
　　(*plant whose berries or seeds have a hot, stinging taste*), 137, 397, 513, 637.

perch, *n.* (PERCHES), 398.

perfect, *adj.*, 398.

perfectly, *adv.*, 288, 398.

perhaps, *adv.*, 331, 338, 398, 418, 541.

period, *n.* (PERIODS) (*division of time*), 398.
　　(*dot used in writing and printing*), 152, 398.

permit, *v.* (PERMITTED, PERMITTED, PERMITTING), 86.

person, *n.* (PERSONS), 18, 44, 70, 75, 94, 96, 97, 99, 104, 105, 106, 126, 135, 139, 149, 158, 160, 167, 168, 171, 177, 180, 181, 185, 187, 199, 211, 224, 239, 240, 266, 273, 286, 304, 305, 314, 324, 333, 339, 340, 352, 353, 354, 355, 356, 358, 360, 361, 362, 373, 380, 385, 386, 390, 392, 397, 398, 403, 407, 409, 410, 411, 432, 442, 446, 460, 479, 493, 496, 501, 506, 507, 509, 537, 554, 555, 563, 566, 570, 580, 582, 585, 593, 603, 610, 611, 622, 624, 630, 631, 639, 641, 653.

Peru, *n.*, 510, 524.

pet, *n.* (PETS), 73, 89, 139, 149, 292, 399, 460, 508, 651.

petal, *n.* (PETALS), 134, 328, 388, 399, 428, 655.

petunia, *n.* (PETUNIAS), 399, 407, 475.

pharmacy, *n.* (PHARMACIES), 399.

phone, *n.* (PHONES), 399.

photograph, *n.* (PHOTOGRAPHS), 399, 401.

piano, *n.* (PIANOS), 23, 44, 180, 252, 291, 296, 319, 349, 398, 400, 408, 424, 426, 590, 624.

pick, *n.* (PICKS), 111, **400.**
　　v. (PICKED, PICKED, PICKING) (*to choose or select*), 101, 169, 378, **400,** 496, 506.
　　(*to dig with a pick*), **400.**
　　(*to gather*), **400.**
　　(*to lift*), 50, 169, 196, 209, 222, 305, 352, 396, **400,** 439, 442, 587.
　　(*to pluck, gather or pull*), 74, 221, 260, 325, 332, 449, 483, 565.

pickle, *n.* (PICKLES), 36, 129, 237, 282, **401.**

picnic, *n.* (PICNICS), 13, 164, 173, 208, 219, 227, 321, 377, 390, **401,** 406, 481, 516, 517, 550, 562.

   v. (PICNICKED, PICNICKED, PICNICKING), **401.**

picture, *n.* (PICTURES), 23, 33, 59, 81, 107, 116, 119, 125, 142, 154, 155, 156, 169, 184, 215, 216, 246, 273, 274, 278, 286, 302, 308, 327, 346, 347, 357, 372, 384, 385, 386, 393, 399, **401,** 422, 429, 491, 515, 524, 548, 554, 556, 615, 630, 637, 640, 648.

   v. (PICTURED, PICTURED, PICTURING), **401.**

pie, *n.* (PIES), 10, 20, 25, 32, 53, 102, 119, 174, 209, 243, 308, 348, 354, 379, 387, **401,** 402, 431, 446, 522, 553, 639.

piece, *n.* (PIECES), 19, 49, 50, 51, 52, 57, 64, 67, 85, 94, 95, 96, 100, 101, 103, 113, 115, 124, 125, 132, 152, 166, 168, 174, 177, 195, 201, 220, 221, 230, 233, 236, 243, 245, 255, 262, 265, 277, 285, 291, 309, 315, 319, 321, 336, 344, 348, 352, 353, 355, 376, 391, 393, 397, **402,** 408, 409, 429, 436, 437, 444, 451, 454, 461, 464, 471, 476, 480, 484, 498, 499, 503, 504, 511, 514, 516, 522, 527, 529, 530, 533, 535, 550, 554, 559, 569, 574, 575, 577, 579, 582, 594, 635, 645.

pieman, *n.* (PIEMEN), 616.

pierce, *v.* (PIERCED, PIERCED, PIERCING), 402, 479.

pig, *n.* (PIGS), 30, 34, 68, 101, 184, 187, 239, 243, 259, 262, 301, 396, **402,** 417, 519, 549, 575.

pigeon, *n.* (PIGEONS), 152, 211, **402.**

piggy bank, *n.* (PIGGY BANKS), **402.**

pile, *n.* (PILES), 114, 156, 176, 250, 251, **403,** 495, 508, 520.

   v. (PILED, PILED, PILING), **403.**

pill, *n.* (PILLS), 333, **403,** 548.

pillow, *n.* (PILLOWS), 131, 190, 383, 386, **403,** 505, 536, 578.

pilot, *n.* (PILOTS), 24, 27, 205, **403,** 565.

pin, *n.* (PINS) (*pointed piece of stiff wire*), 91, **404,** 416, 483, 528.

   (*jewelry*), 284.

pine, *n.* (PINES), 118, 177, 355, **404,** 583.

pineapple, *n.* (PINEAPPLES), **404.**

pink, *adj.* (PINKER, PINKEST), 58, 96, 110, 134, 183, 399, **404,** 447, 619.

   n., **404.**

pint, *n.* (PINTS), **404,** 431.

pipe, *n.* (PIPES) (*long tube for carrying water, gas, etc.*), 204, 260, 304, **405,** 411, 419, 506, 520, 588.

   (*toy for making bubbles*), 69.

   (*tube with a small bowl at one end in which tobacco is smoked*), 23, 193, **405,** 502.

pitch, *v.* (PITCHED, PITCHED, PITCHING), 147, **405.**

pitcher, *n.* (PITCHERS) (*container used for pouring out liquids*), 245, **405.**

   (*player in a baseball game who throws the ball to the batter*), **405.**

place, *n.* (PLACES) (*city, town, or country, or other region, or location; part;*

place *(Cont'd.)*

   spot), 72, 92, 96, 104, 135, 142, 145, 147, 171, 173, 234, 255, 261, 266, 278, 298, 311, 321, 329, 341, 347, 353, 364, 368, 371, 390, 403, **405,** 412, 413, 418, 422, 454, 469, 479, 487, 507, 516, 524, 530, 561, 579, 581, 582, 585, 599, 601, 602, 603, 628, 640, 656.

   (*where something or someone belongs, or usually is*), 5, 9, 19, 25, 27, 32, 34, 45, 46, 81, 115, 141, 153, 178, 210, 226, 227, 256, 264, 281, 310.

   v. (PLACED, PLACED, PLACING), 37, **405,** 428, 510.

plain, *adj.* (PLAINER, PLAINEST) (*clear; easily understood*), **406.**

   (*not good-looking*), **406.**

   (*simple; ordinary*), 186, **406.**

   n. (PLAINS), **406** (*adv. See* plainly).

plainly, *adv.,* 21, 406, 423.

plan, *n.* (PLANS), **406.**

   v. (PLANNED, PLANNED, PLANNING), 4,6.

plane, *n.* (PLANES) (*airplane is often called a plane*), 2, 205, 284, 392, **406.**

   (*tool with a sharp blade used to smooth wood and metal*), 87, 244, **406.**

   v. (PLANED, PLANED, PLANING), **406.**

planet, *n.* (PLANETS), 368, 407, 510, 556, 604.

plant, *n.* (PLANTS) (*factory with machinery and tools for making things*), **407.**

   (*tree, shrub, grass, flower or other living thing that grows in the earth, water, or air*), 10, 16, 39, 43, 56, 71, 74, 92, 100, 103, 107, 110, 113, 120, 121, 135, 142, 177, 205, 223, 224, 229, 233, 234, 236, 238, 253, 274, 305, 311, 315, 344, 353, 371, 381, 388, 395, **407,** 428, 447, 454, 465, 475, 482, 521, 526, 538, 540, 554, 565, 574, 583, 591, 608, 609, 610, 616, 619, 623.

   v. (PLANTED, PLANTED, PLANTING), 12, 144, 161, 237, 300, **407,** 411, 475, 510, 518.

planter, *n.* (PLANTERS), **407.**

plastic, *adj.,* **407.**

   n. (PLASTICS), 89, 263, **407,** 456, 533.

plate, *n.* (PLATES) (*flat dish that has slightly turned up edges*), 105, 124, 147, 167, 354, **408,** 442, 446, 563.

   (*thin, flat piece of metal*), **408.**

platform, *n.* (PLATFORMS), **408.**

play, *n.* (PLAYS), 4, **408.**

   v. (PLAYED, PLAYED, PLAYING) (*to act a part in a play*), 391, 452.

   (*to make believe*), **408.**

   (*to make music on a musical instrument*), 159, 319, 328, 335, 349, 377, **408,** 424.

   (*to take part in a game or activity from which one gets fun*), 4, 11, 36, 43, 94, 114, 138, 141, 145, 149, 156, 176, 197, 208, 225, 242, 254, 262, 272, 292, 379, 390, 400, **408,** 409, 489, 516, 554, 601, 625.

   (*to toy with; to fool with; to handle*), 90, 409, 617.

player, *n.* (PLAYERS), 37, 157, 207, 405, 409, 545, 549, 554, 568, 588, 591.

playful, *adj.,* 409 (*adv.* PLAYFULLY).

playground, *n.* (PLAYGROUNDS), **409,** 499, 651.

playhouse, *n.* (PLAYHOUSES), **409.**

playmate, *n.* (PLAYMATES), **409.**

plaything, *n.* (PLAYTHINGS), **409.**

pleasant, *adj.,* 97, 222, 230, 245, 349, 358, 369, 410, 454, 543, 621, 639 (*adv.* PLEASANTLY).

please, *v.* (PLEASED, PLEASED, PLEASING), 6, 17, 100, 108, 118, 131, 146, 179, 192, 253, 258, 290, 320, 332, 348, 349, **410,** 445, 446, 449, 465, 488, 489, 514, 520, 522, 528, 530, 539, 545, 561, 570, 632, 643. (*See also* pleased; pleasing).

pleased, *adj.,* 424, 427, 559, 633.

pleasing, *adj.,* 369, 410.

pleasure, *n.* (PLEASURES), 141, 312, 328, **410,** 424.

plentiful, *adj.,* 410 (*adv.* PLENTIFULLY).

plenty, *n.,* 116, 275, **410.**

plow, *n.* (PLOWS), **411.**

   v. (PLOWED, PLOWED, PLOWING), 381, **411.**

plum, *n.* (PLUMS), 102, **411.**

plumber, *n.* (PLUMBERS), **411,** 576.

plump, *adj.* (PLUMPER, PLUMPEST), **412,** 431.

plus, *prep.* (*added to*), 373 (*See also* add) (For use of the plus sign "+," see pages 4, 12, 243, 266, 359, 360, 480, 495, 557, 559, 564, 565, 566, 572, 593, 646, 655).

Pluto, *n.,* 407, 604.

pocket, *n.* (POCKETS), 53, 171, 202, 245, 280, 284, 290, 295, **412,** 589, 615, 618.

pocketbook, *n.* (POCKETBOOKS), **412,** 427.

pod, *n.* (PODS), 39, 112, 394, **412,** 485.

poem, *n.* (POEMS), 314, 343, **412,** 445, 446, 575, 608.

point, *n.* (POINTS) (*dot or period*), **413.**

   (*meaning or idea in something spoken or written*), **413.**

   (*narrow tip; sharp end*), 355, 404, **413,** 483, 527, 565, 577.

   (*place*), **413.**

   v. (POINTED, POINTED, POINTING), 8, 164, 196, 244, 307, **413,** 509 (*See also* pointed).

pointed *adj.,* 23, 84, 118, 352, 389, **413,** 558, 592 (*See also* point).

poison, *n.* (POISONS), **413.**

poke, *n.* (POKES), **413.**

polar bear, *n.* (POLAR BEARS), **413.**

pole, *n.* (POLES), 367, **414,** 452, 498, 521, 558, 632.

police, *n.,* **414.**

policeman, *n.* (POLICEMEN), 64, 110, 116, 141, 201, 240, 281, 303, 376, **414,** 421, 461, 494, 500, 530, 553, 563.

polite, *adj.,* 166, 179, 222, 236, 282, 298, 326, 390, 410, **414,** 456, 523 (*adv.* POLITELY).

pond, *n.* (PONDS), 41, 210, 215, 398, **414,** 496, 544.

Pontiac, *n.,* 99.

pony, *n.* (PONIES), 29, 399, **415.**
pool, *n.* (POOLS), **415,** 424.
poor, *adj.* (POORER, POOREST), 130, 145, **415,** 436, 447, 451, 480, 524, 631 (*adv.* POORLY).
pop, *n.* (POPS), 416.
    v. (POPPED, POPPED, POPPING), **416.**
popcorn, *n.* (POPCORNS), **416.**
poplar, *n.* (POPLARS), **416.**
poppy, *n.* (POPPIES), **416.**
popular, *adj.,* **416** (*adv.* POPULARLY).
population, *n.* (POPULATIONS), **416.**
porch, *n.* (PORCHES), **417.**
pork, *n.,* 101, 209, 333, 402, **417,** 469.
porridge, *n.,* **417.**
porter, *n.* (PORTERS), 31, **417.**
Portuguese, *adj.* and *n.* (PORTUGUESE), 300.
possible, *adj.,* 25, 93, 94, 268, 331, 398, 417 (*adv. See* possibly).
possibly, *adv.,* **418.**
post, *n.* (POSTS), 258, 418, 513, 577.
post, *v.* (POSTED, POSTED, POSTING), **418.**
postcard, *n.* (POSTCARDS), 5, 85, 324, **418.**
poster, *n.* (POSTERS), **418.**
postman, *n.* (POSTMEN), 5, 325, **418.**
post office, *n.* (POST OFFICES), 324, 325, **418.**
pot, *n.* (POTS), 13, 58, 104, 106, 113, 123, 146, 236, 237, 245, 264, 291, 310, 417, **419,** 505, 528, 635.
potato, *n.* (POTATOES), 216, 220, 259, 396, **419,** 462, 530, 624, 643.
pound, *n.* (POUNDS), 332, **419,** 576, 624.
    v. (POUNDED, POUNDED, POUNDING), 419, 440, 569.
pour, *v.* (POURED, POURED, POURING), 189, 314, 370, 405, **419,** 428, 531, 554.
powder, *n.* (POWDERS), 112, 204, 333, **420,** 425, 505.
    v. (POWDERED, POWDERED, POWDERING), **420.**
practice, *v.* (PRACTICED, PRACTICED, PRACTICING), 157, 180, 286, **420.**
praise, *v.* (PRAISED, PRAISED, PRAISING), **420.**
pray, *v.* (PRAYED, PRAYED, PRAYING), 102, **420,** 642.
prayer, *n.* (PRAYERS), 45, 63, 242, 294, **420.**
prepare, *v.* (PREPARED, PREPARED, PREPARING), 14, 209, 293, 325, **420,** 442, 529.
present, *adj.,* 3, 255, **421.**
    n. (PRESENTS), 48, 102, 116, 179, 224, 256, 329, **421,** 443, 512, 559, 608, 644.
president, *n.* (PRESIDENTS), 97, 99, 235, 257, 273, 292, 315, **421,** 442, 478, 611.
press, *n.* (PRESSES), 421, **422.**
    v. (PRESSED, PRESSED, PRESSING), 169, 226, 244, 277, 293, **421,** 422, 456, 503, 519.
pretend, *v.* (PRETENDED, PRETENDED, PRETENDING), 45, 149, 180, 324, 325, 391, **421,** 452.
pretty, *adj.* (PRETTIER, PRETTIEST), 5, 24, 30, 132, 134, 135, 139, 140, 143, 175, 215, 231, 282, 298, 302, 307, 324, 344, 371, 384, 406, **421,** 447, 457,

pretty *(Cont'd.)*
    485, 497, 503, 515, 585, 589, 597, 607, 615, 644, 648 (*adv.* PRETTILY).
price, *n.* (PRICES), 178, 320, **422,** 449, 462, 549, 607.
prince, *n.* (PRINCES), **422.**
princess, *n.* (PRINCESSES), **422.**
print, *n.* (PRINTS), **422.**
    v. (PRINTED, PRINTED, PRINTING), 12, 52, 421, **422,** 522, 558, 592.
prison, *n.* (PRISONS), **422.**
prize, *n.* (PRIZES), **422.**
problem, *n.* (PROBLEMS) (*question to be worked out and answered; something for which it is hard to find an answer*), 350.
promise, *n.* (PROMISES), **423.**
    v. (PROMISED, PROMISED, PROMISING), **423.**
promote, *v.* (PROMOTED, PROMOTED, PROMOTING), **423.**
prompt, *adj.,* **423** (*adv.* PROMPTLY).
pronounce, *v.* (PRONOUNCED, PRONOUNCED, PRONOUNCING), 227, **423.**
propeller, *n.* (PROPELLERS), 2, 9, 172, 253, **423.**
proper, *adj.,* **424,** 448 (*adv.* PROPERLY).
protect, *v.* (PROTECTED, PROTECTED, PROTECTING), 22, 23, 35, 43, 239, 303, 352, 414, **424,** 485, 486, 506, 563.
proud, *adj.* (PROUDER, PROUDEST), **424** (*adv. See* proudly).
proudly, *adv.,* **424.**
prune, *n.* (PRUNES), **424.**
pudding, *n.* (PUDDINGS), 312, **424,** 441, 502, 516, 626.
puddle, *n.* (PUDDLES), **424.**
Puebla, *n.,* 353.
puff, *n.* (PUFFS), **425.**
    v. (PUFFED, PUFFED, PUFFING), **425.**
pull, *n.* (PULLS), 283, **425.**
    v. (PULLED, PULLED, PULLING), 16, 26, 62, 85, 87, 88, 102, 111, 122, 145, 154, 156, 162, 248, 249, 263, 320, 324, 381, 411, **425,** 444, 464, 481, 499, 510, 514, 528, 534, 543, 554, 575, 577, 580, 581, 584, 589, 601, 613, 623, 640.
pump, *n.* (PUMPS), **425.**
    v. (PUMPED, PUMPED, PUMPING), 425, 634.
pumpkin, *n.* (PUMPKINS), 185, 280, **426,** 446.
punish, *v.* (PUNISHED, PUNISHED, PUNISHING), 128, 171, 422, **426.**
pupil, *n.* (PUPILS), **426,** 449, 469, 610, 611.
puppet, *n.* (PUPPETS), **426,** 489.
puppy, *n.* (PUPPIES), 63, 225, 238, 249, 286, 317, 350, 352, **426.**
pure, *adj.,* **427** (*adv.* PURELY).
purple, *adj.,* 10, 53, 234, 275, 399, 411, **427,** 440, 610.
    n. (PURPLES), **427.**
purpose, *n.* (PURPOSES) (*something a person wants or intends to get or do*), 574.
purr, *n.* (PURRS), **427.**
    v. (PURRED, PURRED, PURRING), **427.**
purse, *n.* (PURSES), 412, **427,** 448, 503.
push, *v.* (PUSHED, PUSHED, PUSHING), 26, 54, 70, 82, 84, 87, 88, 109, 127, 151,

push *(Cont'd.)*
    252, 280, 284, 287, 305, 364, 391, 423, **427,** 442, 461, 503, 548, 563, 589, 627.
pussy, *n.* (PUSSIES), 47, 145, **428.**
pussycat, *n.* (PUSSYCATS), 145.
pussywillow, *n.* (PUSSYWILLOWS), **428.**
put, *v.* (PUT, PUT, PUTTING), 4, 8, 21, 31, 40, 59, 74, 89, 96, 99, 101, 107, 109, 112, 119, 131, 137, 144, 146, 159, 185, 191, 198, 208, 219, 221, 244, 248, 250, 252, 255, 260, 265, 269, 291, 309, 311, 329, 402, 412, **428,** 443, 460, 476, 477, 478, 484, 513, 515, 522, 538, 548, 570, 585, 609, 613, 618, 622, 626, 632, 640, 653.
putter, *n.* (PUTTERS), **428.**
    v. (PUTTERED, PUTTERED, PUTTERING), **428.**
puzzle, *n.* (PUZZLES), 324, **429,** 447.

Q

Q, q, *n.* (Q'S, Q'S) (*seventeenth letter of the alphabet*), 12, 170, 309, **430,** 558, 592.
quack, *n.* (QUACKS), 160, **431.**
    v. (QUACKED, QUACKED, QUACKING), **431.**
quail, *n.* (QUAILS), **431.**
quarrel, *v.* (QUARRELED or QUARRELLED, QUARRELED or QUARRELLED, QUARRELING or QUARRELLING), **431.**
quarry, *n.* (QUARRIES), **431.**
quart, *n.* (QUARTS), 219, 259, 404, **431.**
quarter, *n.* (QUARTERS), 150, 342, **431.**
quartet, *n.* (QUARTETS), **432.**
queen, *n.* (QUEENS), 128, 173, 293, 386, 432, 452, 567.
queer, *adj.* (QUEERER, QUEEREST), **432** (*adv.* QUEERLY).
question, *n.* (QUESTIONS), 17, 24, 130, 232, 390, 429, **432,** 445, 501, 564, 593, 626.
    v. (QUESTIONED, QUESTIONED, QUESTIONING), **432.**
quick, *adj.* (QUICKER, QUICKEST), 95, 148, 239, 280, 283, 312, 425, **432,** 503, 538 (*adv. See* quickly).
quickly, *adv.,* 22, 23, 55, 74, 107, 155, 164, 188, 197, 203, 205, 220, 225, 232, 268, 271, 283, 284, 287, 330, 343, 372, 392, 396, 417, **433,** 440, 458, 468, 482, 487, 503, 515, 518, 520, 544, 573, 621, 635.
quiet, *adj.* (QUIETER, QUIETEST), 44, 77, 138, 227, 269, 290, 319, 320, 386, 395, **433,** 479, 528, 569 (*adv. See* quietly).
quietly, *adv.,* 433, 458, 492.
quill, *n.* (QUILLS), **433.**
quit, *v.* (QUIT, QUITTED, QUITTING), **433.**
quite, *adv.,* **433.**

R

R, r, *n.* (R's, R's) (*eighteenth letter of the alphabet*), 12, 170, 309, **434**, 558, 592.

rabbit, *n.* (RABBITS), 8, 73, 95, 141, 247, 258, 262, 278, 290, 292, 324, 342, 432, **435**, 488, 559, 584.

raccoon (*See* racoon).

race, *n.* (RACES) (*contest of speed*), 40, 304, 338, **435**, 440, 537, 544, 567, 570, 633, 638.

(*large group of people with the same skin color, kind of hair, and other common characteristics*), **435**.

v. (RACED, RACED, RACING), 110, 650.

racoon or **raccoon,** *n.* (RACOONS or RACOONS), 387, **435**, 551.

radio, *n.* (RADIOS), 66, 169, 314, 337, 357, **436**, 524, 588, 598.

radish, *n.* (RADISHES), 112, **436**, 454, 535.

rag, *n.* (RAGS), 388, **436**, 456, 482.

ragged, *adj.,* **436**, 621.

rail, *n.* (RAILS), **437**.

railroad, *n.* (RAILROADS), 85, 341, **437**, 524, 530, 580, 581.

railway, *n.* (RAILWAYS), 111, **437**.

rain, *n.* (RAINS), 89, 91, 109, 158, 177, 208, 272, 394, 424, **438**, 485, 488, 489, 498, 503, 518, 531, 558, 597, 626, 634.

v. (RAINED, RAINED, RAINING), 10, 13, 27, 89, 93, 146, 161, 173, 177, 265, 272, 278, 288, 331, 415, **438**, 439, 444, 456, 489, 562, 564, 597, 626, 628.

rainbow, *n.* (RAINBOWS), 317, **438**.

raincoat, *n.* (RAINCOATS), 407, **438**, 439.

raindrop, *n.* (RAINDROPS), 242, **438**.

rainy, *adj.* (RAINIER, RAINIEST), 95, **438**, 621.

raise, *v.* (RAISED, RAISED, RAISING) (*to grow*), 88, **439**.

(*to increase in degree, amount, intensity, etc.*), 266, 321, 408.

(*to pick up*), 311, **439**.

(*to put up*), **439**, 457.

(*to take care of*), 100, **439**, 440.

raisin, *n.* (RAISINS), **439**.

rake, *n.* (RAKES), **439**.

v. (RAKED, RAKED, RAKING), **439**.

ran, *v.* (*past tense of* RUN), 3, 4, 22, 23, 27, 108, 304, 337, 435, 439, 446, 549, 567, 570, 573, 625, 638, 652 (*See also* run).

ranch, *n.* (RANCHES), 124, **440**, 522.

rang, *v.* (*past tense of* RING), **440**, 449, 458.

rap, *n.* (RAPS), **440**.

v. (RAPPED, RAPPED, RAPPING), **440**.

rapid, *adj.,* 247, **440** (*adv. See* rapidly).

rapidly, *adv.,* 103, 594.

rare, *adj.* (RARER, RAREST), 193 (*adv.* RARELY).

raspberry, *n.* (RASPBERRIES), **440**.

rat, *n.* (RATS), 5, 47, 89, 95, 250, 280, **441**.

rather, *adv.,* **441**, 551.

rattle, *n.* (RATTLES), **441**, 457.

raven, *n.* (RAVENS), **441**.

raw, *adj.,* **441**, 462.

razor, *n.* (RAZORS), **441**, 483.

reach, *v.* (REACHED, REACHED, REACHING), 164, 256, 298, **442**, 534.

read, *v.* (READ, READ, READING), 2, 12, 13, 17, 50, 57, 59, 82, 84, 141, 142, 143, 161, 185, 216, 223, 271, 276, 306, 309, 310, 352, 357, 377, 384, 388, **442**, 469, 476, 492, 506, 541, 563, 568, 573, 574, 643.

ready, *adj.* (READIER, READIEST), 118, 135, 177, 242, 277, 354, 386, **442**, 449, 508, 633, 652.

real, *adj.,* 170, 180, 185, 186, 223, 230, 330, 389, **442**, 532, 637 (*adv. See* really).

really, *adv.,* 45, 274, 327, 341, 421, 433, **442**, 523, 587.

rear, *n.* (REARS) (*back part*), 284.

reason, *n.* (REASONS), 178, 402, **443**, 474, 561, 631.

receive, *v.* (RECEIVED, RECEIVED, RECEIVING), 102, 223, 224, 231, 421, **443**, 611, 643.

recess, *n.* (RECESSES), **443**.

red, *adj.* (REDDER, REDDEST), 13, 30, 60, 83, 84, 102, 114, 115, 136, 212, 275, 328, 374, 411, 436, 440, 442, **443**, 508, 533, 553, 555, 619.

n. (REDS), 97, 201, 203, **443**, 607.

refrigerator, *n.* (REFRIGERATORS), 99, 119, 212, 215, **443**, 458, 468, 509, 515.

refuse, *v.* (REFUSED, REFUSED, REFUSING), **444**.

reindeer, *n.* (REINDEER or REINDEERS), **444**, 464.

remain, *v.* (REMAINED, REMAINED, REMAINING), **444**, 525.

remember, *v.* (REMEMBERED, REMEMBERED, REMEMBERING), 208, 343, **444**, 653.

remove, *v.* (REMOVED, REMOVED, REMOVING), 106, **445**, 550.

rent, *n.* (RENTS), **445**.

v. (RENTED, RENTED, RENTING), **445**.

repeat, *v.* (REPEATED, REPEATED, REPEATING), **445**.

reply, *n.* (REPLIES), **445**.

v. (REPLIED, REPLIED, REPLYING), **445**.

report, *n.* (REPORTS), **446**.

v. (REPORTED, REPORTED, REPORTING), **446**.

reside, *v.* (RESIDED, RESIDED, RESIDING), 260, **446**.

resident, *n.* (RESIDENTS), **446**.

rest, *n.* (RESTS) (*ease after work; relaxation; sleep*), 94, 116, 142, **446**, 498, 573.

(*what is left over; remainder*), 343, 377, 391, **446**, 463, 521.

v. (RESTED, RESTED, RESTING), 29, 51, 275, 359, **446**, 621.

restaurant, *n.* (RESTAURANTS) (*public place where food can be bought and eaten*), 118.

return, *v.* (RETURNED, RETURNED, RETURNING), 29, 158, 315, **446**, 604, 614.

rhyme, *n.* (RHYMES), **446**.

v. (RHYMED, RHYMED, RHYMING), **446**.

ribbon, *n.* (RIBBONS), 295, **447**, 549, 570, 650.

rice, *n.,* 93, 100, 282, 424, **447**.

rich, *adj.* (RICHER, RICHEST), 284, 326, **447**, 568, 621.

rid, *v.* (RID or RIDDED, RID or RIDDED, RIDDING), 301, **447**, 519.

ridden, *v.* (*past participle of* RIDE), **447**, 448.

riddle, *n.* (RIDDLES), 429, **447**, 551.

ride, *n.* (RIDES), 91, 157, 278, 410, **448**, 553, 588, 650.

v. (RODE, RIDDEN, RIDING), 11, 26, 29, 50, 58, 60, 81, 87, 104, 124, 187, 222, 261, 263, 447, **448**, 460, 471, 475, 522, 526, 534, 550, 552, 569, 588, 618, 633, 637.

ridiculous, *adj.,* **448** (*adv.* RIDICULOUSLY).

right, *adj.* (*correct*), 120, 123, 200, 288, 424, 429, **448**, 476, 513, 646.

(*good, proper, decent, or lawful*), 230, 410.

(*on or toward the side opposite your left hand*), 21, 131, 290, 307, 362, **448**, 482, 509, 523, 585.

adv., 208, 389, 551.

n. (RIGHTS), 591.

right away and **right now** (*immediately*), 6, 27, 140, 231, 273, 358, 373.

rind, *n.* (RINDS), 396, **449**, 619.

ring, *n.* (RINGS) (*any round band*), 93.

(*circle*), 103, **449**, 644.

(*round band worn on a finger*), 143, 223, 229, 284, **449**, 511, 525, 529, 571, 607.

v. (RANG, RUNG, RINGING), 17, 45, 62, 104, 145, 151, 197, 264, 335, 362, 440, **449**, 458, 492, 566, 572, 579, 614, 652.

ripe, *adj.* (RIPER, RIPEST), 410, **449**.

rise, *v.* (ROSE, RISEN, RISING), 3, 33, 165, 307, **449**, 525, 619, 625.

river, *n.* (RIVERS), 34, 39, 82, 134, 176, 192, 327, 354, 368, 398, 440, **450**, 461, 463, 533, 590, 606, 619.

road, *n.* (ROADS), 47, 60, 131, 140, 145, 158, 300, 353, 413, 437, **450**, 455, 534, 552, 553, 580, 590, 620.

roam, *v.* (ROAMED, ROAMED, ROAMING) (*to wander about*), 558.

roar, *n.* (ROARS), **450**.

v. (ROARED, ROARED, ROARING), 313, **450**.

roast, *adj.,* 147, 287.

n. (ROASTS), 42, 189, 305, 379, **451**, 499.

v. (ROASTED, ROASTED, ROASTING), 113, 118, **451**, 590.

rob, *v.* (ROBBED, ROBBED, ROBBING), **451**.

robber, *n.* (ROBBERS), 281, **451**.

robin, *n.* (ROBINS), 80, 128, 190, 205, 302, **451**.

rock, *n.* (ROCKS), 67, 77, 111, 203, 207, 220, 247, 287, 311, 315, 320, 344, 439, **451**, 455, 494, 505, 529, 536, 540, 568, 618.

v. (ROCKED, ROCKED, ROCKING), 125, 209, **451**.

rocket, *n.* (ROCKETS), 155, 188, **452**, 465, 491, 510.

rod, *n.* (RODS), **452.**

rode, *v.* (*past tense of* RIDE), 447, 448, **452.**

role, *n.* (ROLES), **452.**

roll, *n.* (ROLLS) (*bread*), 72, 416, **453.**
(*cylinder*), 103, 212, **453,** 579.
v. (ROLLED, ROLLED, ROLLING) (*to turn over and over*), 39, **453.**
(*to pass*), 498.
(*to wrap around and around itself*), 103, **453,** 535.

roller, *n.* (ROLLERS), **453,** 496.

roof, *n.* (ROOFS), 25, 107, 242, 256, 298, 417, **453,** 498, 609.

room, *n.* (ROOMS) (*one of the inside divisions or parts of a building*), 12, 14, 18, 19, 24, 25, 30, 42, 44, 52, 74, 77, 92, 95, 105, 106, 108, 120, 121, 127, 136, 141, 145, 151, 153, 170, 174, 177, 199, 204, 243, 264, 269, 278, 281, 293, 304, 345, 361, 376, 388, 391, 403, 406, 421, 433, 449, **453,** 470, 474, 477, 481, 501, 502, 521, 522, 532, 548, 569, 570, 584, 585, 601, 606, 615.
(*space*), 195, 200, 275, **453,** 510.

rooster, *n.* (ROOSTERS), 98, 112, 115, 127, 254, **454,** 549.

root, *n.* (ROOTS), 43, 71, 88, 224, **454,** 591.

rope, *n.* (ROPES), 11, 32, 104, 166, 283, 285, 295, **454,** 484, 497, 535, 558, 589.

rose, *n.* (ROSES), 56, 205, 369, 371, 399, **454, 455,** 501, 503, 543, 565.
(*past tense and past perfect of* RISE), 449.

rosebush, *n.* (ROSEBUSHES), 407, **455,** 565.

rotten, *adj.,* 405, **455,** 501, 515.

rough, *adj.* (ROUGHER, ROUGHEST), 121, 150, 191, 195, 259, 281, 330, 404, 450, **455,** 502, 552, 574, 609, 615 (*adv.* ROUGHLY).

round, *adj.,* 21, 33, 36, 39, 63, 82, 93, 97, 118, 152, 194, 207, 234, 343, 353, 355, 375, 387, 394, 395, 404, **455,** 482, 516, 577, 591, 627, 629.

row, *n.* (ROWS), 168, 253, 314, **455,** 558, 564, 565, 592, 593.
v. (ROWED, ROWED, ROWING), 367, **455,** 456.

rowboat, *n.* (ROWBOATS), 58, 367, **456.**

rub, *v.* (RUBBED, RUBBED, RUBBING), 175, 226, 236, 310, **456,** 472, 636.

rubber, *n.* (RUBBERS), 60, 62, 175, 263, **456,** 465, 534, 573.

rubbers, *n.,* **456,** 550.

rude, *adj.* (RUDER, RUDEST), **456** (*adv.* RUDELY).

ruffle, *n.* (RUFFLES), **457.**

rug, *n.* (RUGS), 67, 87, 204, 299, 311, 330, **457,** 482, 487, 585, 606, 622, 644.

ruin, *v.* (RUINED, RUINED, RUINING), **457,** 515.

rule, *n.* (RULES) (*direction telling what may and what may not be done*), 64, 67, 219, 414, **457.**
(*flat stick, marked with evenly spaced lines, used for measuring*), 641.
v. (RULED, RULED, RULING), **457.**

ruler, *n.* (RULERS), 4, 228, 308, 317, 432, **457,** 567.

run, *v.* (RAN, RUN, RUNNING) (*to flow*), 204, **458.**
(*to go*), 260.
(*to go by moving the legs faster than in walking*), 5, 6, 23, 44, 65, 90, 95, 108, 140, 188, 191, 192, 219, 247, 300, 304, 372, 388, 435, 439, **458,** 468, 543, 544, 559, 570, 632, 633, 651.
(*to operate*), 111, 219, 227, 246, 346, 354, 371, 437, 443, **458,** 525, 534, 583, 588, 634, 638, 643.

rung, *v.* (*nonstandard past tense and standard past participle of* RING), 449, **458** (*See also* ring).

rush, *n.* (RUSHES), **458.**
v. (RUSHED, RUSHED, RUSHING), 74, **458.**

rye, *adj.,* **458.**
n. (RYES), 53, 204, 233, 234, **458,** 533.

S

S, s, *n.* (S's, s's) (*nineteenth letter of the alphabet*), 12, 170, 309, **459,** 558, 592.

sack, *n.* (SACKS), 55, 280, **460.**

Sacramento, *n.* 353.

sad, *adj.* (SADDER, SADDEST), 2, 57, 144, 172, 177, 184, 191, 196, 227, 265, 316, 317, 341, **460,** 474, 508, 577, 599, 633 (*adv. See* sadly).

saddle, *n.* (SADDLES), **460.**

sadly, *adv.,* **460,** 560.

sadness, *n.* (SADNESSES), 604.

safe, *adj.* (SAFER, SAFEST), 22, 30, 136, 414, **460,** 512, 599, 656 (*adv. See* safely).
n. (SAFES), **460,** 474.

safely, *adv.,* 303, 389, **461,** 576.

safety, *n.* (SAFETIES), **461,** 656.

said, *v.* (*past tense and past participle of* SAY), 6, 14, 18, 25, 44, 54, 77, 95, 116, 122, 142, 144, 150, 166, 183, 210, 236, 243, 254, 261, 272, 290, 303, 364, 377, 410, **461,** 494, 515, 538, 545, 560, 575, 606, 624, 643 (*See also* say).

sail, *n.* (SAILS), **461.**
v. (SAILED, SAILED, SAILING), 38, 82, 414, **461,** 462, 473, 486.

sailboat, *n.* (SAILBOATS), 401, **461,** 650.

sailor, *n.* (SAILORS), 84, 85, 333, 354, **462,** 599, 616.

Saint Nicholas, *n.,* 464.

Saint Valentine's Day, *n.,* 606.

sake, *n.,* 462.

salad, *n.* (SALADS), 101, 129, 209, 310, 441, **462,** 609.

sale, *n.* (SALES), **462,** 616, 648.

salmon, *n.* (SALMON OR SALMONS), **462.**

salt, *n.* (SALTS), 30, 73, 152, 196, 367, 368, 401, **463,** 473, 528, 553, 584.

salty, *adj.* (SALTIER, SALTIEST), 368, **463,** 475, 553, 555.

same, *adj.,* 10, 30, 32, 51, 52, 68, 88, 96, 103, 105, 174, 176, 223, 237, 243, 296, 304, 312, 315, 328, 352, 373,

same (*Cont'd.*)
375, 378, 386, 390, 393, 402, 448, 458, **463,** 494, 513, 514, 519, 529, 570, 572, 585, 594, 599, 603, 633, 642.

sample, *n.* (SAMPLES), **463.**

sand, *n.* (SANDS), 31, 39, 176, 207, 226, 233, 249, 403, 409, **463,** 464.

sandwich, *n.* (SANDWICHES), 97, 244, **464,** 633.

sandy, *adj.* (SANDIER, SANDIEST), 39, 142, **464.**

sang, *v.* (*past tense of* SING), 87, 319, 321, 400, 424, **464,** 493, 585, 628 (*See also* sing).

sank, *v.* (*past tense of* SINK), **464,** 494.

Santa, *n.* (*short form for* SANTA CLAUS) 159 (*See also* Santa Claus).

Santa Claus, *n.,* 116, 179, 259, 405, 444, **464** (*See also* Santa).

sap, *n.* (SAPS), 327, 456, **465,** 546.

sardine, *n.* (SARDINES), **465.**

sat, *v.* (*past tense and past participle of* SIT), 43, 102, 185, 255, 283, 375, 391, 433, **465,** 615, 616.

satellite, *n.* (SATELLITES), **465.**

satisfy, *v.* (SATISFIED, SATISFIED, SATISFYING), 118, **465.**

Saturday, *n.* (SATURDAYS), 137, 194, 199, 213, 272, 342, 376, **465,** 474, 479, 495, 539, 569, 589, 623, 635, 640.

Saturn, *n.,* 407.

sauce, *n.* (SAUCES), 90, **465,** 513.

saucer, *n.* (SAUCERS), 147, 244, **466.**

sauerkraut, *n.,* **466.**

sausage, *n.* (SAUSAGES), 212, **466,** 594.

save, *v.* (SAVED, SAVED, SAVING), 311, 333, **466.**

saw, *n.* (SAWS), 87, 244, **467.**
v. (SAWED, SAWED, SAWING), **467.**

saw, *v.* (*past tense of* SEE), 79, 82, 91, 94, 128, 137, 147, 155, 156, 157, 158, 179, 184, 196, 201, 202, 203, 208, 222, 236, 237, 255, 257, 258, 293, 300, 302, 324, 329, 336, 337, 354, 357, 361, 362, 381, 386, 392, 408, 441, 446, 461, **467,** 472, 474, 481, 487, 497, 511, 518, 521, 525, 529, 540, 551, 561, 572, 576, 580, 607, 609, 631, 638, 648 (*See also* see).

sawdust, *n.,* **467.**

say, *v.* (SAID, SAID, SAYING), 24, 25, 44, 56, 68, 89, 106, 118, 127, 138, 145, 149, 179, 227, 230, 236, 242, 266, 300, 321, 332, 339, 361, 387, 410, 423, 436, 442, 454, **467,** 487, 512, 524, 557, 562, 587, 604, 640, 655.

scale, *n.* (SCALES), 32, **467,** 624.

scamper, *v.* (SCAMPERED, SCAMPERED, SCAMPERING), **468.**

scarcely, *adv.,* 35, **468.**

scare, *v.* (SCARED, SCARED, SCARING), 5, 9, 190, 214, 440, **468,** 487.

scarecrow, *n.* (SCARECROWS), **468.**

scared, *v.,* **468** (*See also* scare).

scarf, *n.* (SCARFS OR SCARVES), **469.**

scatter, *v.* (SCATTERED, SCATTERED, SCATTERING), **469,** 510, 514.

scene, *n.* (SCENES), **469,** 609.

scent, *n.* (SCENTS), **469.**

school, *n.* (SCHOOLS), 4, 6, 8, 9, 13, 19, 21, 23, 25, 41, 53, 64, 67, 73, 84, 88, 94, 105, 114, 140, 144, 147, 153, 155, 160, 166, 179, 184, 186, 188, 227, 228, 230, 232, 237, 243, 249, 257, 268, 271, 272, 273, 277, 280, 281, 288, 290, 292, 293, 296, 302, 304, 306, 307, 314, 316, 321, 333, 338, 363, 364, 365, 368, 373, 374, 392, 393, 398, 404, 409, 415, 416, 418, 423, 426, 439, 443, 446, 448, 449, 452, 458, 467, **469,** 500, 501, 513, 521, 523, 541, 550, 553, 562, 575, 581, 603, 604, 606, 608, 611, 625, 628, 631, 637, 652.

schoolhouse, *n.* (SCHOOLHOUSES), **469.**

schoolroom, *n.* (SCHOOLROOMS), **470.**

scissors, *n.,* 470, 483, 484.

scold, *v.* (SCOLDED, SCOLDED, SCOLDING), **470.**

scoop, *n.* (SCOOPS), 147, **470.**

   v. (SCOOPED, SCOOPED, SCOOPING), **470.**

scooter, *n.* (SCOOTERS), **471.**

scour, *v.* (SCOURED, SCOURED, SCOURING), **471.**

scout, *n.* (SCOUTS), **471.**

scrap, *n.* (SCRAPS), **471.**

scrape, *v.* (SCRAPED, SCRAPED, SCRAPING), 147, **471,** 508.

scratch, *n.* (SCRATCHES), 268, **472.**

   v. (SCRATCHED, SCRATCHED, SCRATCHING), 203, 330, 405, 427, **472,** 561.

scream, *n.* (SCREAMS), **472.**

   v. (SCREAMED, SCREAMED, SCREAMING), 361, **472.**

screw, *n.* (SCREWS), 71, 87, **472,** 641.

   v. (SCREWED, SCREWED, SCREWING), **472.**

scrub, *v.* (SCRUBBED, SCRUBBED, SCRUBBING), 38, **471,** 472, 528.

sea, *n.* (SEAS), 38, 111, 173, 369, **473,** 486, 487, 494, 533, 611, 615, 626.

sea gull, *n.* (SEA GULLS), **473.**

seal, *n.* (SEALS), 35, **473,** 572, 584, 615.

seashore, *n.* (SEASHORES), 111, 395, **473,** 487.

season, *n.* (SEASONS), 26, 185, **473,** 518, 539, 636.

seat, *n.* (SEATS), 74, 85, 94, 95, 335, 393, 405, 460, **474,** 530, 550, 603.

second, *adj.,* 35, 105, 190, 194, 199, 204, 211, 213, 332, 342, 377, 423, 465, **474,** 479, 495, 539, 553, 564, 569, 589, 602, 623.

   adv., 302.

   n. (SECONDS), 264, 340, 571.

secret, *adj.,* 412, **474.**

   n. (*secrets*), 350, **474** (*adv.* SECRETLY).

see, *v.* (SAW, SEEN, SEEING) (*to encounter; to visit*), 151, 242, 298, 309, **474,** 482, 490, 610, 624.

   (*to look at; to notice with the eyes; to have power of sight; to view*), 3, 11, 40, 55, 65, 72, 81, 110, 124, 141, 170, 194, 204, 210, 221, 230, 281, 317, 337, 343, 362, 371, 396, 406, 467, **474,** 476, 500, 514, 520, 551, 565, 598, 602, 609, 643.

   (*to make certain*), **474.**

   (*to understand; to learn; to find out; to know*), 167 255, 383, 435, **474,** 583.

seed, *n.* (SEEDS), 4, 39, 47, 53, 71, 97, 113, 118, 121, 135, 137, 194, 233, 280, 315, 338, 367, 394, 395, 397, 407, 411, 412, 416, 440, 447, 469, **475,** 510, 513, 518, 529, 540, 567.

seem, *v.* (SEEMED, SEEMED, SEEMING), 4, 20, 275, 324, 370, **475,** 509, 511, 556.

seen, *v.* (*past participle of* SEE), 20, 129, 177, 181, 223, 278, 340, 483, 491, 493, 509, 537, 606, 607 (*See also* see).

seesaw, *n.* (SEESAWS), 409, **475.**

seize, *v.* (SEIZED, SEIZED, SEIZING), **475.**

seldom, *adv.,* 25, **475,** 601.

select, *v.* (SELECTED, SELECTED, SELECTING), **476.**

self, *n.* (SELVES), **476.**

selfish, *adj.,* 178, **476** (*adv.* SELFISHLY).

sell, *v.* (SOLD, SOLD, SELLING), 32, 75, 107, 184, 219, 335, 338, 462, **476,** 580.

send, *v.* (SENT, SENT, SENDING), 66, 148, 169, 174, 237, 252, 337, 452, 465, **476,** 477, 522, 568.

sense, *n.* (SENSES) (*feeling; awareness*), **476,** 578.

   (*judgement or intelligence*), 207, 323, 370, 443, **476,** 501, 537.

sensitive, *adj.,* **477** (*adv.* SENSITIVELY).

sent, *v.* (*past tense and past participle of* SEND), 85, 106, 324, 418, 476, 477, 487, 555, 556.

sentence, *n.* (SENTENCES), 152, 271, 398, 432, **477.**

separate, *adj.,* 211, 226, 477 (*adv.* SEPARATELY).

   v. (SEPARATED, SEPARATED, SEPARATING), 49, 148, 391, **477,** 508.

September, *n.* (SEPTEMBERS), 20, 343, 478, 606, 651.

serious, *adj.,* 86, 147, **478** (*adv.* SERIOUSLY).

servant, *n.* (SERVANTS), 324, 447, **478.**

serve, *v.* (SERVED, SERVED, SERVING) (*to bring food to*), **478,** 548, 614.

   (*to do good for*), **478.**

set, *n.* (SETS) (*group of articles used together*), 117, **478,** 539.

   (*television*), 339, **478,** 556.

   v. (SET, SET, SETTING), 53, 428, 442, 466, **478,** 569, 601, 625.

settle, *v.* (SETTLED, SETTLED, SETTLING), **479.**

seven, *adj.,* 127, 137, 139, 168, 273, 372, 438, **479,** 480, 623.

   n. (SEVENS), 122, 167, 170, 200, 210, 369, **479,** 495, 557.

seventeen, *adj.,* 167.

   n. (SEVENTEENS), 211, **479,** 495.

seventeenth, *n.* (SEVENTEENTHS), 170, 479.

seventh, *adj.,* 168, 194, 199, 213, 287, 342, 465, 474, **479,** 495, 539, 569, 589, 623.

seventy, *n.* (SEVENTIES), **480.**

several, *adj.,* 60, 237, **480,** 506, 515, 537, 641.

severe, *adj.* (SEVERER, SEVEREST), **480** (*adv.* SEVERELY).

sew, *v.* (SEWED, SEWED *or* SEWN, SEWING), 23, 76, 110, 287, 318, 325, 334, 355,

sew (*Cont'd.*)
   393, 412, 458, **480,** 489, 528, 544, 554, 563, 566, 575.

shabby, *adj.* (SHABBIER, SHABBIEST), **480** (*adv.* SHABBILY).

shade, *n.* (SHADES) (*shadow or partial darkness made by something blocking the light*), 171, 327, **481.**

   (*something made to shut out light*), 320, **481.**

   v. (SHADED, SHADED, SHADING), 326, **481.**

shadow, *n.* (SHADOWS), **481.**

shake, *v.* (SHOOK, SHAKEN, SHAKING) (*to clasp hands*), **482.**

   (*to jerk; to move quickly up and down or to and fro*), 103, 282, 441, **482,** 506.

   (*to tremble*), 486, 583.

shall, *v.* (SHOULD), 7, 22, 200, 223, 254, 265, 272, 317, 336, 448, 451, **482,** 625, 628, 631, 640.

shamrock, *n.* (SHAMROCKS), **482.**

shape, *n.* (SHAPES), 21, 76, 106, 194, 195, 209, 220, 226, 314, 416, 474, **482,** 503, 525.

   v. (SHAPED, SHAPED, SHAPING), 103, 106, 212, 402, 407, **482.**

share, *n.* (SHARES), 236, 391, **483.**

   v. (SHARED, SHARED, SHARING), 222, 247, **483.**

sharp, *adj.* (SHARPER, SHARPEST), 27, 53, 86, 105, 107, 132, 161, 166, 236, 295, 350, 355, 404, 411, 413, 467, 470, **483,** 503, 519, 527, 565, 651, 653 (*adv.,* SHARPLY).

shave, *n.* (SHAVES), 34, 40, 340, 441, **483,** 629.

shawl, *n.* (SHAWLS), **483.**

she, *pro.,* 4, 6, 23, 30, 42, 48, 73, 84, 101, 104, 109, 121, 128, 137, 145, 171, 180, 184, 191, 211, 225, 238, 249, 256, 272, 282, 294, 303, 311, 316, 329, 335, 361, 371, 378, 392, 406, 420, 424, 432, 440, 451, 460, 475, 482, 484, 485, 491, 505, 519, 559, 563, 569, 593, 602, 614, 622, 625, 628, 643, 645, 652, 653.

shears, *n.,* 484.

shed, *n.* (SHEDS), **484.**

shed, *v.* (SHED, SHED, SHEDDING) (*to cause something to flow*), 128.

she-deer, *n.* (SHE-DEER) (*female deer*), 149.

sheep, *n.* (SHEEP), 15, 29, 44, 149, 187, 203, 299, 439, 440, **484,** 640.

sheet, *n.* (SHEETS) (*broad, thin piece of anything*), 59, 402, **484,** 548.

   (*piece of cloth big enough to cover a bed*), 206, 484, 598.

shelf, *n.* (SHELVES), 18, 61, 101, 130, 228, 256, 307, 372, 442, **484,** 510, 534.

shell, *n.* (SHELLS), 365, 412, 426, **485,** 487, 502, 578, 592, 615.

she'll, *pro.* and *v.* (*contraction for* SHE SHALL *or* SHE WILL), 428, **485.**

shelter, *n.* (SHELTERS), **485,** 580.

shepherd, *n.* (SHEPHERDS), **485.**

she's, *pro.* and *v.* (*contraction for* SHE IS), **485.**

shine, *v.* (SHINED *or* SHONE, SHINED *or* SHONE, SHINING), 13, 55, 184, 194,

shine (*Cont'd.*)
343, 344, 378, 392, 410, 438, 456, 481, **485**, 487, 497, 511, 523, 539, 620, 621.

shiny, *adj.* (SHINIER, SHINIEST), 66, 143, 226, 229, 353, 420, 441, 472, **485**, 492, 493, 585.

ship, *n.* (SHIPS), 2, 58, 86, 354, 462, 473, **486**, 494, 525, 526.

shirt, *n.* (SHIRTS), 109, 187, 277, 330, 334, 360, 386, 428, **486**, 516, 519, 523, 528, 621.

shiver, *v.* (SHIVERED, SHIVERED, SHIVERING), 47, 99, 480, **486**.

shoe, *n.* (SHOES), 35, 47, 48, 60, 61, 63, 109, 179, 191, 200, 253, 262, 288, 298, 306, 318, 330, 342, 348, 372, 386, 456, 485, **486**, 496, 500, 504, 506, 511, 528, 529, 533, 550, 568, 571, 577, 621, 642.

shoemaker, *n.* (SHOEMAKERS), **486**, 576.

shone, *v.* (*past tense and past participle of* SHINE), 358, 485, 487.

shoo, *interj.*, **487**.

shook, *v.* (*past tense of* SHAKE), 482, 487 (*See also* **shake**).

shoot, *v.* (SHOT, SHOT, SHOOTING), 62, 240, 267, 431, **487**, 488, 511.

shop, *n.* (SHOPS) (*place where things are made*), **487**.
(*small store*), **487**.
v. (SHOPPED, SHOPPED, SHOPPING), 89, 329, **487**, 603.

shore, *n.* (SHORES), 156, 239, 463, **487**.

short, *adj.* (SHORTER, SHORTEST), 26, 40, 73, 80, 84, 107, 187, 202, 220, 247, 280, 290, 303, 311, 317, 318, 340, 342, 353, 363, 374, 375, 435, **488**, 497, 503, 505, 516, 519, 548, 551, 569, 572, 592, 645, 648 (*adv.* SHORTLY).

shot, *v.* (*past tense and past participle of* SHOOT), 23, 487, **488** (*See also* **shoot**).

should, *v.* (*past tense of* SHALL), 13, 29, 39, 91, 105, 121, 142, 166, 238, 303, 306, 310, 321, 349, 353, 355, 410, 415, 420, 431, 448, 457, 476, 478, **488**, 538, 541, 559, 561, 578, 587, 588, 644.

shoulder, *n.* (SHOULDERS), 84, 362, 370, 377, 483, **488**, 509, 530, 552.

shouldn't, *v. and adv.* (*contraction for* SHOULD NOT), **488**.

shout, *n.* (SHOUTS), 80, 97, 128, **489**.
v. (SHOUTED, SHOUTED, SHOUTING), 80, 97, 268, **489**.

shovel, *n.* (SHOVELS), 147, 355, 470, **489**, 511.
v. (SHOVELED or SHOVELLED, SHOVELED or SHOVELLED, SHOVELING or SHOVELLING), **489**.

show, *n.* (SHOWS), 104, 131, 408, 426, **489**, 569.
v. (SHOWED, SHOWED, SHOWING), 4, 16, 23, 80, 111, 116, 126, 128, 129, 136, 171, 240, 252, 261, 304, 305, 307, 319, 327, 329, 347, 377, 406, 413, 463, **489**, 554, 603, 620.

shower, *n.* (SHOWERS), 38, 285, **489**.
v. (SHOWERED, SHOWERED, SHOWERING), **489**.

shut, *adj.*, 421, 615.
v. (SHUT, SHUT, SHUTTING), 108, **489**, 635.

sick, *adj.* (SICKER, SICKEST), 3, 20, 30, 41, 49, 68, 93, 97, 130, 140, 144, 148, 159, 184, 192, 207, 223, 251, 264, 268, 272, 323, 341, 365, 374, 385, 413, 415, 475, **490**, 508, 509, 582, 586, 617, 624, 642.

sickness, *n.* (SICKNESSES), 130, 147, **490**, 621.

side, *n.* (SIDES) (*lateral surface; opposite part; edge*), 4, 6, 11, 22, 30, 32, 48, 49, 57, 59, 79, 91, 96, 101, 125, 127, 166, 169, 173, 183, 195, 244, 257, 275, 290, 300, 307, 318, 451, 471, **490**, 519, 523, 568, 584, 592, 613, 615, 629, 637.
(*team*), **490**.

sidewalk, *n.* (SIDEWALKS), 114, 329, 353, 373, 394, 489, **490**, 508, 544.

sigh, *n.* (SIGHS), **491**.
n. (SIGHED, SIGHED, SIGHING), 2, **491**.

sight, *n.* (SIGHTS), 21, 116, 146, 282, 387, 487, **491**, 591, 607, 610.

sign, *n.* (SIGNS), 4, 23, 117, 150, 174, 418, **491**, 492, 572, 648.
v. (SIGNED, SIGNED, SIGNING), **491**.

signal, *n.* (SIGNALS), 201, 345, **492**.

silence, *n.* (SILENCES), 269, **492**.

silent, *adj.*, **492** (*adv. See* **silently**).

silently, *adv.*, **492**.

silk, *adj.*, 100, 196, **492**, 608.
n. (SILKS), 370, **492**, 650.

silkworm, *n.* (SILKWORMS), 100, **492**.

sill, *n.* (SILLS) (*ledge or shelf across the bottom of the frame of a window, door, or building*), 635 (*See also* **window sill**).

silly, *adj.* (SILLIER, SILLIEST), 95, 110, 224, 397, 448, **493**.

silver, *adj.*, 53, 456, 585.
n., 284, 333, 336, 359, **493**.

simple, *adj.* (SIMPLER, SIMPLEST) (*easy to understand*), 406, 616 (*adv.* SIMPLY).

since, *conj.*, 14, 118, 224, 273, 280, 290, **493**.
prep., **493**.

sing, *v.* (SANG *or* SUNG, SUNG, SINGING), 11, 15, 23, 30, 53, 89, 105, 110, 111, 179, 251, 302, 317, 321, 335, 349, 464, **493**, 504, 507, 608, 625.

singer, *n.* (SINGERS), **493**.

single, *adj.* (*one*), 195.

sing-song *or* **singsong**, *adj.* (*characterized by a rising and falling tone in a monotonous rhythm*), 335.

sink, *n.* (SINKS), 38, 69, 419, **494**, 514, 645.
v. (SANK *or* SUNK, SUNK, SINKING), 203, 540.

sir, *n.* (SIRS), 148, 173, 349, **494**.

sister, *n.* (SISTERS), 3, 13, 15, 23, 26, 68, 102, 107, 135, 191, 225, 259, 306, 314, 352, 353, 371, 421, 424, 441, 455, 484, 485, 488, **494**, 594.

sit, *v.* (SAT, SAT, SITTING), 46, 48, 63, 77, 94, 108, 124, 131, 141, 142, 153, 168,

sit (*Cont'd.*)
171, 197, 214, 249, 254, 301, 312, 428, 451, 465, 474, 475, 479, 481, 494, 522, 537, 548, 550, 561, 616.

six, *adj.*, 88, 191, 275, 296, 308, 372, 453, 480, **495**, 513, 564, 565.
n. (SIXES), 122, 167, 170, 176, 200, 210, 340, 364, 369, 479, **495**, 557.

sixpence, *n.* (*coin representing six pence or half a shilling*), 53.

sixteen, *adj.*, **495**.
n. (SIXTEENS), 479.

sixteenth, *adj.*, **495**.

sixth, *adj.*, 194, 199, 213, 287, 342, 465, 474, 479, **495**, 539, 569, 589, 623.

sixty, *adj.*, 264, 338, 340, 474.
n. (SIXTIES), 46, **495**.

size, *n.* (SIZES), 76, 174, 176, 200, 243, 274, 288, **496**, 571.

skate, *n.* (SKATES), 453, **496**.
v. (SKATED, SKATED, SKATING), 271, 453, **496**.

skater, *n.* (SKATERS), **496**.

skin, *n.* (SKINS), 6, 68, 132, 169, 197, 212, 217, 256, 306, 396, 404, 419, 420, 449, **496**, 543, 558, 574, 578, 622, 632.

skip, *v.* (SKIPPED, SKIPPED, SKIPPING), 110, 166, 335, **497**.

skirt, *n.* (SKIRTS), 109, **497**.

sky, *n.* (SKIES), 3, 22, 106, 109, 136, 164, 184, 202, 203, 205, 222, 250, 265, 298, 312, 413, 438, 452, 491, **497**, 504, 523, 539, 540, 594, 597, 621, 626, 641.

skyscraper, *n.* (SKYSCRAPERS), 358, **497**.

slant, *adj.*, **498**, 526.
n., 305, **498**.
v. (SLANTED, SLANTED, SLANTING), **498**, 572.

slap, *n.* (SLAPS), **498**.
v. (SLAPPED, SLAPPED, SLAPPING), **498**.

sled, *n.* (SLEDS), 111, 249, 257, 400, 444, **498**, 499.

sleep, *v.* (SLEPT, SLEPT, SLEEPING), 17, 24, 29, 42, 116, 125, 138, 155, 184, 196, 231, 264, 293, 304, 306, 321, 345, 353, 359, 379, 386, 403, 420, 451, 484, **498**, 499, 505, 558, 573, 602, 614, 637.

sleepy, *adj.* (SLEEPIER, SLEEPIEST), 150, 159, 353, 361, **498**, 617.

sleet, *n.*, **498**, 503.

sleeve, *n.* (SLEEVES), 84, 108, 168, **498**, 499, 528, 608.

sleigh, *n.* (SLEIGHS), 464, **499**.

slept, *v.* (*past tense and past participle of* SLEEP), 299, 498, **499**.

slice, *n.* (SLICES), 64, 464, **499**, 574.
v. (SLICED, SLICED, SLICING), 401, **499**.

slid, *v.* (*past tense and past participle of* SLIDE), 257, 400, **499** (*See also* **slide**).

slide, *n.* (SLIDES), 409, **499**.
v. (SLID, SLID, SLIDING), 111, 154, 437, 498, **499**, 500.

slip, *n.* (SLIPS), 109, **500**.
v. (SLIPPED, SLIPPED, SLIPPING), **500**.

slipper, *n.* (SLIPPERS), 48, 109, **500**.

slow, *adj.* (SLOWER, SLOWEST), **500**.
adv., 131 (*See also* **slowly**).

slowly, *adv.,* 83, 98, 155, 184, 188, 347, 389, 423, 474, **500,** 502, 616.

sly, *adj.* (SLIER or SLYER, SLIEST or SLYEST), 212, **500.**

small, *adj.* (SMALLER, SMALLEST), 12, 43, 51, 63, 79, 97, 101, 119, 121, 125, 128, 130, 132, 137, 201, 234, 245, 259, 269, 298, 320, 327, 337, 358, 380, 389, 394, 403, 418, 427, 436, 456, 470, 480, **501,** 513, 542, 549, 555, 572, 610, 623.

smart, *adj.* (SMARTER, SMARTEST), 45, 66, 467, **501,** 537, 636 (*adv.* SMARTLY).

   v. (SMARTED, SMARTED, SMARTING), **501.**

smell, *n.* (SMELLS), 369, 454, 469, **501,** 543.

   v. (SMELT or SMELLED, SMELT or SMELLED, SMELLING), 285, 362, 369, 381, 476, **501,** 503, 535.

smile, *n.* (SMILES), 97, **501.**

   v. (SMILED, SMILED, SMILING), 247, **501.**

smog, *n.* (SMOGS), **501.**

smoke, *n.* (SMOKES), 99, 405, 425, 501, **502,** 602.

   v. (SMOKED, SMOKED, SMOKING) (*tobacco*), 103, 405, **502,** 568, 574.

smokestack, *n.* (SMOKESTACKS) (*tall chimney or pipe to let out smoke from a furnace*), 520.

smoky, *adj.* (SMOKIER, SMOKIEST), 30, **502.**

smooth, *adj.* (SMOOTHER, SMOOTHEST), 53, 115, 176, 191, 195, 205, 226, 271, 277, 352, 406, 421, 450, 455, **502,** 578 (*adv. See* smoothly).

smoothly, *adv.,* 371, 499.

snail, *n.* (SNAILS), 63, **502.**

snake, *n.* (SNAKES), 249, **502.**

snap, *n.* (SNAPS), **503.**

   v. (SNAPPED, SNAPPED, SNAPPING), **503.**

snatch, *v.* (SNATCHED, SNATCHED, SNATCHING), 164, **503.**

sneeze, *v.* (SNEEZED, SNEEZED, SNEEZING), 114, 254, **503.**

sniff, *n.* (SNIFFS), **503.**

   v. (SNIFFED, SNIFFED, SNIFFING), 369, **503.**

snow, *n.* (SNOWS), 54, 60, 114, 146, 175, 249, 264, 272, 397, 411, 412, 422, 451, 485, 489, 499, 500, **503,** 504, 531, 580, 630.

   v. (SNOWED, SNOWED, SNOWING), 94, 368, 498, **503,** 538, 561, 562, 628.

snowball, *n.* (SNOWBALLS), 453, **503,** 536.

snowflake, *n.* (SNOWFLAKES), 201, 503, **504.**

snowman, *n.* (SNOWMEN), 630.

snowstorm, *n.* (SNOWSTORMS), **504,** 531.

Snow White, *n.,* 391.

snug, *adj.* (SNUGGER, SNUGGEST), **504** (*adv.* SNUGLY).

so, *adj.,* **504.**

   adv., 3, 13, 21, 47, 110, 138, 169, 193, 215, 247, 272, 324, 340, 355, 413, 424, **504,** 583, 594, 640, 653.

   conj. (**so that:** *to the end that; in order that; with the view, purpose, or intention that; with the result or effect that*), 55, 81, 107, 175, 206, 306, 376, 392, 440, 445, 461, 478, 485, 498, **504,** 510, 522, 532, 618, 625.

soap, *n.* (SOAPS), 34, 38, 69, 79, 96, 106, 201, **505,** 538, 617.

sob, *v.* (SOBBED, SOBBED, SOBBING), **505.**

soccer, *n.,* 207.

sock, *n.* (SOCKS), 35, 109, 191, 253, 386, **505.**

soda, *n.* (SODAS), 201, 224, 226, 371, **505.**

soft, *adj.* (SOFTER, SOFTEST), 30, 83, 94, 135, 141, 190, 191, 192, 205, 222, 226, 247, 287, 304, 319, 320, 342, 344, 359, 386, 403, 424, 428, 449, 455, 457, 492, 502, 503, **505,** 516, 518, 536, 543, 555, 557, 572, 608, 620, 640, 641 (*adv. See* softly).

softly, *adv.,* 29, 321, 573.

soil, *n.* (SOILS), **505.**

   v. (SOILED, SOILED, SOILING), 107, **505.**

sold, *v.* (*past tense and past participle of* SELL), 32, 476, **506,** 530.

soldier, *n.* (SOLDIERS), 22, 70, 84, 85, 88, 116, 117, 172, 194, 209, 210, 234, 239, 285, 328, 333, 376, 389, 462, 494, **506,** 535, 537, 553, 616, 643.

sole, *n.* (SOLES), **506.**

solid, *adj.,* 103, 199, 220, 260, 407, **506** (*adv.* SOLIDLY).

some, *adj.,* 5, 15, 36, 48, 53, 62, 70, 82, 93, 111, 134, 154, 161, 175, 183, 200, 216, 237, 239, 244, 250, 260, 271, 301, 323, 331, 344, 353, 361, 391, 401, 407, 436, 446, 461, 490, 502, **506,** 507, 519, 532, 535, 558, 581, 608, 620, 638, 651.

   pro., 361, 370, 417.

somebody, *pro.,* 18, 26, 151, 179, 183, 230, **506,** 523, 525, 602, 606, 651.

someone, *pro.,* 10, 16, 18, 67, 128, 136, 165, 169, 172, 207, 239, 251, 252, 254, 295, 309, 378, 390, 421, 440, 472, 476, 477, **507,** 522, 559, 603, 618, 624.

something, *adv.* (*in some degree; somewhat*), 399, 542, 618, 638, 655.

   pro., 18, 43, 50, 58, 100, 123, 131, 143, 155, 179, 186, 206, 223, 231, 246, 251, 268, 286, 309, 314, 330, 336, 344, 371, 403, 410, 421, 432, 461, 474, 492, **507,** 510, 525, 549, 564, 570, 585.

sometime, *adv.,* 84, **507.**

sometimes, *adv.,* 3, 8, 14, 17, 33, 34, 35, 36, 39, 40, 46, 51, 58, 64, 66, 67, 68, 70, 72, 76, 79, 88, 97, 101, 104, 109, 110, 111, 118, 119, 120, 125, 128, 137, 141, 151, 152, 157, 167, 173, 186, 193, 198, 199, 201, 211, 212, 216, 224, 226, 230, 232, 252, 254, 259, 260, 263, 273, 275, 284, 285, 304, 305, 307, 310, 312, 324, 325, 326, 328, 330, 331, 338, 340, 341, 346, 347, 352, 362, 389, 393, 403, 406, 407, 416, 417, 427, 428, 435, 437, 441, 450, 460, 462, 463, 464, 473, 483, 492, 503, **507,** 509, 519, 522, 524, 531, 541, 555, 556, 557, 587, 590, 597, 598, 607, 609, 613, 624, 637, 640, 645, 646, 650.

somewhere, *adv.,* 2, 489, **507,** 542.

son, *n.* (SONS), 38, 137, 422, **507,** 529.

song, *n.* (SONGS), 53, 87, 228, 251, 302, 319, 321, 334, 493, **507,** 585, 590, 608, 625, 645.

soon, *adv.* (SOONER, SOONEST), 6, 13, 29, 80, 101, 128, 129, 165, 197, 215, 268, 309, 387, 507, **508,** 561, 562, 568, 586, 601, 621, 625, 642.

as soon as (*when*), 508.

sore, *adj.* (SORER, SOREST), **508,** 567.

   n. (SORES), 58, 73, **508,** 528.

sorrow, *n.* (SORROWS), 460, **508.**

sorry, *adj.* (SORRIER, SORRIEST), 390, 415, **508.**

sort, *n.* (SORTS), **508.**

   v. (SORTED, SORTED, SORTING), **508.**

soul, *n.* (SOULS) (*person*), 193, **509.**

   (*vital and sensitive part of a person*), 420, **509.**

sound, *adj.,* **509.**

   n. (SOUNDS), 35, 60, 72, 77, 104, 124, 147, 164, 169, 201, 238, 242, 251, 259, 266, 284, 303, 337, 349, 361, 423, 427, 436, 449, 450, 487, 503, **509,** 519, 524, 528, 569, 572, 610, 630, 651.

   v. (SOUNDED, SOUNDED, SOUNDING), 111, 446, **509.**

soup, *n.* (SOUPS), 63, 88, 125, 137, 145, 252, 387, 475, 478, **509,** 528, 584, 603, 637.

sour, *adj.,* 76, 97, 234, 308, 401, 466, **509,** 543, 553, 609 (*adv.* SOURLY).

   v. (SOURED, SOURED, SOURING), **509.**

south, *adj.,* 336, 634.

   n., 362, 509.

South America, *n.,* 14, 93, 274, **510.**

South Pole, *n.,* 397.

sow, *v.* (SOWED, SOWED, SOWING), 510.

space, *n.* (SPACES) (*area; room*), 25, 79, 120, 147, 187, 345, 453, 510, **522.**

   (*region beyond earth*), 24, 343, 368, 376, 465, **510.**

spaceship, *n.* (SPACESHIPS), 24, 403, **510,** 641.

spade, *n.* (SPADES), **511.**

Spanish, *n.,* 300, 336.

spank, *v.* (SPANKED, SPANKED, SPANKING), 426, **511.**

spare, *adj.,* **511.**

spark, *n.* (SPARKS), **511.**

sparkle, *n.* (SPARKLES), **511.**

   v. (SPARKLED, SPARKLED, SPARKLING), **511,** 594.

sparrow, *n.* (SPARROWS), 51, 302, **511.**

speak, *v.* (SPOKE, SPOKEN, SPEAKING), 50, 162, 173, 278, 300, 336, 349, 373, 378, 389, 420, 423, 449, 457, 467, 492, 494, **512,** 515, 557.

special, *adj.,* 84, 113, 176, 412, **512,** 656 (*adv. See* specially).

specially, *adv.,* 344.

speck, *n.* (SPECKS), **512.**

speckle, *adj.,* **512.**

   n. (SPECKLES), **512.**

speed, *n.* (SPEEDS), 400, 433, **512,** 570.

   v. (SPEEDED or SPED, SPEEDED or SPED, SPEEDING), **512.**

spell, *v.* (SPELLED or SPELT, SPELLED or SPELT, SPELLING), 27, 90, 119, 175, 230, 398, **513,** 640.

spelling, *n.* (SPELLINGS), 96, 175, 398.

spend, *v.* (SPENT, SPENT, SPENDING), 138, 466, **513.**

story *(Cont'd.)*
296, 303, 314, 357, 370, 372, 392, 408, 413, 422, 431, 433, 442, 446, 460, 469, **531**, 550, 557, 573, 575, 643, 646.

storybook, *n.* (STORYBOOKS), **531.**

stout, *adj.* (STOUTER, STOUTEST), **531.**

stove, *n.* (STOVES), 73, 216, 217, 220, 304, 456, **532.**

straight, *adj.* (STRAIGHTER, STRAIGHTEST), 103, 126, 130, 131, 175, 202, 303, 329, 526, **532**, 619.
adv., 253, 498, 530, **532**, 591.

strange, *adj.* (STRANGER, STRANGEST), 246, **532** (*adv.* STRANGELY).

strap, *n.* (STRAPS), 248, 306, **533**, 618.
v. (STRAPPED, STRAPPED, STRAPPING), **533.**

straw, *n.* (STRAWS) (*drinking*), **533.**
(*hay*), 51, 71, 169, 248, **533.**

strawberry, *n.* (STRAWBERRIES), 47, 216, 226, 271, 281, 401, 402, 505, **533.**

stream, *n.* (STREAMS), 41, 67, 126, 134, 204, 450, 487, **533.**

street, *n.* (STREETS), 2, 4, 11, 12, 26, 55, 77, 86, 120, 127, 136, 157, 158, 161, 194, 197, 257, 269, 272, 290, 303, 335, 411, 418, 460, 461, 490, 492, 497, 507, **534**, 550, 562, 580, 601, 625, 651.

streetcar, *n.* (STREETCARS), 117, **534.**

stretch, *v.* (STRETCHED, STRETCHED, STRETCHING), 311, 442, 517, **534.**

strike, *v.* (STRUCK, STRUCK *or* STRICKEN, STRIKING), 40, 291, 396, 400, **534, 536.**

string, *n.* (STRINGS), 39, 62, 83, 119, 293, 295, 412, 425, 426, **535**, 570, 589, 594, 595, 600, 610, 634.
v. (STRUNG, STRUNG, STRINGING), **535.**

strip, *n.* (STRIPS), 34, 36, 46, 469, **535**, 570, 585, 622, 644.
v. (STRIPPED, STRIPPED, STRIPPING), **535.**

stripe, *n.* (STRIPES), 72, 101, 360, 370, **535**, 570, 655.

strong, *adj.* (STRONGER, STRONGEST), 13, 119, 132, 180, 199, 223, 250, 258, 268, 273, 348, 435, 454, 506, 513, 526, **535**, 609, 621, 651.

struck, *v.* (*past tense and past participle of* STRIKE), 105, 108, 534, **536.**

strung, *v.* (*past tense and past participle of* STRING), 535.

stuck, *v.* (*past tense and past participle of* STICK), 348, 527, 528, **536**, 594, 643.

student, *n.* (STUDENTS) (*person who studies; pupil; one who goes to school*), 23, 105.

study, *v.* (STUDIED, STUDIED, STUDYING) (*to try to learn by reading, going to school, etc.*), 105, 232, 314.

stuff, *n.* (STUFFS), **536.**
v. (STUFFED, STUFFED, STUFFING), **536.**

stumble, *v.* (STUMBLED, STUMBLED, STUMBLING), 338, **536**, 585.

stump, *n.* (STUMPS), **537.**

stung, *v.* (*past tense and past participle of* STING), 528, **537** (*See also* 'sting).

stupid, *adj.* (STUPIDER, STUPIDEST), 161, **537** (*adv.* STUPIDLY).

subtract, *v.* (SUBTRACTED, SUBTRACTED, SUBTRACTING), 443, 469, **537.**

succeed, *v.* (SUCCEEDED, SUCCEEDED, SUCCEEDING), **537**, 588.

such, *adj.*, 207, 286, **537**, 610.
adv., 110, 228, 443, 465, 493, 504, **537.**
such as (*for example*), 93.

suck, *v.* (SUCKED, SUCKED, SUCKING) (*to draw or bring into the mouth*), 405.

sudden, *adj.*, 2, 121, 285, 440, 523, **538.**
all of a sudden (*suddenly; in a sudden manner*), **538.**

suddenly, *adv.*, 74, 184, 185, 202, 393, 503, **538.**

suds, *n.*, **538.**

suffer, *v.* (SUFFERED, SUFFERED, SUFFERING), 268, **538.**

sugar, *n.* (SUGARS), 43, 79, 83, 112, 215, 225, 271, 281, 283, 306, 308, 321, 327, 334, 341, 376, 463, 465, 509, **538**, 543, 546, 549, 553, 584.

suggestion, *n.* (SUGGESTIONS), 5, **538.**

suit, *n.* (SUITS), 106, 397, **539.**
v. (SUITED, SUITED, SUITING), **539.**

suitcase, *n.* (SUITCASES), 31, 306, 311, 320, 383, 533, **539**, 563.

summer, *n.* (SUMMERS), 26, 90, 121, 185, 238, 242, 299, 317, 407, 415, 469, 473, 518, **539**, 585, 606, 616, 623, 636, 643.

summertime, *n.* (SUMMERTIMES) (*in the summer season*), 344.

sun, *n.* (SUNS), 13, 55, 66, 68, 112, 156, 165, 184, 228, 250, 252, 256, 285, 307, 311, 334, 343, 344, 358, 362, 376, 378, 379, 392, 393, 407, 410, 438, 478, 481, 485, 497, 509, 510, 523, **539**, 540, 541, 587, 604, 621, 625, 651.

Sunday, *n.* (SUNDAYS), 45, 116, 137, 138, 149, 166, 186, 194, 199, 213, 341, 342, 375, 376, 465, 474, 495, 539, 569, 589, 623, 651.

sunflower, *n.* (SUNFLOWERS), **540.**

sung, *v.* (*past tense and past participle of* SING), 228, 493, 507 (*See also* sing).

sunk, *v.* (*past tense and past participle of* SINK), 494, 536, **540** (*See also* sink).

sunlight, *n.*, 343, 511, **540**, 587.

sunny, *adj.* (SUNNIER, SUNNIEST), 95, 97, 134, 171, 196, **540.**

sunrise, *n.* (SUNRISES), **540.**

sunset, *n.* (SUNSETS), 6, **540**, 652.

sunshine, *n.*, 481, 540, **541**, 635.

supper, *n.* (SUPPERS), 273, 277, 303, 336, 391, 420, 424, 458, **541**, 607, 620.

suppose, *v.* (SUPPOSED, SUPPOSED, SUPPOSING), 273, **541.**

sure, *adj.* (SURER, SUREST), 93, 260, 331, 344, 412, 414, **541** (*adv. See* surely).

surely, *adv.*, 93, 123, **541.**

surprise, *n.* (SURPRISES), 541, 638, 652.
v. (SURPRISED, SURPRISED, SURPRISING), 22, **541**, 624, 639, 653.

swallow, *n.* (SWALLOWS) (*bird*), **542.**

swallow, *v.* (SWALLOWED, SWALLOWED, SWALLOWING), 157, 166, 240, 529, **542.**

swam *v.* (*past tense of* SWIM), 145, **542**, 544.

swan, *n.* (SWANS), **542.**

swarm, *n.* (SWARMS), **542.**

sweat, *n.*, **543.**

sweater, *n.* (SWEATERS), 109, 154, **543**, 640.

sweep, *v.* (SWEPT, SWEPT, SWEEPING), 67, 204, 208, 254, 284, 356, 373, 394, 423, 543, 544, 640.

sweet, *adj.* (SWEETER, SWEETEST), 72, 83, 97, 119, 125, 137, 142, 143, 215, 240, 261, 271, 285, 287, 327, 334, 395, 401, 419, 424, 449, 463, 509, 538, **543**, 546, 553, 610, 645 (*adv.* SWEETLY).

swell, *adj.*, **544.**
v. (SWELLED, SWELLED *or* SWOLLEN, SWELLING), **544.**

swept, *v.* (*past tense and past participle of* SWEEP), 25, 151, 208, 543, **544.**

swift, *adj.* (SWIFTER, SWIFTEST), 440, **544** (*adv. See* swiftly).

swiftly, *adv.*, 84.

swim, *v.* (SWAM, SWUM, SWIMMING), 6, 94, 122, 126, 160, 228, 247, 294, 299, 300, 323, 331, 374, 397, 415, 432, 473, 514, 542, **544**, 546, 587, 622, 636, 643, 652.

swing, *n.* (SWINGS), 104, 409, 535, **545.**
v. (SWUNG, SWUNG, SWINGING), 104, **545**, 546.

switch, *n.* (SWITCHES) (*device used to open or to close an electric circuit*), 372, **545.**
(*whip*), 545.
v. (SWITCHED, SWITCHED, SWITCHING) (*to put a light, motor, etc., on*), 545.
(*to whip*), 545.

swollen, *adj.* and *v.* (*past participle of* SWELL), 72, 545 (*See also* swell).

sword, *n.* (SWORDS), **546.**

swum, *v.* (*past participle of* SWIM), 544, **546** (*See also* swim).

swung, *v.* (*past tense and past participle of* SWING), 545, **546** (*See also* swing).

syrup, *n.* (SYRUPS), 261, 327, 465, 505, **546.**

T

T, t, *n.* (T'S, T'S) (*twentieth letter of the alphabet*), 12, 170, 390, **547**, 558, 592.

table, *n.* (TABLES), 3, 10, 12, 18, 46, 68, 69, 87, 88, 92, 106, 120, 128, 139, 147, 154, 166, 202, 217, 220, 227, 230, 232, 298, 304, 308, 311, 318, 320, 325, 327, 330, 331, 332, 334, 347, 353, 368, 370, 375, 379, 385, 397, 408, 410, 419, 420, 424, 425, 442, 445, 478, 506, 512, 514, 520, **548**, 552, 561, 569, 572, 601, 614, 628, 638, 641.

tablecloth, *n.* (TABLECLOTHS), **548.**

tablespoon, *n.* (TABLESPOONS), **548.**

tablet, *n.* (TABLETS), **548.**

tack, *n.* (TACKS), **548.**
v. (TACKED, TACKED, TACKING), **548.**

tadpole, *n.* (TADPOLES), **548.**

taffy, *n.*, **549.**

tag, *n.* (TAGS) (*small piece of cardboard fastened to anything to give a name, directions, price, etc.*), **549.**
(*game in which one player chases the other*), **549.**
v. (TAGGED, TAGGED, TAGGING), **549.**

tail, *n.* (TAILS), 3, 16, 20, 40, 41, 44, 63, 73, 75, 228, 247, 267, 268, 290, 342, 389, 435, 484, 520, 546, 548, **549,** 613, 645.

tailor, *n.* (TAILORS), **549.**

take, *v.* (TOOK, TAKEN, TAKING) (*to carry; to bring*), 65, 148, 265, 307, 324, 447, 448, 505, **550,** 553.
(*to choose*), 18, 101, 168, **550.**
(*to get engaged or involved in*), 31, 38, 135, 153, 175, 258, 311, 328, 353, 489, 496, 527, 585, 588, 637.
(*to hold; to get; to receive*), 114, 160, 171, 209, 232, 259, 261, 277, 291, 301, 341, 420, 421, 429, 470, 482, 525, 534, **550,** 567, 576, 650.
(*to need; to be required of someone or something*), 338, 376, 474, **550,** 643, 651.
(*to ride on*), **550.**
(*to use; eat or drink; to consume*), 166, 333, 371, 403.

take a picture (*to photograph*), 81, 648.

take away (*to deprive; to remove*), 309, 426, 451, 503, 573, 614.

take care of (*to assume responsibility for the maintenance, support, etc., of*), 61, 86, 138, 173, 189, 281, 290, 345, 365, 399, 424, 437, 439, 478, 485.

take off (*to go into the air*), 9, **550.**

take off (*to remove*), 374, 396, 445, 535, **550,** 600.

take one's seat (*to sit down in one's chair*), **550.**

take part in (*to join in; to participate in*), 391, 408 (See also **taken; took**).

taken, *v.* (*past participle of* TAKE), 44, 120, 340, 363, 431, **550** (See also **take**).

tale, *n.* (TALES), 170, 442, 531, **550,** 637.

talk, *n.* (TALKS), 95.
v. (TALKED, TALKED, TALKING), 17, 29, 58, 66, 95, 100, 122, 161, 179, 186, 259, 269, 283, 290, 294, 300, 331, 336, 337, 341, 347, 379, 390, 433, 504, 512, 515, 516, **551,** 556, 620, 630.

tall, *adj.* (TALLER, TALLEST), 2, 89, 99, 118, 120, 170, 175, 191, 223, 224, 229, 253, 256, 298, 375, 488, 497, 540, **551,** 579.

tame, *adj.* (TAMER, TAMEST), 89, **551,** 632.

tan, *adj.* (TANNER, TANNEST), 68, 212.
n. (TANS), **551.**
v. (TANNED, TANNED, TANNING), **551.**

tangle, *n.* (TANGLES), **552.**
v. (TANGLED, TANGLED, TANGLING), 330, **552.**

tank, *n.* (TANKS), 20, 219, 535, **552,** 638.

tap, *n.* (TAPS) (*faucet*), **552.**
(*light knock*), 393, 394, **552.**
v. (TAPPED, TAPPED, TAPPING), **552.**

tardy, *adj.* (TARDIER, TARDIEST), 302, **552.**

tart, *n.* (TARTS), **553.**

task, *n.* (TASKS), **553.**

tassel, *n.* (TASSELS), **553.**

taste, *n.* (TASTES), 463, 535, 584.
v. (TASTED, TASTED, TASTING), 52, 101, 141, 240, 381, 397, 465, 475, 513, 521, **553,** 576, 588.

tasty, *adj.* (TASTIER, TASTIEST) (*pleasing to the taste; that tastes good*), 164, 215, 224, 271.

taught, *v.* (*past tense and past participle of* TEACH), **553.**

tax, *n.* (TAXES), 303, **553.**

taxi or **taxicab,** *n.* (TAXIS or TAXICABS), **553.**

tea, *n.* (TEAS), 100, 157, 291, 477, **554,** 555.

teach, *v.* (TAUGHT, TAUGHT, TEACHING), 23, 25, 105, 106, 143, 157, 166, 271, 309, 469, 551, 553, **554,** 575, 581.

teacher, *n.* (TEACHERS), 12, 17, 23, 25, 44, 53, 85, 88, 94, 95, 102, 105, 106, 107, 111, 114, 137, 150, 179, 180, 183, 195, 221, 222, 224, 225, 258, 265, 269, 272, 277, 290, 292, 304, 309, 314, 323, 325, 329, 333, 339, 361, 363, 394, 398, 406, 408, 415, 420, 422, 423, 439, 446, 449, 457, 469, 492, 501, 507, 521, 522, 550, **554,** 559, 598, 601, 652.

team, *n.* (TEAMS), 7, 8, 37, 48, 85, 97, 111, 207, 268, 304, 318, 361, 490, **554,** 588, 591.

tear, *n.* (TEARS), 380, 393, **554,** 565, 616.
v. (TORE, TORN, TEARING), **554,** 577, 578.

tear, *n.* (TEARS), 96, 126, 128, 373, **555.**

tease, *v.* (TEASED, TEASED, TEASING), **555.**

teaspoon, *n.* (TEASPOONS), **555.**

teddy bear, *n.* (TEDDY BEARS), 117, **555.**

teeth, *n.* (*plural of* TOOTH), 16, 41, 52, 69, 98, 124, 142, 157, 169, 186, 242, 271, 313, 325, 347, 371, 467, **555,** 577 (See also **tooth**).

telegram, *n.* (TELEGRAMS), **555.**

telephone, *n.* (TELEPHONES), 17, 62, 107, 379, 508, 551, **556,** 566, 636.
v. (TELEPHONED, TELEPHONED, TELEPHONING), 80.

telescope, *n.* (TELESCOPES), 164, 368, **556.**

television, *n.* (TELEVISIONS), 66, 169, 223, 339, 363, 478, 479, 524, **556,** 592, 631 (See also **TV**).

tell, *v.* (TOLD, TOLD, TELLING), 5, 6, 23, 30, 41, 50, 58, 59, 80, 105, 108, 134, 137, 139, 142, 146, 151, 164, 179, 184, 214, 239, 244, 247, 261, 264, 286, 293, 294, 296, 303, 309, 310, 325, 332, 333, 339, 340, 350, 357, 364, 367, 372, 402, 442, 446, 457, 467, 477, 484, 491, 492, 531, 551, **557,** 559, 571, 572, 575, 579, 587, 600, 606, 607, 617, 632, 646, 655.

ten, *adj.* (7, 11, 18, 49, 92, 95, 145, 150, 151, 152, 168, 174, 193, 194, 208, 209, 219, 225, 239, 246, 247, 265, 266, 306, 309, 314, 320, 323, 325, 339, 370, 433, 462, 530, 534, **557,** 559, 566, 611, 624, 643.
n., (TENS), 122, 167, 170, 200, 339, 360, 480, **557,** 558, 572, 593, 655.

tender, *adj.* (TENDERER, TENDEREST), 222, **557,** 558 (*adv.* TENDERLY).

tennis, *n.,* 356, **557.**

tent, *n.* (TENTS), 81, 104, **558.**

tenth, *adj.,* 368, **558.**

tepee, *n.* (TEPEES), **558.**

terrible, *adj.,* 155, **558** (*adv.* TERRIBLY).

test, *n.* (TESTS), 46, 48, 96, 232, 290, 292, **559,** 583.

than, *conj.,* 3, 6, 36, 43, 46, 48, 49, 50, 77, 147, 178, 181, 188, 219, 222, 223, 234, 236, 247, 254, 257, 301, 306, 309, 317, 318, 320, 323, 335, 343, 348, 372, 374, 379, 381, 395, 435, 441, 462, 488, 500, 511, 521, 523, 544, **559,** 567, 570, 576, 611, 633, 637, 642.

thank, *v.* (THANKED, THANKED, THANKING), 21, 45, 166, 414, **559,** 560, 624.

thankful, *adj.,* **559** (*adv.* THANKFULLY).

thanks, *n.,* **559.**

Thanksgiving Day, *n.* (THANKSGIVING DAYS), 190, **559, 560,** 590.

that, *adj.,* 469, **561.**
conj., 102, 180, 197, 215, 242, 273, 286, 294, 324, 331, 341, 480, 521, **560,** 586, 643.
pro., 84, 97, 119, 124, 140, 158, 168, 213, 243, 244, 250, 300, 316, 354, 361, 373, 386, 407, 441, 502, 533, **560,** 580, 608, 630, 635, 640.
so that (See **so**).

that's, *pro. and v.* (*contraction for* THAT IS), 25, 63, 88, 96, 110, 169, 173, 215, 225, 327, 343, 486, **560,** 610.

their, *adj.,* 34, 41, 42, 44, 51, 53, 59, 63, 68, 85, 86, 88, 90, 104, 110, 111, 115, 123, 124, 125, 134, 164, 175, 179, 186, 187, 194, 202, 203, 212, 225, 239, 245, 255, 258, 263, 313, 319, 323, 333, 338, 352, 356, 361, 364, 365, 371, 388, 397, 405, 414, 426, 439, 446, 464, 467, 484, 499, 507, 522, 524, 542, 551, **560,** 578, 583, 588, 592, 606, 620, 635, 641, 645, 655.

theirs, *pro.,* **560.**

them, *pro.,* 15, 19, 25, 33, 40, 51, 59, 65, 74, 84, 92, 109, 142, 152, 164, 166, 168, 173, 176, 194, 198, 206, 212, 216, 229, 232, 245, 249, 275, 287, 310, 329, 335, 352, 359, 377, 402, 439, 446, 454, 480, 500, **561,** 568, 593, 606, 632, 652.

themselves, *pro.,* 16, 68, 126, 427, **561,** 609.

then, *adv.,* 22, 25, 30, 40, 51, 60, 114, 123, 144, 174, 209, 225, 226, 232, 253, 280, 281, 290, 294, 295, 309, 335, 364, 405, 419, 456, 460, 475, 479, 507, 519, **561,** 571, 572, 578, 591, 609, 645.

there, *adv.,* 3, 130, 142, 299, 340, 447, **561,** 652.
expletive: an introductory word or phrase used merely to fill out a sentence, 10, 20, 38, 47, 50, 60, 70, 82, 94, 108, 164, 171, 184, 194, 200, 208, 219, 228, 237, 243, 252, 264, 273, 280, 302, 312, 334, 355, 383, 390,

there *(Cont'd.)*
404, 412, 418, 428, 437, 463, 474, 486, 491, 495, 506, 515, 521, 531, 534, 553, **561**, 562, 571, 576, 593, 602, 613, 623, 641, 655.
interj., **561**.

therefore, *adv.,* **562**.

there's, *expletive* and *v.* *(contraction for* THERE IS), 193, 233, 275, **562**.

these, *adj.,* 19, 33, 36, 37, 87, 100, 138, 152, 261, 262, 307, 309, 335, 344, 372, 404, 427, 435, 437, 442, 446, 480, 516, 524, 527, 539, 541, 556, **562**, 590, 593, 599.
pro., 39, 41, 53, 63, 70, 115, 134, 135, 137, 226, 305, 313, 346, 422, 432, 496, 500, 545, **565**, 630, 636.

they, *pro.,* 11, 17, 25, 35, 42, 45, 53, 72, 88, 101, 110, 122, 138, 149, 166, 179, 183, 190, 205, 216, 225, 231, 238, 258, 283, 287, 315, 328, 335, 341, 347, 359, 376, 392, 409, 415, 435, 462, 471, 476, 483, 492, 502, 515, 522, 531, 539, 559, **562**, 570, 586, 609, 619, 632.

they'll, *pro.* and *v.* *(contraction for* THEY WILL *or* THEY SHALL), 44, 484, **562**.

they're, *pro.* and *v.* *(contraction for* THEY ARE), 21, 92, 388, **562**.

they've, *pro.* and *v.* *(contraction for* THEY HAVE), 291.

thick, *adj.* (THICKER, THICKEST), 71, 75, 89, 126, 281, 290, 513, 546, **562**, 563, 569, 608, 629 (*adv.* THICKLY).

thief, *n.* (THIEVES), 451, 503, 529, 563 (*See also* thieves).

thieves, *n.* (*plural of* THIEF), 451, 525, 563 (*See also* thief).

thimble, *n.* (THIMBLES), **563**.

thin, *adj.* (THINNER, THINNEST), 71, 103, 119, 124, 125, 189, 196, 201, 224, 352, 355, 375, 389, 397, 408, 466, 499, 502, 521, 527, 531, 562, **563**, 588, 592, 610, 633, 641, 645 (*adv.* THINLY).

thing, *n.* (THINGS), 4, 16, 25, 30, 52, 65, 72, 81, 106, 129, 140, 171, 180, 191, 213, 222, 235, 245, 254, 261, 273, 295, 298, 303, 315, 321, 331, 342, 354, 380, 390, 403, 412, 427, 432, 442, 452, 467, 470, 489, 493, 507, 512, 527, 535, 541, 553, 559, **563**, 572, 580, 587, 606, 615, 622, 636, 639, 644.

think, *v.* (THOUGHT, THOUGHT, THINKING), 7, 25, 42, 45, 136, 146, 271, 273, 330, 331, 339, 349, 438, 440, 443, 444, 458, 476, 489, 509, 541, 563, **564**, 566, 587, 633, 640 (*See also* thought).

third, *adj.,* 194, 199, 204, 211, 213, 232, 302, 327, 332, 342, 465, 474, 479, 495, 539, **564**, 569, 589, 623.

thirst, *n.* (THIRSTS), **564**.

thirsty, *adj.* (THIRSTIER, THIRSTIEST), 160, 301, 564.

thirteen, *adj.,* 535, **564**, 565.
n., (THIRTEENS), 211, **564**.

thirteenth, *adj.,* **565**.

thirtieth, *adj.,* 593.

thirty, *adj.,* 20, 343, 364, 379, 478, **565**, 611.
n., (THIRTIES), **565**, 593.

thirty-one, *adj.,* 26, 139, 281, 287, 327, 331, 343, 368, **565**.

thirty-six, *adj.,* 650.

this, *adj.,* 17, 46, 52, 60, 77, 131, 175, 180, 207, 220, 233, 250, 255, 272, 295, 316, 340, 358, 378, 399, 420, 431, 445, 452, 474, 503, 510, 539, **565**, 566, 573, 576, 608, 613, 625, 631, 652.
pro., 4, 23, 31, 84, 96, 107, 120, 142, 150, 160, 165, 186, 195, 214, 230, 282, 301, 327, 335, 370, 489, 560, 586, 631, 644, 655.

thorn, *n.* (THORNS), 454, **565**.

those, *adj.,* 121, 172, 352, 378, 560, 562, **565**, 598.
pro., **565**.

though, *adv.,* 441.
conj., 13, 84, 272, **566**.

thought, *n.* (THOUGHTS), 271, **566**.
v. (*past tense and past participle of* THINK), 162, 406, 564, **566**.

thoughtful, *adj.,* 414, **566** (*adv.* THOUGHT-FULLY).

thoughtless, *adj.,* **566** (*adv.* THOUGHT-LESSLY).

thousand, *adj.,* 339.
n. (THOUSANDS), 339, **566**.

thread, *n.* (THREADS), 100, 121, 196, 287, 295, 298, 355, 457, 480, 492, 514, 516, 528, **566**, 622, 636, 650.
v. (THREADED, THREADED, THREADING), **566**.

three, *adj.,* 4, 10, 90, 99, 106, 110, 121, 139, 156, 157, 158, 160, 188, 193, 201, 204, 231, 283, 296, 298, 301, 302, 332, 337, 343, 370, 399, 414, 426, 435, 444, 447, 453, 482, 484, 499, 509, 518, 522, 560, 561, 563, 565, 583, 584, 585, 628, 636, 637, 642, 650.
n. (THREES), 12, 15, 50, 77, 122, 167, 170, 200, 210, 309, 364, 369, 479, **567**, 572, 655.

thresh, *v.* (THRESHED, THRESHED, THRESH-ING), **567**.

threw, *v.* (*past tense of* THROW), 25, 68, 91, 286, 320, 374, **567**.

throat, *n.* (THROATS), 121, 238, 239, 385, 529, 542, 564, **567**, 570, 610.

throb, *v.* (THROBBED, THROBBED, THROB-BING), **567**.

throne, *n.* (THRONES), **567**.

through, *adj.,* **568**.
adv., **568**.
prep. (*among; in the midst of; between; within*), 8, 84, 85, 109, 115, 124, 203, 205, 293, 304, 384, 436, 464, 510, 544, **568**, 588, 606, 616, 641.
(*because of*), **568**.
(*by means of*), 65, 71, 169, 174, 299, 362, 418, 503, **568**.
(*during; throughout*), 56, **568**.
(*in one side and out the other; from one end to the other end of*), 39, 53, 82, 83, 127, 137, 142, 151, 166, 226, 239, 240, 243, 252, 260, 263, 305, 355,

through *(Cont'd.)*
396, 397, 405, 438, 458, 465, 480, 483, 506, 516, 528, 533, 543, 556, 566, **568**, 584, 590, 630, 635, 636.

throughout, *prep.,* 449, **568**, 583.

throw, *v.* (THREW, THROWN, THROWING), 111, 137, 160, 198, 287, 405, 511, 514, 529, 567, **568**, 603 (*See also* threw).

thrown, *v.* (*past participle of* THROW), 220, 473, 568, 618, 621, (*See also* throw).

thumb, *n.* (THUMBS), 102, 226, 244, 341, 548, **569**.

thumbtack, *n.* (THUMBTACKS), 548.

thump, *n.* (THUMPS), 40, 252, **569**.
v. (THUMPED, THUMPED, THUMPING), 569.

thunder, *n.* (THUNDERS) (*sound that follows a flash of lightning*), 60, 105, 214, 251, 312, 531, 558.

Thursday, *n.* (THURSDAYS), 137, 194, 199, 213, 342, 376, 465, 474, 479, 495, 539, 569, 589, 623.

tick, *n.* (TICKS), 569.

ticket, *n.* (TICKETS), 9, 117, 569.

tickle, *n.* (TICKLES), 570.
v. (TICKLED, TICKLED, TICKLING), 505, 570.

tidy, *adj.* (TIDIER, TIDIEST), **570** (*adv.* TIDILY).

tie, *n.* (TIES) (*equality of scores in a contest*), 570.
(*necktie*), 52, 330, 355, 539, 570.
v. (TIED, TIED, TYING), 32, 47, 49, 73, 119, 258, 293, 295, 298, 318, 355, 535, 595, 600.

tiger, *n.* (TIGERS), 8, 104, 288, 312, 570, 632.

tight, *adj.* (TIGHTER, TIGHTEST), 32, 79, 131, 258, 265, 299, 318, 497, 571 (*adv. See* tightly).

tightly, *adv.,* 32, 103, **571**.

till, *conj.,* 386, 553, **571**.
prep., 137, **571** (*See also* until).

time, *n.* (TIMES), 6, 7, 9, 13, 26, 27, 42, 43, 44, 60, 63, 74, 75, 76, 81, 83, 94, 102, 108, 111, 127, 137, 138, 149, 159, 161, 177, 184, 200, 202, 216, 221, 224, 225, 228, 242, 244, 247, 248, 264, 268, 277, 286, 288, 290, 294, 302, 311, 317, 340, 342, 343, 357, 359, 364, 372, 373, 376, 377, 378, 390, 392, 423, 433, 443, 444, 445, 448, 458, 465, 469, 474, 493, 500, 507, 508, 513, 523, 534, 561, 562, 570, **571**, 574, 579, 585, 601, 603, 604, 606, 614, 623, 627, 628, 640, 650, 651, 652, 655.

times, *v.* (*multiplied by*), 572.

timid, *adj.* (TIMIDER, TIMIDEST) 572 (*adv.* TIMIDLY).

tin, *n.* (TINS), 82, 242, 408, 572.

tinkle, *n.* (TINKLES), 572.
v. (TINKLED, TINKLED, TINKLING), 284, 572.

tiny, *adj.* (TINIER, TINIEST), 25, 76, 98, 137, 143, 158, 194, 198, 223, 233, 236, 275, 299, 344, 389, 426, 463, 465, 467, 470, 498, 504, 505, **572**, 623.

tip, *n.* (TIPS) (*end*), 32, 330, 413, **572,** 573.
    v. (TIPPED, TIPPED, TIPPING), **572.**
    tip over (*upset*), 602.
tiptoe, *n.* (TIPTOES), **573.**
    v. (TIPTOED, TIPTOED, TIPTOEING), **573.**
tire, *n.* (TIRES), 8, 202, 456, **573.**
tire, *v.* (TIRED, TIRED, TIRING), **573** (*See also* tired).
tired, *adj.,* 231, 252, 299, 305, 386, 475, 491, 498, 544, 546, **573,** 621, 641, 650 (*See also the verb* tire).
title, *n.* (TITLES), **573.**
to, *prep.,* (*along with*), **574.**
    (*as far as; terminating in*), 134, 193, 413, **574,** 640.
    (*for; for the purpose of*), 219, 227, 268, 303, 463, 562.
    (*in relation to; with regard to*), 2, 275, 344, 375.
    (*in the direction of*), 38, 91, 175, 413, 450, **574.**
    (*on; in contact with*), 83, 355, 526, 549, **574.**
    (*with a specific person or thing as recipient or indirect object of an action; for the benefit of*), 324, 332, 470, 509, 549, **574,** 600.
    to: a sign of the infinitive, 2, 11, 24, 43, 59, 65, 74, 83, 91, 105, 128, 134, 145, 154, 161, 175, 181, 208, 219, 242, 259, 268, 275, 298, 303, 324, 332, 355, 361, 375, 383, 413, 429, 441, 463, 470, 486, 499, 518, 531, **574,** 577, 592, 600, 607, 615, 622, 640.
toad, *n.* (TOADS), 548, **574.**
toast, *n.* 281, 283, 517, **574.**
    v. (TOASTED, TOASTED, TOASTING), 169, **574.**
toaster, *n.* (TOASTERS), 169.
tobacco, *n.* (TOBACCOS or TOBACCOES), 103, 324, 405, 502, **574.**
today, *adv.,* 7, 42, 51, 57, 60, 70, 85, 87, 94, 102, 105, 111, 126, 127, 154, 156, 159, 160, 191, 200, 210, 221, 225, 231, 253, 255, 265, 268, 272, 309, 311, 323, 331, 420, 461, 476, 489, 499, 504, 514, 518, 544, **575,** 576, 617, 620, 621, 625, 642, 646, 655.
    n. (TODAYS), 25, 80, 95, 315, 571, **575,** 640, 651.
toe, *n.* (TOES), 207, 352, 573, **575,** 594, 622, 653.
toenail, *n.* (TOENAILS), 352, **575.**
together, *adv.,* 4, 12, 14, 15, 21, 32, 36, 40, 58, 59, 71, 72, 73, 93, 104, 105, 107, 114, 120, 137, 145, 152, 185, 201, 204, 206, 221, 227, 236, 237, 261, 281, 285, 292, 295, 298, 328, 330, 334, 341, 348, 352, 360, 378, 386, 391, 393, 402, 404, 427, 428, 429, 435, 439, 454, 456, 457, 464, 470, 478, 480, 501, 503, 527, 528, 539, 542, 548, 554, 562, 572, **575,** 581, 599, 608, 615, 620, 622, 634, 637, 640.
toilet, *n.* (TOILETS), 38, **575.**
Tokyo, *n.,* 282.
told, *v.* (*past tense and past participle of* TELL), 2, 4, 44, 45, 88, 158, 180, 186,

told (*Cont'd.*)
    211, 224, 255, 258, 269, 285, 296, 309, 310, 333, 336, 354, 376, 378, 392, 394, 399, 413, 423, 448, 460, 461, 504, 512, 522, 550, 557, 559, 575, 587, 624.
tomato, *n.* (TOMATOES), 82, 213, 287, 464, 465, 509, 513, 519, **575,** 609.
tomorrow, *adv.,* 25, 105, 254, 329, 338, 482, 610, 625, 637.
    n. (TOMORROWS), 160, 161, 315, **575.**
ton, *n.* (TONS), 332, **576.**
tongue, *n.* (TONGUES), 202, 301, 310, 347, **576,** 610.
tonight, *adv.,* 144, 336, 398, 428, **576.**
    n. (TONIGHTS), 576.
too, *adv.,* 7, 13, 14, 16, 24, 26, 30, 34, 35, 41, 47, 55, 59, 64, 68, 73, 83, 92, 102, 105, 109, 112, 117, 123, 129, 159, 170, 179, 187, 190, 192, 196, 200, 217, 219, 220, 228, 229, 233, 234, 238, 253, 256, 260, 268, 281, 288, 318, 338, 341, 348, 357, 358, 362, 379, 387, 388, 390, 401, 409, 410, 418, 455, 475, 476, 478, 489, 493, 494, 501, 504, 512, 514, 515, 516, 526, 529, 535, 545, 551, 553, 554, 562, 563, 571, **576,** 579, 584, 586, 597, 608, 611, 616, 617, 618, 621, 623, 632, 639, 642, 646, 651.
took, *v.* (*past tense of* TAKE), 19, 23, 35, 52, 91, 102, 135, 139, 153, 156, 184, 213, 214, 219, 237, 246, 268, 280, 286, 304, 309, 339, 341, 370, 392, 396, 400, 405, 410, 445, 483, 529, 550, 553, **576,** 582, 584, 591, 614, 648.
tool, *n.* (TOOLS), 87, 98, 117, 244, 259, 411, 439, 467, 484, 489, **576,** 641, 645.
toolbox, *n.* (TOOLBOXES), 244.
tooth, *n.* (TEETH), 385, 477, 480, 555, 577, 588, 592.
toothache, *n.* (TOOTHACHES), 385, **577.**
toothbrush, *n.* (TOOTHBRUSHES), 69, 577, 588.
toothpaste, *n.* (TOOTHPASTES), 588.
top, *adj.,* 43, 442, 484, 534.
    n. (TOPS) (*cover*), 588.
    (*highest or upper part*), 61, 82, 92, 115, 123, 126, 153, 171, 202, 204, 216, 244, 251, 253, 310, 387, 452, 453, 469, 502, 510, 537, 548, 575, 577, 601, 609.
    (*toy*), 512, 514, 518, **577.**
    on top of (*on or at the uppermost part or side of*), 374, 379.
tore, *v.* (*past tense of* TEAR), 334, 393, 506, 554, 577, 609.
torn, *v.* (*past participle of* TEAR), 242, 436, 480, 554, **578.**
tortoise, *n.* (TORTOISES), **578.**
toss, *v.* (TOSSED, TOSSED, TOSSING), **578.**
touch, *v.* (TOUCHED, TOUCHED, TOUCHING) (*to come in contact with*), 7, 73, 368, 549, 552, 570.
    (*to feel something*), 92, 100, 191, 192, 245, 368, 476, **578.**
tough, *adj.* (TOUGHER, TOUGHEST), 557, 578.

toward, *prep.,* 81, 91, 116, 156, 183, 276, 317, 362, 425, 533, **578,** 579, 583, 620, 625, 633.
towards, *prep.,* 579.
towel, *n.* (TOWELS), 96, 206, 453, **579,** 636, 646.
tower, *n.* (TOWERS), 45, 89, 229, 579.
town, *n.* (TOWNS), 49, 104, 138, 153, 198, 257, 310, 327, 338, 370, 409, 416, 501, 534, **579,** 586, 609, 632.
toy, *n.* (TOYS), 18, 97, 101, 149, 305, 383, 409, 441, 483, 555, 577, **579,** 643.
track, *n.* (TRACKS) (*footprint*), 580.
    (*steel rail*), 437, 530, 534, **580.**
    v. (TRACKED, TRACKED, TRACKING), 580.
tractor, *n.* (TRACTORS), 183, 411, **580.**
trade, *n.* (TRADES), 580.
    v. (TRADED, TRADED, TRADING), 580.
trader, *n.* (TRADERS), 580.
traffic, *n.,* 140, 303, 491, 492, 530, 580.
trailer, *n.* (TRAILERS), 122, **581,** 627.
train, *n.* (TRAINS), 2, 31, 77, 85, 86, 90, 111, 117, 213, 341, 392, 417, 437, 448, 452, 524, 530, 534, 550, 568, 569, 580, **581,** 590, 614, 625, 652.
    v. (TRAINED, TRAINED, TRAINING), **581.**
tramp, *n.* (TRAMPS), 161, **581.**
    v. (TRAMPED, TRAMPED, TRAMPING), **581.**
trap, *n.* (TRAPS), **582.**
    v. (TRAPPED, TRAPPED, TRAPPING), **582.**
travel, *v.* (TRAVELED or TRAVELLED, TRAVELED or TRAVELLED, TRAVELING or TRAVELLING), 2, 9, 81, 104, 111, 121, 131, 142, 169, 286, 288, 316, 338, 343, 376, 392, 407, 437, 450, 465, 490, 510, 534, 539, 552, 580, 581, 582, 590, 603, 604, 611, 620.
traveler, *n.* (TRAVELERS), 275, 345, **582.**
tray, *n.* (TRAYS), **582.**
treasure, *n.* (TREASURES), **582.**
treat, *n.* (TREATS), 47, 164, 215, 220, 250, 271, 327, 583, 610.
    v. (TREATED, TREATED, TREATING), **583.**
tree, *n.* (TREES), 4, 12, 20, 33, 55, 90, 97, 100, 101, 134, 140, 144, 158, 168, 179, 224, 234, 258, 267, 288, 305, 307, 311, 326, 329, 344, 354, 367, 390, 395, 402, 407, 416, 435, 465, 481, 513, 515, 530, 537, 546, 565, 576, **583,** 609, 633.
treetop, *n.* (TREETOPS), 380.
tremble, *v.* (TREMBLED, TREMBLED, TREMBLING), 416, **583.**
trial, *n.* (TRIALS), **583.**
triangle, *n.* (TRIANGLES), **584.**
tribe, *n.* (TRIBES), **584.**
trick, *n.* (TRICKS) (*clever act; stunt*), 286, 324, 581, **584.**
    (*joke*), **584.**
    v. (TRICKED, TRICKED, TRICKING), 207, 324.
tried, *v.* (*past tense and past participle of* TRY), 116, 127, 167, 230, 233, 281, 317, 320, 448, 451, 492, 503, 525, 537, 583, **584,** 588.
tries, *v.* (*third person singular, present indicative of* TRY), 31, 37, 44, 230, 267, 314, 367, 566.

trim, *adj.* (TRIMMER, TRIMMEST), **585.**
    v. (TRIMMED, TRIMMED, TRIMMING) (*to cut and make neat*), 470, **585.**
    (*to decorate*), 139, 186, 212, **585.**
trio, *n.* (TRIOS), **585.**
trip, *n.* (TRIPS), 31, 175, 286, 296, 320, 446, 448, 461, 512, 538, 550, 557, **585,** 606, 611, 614, 639.
    v. (TRIPPED, TRIPPED, TRIPPING), **585,** 618.
trot, *v.* (TROTTED, TROTTED, TROTTING), 448, **585.**
trouble, *n.* (TROUBLES) (*extra work*), 165, **586.**
    (*matter; problem*), 331.
    (*worry*), 61, 185, **586.**
trousers, *n.,* 46, 380, 388, 393, 539, **586.**
truck, *n.* (TRUCKS), 86, 127, 158, 192, 213, 225, 249, 315, 316, 321, 411, 443, 458, 490, 580, 581, **586,** 607.
true, *adj.* (TRUER, TRUEST), 45, 183, 186, 310, 321, 442, 448, 504, 531, 541, **587** (*adv. See* truly).
truly, *adv.,* **587.**
trunk, *n.* (TRUNKS) (*luggage*), 31, 320, **587.**
    (*snout of an elephant*), 169, **587.**
    (*stem of a tree*), 63, 316, 583, **587.**
trust, *v.* (TRUSTED, TRUSTED, TRUSTING), 45, 185, **587.**
truth, *n.* (TRUTHS), 184, 261, **587,** 646.
try, *v.* (TRIED, TRIED, TRYING), 8, 47, 90, 119, 166, 167, 180, 185, 194, 196, 205, 239, 256, 272, 283, 290, 295, 307, 314, 317, 320, 341, 391, 402, 415, 420, 427, 429, 442, 534, 581, 583, **588,** 591, 598, 633 (*See also* tries).
tryout, *n.* (TRYOUTS), 583, **588.**
tub, *n.* (TUBS), 38, 103, **588,** 617.
tube, *n.* (TUBES) (*electronic piece of equipment*), **588.**
    (*pipe; hollow piece of rubber, metal, glass, etc.*), 263, 405, 466, 567, **588.**
    (*round container of plastic, thin metal, etc., with a top that screws on*), **588.**
tuck, *v.* (TUCKED, TUCKED, TUCKING), **589.**
Tuesday, *n.* (TUESDAYS), 137, 144, 194, 199, 213, 231, 342, 372, 375, 376, 465, 474, 479, 495, 539, 569, **589,** 623.
tug, *v.* (TUGGED, TUGGED, TUGGING), **589.**
tulip, *n.* (TULIPS), 42, 71, 205, **589.**
tumble, *v.* (TUMBLED, TUMBLED, TUMBLING), 384, **590.**
tumbler, *n.* (TUMBLERS), **590.**
tune, *n.* (TUNES), **590,** 630.
tunnel, *n.* (TUNNELS), 165, 568, **590.**
turkey, *n.* (TURKEYS), 228, 560, **590,** 624.
turn, *n.* (TURNS) (*chance; opportunity; time*), 94, 138, 358, **591.**
    v. (TURNED, TURNED, TURNING) (*to become*), 41, 129, 276, 299, 307, 551, **591.**
    (*to change direction*), 22, 29, 317, 532, **591.**
    (*to move, or to make move, around or partly around*), 107, 189, 196, 245, 411, 419, 552, 646.

turn (*Cont'd.*)
    (*to move, or to make move, round as a wheel does*), 2, 46, 148, 192, 335, 453, 472, 591, 629, 634.
    turn off (*to stop; to make some machine, appliance, tap, etc., cease to function*), 370.
    turn on (*to start; to make some machine, appliance, tap, etc., begin to function*), 77, 311, 339, 372, 545, 552, 591.
turnip, *n.* (TURNIPS), **591.**
turpentine, *n.* (TURPENTINES), **592.**
turtle, *n.* (TURTLES), 347, 485, 559, 578, 592.
tusk, *n.* (TUSKS), **592,** 615.
TV, *n.* (TV's), 556, **592.**
Twain, Mark, *n.,* 370.
tweedle-dee, 193.
twelfth, *adj.,* 139, **592.**
twelve, *adj.,* 153, 174, 191, 207, 274, 308, 317, 343, 571, 593, 651.
    n. (TWELVES), 557, 592.
twentieth, *adj.,* **593.**
twenty, *adj.,* 53, 150, 338, 348, 611.
    n. (TWENTIES), 360, 495, 593.
twenty-eight, *adj.,* 190, 343.
    n. (TWENTY-EIGHTS), 593.
twenty-fifth, *adj.,* 593.
twenty-first, *adj.,* 593.
twenty-five, *adj.,* 82, 306, 422, 431.
    n. (TWENTY-FIVES), 593.
twenty-four, *adj.,* 137, 264, 571.
    n. (TWENTY-FOURS), 593.
twenty-fourth, *adj.,* 593.
twenty-nine, *adj.,* 190, 343.
    n. (TWENTY-NINES), 190.
twenty-ninth, *adj.,* 593.
twenty-one *n.* (TWENTY-ONES) 593.
twenty-second, *adj.,* 593.
twenty-seven, *adj.,* 632.
    n. (TWENTY-SEVENS), 593.
twenty-seventh, *adj.,* 593.
twenty-six, *adj.,* 12, 309.
    n. (TWENTY-SIXES), 593.
twenty-sixth, *adj.,* 170, 593.
twenty-third, *adj.,* 593.
twenty-three, *n.* (TWENTY-THREES), 593.
twenty-two, *n.* (TWENTY-TWOS), 593.
twice, *adv.,* 142, 431, 528, **594.**
twig, *n.* (TWIGS), 36, **594.**
twin, *n.* (TWINS), **594.**
twinkle, *n.* (TWINKLED, TWINKLED, TWINKLING), **594.**
twirl, *v.* (TWIRLED, TWIRLED, TWIRLING), 594.
twist, *v.* (TWISTED, TWISTED, TWISTING), 344, 454, 514, 519, 552, 594, 645, 646.
two, *adj.,* 4, 21, 29, 37, 49, 50, 52, 61, 68, 73, 81, 87, 105, 106, 114, 120, 123, 144, 145, 152, 153, 161, 166, 168, 169, 175, 176, 178, 188, 191, 194, 195, 205, 207, 223, 229, 233, 235, 243, 244, 246, 253, 266, 274, 280, 285, 302, 308, 312, 315, 317, 337, 345, 352, 354, 368, 381, 386, 391, 402, 404, 405, 413, 431, 444, 447, 458, 464, 470, 471, 476, 477, 480, 523, 527, 529, 554, 575, 576, 577, 594, **595,** 602, 627, 635, 638, 652.

two (*Cont'd.*)
    n. (TWOS), 12, 15, 122, 167, 170, 200, 210, 309, 340, 364, 369, 479, 495, 541, 557, 567, 572, 655.
tying, *n.* (*present participle of* TIE), 285, 298, 454, 570, **595.**
typewriter, *n.* (TYPEWRITERS), 107, 323, 371, **595.**

U

U, u, *n.* (U's, U's) (*twenty-first letter of the alphabet*), 12, 170, 309, 558, 592, 596.
ugly, *adj.* (UGLIER, UGLIEST), **597,** 637.
umbrella, *n.* (UMBRELLAS), 208, 265, 379, 439, 485, 488, 597.
uncle, *n.* (UNCLES), 26, 123, 173, 186, 187, 231, 263, 290, 306, 311, 315, 334, 335, 341, 384, 398, 461, 493, 524, 563, 565, 597, 613, 631.
under, *prep.,* 25, 47, 61, 74, 91, 92, 111, 159, 171, 179, 196, 224, 255, 256, 330, 395, 405, 439, 451, 454, 500, 540, 590, **597,** 598, 622, 639.
underclothes, *n.,* 598.
underneath, *prep.,* 598.
underparts, *n.,* 203.
understand, *v.* (UNDERSTOOD, UNDERSTOOD, UNDERSTANDING), 106, 180, 332, 341, 349, 350, 406, 598.
underwear, *n.,* 598.
undress, *v.* (UNDRESSED, UNDRESSED, UNDRESSING), **598.**
uneven, *adj.,* 318 (*adv.* UNEVENLY).
unfold, *v.* (UNFOLDED, UNFOLDED, UNFOLDING), **598.**
unhappiness, *n.,* 340.
unhappy, *adj.* (UNHAPPIER, UNHAPPIEST), 23, 52, 185, **599,** 642.
uniform, *n.* (UNIFORMS), 506, 599.
United Nations, *n.,* 599.
United States, *n.,* 14, 70, 82, 99, 104, 113, 122, 211, 235, 239, 260, 273, 292, 300, 336, 353, 358, 362, 368, 395, 406, 421, 442, 478, 524, 535, 576, **600,** 617.
United States Army, *n.,* 285.
United States Coast Guard, *n.,* 239.
United States of America (*See* **United States**).
unkind, *adj.* (UNKINDER, UNKINDEST), **600** (*adv.* UNKINDLY).
unknown, *adj.,* **600.**
unpleasant, *adj.* (UNPLEASANTER, UNPLEASANTEST), 361 (*adv.* UNPLEASANTLY).
unless, *conj.,* 242, 247, **600.**
unlock, *v.* (UNLOCKED, UNLOCKED, UNLOCKING), 291, **600.**
untie, *v.* (UNTIED, UNTIED, UNTYING), **600.**
until, *conj.,* 118, 128, 195, 226, 236, 249, 276, 340, 356, 372, 425, 438, 444, 447, 451, 456, 491, 519, 522, 549, **601,** 614, 642, 643.
    prep., 172, 498, 525 (*See also* **till**).
unusual, *adj.,* 246, 601 (*adv.* UNUSUALLY).

up, *adj.,* **601.**
    adv. (above the ground), 134, **601.**
    (awake; out of bed), 231, 302, **601.**
    (on one's feet), 449, **601.**
    (out of the ground), **601.**
    (to a higher place; in an upright position; away from the earth), 3, 21, 46, 112, 210, 475, 509, 536, 578, 587, **601.**
    intensifier with a verb, 63, 73, 99, 103, 141, 158, 201, 282, 326, 341, 552, 595, 638.
    prep. (along), **601.**
    (to the top of), 15, 384, 527, **601, 602.**
    (toward or near a point closer to the beginning), 198.
    (until) (used with "to," i.e., **up to**), 652.
    blow up *(to expand),* 54.
    eat up *(to eat until one is finished),* **601.**
    make up *(to compose),* 623.
    pick up *(to take hold of and lift up),* 169, 352, 396, 439.
upon, *prep.,* 96, **601.**
upper, *adj.,* 14, 168, 243, 294, 313, 373, 577, **601,** 629.
upset, *adj.,* **602.**
    v. (UPSET, UPSET, UPSETTING), **602.**
upstairs, *adv.,* 153, 170, 521, **602,** 606.
upward, *adv.,* **602,** 609.
Uranus, *n.,* 407.
Uruguay, *n.,* 510.
us, *pro.,* 9, 12, 22, 23, 42, 45, 50, 66, 68, 80, 85, 86, 97, 102, 105, 118, 124, 139, 141, 143, 148, 158, 166, 169, 180, 189, 197, 198, 223, 237, 252, 254, 255, 258, 268, 272, 286, 294, 303, 304, 305, 309, 315, 324, 332, 335, 340, 343, 344, 347, 354, 357, 364, 370, 372, 376, 377, 378, 392, 394, 396, 398, 406, 408, 410, 414, 418, 431, 432, 442, 445, 446, 448, 457, 461, 462, 463, 485, 491, 492, 512, 514, 519, 532, 550, 551, 553, 555, 559, 560, 571, 572, 583, 590, 598, 600, **602,** 603, 610, 614, 616, 620, 624, 625, 633, 640, 655.
U.S.A., *n.,* 362 (*See also* **United States**).
use, *n.* (USES), **602.**
use *v.* (USED, USED, USING) *(to consume or expend the whole of; to deplete or exhaust),* 513, **603,** 618.
    (to make a practice of), **603,** 620.
    (to employ for some purpose; to put to work), 4, 27, 31, 41, 45, 50, 60, 67, 69, 83, 86, 87, 101, 107, 108, 113, 125, 129, 143, 145, 168, 170, 185, 188, 197, 198, 207, 209, 225, 227, 245, 250, 252, 253, 259, 262, 275, 301, 308, 331, 337, 353, 371, 379, 383, 385, 389, 393, 433, 443, 463, 467, 470, 471, 505, 530, 538, 545, 556, 564, 576, 579, 582, **603,** 607, 617, 637, 645, 650.
useful, *adj.,* **603** (*adv.* USEFULLY).
usher, *n.* (USHERS), **603.**
usual, *adj.,* 181, 242, 462, **603,** 604.
usually, *adv.,* 36, 134, 143, 244, 246, 263, 273, 290, 302, 305, 312, 327, 336, 401, 424, 440, 450, 462, 591, **604,** 607, 615, 621.

utmost, *adj.,* **604.**
utter, *v.* (UTTERED, UTTERED, UTTERING), **604.**
utterly, *adv.,* **604.**

V

V, v, *n.* (V's, v's) *(twenty-second letter of the alphabet),* 12, 170, 309, 558, 592, **605.**
vacation, *n.* (VACATIONS), 81, 260, 317, 383, 539, **606.**
vacuum cleaner, *n.* (VACUUM CLEANERS), 323, 457, **606.**
valentine, *n.* (VALENTINES), **606.**
valley, *n.* (VALLEYS), 260, **606,** 609.
valuable, *adj.,* 273, **607** (*adv.* VALUABLY).
value, *n.* (VALUES), 582, **607.**
van, *n.* (VANS), 586, **607.**
vanish, *v.* (VANISHED, VANISHED, VANISHING), **607.**
vase, *n.* (VASES), 54, 379, 602, **607.**
veal, *n.,* 101, **607.**
vegetable, *n.* (VEGETABLES), 39, 43, 48, 79, 88, 92, 129, 166, 187, 206, 209, 220, 242, 287, 295, 310, 328, 329, 373, 378, 394, 395, 396, 397, 407, 419, 436, 462, 509, 514, 515, 519, 591, **608,** 623.
velvet, *n.* (VELVETS), 344, **608.**
Venezuela, *n.,* 510.
Venus, *n.,* 407.
verse, *n.* (VERSES), **608.**
very, *adv.,* 6, 15, 32, 40, 52, 71, 99, 111, 114, 126, 132, 141, 152, 164, 175, 184, 194, 201, 213, 224, 231, 235, 250, 271, 282, 292, 316, 320, 333, 354, 370, 397, 410, 421, 424, 435, 444, 463, 473, 484, 491, 515, 531, 544, 551, 568, 572, 579, 590, **608,** 618, 636, 646, 655.
vest, *n.* (VESTS), **608.**
view, *n.* (VIEWS) *(scene),* 300, 469, **609.**
    (sight; range of vision), 607.
    v. (VIEWED, VIEWED, VIEWING), **609.**
village, *n.* (VILLAGES), **609.**
vine, *n.* (VINES), 129, 216, 334, 344, 394, 426, 519, 533, **609,** 619.
vinegar, *n.* (VINEGARS), 90, 129, 401, 549, 553, **609.**
violent, *adj.,* **609** (*adv.* VIOLENTLY).
violet, *n.* (VIOLETS), 260, **610.**
violin, *n.* (VIOLINS), **610.**
visit, *n.* (VISITS), 80, 142.
    v. (VISITED, VISITED, VISITING), 27, 45, 117, 239, 254, 364, 378, 390, 391, 394, 398, 405, 445, 474, 482, 507, 560, **610,** 624, 628.
visitor, *n.* (VISITORS), **610.**
visual, *adj.,* **610** (*adv.* VISUALLY).
voice, *n.* (VOICES), 30, 106, 169, 184, 222, 238, 259, 266, 326, 337, 378, 464, 493, 505, 543, **610,** 630.
vote, *n.* (VOTES), 169, **611.**
    v. (VOTED, VOTED, VOTING), 169, **611.**

voter, *n.* (VOTERS), **611.**
voyage, *n.* (VOYAGES), **611.**

W

W, w, *n.* (W's, w's) *(twenty-third letter of the alphabet),* 12, 170, 309, 558, 592, **612.**
wade, *v.* (WADED, WADED, WADING), **613.**
wag, *v.* (WAGGED, WAGGED, WAGGING), 44, **613.**
wage, *n.* (WAGES), **613.**
wages, *n.* (*plural of wage*), **613.**
wagon, *n.* (WAGONS), 88, 154, 248, 278, 283, 374, 381, 425, 427, 554, 581, 589, **613,** 644.
waist, *n.* (WAISTS), 46, 301, 497, **613.**
wait, *n.* (WAITS), **614.**
    v. (WAITED, WAITED, WAITING), 165, 180, 210, 273, 275, 317, 377, 438, 440, 513, 524, 530, 541, 571, 591, **614,** 628, 652, 656.
waiter, *n.* (WAITERS), **614.**
wake, *v.* (WAKED or WOKE, WAKED, WAKING), 27, 70, 127, 150, 223, 420, 492, 573, 597, **614,** 637.
walk, *n.* (WALKS) *(pathway),* 67, 300, 326, 543.
    (trip on foot), 19, 231, 338, 374, 383, 523, 550, **614,** 637.
    v. (WALKED, WALKED, WALKING) *(to go forward on foot),* 4, 10, 12, 22, 29, 30, 32, 35, 44, 49, 83, 85, 104, 118, 125, 160, 184, 188, 190, 191, 195, 207, 209, 243, 249, 257, 258, 294, 300, 304, 306, 326, 328, 343, 347, 372, 373, 425, 488, 490, 492, 521, 526, 527, 531, 532, 562, 573, 574, 575, 578, 581, 591, 601, 603, 613, **614,** 616, 637, 653.
wall, *n.* (WALLS), 3, 11, 65, 89, 90, 120, 124, 134, 185, 199, 221, 246, 281, 305, 372, 374, 388, 408, 472, 481, 530, 548, 562, 579, 606, 609, **615,** 635.
wallet, *n.* (WALLETS), 415, **615.**
wallpaper, *n.* (WALLPAPERS), **615.**
walnut, *n.* (WALNUTS), 462, **615.**
walrus, *n.* (WALRUSES), **615.**
wander, *v.* (WANDERED, WANDERED, WANDERING), **616.**
want, *v.* (WANTED, WANTED, WANTING), 3, 6, 18, 67, 86, 101, 130, 141, 144, 150, 164, 175, 178, 200, 208, 236, 246, 254, 260, 267, 269, 273, 276, 300, 311, 330, 333, 341, 348, 356, 361, 364, 371, 390, 410, 435, 442, 448, 457, 467, 476, 490, 498, 506, 515, 518, 522, 538, 550, 559, 564, 573, 576, 588, 602, 611, **616,** 620, 623, 626, 636, 643, 651.
war, *n.* (WARS), 22, 194, 210, 333, 340, 395, 462, 506, 599, **616.**
ware (*See* **wares**).
wares, *n.* (*plural of* WARE), **616.**

warm, *adj.* (WARMER, WARMEST), 11, 26, 50, 54, 70, 73, 95, 107, 111, 112, 114, 119, 123, 124, 191, 194, 197, 199, 234, 249, 252, 264, 265, 273, 285, 323, 325, 334, 341, 362, 387, 404, 428, 447, 451, 456, 469, 483, 504, 532, 591, **616**, 620, 621, 640 (*adv.* WARMLY).

warn, *v.* (WARNED, WARNED, WARNING), 9, **617.**

was, *v.* (*first and third persons singular, past tense, indicative of* BE), 2, 14, 41, 47, 52, 64, 74, 86, 94, 101, 119, 136, 145, 159, 173, 184, 193, 208, 228, 246, 256, 259, 272, 282, 294, 304, 318, 323, 332, 336, 350, 358, 371, 376, 383, 390, 398, 405, 415, 422, 436, 439, 443, 448, 463, 467, 480, 490, 493, 504, 510, 515, 526, 530, 541, 552, 558, 563, 570, 577, 583, 609, 614, **617**, 625, 635, 642, 645, 651, 653.

wash, *v.* (WASHED, WASHED, WASHING), 38, 69, 109, 140, 169, 201, 214, 226, 233, 237, 271, 303, 340, 346, 370, 392, 436, 472, 478, 489, 494, 496, 512, 523, 538, 552, 588, **617**, 619, 628, 636, 640, 643.

washing machine, *n.* (WASHING MACHINES), 346, **617.**

Washington, D.C., *n.,* **617.**

Washington, George, *n.,* 137, 235, 273, 421, 442, **617.**

washtub, *n.* (WASHTUBS), 588, **617.**

wasn't, *v.* and *adv.* (*contraction for* WAS NOT), 410.

wasp, *n.* (WASPS), **618.**

waste, *n.* (WASTES), **618.**

    v. (WASTED, WASTED, WASTING), 618.

wastepaper, *n.* (WASTEPAPERS), **618.**

watch, *n.* (WATCHES), 93, 229, 335, 350, 448, 485, 509, 518, 560, 569, **618**, 643, 646.

    v. (WATCHED, WATCHED, WATCHING), 52, 73, 101, 131, 141, 185, 191, 204, 205, 219, 223, 232, 239, 283, 300, 301, 306, 324, 328, 358, 426, 440, 449, 479, 483, 494, 503, 540, 584, 613, **618.**

watchful, *adj.,* 618 (*adv.* WATCHFULLY).

water, *n.* (WATERS), 10, 11, 38, 39, 41, 58, 60, 65, 67, 69, 81, 82, 84, 89, 106, 113, 119, 126, 134, 136, 137, 142, 143, 145, 152, 158, 159, 160, 169, 173, 195, 198, 199, 203, 204, 210, 212, 214, 215, 220, 263, 269, 271, 276, 277, 282, 291, 299, 300, 301, 308, 314, 334, 348, 367, 368, 370, 384, 393, 401, 405, 415, 419, 424, 425, 427, 428, 437, 438, 454, 458, 473, 494, 502, 505, 509, 514, 517, 518, 519, 520, 525, 531, 533, 538, 540, 544, 549, 552, 554, 555, 568, 591, 592, 608, 613, 617, **619**, 624, 626, 634, 645, 646.

    v. (WATERED, WATERED, WATERING), 220, 250, 263, **619.**

water lily, *n.* (WATER LILIES), **619.**

watermelon, *n.* (WATERMELONS), 334, **619.**

wave, *n.* (WAVES), **619.**

    v. (WAVED, WAVED, WAVING), 202, **619.**

wax, *n.,* 83, 89, 226, 261, **620.**

    v. (WAXED, WAXED, WAXING), **620.**

way, *n.* (WAYS) (*direction*), 84, 146, 155, 160, 189, 240, 280, 305, 318, 527, **620.**

    (*distance*), 187, 439, 506, 575, **620.**

    (*fashion; style; habit of life*), 317, 354, **620.**

    (*how; manner*), 23, 27, 82, 88, 175, 216, 222, 224, 228, 265, 271, 301, 304, 326, 335, 341, 348, 369, 377, 390, 398, 422, 429, 445, 460, 572, **620**, 640.

    (*road*), 300, 307, 450, 590, **620.**

    (*what one wants*), **620.**

we, *pro.,* 3, 4, 13, 21, 39, 49, 56, 60, 73, 83, 91, 98, 109, 112, 129, 136, 145, 150, 165, 186, 191, 197, 203, 206, 211, 220, 224, 231, 236, 243, 247, 256, 268, 277, 290, 299, 310, 328, 332, 340, 343, 354, 367, 376, 397, 420, 432, 443, 447, 451, 460, 478, 490, 498, 517, 523, 534, 538, 550, 559, 580, 586, 598, 614, **620**, 624, 632, 645, 652.

weak, *adj.* (WEAKER, WEAKEST), 184, 190, 535, **621** (*adv.* WEAKLY).

wealthy, *adj.* (WEALTHIER, WEALTHIEST), 165, **621.**

wear, *v.* (WORE, WORN, WEARING), 20, 24, 39, 46, 52, 59, 60, 84, 108, 109, 118, 128, 143, 155, 186, 226, 232, 236, 243, 248, 280, 284, 330, 341, 342, 345, 352, 359, 363, 372, 380, 386, 393, 397, 438, 457, 483, 497, 500, 504, 506, 543, 551, 568, 570, 572, 586, 618, **621**, 628, 640, 642.

weary, *adj.* (WEARIER, WEARIEST), 573, **621** (*adv.* WEARILY).

weather, *n.,* 11, 26, 33, 41, 70, 94, 95, 107, 234, 248, 252, 263, 280, 288, 404, 410, 432, 447, 522, 615, **621**, 634, 635.

weave, *v.* (WOVE, WOVEN, WEAVING), **622**, 644.

weaver, *n.* (WEAVERS), **622.**

web, *n.* (WEBS), 513, 514, **622** (*See also* webbed).

webbed, *adj.,* **622** (*See also* web).

wed, *v.* (WEDDED, WEDDED, WEDDING), **623.**

Wednesday, *n.* (WEDNESDAYS), 137, 194, 199, 213, 342, 363, 376, 465, 474, 479, 495, 539, 569, 589, **623.**

wee, *adj.* (WEER, WEEST), 575, **623.**

weed, *n.* (WEEDS), 15, 259, 407, 601, 623, 640.

    v. (WEEDED, WEEDED, WEEDING), **623.**

week, *n.* (WEEKS), 39, 80, 96, 137, 177, 194, 199, 213, 231, 264, 273, 294, 302, 325, 342, 347, 376, 392, 401, 465, 474, 479, 484, 569, 589, 613, 621, **623.**

weep, *v.* (WEPT, WEPT, WEEPING), **623**, 625, 633.

weigh, *v.* (WEIGHED, WEIGHED, WEIGHING), 32, 467, 576, **624.**

weight, *n.* (WEIGHTS), 13, 174, 419, 576, **624.**

welcome, *adj.,* **624.**

well, *adj.,* 21, 130, 148, 159, 236, 264, 265, 272, 333, 475, 490, 561, 586, 617, **624**, 642.

    adv., 30, 44, 82, 107, 135, 138, 143, 155, 157, 180, 213, 231, 258, 286, 291, 318, 319, 324, 330, 416, 420, 422, 424, 426, 445, 451, 473, 491, 493, 499, 515, 537, 542, 581, 584, 588, 610, 623, **624**, 625.

    interj., **624.**

    n. (WELLS), 140, 145, 425, **624.**

we'll, *pro.* and *v.* (*contraction for* WE WILL *or* WE SHALL), 291, 586, 625.

went, *v.* (*past tense of* GO), 13, 15, 43, 52, 82, 89, 91, 114, 130, 145, 146, 147, 153, 157, 165, 166, 175, 177, 193, 201, 202, 203, 208, 227, 231, 239, 244, 246, 260, 264, 268, 271, 275, 276, 278, 300, 302, 307, 323, 339, 356, 377, 378, 379, 384, 392, 402, 408, 410, 412, 448, 461, 464, 466, 474, 489, 497, 529, 533, 539, 540, 551, 561, 568, 569, 574, 575, 583, 601, 603, 606, 614, 620, **625**, 632, 641, 650.

wept, *v.* (*past tense and past participle of* WEEP), **625.**

were, *v.* (*second person singular; first, second, and third person plural, past tense, indicative of* BE), 23, 35, 52, 63, 64, 67, 70, 76, 91, 105, 130, 135, 136, 139, 168, 177, 184, 201, 211, 231, 232, 237, 246, 273, 274, 276, 281, 304, 318, 325, 343, 361, 362, 372, 375, 378, 379, 397, 406, 415, 424, 436, 444, 455, 462, 471, 480, 487, 492, 497, 504, 532, 534, 538, 551, 561, 568, 580, 591, 594, 602, 609, 623, **625**, 631, 648.

we're, *pro.* and *v.* (*contraction for* WE ARE), 447, 625.

west, *adj.,* 368, 370, 634.

    adv., **625**, 632.

    n., 146, 406, 478, **625.**

wet, *adj.* (WETTER, WETTEST), 27, 91, 109, 135, 156, 160, 202, 208, 209, 223, 348, 438, 519, 527, **626**, 634, 645, 646.

    v. (WET *or* WETTED, WET *or* WETTED, WETTING), **626.**

wetness, *n.,* 156, **626.**

whale, *n.* (WHALES), **626.**

what, *adj.,* 15, 27, 104, 145, 170, 181, 217, 292, 331, 508, 512, 628, 630, 631.

    adv., 134.

    pro., 5, 7, 23, 25, 32, 41, 44, 45, 63, 75, 77, 88, 155, 166, 225, 238, 261, 314, 331, 332, 339, 340, 342, 350, 352, 357, 363, 367, 429, 432, 451, 457, 463, 467, 474, 558, 564, 587, 594, 600, 607, 609, 620, **626**, 627, 636.

whatever, *adj.,* **626.**

    pro., 470, **626.**

what's, *pro.* and *v.* (*contraction for* WHAT IS), 210, 383, **627.**

wheat, *n.,* 93, 193, 204, 233, 234, 338, 510, 533, 567, **627.**

wheel, *n.* (WHEELS), 2, 46, 50, 85, 88, 192, 453, 471, 496, 526, 573, 581, 613, **627.**

wheelbarrow, *n.* (WHEELBARROWS), **627.**

when, *conj.,* 2, 16, 23, 35, 45, 63, 67, 75, 84, 94, 104, 123, 135, 140, 156, 166, 185, 196, 323, 407, 475, 523, 544, **627,** 642, 646, 655.

whenever, *conj.,* 96, 380, **627,** 642.

where, *adv.,* 41, 230, **628.**

    conj., 5, 19, 96, 153, 193, 210, 255, 264, 293, 318, 332, 371, 379, 388, 405, 412, 422, 444, 515, 524, 530, 553, 597, 615, 623, 640, 656.

wherever, *adv.,* **628.**

whether, *conj.,* 139, 272, **628,** 642.

which, *adj.,* 446, 490, 593, **628.**

    pro., 14, 32, 49, 83, 88, 94, 111, 128, 154, 158, 192, 211, 248, 280, 284, 293, 324, 330, 353, 383, 385, 407, 497, 518, 525, 549, 586, 603, **628,** 632, 645, 655.

while, *conj.,* 23, 76, 100, 134, 155, 161, 202, 219, 259, 318, 328, 336, 339, 342, 349, 353, 375, 379, 386, 400, 492, 506, **628.**

    n., 30, 55, 113, 273, 303, 308, 315, 489, 568, 597, 614, **628.**

whip, *n.* (WHIPS), **629.**

    v. (WHIPPED, WHIPPED, WHIPPING), 126, 545, **629.**

whirl, *v.* (WHIRLED, WHIRLED, WHIRLING), 148, **629.**

whisker, *n.* (WHISKERS), 441, **629.**

whisper, *v.* (WHISPERED, WHISPERED, WHISPERING), 320, 336, 505, **630.**

whistle, *n.* (WHISTLES), 2, 54, **630.**

    v. (WHISTLED, WHISTLED, WHISTLING), 2, 81, **630.**

white, *adj.* (WHITER, WHITEST), 40, 43, 60, 73, 79, 96, 97, 106, 109, 110, 112, 115, 118, 121, 129, 134, 135, 229, 278, 285, 291, 299, 311, 312, 321, 327, 338, 360, 379, 387, 399, 412, 413, 419, 425, 436, 441, 448, 463, 493, 503, 516, 519, 525, 535, 538, 555, 577, 610, 619, 621, **630,** 655.

    n. (WHITES), 57, 201, 375, 397, **630.**

who, *pro.,* 6, 17, 27, 29, 44, 45, 47, 54, 70, 73, 75, 87, 94, 96, 99, 102, 104, 106, 124, 131, 135, 136, 142, 145, 151, 158, 160, 162, 171, 172, 173, 180, 187, 200, 207, 222, 239, 240, 244, 260, 267, 281, 286, 304, 305, 314, 324, 330, 333, 335, 338, 339, 345, 348, 354, 356, 357, 370, 380, 385, 391, 403, 409, 411, 414, 415, 417, 426, 435, 437, 446, 447, 448, 451, 462, 485, 486, 493, 496, 511, 537, 549, 552, 554, 558, 563, 580, 581, 582, 603, 610, 611, 614, 622, **630,** 632, 633, 638, 639, 641.

whole, *adj.,* 10, 87, 174, 177, 195, 294, 354, 621, **630,** 641.

whom, *pro.,* 45, 77, 102, 252, 268, 389, 409, 549, 611, **631.**

whose, *pro.,* 391, 428, **631.**

why, *adv.,* 41, 179, 200, 275, 303, 443, 474, 541, **631.**

wicked, *adj.,* **631** (*adv.* WICKEDLY).

wide, *adj.* (WIDER, WIDEST), 26, 66, 259, 300, 353, 388, 523, 617, **631,** 650.

wife, *n.* (WIVES), 26, 268, 329, 426, 432, 531, **632.**

wig, *n.* (WIGS), **632.**

wigwam, *n.* (WIGWAMS), **632.**

wild, *adj.* (WILDER, WILDEST), 40, 70, 141, 193, 212, 261, 288, 313, 332, 551, 570, **632,** 638, 655, 656 (*adv.* WILDLY).

will, *v.* (*past tense:* WOULD), 4, 16, 25, 32, 45, 55, 66, 81, 97, 103, 119, 125, 134, 141, 151, 160, 179, 185, 198, 209, 219, 227, 237, 245, 255, 271, 285, 293, 305, 313, 323, 331, 348, 357, 369, 376, 398, 405, 413, 427, 439, 447, 458, 465, 472, 481, 497, 503, 511, 522, 533, 544, 553, 561, 573, 585, 598, 618, 627, **633,** 645, 653.

willing, *adj.,* 7, 222, **633,** 643 (*adv.* WILLINGLY).

willow, *n.* (WILLOWS), **633.**

win, *v.* (WON, WON, WINNING), 8, 37, 48, 94, 194, 318, 361, 537, 588, **633,** 638.

wind, *n.* (WINDS), 2, 65, 109, 124, 135, 156, 161, 205, 293, 305, 451, 461, 517, 531, 535, 558, 621, 626, 629, **634,** 635.

wind, *v.* (WOUND, WOUND, WINDING), 130, 594, **634,** 643.

windmill, *n.* (WINDMILLS), **634.**

window, *n.* (WINDOWS), 8, 67, 74, 77, 131, 189, 215, 225, 226, 278, 307, 317, 320, 394, 440, 474, 481, 482, 540, 561, 574, 631, **635,** 643.

window sill, *n.* (WINDOW SILLS), **635.**

windstorm, *n.* (WINDSTORMS), 132, 268.

windy, *adj.* (WINDIER, WINDIEST), **635.**

wing, *n.* (WINGS), 9, 37, 42, 43, 51, 53, 57, 76, 164, 202, 203, 205, 275, 363, 451, 517, **635.**

wink, *v.* (WINKED, WINKED, WINKING), **635.**

winter, *n.* (WINTERS), 26, 54, 112, 114, 155, 183, 185, 205, 260, 317, 362, 432, 473, 487, 489, 496, 518, 530, 531, 539, 561, 583, 616, **636.**

wipe, *v.* (WIPED, WIPED, WIPING), 161, 245, 330, 353, 579, **636.**

wire, *n.* (WIRES), 36, 71, 79, 104, 107, 119, 169, 192, 246, 262, 299, 436, 516, 555, **636.**

wise, *adj.* (WISER, WISEST), 165, 207, **636** (*adv.* WISELY).

wish, *n.* (WISHES), 234, **636.**

    v. (WISHED, WISHED, WISHING), 172, 263, **636.**

wishes, *n.,* **637.**

witch, *n.* (WITCHES), 180, **637.**

with, *prep.,* 2, 9, 15, 22, 37, 42, 53, 68, 75, 83, 90, 98, 112, 119, 132, 144, 155, 165, 181, 193, 206, 212, 220, 225, 231, 245, 250, 255, 266, 275, 280, 285, 292, 295, 299, 309, 320, 327, 337, 345, 350, 371, 393, 399, 402, 406, 419, 422, 424, 433, 441, 455, 462, 467, 480, 487, 498, 507, 511, 518, 528, 530, 534, 545, 550, 554, 562, 573, 578, 584, 600, 614, 625, 632, **637,** 640, 650.

within, *prep.,* 88, **637.**

without, *prep.,* 9, 27, 32, 35, 47, 52, 81, 136, 140, 156, 157, 172, 273, 287, 307, 341, 347, 352, 398, 433, 436, 457, 458, 488, 500, 502, 503, 528, 530, 532, 608, **637.**

woke, *v.* (*past tense and past participle of* WAKE), 231, 282, 614, **637.**

wolf, *n.* (WOLVES), 316, **638.**

wolves, *n.* (*plural of* WOLF), **638.**

woman, *n.* (WOMEN), 5, 225, 244, 268, 298, 324, 329, 345, 348, 432, 632, 637, **638** (*See also* **women**).

women, *n.* (*plural of* WOMAN), 104, 225, 266, **638** (*See also* **woman**).

won, *v.* (*past tense and past participle of* WIN), 40, 48, 97, 268, 338, 422, 435, 570, **638.**

wonder, *v.* (WONDERED, WONDERED, WONDERING), 255, 256, 383, 472, 541, 594, **638,** 642.

wonderful, *adj.,* **639** (*adv.* WONDERFULLY).

won't, *v.* and *adv.* (*contraction for* WILL NOT), 602, 638, **639.**

wood, *n.* (WOODS), 17, 27, 35, 36, 54, 57, 71, 87, 100, 192, 195, 203, 244, 262, 285, 293, 327, 331, 367, 388, 397, 403, 406, 437, 467, 471, 472, 506, 515, 516, 525, 527, 530, 532, 582, 583, 615, 635, **639.**

woodcutter, *n.* (WOODCUTTERS), **639.**

wooden, *adj.,* 27, 75, 87, 110, 262, 335, 367, 465, 494, 639, 648.

woodpecker, *n.* (WOODPECKERS), 203, 396, **639.**

woods, *n.,* 122, 128, 140, 208, 269, 305, 318, 346, 383, 401, 607, 616, **640.**

wool, *n.* (WOOLS), 32, 203, 484, 514, **640,** 650.

woolen, *adj.,* 483, **640.**

woolly, *adj.* (WOOLIER, WOOLIEST), 299.

word, *n.* (WORDS), 12, 26, 52, 96, 138, 142, 143, 175, 180, 220, 250, 271, 300, 309, 314, 326, 332, 341, 389, 391, 398, 406, 422, 423, 429, 431, 442, 446, 447, 467, 470, 477, 507, 512, 513, 551, 557, 575, 598, 604, 610, 620, 626, **640.**

wore, *v.* (*past tense of* WEAR), 102, 342, 463, 616, 621, 632, **640.**

work, *n.,* 72, 86, 88, 139, 144, 148, 149, 150, 157, 165, 169, 181, 197, 230, 254, 272, 284, 309, 323, 324, 358, 370, 371, 391, 415, 443, 445, 446, 467, 470, 491, 497, 539, 553, 573, **640.**

    v. (WORKED, WORKED, WORKING), 8, 20, 42, 51, 75, 117, 138, 142, 144, 149, 165, 167, 169, 183, 184, 187, 189, 216, 227, 228, 230, 246, 247, 249, 250, 263, 265, 273, 292, 304, 323, 324, 339, 355, 371, 376, 380, 381, 392, 394, 417, 425, 426, 439, 446, 458, 521, 532, 537, 568, 573, 580, 588, 598, 599, 606, **640,** 641.

work of art, 23, 640.

workbench, *n.* (WORKBENCHES), 46, **641.**

worker, *n.* (WORKERS), 358, **641.**

workman, *n.* (WORKMEN), **641.**

world, *n.* (WORLDS), 60, 86, 150, 211, 228, 354, 357, 358, 471, 594, 599, **641.**

worm, *n.* (WORMS), 31, 90, 100, 165, 302, 492, 574, **641.**

worn, *adj.,* 480.

   v. (*past participle of* WEAR), 128, 355, 386, 539, 570, 621, 632, **642.**

worn-out, *adj.,* 242, 568, 642.

worry, *n.* (WORRIES), 86, 597, **642.**

   v. (WORRIED, WORRIED, WORRYING), 586, 602, **642.**

worse, *adj.* (*comparative degree of* BAD), **642**

   adv., 642 (*See also* **bad; worst**).

worship, *v.* (WORSHIPED or WORSHIPPED, WORSHIPED or WORSHIPPED, WORSHIP- ING or WORSHIPPING), 102, **642.**

worst, *adj.* (*superlative degree of* BAD), **642** (*See also* **bad; worse**).

worth, *adj.,* 50, 121, 174, 230, 359, 397, 431, 607, **643.**

   n., **643.**

would, *v.* (*past tense of* WILL), 48, 136, 175, 273, 274, 331, 335, 374, 375, 392, 398, 401, 402, 405, 423, 437, 441, 442, 461, 466, 480, 481, 500, 515, 583, 584, 616, 625, 636, **643.**

wouldn't, *v.* and *adv.* (*contraction for* WOULD NOT), 349, 532, **643.**

wound, *n.* (WOUNDS), 34, 73, 268, **643.**

   v. (WOUNDED, WOUNDED, WOUNDING), **643.**

wound, *v.* (*past tense and past participle of* WIND), 516, 634, **643.**

wove, *v.* (*past tense and past participle of* WEAVE), 622, **644.**

wrap, *n.* (WRAPS), **644.**

   v. (WRAPPED or WRAPT, WRAPPED or WRAPT, WRAPPING), 34, 36, 383, 388, 453, 634, 643, **644.**

wreath, *n.* (WREATHS), **644.**

wreck, *n.* (WRECKS), **644.**

   v. (WRECKED, WRECKED, WRECKING), **644.**

wren, *n.* (WRENS), 250, **645.**

wrench, *n.* (WRENCHES), 641, **645.**

wring, *v.* (WRUNG, WRUNG, WRINGING), 645, 646.

wrinkle, *n.* (WRINKLES) (*crease in the skin*), 372, **645.**

   (*small furrow in a normally smooth surface*), 277, 421, **645.**

   v. (WRINKLED, WRINKLED, WRINKLING), **645.**

wrist, *n.* (WRISTS), 618, **646.**

write, *v.* (WROTE, WRITTEN, WRITING), 7, 53, 82, 84, 94, 138, 142, 175, 196, 257, 275, 276, 300, 304, 306, 307, 314, 323, 348, 373, 383, 388, 396, 397, 413, 422, 435, 467, 469, 484, 491, 500, 548, 555, 572, 626, **646,** 648, 655.

writing, *n.* (WRITINGS), 314.

wrong, *adj.,* 23, 138, 146, 178, 179, 189, 239, 251, 331, 341, 398, 426, 508, 529, **646** (*adv.* WRONGLY).

wrote, *v.* (*past tense of* WRITE), 5, 174, 309, 336, 363, 422, **646.**

wrung, *v.* (*past tense and past participle of* WRING), **646.**

X

X, x, *n.* (X'S, x's) (*twenty-fourth letter of the alphabet*), 12, 170, 309, 558, 592, 647.

Xmas, *n.* (XMASES), **648.**

X ray, *adj.* (*adjective spelt with hyphen:* X-RAY), **648.**

   n. (X RAYS), **648.**

xylophone, *n.* (XYLOPHONES), **648.**

Y

Y, y, *n.* (Y'S, Y'S) (*twenty-fifth letter of the alphabet*), 12, 170, 309, 558, 592, 649.

yacht, *n.* (YACHTS), **650.**

yard, *n.* (YARDS) (*area shut in by a fence or a wall*), 35, 396, 443.

   (*space, lawn, or ground around a house*), 51, 74, 99, 142, 143, 161, 165, 194, 234, 250, 251, 303, 403, 439, 484, 563, 633, 640, **650.**

   (*unit of measure equal to 3 feet*), 274, **650.**

yarn, *n.* (YARNS), 95, 543, 554, 640, 643, **650.**

yawn, *v.* (YAWNED, YAWNED, YAWNING), **650.**

year, *n.* (YEARS), 7, 20, 26, 44, 51, 60, 70, 71, 80, 116, 122, 137, 139, 142, 146, 177, 190, 199, 211, 225, 232, 238, 264, 281, 287, 315, 327, 331, 332, 343, 357, 364, 368, 372, 393, 404, 410, 411, 439, 442, 444, 473, 477, 478, 487, 539, 571, 583, 603, 625, 636, 644, **651,** 653.

yell, *n.* (YELLS), **651.**

   v. (YELLED, YELLED, YELLING), 9, 25, 361, 489, **651.**

yellow, *adj.,* 17, 21, 60, 64, 66, 72, 76, 110, 126, 134, 135, 198, 229, 234, 236, 248, 273, 275, 285, 308, 328, 329, 353, 395, 396, 411, 419, 440, 486, 498, 519, 540, 562, 564, 570, 610, 619, 620, 635, **651,** 652.

yellow (*Cont'd.*)

   n. (YELLOWS), 203, 214, 311, 607, **651.**

yelp, *n.* (YELPS), **651.**

   v. (YELPED, YELPED, YELPING), **651.**

yes, *adv.,* 14, 18, 148, 251, 274, 294, 361, 389, 445, 494, 498, 538, **651.**

yesterday, *adj.,* 353.

   adv., 25, 47, 60, 80, 102, 148, 157, 205, 225, 237, 255, 292, 310, 324, 419, 452, 474, 499, 528, 542, 550, 561, 576, 617, 634, 644, 646, **651.**

   n. (YESTERDAYS), 184, 438.

yet, *conj.,* **652.**

   adv., 75, 99, 176, 451, **652.**

yolk, *n.* (YOLKS), **652.**

yonder, *adv.,* **652.**

you, *pro.,* 4, 11, 15, 21, 39, 51, 59, 71, 80, 97, 107, 121, 126, 130, 142, 151, 164, 167, 172, 181, 191, 202, 210, 216, 228, 239, 251, 254, 262, 267, 281, 292, 306, 323, 335, 342, 352, 361, 368, 373, 387, 398, 410, 420, 431, 440, 447, 453, 463, 476, 488, 497, 506, 517, 523, 533, 539, 551, 557, 564, 569, 578, 588, 601, 617, 622, 630, 632, 644, **652.**

you'll, *pro.* and *v.* (*contraction for* YOU SHALL or YOU WILL), 233, **652.**

young, *adj.* (YOUNGER, YOUNGEST), 29, 99, 101, 225, 271, 292, 324, 372, 373, 402, 526, **653.**

youngster, *n.* (YOUNGSTERS), **653.**

your, *adj.,* 7, 32, 72, 98, 121, 146, 172, 207, 254, 286, 304, 329, 349, 362, 378, 409, 422, 443, 457, 472, 488, 499, 508, 523, 536, 550, 567, 575, 585, 597, 614, 626, 642, 644, 646, 648, **653.**

you're, *pro.* and *v.* (*contraction for* YOU ARE), 247, **653.**

yours, *pro.,* 349, 562, 628, 631, **653.**

yourself, *pro.* (YOURSELVES), 340, 476, 479, 489, 617, **653.**

Z

Z, z, *n.* (Z'S, Z's) (*twenty-sixth letter of the alphabet*), 12, 170, 309, 558, 592, **654.**

zebra, *n.* (ZEBRAS), **655.**

zero, *n.* (ZEROS or ZEROES), 363, 413, **655.**

zest, *n.,* **655.**

zinnia, *n.* (ZINNIAS), 475, **655.**

zone, *n.* (ZONES), **656.**

zoo, *n.* (ZOOS), 11, 23, 40, 79, 141, 191, 272, 441, 446, 450, 551, 632, 638, 639, **656.**

THE SENTENCE AND EIGHT PARTS
OF SPEECH

To help parents, teachers, and adults learning the English language both to teach and to understand the usage of words in The International Visual Dictionary, *the following explanations of the parts of speech are supplied. This section is not designed to provide the reader with a detailed grammatical treatment of these terms, but only to present him, by way of introduction or review, with the basic elements of their meaning.*

THE SENTENCE

A sentence is *a group of words that tells us, or expresses, a complete thought.* Here are some sentences:

Jack gave candy to Mary.
Who gave candy to Mary?
What a big piece of candy Mary has!
Give the candy to Mary.

In a sentence, words can be used in eight different ways. Each of these ways is called a *part of speech.* The eight different parts of speech are these: *noun, pronoun, verb, adjective, adverb, preposition, conjunction,* and *interjection.*

THE NOUN

Nouns are *names of persons, places, things, or ideas.*

Names of persons: John, Mary, girl, boy, nurse.
Names of places: Mexico, Paris, Nile River, Africa.
Names of things: cat, dog, candy, brush, house, lake.
Names of ideas: love, fear, sorrow, safety, wetness.

THE PRONOUN

A pronoun is *a word that is used in place of a noun.* A pronoun can take the place of a person, a place, a thing, or an idea. Here are some words which you will understand. You will find nouns among these words, but you will not find pronouns. Can you pick out the nouns?

Jack gave candy to Mary.

Now we will talk about the same persons and thing, but we will use pronouns instead of nouns. Do you know which nouns these pronouns take the place of?

He gave *it* to *her.*   (He = Jack; it = candy; her = Mary)

The pronouns of this kind are: *I, me*   *we, us*
         you   *you*
         he, him, she, her, it   *they, them*

Showing Ownership

In the sentences below, you will see an example of a pronoun showing ownership.

John has his own book, but Joe has Mary's book.
John has his own book, but Joe has *hers.* (hers = Mary's book)

The pronouns of the above kind are: *mine*   *ours*
         yours   *yours*
         his, hers, its   *theirs*

All in the Same Sentence

In the sentences below, you will see examples of a pronoun with a verb of its own. This kind of pronoun takes the place of a noun or another pronoun already expressed in the same sentence.

John is reading the book.
John is reading the book *which* is blue. (which = the book)

Give the candy to the person *who* wants it.
Give the candy to *whomever* wants it. (whomever = the person who)

The pronouns of the above kind are: *that, who, which, what, whoever, whichever, whom, whomever.*

Pointing Out People and Things

In the sentences below, you will see an example of a pronoun which points out.

John gave Mary the blue book here on the table.
John gave Mary *this.* (this = the blue book here on the table)

The pronouns of the above kind are: *this, these; that, those.*

Asking Questions

In the sentences below, you will see an example of a pronoun which asks a question.

Mary is reading.
Who is reading? (who = Mary)

The pronouns of this kind are: *who, whose, whom, which, what.*

THE VERB

ACTION WORDS

Verbs are *words which tell us what we can do.* What can you do? What can people do? What can things do? Verbs are *action words.*

I *sing*	Mother *cooks.*	The cat *runs.*
I *talk.*	Father *works.*	The fish *swims.*
I *think.*	Grandfather *smokes.*	The dog *barks.*
I *live.*	Grandmother *sews.*	The top *spins.*

Can you pick out the verbs from the sentences above? Can you find the words that tell us what people and things can do?

WHAT IS, WHAT WAS, AND WHAT WILL BE

Verbs also are words that tell about what is, what was, and what will be. The most used word of this kind is the verb *to be.* It is a very interesting word. The verb *to be* can look very different when it is used in different ways. Here are some examples of the verb *to be* in the *present tense* (the time now), in the *past tense* (the time before, the time in the past, the time gone by), and in the *future tense* (the time that will come, the time that has not yet come):

Verb "To Be"

Present Tense		*Past Tense*	
I *am*	we *are*	I *was*	we *were*
you *are*	you *are*	you *were*	you *were*
he, she, it *is*	they *are*	he, she, it *was*	they *were*

Future Tense

I shall (will) *be*	we shall (will) *be*
you will (shall) *be*	you will (shall) *be*
he, she, it will (shall) *be*	they will (shall) *be*

The verb *to be* can also look like this: *being* (present participle) and *been* (past participle).

To Be: a Verb That Connects

The verb *to be* links, or joins, things together. It is a verb that *connects* things.

The Same As: Is Equal To

The verb *to be* shows that one part of a sentence is equal to, or is the same as, the other part of a sentence. Study these sentences:

Mr. Jones *is* the principal.	(Mr. Jones = the principal)
That boy *is* my cousin.	(that boy = my cousin)
I *am* the leader.	(I = the leader)

To Have a Place

The verb *to be* also means *to have a place*. Study these sentences:

I *am* (have a place) here.
The Empire State Building *is* (has a place) in New York City.
The Panama Canal *is* (has a place) in the country of Panama.
We *were* (had a place) in the park yesterday.
Mother and Father *are* (have a place) at the movies.

To Belong to a Group

The verb *to be* also means *to belong to a group called*. Study these sentences:

A rose *is a* (belongs to a group called) plant.
Mr. Lopez *is a* (belongs to a group called) teacher.
The earth *is a* (belongs to a group called) planet.

To Have the Quality or Trait

Many things make us what we are. Let's talk about a boy named John.

John *is* tall.
John *is* fat.
John *is* smart.
John *is* kind.

From the above sentences, we know that John is tall, fat, smart, and kind. All these things that we have said about John are called *qualities* or *traits*. These qualities are some of the things that make John what he is. Study the sentences below and notice how the verb *to be* is used.

John *is* tall. (John has the quality of tallness.)
John *is* fat. (John has the quality of fatness.)
John *is* smart. (John has the quality of smartness.)
John *is* kind. (John has the quality of kindness.)

If we know more qualities of John, we are able to know John better: We are able to know better who John is. The verb *to be*, then, can mean *to have the quality of.*

THE ADJECTIVE

An adjective is *a word that gives us more information about the meaning of a noun or a pronoun.* It adds something extra to the meaning. An adjective describes a noun or a pronoun. It tells us something about a noun or a pronoun. Adjectives answer such questions as: *What kind? Which one? How many?* In the sentences below, can you pick out the adjectives?

Mary has a *beautiful* dress. (**What kind** of dress does Mary have?)
That boy standing in the corner is Paul. (**Which one** is Paul?)
Ten apples are in the basket. (**How many** apples are in the basket?)

Nouns Used as Adjectives

Sometimes nouns are used as adjectives. Here are some examples of nouns that are used as ajdectives: *radio* station, *school* books, *baseball* game.

Verbs Used as Adjectives

Verbs can also be used as adjectives. When verbs are used as adjectives, they are called *participles*. Here are some examples:

playing children	(children who are playing)
working men	(men who are working)
broken glass	(glass which has been broken)

The Article: a Special Adjective

An article is a kind of adjective. *A, an,* and *the* are articles.

USING "A" AND "AN"

When we *are* **not** *talking about something or somebody special,* we use the articles *a* or *an.*

A boy came late.

In the sentence above, we show that we do not know who the boy is. We only know that it is somebody who is *a* boy. Below is a little talk between Martha and Thomas. It will help you to understand the meaning and use of the words *a* and *an.*

Martha said, "*A* boy came late for school."
Thomas asked, "Who was late? What is that boy's name?"
Martha answered, "I do not know. I only know that *a* boy was late for school. I saw some boy arrive at school after the bell had rung."

We use *an* before words beginning with a vowel *(vowels = a, e, i, o, u): an* apple, *an* airplane, *an* automobile. We use *a* before words which do not begin with a vowel: *a* boy, *a* girl, *a* desk, *a* hat, *a* zebra.

USING "THE"

When we *are talking about something or somebody special,* we use the article *the.*

The boy came late for school.

In the above sentence, we show that we know who *the* boy is. We can tell others something about *the* boy. Below is a little talk between Mark and Sally. Notice carefully how the article *the* is used.

Mark said, "*The* boy came late for school."
Sally asked, "Who was late? What was that boy's name?"
Mark answered, "*The* boy is called Robert Brown. *The* boy is in the second grade. *The* boy is short. *The* boy lives on Oak Street. He is *the* boy who came late for school."

THE ADVERB

An adverb is *a word that gives us more information about the meaning of a verb, an adjective, or another adverb.* It adds something extra to the meaning of a verb, an adjective, or another adverb. Adverbs answer the questions: *How? When? Where? How much?*

How? *quickly, slowly, carefully, difficultly.*
When? *often, now, soon, yesterday.*
Where? *here, there, away, inside, outside.*
How much? *very, more, quite, exactly.*

Adverbs and Verbs

Look carefully at these sentences:

Walk to your desk.
Walk *slowly* to your desk.

In the second sentence above, the adverb *slowly* gives us more information about the meaning of the verb *walk.* Do not just walk, but walk *in a slow manner,* walk *in a slow way. Slowly* answers the question: **How?**

Adverbs and Adjectives

Look carefully at these sentences:

I have a better toy than you.
I have a *much* better toy than you.

In the second sentence above, the adverb *much* adds something extra to the meaning of the adjective *better.* The toy is not only better, but it is better *by much, by a lot, by plenty, by a great deal. Much* answers the question: **How much?**

Adverbs and Other Adverbs

Look carefully at these sentences:

We always have a pet.
We *almost* always have a pet.

In the second sentence above, the adverb *almost* gives us more information about the meaning of the adverb *always.* Most of the time we have a pet, but not always. Nearly always we have a pet, but not always. *Almost* answers the question: **How much?** Do you know what question the adverb *always* answers?

What Do Adverbs Look Like?

Many adverbs are made by adding *ly* to adjectives. Some adverbs do not end in *ly.* Here are some examples: *often, always, there, here, inside, away, soon, quite.*

THE PREPOSITION

A preposition is *a word that is placed before a noun or a pronoun.* A preposition allows us to understand how a noun or a pronoun is connected to some other word in a sentence. Let us say this same thing another way: A preposition is *a word that stands before a noun or a pronoun to show the relationship of the noun or pronoun to some other word in the sentence.*

> Paul gave the book *to* Sandra. (A preposition is placed before a *noun.*)
> Paul gave the book *to* her. (A preposition is placed before a *pronoun.*)

Here is a list of words that are often used as prepositions:

about	between	of	toward
above	by	off	under
across	down	on	underneath
after	during	over	until
around	except	past	up
at	for	since	upon
before	from	through	with
beneath	in	throughout	within
beside	into	to	without

In the sentences below, you can see how important prepositions are. Notice how the meaning changes when a different preposition is used.

> John put his book *on* the desk.
> John put his book *beside* the desk.
> John put his book *in* the desk.
> John put his book *under* the desk.

THE CONJUNCTION

A conjunction is *a word that connects words or groups of words.*

Connecting Words of Equal Value

Some conjunctions connect words, or groups of words, of equal value. Look carefully at the following sentence:

> Louise *and* Helen ran to school.

The *two words of equal value* are: **Louise; Helen**
The *conjunction* connecting these words is: **and**

Here is another example:

> Edward works *and* plays at school.

The *two words of equal value* are: **works; plays**
The *conjunction* connecting these words is: **and**

Below we have a sentence with two *groups* of words of equal value:

Alice went to the store, *but* Susan stayed home.

The *two groups of words of equal value* are: **Alice went to the store**
Susan stayed home

The *conjunction* connecting these two groups is: **but**

Two Separate Conjunctions

Some conjunctions are made up of two *separate* words, or two separate groups of words. These words connect like parts of the same sentence.

SEPARATE WORDS

Look closely at the following sentence:

Either he *or* I will go to the store.

The *like parts* of the same sentence are: **he; I**
The *two conjunctions* connecting these words are: **either . . . or**

SEPARATE GROUPS

Here is an example of conjunctions in two separate groups.

Not only will I come, *but also* I will bring a gift.

The *like parts* of the same sentence are: **will I come; I will bring a gift**
The *two conjunctions* connecting these words are: **not only . . . . but also**

The most often used conjunctions of this kind are: *either . . . or, neither . . . nor, both . . . and, not only . . . but also, whether . . . or.*

One Group of Words Needs Another

Finally, there is another kind of conjunction that makes the group of words following it need another group of words. As soon as we see this kind of conjunction, we know that the part of the sentence following the conjunction needs another group of words. We need this second group of words to understand the meaning of the sentence. If, for example, someone said

"When John saw me,"

you would not know what was meant. You would be waiting for more words. But if someone said

"When John saw me, he laughed,"

you would know exactly what was meant. From the above example we can see three things:

A *group of words that needs another group:* **When John saw me**
A *conjunction* beginning this group of words: **When**
The *needed group* of words that can stand alone: **he laughed**

Can you find the conjunctions in these sentences?

> *After* the baseball game, we went home.
> *If* it rains, we will not take a walk.
> Tim goes swimming often *because* he lives near a lake.
> *While* it was snowing, we were in the car.

Some often used conjunctions are: *as, while, until, before, since, after, so, because, for, if, unless, otherwise, that, in order that.*

THE INTERJECTION

An interjection is *a word that shows strong and sudden feeling.* Interjections are separated from the rest of the sentence. Here are some sentences. Can you pick out the interjections?

> *Hurrah!* We won the football game.
> *No!* You may not go out in the rain.
> *Hush!* The baby is sleeping.
> *Ouch!* The bee's sting hurts.

ASIA